A Cultural HISTORY of Theatre

Jack Watson
Grant McKernie

University of Oregon

Longman
New York & London

A Cultural History of Theatre

Longman, 10 Bank Street, White Plains, N.Y. 10606

Associated companies:
Longman Group Ltd., London
Longman Cheshire Pty., Melbourne
Longman Paul Pty., Auckland
Copp Clark Pitman, Toronto

Acquisitions editor: Kathleen Schurawich
Sponsoring editor: Gordon T. R. Anderson
Development editor: Virginia L. Blanford
Production editor: Halley Gatenby
Text design concept: Walter Norfleet
Cover design: Joseph DePinho
Cover illustrations: from Torii Kiyomasu I, *Warriors in Combat,* The
   James A. Michener Collection, The Honolulu Academy of Arts; *The
   Fire Dancer,* a production of the Arabesque Ballet Studio, Sofia,
   copyright U.N. Mission of Bulgaria.
Production supervisor: Joanne Jay

Library of Congress Cataloging-in-Publication Data

Watson, Jack (Jack Clair)
   A cultural history of theatre / by Jack Watson & Grant McKernie.
       p.   cm.
   Includes bibliographical references and index.
   ISBN 0-8013-0618-3
   1. Theater—History.   2. Theater and society.   I. McKernie, Grant
Fletcher, [Date] .   II. Title.
PN2100.W38   1992
792'.09—dc20   92-11258
                                                CIP

 3 4 5 6 7 8 9 10-CRW-9695

Contents

Illustrations

Preface

A Cultural History of Theatre is intended as a primary text for theatre history courses. We present the history of theatre within a framework of cultural and social ideas because we believe that theatre occurs in a cultural context. This belief is based on several underlying assumptions: that any social institution serves a social function for its participants, that a definable cultural milieu exists in any given society, and that the cultural characteristics of a society are worth studying.

We have based our work on two other assumptions as well: first, since theatre occurs at the time of performance, the study of theatre history is always to some extent an act of informed imagination; and second, attempts to systematize the study of theatre lead inevitably to reductionism. In the interest of providing a comprehensive, globally focused text, we have had to make choices. We hope we have chosen wisely, but we have no doubt that some of you will disagree with some of our choices. We have focused largely on Western theatre, and we have included movements, individuals, structures, and plays that have been most influential or that students are most likely to encounter in performance. We have organized our text more or less chronologically, and we have selected some consistent categories for analysis. Throughout, we have supplemented our primary choices with *inserts* that focus on people, places, and events that we feel are particularly significant, with *charts* to provide factual detail, and with *Global Perspectives* that provide snapshots of theatrical events in other cultures.

Our chapters are built on the following structure:

1. The *introduction* provides a brief narrative perspective for the material that follows.

2. *Social ideas* that emerge from the history of the period and that we find influential in the development of theatre are investigated. Key historical events and personalities are included in the *time lines* that appear at the beginning of the chapters. These sections are necessarily highly selective; we have tried to highlight ideas that are historically prominent and relevant to theatre.

3. *Arts ideas* that illustrate or explicate the same aesthetic concepts current in the theatre are explored. Material from painting, sculpture, architecture, music, and dance is included, although not all forms are considered in every chapter. Works cited are those that are generally regarded as typical,

those that are likely to be experienced in other classes, and those that reflect ideas in the theatre.

4. *Theatre history* is organized through a study of six elements: occasion, location, performers, audience, standards of judgment, and dramatic literature. *Occasion* seeks to determine when theatre occurred within a given society, the purpose or function of the performance, and the organizational methods that led to presentation. The relationship of the performance to other social/political/cultural events is also noted. *Location* investigates not only theatre architecture but the placement of theatre within the physical structure of the community. Of particular interest in this area is the relationship such structures created between the performer and the audience. *Performers* refers to the entire range of theatrical practitioners: actors, designers, technicians, dancers, managers, and so forth. The focus is not simply on knowledge of names but on the standards and styles of work created and how they interrelated in the creation of theatre. *Audience* examines the composition of the audience to determine for whom a given form was created and who was excluded. Audience attitudes and behaviors are also of interest. *Standards of judgment* assess the rules by which a theatre piece was judged, as expressed through the critical writings of the period.

5. *Dramatic literature* is an extended study of the major dramatic forms and styles of the period with a focus on plays that the student is most likely to encounter in performance. At least one play is analyzed in some detail, anticipating that students will read at least one play from each period, recognizing as they do so that the reading of a play is a textual "performance" in itself. The reader must interpret not only the dialogue but all the possibilities of performance discovered in the study of the culture. Imagination is required in this integration of elements, and the responsibility for this act belongs to the individual reader.

6. A study of *connections* identifies major contributions of the period and notes the presence of those contributions in contemporary theatre, television, and film. These sections are necessarily brief, and students are encouraged to explore their own experience of modern theatrical forms to recognize connections beyond those described in the text.

ACKNOWLEDGMENTS

We wish to express our gratitude to the following reviewers, whose thoughtful suggestions aided us greatly in writing this book.

Maarten Reilingh, McNeese State University, Louisiana;

Jerry Dickey, University of Arizona;

Freda Scott Giles, State University of New York/Albany;

Attilio Favorini, University of Pittsburgh; and

Lani Johnson, Central Connecticut State University.

The editorial staff at Longman Publishing Group has been most supportive. In particular we wish to acknowledge the late Gordon (Tren) Anderson, who was the first to encourage us in this effort; Kathy Schurawich, for continued optimism; Ginny Blanford, for positive guidance when it was most needed; Halley Gatenby, for fortitude; and, most important, David Fox, for patience throughout the project.

In addition, we wish to thank other individuals who contributed to or in other ways supported our work on this book: Rick Turnbow, Molly Eness, Barbara Embree, Annie McGregor, Teresa Mason, Steve McGillivray, Ginger Cochran, Dennis Smith, Karen Falise, and Mary Pheifer. Special thanks to our colleagues at the University of Oregon, and particularly to Sandy Bonds and Jerry Williams for sharing their art. Our gratitude, also, to the many students who tolerated the book in its formative stages and provided valuable feedback and welcome encouragement.

1

Introduction

In a high school auditorium in McMinnville, Oregon, a nervous group of students huddles backstage around their teacher just moments before the opening performance of their production of *The Miracle Worker*. An audience of parents and friends sits on folding chairs, chatting amiably as they anticipate this annual event.

An energetic group of people in a remote village in Brazil loudly offers possible choices for a character in a play that deals with the economic situation of their own village. They argue among themselves as several possible alternatives are explored by the actors, seeking agreement on the best solution.

On an idyllic beach on Bali, a masked demon is attacked by villagers armed with sharp knives. In a trance and under the curse of the evil figure, they turn the knives on themselves but suffer no physical harm. The other villagers cluster closely, staying after the performance to tend to the exhausted performers.

In Europe, an elegantly dressed audience quiets down as the house lights dim and turns its attention to the stage. The curtain rises on a formal living room as the Comédie-Française of Paris presents Molière's play *Tartuffe*—the script and gestures closely paralleling those that have been performed there for more than a hundred years.

One of the joys of any study of theatre is the remarkable variety such a study presents. The four examples above do not represent a historical cross section; they are examples of recent theatrical events. Indeed, a similar diversity will occur on the very day you read this chapter. The problem in studying theatre history lies not in finding interesting things to study, but in limiting such a study in a meaningful fashion.

To some people the theatre is nothing more than a commercial venture. Yet for every entrepreneur there is another person who feels the theatre is a place of reverence and social bonding. Indeed the theatre has been a religiously oriented art form in a number of societies, while in others it has been at best a source of amusement and diversion. Further, the meaning of theatre is different for those who practice and create it, and those who see it. It also varies from one society to another. In this century, the definition of theatre has been made still more difficult by the creation of new theatre forms, television, and film. Each of these perspectives provides only a partial understanding of what theatre is.

Theorists often argue about the precise definition of the term *theatre*. It is derived from a Greek word, *theatron*, meaning "a place from which to view," and in its broadest definition might include such diverse activities as the spoken drama, opera, dance, film, television, the circus, and sporting events. Since such a range is obviously beyond the scope of any one book, this text focuses on the spoken drama, although references to other forms are included.

THEATRE AND ITS ORIGINS

Part of the difficulty in defining theatre is that no one knows for sure how or why theatre originally developed. If the sources of theatre could be traced to a single location in time and space, it would be fairly easy to determine the factors in that situation that led to the creation of theatre. No such moment has been found, however. Instead, theatre historians have had to rely on different kinds of information from different sources and have reached different conclusions about the origin of theatre.

Aristotle

The oldest account of the origin of theatre is found in Aristotle's essay *Poetics*, written in Greece about 330 BCE and studied by theatre historians ever since. In a brief passage, Aristotle reported that tragedy and comedy at first were presented in improvisations. That is, they were spontaneous creations of the moment, presumably with no script and little preplanning. He then suggested that the theatre advanced slowly until it found its natural form and then stopped. Aristotle had no way of knowing that the theatre after his time would continue to evolve in several different directions, rendering his concept of "natural form" somewhat limited. He also could not know that theatre in non-Western cultures also developed in very different directions from that of ancient Greece.

However, Aristotle also stated that tragedy evolved from the desire in human-kind to imitate. He asserted that this desire is instinctive in all humans. Later writers have expanded this by explaining that imitation is a means by which we take control of the world around us. When we imitate life experience, we are giving it shape and thereby giving it meaning. We may be acting out the way we want something to happen (a group of hunters imagines how they will kill their prey). We may be retelling an event that already has happened (the returning hunters report their kill). Or we may be repeating an experience in order to convince ourselves that it really happened (the hunters repeat the death of their friend in order to realize fully that their friend is dead). We might even retell an event in the hope that the success of a previous venture will be repeated (the hunters portray a successful hunt before leaving the village). In these and other ways, imitation is a means of structuring experience according to our emotional and social needs. While Aristotle did not cite these specific examples, he did identify imitation as the key element in human nature, and later writers have used it to explain the appeal of theatre. Because Aristotle's analysis of tragedy as a form is so meaningful, it is tempting to assume that what he wrote about the origins of theatre is equally valid. Unfortunately, little corroborating evidence has been found to support some of his assertions. As a result, the quest to find the roots of theatre continued beyond his account.

Ritual Theories

A second theory of the origins of theatre was particularly prominent at the end of the 19th century. Several anthropologists searched for the origins of theatre in the form in which theatre exists. They collected thousands of examples of cult worship, rituals, and magic practices in hundreds of societies. They then looked for com-monalities in those examples, they were united in their conviction that theatre is based on ritual.

These theorists presented an impressive array of cross-cultural evidence to de-velop their theory that there is a recurring pattern in the ritual practices of most societies. Rituals include a contest, usually between death and life in the guise of winter and spring or darkness and light. Fertility symbols are common, for the victory of light and spring means that the society will be sustained by new crops. Harvest festivals honor the fertility symbols for granting a good harvest. Theorists also noted that societies hold contests for leadership that involve rejecting the old and heralding the new. Here again, fertility is important, for the new leader symbolically possesses the society's fertility symbol. Associated with these ritual contests is some lamentation for the past and hope for the future. Further, the contest involves a discovery or realiza-tion that the society is better for having had the defeat of the old and the victory of the new.

This very brief account of the ritual origins of theatre points to the key contribu-tion of the ritual theorists. There does seem to be a recurring pattern of action in every drama that includes a contest, a defeat, a discovery, and a resolution. Unfortunately, the theorists could not prove that a specific ritual of this kind was the source of theatre. They did, however, identify an emotional and social need felt in several cultures across time: the desire to begin life anew and the need to find some way of expressing that desire.

Gerald Else

A very different approach to the search for theatre's origins is found in the writings of Gerald Else (1965). Else turned away from the (so far) unprovable theories of ritual and asserted that the origins of theatre lie in the work of two individuals. The origin of tragedy, he believed, was not so much a gradual development as a sequence of two creative leaps, one by Thespis and a second by Aeschylus. Thespis was the actor who stepped out of the chorus and took on the role of a god. Aeschylus created the second actor, who could interact with the first and thereby give the theatre dramatic immediacy. He also is credited with creating scene painting and therefore developing the theatre as a visual illusion.

Else identified another important component in the appeal of theatre. Theatre is a creative act done by artists. Individuals make theatre happen. Theatre may evolve from social and religious needs, but it achieves its form and impact from individuals who shape it to that form. Imagination and invention have social roots, to be sure, but it requires individuals to give their own personal imagination the shape and substance of the culture. Else's theory is at least a reminder of the importance of the individual artist in the development of theatre.

Theatre and Faith

One way of answering the question, What is theatre? is to look to its origins and determine how and why theatre developed as it did. A second way is to understand why the theatre has appeal. No social institution exists over time unless it is providing some positive function for the individuals connected to that institution. The fact that theatre has survived for centuries, in spite of recurring attempts to prohibit it, is itself illuminating. It suggests that theatre is more than a pastime or a luxury. It is, in some manner, a response to the felt needs of the audience and the society from which that audience comes.

Many people who have studied the theatre believe that there is a close association between the shaman or priest in tribal societies and the actor in the theatre. The shaman disguises himself to remove his identity as a typical member of society. He then acts on behalf of the society as an intermediary between that society and the powers of the universe. He represents the interests of the community, asking or praying for the community's health and welfare. In speaking for the society, he repeats actions and words that have been used in the past to achieve the same result. In other words, he follows a ritual that the community understands is appropriate for the occasion.

One function of the shaman is to express the faith of the community. By representing the whole community, he is a symbol of those feelings and beliefs that

MASKS
IN THE
THEATRE

*I*n many cultures, a masked figure plays a major role in important community rituals. In Bali the ritual mask of Rangda possesses magical powers and must be covered until the moment of performance. Among the Seneca Indians of New York State, "False Face" masks carved from tree trunks have curative powers. During Carnival in many parts of the world masked figures break established social taboos with impunity. On October 31, American children don masks and go door to door, inviting neighbors to give them "treats" to avoid some potential "trick."

In these instances, as in many forms of drama, the mask has special properties. Masks may be used during rites of passage, as part of funerary rites, or as an element of religious observance. They may be beneficent or evil, frightening or funny. Whatever the occasion and whatever the use, they possess the power of transformation, of allowing an individual to seem something "other," something "more." Some anthropologists describe this process as providing a flow between the spiritual and the material worlds. The power of the mask is a key to a raised level of understanding, and some anthropologists consider the ability to understand the function of the mask as key to understanding societies.

Masks have been used in drama throughout its history—in the ancient Greek theatre and in classical Japanese drama, in the Italian commedia dell'arte and in contemporary theatre groups such as the Bread and Puppet Theatre. In the modern theatre, masks are frequently used in actor training as well. For example, neutral masks worn by the acting student are used to allow the actor to reveal and then overcome habitual patterns of gesture, speech, and movement. The presence of the mask reorders the senses and alters the means of conveying and receiving information, challenging the actor to rely no longer on facial expression and vocal inflection. Freed from these limitations, the actor is encouraged to explore a full range of expressive capability. Character masks, commedia half-masks, and clown faces are similarly used to enable the actor to escape the limitations of a socially defined "persona" and explore possibilities that might not be available in an unmasked situation.

For the spectator, the mask denies the individual presence of the human actor and allows the drama to escape limitations of time and place. For both actor and spectator, the sense of transformation is crucial to the use of mask in drama. The mask, whether lifelike or grotesque, displaces the identity of the wearer and creates an altered form of communication. Although some sources will discuss Greek drama masks as huge grotesque images with built-in megaphones, this development occurred several hundred years after the 5th century. Rather than merely creating towering godlike figures, the masks were important in allowing the dramatist, the actors, and the spectators to move beyond the particular time and place in which the performance occurred and let them explore mythical stories and abstract concepts.

the community has in common. His very existence is a visual reminder that the community has these feelings and beliefs. When he leads the community through its rituals, he brings its individual members together and reminds them of what it is they share. Because the rituals have been performed in previous generations, he also reminds the community of its shared history and its connection to the communities of the past. It is also implied that he will perform these rituals again in the future, giving the community a sense of identification with the future as well as the past. (For further reading on the shaman and ritual, see Kirby, *Ur-Drama*.) Implicit in this is the notion that individuals want to belong to something beyond the self. The function of ritual in this context is to give each person in the society a feeling of connection to the world around them. Almost all human beings seek some identification with the outside world—even the hunter who prefers to live alone with nature. Most people do not feel completely whole as human beings unless they are part of some larger scheme or plan of life. Such a scheme may be familial, social, religious, or all of these. The shaman enacts the desire of the individuals in a community to reach out beyond themselves in order to feel a sense of completion in themselves.

The theatre has this same inherent capacity for many people. For them, theatre is a celebration of the social nature of human existence. It is a ritual reenactment of what the community believes. It is a reminder of the need to reach beyond the self to understand the self. The characters in tragedy who fail to achieve their goals help us to understand the limits of human potential. The characters in comedy who succeed are joyful reminders of ways to make our lives worthwhile. Most important, these realizations come while we are witnessing these characters in a group. Their experience has meaning not just for us but for everyone in the audience. It is a shared, communal experience, a ritual reenactment of our faith that life has value.

For many people, the modern theatre is a rejection of that faith. Some plays appear to have no universal meaning because they present bizarre incidents that could not happen to anyone other than the characters. Other plays seem bereft of any faith in the future of humankind. Still others seem intent on attacking the audience rather than expressing what it believes. The reasons for the appearance of such plays in the 20th century will be explored in the last chapters of this book. The existence of such plays does not deny the concept that theatre is a communal act of faith. It only points to the difficulty of having faith in the modern world.

THEATRE AND SOCIETY

Theatre serves as something depending on society tera rchanges

Perhaps few people in our modern world who write a play or perform in one think consciously of the social function they are serving. Yet through the centuries history reveals that theatre has served a variety of purposes that directly influence the nature of the dramas and their performances. These functions further expand our appreciation of what theatre is.

Some societies have used the theatre to teach moral lessons, whether the lessons be religiously based as with the medieval European societies, mythologically derived as in the shadow puppets of Southeast Asia, or philosophically oriented as with much of Renaissance literature. In such plays, the final outcome of the action is geared to punishing vice and rewarding virtue. In other societies, theatre has been more concerned with clarifying the individual's role in society. Ancient Greek theatre articulated the worth of human beings, especially through its development of the tragic hero. (In doing so, it also served the broader social function of integrating the community.) Romanticism provided an alternative model of heroism for 19th-century audiences in Europe, focusing on the emotional and rebellious outcast. In fact, the search for truths in human behavior has been a recurrent theme of all theatres, and history reveals that all great plays share this purpose.

More recently, the rise of realism in Western Europe and America has been accompanied by the use of theatre to identify and discuss social and political problems. Theatres in socialist societies present plays that suggest ways of thinking about matters of concern to the audience. Another variation of this social function is for a play to confront an audience and demand action about a social problem. During the 1960s in the United States, for example, street theatres opposing the government's policies in Vietnam gained notoriety. In contrast, the 17th- and 18th-century theatres of Continental Europe were usually intended to glorify the authority of the state, not challenge it. Similarly, the ancient Roman theatres were used to divert the attention of Romans from the politics and problems of the Empire.

Theatre can therefore serve many functions related to the individual and to society. Any effort to define theatre according to these functions, therefore, reveals once again the scope and complexity of theatre as an institution. Comparing theatre to its related arts offers an alternative approach to understanding the theatre and some of the reasons for its continuing popularity.

THE STUDY OF THEATRE HISTORY

Two factors concerning the study of theatre history must be considered at the outset. First, theatre is an event that occurs at the time of performance. Although it can be preserved in some fashion through a script, a review, a photograph, or a videotape, theatre itself cannot exist outside of the performance. The study of theatre history then is the act of an informed imagination. This book presents cultural concepts, known facts or theories of theatre history, and an analysis of drama. The combination of these factors into a sense of *theatre* cannot be accomplished on the written page and demands the active participation of the reader. The total effect of author, director, scene designer, costumer, lighting, music, scenery, actor, auditorium, audience, and surrounding cultural milieu lies beyond our ability to re-create, but it is our challenge to approximate it.

Second, attempts to systemize the study of theatre lead inevitably to some form of reductionism. In this book, two systems of study are used that artificially limit our knowledge. First, the book is divided into chapters that identify cultural "periods." These divisions are arbitrary in themselves and the discussion of theatre within these periods is necessarily generalized. And while this book attempts to present an idea of the range of theatrical forms, including those that were most successful and, thus, most influential, alternative forms of theatre to those discussed almost certainly existed. Similarly, the book attempts throughout to present current concepts and ideas, but such information is subject to change as new discoveries or insights are achieved.

Further, the establishment of "categories" of investigation is also limiting. Categories are used here to offer the beginning scholar a framework for comparison and contrast. It is hoped that such knowledge will invite further study in areas of special interest, and that such study will transcend the limitations that our categories impose. It is important to recognize that any survey of this nature is automatically a summary, and that the view it presents of a given topic is limited in scope. Such study remains important, however, because ultimately the importance of any knowledge of history rests not only in what you know about another time period, but what you learn about yourself.

The study of theatre history can take a variety of forms, and historians utilize a fascinating array of techniques and formats with which to obtain and interpret knowledge about the past. Traditional methodology tended to focus on one particular form of artifact. For those who took an archaeological focus, this might involve a detailed measuring of the ruins of ancient Greek theatres. From those measurements, reasoned guesses could be made at the structure of the entire theatre. Anthropologists found comparisons between theatre and other social structures or events and sought to derive the possibilities of theatre performance by applying one field to the other. Other researchers adopted a literary focus, searching through dramatic texts for clues that would offer possibilities of understanding performance.

Recent movements have greatly expanded the techniques available to the theatre historian. Although these studies may vary widely in philosophical basis and in their particular vocabularies, they share an interest in the theatre as a part of a larger social construct and recognize that our perception of that culture is colored by our own biases and those of the people who have recorded the history. Such studies may present concepts of cultural hegemony, of feminist perspectives, economic analysis, or intercultural influences. They may focus on specific relationships within a culture, on specific groups determined by class, genre, or ethnic background, or they may seek to find relevance in the common or in the bizarre. In most cases, however, theatre historians today deal with theatre as a social phenomenon that creates, communicates, and reflects the culture within which it occurs.

Focus of the Text

This book, then, presents theatre in a cultural context, discussing the confluence of theatre and the social and cultural institutions and values around it. In doing so, it seeks to explain theatrical practices and literary concepts by showing their social origins and by illustrating them with examples from other arts. The characters of plays live in worlds that at least partially reflect the playwright's world, and their customs and habits are often best understood by explaining the social customs and practices of that world. Likewise, the theatrical practices of each era often share aesthetic assumptions with the other arts that can be readily illustrated with visual and aural examples from art and music. Additionally, discussion of theatre and drama in their cultural context helps to identify the attitudes and backgrounds of the audiences for whom the plays were initially intended.

Such an approach presupposes a number of assumptions worth noting because they clarify the approach itself. First, it assumes that any social institution serves some kind of social function for those who participate in it. Because the participants in theatre (both the audience and the presenters) are social beings, they bring their values to the theatre and participate within an established set of value limitations. To isolate the theatre from its socio-historical context is to miss this simple but essential factor. It also results in a failure to consider how the theatre affects society, through either challenging or changing the values that the audience brings with it. If the theatre were not socially functional in some way, it would eventually disappear, something it has done in different time periods. The cultural approach looks at the social values found in the theatre and drama and at the way theatre and drama affect those values.

Second, the cultural approach assumes the existence of a cultural milieu in any given society—an artistic context with dominant aesthetic characteristics. Often these characteristics are discernible only in retrospect, and important and frequent exceptions to them can always be noted. Nevertheless, these recurring characteristics can usually be identified in more than one art form, and most commonly they are found in a range of arts experiences. Taken together, their presence suggests that there is a set of commonly held values about life and art in that society. These values, frequently distilled or even warped, form the heritage of later societies. Of course, each artwork stands by itself with its own set of aesthetic assumptions and intents, just as each creative artist is creative precisely because she or he brings a unique perspective to bear on an art form. Yet, when the same sets of assumptions are found in a large number of significant works in a given time period, then a generalization can be made about that period's artistic style. The danger with this is the tendency to look for shared characteristics and to see them where they do not necessarily exist. Such history is prescriptive rather than descriptive, and it is ultimately ethnocentric. One can, however, be on guard against such a danger by frequent reference to the analysis of experts. As our knowledge of theatre history is in a constant state of flux, just so our conclusions must be similarly tentative and always open to revision.

Third, cultural characteristics are worth studying. Not only are they part of our heritage, the basis of many of the assumptions by which we live today, but they are also valuable lessons about human nature and the human condition. The study of theatre is one of the greatest proofs that peoples of all societies and time periods

finding similarities
can B dangerous

have in common the process of human growth and change. Learning how other cultures have coped with that process helps us become more aware of the choices available to us.

The world of theatre is complex, existing on many levels simultaneously. The world of the playwright, that of the characters, and that of the audience (or the reader) are woven together by a remarkable conglomeration of values and artistic ideas, some representative of earlier cultures and some dominant in our own. Experiencing the world of theatre enables us to identify the basis of our commonly held culture and forces us to think about ourselves, our heritage, and our society. We may not always enjoy the theatres of different periods, but we are always indebted to them for what they tell us of our past, for the manner in which they have influenced our present, and for the insights they can give to our future. In studying the theatre culturally, then, we share the past with the present in hopes of benefiting the future.

SOURCES FOR FURTHER STUDY

Aristotle. *Poetics.* Trans. Ingram Bywater. New York: Modern Library, 1954.
Else, Gerald. *The Origin and Early Form of Greek Tragedy.* Cambridge: Harvard University Press, 1965.
Harrison, Jane Ellen. *Themis.* New York: World Publishing, 1912.
Kirby, Ernest Theodore. *Ur-Drama.* New York: New York University Press, 1975.

C H A P T E R

2

General
Events

Iliad and *Odyssey*
BCE 950–800

Arts
Events

Classical Athens

Theatre
History
Events

The boy has hardly slept, for he has eagerly awaited the performance of plays at the City Dionysia—the main civic event of the Athenian year. The mother waves goodbye to her husband and child; although some women might be going to the theatre, most of her friends will remain at home as she does. Walking to the theatre, the boy's father encounters other citizens who have been discussing what they have heard about the plays being performed that day. Anticipation is high, for the process of selecting the three tragic poets for the competition was made 11 months ago, shortly after the last City Dionysia. The entire community has known of the participants for the day's plans and has debated their relative merits. Of course, the competition between the poets dictates some secrecy in rehearsal. It increases the excitement and ensures that the opposition does not learn of special theatrical devices that may be employed. Anticipation has continued to build through the first several days of the festival, and now the day of performance is here.

As the young boy climbs along the path leading to the theatre itself, he is joined by friends, relatives, and neighbors. Close to half of all Athenian citizens are clamoring for seats in the theatre, and front-row seats are reserved for civic officials, priests, and honored guests. The boy and his father aren't worried about their choice of seats because the shape of the amphitheatre means that most seats are equally good, and the acoustics of the theatre are so effective that the slightest sounds can be heard in the last rows. Once they

Timeline

First Olympiad	Solon	Battle of Marathon	Athenian democracy	Athens falls	Alexander the Great
BCE 776	638–558	490	490–429	431–404 404	336–323

Peloponnesian War

	Temple of Zeus, Olympia	Parthenon begun		
500	470–456	450–440 448	380	

Pindar's *Odes* — Polykleitos's "Doryphoros" statue — Plato's *Republic*

City Dionysia	Comedy officially recognized	Sophocles introduced third actor	Dithyramb contests	Aristotle's *Poetics*
BCE c. 534	c. 499 c. 487 484	471–468 449	400	c. 335–323

Theatre of Dionysus — Aeschylus's first victory — Contest of tragic actors

find seats halfway up, they have a good perspective on the playing area as well as an excellent view of the landscape beyond. When the chorus refers to geographical locations in its speeches, the young boy can look off toward that place in the distance.

The sun has not yet risen when the audience finds its places on the stone bleachers of the theatron, crowding together to enable as many as 17,000 to witness the plays. Because four plays are to be given on this day, the boy and his father have brought food and wine with them. When they eat their food will depend quite likely on the quality of the productions; if the play is engrossing, they will wait until it has ended. If the play is bad, the audience is quite capable of using its food to comment on the play. However, any carousing or other audience commentary on the action is unlikely to occur during the tragedies.

Just before dawn, with the temperature still quite cold (it is late March), two actors, both portraying women, rush out from the building behind the stage. They conspire against their king, Creon. One of them decides not to participate in the plot and returns to the building, while the other escapes down the path away from the city. While our young boy wonders what is the meaning of this prologue to Sophocles' play *Antigone,* the chorus enters singing and dancing from the right. At the moment they sing their first choral ode to the arrival of a new day in Thebes, where the play takes place, the sun

The theatre at Epidauros, the best-preserved theatre ruin in Greece. *Courtesy Alison Frantz Photographs*

makes its first appearance in the eastern skies of Athens. The performance of tragedies has begun.

This imaginary trip to the theatre in Classical Athens begins our journey to one of the most remarkable eras in European history. In the brief period from 480–404 BCE Athens was an intellectual and artistic center unrivaled not only in its own time but quite possibly at any other time. The theatre, as well as sculpture, architecture, philosophy, and history, attained new dimensions that dominate Western European traditions in those fields to the present day. To understand the development of theatre in Athens, it is necessary to know something of the culture in which that theatre flourished, for the theatre helped to shape Athenian culture just as the political and artistic ideas of the age helped to shape the theatre.

Athens did not come into its own as a dominant political force in the region of the eastern Mediterranean until the 400s BCE. However, [...] ant achievements prior to that time helped to give Athens its partic [...] orientation. Solon (640–558 BCE) is credited with developing Athenian [...] concept of justice for all citizens. (It must be noted that of the approxim [...] ple living in Athens in the 400s, only some 40,000 were citizens, ar [...] was made up of women, foreign-born residents, and slaves.) Solon's la[...] ement for debts and originated the concept of a popular assembly th[...] ble for the establishment of laws. Kleisthenes (fl. 520–500 BCE) elabor[...] of government that broke up loyalties among ancient tribes and he [...] the polis or city-state. The Council of 500, chosen by lot, was establis[...] with issues of finance and foreign affairs. This council, along with an assem[...] zens, ran most of the civic affairs of Athens.

(handwritten note: democracy based on justice unifying tribes)

The democratic nature of Athenian government is cruc[...] development of the theatre, for it provided a political environment in which i[...] d and should be freely expressed. The Athenians were accustomed to coming t[...] o debate openly the issues of the day. Public speaking was one of the m[...] ortant and most appreciated of skills; the dominance of many politicians of the age was due to their ability to sway the assembly with their power of speech. It is little wonder that the Greeks would create an art form in which all the citizens could come together to hear characters speak (and sing) eloquently of the nature of life.

Also contributing to the shape of Greek drama was the military standing of Athens in the 400s BCE. Athens' rise to power was the result of the victory of Greek forces over the Persians in a series of battles in the 480s. Athenian power at sea was one of the keys to Greek victory, and Athens used her new prestige to solidify and then dominate alliances with other islands and city-states in the region. The drama of the period following the defeat of the Persians often reflects the confidence of Athens in its greatness and the disdain for anyone not born a Greek (the words *Greek* and *Greece* were not in use at the time; they referred to themselves as Hellenes).

Athens was at war in all but a few of the years of the century. Many of the greatest plays of the period were written during the Peloponnesian wars (431–404 BCE), which pitted Greek against Greek, as Sparta, another Greek city, resisted Athens' growing attempts at domination and imperialism. That two of the greatest playwrights of the century, Euripides and Aristophanes, could write of their opposition to the tactics employed in the wars attests to the openness of public debate and the willingness of Athenians to listen to all sides of an argument.

SOCIAL IDEAS

Greek Religion

Theatre and drama in Greece were in part an outgrowth of Greek ritual and religious practice. The structure of the plays bears some resemblance to their religious festivals. The characters of many dramas are religious figures. The tragic ideas of the playwrights include a conception of tragedy based on the religious views of the time period. A brief

DIONYSUS

*H*e was the god of wine and intoxication and of ecstasy and insight. He could transform himself from the handsomest man in Greece into a lion, a bull, or a rapidly growing vine. He demanded that people acknowledge his power or he would drive them into a frenzy, even to the point of having them kill their own children. He was Dionysus, the god for whom the major theatre and theatre festival in Athens were named. To tell his story is to gain insight into the function of the theatre for the Greeks.

Dionysus was the result of the union of the chief god, Zeus, and a mortal named Semele. So in love with Semele was Zeus that when she asked him to grant her a favor, he agreed. She asked to see him in his true godlike form; although Zeus knew the consequence, he revealed himself to this mortal. Instantly she burned to death. Zeus took the fetus of Dionysus and sewed it into his thigh, where it matured. The son of the great god Zeus was a threat to all the other gods, however, and when the child was born, they destroyed it. Some of the baby's blood fell on the earth, and a pomegranate tree grew from that spot. Zeus's mother was able to bring Dionysus back to life again from that tree. Dionysus was thus born three times—once from his mortal mother, once from his immortal father, and once from the wisdom of the earth.

As a mature god in his own right, Dionysus was demanding and impetuous. His most famous encounter, told by the playwright Euripides, was with Pentheus, who ruled the land of Thebes where Dionysus was born. Pentheus denied the god's power and insisted that the people of the region should not worship him, even though his own mother was a leader of the Dionysian cult. Dionysus first resisted arrest when he appeared to Pentheus, then convinced Pentheus to spy on his mother and her fellow worshippers. In their religious ecstasy, they mistook Pentheus for an animal and ripped him apart. Once the mother realized what she had done, she was banished from Thebes, and Dionysus issued a warning to all never to underestimate his power.

Dionysus was not all vengeance and destruction, however. He fell in love with Ariadne and married her. They had several children and were happy until she died. He also mourned for the fact that he never knew his mother, so he went on a dangerous trip to the underworld, where he rescued his mother and brought her back to the world of the gods. Dionysus himself was honored by the other gods when he was given the seat at the right hand of Zeus.

The characteristics of Dionysus help us to understand his close association with the theatre. Dionysus represents the power of the nonrational or the emotional side of life. His warnings to heed him are a reminder that no matter how much we seek to control and understand life, emotional experiences will occur. Whether it be love, death, war, despair, or ecstasy, Dionysus represents the intrusion of the unexpected into people's lives and the realization that we cannot control all that happens to us. The theatre from the time of Aeschylus has focused on precisely these issues.

Dionysus, like other Greek gods, was capable of transformation, and that transformation is symbolic of the change undergone by the actor who takes on the mask (or makeup) of another person. The Greeks created in the Western world the alteration of an individual from one person to another with the intent of showing us some truth of life. This is exactly what Dionysus did with Pentheus.

The cult of Dionysus persisted at least from the 15th century BCE. It gave the theatre many of its formative features: the concept of transformation of the individual, the use of masks, the satyr plays (satyrs were one kind of followers of Dionysus), the dithyrambs (the songs sung in honor of Dionysus that preceded the drama), and four Greek festivals held in his honor. His followers and their religion had a definite impact on the development of the theatre in Classical Greece.

Gods interracted w/ people

understanding of Greek religion in the 5th century BCE, therefore, will be a helpful beginning for a discussion of tragedy.

The specifics of ancient religious history are lost. What is known is that the people who inhabited the region now called Greece were flexible in their religious views. They adapted to new influxes of religious thought, and they accepted the gods of other races that invaded their territory. From this they evolved a polytheistic faith, or belief in many gods, which emphasized the relationship of the Hellenes to the world around them. They accepted the presence of a force beyond them and they articulated that presence by giving it names for each situation. Thus, the universal power of life could appear in a location (such as the sea or the mountains), in the actions of human beings (such as war or harvesting), in the processes of nature (such as fertility), or in universal characteristics of human beings (rationality, wisdom, or revenge). To express these forces of nature, the Hellenes gave them the names and characteristics of gods. That the characters of Greek drama so frequently appeal to the gods, then, was not the desire to blame somebody else for their actions. Instead, it was a genuine acknowledgement that individuals are not isolated in the world, but are part of an organic whole that includes forces beyond human understanding.

Many modern readers are disturbed that the gods often appear as mortals in Greek literature, and not as very good mortals at that. That the gods are anthropomorphic, having human attributes, means only that they were accessible to humans. It does not mean that they were human themselves. The familiarity of the Hellenes for their gods means that these people believed that divine beings were concerned with the fate of mortals. Further, the gods could make mistakes because the Greeks realized that nothing in life or nature follows a perfect or predictable pattern.

The arrival of one particular god (perhaps in the 15th century BCE) and his religious followers further impelled the Hellenes toward the drama. Dionysus was the god of wine and fertility, but his followers worshipped the nonrational forces in human nature. The worship of Dionysus was a means of expressing the ability of human beings to lose themselves in uncharacteristic behavior, whether through drunkenness (the simplest of means) or physical ecstasy. When people feel that they have lost themselves, they are free to assume another role. Dionysian worship encouraged followers to create such ecstatic states, and this in turn encouraged the concept of becoming someone else. While some religions see such behavior as morally unaccept-able (because a person can deny responsibility for his actions), the worship of Dionysus actually fostered the art of acting.

Equally important, the religion of Dionysus involved a ritual that bears striking resemblance to the form of primitive manhood rituals and to the eventual structure of the drama. Traditionally, Dionysus was said to have been born twice, once from the thigh of the god Zeus, and once from a mortal. He was killed, dismembered, and then reborn again. Worshippers reenacted this process in festivals. A pole bearing a mask of the god would be carried through the town to an altar, usually outside the city. Spectators were encouraged to join in the procession, their participation in drunken revelry and sexual activities varying according to the degree of wine and ecstasy they felt. When the spectators reached the altar, a goat or bull would be sacrificed to symbolize the death of the god. The return to the city symbolized the god's rebirth in the presence of that community.

Eventually, the hymns were organized into choruses from each tribe or section of the community. They were sung in honor of (but not necessarily about) Dionysus. These choral odes, or dithyrambs, were important antecedents to the drama because they distinguished participants from spectators, encouraged organization and rehearsal (there were 50 in each chorus), and promoted artistry and creativity because each dithyramb was different. That they were sung either on the same day or on successive days only fostered the Greek love of competition, and by 535 BCE winners were selected and honored at the festivals. Some historians suggest that Thespis (dates uncertain) emerged from one such dithyrambic chorus to further the evolution of the drama. By setting himself apart from the chorus as a solo performer, Thespis is generally considered to be the first actor in the Western theatre.

Conception of the Individual

The development of Greek religion and particularly of the worship of Dionysus is only one of the critical elements in the formation of the drama. The origin and form of the drama might have come from religious rituals, but the subject matter of the great Greek dramas came from the Hellenic conceptions of the individual and of the social commu-nity to which he or she belonged. What distinguished Greek drama was its unique emphasis on character. At the core of every tragedy was a person attempting to understand the nature of the human individual in a specific situation. This distinctive feature was a reflection of the Greek search to know oneself. The Hellenes took great pride in their freedom and potentiality as individuals. Whether in the time of Homer (c. 8th century BCE) or that of Classical Athens, the conception of what it means to be a human being was suffused with joy and vitality. The Greeks loved life and they loved to participate in life, whether it be in games or war. They believed that the best way to know themselves was through action—by participating in the world around them. Their philosophy sprang from experience and their ideals were tempered by practicality. When the communities became too large for each person to engage in every activity, they created vicarious forms of experience, including the drama.

In addition, the Greeks thought of themselves differently from modern individuals. They were never isolated from the world around them. They saw themselves as part of a natural order and part of a social order (the city-state). Their freedom derived from their ability to think clearly. They defined themselves by the characteristics they had in common with others, not by those that distinguished them from others. Their civic duty was a *natural* component of their personality (the word *idiot* originally meant "one who does not participate in civic affairs"). Finally, they strove for excellence and beauty in all things, including personal behavior.

Conception of Justice

The Greeks (until 420 BCE, at least) believed that there was an order in the universe and an order in human affairs. They used the gods to express the first of these. They used *dike* (pronounced dee-kay), their conception of justice, to express the second. Today, the term *dike* is translated as "justice," but originally it meant much more than that which is legally fair or correct. It meant determining the due share of each person, not determining which person was right. It implied an equality of all men in civic life, deriving from their equal responsibility to one another.

Dike was also based on a principle of balance and proportion in the universe. To the Greeks, the natural as well as the social worlds existed in equilibrium. When a natural catastrophe or human error occurred, there was an inevitable redress of the "imbalance." The return of the equilibrium was justice or *dike*. *Hubris* was an action that upset the natural order of things. The tragedies of Sophocles deal primarily with actions of *hubris* followed by a return to balance or *dike*.

ARTS IDEAS

Conception of Beauty

The Greek conception of character included the concept of beauty. Characteristically, the Greek's best theories of what is beautiful were practical applications of aesthetic principles, not philosophical treatises. Just as beauty is realized in an individual's actions, beauty in art is realized in artworks, not discussions of art. To the Greeks, beauty was the result of several things, including rationality, idealism, proportion, and balance. These principles are best realized in a Greek temple and in a sculpture of a male athlete.

Temple.   What strikes the visitor to a Greek temple such as the Parthenon in Athens are its location and structure. Housing the images of the patron god or goddess of the community, the temple was placed at the top of a hill, or an acropolis, overlooking the remainder of the city. It was a symbolic assertion of civic pride, for it could be seen from great distances by people approaching the city.

In every detail the temple reflects the Greek conception of beauty. The interior section, which housed the god's statue, was usually surrounded with one or two rows of columns tapering gently toward the sky. Each column was built with mathematical precision by virtue of the ratio of width, height, and distance between columns. On top of the columns going around the entire temple rested a marble ribbon called a frieze, on which were carved sculptures. The interior section also had a frieze around the top. The friezes show scenes of the victory of human ideals and the establishment of the god's power. Each component of the temple had a function that is clearly and beautifully articulated.

Sculpture.   The Greek search for the ideal as realized in the human is found in freestanding sculpture as well as in the theatre. In the euphoria of victory over the Persians in 490 BCE, Athenian artists found new means of articulating the human form and rendering it lifelike and vital. Two sculptors sculpted bronze and marble statues of gods and athletes that still rank as representations of the ideal in human form. The sculptures on the Parthenon were organized and supervised by Phidias (490–c. 432 BCE), who effectively filled each available space, and maintained variety and continuity throughout the friezes and pediments. Polykleitos (fl. 450–430 BCE), working almost exclusively with the male athlete form, used a canon of proportion to suggest musculature in motion. His *Doryphorus*, or *Spear-Bearer* (see photo), displays monumental power in its bulk balanced by sensitive fluidity of the curves of the body. Each section of the body balances another (note, for example, the relaxation in the right arm and the left leg) to create a unity of design. This athlete is at once real and ideal; Polykleitos expressed the spirit of the athlete through human form. We would not expect to meet such a person in real life, yet we can contemplate the human potential through this figure. For Polykleitos, the best work of art was one that engaged the mind as well as the eye. Beauty did not exist for its own sake, but as a guide to truth concerning human nature.

Like the sculptors, Greek dramatists invented new techniques to meet the needs of their ideas, and these ideas always concerned the impact of events on the life of the community. The Hellenes developed the drama for a particular purpose: they were a social people committed to learning about themselves and their world. They realized that their survival depended not only on military powers but on a sense of group identity and social cohesion. To achieve these, they relied on art forms to remind them of who they were and who they could be. As long as the community remained committed to its own integration, drama flourished as it would seldom do again in Western culture.

Doryphoros (Spear-Bearer) by Poly-kleitos, c. 450 BCE.   *National Museum, Naples*

GREEK THEATRE

Occasion

The communal nature of the Greek theatre determined the occasion of performance. Unlike the theatre of today, in Periclean Athens performances were not given every night at a variety of theatres throughout the city. Instead, they were held in conjunction with religious/social/political festivals sponsored by the city-state throughout the year. Plays were performed at three of these festivals. The *Lenaia*, held each January, featured comic performance; the *Rural Dionysia*, held in December, seems to have been more important outside of Athens. Although all of them honored Dionysus, it was at the *City* or *Great Dionysia* held at the end of March that the great dramatists competed. Planning for the festival occupied much of the year.

The close connection between the theatre and its culture in Athens is evidenced by the activities preceding the performance of the plays. The theatre itself was the site of the presentation of awards to leading citizens, the greeting of visiting dignitaries, and the presentation of the wealth of Athens (literally placed in front of the audience).

The 10 generals responsible for Athens's safety poured libations on the altar, one of the few times in the year that they appeared in a public celebration together. Civic pride was also expressed by the appearance of children of those who had died in war and by the presentation of the sons of deceased soldiers who had been raised by Athens. The *City Dionysia* was a point of intersection of civic awareness and the theatre. From this perspective, the theatre was a deeply social and political experience for the Greeks, suggesting that the plays addressed issues of concern to the community as a whole.

The selection of plays to be performed was made by a leading civic official, the *archon*. At the same time he also appointed a *choregos*, or wealthy citizen, to underwrite each production of the tragedians. The *choregos* paid for all aspects of his production, including the training of the chorus. The success of the playwright could obviously depend on the generosity of the *choregos* assigned him, but it was a matter of pride for the productions to succeed. In fact, the prize for the best group of tragedies was shared by the playwright and the *choregos*. The *archon* also appointed the leading actors for each production, although the playwright himself took the lead role in the early days of the festival.

Location

The fact that information concerning the theatre structure itself is largely based on information gained from theatres built 200 years after the Periclean age makes it difficult to know the precise nature of those structures. Although debate continues today over the precise size and shape of the various elements of the structure that housed theatre, an understanding of the theatre space is an important element in understanding the presentation of theatre. Enough information exists to provide a good idea of the theatre that housed Greek drama.

Originally, theatre events occurred in the *agora*, the marketplace of the city, and wooden benches or scaffolding were erected for spectators. Ancient records speak of the collapse of such a structure (c. 499 BCE), and that event may have led to the development of the stone theatre structures that provide the basis for most of our knowledge, since many ruins of theatres still exist in Greece.

At an early date the theatre was moved from the marketplace and located within the precincts of the temple. Typically, the theatre was located in a natural amphitheatre with the seats progressing up the hillside and the "stage" located on level ground at the foot of the hill. This location influenced the theatre in several ways.

On a purely physical level, the location allowed for a large audience, for sightlines and acoustics were both naturally good. Many visitors to Greek theatres are astonished when a word spoken softly on the stage is clearly heard in the top row. Spiritually, the placement of the theatre within the temple precinct indicates that theatre is concerned with important issues and that its societal role is more than entertainment. Finally, the theatre is set within nature, with a panoramic backdrop clearly placing the action of the play within the natural world. This sense of integration of humans and nature is a key concept in the experience of the classical Greek theatre.

The theatre structure itself reflects the Greek ideals of beauty: unity, proportion, and balance. Three important segments are integral to a Greek theatre structure: the *théatron* (viewing place), or seating area; the *orchestra*, a flat playing space; and the *skene*, or stage house located behind the *orchestra.* Each of these varies from theatre to theatre, but in every case the three segments are unified through design and construction materials, creating a self-contained structure that still maintains a harmonious relationship with the world around it.

The *theatron* apparently began as simply a hillside to which wooden benches were added for comfort. Later the wood was replaced by stone benches that generally formed a semicircle around one side of the acting space. The seating capacity varied as well, although the remains of the theatre at Epidauros indicate a seating capacity of approximately 17,000, and this is not considered unusual. The seating area was undivided so that seating was essentially democratic, although some special seats in the front rows were constructed for priests and dignitaries. One could enter the seating area from either the top or the bottom, and an audience member would pass many members of the community while moving to a chosen spot. Thus, a large portion of the citizens could attend a given performance, and the theatre structure helped to establish the sense of community that was an essential ingredient in Greek life.

The *orchestra* is a large area between the seating area and the "stage." In our contemporary theatre this area is used for seating (or, perhaps, for musicians), but the *orchestra* was an important performance area for the Greeks. Although some early

Theatre Dionysus in Athens.   *Courtesy Alison Frantz Photographs*

examples may have been either circular, rectangular, or free-formed, most historians agree the circular shape was generally used by the 5th century. By the 3rd century BCE the Theatre of Dionysus in Athens had a circular *orchestra* that measured 66–70 feet in diameter with an altar, or *thymele*, placed in the center. On either side, between the *orchestra* and the *skene*, two openings called *paradoi* allowed easy access to the acting area. It was conventionally accepted that one *parados* led to the city and the other to foreign places.

No one knows precisely how the *skene* developed. The earlier plays of 5th-century Greece occurred before natural backdrops, but by 458 BCE most plays were set in front of a temple or other building. No secure architectural records exist, but the lack of clear foundations indicate that the earliest forms of the *skene* were built of wooden timbers and may have been temporarily erected for each festival, primarily to provide a room for changing costumes and to hide any apparatus necessary for the perform-ance. Later structures indicate a large *skene* with an acting area raised above the orchestra, three permanent architectural doors, two side wings with additional doors (*paraskenae*), and a roof that could be used by actors as well. In addition, some form of machinery was used to lift and lower actors in plays that called for flying. The precise arrangement that existed in 5th-century Athens remains unknown, but historians agree that the structure was considerably less developed than those found in the remains of theatres built 100 to 200 years later. When reading the drama, one can assume the presence of a *skene* that provided, at the very least, a backdrop for the performance, one to three doors for exits and entrances in addition to the *paradoi*, and an acting area that was separate from the orchestra. This acting area may or not have been raised above the orchestra, but in either case movement between the two areas was easily accom-modated.

Performers

The theatre structure as we know it would allow scenic support for the theatre presentation, and many of the plays seemed to demand it. Since no records remain, precise knowledge of the type of scenic presentation used by the Greeks is impossible, and present-day historians debate whether scenic devices were illusionistic and tried to create a sense of reality or whether they were conventional and merely served to communicate necessary information for the spectator.

Those who favor the illusionistic theory cite the existence of multiple locations in one play or the fact that the presentation of three plays on a given day demanded a different background, which the Greeks certainly had the artistic ability to create. Writings of the period do indicate the existence of *pinakes*, or painted panels, similar to the modern stage flat. The illusionistic theory claims that these panels were painted specifically for each scene or play and were possibly mounted on the front of the *skene*. In later times, records indicate the development of a more elaborate structure known as the *periaktoi*. For many years they were thought to be a three-sided structure with three separate painted scenes that could rotate to indicate a change of scenery, although some modern scholarship disputes this interpretation of the word.

Conventional theorists, on the other hand, argue that *pinakes*, when they were used, were painted only in architectural designs to serve as appropriate backdrops.

Changes in location, according to this theory, were achieved either through entrances and exits, through choreography, or through the spoken words of the play. The eventual erection of a permanent stone *skene* that served as a backdrop for all plays is a convincing argument for the conventional theory.

Perhaps the truth lies somewhere in between. Rather than strictly observing our modern concepts of illusion or convention, the Greeks may have felt free to mix the two, utilizing a realistic scene where it seemed appropriate and relying on a conventional backdrop when that was most effective.

Two important devices of scenic support must be noted. The *ekkyklema* was a large rolling platform that could be moved through the central door to present a tableau illustrating action (often killing or death) that had occurred offstage. Some historians believe that it was pivoted into position rather than rolled, and some claim that it was located on the upper story or roof of the *skene*, but its function is generally accepted. The *mechane*, a simple crane device located behind or on top of the *skene*, was used to show creatures in flight or ascending/descending to or from the earth. The depiction of characters riding chariots through the sky or riding on the backs of flying creatures could be achieved through this simple mechanism, and such devices allowed the playwrights to explore freely the traditional myths. Since the *mechane* was visible to the audience, its use supports the theory of conventional rather than realistic presentation. Although furniture was almost never used, it seems likely that properties were present on stage. Altars, chariots, carpets, funeral biers, and couches all appear in the tragedies, and the comedies are filled with properties of all descriptions. Unfortunately, we have no means of determining whether realistic props were developed or whether simple representational items were used.

The patriarchal nature of society is reflected in the sole use of male performers in the theatre. Just three actors, all male, played all the speaking roles. The first of these, called the protagonist, was extremely important, for it was his acting that was the core of the drama. He always played the central role, leaving to change masks and take a minor role only at the end of a play if his character died. Only he could win the prize for acting. The second and third actors divided the remaining roles between them, either according to logistics or to their abilities. Other actors could appear in the play, but they almost never had any lines to speak. They were supernumeraries or extras who played guards or citizens; in fact, they were human scenery. A man who chose to be an actor worked his way up from extra to third actor and then to second actor. Only then did he get to play major roles.

Because the actors played the parts of women and gods as well as men, the acting style was most likely not realistic in the modern sense. All actors were masked, and one modern historian has argued that the very nature of the masked actor leads to an acting style that is not realistic but is more dependent on gesture and tone. An actor had to portray real emotions and actions, but he also had to sing some of his long speeches and intone others. Also, the playwright seldom provided the details of ordinary life in the incidents of the plays. Actors, therefore, could not immerse themselves in realistic moments as they might in life. Instead, like the sculptor, the actor created a figure that was both real and ideal.

Interesting recent research indicates that the actor became more and more important in the theatre during the 5th century. In the middle of the century (449), a contest for actors was initiated alongside the competition for playwrights, indicating a growing recognition of the actor's importance in the presentation of the play and an ability to distinguish excellence. A tradition of father-son actor combinations indicates the probability that actors learned their trade through apprenticeship. Of specific acting techniques we know very little, although a 4th-century source describes an actor using his own son's ashes as a prop to increase the emotional power of his performance.

A major performance feature was the use of a chorus. Accompanied by a flute player (the musical instrument was akin to a double oboe), the chorus remained in the playing area throughout the play. It was probably composed of twelve members for the plays of Aeschylus and fifteen for later playwrights. The chorus sang an ode between each incident of the action and occasionally split into two groups to alternate singing the stanzas of the ode. During the incidents themselves, lines were delivered by a chorus leader. The chorus was dressed according to its role in the play, for it was always integrated into the action. The dramatic impact of the Greek chorus is difficult for a reader to comprehend because most of their odes were sung and danced. Few records remain of the nature of either the music or the movement, but the fact that choruses were used long after their dramatic utility had waned suggests that they contributed considerably to the visual spectacle of the plays. The Greek word for chorus is akin to the word for dance, and some modern critics think this indicates a highly physical, choreographed role.

The functions of the chorus varied from one playwright to the next and also varied according to the action of a particular play. In general, its importance was considerably greater than that of the chorus of a modern musical comedy, for example. The presence of the chorus emphasized the communal nature of Athenian life and theatre. Chiefly, the chorus represented the people most interested in and affected by the action of the play. As such, their commentary developed the broader implications of the action, giving it a moral and communal framework. Often, the chorus summarized the action and explored the relationship of that action and the concepts of justice. Their presence reminded the audience that what was taking place had meaning for them as well as for the people in the play. Also, the chorus frequently participated in the action, urging the protagonist to follow a particular course of action or withholding information from another character. The chorus almost always associated its fate with that of the protagonist. Finally, the use of the chorus provided visual and aural variety. The rhythms of the poetry in which the tragedies were written was such that each component of the play was carefully structured to achieve an effect through sound and movement as well as meaning. The chorus offered a good playwright an excellent opportunity to elaborate on those rhythms.

Another difference between the Hellenic and modern theatres was costume, particularly the use of masks. The masks were built of linen, cork, or wood. There was little distortion in the face (except the mouth for audibility). Painted wrinkles, eyebrows, and the like were common. Most masks covered the entire face and included hair appropriate to the character. Apart from the mask, the actor customarily wore clothes similar to daily wear, although they would be appropriate to the character being portrayed. The basic garment was a *chiton*, a richly patterned full-length tunic with long sleeves. Its color and detail varied according to the character but could be highly elaborate, particularly for tragedy. The long sleeves helped to cover the actor's identity

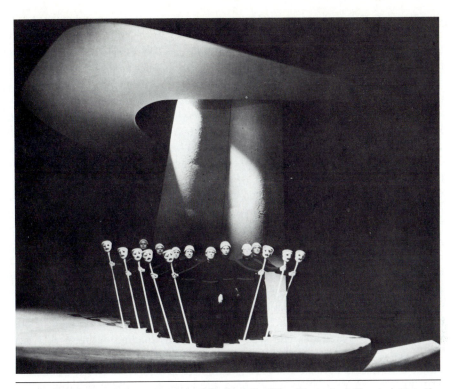

The chorus in a modern production of *Oedipus the King* (Darmstadt Theatre). Note the use of masks.   *Courtesy German Information Center. Photo: Pit Ludwig*

and allowed him to play multiple roles. When an actor changed roles, he would put on a different mask but not change his chiton. He might, however, add a shawl, or *himation*, to vary his costume. A soft leather boot, or *kothornos*, with no heel that extended to the calf was worn on the foot.

At times, however, the plays seem to call for very particular and unusual costumes. The scripts refer to armor, special cloaks, and other distinctive personal items. In addition, the chorus in some cases represented animals or special classes of people, and it seems likely that special costumes were developed for those plays.

Audience

The audience that gathered to watch these plays represented a cross section of the populace. Nearly one-tenth of the population could attend the theatre on a given day, and there is some indication that tickets were issued and possibly an admission fee was charged. A fund was established to provide tickets for the poor, and dignitaries, men, women, boys, and slaves all were allowed to attend. Priests, visiting dignitaries, civic officials, and those who were receiving honors from the city were seated in the front rows. Others were seated in sections along with their "tribes," although precise seats were not assigned.

Standards of Judgment

Few critical writings from the period exist at all. The Greek philosopher Aristotle (384–322 BCE), writing more than 100 years later, developed a theory of theatre in his *Poetics* (c. 335–323 BCE) that refers to the plays of the earlier period as examples of good drama. The *Poetics* has been a standard for criticism throughout history, and widely varying interpretations have developed in different time periods. Although we cannot know if Aristotle reflects the attitudes and tastes of the 5th century, he presents the clearest statement of a critical standard available and has been highly influential.

Aristotle asserted that tragedy is the imitation of an action that is serious, has magnitude, and is complete in itself. Also, tragedy is in dramatic form, arouses feelings within us, and resolves those feelings in its conclusion. By imitation, Aristotle did not mean mimicry. Rather imitation referred to the re-creation of a full and complete action that is drawn from life experience. An effective action therefore is one with consequences for the character and with potential meaning for the audience. Falling on a banana peel is an action, but it tells little of the person who fell except that he or she is clumsy. It also says little to the audience about life, except to beware of banana peels. Aristotle believed that tragedy is serious when it deals with subjects that have a certain magnitude. The subjects are serious because they have scope and dimension beyond the confines of the story itself. The characters learn from the action and the audience learns with the characters. The action therefore has magnitude because it has been developed to the point that the universal significance of the action is evident. This significance occurs because the play is complete in itself. That is, it provides all the elements that are needed for an audience to comprehend the play fully.

Tragedy is dramatic in form, not narrative. It doesn't tell a story in the past tense. It re-creates the action in the present tense. It creates the illusion of virtual time and space, arousing in the audience the sensation of experiencing the action itself. For Aristotle, these feelings were pity and fear: pity that the action had to occur, and fear that the action could also happen to them. Finally, Aristotle believed that tragedy must resolve those feelings by its conclusion. In the resolution, the audience comes to a new understanding of itself and the world. It learns from the emotional changes that have occurred during the action. It has been generally accepted that Aristotle's conception of theatre has provided a starting point for the development of theories of theatre by later writers.

The creative combination of these elements allowed Greek theatre to achieve its greatness. After a lengthy period of preparation by all concerned, these elements combined to produce the theatre as an important community event. The *City Dionysia* began with a Dionysian processional, celebrated by the entire city. The return of the procession to the city was followed by the performance of 10 dithyrambs by the 10 tribes of Athens. Five were performed by choruses of men and five by boys, with each chorus composed of 50 members. After 487 BCE, five comedies by different authors were performed on the second day. Three days were then devoted to tragedies, with four plays written by a single author being given each day. Three of these plays were tragedies, often revolving around one subject or theme, while the fourth was a satyr play, a burlesque treatment of a mythical theme featuring a chorus of half-human, half-animal followers of Dionysus. Following these three days for the tragic playwrights, an assembly was held on the last day to award prizes and discuss any problems that occurred during the festival.

The theatre provided an opportunity for the citizenry to come together to reaffirm its ethical foundation through the religious procession and dithyrambs, through the dramatic ideas of the playwrights, and at the final assembly. In part, the greatness of Greek drama lay in its ability to express the ideas of the community and thereby bring its citizens closer together. Its greatness also lay in the achievements of its individual playwrights, who developed the unique combination of religious ritual, ethical ideas, and creative imagination that resulted in our Western concept of drama.

DRAMATIC LITERATURE

The brothers of Antigone and Ismene have been killed in battle, one defending Thebes and the other attacking it. The new Theban ruler, Creon, has decreed that the body of the brother who attacked the city should be left unburied as punishment for his action. Antigone believes it sacrilegious to leave her brother's body to rot in the open air. She believes in a law higher than human decree, and that law forbids her from leaving his body uncleansed. Creon insists that to disobey him is to invite an end to civic law and order. When Antigone cares for the body, Creon condemns her to die in a cave. His own son argues for her pardon, but to no avail. The chorus speaks on her behalf, also without success. Finally, a prophet convinces Creon that he has been too harsh. Creon realizes he has upset the balance in life by caring more about his own status than about justice. He rushes to the cave, but he arrives to find that Antigone has hanged herself. His son, who was betrothed to Antigone, tries to kill Creon, but kills himself when he fails. Further tragedy befalls Creon when his wife dies because of her sorrow over their son's death. As the play ends, Creon is left alone in this world to ponder the tragedy of human existence.

When Sophocles wrote *Antigone,* tragic drama had been in existence for less than a century. Yet in those few decades the Greeks provided the world with the outlines of tragedy that would continue in use to the present day. In the works of Aeschylus, Sophocles, and Euripides, they also created three distinct conceptions of the meaning of tragedy. Equally important, the classical Greeks invented the theatrical means by which to visualize their tragedies. Virtually all scenic and staging practices in Western history can be traced to this period of Greek theatre.

A Global Perspective

Early Drama: The Egyptian Evidence

*A*lthough it is safe to say that dramatic performances occurred long before the Athenian civilization, scholars have had difficulty identifying precisely when a ritual or other dramatic event becomes a play. Certainly, many cultures in Asia and Africa had early rituals that included dramatic segments. Some of the most fascinating evidence comes from Egypt.

No evidence exists of a theatre building in Egypt, but texts that might be interpreted as plays do exist. The Abydos Passion Play (named long after its use by those who discovered it) deals with the death of the god Osiris and his eventual descent to the underworld. The text seems to indicate some mimed actions, at least, which has led some scholars to see it as a prototypical drama. This ritual was performed annually as early as 2500 BCE and perhaps as late as 550 BCE.

The so-called Pyramid Texts—writings discovered on the walls of pyramids—also seem to offer dramatic possibilities. Some claims have been disputed on the grounds that fragments were assembled incorrectly or because of a lack of complete texts. One, *The Triumph of Horus*, is the only existing text that might represent a complete drama, although some scholars dispute this claim as well. The text commemoerates the victory of Horus over his enemies and his coronation as king of a unified Egypt and was apparently performed annually for hundreds of years.

The text as transcribed includes a chorus, solo speeches, musical passages, narrative, and pantomimed action, along with several passages of stage directions and possible indications of audience participation. Although dating is nearly impossible, some scholars feel the play may have been composed as early as 1200 BCE. This may be the only Egyptian drama to have been performed in modern times: a performance was mounted by the Padgate College of Education in June, 1971.

Aeschylus (525–456 BCE)

Despite our very limited knowledge of Aeschylus, such information as does exist warrants labeling him both the first dramatist in Western culture and one of the most significant of any age. So revered was he by Athenians that a century after his death anyone wishing to produce one of his plays in the festivals was automatically accorded the opportunity to do so. Only seven of his plays still exist, three of them part of a single trilogy, *The Oresteia* (458–457 BCE). Yet they contain enough of his ideas of life, of drama, and of theatre to fascinate critics and writers in every succeeding age.

The drama of Aeschylus is played out on two planes, one being the realm of the gods in which the pattern of universal justice is articulated, and the other being the city-state in which the pattern of human justice is measured against universal justice. The function of the Aeschylean drama is to elaborate that organic connection to the world that is characteristic of Greek thought in his lifetime. Aeschylus included gods in his plays because the dramatic convention of the gods enabled him to discuss the nature of universal justice *(dike)*.

Aeschylus dramatized the capacity of both humans and gods to suffer. He believed that suffering is universal. He also believed that out of suffering comes

Aeschylus by Lycurgus.   *Phots. Mus. Berlin*

wisdom. Each tragic experience is a component of universal justice; to understand the experience is to understand justice. Because suffering can rarely be avenged or explained at the moment it occurs, Aeschylus expanded the dramatic action onto a vast panorama of interaction between gods and humans and between one generation and another. He reaffirmed the conviction that eternal justice exists, but his affirmation required the scope of human destiny for its explanation. Aeschylus repeatedly created situations in which sin led to sorrow, the experience of sorrow provoked a search for justice, and the search for justice resulted in wisdom. No heinous act went unpunished, even though years might pass before the act was avenged.

This version of reality has a number of dramatic consequences. First, Aeschylus wrote his three tragedies as a single grouping, or trilogy, to demonstrate the ways in which justice reveals itself through human destiny from one year to another. Second, Aeschylus used Greek myths to tell his stories because they evoke a world without time or specificity. However, he adapted the myths to his own needs; he did not simply retell them as they had been told by Hesiod before him. He refashioned them to illuminate the concepts of Athenian law that interested him.

In addition, Aeschylus reduced the size of the chorus from the 50 used in the dithyrambs to a much smaller number, probably only 12. The smaller chorus enabled him to bring them closer to the action. Also, it could share its feelings with the characters and occasionally participate directly in the action. Finally, Aeschylus increased the number of actors from one to two. The first actor had established a question-and-response interchange in the drama; a second actor extended the play across time by announcing offstage actions, leaving and then returning to report new events. The second actor could reappear as another character and thereby develop the protagonist in relationship to a new person. Both of these served Aeschylus's dramatic purposes. The one gave him the dramatic time he needed for his conception of destiny, and the other expanded the possibilities of revealing human suffering.

Aeschylus's sense of theatricality was equal to his philosophy. His ideas are important precisely because they occur in the drama. His belief that universal justice exists in the actions of individuals is effective because the audience witnesses the suffering. Aeschylus wrote plays because he could not express his philosophy any other way. He made his audiences share the tragedies of others and thereby understand themselves and their world more fully.

The Oresteia dramatizes the story of the murder of Agamemnon by his wife, Clytemnestra (the subject of the first play in the trilogy), the revenge of the murder by their son, Orestes (the subject of the second play), and then, in the third play, the determination of the punishment of Orestes for his crime. Aeschylus opposes an old conception of justice, in the chorus of Furies who chase Orestes for his mother's murder, against a new conception of justice in which the patron goddess Athena establishes the first jury of citizens to decide Orestes' fate. When Athena casts the deciding vote in favor of Orestes against the Furies, the drama explodes in a magnificent theatrical celebration with a second chorus bearing torches and singing joyfully of the dawn of a new era of civic justice. The playwright's theatricality is also demonstrated in the horrifying murders of the first two plays, the appearance of the ghost of Clytemnestra in the third play, and the use of the chorus as Furies.

Sophocles (496–406/5 BCE)

Sophocles presented a different tragic vision. For him, tragedy came not from the suffering requisite to wisdom but from the realization of the inevitability of suffering. He believed that the magnificence of the human spirit is its ability to recognize the pattern of universal justice in one's life. He therefore focused the drama on a single individual. His protagonists realized the causes of their tragedy during the action of the play. In fact, this awareness made them tragic heroes, for in their desire to know the truth they gained heroic stature. They realized that justice had been served by their suffering and they accepted that fate.

Sophocles' tragic vision was that a rational justice prevails in the universe and justice is revealed through the destinies of individuals. The only way to understand that justice is to realize and accept one's own personal destiny. Although the hero should count himself lucky if no sorrow befalls him, he must accept sorrow if it comes. In that way he learns both about himself and about the nature of universal justice. Sophocles, then, shifted the dramatic focus from an overall pattern of existence to individual destiny. He knew the entire myth of Oedipus, for example, but his play included only the moment when Oedipus must confront the truth of his past actions. The power of the play lies in experiencing Oedipus's realization and in witnessing the impact it has on him. The audience may be saddened by Oedipus's fate, but his handling of that fate enriches them.

Sophocles' conception of character is more akin to the psychological orientation of the modern reader. Living in the age that first sought to define the nature of the soul (psyche), Sophocles probed the depths of human motivation with great insight and determination. He accepted the fallibility of human nature, but he also admired its potentiality. He recognized that the soul possesses the capacity for error (hamartia) and he believed that tragedy derives from such errors in spite of the overriding goodness of the individual. To illustrate this dramatically, Sophocles first limited the scope of the action of a play to the single error that the hero has committed. To create tension, he withheld the final revelation of that error until the character had been fully developed. To give the final tragedy greater impact, he developed the hero's basic goodness, making his downfall more poignant. In developing this goodness, Sophocles revealed his belief that the human soul is capable of rational balance and harmony. Sophocles invested his hero with nobility of soul marred by a fatal error. This error mars the symmetry and proportion of the character, and these qualities are as essential to a human life as they are to an artistic creation.

In dramatizing the tragedy of the individual, Sophocles made a number of important changes in dramatic structure. First, he discarded the trilogy; instead, he wrote distinct single plays. Second, he added a third actor to give himself more dramatic flexibility. With the third actor, he could introduce more characters who would challenge the protagonist more fully and show the impact of the tragedy on more than one life. A third change was to increase the size of the chorus to 15 and to modify its function. The chorus still participated in the action (they are the citizens of Thebes in *Oedipus*, suffering because there is a plague in the city), but they did so as

A scene from a modern production of *Antigone* (University of Oregon).

witnesses more than as agents of change. Their choral odes are primarily transitions between the separate incidents of the action.

The theatrical effectiveness of Sophocles results from many elements. He sharply delineated his characters by giving each of them a complex set of motives. He demonstrated how character can be revealed through interaction with other characters. He developed the first three-character scenes in which the audience watches how different people respond to news from their own private perspectives. This in turn led to his use of dramatic irony, in which one person's joy is another's unhappiness. He virtually created the modern conception of the tragic hero, and tragedy today owes as much to Sophocles as to any other individual.

Euripides (c. 485–406 BCE)

Euripides, writing between 440 and 406, reflects the vast changes that took place in Athenian thought and politics after the death of Aeschylus. His plays are filled with mistrust of universal logic. His dramatic techniques include pessimism, cynicism, and despair. Euripides found no balance or proportion in the universe, nor did he see a harmonious rhythm between universal order and human action. His characters yearn for spiritual beauty, but they seldom find it in their destinies or in the actions of others. They are, for the most part, victims of irrational forces that swirl around and within them. The chaos in their lives offers little opportunity for self-awareness or understanding. Whether Euripides was religious or cynical (and critics have argued both), his plays were studies of passion unchecked by logic.

Euripides expressed the passionate nature of human beings by giving his characters conflicting feelings, unleashed desires, and subconscious motives. Some feel overwhelmed by their feelings because they are unable to control them. Others pursue a single goal without realizing the consequences of doing so. Whatever their situation, the characters are dramatized at their moment of greatest passion. The climax of tragedy for Euripides is the moment when circumstances have evoked the full extent of human emotion.

For example, Medea (*Medea*, 431 BCE) murders her brother and leaves her homeland to be with her husband, Jason. Euripides begins the dramatic action when Jason spurns Medea for another woman. He gives voice to Medea's fury and to her determination for revenge. When she fails to convince Jason to modify his decision, she kills their two children in order to wound Jason as deeply as she can. Despite her own love of the children, Medea must find some means of expressing her passion.

Euripides' contributions to the drama are considerable, despite his dismal view of life, or perhaps because of it. He expanded the possibilities of characterization to reveal the complexity of human passion. His language evoked the irrational forces in human nature. He visualized the plight of the victims of tragedy, drawing attention to their justified anger at the gods. He broke the link between the drama and the gods, proving that tragedy is great even if it has no explanation in the universe. As such, many critics regard him as the first realist in drama, because he presented human situations as they actually occur. He did not express the ideals of his age, but he expressed its concerns. He showed people struggling to survive in a hostile world where events are beyond their control. At times, they succeed, as in his version of the story of Helen of Troy (*Helen*, 412 BCE). When they fail, as in *Medea* or *The Trojan Women* (415 BCE), the audience is left to ponder the injustices done to them. Euripides provides few answers to these situations, for he was the first playwright in history to sense the loneliness of the soul and the precariousness of human existence.

Comedy and Aristophanes (c. 447–c. 380 BCE)

The creative genius of Aeschylus, Sophocles, and Euripides has given Athens its place as the first home of tragedy. The Hellenes, however, were no less able to laugh at themselves, and the development of comedy also occurred there. It would therefore be inappropriate to leave Classical Athens without discussing the plays of Athens's great comic writer, Aristophanes. Aristophanes was not the first writer of comedies. In fact, he drew on a long tradition of comic and dramatic experience.

Comedy developed from two sources, the revels surrounding the Dionysian festival and the structure of tragedy. The festivals relied on interaction with the audience, on burlesques of well-known individuals, blunt sexuality, and animal disguises. From tragedy, comedy adopted the use of 3 actors (expanding that to 5 on occasion), a chorus of 12 (doubling that to 24 at times), a series of dramatic incidents with choral odes between them, and a hero who is attempting to bring about some new order of social justice.

Old Comedy, which is the term for the plays of the 5th century, included a prologue delivered to the audience, followed by the development of the plot, and then a long speech by the chorus to the audience called the *parabasis*. This speech reflected

GREEK PLAYWRIGHTS AND PLAYS

Aeschylus (525–456 BCE)

The Persians	472 BCE
The Seven Against Thebes	467 BCE
The Oresteia (Trilogy made up of **Agamemnon,**	458–457 BCE
The Choephori, The Eumenides)	

Sophocles (496–406/5 BCE)

Antigone	c. 441 BCE
Oedipus the King	c. 430 BCE
Electra	c. 415 BCE
Oedipus at Colonus (produced after his death)	401 BCE

Euripides (c. 485–406 BCE)

Medea	431 BCE
The Trojan Women	415 BCE
Electra	c. 413 BCE
Bacchae	c. 406 BCE

Aristophanes (c. 447–c. 380 BCE)

Acharnians	425 BCE
Clouds	423 BCE
Lysistrata	411 BCE
Frogs	405 BCE

Menander (c. 342–c. 291 BCE)

The Grouch	316 BCE

Note: Some dates are approximate, based on available evidence.

the views of the playwright and often did not particularly concern itself with the subject of the play. It was followed by a few loose scenes to bring the plot to a conclusion, then by an epilogue. The parabasis and direct address to the audience in the prologue and epilogue suggest the social and civic orientation of comedy.

Only eleven Aristophanes's plays survive the period, including *The Birds* (414 BCE), *Peace* (421 BCE), and *Lysistrata* (411 BCE). Writing primarily between 425 and 385 BCE, Aristophanes subjected the entirety of Athenian life to his scrutiny and ridicule. He used a variety of comic techniques available to attack virtually every major politician of his age, every literary charlatan, and every self-important philosopher. He burlesqued the lifestyle of farmers and city-dwellers. He laughed at the pretensions of the old and the naiveté of the young. He particularly enjoyed making fun of male-female relationships. Because the objects of attack are diverse, he has been labeled conservative or radical by different critics. More to the point, he attacked authority figures, sometimes because they deserved it and at other times simply because they were authority figures.

His comic techniques included the creation of an elaborate imaginary edifice around which the plot was woven. For example, *The Birds* is the story of a man who convinces the birds to build a new city in the heavens because Athens is not a fit place in which to live. A second comic technique was exaggeration, in which a character or an incident is expanded beyond expectation. *Lysistrata* tells of a decision by the women of Athens to withhold sexual favors from their husbands until the men end a war and return home. A third technique of Aristophanes is sexual humor, with extensive references to the sexual prowess of the characters. Fourth, Aristophanes lampooned prominent Athenians in his plays. For example, he satirized many of the generals who were engaged in the Peloponnesian War. Finally, Aristophanes centered his plays on a single comic hero, someone with base motives whose goal is to make life easier for himself and whose wit and cunning engage the audience on his side.

Modern productions of Aristophanes are presented with two major problems: the objects of his satire are unknown to contemporary audiences, and the overt sexuality of the language and action is more than theatre custom accepts today. Yet, his plays are significant. They provide extensive information about Athenian daily life. They established many of the comic devices used in later ages. They remind us that the Hellenic audience could laugh at itself and its authority figures (including the gods) and that it could respect a playwright who spoke out against the policies of his government. In his combination of social thought and comic technique, Aristophanes is ranked with Shakespeare and Molière as the finest of the comic playwrights in Western culture.

CONNECTIONS

Since the Romans first turned to the Greeks for models of theatre, the influence of Greek concepts has been a major determinant of the development of Western theatre. Although our perceptions of Greek theatre are greatly colored by the interpretations of the Renaissance and other intervening epochs, the traditional stance in Western theatre considers the Greek theatre as the foundation for later developments. While it may be difficult for current practitioners to know what is authentically Greek and what has been altered by centuries of study and criticism, the influence of the Greek theatre continues as a dominant force.

In their love of play and their desire to know the world through action, the Hellenes provided the formative concepts of the drama. They developed both tragedy and comedy to express their understanding of the world. They made theatre a social art by using it to bring the community together to laugh, think, and feel. They realized that the theatre can help to integrate the community through its discussion of universal justice, human nature, and social justice.

The outlines of the Western concept of performance space are also derived from the Greeks. The placement of the audience in Greek theatres remains the norm today. The use of the orchestra as an open playing space in front of the scene is noticeable today as the orchestra pit (or as the forestage of some theatres). Their side entrances for the entrance and exit of the chorus can be seen in many contemporary theatre structures. Also, their scene building and painted scenery were the first efforts in Western culture to give specific location to a dramatic action. The Greeks invented the first stage machinery to enhance the action. They used costumes and masks that continued in use for centuries and are still imitated in many revivals of Greek plays. In sum, every aspect of theatrical production was given particular shape and form by the Greeks in Classical Athens.

The Athenians also provided the outlines for all of Western drama. They unified the dramatic action by advancing the concept of plot, or arrangement of incidents. They conceived of character as a reflection of human nature and experience. They invested their stories with themes of universal and social justice. They were poets who constructed their concepts of action with words. They integrated music both in the sounds of the words and in the use of choral odes and instrumental accompaniment. Perhaps most important, the Greek playwrights added spectacular theatrical effects to visualize their dramatic actions.

Finally, in the work of three writers, the Greeks gave to future generations the outlines of three different tragic visions of life. Aeschylus established the connection between individual human action and the patterns of history and the universe. He recognized the capacity of the soul for suffering, and noted the connection between suffering and free will. Sophocles recognized the tragic consequences of self-knowledge. He saw in the process of human life the search to understand oneself. Euripides provided an awareness of the passionate side of human activity. He dramatized the irrational forces in human nature, and depicted the feelings of individuals lost in a world without meaning.

To say that Western drama is the invention of the Greeks is only a slight exaggeration. No other age would as radically alter the drama until the invention of electronic media in the 20th century. Nevertheless, the contributions of later societies would expand the scope and potentiality of the theatre and drama. In their own way, these alterations would prove as valuable and creative as the original inventions of the Greeks.

SOURCES FOR FURTHER STUDY

Social/Art/Philosophy Background

Becatti, Giovanni. *The Art of Ancient Greece and Rome: From the Rise of Greece to the Fall of Rome.* New York: Harry N. Abrams, n.d.

Charbonneaux, Jean, Roland Martin, and Francois Villard. *Archaic Greek Art.* Trans. James Emmers and Robert Allen. New York: George Braziller, 1971.

Dinsmor, William Bell. *The Architecture of Ancient Greece: An Account of Its Historic Development.* New York: B. T. Batsford, 1950.

Ehrenberg, Victor. *From Solon to Socrates.* London: Methuen & Co., 1967.

Hamilton, Edith. *The Greek Way.* New York: W. W. Norton & Co., 1930.

Jaeger, Werner. *Paedeia: The Ideals of Greek Culture.* Vol. 1. Trans. Gilbert Highet. New York: Oxford University Press, 1965.

Kostof, Spiro. *A History of Architecture: Settings and Rituals.* New York: Oxford University Press, 1985.

Leonard, George. *The Ultimate Athlete.* New York: Viking Press, 1975.

Onians, John. *Art and Thought in the Hellenistic Age.* London: Thames and Hudson, 1979.

Pomeroy, Sarah B. *Goddesses, Whores, Wives, and Slaves: Women in Classical Antiquity.* New York: Schocken Books, 1975.

Greek Theatre

Arnott, Peter. *The Ancient Greek and Roman Theatre.* New York: Random House, 1971.

Bieber, Margaret, *The History of the Greek and Roman Theater.* 2d ed. Princeton, N.J.: Princeton University Press, 1961.

Pickard-Cambridge, A. *The Dramatic Festivals of Athens.* 2d ed. Oxford: Oxford University Press, 1968.

Simon, Erika. *The Ancient Theatre.* Trans. C. E. Vafopoulou-Richardson. London: Methuen, 1972.

Taplin, Oliver. *Greek Tragedy in Action.* Berkeley: University of California Press, 1978.

Trendall, A. D., and T. B. L. Webster. *Illustrations of Greek Drama.* New York: Phaidon, 1971.

Walton, J. Michael. *The Greek Sense of Theatre.* London: Methuen, 1984.

Webster, T. B. *Greek Theatre Production.* London: Methuen, 1970.

Greek Drama

Aristotle. *The Rhetoric and the Poetics.* Trans. W. Rhys Roberts and Ingram Bywater. New York: Modern Library, 1954.

Baldry, H. C. *The Greek Tragic Theatre.* London: Chatto & Windus, 1971.

Hathorn, Richmond Y. *Tragedy, Myth and Mystery.* Bloomington, Ind.: Indiana University Press, 1962.

Kitto, H. D. F. *Form and Meaning in Drama.* London: Methuen & Co., 1956.

————. *Greek Tragedy.* London: Methuen & Co., 1939.

Kott, Jan. *The Eating of the Gods: An Interpretation of Greek Tragedy.* Trans. Boleslaw Taborski and Edward J. Czerwinski. New York: Random House, 1970.

Podlecki, Anthony J. *The Political Background of Aeschylean Tragedy.* Ann Arbor: University of Michigan Press, 1966.

Thomson, George. *Aeschylus and Athens.* London: Lawrence and Wishart, 1941.

CHAPTER

3

General Events	Rome founded BCE 753
Arts Events	
Theatre History Events	

Rome

On a spring day in the year 100 CE the difficulty facing a young Roman citizen was not a lack of entertainment but the problem of choosing from the vast variety of events available. For a few coins, he could spend several pleasant hours at the baths. These vast "cathedrals of paganism" (as one critic called them) were lavish, beautifully decorated with sculptures and mosaics, and warm. Here he could participate in athletics in the gymnasium, bathe in heated pools, languish in a steam bath, and engage in spirited, lively conversation. The baths were a great place for people-watching and gossiping, and a chance to show off or brag of one's achievements.

However, many other diversions were available nearby. Chariot races at the Circus Maximus offered excitement. There he could join with a group of his friends to cheer on their current favorite. Now this might lead to a small encounter with a rival's fans, but that would only add to the excitement.

Even more enticing to some Romans were the gladiator battles at the amphitheatre. Here fans developed great loyalties to favorite combatants, and from time to time a gladiator was exiled because there had been too many riots when he appeared. Crowd favorites were battles in which both gladiators fought to exhaustion and the one left standing turned to the patron for a decision on whether the fallen combatant should live or die. To experience that moment of tension and to see such bravery exhibited by the participants was more than enough reason for attending.

A final choice was the theatre and the spectacle it provided. A production

Roman Republic | First Punic War | Third Punic War; Carthage destroyed | Augustus | Fall of Rome (variously dated)

c. 500 — 264–241 — 218–202 — 150–146 — 49–44 — 27 — CE 4 — 450

Second Punic War | Julius Caesar rules | Birth of Jesus (crucified c. 30 AD)

Vergil's *Aeneid* — Ovid's *Metamorphoses*

c. 27 — c. 16 — CE c. 5 — 80

De Architectura; Horace, *Odes* — Colosseum

First theatrical performance: Rome | Livius Andronicus | Terence's *The Menaechmi* | Pantomime

BCE 364 — 264 — c. 240 — c. 205 — c. 165 — 75 — 22

First gladiatorial contest | Plautus's *The Braggart Warrior* | First permanent theatre

of *Clytemnestra* boasted that more than 600 mules were used in the production, and nearly every performance included at least one major battle scene of some sort. For a lighter mood, the mimes offered bawdy farce performed in an athletic style. Further diversion was presented by the jugglers, high-wire performances, fire-eaters, and acrobats. Fretting over the choice of entertainment was unnecessary. If you didn't like one activity, you were free to leave and go to another.

This spectrum of entertainment was common in the days of the Roman Empire. However, in discussing the theatres of Rome, two very contrasting periods in Roman history must be distinguished: the republican period (from approximately 500 BCE to the reign of Augustus in 27 BCE) and the imperial period (the era of the emperors to the fall of Rome in the mid-400s CE). Much of what is commonly thought or believed about the society of Rome is derived from the empire: the images of gladiators, huge spectacles, Roman soldiers encamped in foreign countries, mad or vengeful emperors, and so forth. The comedies of ancient Rome, however, derive from the republican era, more than 150 years before the first emperor.

Family life among the citizens of the Roman Republic was vastly different from that of the modern American family. The *pater familias*, or head of the family, was usually the senior male in the family, although a son could establish his independence and exercise control over his own family. The power of this male is astonishing by modern standards. Legally, the father determined the lives of the rest of the family. He even had the right to kill a new-born child by leaving it to die unattended in the open air.

Once a child had grown, the *pater familias* could not kill his offspring, except under rare circumstances. However, he did have the right to sell them into slavery or marry them to whomever he wished. He could even choose to marry a daughter to someone but keep her within his authority. In the early republic, remaining in the hands of the *pater familias* was advantageous to sons or daughters because it insured their continued financial and familial protection. If a girl were married without power shifting to her husband, she continued to worship the gods of her father rather than those of her husband. Even if she was placed under the power of her husband, her parents could still take a great interest in her well-being.

As a result, the welfare of a potentially large number of people was dependent on the head of the family. He alone controlled the expenditure of money to anyone who was legally "in his hands." Consequently, Roman plays are filled with young men who are destitute of funds and scheming with their slaves to get money, usually to buy a courtesan. These young men are not poor, however; they are merely dependent on their fathers for their income. To slight the father is to risk losing all financial independence (and being stricken from the will). One of the classic situations in Roman comedy occurs when a young man wants to get money from his father to buy a woman, only to discover that the father has decided to buy her, too. The young man cannot easily compete with his father, for to incur his wrath may cost him his financial freedom.

The primary function of the women was to marry and bear children. However, the Roman matron could receive some education and she was frequently appreciated for her knowledge and intelligence. Also, the central role played by the family in the affairs of the citizens gave informal authority to mothers who understood their children and could communicate effectively about them with their husbands. This led to two types of mothers in comedy. One was the stereotyped image of the nagging wife often found in Roman comedy. The other was the Roman matron, one of the most endearing and sensitive characters in Roman literature. Husbands may have complained about their wives, but children almost always honored and cherished their mother's love and opinion.

Religion

The Romans seem not to have been in awe of the universe, nor particularly in love with it. They accepted it on its own terms, looking for ways to adjust and adapt to it. They knew that they did not control their own destinies, but this led them to ask how to cope with that fact rather than to ask why it was so. As a consequence, the Romans were less inclined than the Greeks to perceive a rational justice in the universe; instead, they perceived the events of life to be fickle, uncertain, and indifferent.

In addition, Roman religious practice was characterized by a proliferation of gods and cults adopted from conquered peoples. No one belief system dominated Rome. Instead, each family worshipped its own gods. Consequently, religious festivals were not a time for the whole community to come together. They were state occasions with little shared religious meaning.

No discussion of religion in the Roman era can ignore the history of the Christians. From a small persecuted group on the fringes of the empire in the century following Jesus' death, Christianity grew until it was legalized by the Edict of Milan in 313 CE. The growth was neither steady nor easy: the emperors Domitian (in 93 CE), Trajan (in 111 CE), Decius (in 250 CE), and Diocletian (in 302 CE) were particularly severe in their persecution of this relatively new religious sect. In 395 CE, however, Christianity was declared the official and only religion of Rome by Theodosius.

Because the festivals were the location of the theatrical performances as they had been for the Greeks, this reduction in the religious component of the festivals had great consequences for the drama. The theatre lost its moral perspective. The imagery of gods and justice was replaced with imagery of the home and civil law. Characters rarely discussed ethical issues or questioned the meaning of life. No choruses existed to draw meaning from the events of the play. Characters lived in the streets of Rome; they were not drawn from religious myths or history. The playwrights seldom stopped the action to point out the relation between the plot and a problem in society. Roman theatre was not the world of the Greeks, where the limits of a person's power were tested. In the world of the Roman citizen the ordinary and the mundane were uppermost in the minds of the characters.

Law

The minor role of religion in the life of the non-Christian Roman is countered by the primacy and supremacy of law. The complexity of Roman civilization and the vast variety of peoples it included (as the result of the Punic Wars in the Republic and the conquering of foreign lands during the empire) made the establishment of a permanent set of "rules" impossible. The growth of a huge urban center necessitated new approaches to the organization of society. Instead of concepts of right and wrong, Roman law developed as a system of regulations. Rather than an ideal, justice was a process.

The law was created by humans and could be changed by humans. Senators, assemblymen, philosophers, judges, and lawyers all contributed to the development of the law. And the law covered every aspect of Roman life: marriage, land, slavery, travel, and even entertainment. The law applied to all people (even slaves were protected against unjust cruelty and the emperor was also subject to the law).

The basic "fairness" of this law and the Roman ability to adapt to a constantly changing world were essential to the development of the Roman Empire. Indeed, Roman law is the basis for the legal systems of most of the countries of the Western world.

THE THEATRE
AND THE
CHRISTIAN
CHURCH

*T*he ostentatious and violent entertainments of Rome inevitably came into conflict with the more conservative leaders of the early Christian church. The church viewed the spectacles and games of wealthy Rome as dangerous diversions that were certain to lead people astray from the rigorous simplicity of the Christian perspective. Christian authors criticized the unruly behavior of spectators, the temptation away from proper concerns, the lewd and violent content of the entertainments, and the inhumanity of the slaughters.

The dominant Christian position is best summarized in the writings of Tertullian. An African writer from Carthage, Tertullian was a priest for a major portion of his life, and his writings generally were composed between 196 and 212 CE. One of his earliest works, *De Spectaculis*, referred most directly to the theatre, and further attacks on the theatre are contained in many of his other writings.

Tertullian was writing to fellow Christians—both those of long standing and those newly converted. He warned that attendance at the spectacles would lead to sin and cited two specific reasons. First, the spectacles originated in idolatrous worship, and to participate in them would deny one's own Christian faith. He noted that the earliest plays were folk festivals in honor of Liber, a Greek god closely related to Dionysus, and the Circus, a major site of the games, was a temple to the Sun. Secondly, attendance at the plays undermined morality because the plays roused violent passions that were best controlled. He noted that Christians are urged to deal in tranquillity, gentleness, quiet, and peace and to avoid frenzy, anger, and grief. He wrote that "the theatre's greatest charm is above all produced by its filth . . ." and cited cases in which attendance at the theatre resulted in demonic possession and even death. He recognized the lure of theatre, but urged his readers to consider all temptations of the spectacles ". . . whether manly or honorable or sonorous or melodious or tender . . . [as] drippings of honey from a poisoned cake. . . ." The true Christian, he asserted, will turn away from the circus, the theatre, and the stadium and focus on the teachings of Christ, which will provide even greater delight, awaiting the greatest spectacle of all—the Last Judgment.

Although Tertullian's writings are persuasively written, they appear to have had little effect on the theatre. Church decrees urged Christians to stay away from the theatre and even threatened excommunication to any who attended on Holy Days instead of going to church, but no ruler ever issued an official ban on theatre, and performances continued until the fall of Rome.

The Christian opposition to theatre was maintained by later councils and individual writers. St. Augustine, writing in the 5th century CE, condemned the drama for creating plays that honored false gods. The Canons of Concilium Trullanum, a church edict issued in 692, spoke against mimes, theatres, dancing, bear-baiting, and comic and satyric masks. By 813, clergy were banned from attending any form of secular theatre performance, and actors were banned from membership in the church. *

Interestingly, these edicts and treatises against theatre were apparently unsuccessful, for similar statements continued to be made for hundreds of years. Indeed, the protests of the church against the theatre prove the existence of theatre through these "dark ages." Although theatre was not officially sanctioned and therefore apparently purged from any formal records or sanctioned writings, the constant worry about the dangers of theatre argues convincingly that an active theatre tradition existed.

ARTS IDEAS

Domestic Art

The ordinary and mundane were also the concern of the visual arts. Rome constructed heroic arches and columns to honor its emperors in the Empire period, but in the Republic period the focus was on domestic life. Art was not created for the entire community, but for the individual family. Throughout the home of a wealthy citizen, portrait busts, portraiture, sculpture, and wall paintings proliferated. These objects were status symbols of the owners, but their larger purpose was to honor and solidify the family. Prominent family members, including the *pater familias* and the matron, were rendered in busts and portraiture. Scenes of daily activities, including the theatre, could also be found in wall paintings. The extensive use of art to adorn the homes of Roman citizens suggests that the acquisition of property was a positive virtue. It illustrates once again the power of the family. Roman comedy's emphasis on domestic life is therefore part of a much broader interest expressed through other arts.

Sculpture

The artistic style that dominated the domestic arts of Rome showed a preference to re-create things as they are rather than as they ought to be. This art appeals more to the memory than the mind. Even when depicting that which does not exist—images of gods, for instance—naturalism renders the nonexistent in the language of the real

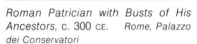

Roman Patrician with Busts of His Ancestors, c. 300 CE. *Rome, Palazzo dei Conservatori*

and possible. It is more likely, however, that naturalism will depict living individuals. Portrait busts of Roman *pater familias* are filled with the wrinkles and warts of reality; they are not refined or smoothed over to suggest the moral or personal qualities of the individual.

Typical of this style is the *Roman Patrician with Busts of His Ancestors,* sculpted about 300 BCE. The face of the patrician is individualized: each facet of the sitter's face is reproduced without any attempt to improve or enhance it. One would expect to meet this individual and not stand in awe of his position in life. The toga is drawn together at the waist with no effort to flatter his physique. Each of the folds is reproduced in spite of their intersecting lines and the overall shapelessness that results. The toga clings to the legs more to suggest the reality of the body than to actually duplicate the skeletal features of the legs. The busts the patrician holds reveal family resemblances and provide the chief integrating feature of the total composition.

With this aesthetic ideal, Roman drama evolved into a style very different from the Greek. Using Greek plays as their base, the playwrights depicted characters who are carefully individuated. They are neither distillations of essential features nor representations of all humans. They are ordinary and mundane, not idealized. Their concerns are those of people of all ages: love, romance, financial security, and domestic strife.

ROMAN THEATRE

The term *theatre* has a broader application when considering Roman performance, as a greater diversity of forms is apparent. Although the spoken drama is still evident, other forms, ranging from dance to athletics, were important and popular theatrical events.

Occasion

As in the Greek theatre, performances of plays were held as part of huge civic festivals. Plays were performed at only four festivals, and this indicates that between 11 and 17 days out of the year were used for theatre performances. However, the actual number is somewhat higher because successful plays were often purchased for performance at special festivals held for religious or civic reasons, and occasionally at games held to honor an individual.

Roman festivals were markedly different from their Greek counterparts, however. Although the four major festivals were ostensibly religious, the worship of the gods was minimized, and participants seldom felt they were participating in a religious ceremony. Rather the mood seems more similar to modern holidays in which the sense of freedom and release from daily chores dominates. In fact, these games, including the drama, were provided by the government specifically to please and placate the populace. The games of the festivals were financed by the government, and the play was only one attraction among many, including athletic contests, circus-type performances, and processions. Admission to all events was free, giving liberty to the spectators to come and go as they wished.

When plays were to be offered as part of the games, officials in charge contracted with a producer, the *dominus gregis*, who purchased a play from a writer for use by his company of actors. The play was thereafter in the hands of the producer, and the playwright received no further benefit from its production. The *dominus* accepted full responsibility for the presentation of the play, knowing that a successful presentation might result in future contracts.

Location

No permanent theatre structures existed in republican Rome. Instead, theatre was performed in a variety of locations, including arenas such as the Circus Maximus, a long oval-shaped outdoor arena also used for chariot competitions and gladiatorial combats. Inside, a temporary stage was constructed on a wooden platform with, in some cases, a short staircase to the ground at the center. The stage itself was long and shallow, perhaps 60 yards wide, with no curtain or other staging devices. Short wings at the sides provided entrances, with one wing representing the way to town, the other the way to the harbor or to the country. Spectators, sometimes numbering in the thousands, crowded around the stage, standing or even bringing their own seats to a play, although special seats for senators and civic officials may have been constructed for certain performances.

Because the theatres were temporary, a basic stage plan was used for all comedies, and no scenery changes occurred. The stage depicted a street represented by painted boards. In contrast to Greek theatre with its action in front of a palace or community structure, the Roman comedies took place in front of the facade of one, two, or three houses with a total of three doors for entrances and exits. The doors were recessed into the wall, creating a small vestibule that probably proved valuable for eavesdropping. Actors entered through the doors or from the sides. Because the stage was long, an actor at one end of the stage could whisper something to the audience about an approaching character without destroying the illusion that that character was unable to overheard what was said. Roman comedies called for more props than were used in Greek drama, especially baggage for returning travelers and items used by the professions of the characters. However, no permanent set pieces or furniture were used on the stage, the audience's imagination being called on to provide more particular settings.

Performers

As many as 14 characters, almost always including a *pater familias*, appear in the comedies, but probably no more than 5 to 7 actors played the roles, although experts dispute the precise means of doubling that were used. In the 3rd century BCE, the playwright took the leading role, but this practice had disappeared by the time of the comedies discussed here. Instead, the *dominus gregis* was the chief actor. He had to be a good singer and an agile athlete and dancer. The rest of the company were either freedmen or slaves. Because of the few number of performances they would give in a year, they received limited training. All the actors were men, but the first appearance of women occurred at about this time in another dramatic form, the mime.

The social status of Roman performers was generally quite low. (The term *grex* used to refer to a troupe of actors also referred to a herd of sheep.) Rather than functioning as community representative in an important ritual as in Greek theatre, the actor was an entertainer. Theatre was a commercial enterprise, and the short playing season indicates that acting was not a profession that would bring in great wealth. Near the end of the Republic, records indicate that a few star performers did accumulate fortunes, but much of this may have come as gifts from admiring patrons rather than as salary.

The acting style of the period can be deduced from the stage conventions and from the lines of the plays. Roman comedy utilized a presentational method of acting, in which the characters turn the action directly out to the audience, recognizing and acknowledging its presence. In some plays, the characters could even break character; that is, they could talk to the audience as actors and then return to portraying their character. Given that the play was performed outdoors before a very large audience by actors impersonating more than one character, the acting style likely included broad gestures, considerable physical action, and frequent looks to the audience for support or asides.

Records indicate that actors were trained in placement of the head and feet, use of the hands, and intonation, particularly in the performance of farce. Each character type had its own specific mannerisms that the audience could recognize. Many of the plays relied on comic devices to fill the size of the stage, including characters running

A tragic actor of the imperial period.
Musées de la Ville de Paris © by SPADEM 1992

breathlessly across stage or shouting for another character who is standing directly behind them.

The plays were performed without act breaks or other intended interruptions. They were adapted from Greek originals that had divided the action by having choral interludes between episodes. When these were cut by the Roman playwrights, monologues or songs were inserted. The comedies did not have a chorus as in Greek Old Comedy, but musical accompaniment throughout portions of the action was common. A double pipe was used to accompany songs, to bridge the action from one scene to another, and indicate a change in the poetic rhythms of the language. Songs were not like those of modern times with repeated melodic lines and short poetic phrases; they were complex lyrical passages, predominantly sung by the lead actor.

The comedies were known as *fabula palliata, fabula* meaning "play" and the latter word referring to the costumes of the actors that were modeled on the Greek New Comedy. Each character wore a Greek-styled tunic (similar to the *chiton*) with a shawl over the shoulders. The length of the tunic varied according to the social station of the character. Female characters wore a long, flowing long-sleeved garment regardless of their social stature. A soft slipper, or *soccus*, was worn on the foot. There is considerable debate whether masks were worn in this time period. Wigs of differing colors and shapes were almost certainly worn and were possibly attached to facial masks that exaggerated the features of the face according to type of character portrayed. The mouth and eyes are particularly prominent in these masks.

Audience

The Roman audience included a wide cross section of Roman society, with men and women both attending, although they were seated separately. Evidence from the prologues and the plays themselves suggests that the audience was extremely active and vocal. In the audience might be a group hired particularly by the producer to react favorably to the play, since crowd reaction could influence officials to hire the troupe again. Acoustics were a problem, and people far from the stage had difficulty hearing. Prologues mention gossiping wives, crying children, and misbehaving slaves, and on more than one occasion huge portions of an audience left during the performance to attend a more entertaining event. For the audience, the theatre was a diversion rather than a ritual obligation.

The Imperial Theatre, c. 200 CE

Two hundred years after the Republic, the Roman theatre was strikingly, even shockingly, different. In some ways the theatre was more popular than it had been. Performances were held on as many as 100 days of the year, and a few actors had achieved great fame and fortune. Permanent theatre buildings were erected to seat as many as 25,000 people in one location, and the variety of theatrical entertainments had increased. However, counter-trends also existed: most actors were barred from full citizenship, virtually no new plays were being written, aristocrats wrote of their disdain for the theatre, and the popularity of the theatre relative to the games had actually declined.

Roman imperial theatre cannot be overlooked, however, because during this time the theatre building developed many elements still found in the theatre today. The first permanent theatre was built in Pompeii about 75 BCE, with the first theatre in Rome coming 20 years later. The Romans primarily attached civic, not religious, significance to the theatre. They therefore built their theatres wherever convenient, often on level ground in the central section of the city.

This site required a building quite different from the Greek theatres that still existed in some locations. Rather than the open amphitheatre, the imperial Roman theatre was one complete structure including the stage house, the stage, and the audience area. The most striking features of the Roman theatre were related to the stage. The orchestra had been reduced to a small semicircle behind which was a raised stage on which the action took place. The stage itself *(pulpitum)* was no more than five to seven feet above the ground, but stretched as wide as the orchestra. The front of the scene building, or *scaenae frons,* was a magnificently decorated facade, two to three stories high, with columns, statues, niches, and porticoes. The number of doors varied, but Romans apparently found it more important to have a beautiful architectural view than to have a flexible stage that would meet the needs of different plays.

Seating was semicircular as in the Greek theatre, but different galleries existed to distinguish the social status of the audience. Tunneled entry ways *(vomitoria)* created easy access to various locations in the audience area. Box seats near the stage were provided for special guests and for those who had paid for the performances, and special boxes to the side of the stage were provided for the tribune. The top row of the audience was the same height from the ground as the top of the stage house, so

Model of the Theatre of Pompey, c. 55 CE.   *Reprinted by Permission of Methuen London*

the entire theatre formed a unified structure, although a clear distinction existed between audience area and performance area.

Two other features of the Roman theatre deserving mention are the addition of a curtain at the front of the stage to open and close the play. Originally, this curtain was most likely in place at the beginning of the show and was dropped into a trench in the floor to indicate the beginning of the performance, but in later days it functioned much like a front curtain does in contemporary theatre. A *velum*, or roof, over a portion of the seating area and stage served as some protection against weather and also helped unify the different elements still further.

On festival days for theatre performances, each of the theatres in Rome would hold entertainments, meaning that as many as 50,000 people witnessed the shows (in contrast to the 250,000 who saw the games in the Colosseum). The theatre competed for the attentions of the spectators with a variety of games that defy belief. Chariot races were held in the circuses, usually 24 per day. Gladiators were trained in a variety of combats to kill one another. A victorious athlete had to prove himself at many games before hoping to win his freedom. Animals were brought into the amphitheatres to fight one another or be slaughtered by human beings. Occasionally the arenas were filled with water to hold *naumachae*, or naval battles, in which ships of defeated enemies fought against and killed one another. At the end of the day, a banquet was given to appease those who lost their savings on gambling and to retain the loyalty of the citizenry.

A TRIP TO THE
ROMAN
THEATRE

---

*I*t is the year 165 BCE. The third Macedonian War within 50 years ended only 3 years ago. Rome is a republic dominated by the patricians. In drama, the great comic writer Plautus died almost 20 years ago, and a new playwright is being talked about as his successor.

A young girl receives permission from her parents to attend the performance of a play with her father and her nurse. A few years ago, she saw her first play at the funeral games held for the death of a distant relative and she loved it.

The occasion for these activities is the *ludi Romani*, or public festival held in honor of Jupiter each September. She adores this time of year, for the city is alive with activity—not only the play but several other amusements occur as well. On the way to the theatre, the trio stop several times to watch street vendors, jugglers, and acrobats. They are jostled repeatedly as slaves run errands for their masters, and wealthy citizens are carried through the streets in individual curtained litters. The girl's father complains about going to the theatre. He is tired of the comedies, mostly because he thinks they are becoming too Greek. When a friend wanders by, the father decides to skip the play and seek some other form of entertainment. He convinces the nurse to take his daughter to the play while he and his friend head for the arena.

The old nurse does not look forward to the play because Terence is the author and everyone knows he is an upstart slave turned playwright who has found favor with an elite group of young aristocrats. She bemoans the passing of the old days when the matron allowed her to see the plays of Plautus. His plays were much funnier, and they always told you what was going to happen so that you didn't have to concentrate so hard.

The nurse and young girl arrive at the Circus Maximus. Recognizing no one they know, they notice that the front rows reserved for the wealthy are already full. The nurse explains that friends and enemies of the playwright come early so that they can make their opinions obvious. The girl and her nurse settle for seats near the back, even though they know it will be difficult to hear the actors over the noise of the audience. As with any outdoor attraction, distractions abound: babies cry, people gossip, children wander around, and people leave and then return again. The girl wonders why people even come to the play if they aren't going to pay attention! An actor enters from the side of the stage and addresses

Theatre masks from the time of Terence. *Courtesy Foto Biblioteca Vaticana*

the audience. He asks them to like the play and defends the author against his literary critics and the jeers of some rowdies seated near the stage. When he finishes, the friends of the author in the front rows applaud mightily, while to one side a roar of approval comes from a cluster of people hired to praise the play.

The play is full of energy and life, and the young girl delights in the confusion of the characters resulting from mistaken identity and at the physical antics of the slave character. The nurse admires the magnificent vocal quality of the lead actor, but the girl waits anxiously for the slave to return, for it his physical stamina and acrobatic skills that make the play exciting. One humorous situation follows another, and the combination of physical action, comedy, and music presents a lively scene that keeps most of the audience's attention easily. The time flies by. When the play is over the girl notices that the nurse didn't even fall asleep.

On their way home, they meet the girl's father, who is in a good mood because he has won a considerable sum of money at a boxing match. As he listens to his daughter recite her favorite moments from the play, he shakes his head at what a sad state Roman comedy is in. What he doesn't know is that the golden age of literature is coming to an end and that Rome will never again produce playwrights of the reputation of Livius Andronicus, Plautus, or Terence.

Standards of Judgment

We cannot be certain as to the critical attitudes that were applied to these diverse forms of performance. It seems that often the patron or emperor was the sole source of approval or disapproval. Spectacle and action, however, seemed to have been of more importance than literary quality.

One important statement of literary standards was written by the poet Horace (65–8 BCE) about 19 BCE. Although Horace's advice seems to have been only partially followed by his contemporaries, his theories were extremely influential on later writers, particularly in the Renaissance.

Horace's concepts of the drama are contained in *Ars Poetica*. The major concern for the dramatist is plausibility, a concern closely allied to the Roman preference for naturalism. Horace maintains that traditional character traits work best, but if originality is used the character must remain consistent throughout the drama. Similarly, a character's words must be suited to the character's age and station in life. Plausibility also demands that gods not be introduced into the action unless absolutely necessary, and that the writer not strive for special effects either in action or language.

Horace also notes the primacy of action, urging authors to avoid lengthy descriptions of off-stage action since appeals to the eye are more powerful than those to the ear. Only those events that might disgust the viewer should be avoided.

Horace further states that plays should be written in five acts, should be brief, and must prove both delightful and useful. Finally he urges the author of drama to rely on the Greeks as models for their plays.

Throughout Roman times, the theatre functioned as a diversion. It did not serve as a means of unifying the citizenry, but rather it served to entertain them or, as one critic attests, to tranquilize them. In an urban situation in which the individual was removed from the sources of power, and cultural unity such as the Athenians knew was absent, theatre served to placate the populace through the provision of entertainment. The theatre's focus on the family strengthened that social structure, and the presentation of athletes from conquered lands demonstrated the glory of Rome. No longer connected to religious practice, the theatre was free to develop in many directions, and a multiplicity of theatrical events developed. Similarly, with the emphasis no longer on the presentation of philosophical ideas, spectacle became a more important element. In the later years, the script itself diminished in importance and the performer became the central focus of the drama.

DRAMATIC LITERATURE

A young man storms out of his house, shouting back at his wife that she is a good-for-nothing. He rushes straight to the audience to complain of the ill treatment he receives from her. He then goes for comfort to his next-door neighbor, his mistress, Erotium. Later, the young man's long-lost twin brother arrives in town in search of him. Everyone mistakes him for his brother, including the wife who nags at him and the mistress who invites him into her home. This long-lost brother is quite convinced that everyone in the town is mad. Meanwhile the first brother wonders why everyone acts as though they have seen him on occasions when he wasn't there. Eventually, the brothers are re-united and the cases of mistaken identity cleared. The young man who had complained of the problems of domestic life at the beginning of the play decides to dispose of his wife and property. He goes off to live with his twin brother in another town. The audience is delighted; they have seen nothing to surprise or shock them. Even the young man's decision to leave his wife forever is accepted as part of the comic conclusion of the play.

The Menaechmi (no date) by Plautus is typical of Roman comedy. The plot revolves around mistaken identity and chance encounters. Rather than discuss philosophical issues, characters complain about daily living. Marital problems, love affairs, and mistresses abound. Buffoonish characters are added to the story solely for the sake of merriment. The audience shares the woes of the major character as if those woes were a part of their lives as well. The world of Roman comedy is the world of domestic theatre, peopled with characters who are concerned with satisfying the basic needs of romance, money, and household tranquillity. So acute were the Roman writers in their perceptions of these concerns that their situations and characters have survived for centuries in adaptations by later writers.

In the Roman Republic, theatre practices were largely an outgrowth of comic mimes and literary comedy. Although the mimes were important of themselves, the written comedies were more so, as they influenced the remainder of Western theatre history. They crystallized in literary form a great number of comedic elements that served as the models for comic writers from Shakespeare and Molière through to the days of television situation comedies. Despite the greatness of Aristophanes' fantasies, medieval and Renaissance writers turned to the plays of Plautus and Terence for their comic characters and plots.

The golden age of Roman comedy came after centuries of popular entertainments. Improvised humor at harvests, dances from the earlier Etruscan culture, and musical medleys are known to have existed in the early days of the Republic. In Southern Italy, farces with masked actors were performed on makeshift wooden stages. In the town of Atella, short verses (called *fabula Atellana*) presented images of daily life in the country. Mimes made their first appearance in Rome around 211 BCE. Because all of these forms were nonscripted, few details survive of their exact nature. They suggest, however, that a strong tradition of comic performance existed in Italy when the first written works appeared.

Literary drama did not begin until Livius Andronicus (d. 204 BCE) first presented plays known as *fabula palliata* (comedies based on Greek subjects) in Rome in 240 BCE. Gnaeus Naevius wrote the first Roman historical plays, known as *fabula praetexta*, which also adapted Greek originals to Roman settings. For the comedies, Livius, Plautus, and Terence all borrowed extensively from the Greek writer Menander (c. 342–c. 291 BCE).

Menander wrote for Athenian audiences near the end of the 300s BCE. Plays of

MIME
AND
PANTOMIME

*O*ften, artistic forms that are the focus of history are not the most popular in their own time. From a literary standpoint, Roman comedy and tragedy are important contributions to theatre history. From a popular standpoint, they were at best the second choice among the people who attended the theatre. From late republican times through the Empire, mime was clearly the favorite form of theatre in Rome.

The Roman mime began as early as 212 BCE and possibly even earlier. Clearly established as a separate literary form during republican Rome, it dominated the stage during the years of the Empire, far surpassing the popularity of traditional drama.

Mime was not the silent, abstract art form popularized in this century by Marcel Marceau. Roman mime used spoken dialogue, although a good deal of the script was probably improvised. The plays tended to be short sketches, with themes ranging from travesty versions of myths to intrigue and poisoning. Adultery, however, was by far the most popular theme. If, as Aristotle stated, tragedy attempts to show people as better than they are and comedy attempts to show people as worse than they are, mime simply tried to show people as they really are. Typically, a Roman mime was the story of an old man who is shown to be a fool by his young wife and her lover. The incident was treated as broad farce and often included indecent situations, obscene gestures, and bawdy language.

Some plays seem to have required as many as twenty actors, and the companies included both men and women. Perhaps as many as sixty performers might have participated in a single performance, with many of them being jugglers, acrobats, and tight-rope walkers. Records mention specific names of actors and actresses, and it appears that popular mimes could be respected and wealthy. Indeed, one actress, Theodora (d. 548), married the Emperor Justinian (483–565) and ruled with him for many years.

In their earliest form, the mimes were presented as afterpieces to regular drama, but as their popularity grew they became the featured performance. Details of performance style are not known, but the mimes relied on gesture and mimicry rather than on dialogue. Although some characters may have been masked, the main character apparently was not, since facial gesture is a noted skill of the best actors.

Mime was not popular with all of Rome, for many viewed it as indecent. The theme of adultery was one problem, but Christian writers in particular attacked the basic indecency of both theme and presentation, referring not only to obscene gestures and language but to nudity on the stage. This claim is disputed by many, although it seems likely that the mime actress wore clothes that were less conservative than those worn by the typical Roman woman. Not everyone found the mimes offensive. Seneca accuses the mimes of being too careful and not presenting some vices that occur all too often in Roman life.

The hallmark of the mime tradition was freedom, and their response to Christian complaints was predictable. In retaliation, the mimes began to mock Christian sacraments as a part of their plays. However, the Christian complaints seem justified. Records indicate that the Emperor Heliogabulus insisted on realistic portrayal of sex on the stage. This, of course, made the situation more volatile. In the 6th century, the theatres were officially closed, but it appears that mime lived on in private performances, surviving well into the medieval period.

A second form of theatre popular among a segment of the populace was pantomime, which was essentially an interpretative dance performed to recitation and music. A Greek writer, Lucian (c. 120–200 CE), listed pantomime among the great arts. He described the artists as possessing the skills of music, rhythm, poetry, philosophy, rhetoric, painting, and sculpture.

Pantomime was typically a solo performance with one actor playing several different roles, using masks to portray different characters. At times a solo musician or vocalist might accompany the dancer, and some performances apparently used a chorus of voices. Themes ranged from myth to farce, although in both cases the pantomimes tended to focus on the sensual aspects of the story.

Writers of the day remark on the skills of the performers who could "make the limbs speak when the tongue is silent," and rave about the abilities of the performers to make the meaning perfectly clear without uttering a word. Of the two most famous rivals in the 1st century BCE, Pylades was known for his serious tragic style, while Bathyllus was admired for his skill with comedy. Pantomime was favored by the elite (and apparently not by the general populace) and was dependent on the favor of the emperor for its existence. Royal disfavor could result in banishment (Augustus exiled the famous Pylades for embarrassing a royal friend). Caught up in the political fortunes of court factions, pantomime was unable to maintain its important role in the social life of the court and eventually disappeared.

this time are known as Greek New Comedy to contrast them with the works of Classical Athens. New Comedy is characterized by greater emphasis on love stories, the personal problems of characters, stock character types, and the language of everyday life. Menander usually began his plays with a prologue that set out the story line of the play, including the conclusion. Virtually all of his plays were love stories in which a boy pursues a young girl (who need not even appear until the end of the play). The plays were comic more for their happy endings than for any reliance on jokes, however. Although he relied on stock characters and frequently repeated his basic love-story situation, Menander was copied because of his realistic language, his plot construction, and, above all, his careful delineation of character.

Plautus (c. 254–c. 184 BCE)

In translating the plays of Menander and other Greek writers, Plautus adopted many of their characters and plot situations. Plautus kept the location of the plays in Athens to allow him to make jokes that would have appeared unseemly coming from a Roman character. Among the comic changes Plautus made in adapting Menander's plays were (1) his use of *cantica*, or lyrical songs, which in part replaced the choral interludes of Greek plays; (2) expansion of the characters to emphasize their comic qualities; (3) addition of jokes and comic routines that would appeal to Roman audiences; and (4) greater reliance on characters from the lower classes, including slaves, prostitutes, slavedealers, and parasites. These characteristics are evident in the 21 extant plays of Plautus, including *The Braggart Soldier, The Comedy of Asses,* and *Pot of Gold.* (There are no certain dates for his plays.) Plautus's comic devices included plays on words, the invention of words that sound comical, lampooning Greek mythological characters, exchanges of insults and threats between two impotent characters, and considerable use of sexual innuendoes. The overall impact of the plays was based on quickpaced encounters between characters who are brought onstage to add to the merriment of the moment. The plays were larger-than-life in their gestures, actions, characterizations, and humor. The goal of Plautus was to please his audience by giving them what he thought would make them laugh. Plautus gave to the development of comedy in the Western world a comic form that emphasized foreknowledge by the audience, a preference for jokes for their own sake, and a close association between physical humor and character type.

Terence (c. 190–159 BCE)

Terence, a black writer from Roman Africa, wrote only 6 plays, all of which survive today (in contrast to 21 surviving plays of the 100 that Plautus wrote). His best-known plays today include *Phormio* and *The Brothers,* both written around 160 BCE. Roman writers praised Terence for his *humanitas,* or sense of humanity. By reducing the number of puns, linguistic inventions, and one-liners, Terence shifted the focus of his plays toward the emotional reactions of his characters to their situations. The initial story lines may seem contrived (a father gives one of his sons to his brother to raise), but the complicating episodes that follow are logical and sensitive. Terence used the prologue to defend the literary merit of his plays rather than to tell the story line of the play to follow. As a result, the audience had to follow his plays more closely than

The Roman theatre at Aspendus, Turkey.   *Courtesy Alison Frantz Photographs*

those of Plautus. Other characteristics of Terence include his preference for double plots (two connected stories at the same time), his use of the comic device of mistaken identity, his avoidance of obscene jokes and coarse language, and his use of scenes from two Greek plays in a single translation.

The plays of Terence greatly influenced the structure and style of comedy through the medieval and Renaissance periods, and even into the 17th and 18th centuries as well. Their appeal derives from Terence's ability to give the problems of ordinary people sensitive treatment within a comic framework. He does not ridicule his characters, but he persuades them to reform. He does not pander to his audience, but he respects them by making them follow the action closely. He points the way for comedy to become a mode of moral instruction, but he is never stern or condescending. Like Menander before him, Terence demonstrates that life can have happy endings through intelligence, wit, and resolution. The joy of life for Terence is in making those endings believable, rather than in ridiculing the excesses of people. His plays were not very popular during his lifetime, for Roman audiences were more accustomed to the ribaldry of the mimes. Posterity has accorded him due honor, however, for audiences still appreciate his gentility and subtlety. Audiences laugh raucously at Plautus; they smile knowingly with Terence.

Nature of Roman Comedy

Despite the stylistic differences between Plautus and Terence, an outline of the nature of Roman comedy can be constructed. The Roman emphasis on domestic life led to the development of characters who reflected the social customs of the Republic. The functions they served in the household and in public defined their basic natures. The world of Roman comedy was peopled with characters who accept who they are, take life on its own terms, and seek only to find leisure, pleasure, and happiness within the limitations of their social standing.

As a result, the humor of the play lies in the often needless frustrations of the characters as they seek their happiness. It also lies in the conflict between character types. Audiences enjoy watching familiar characters stumble over the same domestic problems that confront them in their own lives, especially when they know that the problems can and will be resolved. The comic devices, slapstick humor, one-liners, and verbal jokes are important to the festive mood of the plays, but at the heart of the plays are the characters and their interactions. That the character types often retain the same name from one play to another indicates the sustained popularity of particular character personalities.

Most of the plays focus on a young son hoping to win the love of a neighbor girl or a courtesan. Because he falls under the power of his father, the son is helpless to win his lover without the father's money or blessing. The son is young, handsome, and something of a rascal. He begs the audience, and any character who passes by, to help him devise a plan that will secure his love. The heroine is traditionally so modest and passive that she frequently doesn't appear until the end of the play. She is stereotypically quiet, demure, and very lovely. By themselves, these lovers would not make for very funny or interesting comedy, for all they want to do is fall in love and live happily ever after. Playwrights wish them success, but usually focus on other more enjoyable characters.

The *senex* is an old man, usually a father or guardian, whose greatest problem in life is that his household is in disorder. His wife is nagging, his daughter is pregnant, his son is in debt, his slaves are impudent, and everyone seems to feel free to spend his money. He is overwhelmed by the authority he holds, and no one seems to sympathize with his situation. Three distinctive types of fathers emerge from this. The miser keeps his money from the family and friends at all costs. The grouch pretends to dislike everyone. The lecher decides to find happiness by taking the heroine for himself. All three of these types can exist in the same drama, but usually only one is the father, and the others are neighbors. Not all fathers exhibit these negative qualities, however; many are very caring for their sons and daughters. However, most of them manage in spite of themselves to foil the young lover's plans and prolong the comic situation.

The matron or mother is in a difficult position, as she was in actual Roman society. On the one hand she had no power, but the importance of the family and the role of the mother in raising that family gave her an informal respect and love that the father frequently envies. Thus, two distinctive mother types emerge. One is the nagging wife who is always berating the father for his stinginess and indifference. The other is the matron who commands loyalty and reverence. The former appear in comedies to harass the father and add to the general confusion of the situation. The matron, however, is not a particularly funny creation, and therefore she usually appears only near the end of the play to help unravel the plot and give her blessing to the union of the lovers.

Roman slaves, or *zanni*, did the work of the household and were indispensable to domestic Rome. Not surprisingly, then, they frequently play a major role in the Roman comedies. At the very least they are minor characters performing the functions of servants, messengers, or baggage carriers. More frequently, they are friends of the hero who listen to his woes and help him reach his goal. Occasionally, Roman slaves are pesky and sly rascals who confound their masters and complicate the plot situation. They agree to help their heroes win the heroine, but only if they get their freedom or money. They purposely increase the general confusion in order to enjoy the situation to the fullest and to satisfy themselves that they alone are capable of making society work correctly. At no time, however, does their insolence border on rebellion. The slave, like all Roman characters, is basically satisfied with who he is. He may seek to improve his financial situation and win his freedom, but he does not attempt to change the social order.

A host of other characters, frequently called buffoons, are added to the plots of Roman comedy to insure that merriment and laughter abound. The *miles* is a braggart soldier who boasts, often falsely, of his military and amorous conquests. Unlike his Greek comic counterpart, however, he never represents an actual military faction in the Roman government. His humor comes from his bloated self-importance and unjustified self-confidence. The *cook* is an effeminate busybody, trailing a string of young boy servants after him as he rushes between the kitchen, the marketplace, and the banquet table. Inevitably, someone ruins his culinary plans and sends him into a tailspin. The *parasite* is what his name implies; he leeches off his friends, flattering them in order to wrangle an invitation to dinner. Finally, the slave dealer *(leno)* appears in many comedies. He is the owner of a courtesan desired by the hero and therefore is an obstacle to be overcome. Consequently, he is depicted as greedy, foolish, or untrustworthy. He is included to provide a butt for jokes and complicate the plot.

Seneca (c. 4 BCE–65 CE) and Roman Tragedy

Although Roman drama is dominated by the wealth of comedy, serious drama of the period is also worthy of consideration. In particular, the writings of Seneca are important documents of the period and were highly influential in later years.

Born in Spain around 4 BCE to an influential family, Seneca spent most of his life in Rome. He served as a government official, finally rising to the rank of senator, and was also a famous orator. Although he wrote both prose and poetry, his tragedies are of major interest.

Fortunately, actual manuscripts of the plays exist, and scholars generally agree that nine plays were authored by Seneca. These are all tragedies based on well-known myths, but they are far from slavish imitations of Greek plays. Senecan tragedy is distinct in its focus on the passions of the characters and the inward, introspective nature of the speeches. Rather than focusing on exterior actions, the plays explore inner thoughts and realities. In Shakespeare's day this developed into soliloquies and asides. In modern drama, this relates to the concept of subtext.

This focus on interior thought and emotion was achieved through the use of long, elaborate speeches. A full exploration of an emotional response to a tragic situation

A Global Perspective

Sanskrit Drama in India

*I*t may have been influenced by Greek theatre brought to India during the conquests of Alexander the Great, or it may have evolved from early dance forms. Whatever its origins, Sanskrit drama evolved into a highly developed form of theatre by 500 CE.

The aim of Sanskrit drama was to arouse the spectators' emotions in such a manner as to lead them to an understanding of higher values or sentiments *(rasa)*. Staged as part of temple celebrations, performances followed a detailed set of rules provided in the *Natyasastra*, an elaborate aesthetic theory written by Bharata some time between 2000 BCE and 200 CE. Besides providing a divine origin for drama (as an imitation of the emotional state of the entire universe), the *Natyasastra* discusses every aspect of theatre practice, from playwriting to theatre management.

Performances of the Sanskrit drama were held in specially constructed buildings, erected near or within the temple grounds according to strict rules in terms of location and materials. Frequently, astrologers were consulted to aid in choosing the site.

Performances were given for various religious and ceremonial occasions, with the audience seated by social caste. The most common theatre seated approximately 1;000 people, with a rectangular raised stage occupying one-half of the building.

Stories were usually taken from ancient texts and focused on a particular theme. The plays were long, with extended verse passages alternating with prose dialogue and occasional musical interludes. The lyrical verse passages were often descriptive or evocative, providing the author and the performer with an opportunity to display their art.

The performance style was based on elaborate conventions, placing great demands on performers and audience alike. Little scenic reinforcement was used; a curtain between front and back provided for quick entrances and exits. Actors, highly trained in physical and vocal performance, utilized specific gestures of the hands, head, and arms, combined with intricate postures, to communicate.

The Sanskrit drama remained popular until the 10th century CE, when a changing society and Muslim invasions resulted in a decline in theatre presentation and the gradual abandonment of the Sanskrit style.

often resulted in long speeches filled with imagery and passion. Given Seneca's reputation as an orator, his use of speech in this manner does not seem surprising.

The myths considered are remote from Roman times and, in contrast to the comedy, seem to make few references to contemporary issues and situations. Instead, Seneca's tragedies present titanic clashes of morality and rapid shifts in emotion. In *Phaedra* (c. 45–55 CE), when Theseus returns from the dead to find his wife, Phaedra, apparently threatening suicide, he is stricken with remorse and tears. These tears change instantly to rage as he threatens to torture Phaedra's nurse to tell him why Phaedra is so upset. When Phaedra tells him, untruthfully, that she was raped by her stepson, Hippolytus, Theseus immediately believes the story and vows revenge. This heightened emotional tone separates Seneca's plays from the Greek. This tone also makes the plays seem artificial to some contemporary readers.

Another innovation of Senecan tragedy was the emphasis on magic, death, the supernatural, and violence. The emotional excess of the characters frequently led to physical violence that apparently was graphically illustrated on stage. (Although no documentation refers to any of Seneca's plays, descriptions of other tragedies indicate that slaves condemned to die were cast in certain roles so that the execution could be incorporated in the drama.)

Seneca's moral stance is not entirely clear. Although some critics attack him as a stern moralist, his plays seem to indicate that questions of right and wrong are difficult and tenuous. At times Seneca's plays seem to indicate that the evil is all-powerful. At other times, they seem to point to the inevitable triumph of good. This moral flux and the question it raises concerning the basis of human behavior make Seneca's plays more complex than they might seem on first reading.

Seneca's plays are not often performed today, and debate continues over whether or not the plays were produced in Rome. Tragedy was not often performed in Seneca's time, for the stage was dominated by comedy and by paratheatrical forms. It would also have been most unusual for a person of Seneca's rank to write for the theatre, since most playwrights wrote for the financial rewards—there was no literary merit attached to the drama at this time. Recent scholars, however, argue convincingly that the plays were meant for presentation, since they are clearly not meant for recitation by a single reader. The intellectual quality of the plays makes it possible that they were meant for presentation at small, private gatherings of Seneca's elite circle of acquaintances rather than in public theatres.

Whether or not they were performed in imperial Rome, the plays of Seneca became highly influential during the Renaissance. Scholars of that day adopted the Senecan tragedy, not the Greek, as the "classic" form, and Renaissance drama throughout the Western world came to be modeled on these plays.

CONNECTIONS

One indication of the significance and greatness of Roman comedy is the endurance of its comic characters throughout literary history. These same types appear, with their characteristics virtually intact, in the Italian commedia dell'arte in the 16th century. Some historians have conjectured that they were "kept alive" by wandering players during the medieval period. The renewed interest in Latin literature in the Renaissance led to the study of Roman comedy and therein provided a surer connection, however. From the commedia, they appeared throughout Europe in the plays of Molière and occasionally in the comedies of Shakespeare. These same types can be identified in the English comedy of manners, in the melodrama, and even in modern television situation comedies.

"All in the Family," for instance, had a typical grouch (Archie), a wife (Edith) who nags him (from his point of view), and a young daughter and son-in-law whose lives are complicated by the father figure. "Murphy Brown" includes a *miles* (he is even named Miles), a parasite (Corky), and a pedantic grouch (Jim). Buffoon types are also present in Phil, the bar owner, and the rustic Eldin, Murphy's house painter. Only the heroine is changed to meet the perceptions of the modern woman. Virtually every television comedy has identifiable characters who embellish the stock characteristics developed in the Roman era.

Other aspects of Roman comedy have survived the centuries and contributed to the elaboration of comic forms. Plautus and Terence used comic devices still popular today: characters who eavesdrop, asides to the audience, mistaken identity, misinformation, delayed reactions, and cascades (that is, difficulties that involve more and more people). They articulated a vast range of comic possibilities from the burlesques of some of Plautus's characters to the reflective monologues of Terence. They used tricks, lies, and deceptions to win the girl for the boy; many of these were later used by Molière and Shakespeare. Finally, they took incidents from daily life and gave them both believability and humor. They proved that the actions of ordinary people were worth dramatizing, and that the problems everyone faces in daily life are rich with comic possibilities. They thereby accorded to the average individual a dignity and respect that derived from his or her ability to overcome all obstacles. The buffoons may be ridiculed in Roman comedy, but the family members more frequently survive their ordeals with their self-respect. They are changed, to be sure, but they are changed for the better. Plautus and Terence are therefore major contributors to the dignity and humanity of the common person in Western literature.

The Roman theatre represents a time when the theatre clearly moved away from a religious basis and began to focus on the concept of entertainment. The multiplicity of theatrical forms, the growth of spectacle, and the ascendency of comedy all testify to a theatre that was firmly focused on providing diversion and pleasure for its audiences.

SOURCES FOR FURTHER STUDY

Social/Art/Philosophy Background

Carcopino, Jerome. *Daily Life in Ancient Rome.* Trans. E. O. Lorimer. New Haven: Yale University Press, 1940.

Frank, Tenney. *Life and Literature in the Roman Republic.* Berkeley: University of California Press, 1930.

Grant, Michael. *The World of Rome.* New York: Mentor Books, 1960.

Hamilton, Edith. *The Roman Way.* New York: Avon Books, 1932.

Jenkins, Ian. *Greek and Roman Life.* Cambridge, Mass.: Harvard University Press, 1986.

Kostof, Spira. *A History of Architecture: Settings and Rituals.* New York: Oxford University Press, 1985.

Maguiness, W. S. *The Civilization of Rome.* New York: Simon and Schuster, 1963.

Pomeroy, Sarah B. *Goddesses, Whores, Wives, and Slaves: Women in Classical Antiquity.* New York: Schocken Books, 1975.

Veyne, Paul, ed. *A History of Private Life: From Pagan Rome to Byzantium.* Trans. Arthur Goldhammer. Cambridge, Mass.: Harvard University Press, 1987.

Roman Theatre

Arnott, Peter. *The Ancient Greek and Roman Theatre.* New York: Random House, 1971.

Beare, W. *The Roman Stage: A Short History of Latin Drama in the Time of the Republic.* Cambridge, Mass.: Harvard University Press, 1951.

Bieber, Margarete. *The History of the Greek and Roman Theatre.* 2d ed. Princeton, N.J.: Princeton University Press, 1961.

Simon, Erika. *The Ancient Theatre.* Trans. C. E. Vafopoulou-Richardson. London: Methuen, 1972.

Slater, Niall W. *Plautus in Performance.* Princeton, N.J.: Princeton University Press, 1985.

Roman Drama

Arnott, W. Geoffrey. *Menander, Plautus, Terence.* Oxford: Clarendon Press, 1975.

Cornford, Francis Macdonald. *The Origin of Attic Comedy.* Cambridge: Cambridge University Press, 1934.

Duckworth, George E. *The Nature of Roman Comedy.* Princeton, N.J.: Princeton University Press, 1952.

Goldberg, Sander M. *The Making of Menander's Comedy.* Berkeley: University of California Press, 1980.

Henry, Denis, and Elisabeth Henry. *The Mask of Power: Seneca's Tragedies and Imperial Rome.* Chicago: Bolchazy-Carducci, 1985.

Konstan, David. *Roman Comedy.* Ithaca, N.Y.: Cornell University Press, 1983.

Rosenmeyer, T. G. *Senecan Drama and Stoic Cosmology.* Berkeley: University of California Press, 1989.

Sandbach, F. H. *The Comic Theatre of Greece and Rome.* New York: W. W. Norton & Co. 1977.

C H A P T E R

4

The Medieval Era

When the Devil tempts Adam to eat of the fruit of the tree of knowledge, Adam refuses because he believes the Devil will separate him from God. Before the Devil visits Eve, he goes out among the audience. No lines are written for him, but his purpose is clear: to taunt individual members of the audience just as he is taunting Adam and Eve. He doesn't offer an apple, but with ingratiating seriousness he offers eternal power and knowledge. The audience knows how to respond because it knows the outcome of the story. Yet when the Devil returns to the stage to tempt Eve, the audience members have become accomplices. They know they would have accepted the Devil if they didn't know the story, just as Eve will accept the Devil because she does not realize the consequences. It does not matter that the dramatic action has been broken while the Devil walked among us; the dramatic idea has been intensified. The playwright of *The Representation of Adam* (12th century) wants to demonstrate the inseparable link between the human condition of the audience and that of Adam and Eve. Through one small stage direction—"the Devil walks among the people"—he creates a new dramatic experience in which Biblical time and medieval time become the same and the reality of the present is indistinguishable from the reality of the past.

	Magna Carta	Crusades			Black plague		
1150–1170	1215	1096–1291		1337	1348–1353		1378–1417
University of Paris founded				Hundred Years' War begins		Papal Schism	

	Notre Dame of Paris	Chartres cathedral	Gothic style		Giotto's "Death of St. Francis"		The Triumph of Death	The Canterbury Tales
	1163–1250	1194–1260	1200–1400	1314–1321	c. 1318–1320	1348–1352	c. 1354	c. 1387
				Divine Comedy		Decameron		

	Feast of Corpus Christi established	Cycle plays prominent		Miracle plays prominent	Morality plays popular
	1264	1300–1450	1377	c. 1350–1575	1400–1550
		Courtly entertainment with elaborate scenery			

The medieval theatre was a theatre of faith. It used the conventions of performance and stage practice to express for the audience its commitment to the Catholic religion. In theatre and drama, as well as in art and architecture, the medieval audience found visual and aural representation of its ideals. The arts transmitted and translated the faith of the Church. They explained present unhappiness by re-creating the past and giving hope for the future. The medieval arts collapsed real time in order to illustrate the faith that gave meaning to all earthly contradictions. The biblical past, the medieval present, and the heavenly future appeared beside one another in most works of art. The chaos of earthly life became rational when placed in the history of God's plan. To understand this theatre of faith, the nature of medieval life, the faith of the church, and the means by which artists blended those together must be appreciated.

SOCIAL IDEAS

Daily life in medieval Europe in 1400 was violent, cruel, passionate, and rough. War, crime, death, and diseases have existed in every epoch, but in 1400 both their nature and their intent were more severe. Wars were often won by starving cities into submission. Famine swept across Europe periodically, leaving many with insufficient food to survive harsh winters in small hurts or crowded villages. One-third of all the people in Europe died in the black death, or bubonic plague, between 1348 and 1353. In such conditions, medieval people, not surprisingly, sought for and created systems of order and structure that would provide a logic for this chaos of death and destruction.

Hierarchism

Where the medieval mind found uncertainty, it imposed order. The movements of the planets and stars were codified in astrology. Numerology was popular, with associations frequently made between the seven virtues, the seven deadly sins, and the seven days of creation. Chivalry was a stringent behavior code governing matters of love and heroism. Symmetry in art or nature was regarded as reflective of some eternal truth. The Catholic Church carefully organized the calendar of worship for each day as well as for the year. Church and monastery bells rang throughout the day to tell the faithful what activities to engage in.

The Church also asserted a hierarchy of relationships between its own members (bishops and priests) and between religious leaders and secular authority. Clear lines of authority reached from pope to commoner and from king to commoner. These relationships were frequently strained, especially between the two lines, and in fact, order was something to be desired more than something readily achieved.

Feudalism

In addition, feudalism organized the lives of most people in the medieval period. Feudalism was a system of mutual obligations primarily between a lord, his vassals, and the serfs. The lord administered justice and maintained peace within his lands and waged war against enemies. The vassal swore allegiance to the lord and demonstrated his fealty through military service, taxes, and various social obligations. The serfs worked the land, gave a fixed percentage of their crops to the lord, and paid other duties to the lord. In return, the vassals and serfs received the protection of the lord.

The Catholic Church

Catholicism in the medieval era was not the same set of beliefs as those that are held in the 20th century, despite the obvious historical connection. In 1400, the Church had not been seriously challenged either by the Reformation or by the developments of science. It was an unquestioned authority on all matters of faith and on many matters of daily life. It stood in uneasy alliance with the kings and lords of Europe, with informal power flowing from one side to the other depending upon the personalities of a particular geographical region.

Five characteristics of the Catholic Church influenced the development of drama and are discussed here because they offer insight into the nature of medieval drama. First, Jesus expressed his teachings through parables, or stories that illustrated a concept and taught a moral lesson. The Church adopted this method of illustration in both art and drama. The windows and niches of the cathedrals were spaces for the presentation of scenes from the Bible. The drama evolved in part as a vehicle for retelling stories from the Bible, as well as stories of the lives of saints.

Second, the Catholic faith emphasized that the continuation of injustice and unhappiness in this life were part of God's plan. The Church taught acceptance on faith that suffering is part of the mystery of life as it was a part of Jesus' life. This sense of the mystery or spirituality led artists away from the depiction of life as it is and toward the presentation of life as it will be under God's grace. Particularly after 1200, the majority of dramas identified both the need for the message of Jesus and the need to prepare for salvation in death.

Third, the Catholic Church shared in the general medieval belief that contemplation of one's sins and preparation for the next life are desirable activities. For many, this led to asceticism, the rejection of worldly things and goods because they divert the mind from its appropriate duties. Many dramas of the period reflect this view of life by presenting characters who are tempted by vanity and greed.

Fourth, the Church imposed order on its own worship service. Each service (or celebration of the faith) was performed according to Church law in a specific order. In part, this regularity meant that some churches sought means of retaining the interest of the congregation. The most readily available means were the interpolations in the text, that is, the sections where Church law allowed additions to be made. From these sections emerged liturgical drama.

Finally, the Church influenced the development of drama in a negative manner. Throughout the Middle Ages, the voices of clergy were raised against actors and performers who attracted the enthusiasm of people away from the message of the Church. Even though the Church used the drama to tell stories of the Bible and improve the religious fervor of the followers, it vehemently opposed performances that provided entertainment without instruction. The role of instruction in the drama would remain a critical issue for the next several centuries.

ARTS IDEAS

More than any other period in Western history, the medieval era relied on the arts to communicate ideas about human existence and the meaning of life. Illiteracy was only one reason the Catholic Church and secular officials used visual and aural examples to illustrate the structure of the world as they understood it. Equally important was the fact that the medieval vision of reality was based on supra-rational components of faith that could not be explained in words. The fullness of God's plan was realized only in death and through the Judgment Day, both of which lent themselves to visual depiction in lurid and provocative images. The Church relied on stories from the Bible and on the lives of saints to serve as examples of the path to righteousness. Sculptural detail, song, and dramatic presentations demonstrated the vitality and immediacy of those stories, and additionally served as proof of their eternal truth. The skill of the artists made these stories more than mere reiteration or repetition. In the hands of the artists, they became an international language linking people through images of this world and the next.

Medieval music, sculpture, and architecture thus demonstrated the use of the arts to explain the meaning of life. The songs told of the unhappiness and sadness that pervaded daily life and of the need to seek consolation and redemption in the forgiveness of God. Symmetry and regularity of line in sculpture and painting were visual representation of the ultimate harmony of life. The use of symbols in the depiction of the saints and prophets (Saint Paul was always shown with curly hair and a short beard, for example) was a reminder that the true meaning of life is found beyond physical reality. The sculptural plan of a cathedral was a careful pattern to take the spectator through a purposefully organized presentation of the history of the faith. The architecture of a Gothic cathedral was a superb synthesis of religious concept and utility with the Christian symbol of the cross as its spine.

Gothic Cathedral

For breathtaking architectural accomplishment, sculptural variety, complexity, and sheer visual wonder there is no equivalent to a Gothic cathedral. A singular monument to the medieval vision of life, it presents a rich interplay of real, biblical, and imagined scenes that overwhelm the spectator. Yet there is unity in the variety and a synthesis of the contrasting elements of architecture, sculpture, and stained glass. The cathedral is an excellent example of the way the world was envisioned in the late medieval period.

The term *Gothic* refers to cathedrals built from about 1190 to 1450. The Gothic cathedral was built in the center of a city and served as the focal point of civic activity and pride. While the Romanesque cathedral (those built between 1000 and 1200) was

The cathedral at Chartres, France.

constructed as a fortress against the evils of life, the Gothic cathedral was a symbol of ebullient faith. The Gothic architects shifted their emphasis from the squat barrel-vaulted interiors of the Romanesque style to pointed arches that reached toward the heavens. They focused on space as a religious experience intended to uplift the soul. The results were multifunctional buildings that served as a tourist attraction and as a house for religious artifacts and ceremonies. They were also a theatre and a concert hall.

The Gothic cathedral, like its Romanesque predecessor, contained all the elements necessary to a theatre of faith: props (used in the communion service), costumes (the vestments), a story (the Bible), actors (the priests who recite the story), a distinctive space capable of mood and atmosphere (the stained glass windows), and music. The drama that evolved from this was, not surprisingly, a combination of symbolic code (the Garden of Eden can only be suggested, for instance, not re-created) and literal action (lines often taken directly from the Bible). Set in a visual and spatial atmosphere in which every detail of the architecture is an echo of the biblical action, the resulting "performance" was a complete theatrical experience.

The cathedral therefore provided several traditions that influenced medieval theatre. Even though by the year 1400 the bulk of theatre activities were performed outdoors, many of them still used visual and aural spectacle to tell the story of the Catholic faith.

MEDIEVAL THEATRE

A variety of dramatic forms were common throughout Western Europe and England by 1400. An absence of records dating before the year 1000 make it impossible to know definitively what kinds of drama existed during and after the reign of Charlemagne. Yet some forms of nonliterary theatre persisted after the Roman Empire, as indicated by surviving fragments of stories and occasional church edicts against performers. These early secular forms were an outgrowth of the lifestyle of the tribes of Europe, but they also contain remnants of the theatre of the late Roman Empire.

Occasion

Tournaments of various forms focused on athletic competition, and royal entry parades were held to welcome visiting royalty or to welcome one's own royalty home from a voyage. These huge spectacles were highly theatrical forms through which the aristocracy demonstrated their power and their courtly graces, and they became even more highly developed in the Renaissance. A form of entertainment known as mummers' plays were folk dramas that became popular as court entertainment as well. These Christmas plays utilized disguise and masks to tell the story of the death and resurrection of St. George or other popular figures. Mimicry included a variety of entertainment forms ranging from spontaneous imitation to coordinated re-creation. The term refers to masquerading in which villagers went from house to house with warnings to children or gifts for the poor. It also refers to the actors who roamed Europe performing acrobatics, juggling, and dancing.

Mock combats were a form of entertainment in which social relations were acted out in symbolic fashion and victories in battle were ceremoniously repeated. These

A Global Perspective

The Minstrel Tradition in Russia

*A*mong medieval forms of theatre, several were not related to the Church, and one remained steadfastly the enemy of the church. The traveling minstrel was often considered a remnant of old pagan religions and therefore was viewed as an enemy of Christianity. A fine example of the minstrel tradition are the *skomorokhi* of Russia.

The word *skomorokhi* has no clear English translation but roughly means "versatile entertainers." The earliest records of these minstrels are 11th-century church treatises that identify them with pagan worship and witchcraft.

These Russian minstrels participated in many traditional folk festivals and were particularly central to weddings, which were often multiday festivals. They were also central to folk festivals held at various times of the year, including midsummer and harvest times. Attired in a brightly colored costume, the minstrel was the "director" of the event, organizing various activities, assigning "roles" to the participants, and providing music and other entertainment. Eventually groups of *skomorokhi* became traveling professionals, moving from place to place to avoid the censure of the officials.

Music, dance, and song were the primary ingredients of *skomorokhi* entertainments, but trained bears and puppets were also used. The bears were trained to perform comic roles (a young girl in a pretty dress, a devout priest saying prayers), while the puppets were used to prolong a story-telling tradition. Hand puppets were the most common. A puppet stage would be created by wrapping a blanket supported by poles around the puppeteer, who would then present the play by displaying the puppets above the blanket, holding his hands above his head. The primary character was Petrushka, a figure similar to Pulcinella in Italy, Punch in England, and Hanswurst in Germany. The stories, of which 23 still exist, were short comic tales usually involving a heated argument over the purchase of a horse.

The *skomorokhi* were international citizens, and they are known to have traveled to Italy and Germany and possibly through parts of China. Although they were outlawed by the czar in 1648, their influence can be traced in contemporary Russian song, dance, and theatre.

combats took the form of folkplays, in which the villagers acted out a traditional story on some special occasion. Usually costumes were worn, masking the faces of the performers to hide their real identities and give them freedom to behave differently. In central Europe, these symbolic battles and victories of the community were so popular that many later religious dramas were structured as combats or victories for the hero.

Dancing was a prominent form of medieval entertainment that included many theatrical elements. Some dances told stories of love and involved the effort of the lovers to unite despite some hostile force that opposed their union. Other kinds of dances were sword dances, ring dances, and maypole dances. Many of them retained some connection to an event in the calendar of the Catholic Church.

The theatre also was connected to the church calendar, and like most medieval arts provided a means of celebration and communion. Modern criticism usually associates the rise of liturgical drama with the *trope,* a short musical interlude in the church service that was changed for each holiday of the religious calendar. Because these interludes were not repeated daily, they afforded an opportunity for variety and imagination. Probably the first and certainly the most common of the tropes to be developed with dramatic action was the *Quem quaeritis* (c. 950) given during the Easter service. In its entirety, the earliest version of the trope was only four lines long:

ANGELS: Who do you seek in the tomb, O Christians?
MARYS: Jesus of Nazareth, the crucified, O heavenly ones.
ANGELS: He is not here. He is risen.
Go and announce that He is risen from the tomb as foretold.

In the late 10th century, St. Ethelwold in England encouraged the Church to realize the theatrical potential of this trope. He articulated the visual and ritual potential of the lines with attention to the emotional impact they could have on the congregation (*Concordia Regularis,* c. 975).

The staging of these tropes utilized the environment of the cathedral to indicate the location of the action. Statues of characters in the trope (the three Marys, for instance) served as the "home" or station for those characters. These locations were known as *mansions.* The open area between mansions was called the *platea,* or playing area.

Over the years, more elaborate representations followed. Detailed movement was included throughout the church. The figures of Peter and John were added, including Peter and John running through the aisles searching for Jesus. The text was expanded to include lines that were logical connectors between actions noted in the Bible. Costuming became more elaborate when the priests began wearing clothing appropriate to the characters rather than their own vestments. Priests played all the roles, and the scenes were brief and climactic. Nevertheless, a religious drama was created that grew in popularity over the centuries.

While some of the tropes were performed in church, others were more suitable to performance outside, either because of their subject matter or because the theatrical action was too large. Outside the church, scenery became a necessity, special effects were created, and new characters were developed (such as the Devil) that would not have been appropriate in the sanctuary.

Scholars dispute the exact sequence by which tropes developed into drama, but a form that was clearly dramatic began to develop within and without the mass. Soon, a variety of dramatic forms gained popular approval throughout Europe. None of these forms rivaled in size and pageantry the plays performed during the Feast of Corpus Christi, held in late May or early June.

Like medieval life itself, the Feast of Corpus Christi is a study in dualities: religious yet commercial, amateur yet well-prepared, serious yet comic. Above all, a variety of distinctive theatrical elements are unified by the single idea of faith.

The plays of the Feast of Corpus Christi were written and performed very differently in each community of Europe. The purpose of the plays of Corpus Christi was to witness and celebrate the appearance of Jesus Christ on earth as proof of God's forgiveness of humankind's sins, and the possibility of salvation. Such a purpose necessitated presentation of the source of original sin, the predictions of the coming of Jesus, and the entire life of Jesus. It would be impossible to encompass these events in a single play, so individual scenes of plays were written for each of the major events in the story line (or cycle) from original sin to salvation. In England, the York cycle (c. 1376) consisted of 48 plays; the Towneley cycle performed in Wakefield (c. 1580) consisted of 24. Although each play was discrete, it shared with the others in the cycle the common theme of eventual salvation. Sometimes a narrator or herald began each play by pointing out its connection to the entire cycle.

Scripts were written by local clerics or authors and then retained from year to year. Writers were familiar with the needs of the theatre. They were able to develop insight and empathy for biblical characters. They knew how to hold audience interest with visual and topical elements. The combination of shrewd writing, community involvement, and skilled performances resulted in great public enthusiasm.

The Corpus Christi Feast Day, established in 1264 by Pope Urban IV, was a commemoration of the doctrine of transubstantiation and a signal reminder to the faithful that Jesus Christ died for the sins of humankind. Unlike Christmas festivities, which were limited by the weather, and Easter, which was preceded by Lent, the Feast of Corpus Christi could develop into an outdoor festival of joy and thanksgiving. A careful "wedding" of Church and secular authorities, it provided the perfect setting for the development of drama. The plays could be essentially religious, even though they were performed in the vernacular. They took place outside of the Church and were not performed by clergy, but through financial interests it could maintain careful control of the performances. By 1400, Corpus Christi had become an organized presentation of plays involving virtually every segment of a city's population.

Although the dramas and the feast day were religious, the organization of activities was in many locations handled by civic authorities, for there was money to be made from the commercial activity. Not only did communities take pride in their ability to mount a successful festival, but groups within the town vied to present the most effective and elaborate play. Thus, the performance of the drama took place within a context of bustling commercial vitality.

Location

The plays were performed in various locations—in a town square with temporary scaffolds built for the audience, or at different locations throughout the city. The performance area could be circular, square, or rectangular, and in some cases, notably

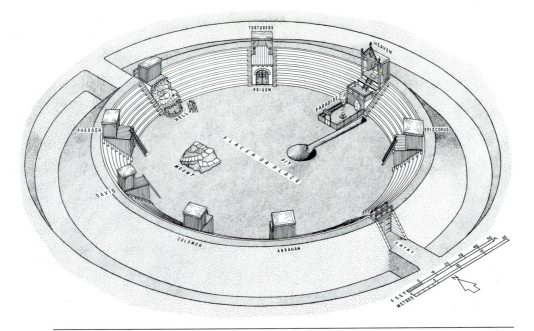

A drawing of a Piran Round in Cornwall (England) as prepared for the first day of a medieval presentation.   *Reprinted by Permission of Methuen London*

in England, the plays were mounted on wagons to be rolled through the town. These pageant wagons were actually quite elaborate, since they carried scenery, special effects, and as many as twenty or more actors and singers. The audience was free to mill around from one wagon to another or to follow a wagon in its course through the city. Some people liked to move close to the play when it began and tried to talk with the performers. The performance situation was obviously casual, fluid, and dynamic. No one production location seemed to dominate; sometimes ancient Roman amphitheatres were used; more often, cathedral interiors; another arrangement included a long playing platform arranged along an exterior wall of a building.

Performers

Settings varied widely in terms of elaboration and detail, but most seemed to follow a basic style. The basic configuration of a central playing area *(platea)* and a set piece *(mansion)* was continued from the tropes. For example, the set on the wagon was a booth-like edifice from which the actors emerged to step onto an open playing area—either the front of the wagon or a second open wagon placed beside the first. The facade of the booth was designed and painted to indicate more than one location. The actors stepped in front of one section, announced they were traveling to another locale, and then walked down the wagon to the area in front of the second location. Some of the booths (or tiring-houses, named because they were the place where the actors retired after their lines) were built with an upper loft to house angels or characters who had gone to heaven.

The stage as prepared for the Valenciennes (France) Passion Play in 1547. *Courtesy Biblio-thèque Nationale*

In other situations, the scenery was all present in one location, with different backdrops set side by side. Reference to a particular scenic unit, called a mansion, was enough to establish a sense of location. The number of mansions used varied greatly from location to location in Europe. In some cases, the presentation of the plays lasted several days, and mansions could be redecorated or altered overnight to serve as a different location on the following day.

Typically, the duties for presentation of the plays was shared, with the cathedral chapter organizing the script, music, costumes, and finances, while the civic officials were responsible for the wagons, scenery, machinery, food, and lodging. Either a church official or civic authority (often a committee organized for the purpose) assigned each play to a different group in the community to produce. Traditionally, the town guilds took most of the plays. Guilds were organizations of laborers or artisans all of whom worked in the same profession. They usually performed that portion of the biblical story that most closely pertained to their profession. For example, the water-drawers might perform the story of Noah's Ark. Each guild performed the same play every year, retaining the costumes and scenery and assigning roles to the same persons. One full copy of the play existed; individual parts were written out for the actors. Yet many actors were illiterate, and the authors wrote their plays in verse, perhaps to make memorization easier.

Rehearsals were usually held early in the morning before work, with part of the production costs going to provide breakfast. The length of rehearsals varied depending on whether new people were performing the roles and whether changes had been made in the script. A new script could result in several rehearsals spread over a full month's time. Construction of the set would be reserved until a few days before the performance. No more than four or five dress rehearsals of each play were held with all elements of the production in place.

The involvement of all the guilds, the inclusion of children in the choirs, and the preparation of food for rehearsals all combined to involve most of the local population. Consequently, there was little need for advance publicity. Even so, a play called the *banns* was frequently performed several days in advance to announce the cycle. Community interest was orchestrated to its fullest potential. If the weather was good, the Feast of Corpus Christi could be expected to draw most everyone in the city to enjoy the festivities and watch the plays.

The staging of medieval drama included many elements of spectacle and excitement. The miracles of the Bible were re-created with ingenious solutions. Sound effects were utilized for the appearance of important characters, and choirs sang during transitions from one scene to another. Especially memorable were the depictions of hell, replete with costumed devils who ran about with noisemakers and forks to poke and frighten the audience. The scenic location of hell was known as the hell-mouth. It was shaped in the image of a fire-breathing monster and was large enough to hold perhaps a dozen actors. Costumes were either borrowed from the Church or constructed by the

A medieval pageant wagon from England in procession.   *Reproduced by Permission of The Huntington Library, San Marino, California.*

CHAMBERS OF RHETORIC

*T*hroughout Europe in the medieval era, guilds or fraternities of men provided one of the chief means of social interaction. The guilds took on the responsibility of providing entertainment and organizing festivals in many areas of the Continent. For example, the meistersingers in Germany were groups devoted to music, while the Confrérie de la Passion in Paris performed plays. For dramatic skill and range of theatrical invention, however, few guilds could match the *rederijkerkamers* or Chambers of Rhetoric in the Low Countries (Holland and Belgium).

First appearing in the 1400s, the chambers came to dominate the civic and cultural landscape of the Low Countries in the 1500s. Most towns had one chamber, but larger cities such as Antwerp had as many as nine. The chambers were devoted to providing visual and intellectual entertainment for the city. They included a chief poet who would write poetry and drama, and a fool who would insure the presence of humor at all civic functions. By the 1500s (due partially to encouragement from Philip the Fair) they organized triumphal entries and building decorations for visiting dignitaries, processions on religious and civic holidays, and competitions in poetry, rhetoric, and drama.

The chambers loved competitions, not only within the membership of each, but between chambers of different cities. While in the 20th century civic rivalry is often expressed through competing professional sports teams, the cities of the Low Countries expressed civic pride through these amateur dramatic and poetry societies. The chamber of a city would decide to host a competition (or *landjuweel*), identifying a theme or subject and then inviting the chambers of other cities to prepare visual and dramatic material exploring that subject. Topics varied from the religious (what is God's greatest miracle?) to humanistic (what can best lead a person to the liberal arts?). Each chamber would answer the question according to its own values and orientation. Prizes were awarded for virtually every aspect of the competition: best presentation of the chambers' emblem, best song, best singer, best poet, best decoration in the city, best fool (apparently one who could drink as well as crack jokes), and, of course, best play.

Of particular note to theatre students were the *tableaux vivants*, or stationary pictures illustrating a particular theme. Architectural facades, often with several entrances and more than one level, were built at the rear of a platform. These facades could be very ornate, with rows of columns, statuary, and decorations along the walls. The purpose of a tableau was to visualize a theme, and since many of the themes were humanistic, the facades reflected an interest in classical architectural features.

Figures would appear in the niches and entrances of the facade and hold a pose while a poet would rhetorically define the theme chosen in answer to the competition's subject. Figures could also speak or read poems, some mime could occur, or short plays could also be performed. Regardless of the extent of movement by the figures, the focus of the presentation was the rhetorical and visual means by which the chamber presented its theme.

The most elaborate of the *landjuweel* occurred in Antwerp in 1561, when a tremendous amount of money was spent to invite nine chambers. Some 23 triumphal chariots and 197 wagons were prepared for the competition, as well as decorations, processionals, and contests—all ornately costumed and rehearsed. Writers of the day believed that the spirit of Classical Athens, in which the citizenry participated together in the exploration of ideas, had come to Belgium and Holland. Unfortunately, the Spanish Inquisition had also come, and the Spanish invaders had little use for the humanistic and reformationist tendencies of the Low Countries. Despite insurrections and revolts against foreign domination, the people and the economies of the cities of the Low Countries were brutally suppressed. Few *rederijkerkamers* survived beyond 1600.

guilds for use in the cycle plays. There was apparently some attempt at realism in the costuming, although God was often dressed as the Pope. Angels wore robes with wings mounted on their backs, and complicated costumes were devised to represent devils as birds of prey, complete with tails, horns, and claws.

In some of the more elaborate cycle plays of England and the Low Countries during the 15th century, the pageant wagons evolved into highly complex theatrical machines with trapdoors, pulleys for flying characters, and devices hidden underneath the wagons. Some wagons even had two separate levels with heaven above and hell below. Others used the roofs of nearby buildings to create flying effects aided by pulleys and winches. These *secrets* required stagecrews of 10 or more for their effective operation, leading to the conclusion that medieval drama was a sophisticated interplay of visual and aural effects intended to surprise and awe the audience. The language of medieval drama may appear simple, but the full impact of the presentation of the plays is one of theatrical splendor and audience involvement.

Although the actors were drawn from members of the guild that was staging a particular play, they were selected for their suitability to the parts and were then retained from one year to the next if they were effective. By 1400, some actors were paid for their roles, suggesting appreciation for their work and some degree of professionalism. Records indicate that particularly good actors were even loaned to other guilds on occasion. The acting style was probably fairly realistic, since stage directions in the play call upon the actor to perform actions "as if" they are actually occurring. Even the presence of a prompter onstage whispering lines would not deter actors from involvement in the scene. The performance level obviously varied from one play to another, but is generally of a professional quality for the times.

One other performance aspect is worth noting. Visual comic elements often were combined with a serious message (one of the prophets, for instance, can't get to the king because his ass won't move, and he stands onstage on some kind of fake donkey trying to get to the other side of the stage). Because these comic moments were external to the biblical stories, they provided an opportunity for the actors to re-create scenes from actual medieval life. Actors imitated their neighbors or commented on real problems of the audience. In doing so, the comedy pointed toward the feeling of joy derived from the central message of salvation. It also distinguished the comic irrelevance of this life against the purity and beauty of the lives of past Christians. The comedy further identifies the irony of the ultimate unimportance of the many struggles of daily life compared to the importance of God's forgiveness.

Audience

The entire community was able to attend the performances of the plays. In some situations, a special viewing station was set up for town dignitaries, but all community members were afforded an opportunity to view the plays. In the typical situation, it would appear that the audience was fluid, moving from place to place to get a better view or to withdraw from a threatening devil. Interaction between the stage and the spectators was common, and the atmosphere was highly charged and exciting.

Standards of Judgment

The Church and the community provided the essential judgment on a play's success, for little criticism exists from this time period. The earliest rediscovery of Aristotle's writing occurred during the medieval period, but the influence of this discovery is more evident in later years. One noted change is the movement away from Tertullian's condemnation of the drama to a point of view that sees theatre as a viable means of communication and of moral instruction.

In summary, the cycle plays celebrated the presence of Jesus Christ in the lives of the faithful. The plays covered the entirety of human history from original sin to the last judgment. The connection between the plays was the message of the Church, expressed through the theatrical representation of heaven, hell, and earth, and through the dramatic representation of past, present, and future. The pageant wagons were filled with surprises and spectacle to tell their stories. The union of church faith and civic pride insured widespread involvement and commitment. When the town banquet was held following the last play, a feeling of satisfaction as well as revelry were evident. The sense of community was one means of combating the rigors of medieval life. At the same time, the plays provided a means of connection between the church and the growing secular concerns.

The theatre helped people forget the violence and death of the times. Drama provided an explanation for the suffering of the world and a reason to go on living.

Life was given meaning through the drama as the community members worked together to express their faith. People displayed their skills as actors and as guildsmen. The message of the plays was that life will be better, but the performance of the plays showed that this life could also be enjoyable and wondrous.

DRAMATIC LITERATURE

Major developments in dramatic literature during this period were the expansion of the biblical plays and the development of alternative genres of religious plays. They were complemented by a variety of secular forms. Only the dominant forms are discussed here.

Liturgical Drama

An example of this expanded liturgical drama is *The Representation of Adam*, described at the beginning of the chapter. This type of play, based on biblical stories, is commonly called a *mystery*. Written in Anglo-Norman French sometime in the 12th century, *Adam* includes more than one biblical scene covering a wide time span. The first section takes place in the Garden of Eden and includes God's commandment, the temptation of Adam, the temptation of Eve, the loss of innocence, and the expulsion. The second section dramatizes the story of Cain and Abel, while in the third section prophets appear to foretell the coming of Jesus. The play is written with characters who have subtle and well-delineated emotions, values, and motivations. The playwright adds directions for facial reactions and gestures to complement the language. The play is also filled with stage effects, climactic actions, and pageantry. Mystery plays are not always serious. The *Second Shepherd's Play*, from the Wakefield Cycle in England, provides contemporary English shepherds as comic material, while *Abraham and Isaac* creates comedy with biblical characters.

The most enduring form of liturgical drama are passion plays. Depicting the last days of the life of Jesus Christ, they were popular throughout Europe. The passion play in Oberammergau, Germany, is known to many Westerners; another play from the period, still performed in Poland, is *History of the Glorious Resurrection of Our Saviour* (1580) by Mikolaj of Wilkowiecka.

Other Religious Forms

The Representation of Adam is but one example of the expansion of and experimentation in liturgical drama in the 12th and 13th centuries. Other forms that were performed in this time period included the consecration of the church, an adoration of the cross, and a variety of Christmas dramas. These latter, including the *Slaughter of the Innocents*, the *Play of Herod*, and the *Play of Daniel* (all 12th century), were performed in the church and relied more on music and gestures than on verse dialogue to tell the story. Adherence to the biblical text was essential in them, but wherever the character was sketchily presented in the Bible (as with Herod, particularly) the authors felt free to use

HROSVIT OF
GANDERSHEIM
(c . 9 3 5 – 9 7 3)

*A*mong the most interesting figures in medieval theatre history was a young Saxon nun, Hrosvit of Gandersheim. The earliest poet known in Germany and the first dramatist after the fall of Rome, Hrosvit was the author of legends, dramas, and poems.

Actually, the term *nun* is misleading, for Hrosvit most likely was a member of a sect that emphasized teaching and education. Although we tend to refer to this period as "the Dark Ages," studies indicate that many parts of the community maintained an emphasis on learning. This included a continued study of the classics and the transfer of critical writings into the vernacular, making them available to more members of the populace. Belonging to a convent freed a woman from usual sexual and familial responsibilities and allowed her to pursue learning.

Our knowledge of Hrosvit's life comes only from her own writings and the deductions of scholars. She was born of noble parents about 935 in a section of modern-day Germany. Typically she would have entered the convent at an early age, and her studies would have included both Latin and Greek. She wrote eight legends, six dramas, three epics, and a poem. These works were rediscovered in 1494, and although scholars of the time were excited, little further notice was given to her writings. Interestingly, it was not till 1923 that the plays were published in English.

The works of the Roman playwright Terence are the obvious structural models for her plays, but her objectives are distinct from his. She writes in one preface that her object is ". . . to glorify within the limits of my poor talent, the laudable chastity of Christian virgins. . . ." Her plays present women as dignified, intelligent, and respectable. Two deal with attempted seduction (by either guile or force) that is resisted. The plays tend to be episodic, made up of many short scenes, and the lines are short and to the point. Her characters, however, are believable and interesting, and the plays have theatrical value and have been produced successfully from time to time.

Controversy exists over whether the plays were ever produced during

Hrosvit's lifetime. Stage directions are included, so it would seem that production was intended, but no records have been discovered. If the plays were produced in the 10th century, they would have been performed by women for an audience of women. In this fashion, as well as in her learning, her talent, and her concerns for the rights of women, Hrosvit provides an intriguing forerunner to contemporary women's theatre.

their imagination in inventing dialogue and motivation. Musical instruments were used for many of these plays, and the long musical sections suggest that the action was spread throughout the entire church, necessitating processionals from one area to another.

In Italy, the best-known religious plays were the *sacre rappresentazioni*. Extensions of the earlier *laudi*, or songs of praise, the plays were performed throughout the Italian peninsula but were most closely identified with Tuscany, the area around Florence. Italian artists brought to these plays the same creative energy for which they became famous in other fields: colorful costumes, complicated stage machinery, and beautifully designed backdrops. One of the first of the *sacre rappresentazioni* was Feo Belcari's *Abraham and Isaac*, performed in 1449.

Miracle and morality plays were other forms of religious drama popular throughout the medieval period. Miracle plays were stories of the lives of saints; they could be developed around saints that were particularly important to a given community. In addition, they offered multiple opportunities for special effects that have immense popular appeal. As such they served to expand the scope of the drama. Jean Bodel's *Play of Saint Nicolas* (1200) is an example of a miracle play, telling of a miracle performed by Saint Nicolas when he was in North Africa.

Morality plays were a later form of religious drama, prominent after 1400. They retained the religious concern with the life to come but shifted the dramatic emphasis to an individual's preparation for that life. The action centered on the classic struggle between good and evil within the human soul. Morality plays were distinguishable from other religious forms because they did not illustrate stories from the Bible or the lives of saints. Instead, they were secular in their emphasis on the problems of living a moral life in this world. The titles from the French plays alone indicate the nature of the moralities: *Just Man and Worldly Man*, *The Blind Man and the Cripple*, and *The Blasphemers*.

The most famous morality play is *Everyman*, written about 1500. When Death comes to take Everyman, he asks time to find someone among his friends who will accompany him. Family, Beauty, Strength, Five Wits, Goods, and Discretion all desert him, though they remind him of the joy they brought him in this life. Only Good Deeds agrees to go with him. Everyman learns that this life is but a preparation for the life to come and that what may seem important is, in the scheme of eternity, often meaningless. Only through a morally just life does an individual find true peace and salvation.

A modern production of *Everyman*.   *Courtesy New York Public Library*

Later Secular Forms

Many of the early secular forms of drama continued to flourish throughout the entire medieval period, retaining their folk origins and loosely scripted structures. During the 1200s, however, a number of plays were written that deal with everyday life but are carefully crafted in the manner of the morality and miracle plays. One type of secular play popular in France was called the farce, because it presented less-than-admirable characters in embarrassing situations that revealed their human fallibility. Farces dramatized situations with broad humor and physical actions. The dialogue and events were usually domestic, with husbands and wives cheating on each other, or merchants and thieves engaging each other. Most of the characters make foolish errors of judgment, with the audience laughing at both the error and the later disclosure of the error. The French farce *Pierre Patelin* (c. 1470) is still read today, as are the plays of the Italian Angelo Beolco (1502?–43).

Variations on farce included *sotties* and *sermons joyeux*. *Sotties* were short comic satires on social, political, or religious subjects, the most famous of which was *The Prince of Fools* (1512). *Sermons joyeux* were burlesque sermons. The *Fastnachtspiel* or Shrovetide plays in Germany introduced stock comic characters in the presentation of social satire intermixed with wild celebration.

Another type of medieval drama appearing in the late 1400s is frequently called humanist drama because it was written by people connected with the development of humanism. Humanist drama is a bridge to the Renaissance, for it anticipates the interest in human institutions such as law and education and concerns itself with the need for social reforms. Unlike farce, which ridicules its characters and situations,

The *Schembartlauf*, a 15th-century German festival in which the ship, protected by demons, is overcome and destroyed.   *Courtesy Stadtbibliothek Nurnberg*

humanist drama focuses on ideas, courtly manners, or human virtues such as wit and science. Frequently, the writing includes classical allusions or linguistic devices. However, the plays are identifiably medieval in their use of stock characters from the morality plays, in their absence of act divisions and classical references, and in their generally didactic tone. Of the surviving humanist dramas, the most famous are *Fulgens and Lucrece* (a romance) by Henry Medwall (fl. 1500), and *I Suppositi* (no date) by Ludovico Ariosto (1474–1533).

CONNECTIONS

The decline or evolution of medieval theatre coincides with disruption in the Church. The weakening of the Church, the challenge to the supremacy of the Pope, and the increase in secular learning were all distinct threats to the Church's position in society. Drama was a powerful weapon—and it could be used as powerfully by the Church's enemies as by the Church itself. Accordingly, Church bans against religious plays began to appear, in the Netherlands in 1530, in Italy in 1547, and in England by 1558, and these sanctions were formalized by the Council of Trent (1545–1563).

Medieval theatre, however, did not decline or disappear so much as evolve into Renaissance forms. The spectacle of the cycle plays were adapted to Renaissance pageantry. The mock combats and dances were integrated into political festivals. Humanist drama evolved into the classical plays written by Renaissance playwrights. Further, the Renaissance retained many elements of medieval drama: the use of drama for moral instruction, the presence of characters who represent virtues and vices, the inclusion of low-life comic characters, and the sense of visual and aural spectacle, among others.

The reasons for this gradual transformation are directly attributable to the rise of the Renaissance. The Catholic Church lost its dominance of European thought with the Protestant Reformation. Martin Luther advocated the use of music in worship, but otherwise opposed extensive reliance on elaborate church decorations that had been the backbone of theatrical spectacle. The mystery of the faith was challenged by new scientific investigations. The power of the monarchy replaced the authority of the bishop. Most important, the message of salvation in the next life was undermined by the humanist search for meaning in this life, and by increased confidence within individuals that they could improve themselves through study and hard work. By 1500, the core of most medieval drama—the promise of a better life after death—had been rendered obsolete by the confidence and exuberance of a new age.

Nevertheless, medieval drama made significant contributions to the history of theatre. It developed new methods of theatrical presentation, including the pageant wagons, stage machinery, and the use of a generalized playing area (the platea). It created new comic characters who survived with different names for centuries (the flamboyant and evil Herod, the pessimistic and nagging Wife of Noah, the ignorant and cuckolded husbands). It developed the possibilities of actors interacting with the audience. It demonstrated the potential of an epic theatre that covers a vast period of time and includes many separate actions.

Perhaps the most important contribution of medieval drama was its creation of a theatre of faith and community. It found the means to express a deeply felt religion in terms that could be appreciated by all people, regardless of their station in life or their learning. It visualized the sense of mystery in that faith without becoming childish or sacrilegious. It illustrated the relationship between events of the distant past and the promise of a future life. It brought the community together to work on a single project filled with civic pride. It gave renewal to the community's belief system. In serving all these functions, it expanded the scope of the theatre as a social institution. Medieval drama illustrates the ability of the theatre to bring a community together to express its faith. Therein lay its vitality.

SOURCES FOR FURTHER STUDY

Social/Art/Philosophy Background

Cantor, Norman. *Medieval History: The Life and Death of a Civilization.* New York: Macmillan Publishing Co., 1969.

Dubruck, Edelgard. *New Images of Medieval Women.* Lewiston, N.Y.: Edwin Mellan Press, 1989.

Duby, Goerges, ed. *A History of Private Life: Revelations of the Medieval World.* Trans. Arthur Goldhammer. Cambridge, Mass.: Harvard University Press, 1988.

Fisher, Sheila, and Janet E. Halley, eds. *Seeking the Women in the Late Medieval and Renaissance Writings.* Knoxville: University of Tennessee Press, 1989.

Focillon, Henri. *The Art of the West in the Middle Ages.* 2 vols. New York: Phaidon, 1969.

Heer, Friedrich. *The Medieval World.* New York: Mentor, 1964.

Huizinga, Johann. *The Waning of the Middle Ages.* Garden City, N.Y.: Anchor Books, 1949.

Leff, Gordon. *Medieval Thought.* Chicago: Quadrangle, 1959.

Male, Emile. *The Gothic Image.* Trans. Dora Nussey. New York: Harper, 1958.

Martindale, Andrew. *Gothic Art.* New York: Praeger Books, 1967.

Oakley, Francis. *The Medieval Experience.* New York: Charles Scribners Sons, 1974.

Tuchman, Barbara W. *A Distant Mirror: The Calamitous 14th Century.* New York: Ballantine Books, 1978.

Medieval Theatre

Chambers, E. K. *The Medieval Stage.* London: Oxford University Press, 1903.

Clopper, Lawrence. *Chester.* Toronto: University of Toronto Press, 1979.

Hardison, O. B., Jr. *Christian Rite and Christian Drama in the Middle Ages: Essays in the Origin and Early History of Modern Drama.* Baltimore: Johns Hopkins University Press, 1965.

Nagler, A. M. *The Medieval Religious Stage: Shapes and Phantoms.* New Haven: Yale University Press, 1976.

Salter, F. M. *Medieval Drama in Chester.* Toronto: University of Toronto Press, 1955.

Tydeman, William. *The Theatre in the Middle Ages.* Cambridge: Cambridge University Press, 1978.

Vince, Ronald W. *A Companion to the Medieval Theatre.* New York: Greenwood Press, 1989.

Wickham, Glynne. *The Medieval Theatre.* New York: St. Martin's Press, 1974.

Medieval Drama

Axton, Richard. *European Drama of the Early Middle Ages.* London: Hutchinson University Library, 1974.

Bevington, David. *Medieval Drama.* Boston: Houghton Mifflin Co., 1975.

Case, Sue-Ellen. "Reviewing Hrosvit." *Theatre Journal* 35:4 (December 1983): 533–542.

Denny, Neville. *Medieval Drama.* New York: Crane Russak, 1973.

Frank, Grace. *The Medieval French Drama.* Oxford: Clarendon Press, 1954.

Wilson, Katharina M., ed. *Hrosvit of Gandersheim: Rara Avis in Saxonia?* Ann Arbor, Mich.: MARC Publishing Company, 1987.

Young, Karl. *The Drama of the Medieval Church.* Oxford: Oxford University Press, 1933.

C H A P T E R

5

General
Events

Arts
Events

Donatello's
David

1430–1432

Theatre
History
Events

Vitruvius's text,
On Architecture,
rediscovered

1414

Visual Spectacle in the Italian Renaissance

A young couple are engaged to be married, but neither wishes the match. The woman, Lepida, is secretly in love with a German nobleman disguised as the family tutor. The man, Lucretio, pines for a lady whom he thinks is dead, but who has actually reappeared in town disguised as a pilgrim. When the lady pilgrim discovers that her beloved is betrothed to another woman, she is upset. When she is told that he has made Lepida pregnant, she is furious. Lepida's father is also upset, especially when he learns that his daughter has been seen in bed with the family tutor. Meanwhile, Lucretio is none too happy either, since he has been falsely accused of being the father of Lepida's child. In fact, the only really happy person in this situation is Targhetta, the household servant. He finds the family's misfortune amusing and delights in telling everyone the awful news. So frustrating is the situation for the father that he determines to tell the prince all his problems. The prince is known for being harsh in his judgment of adulterers, and the father expects the prince will aid him in seeking retribution. He goes off to restore the family's honor. Act IV of *La Pellegrina* (1589) comes to an end.

During the intermission, the audience does not leave the great hall where the play is taking place. The entertainment that has attracted many in the audience is about to begin. The curtain opens to reveal an ocean. Aphrodite, dressed in a fleshtone body stocking adorned with jewels, is towed on a shell across the ocean by two perfume-squirting dolphins. Playful nymphs, precursors of the water-ballet movies of the 1940s, sing to a wedding couple in the audience. Then a ship, carrying between 20 and 40 sailors, enters and

Lorenzo de' Medici	Protestant Reformation begins		Council of Trent	
1469–1492	1517	1527	1545–1563	
		Rome sacked		

Translation of Plato	Leonardo's *The Last Supper*	Michelangelo's Sistine Chapel ceiling		Machiavelli's *The Prince*	Olympic Academy of Vicenza	Monteverdi's *Orfeo*	
1482	1490	1495–1498	1498	1508–1512	1532	1555	1607
Aldine Press	Michelangelo's sculpture *Pièta*						

	La Cassaria by Ariosto	Serlio's *Architettura*	Gelosi's commedia troupe	*La Pellegrina*	Teatro Farnese
	1508	1545	1569 1580	1589	1618
			Teatro Olimpico of Vicenza		

performs several feats, including hoisting full sail. They attack a young man, who jumps overboard. As the ship glides offstage, Arion leaps on the back of a dolphin and is borne away. The music accompanying this intermezzo ends and the curtain descends. The audience settles in for the last act of the serious comedy about two pairs of lovers and their efforts to find happiness.

This performance of *La Pellegrina* combines two characteristic features of Italian Renaissance theatre from 1500 to 1650. The first is the literary tradition, of which the comedy is an example. Renaissance drama was based on classical models, particularly the plays of Plautus and Terence. These models were followed in regard to their structure, their use of similar characters, and their comic devices of disguise and mistaken identity. They were updated by the addition of complications, new characters, and 16th-century Italian dialects and language.

The second feature of the period was the nonliterary tradition that emphasized visual and musical spectacles. Renaissance audiences loved to be amazed by special effects and scenic transformations. They were charmed by theatrical displays of ostentatious wealth. They delighted in the physical humor and pantomimic antics of the comic actors.

Not surprisingly, the visual and the spectacular theatre overwhelmed the literary theatre. Despite the publication of many fine humanist comedies, the theatre of sight and sound dominated the theatre of mind and matter. The story of the Italian Renaissance theatre is the story of the growth of this visual, nonliterary tradition. The between-acts visual entertainments grew in importance and popularity. Scenery and stagecraft became both an art and a science. Theatrical pageants and parades were used to symbolize the power of rulers. Opera was born of the union of visual display and musical excellence. Meanwhile, other audiences embraced the commedia dell'arte, a nonscripted theatre filled with stock characters and physical humor and pantomime. Less than a half-dozen plays of the Italian Renaissance are still performed today, but the period has influenced the modern theatre in architecture, scenery and scenic devices, pageants, and improvisational theatre.

SOCIAL IDEAS

The reasons for the development of visual spectacle in the Italian Renaissance are to be found first in the social history of the period. The pageantry and visual splendor of 16th- and 17th-century theatre is deeply embedded in the phenomenon of the Renaissance. Today scholars trace the beginnings of the Renaissance into the early 14th century. Some writers insist that the Renaissance was a very gradual development of a few ideas, while others hold to the more traditional view that the Renaissance was a sudden awakening of interest in the classics that occurred in Italy around the year 1400 and lasted into the middle 1500s. Whatever its origin, the Renaissance is a period in which several new ideas began to spread through Europe, undermining the assumptions and attitudes associated with medieval institutions and encouraging writers and artists to explore the world in new and revolutionary ways. In literature, the rediscovery of the classics brought new interest in Greek and Roman models of writing. In economics, the evolution of capitalism gave rise to the merchants of Venice. In science, Copernicus (1473–1543) and Galileo (1564–1642) disproved the theory that the earth is the center of the universe. In art, visual artists rendered experience less in symbolic and allegorical terms, and more in natural and mechanical modes. Permeating all these developments were two clusters of ideas and experiences: statecraft and humanism.

Statecraft

The social and political foundation of the Renaissance was the Italian city-state. Unlike medieval kingdoms, the city-states were ruled by princes who held their positions through power rather than through claims of heredity. The princes defended themselves by engaging in complex political intrigues and occasional warfare. The famous advice of Machiavelli (1469–1527) in his book *The Prince* (1513) indicates the means necessary for a prince to hold his crown. When they were not engaged in diplomacy or battles, princes used another tactic to prove their strength—they showed off their wealth in demonstrations of economic power. Hidden wealth never deterred one's enemies or impressed one's friends in the Renaissance. It was necessary to display the riches of the city-state for everyone to see.

The history of the Renaissance theatre is based in large measure on this determination of princes to prove that they were powerful. They commissioned artists and craftsmen to create theatrical spectacles that would awe their subjects and impress their neighbors. Theatrical activities, including pageants, parades, tournaments, and other community festivals, became metaphors for the strength of a city and the personal greatness of its prince. The people created their own theatre, the commedia dell'arte, but the princes relied on their own theatre to provide legitimacy for their rule.

Humanism

What distinguished the Italian princes from other rulers who had used the arts to assert their power was the influence of humanism. Humanists were men and women who studied the classics and discussed great ideas of the ancients. They encouraged the conviction (especially in the princes) that their age was the equivalent in brilliance of Classical Athens, Rome, and Egypt. They identified connections between the ideas of Plato and those of Christianity. They did not reject Christianity, but wed it to philosophers of other ages. In the process, they built up civic pride in the greatness of Italy and in Italy's new princes. They provided the philosophical legitimacy the new princes needed in order to maintain their position. As a result, every court sought the most renowned scholars to advise them. Popes appointed the humanists as cardinals, and princes commissioned them to write new works. These humanists had no loyalty to a native city; they were international citizens, traveling from one court to another in search of support.

The impact of humanism on the theatre was considerable. There was a reawakening of interest in the ideas of Roman and Greek writers and thinkers. For example, Vitruvius's book of architecture, including information on Roman theatres, was rediscovered in 1414. Twelve plays of Plautus were found in 1429. These works were the subject of discussions in courts and universities. By 1500 Aristotle's *Poetics* was published and most of the known plays of Terence and Plautus were also in print.

In addition, humanism fostered a new conception of the individual, which in turn influenced the conception of character in drama. Heroes were given the civilizing characteristics of *virtù*, meaning excellence in all things. In contrast to the medieval characters who generally focused on the world to come, Renaissance characters lived in this world and tested themselves by expanding their capabilities. Court audiences saw themselves in these characters and found them appealing.

Humanism provided a literary and classical foundation for drama. It generated interest in the ancient theatre. It encouraged experiments to re-create the productions of Classical Athens and Rome. In devising these experiments, humanists relied on their love for the visual and the aural.

ARTS IDEAS

The Italian Renaissance is associated in most modern minds not with theatre but with the visual arts. The Renaissance evokes the names of many of the greatest artists in Western culture: Leonardo da Vinci (1452–1519), Michelangelo (1475–1564), Raphael (1483–1520), Titian (c. 1490–1576), and Botticelli (1444–1510), as well as the men

The arch of the City of Florence designed for the entry of Christina of Lorraine, 1589.
Courtesy of the Warburg Institute, University of London

who preceded them: Brunelleschi (1377–1446), Donatello (1386–1466), and Masaccio (1401–1428). The talent of these men, many of whom also designed for the theatre, was to create new means of artistic communication. They articulated the world around them in ways that had not been conceived for centuries. They modeled the human form to give it new expression, feeling, and subtlety. In drawings, oils, frescoes, and sculpture they translated the spirit of the age into palpable form. In doing so, they created a new sensitivity to ways of seeing things. As a result of their influence, a demand was created for the most beautiful and visually spectacular in all things.

Perspective

No single technique or artistic ideas initiated the Renaissance, but the development of perspective transformed the visual arts in the 1400s and dominated composition in both painting and theatre for centuries. Perspective is the process of rendering three-dimensional space on a flat surface. It utilizes the scientific method to organize a picture to suggest depth. The eye perceives objects in the distance to be smaller than those in proximity, and perspective is the method of realizing that gradation on a flat surface.

Andrea Mantegna's rendering of the body of Christ in the tomb (c. 1480) is a stunning example of the effects of perspective. Perspective assumes two points—the point of view of the observer, and the vanishing point or the point in the "distance" to which the painting recedes. The observer is made to feel a part of the scene because the artist has brought the edge of the scene close to the surface of the canvas. The observer cannot treat the scene objectively because he or she is a part of it. The realistic depiction of the body is rendered in several ways. First, vertical lines of the body recede as the eye moves toward the head, which is farther from the observer than the feet. These lines converge at a point behind the head of Christ. This vanishing point, or point at which the images vanish in the distance, also organizes the picture. The focus is on Christ, not on the witnesses surrounding Him. Perspective is also achieved by darkening the colors of those objects farther from the eye of the observer. Finally, perspective is achieved by the use of symmetry, the careful ordering of all elements so that they are equally balanced on either side of the vanishing point, thus keeping the eye focused in the center where the main object of attention rests.

Perspective was adapted to theatre design. All sets had a vanishing point where the lines of the set converged. There also was a single point from which to observe the set, a point reserved for the duke or prince. This "duke's seat" was situated on a straight line directly in front of the vanishing point on the set. Just as Mantegna complimented the observer by organizing all the elements of his picture to create the maximum effect on the observer, the Renaissance designer organized the sets to compliment the person seated in the middle of the auditorium.

Music

In Florence, a group of humanists calling themselves the Camerata Fiorentina (founded in 1576) searched for the musical style of the ancient Greek dramatists. They wanted music that was more personal, more direct, and more human than seemed available to them in medieval music. They wanted to be able to understand the words of the script in order to move the action forward. Also, they wanted melodies that would reflect the words of the texts in both emotion and thought. Finally, they wanted the texts of the music to reflect the classical interest in mythology rather than the Christian Church's emphasis on spirituality and mysticism.

The first work to meet these conditions was *Dafne*, written in 1597 by Jacopo Peri, who called his effort a "musical fable." When he wrote *Euridice* three years later, he labeled the work a musical drama, giving recognition to the flow of dramatic action in the text. The form gained maturity and musical style under the composer Claudio Monteverdi, whose *Orfeo* (1607) and *The Coronation of Poppea* (1642) are still performed today. Monteverdi transformed the Camerata's expectations into a fluid musical style with intense dramatic effect and musical variety. The action of his operas was usually static; events occurred offstage and the singers responded to them rather than engaging in action themselves. However, musical and dramatic interest was sustained by magnificient scenery and believable characters. In Monteverdi's operas, the Italian taste for visual spectacle was combined with an emerging love of musical dramatic expression.

ITALIAN RENAISSANCE THEATRE

The history of Italian Renaissance theatre provides a rare opportunity to place two dissimilar theatrical traditions side by side. Both the traditional scripted theatre and the commedia dell'arte were prominent forms during this period, and the distinct cultural values they embody present an interesting view of the range of ideas that existed in Renaissance Italy.

A setting for *La Pellegrina*, 1589.   *Courtesy of the Warburg Institute, University of London*

Occasion

The distinction between the two forms is evident in nearly every aspect, including the occasion for performance. The "legitimate" or humanist theatre was performed on special occasions as they were determined by a prince. Such an occasion might be the arrival of special guests, the celebration of a birthday or other special event, or simply a "party" for friends and associates. Performances were thus not directly tied to any state or religious calendar, but were given to meet political or social needs.

At first the commedia apparently was performed at fairs or other civic gatherings, but as its popularity increased, performances were given more frequently. Rather than a day being designated for special performances, the arrival of a commedia troupe itself created an occasion. Thus the basis for performance was essentially commercial—it depended on when and where the troupe could draw an audience. This significant change in the occasion for performance is further experienced in the English Renaissance or Elizabethan period.

Location

The two forms similarly represent an extreme diversity in the location of the performance. In Renaissance Italy, the association of theatre with special civic events and festivities actually retarded the building of permanent theatres. When a prince financed

Teatro Olimpico, designed by Palladio and Scamozzi.   *Property of the Commune of Vicenza.*

A TRIP TO THE
RENAISSANCE
THEATRE

Wedding of Christine and Ferdinand: Florence, 1589

As Christine arrives at the performance of *La Pellegrina* at the Uffizi Palace in 1589, she can't decide whether to be excited or just exhausted. She is excited to attend a performance given in her honor, but she is exhausted from the series of theatrical activities she has been attending over the past weeks. It all began with her betrothal to Ferdinand I de' Medici, Grand Duke of Florence. It has taken two months just to travel from her native Lorraine in France to Florence, for she has had to follow a carefully planned route that will consolidate political alliances and impress neutral states. Her wedding is to be celebrated with dozens of theatrical entertainments and a bewildering display of Medici wealth. To the Medici, the wedding of young Christine to a man she has never met is to be the most important wedding of the century. They intend it to be a demonstration of Medici power and wealth. Sometimes Christine feels she is just going along for the ride.

The plans for Christine's wedding are elaborate. When Christine arrives in Florence, her entry into the city and formal meeting with Ferdinand are to be the ostensible climax of a parade, but the glorious history (somewhat fabricated) of the Medici family is the central theme. The event is presented *à la antique,* or in the ancient style of the entry of great military conquerors into a city. In addition to the procession of dignitaries, arches have been erected along the parade route to tell the story of the Medici family and to extol the virtues of this marriage. The arches are made of wood, canvas, and cloth and are adorned with statues of mythological significance. They are painted in perspective and include paintings of great moments in Florentine and Medici history. In addition to the arches and tableaux along the parade route, the procession itself includes musicians, equestrian units, and floats or decorated wagons. In the time since Christine's arrival, each day has been filled with activities specifically held in her honor. One day she attends an athletic event; on another, a *naumachia,* a mock battle of ships in a plaza flooded for the occasion.

Now, nearly two weeks after the parade, Christine and her wedding party gather in the theatre at the Uffizi Palace to witness what rumors claim will be the most spectacular theatrical entertainment in a thousand years. A large crowd of magnificently dressed patrons has gathered for this special occasion, and much of their attention is focused on Christine, not on the play, which is *La Pellegrina,* or *The Lady Pilgrim,* by Giròlamo Bargagli.

As the curtain rises, Christine sees a pleasant, traditional scene design. A single outdoor scene painted in sharp perspective, it depicts three city streets in Pisa that converge at the front of the playing area. It seems nicely painted but Christine finds it not as extraordinary as she had been expecting. Indeed, the play is rather ordinary and Christine begins to feel weary and somewhat disappointed, facing an evening five acts long.

As the first act ends, Christine stirs restlessly, but in just a few minutes the curtain rises again and Christine finds herself transported. Before her is a fantastic scene of clouds in which a huge choir of the Sirens, Fates, and Planets are magically suspended singing, with Harmony, the praises of the wedding couple and expressing their hopes for the success of the marriage. The music, with the full orchestra, the huge scenery, and the lighting, create an ethereal effect, and Christine watches silently, overwhelmed by the spectacle.

As Act II begins Christine finds herself impatient with the play, because she is so anxiously awaiting the next *intermezzo.* The second is even more delightful than the first, as a music contest is held between two groups of women. Christine gasps audibly when a huge mountain suddenly disappears into the stage floor and applauds excitedly when the losers of the singing contest turn into magpies in full view of the audience. She looks around her quickly to see if she has been too demonstrative, but everyone seems thrilled with the performance.

During Act III, Christine pays little attention to the play and has trouble sitting still, becoming alert only as the curtain falls. She is not disappointed. From the very top of the stage, a pasteboard Apollo descends from the skies. Suddenly he becomes a real person who does battle with a gigantic python that has arisen out of the floor. The entire scene is accompanied by orchestra and chorus and the music rises to a climax as the hero slays the python with a gigantic arrow.

The rest of the evening is a blur, and at times Christine wonders if she is dreaming. In the final *intermezzo,* a nightmare vision of a 15-foot Lucifer startles her awake as he appears from Hell to eat children, but a chorus of Heavenly Spirits announces that such activities will stop now that the wedding couple are united. This announcement is followed by beautiful dancing, and Christine finds tears starting to roll down her cheeks.

During Act V Christine has trouble staying awake, for she has paid so little attention to the play she can't even follow the story. She has been at the theatre for nearly seven hours now and she knows that several more days of festivities await her before the actual wedding. For now, however, her only thoughts are of a comfortable bed and a good night's sleep.

a production, it was prepared for a courtyard, banquet hall, or large room converted for the occasion. The salon at the Uffizi Palace where *La Pellegrina* was held is an example of the last.

Not until 1580 was the first permanent theatre commissioned. Andrea Palladio (1509–1580), one of the period's greatest architects, designed the *Teatro Olimpico* to conform to his image of an ancient Roman theatre. At least in part this was based on Palladio's reading of Vitruvius's *De Architectura*, which had been rediscovered and published during this period. In addition to a semielliptical bank of seats, the auditorium, which seats approximately 1,000 people, is unusual for its row of columns and statues around the back of the seating area. What is most striking, however, is the imposing facade across the entire width of the stage, connecting on the sides with the seating. From floor to ceiling the stage is covered by this edifice that has only three portals for entrances and exits. The facade is decorated with columns, with niches holding statues, and friezes across the top. Of special interest are Vincenzo Scamozzi's original perspective street scenes, which are visible through the three portals and are still in position today.

The Teatro Olimpico opened in 1585 with a production of *Oedipus Rex* utilizing some of the best-known theatre artists of the period. Documents from the period indicate that the emphasis throughout was on visual and musical elements intended to dazzle the spectators. Special costumes were designed, considerable attention was paid to the lighting (which was supposed to produce the bright, direct feel of intense sunlight), many extras were used for the crowd scenes, and special music was composed. There is even some indication that perfume was used to indicate the offering of sacrifices to the gods. Oddly, due to expenses and changing styles, the Teatro Olimpico had a very short theatrical life, and for many years it was an architectural "museum," shown to important visitors but not used for performance. However, in the 19th century, opera was once again performed there, and since that time performances have occurred on a fairly regular basis. The excellence of the theatre's design allows the theatre to accommodate and enrich a wide variety of performance. Drama, opera, concerts, and ballet are all accommodated and enriched by the grandeur and elegance of the space.

Another theatre differing greatly from the Olimpico in style and size was built in 1588. Vincenzo Scamozzi (1552–1616), who had completed the Olimpico after Palladio's death, built at Sabionetta a small, intimate theatre seating just 250 people. The theatre at Sabionetta is generally considered to be closer in size and scale to the court theatre of the day. Five rows of seats arranged in a gentle curve front a small sloped orchestra that joins a small, flat, rectangular floor. A small raked stage contains a single vista of houses constructed and painted in perspective. Some accommodation for machinery probably existed above the stage, but generally the theatre is a model of simplicity and intimacy.

In 1618, the Teatro Farnese in Parma provided a model for theatre architecture that allowed for much more flexibility in staging. Designed by Giovanni Battista Aleotti (1546–1636), the auditorium is in a horseshoe shape. The pit area between the seats and the stage could be used for processions or dancing or perhaps filled with water for *naumachia*. The stage has an elaborate proscenium arch, one of the earliest to be permanently built in a theatre. The proscenium arch is the frame that surrounds the stage at the top and sides. Although the exact purpose for the development of the proscenium arch is unknown, it seems related to the traditional "portal" openings of the Greek and Roman theatres and it also seems to provide a "frame" such as those used for perspective paintings. Whatever its purpose, its functions are clear. It hides the stage machinery as well as the actors waiting to go onstage and provides an artificial "border" to the stage picture, creating a greater sense of what we would call "realism." It also separates the audience from the action, thereby enhancing the illusion of the stage as a location distinct from the auditorium. Aleotti is also credited with the invention of the flat-wing system of scenic perspective, which became a dominant form.

The commedia performance space, contrastingly, was an exercise in simplicity. Commedia troupes performed wherever they could find room, often utilizing a simple platform and a cloth backdrop. Records suggest that performances occurred in town squares, in courtyards, and in the streets. Performers were in close proximity to the spectator, and the spectator was free to move about during the performance. This informality of space produces a very different atmosphere for a performance. A modern parallel might be the difference between attending a rock concert in a formal auditorium with reserved seating, and attending one held in a park.

Performers

Not surprisingly, the two theatre forms focus on very different concepts of performance. The traditional theatre leaves few records of actors or actresses but does leave extended treatises on stage design. The commedia offers little information about scenery but is instead a history of actors.

Many of the innovations in scenic conventions in the traditional theatre were the results of the studies of Sebastiano Serlio (1475–1554). Serlio's works were published as *Architettura* in 1537 and were so popular that four new editions were required within seven years and the book was translated into German in 1542. Serlio explored the use of perspective on the stage and defined three basic stage settings: comic, tragic, and satyric (pastoral). The comic scene depicted houses "appropriate to private persons," including a church, a tavern, and the house of a procuress. The tragic scene represented the houses of great persons to reflect the grandeur of the subjects of tragedy. The pastoral scene was composed of "trees, rocks, hills, mountains, herbs, flowers, and fountains, together with some rustic huts. . . ." Additionally, Serlio called for the floor to slope from the front of the stage upward to the back to aid in creating perspective. Serlio was highly practical, noting that space must be maintained at the back of the stage so that actors can cross from one side to the other without being seen and also noting that a combination of three-dimensional relief building with perspective painting produces the best results. His writings also discussed means of producing lighting effect, including color, and special effects ranging from fires to thunder and lightning.

Nicola Sabbattini (1574–1654) was another scene designer whose works were widely distributed through publication. Sabbattini provided even more focus on perspective painting, but he is mainly known for his work with machinery to change sets and create special effects. Serlio's work was essentially stationary, with one set serving for an entire play. By the last quarter of the 16th century, the development of the *intermezzi*—or allegorical episodes that occurred between the acts of the traditional play—called for more and more attention to moveable scenery.

Sabbattini's work is a detailed "how to" book on creating theatre, from the

The setting for tragedy from Serlio's *Architettura*.   *Courtesy Mark J. Millard Architectural Collection,*
© *1992 National Gallery of Art, Washington*

building of the stage through such details as how to design balconies, how to place highlights and shadows, and how to paint the stage floor. For changing scenery, Sabattini developed Aleotti's method of setting flats in grooves both in the floor and in the stage ceiling. A second groove was then placed in front of the first set, and a second set of flats could be slid into place quickly and easily, resulting in a complete change of scenery. Sabattini further experimented with the use of *periaktoi*, in which three scenes could be mounted on three flats attached to one another to form a triangle. Careful placement of these units allowed the front panels to hide those behind. A winch system was then attached to central pivot poles in each unit. When the winch was turned, the units all turned simultaneously, rotating a second set of flats into audience view.

In later years, two other important advances occurred. Giacomo Torelli (1608–1678) is credited with the invention in the 1630s of an understage device for moving all the flat wings and backdrops simultaneously. Improving Sabbattini's groove method, Torelli cut a groove clear through the stage floor to the basement. A pole attached to the flat ran through this groove to a wheeled cart in the basement. Each of these carts was connected to a central wheel, so that a single person could move an entire set of flats in complete unison. This *chariot-and-pole* system reduced the chance of errors and accidents and permitted changes to take place in view of the audience, thus enhancing the scenic "magic" and further demonstrating human mechanical capabilities.

In the 1700s, Ferdinando Bibiena (1657–1743), one of a family of renowned scene designers, introduced the *scena per angolo*, which replaced the single vanishing point of the perspective picture with two or more vanishing points at the sides. This allowed a far more elaborate use of painting that was more effective to various sections of the audience. The spectacle they were able to create was extremely popular, and throughout both the 17th and 18th centuries Italian designers were in demand throughout Europe. The absolutist monarchs who wanted to demonstrate their wealth and power used the same theatrical devices that had been created for the princes of the Italian Renaissance.

The most complete use of these scenic wonders was in the *intermezzi* that were presented between the acts of the comedies. Huge choruses, full orchestras, dancing groups, and massive scenery were combined with numerous special effects to present tales based on mythology. Unrelated to the play, the *intermezzi* were usually related to one another by a theme that could reflect on the occasion of the performance. In this type of theatre a new "performer" was added to the author, the designer, and the actor, for a stage crew of as many as 50 people was needed to create this form of theatrical

Scene design for the first *intermezzo* of *La Pellegrina*.   *Drawing by Diane Tartar, University of Oregon*

magic. When the *intermezzi* are combined with a script, one can easily imagine how grand opera developed and became a dominant theatrical form in Italy for hundreds of years.

Compared to the intricacies of these scenic developments, the commedia stage was extremely simple. Although there is indication of some stage machinery having been used in the commedia, the focus is clearly on the actor rather than on the spectacle. While the actors of the traditional theatre were essentially talented amateurs, the commedia dell'arte performer was the true professional. Commedia was performed by troupes of actors who worked together to learn one another's strengths as performers, and then integrated those elements into their performances. No scripts were written, but the major business of each scene was prepared in outline form. These plot outlines were usually attached to the sides of the stage or the back walls of the scene to remind actors of what was to happen next. Substituting for dialogue were *lazzi*, or prearranged comic actions inserted into the performance. For instance, an actor might be famous for his unusual laugh or his sneeze, and the other actors would then agree to include the laugh lazzo or the sneeze lazzo at a given moment in the script. The other actors had to be ready to perform these or other lazzi at any moment, in case they felt they were losing the interest of their audience.

In addition to being adept at lazzi, most actors were well-read and had studied and memorized set speeches that they could deliver at any moment. These would have been refined over several performances to achieve a particular effect. Some actors kept notebooks of these speeches to be able to use them no matter what troupe they were with or what scenes they were performing. Not all commedia performers were restricted to street performance; some of the most popular were invited to perform in learned comedy as well.

The stories of the commedia ranged from simple encounters of a clown and an abandoned baby to complex intrigues involving several suitors after the same lady. Frequently the stories grew out of situations familiar to the lower classes and embodied their attitudes toward the aristocracy. The plots invariably relied on ribaldry and physical humor. The modern term *slapstick* derives from the stick used to spank wayward characters in commedia. Low humor included coarse jokes and absurd physical actions. The extent of this kind of humor is uncertain, but the performance of commedia dell'arte was certainly direct, gestural, and physical.

The core of the commedia performances were the individual characters. Since the plots were simple and the dialogue improvised, the sustaining appeal of the plays was the appearance of a well-known character. Over time, these characters became stock; that is, they were a part of the basic performance of the company. Actors specialized in a single character and developed lazzi and set speeches to match that character. One character type required another (a doting father needs a daughter to worry about) until a company of characters existed who were loosely interrelated in stage business and comic possibilities. Their names might change from one country to another and also over time, but their comic construction was similar.

Seven characters were especially important. *Harlequin* was a naive and bumbling servant, an ignorant valet who could slide and worm his way into and out of every conceivable situation. He was a master acrobat, depicted as walking on stilts, turning somersaults, and contorting his body. He was the supreme clown who used every part of his body to articulate feelings and extract laughter. *Brighella* was an intruder, a sly and clever parasite who lived off the foibles of others. With a dark beard and a huge, foppish moustache, he was a threat to every fool who walked the Renaissance stage. In later years, he became less cruel. *Pantaloon* was a miser about everything—he counted his money, protected his daughter, and coveted his neighbor's family and fortune. In his long red stockings, black cape, and huge beard, he was always falling in love with some young lady who would escape his amorous advances thanks to Brighella or another servant. *Dottore* was the only companion for Pantaloon, because he, too, shared a love of the young ladies. Whereas Pantaloon was primarily interested in wooing the lady with money and self-conceit, the Doctor was always ready with an impressive quotation badly mangled or a thoroughly irreverent medicinal cure. *Capitano* was the Renaissance figure who satirized Italian soldiers. He wore a mean-looking mask with a protruding nose, and his costume was changed to fit the military insignia of the audience's city. Proud and boastful, arrogant and overbearing, the Capitano was always determined to win the heroine by challenging old Pantaloon to a swordfight. He never won, but he never admitted

Commedia dell'arte figures.   *Photo courtesy Statens Konstmuseer, Stockholm*

defeat. The young *lovers* were always the focus of the attentions of these other characters, for their union, after considerable complications and several setbacks, was the traditional resolution of the commedia plot. He was a handsome young man, and she a beautiful young girl. The use of women to play the female roles was regarded as a scandal by some churchmen of the time, but their talents and beauty endeared them to princes and public alike.

ITALIAN COMMEDIA CHARACTERS

Harlequin—clown	Insolent, cocky, dumb but shrewd; opportunistic; athletic, acrobatic; often a servant who tries to please his master and win a maiden.
	Also known as Arlecchino, Truffaldino, Zanni, and other names.
Scapino—intriguer	Mischievous, plotting, insinuating; a musician; often a servant, but very calculating for his own ends; spontaneous and inventive.
	Also known as Brighello, Mezzetino, Scapin.
Pulcinella—clown	Physical, often violent; few morals; loud, brash, and a seducer of women.
	Also known as Punch (England) and Hanswurst (Germany).
Pierro—servant	Trustworthy, simple, honest, gentle; accepts the blame for everything; loves to cry.
	Also known as Pierrot, Pedrolino, Gilles.
Pantalone—old father	Greedy, conniving, self-important; likes to control everyone around him; wants to get more money or win a young maiden; usually stupid.
	Also known as Pantaloon, given other names by Molière.
Dottore—doctor	Dull, pedantic, overly proud of his knowledge, but actually stupid about life; often a lawyer, teacher, or philosopher (later could be a minister or puritan).
	Also known by his other professions.
Capitano—captain	A military man, a braggart; confident, domineering, loud-mouthed, and insolent; wants to win the young maiden with boasts.
	Also known as Scaramouche, Giangurgolo.
Inamorata—female lover	Gallant, well-mannered; disdains the advances of the men; coy, but also quarrelsome.
	No single name is used for her.
Columbine—maid	Playful, confident, cocky, outspoken; often lusty and earthy; occasionally involved in intrigue to insure the lovers' union.
	Also known as Soubrette.
Ruffiana—gossip	Talkative; usually a yenta or matchmaker; considers herself above reproach yet judges others freely; usually old but thinks she is youthfully attractive.

Each of these characters, except the young lovers, wore a mask covering the upper half of the face, making the character instantly recognizable to the audience. Sometimes actors played specific characters so well that the actor and the character became intertwined. Such was the case with Isabella Andreini, one of the two leaders of a famous commedia troupe, who played the role of the young lover so well the character became known as "Isabella." Commedia performers could play more than one role, however. Commedia troupes performed the traditional comedies on occasion and even performed tragedies as a part of their repertoire. However, it was the improvised comedy that won them international fame.

Commedia troupes appeared throughout Europe. Companies of performers (frequently referred to as "families," although the actors were not necessarily relatives and were known to change troupes for better roles or more money) toured in London and Spain and France. Paris had resident companies of "Italian players" for many years. Indeed, the later history of commedia is more accurately French than Italian.

By the mid-1700s, written comedies in both Italy and France transformed the commedia characters and situations into people and situations suited to the times. Nevertheless, the commedia introduced (or revived) characters who would remain in dramatic literature to the present. It also realized an improvisational theatre form to which professionals would return in every succeeding age. Wherever pantomime, clowns, and street artists perform today, they are continuing the traditions of the commedia dell'arte.

Audience

The audience of the two theatres differed widely. Traditional theatre was performed by the upper class for the upper class. Indeed, attendance at theatrical performances was frequently a political necessity, and the occasions tended to be highly formal. A commedia audience, on the other hand, was composed of everyone else—although a wealthy person or two might be on hand, probably in disguise. Attendance was voluntary and even perhaps somewhat based on chance, but it may be simplistic to consider the event as purely entertainment and "fun." Some critics suggest that the character types of the commedia are subversive in their depiction of the upper class and that the commedia provided a means of social commentary serving to unite and provide identity to the lower classes.

Standards of Judgment

In a commedia performance, audience response was the basic arbiter of good taste. If the audience liked it, it was a good performance, and no set rules of performance were developed. However, the traditional theatre did have set rules that were developed by critics and written down.

Once again, much criticism is based on translations and interpretations of Aristotle. A key concept developed during this period is *verisimilitude*. This concept stresses that the poet's responsibility is to show on stage only that which is true, presented in such a way that the audience will believe it is true. Renaissance critics further determined that the role of drama is to instruct people in such a way that moral improvement will be the outcome.

A maverick among Italian critics was perhaps the most influential of them all. Lodovico Castelvetro's (1505–1571) study of Aristotle, published in 1570, was the first of the commentaries to be widely published, and Castelvetro was not afraid to disagree with Aristotle, altering the Greek ideas to the needs of the Renaissance stage. Castelvetro's theory is based on the concept of *verisimilitude*. He claimed that theatre is aimed not only at the learned population but also at the uncultured masses, that it is not for the reader but for the spectator. For this reason, theatre must be understandable to the least educated member of the audience. Castelvetro stated, therefore, that the events of the play must cover no greater length of time than it takes to perform them, because even the simplest spectator will know that only a few hours have passed, not several days. Similarly, the action must take place in one location, because the audience will know they remain in the theatre, even if the scenery is changed. This rigid definition of the *unities* of time and place were highly influential in later years, although many of Castelvetro's contemporaries disagreed with him.

Castelvetro also claims that tragedy is easier to write and produce than comedy, for the comic writer must invent all the parts of the play, while the tragic writer usually bases the play on an existing myth or legend. This justification of comedy is important, in that it grants validity to comedy even though comedy is largely ignored by Aristotle.

Finally, Castelvetro claims that the purpose of theatre is not to instruct, as Aristotle and others claimed, but simply to delight. Theatre, therefore, is not restricted by its ability to teach but is justified simply by its ability to bring pleasure to the audience. This focus on the psychology of the audience as the determinant of a play's value was an important change in theatre criticism and greatly affected future developments.

DRAMATIC LITERATURE

The *intermezzi* and the commedia dell'arte were the visual and popular forms of theatre in the Italian Renaissance. The literary drama of scripted plays occupied a middle ground between these two forms, appearing with the *intermezzi* and sharing many of the plots and characters of the commedia. At first the plays were written in Latin, in imitation of the Roman comedies, by humanist scholars attached to major ducal courts. A few plays appeared in the 1400s that were neither medieval nor classical imitations; however, the beginnings of the *commedia erudita* (learned comedy) are generally associated with the 1500s.

Structurally, the learned comedies followed classical principles. Each was five acts long with exposition dominating the first act, complications the second and third, lamentations the fourth, and resolutions the last. The plays adhered to the unities of time and place—all the action took place in a single day at a single location. The unity of action was modified to allow for a second pair of lovers to be introduced into the action. (See the next chapter for a discussion of the unities.)

The plays were written in prose, although for several years the writers wrote separate versions in poetry as well. Sources for the plays were the works of Plautus and Terence, Italian novels and tales, and contemporary urban life. Also, many of the plays of the commedia dell'arte featured similar characters and plots, suggesting that the actors of those troupes borrowed from the learned comedies or that the playwrights borrowed from the actors.

The stories of the learned comedy usually involved a young man's pursuit of an inaccessible lady. Normally they want each other but are prevented by her husband or the young man's betrothal to someone else. They are seldom prevented by either's scruples. The action takes one of two general directions: in one version, the lovers hatch a complicated plot to get the husband out of the way while they rendezvous. In the other, they discover at the end of the play that a long-lost relative has reappeared to reveal that they are brother and sister, or that the young man is betrothed to his sister. The writers make frequent use of disguises and mistaken identities, of clever schemes to divert the husband, helpful servants, and scenes of reconciliation. Stock characters common in the plays are foolish doctors, parasites, courtesans, and lawyers.

Bernardo da Bibbiena's *La Calandria*, performed in 1513, is typical of the Renaissance comedies. Lidio and Santilla are twins separated from each other in childhood when Turks attacked their city. Lidio has just learned that his sister is alive, and he has come to find her. As soon as he arrives in town, however, he is diverted from his goal by Fulvia, with whom he falls madly in love. To gain access to Fulvia, who is guarded by a very stupid husband, Lidio dresses up as a woman and gives himself his sister's name. What Lidio does not know is that his sister, living in the same town, has been dressed as a boy ever since she escaped the Turks, and she is known by her brother's name, Lidio. Complications and confusions abound: the twins are mistaken for each other by everyone, leading to all sorts of comic incidents. No wonder, then, that Fulvia's foolish husband, Calandro, gets confused too. He lusts after Lidio dressed-as-Santilla and orders his servant to arrange a rendezvous. The servant convinces him to pretend he is dead so that he can be taken in a trunk to Lidio's house. The husband is skeptical: if he pretends to be dead, how will he come back to life? Easy, says, the servant, just lean your head way back and spit straight in the air. Although he keeps spitting in his own eyes, Calandro is satisfied with this method of instant resurrection, and he goes off to find Lidio-dressed-as-Santilla. Eventually, of course, the twins are reunited and are given suitable partners in marriage.

Niccolò Machiavelli (1469–1527), author, politician, and diplomat, wrote *Mandragola*, probably the most-produced Italian Renaissance piece today. It is characteristic of the learned comedies in its structure, characters, and emphasis on the pursuit of a young woman. His political treatise *The Prince* influenced later dramatists, including Shakespeare, and the Machiavellian villain, with a complete disregard for ethics, became a familiar figure on the stage.

By the end of the 1500s, most of the comedies had lost their broad physical humor and substituted serious sentiments relieved by happy endings. (*La Pellegrina* is an example of this type of comedy.) Only in the 18th century would the spirit of the commedia be revitalized in the writing of Carlo Goldoni.

A Global Perspective

Javanese Shadow Puppets

*T*he performance of shadow puppets is a special event in Java. An open-air pavilion is erected for the invited guests, but other members of the community will stand outside the pavilion to watch. Behind a large rectangular screen, the sole performer arranges the puppets and adjusts the light (originally a torch) that will project the images of the puppets on the screen. Beginning in the late evening, the performance will last until midnight or even dawn, as the audience watches, eats, talks, and even dozes.

Wayang-Kulit is a traditional form of shadow puppets developed in Java sometime during the 13th century, probably reaching its current form sometime in the 17th century. Although this particular form is indigenous to Java, similar forms are also found in India, China, Bali, and Thailand.

The central figure of the *wayang-kulit* is the *dhalang*, the sole performer who is responsible for all narration, dialogue, puppet movement, and various sound effects. Accompanied in most instances by a *gamelan*, an orchestra composed of various percussion instruments and flutes, the *dhalang* will manipulate some 40–50 different puppets to tell a well-known story from the *Mahabharata*, the ancient book of the Hindu religion. More than 400 puppets exist, each a fantasy version of a particular character. The exaggerated outline—developed to avoid prohibitions on human likeness—and bright colors are key elements that help the audience recognize each particular character.

Although the stories are well known, each telling is different, for the performer is free to combine, rearrange, and adapt the details of the story, although the outline remains the same. The various stories may deal with love, magic, or history. Clowns, often used for satirical comment, are also present, as are dancing figures, but in most cases the problem is usually solved on the battlefield, for the battles are the favorite moments in *wayang-kulit* as puppets fly across the screen, utilizing remarkable acrobatics to attack the foe.

Originally used as religious propaganda, contemporary performances are artistic or may be used as part of a celebration, such as a wedding.

CONNECTIONS

Several theatre practices of the Italian Renaissance are still in evidence today. Theatre architecture has been influenced by the horseshoe-shaped auditorium, by the separation of the audience from the stage, and by the proscenium arch as a device to frame the action of the play. Although few sets today employ the severe perspective of Italianate scenery, the overall unity of the scenic components is practised in most large commercial theatres today. Stage machinery and special effects have adapted to new technology and the computer, but the creation of illusion and the effects of surprise scene changes are standard in Broadway productions, particularly in musicals.

Two theatre forms also developed in the Renaissance, opera and the commedia. Renaissance opera evolved into the 18th- and 19th-century operas that are still performed today in leading opera houses throughout the world. Several characteristics of 19th-century grand opera are evident in the *intermezzi* of the Renaissance, including the imposing sets, large choruses, and lavish costumes. In addition, many of the famous opera houses are built on the models of Italian Renaissance theatres.

The commedia form is still alive on the streets, at country fairs, and wherever a group of actors in mask or makeup perform their lazzi while telling nonscripted stories to whatever crowds they can attract. The characters do not have the same names, but they can often be discerned by their stock characteristics.

Perhaps the most popular Renaissance theatre tradition still in evidence today is the pageantry surrounding community festivals. The Italians perfected these festivals by establishing a series of events that are still commonly found in most major festivals in Western culture. The coronation of a European monarch, the inauguration of a U.S. president, the Olympic Games, and the bowl games on New Year's Day all follow a pattern similar to that used by Renaissance princes.

Each festival has a king or queen whose selection is intended to bring beauty and good fortune to the participants. He or she is presented to the community at the end of a great parade that includes local dignitaries, foreign emissaries, floats, music, and dance and equestrian units. The parade commonly has a theme promoting the local commerce; or (as in the case of modern bowl parades) the floats are sponsored by local industries. A contest is usually involved to select the best representatives of the community. In the case of the Renaissance and the modern bowl games, the contest is athletic and symbolic, while in the case of an inauguration the contest is electoral and literal. Both preceding and following the contest, feasts are held to prove that there is a wealth of food and drink for the benefit of the community. Everyone is encouraged to have a good time by participating with others in events of revelry and merriment. This description fits the festivals of the Medici as illustrated by the marriage of Christine and Ferdinand. It also fits the Rose Bowl and Orange Bowl festivities. The structure of these festivals is intended to build symbolic unity and goodwill. While such festivals existed well before the Renaissance, the Italians of the 16th century gave them the shape and form they still retain today.

The visual spectacles of the Italian Renaissance, then, are important because they influenced theatre practices for several centuries and because many are still a part of our culture. The legacy of the Renaissance may not be apparent at first because few plays from the period are still read or produced. But, in every other aspect of the theatre, the Renaissance continues to influence the theatrical activities of the 20th century.

SOURCES FOR FURTHER STUDY

Social/Art/Philosophy Background

Bertell, Sergio, Franco Cardini, and Elvira Garbero Zorzi. *Italian Renaissance Courts.* London: Sedgwick and Jackson, 1986.

Bjurstrom, Per. *Feast and Theatre in Queen Christina's Rome.* Stockholm: Bengtsons, 1966.

Burckhardt, Jacob. *The Civilization of the Renaissance in Italy.* Vol. I. New York: Harper Colophon Books, 1958.

Chamberlin, E. R. *The World of the Italian Renaissance.* London: Allen and Unwin, 1982.

Chartier, Roger, ed. *A History of Private Life: Passions of the Renaissance.* Cambridge, Mass.: Harvard University Press, 1989.

Gordon, D. J. *The Renaissance Imagination.* Berkeley: University of California Press, 1975.

Grout, Donald Jay. *A Short History of Opera.* New York: Columbia University Press, 1947.

Guicciardini, Francesco. *The History of Italy.* New York: Collier Books, 1969.

Muir, Edward. *Civic Ritual in Renaissance Venice.* Princeton, N.J.: Princeton University Press, 1981.

Ross, James Bruce, and Mary Martin McLaughlin, eds. *The Portable Renaissance Reader.* New York: Penguin Books, 1966.

Strong, Roy. *Splendor at Court: Renaissance Spectacle and the Theatre of Power.* Boston: Houghton Mifflin, 1973.

Theatre History

Castelvetro, Lodovico. *Castelvetro on the Art of Poetry* Trans. Andrew Bongiorno. Binghamtom, N.Y.: Medieval and Renaissance Texts and Studies, 1984.

Ducharte, Pierre Louis. *The Italian Comedy.* Trans. Randolph T. Weaver. New York: Dover Publications, 1966.

Gordon, Mel. *Lazzi: The Comic Routines of the Commedia Dell'Arte.* New York: Performing Arts Books, 1983.

Kenard, Joseph Spencer. *The Italian Theatre from Its Beginning to the Close of the Seventeenth Century.* New York: Benjamin Blom, 1932.

Kernodle, George R. *From Art to Theatre: Form and Convention in the Renaissance.* Chicago: University of Chicago Press, 1944.

Luciani, Vincent. *A Concise History of the Italian Theatre.* New York: S. F. Vanni, 1961.

Ogden, Dunbar H. *The Italian Baroque Stage.* Berkeley: University of California Press, 1978.

Oreglia, Giacomo. *The Commedia Dell'Arte.* New York: Octagon Press, 1982.

Pietropaolo, Domenico: *The Science of Buffoonery.* Ottawa: Dovehouse Editions, 1989.

Scholz, Janos, ed. *Baroque and Italian Stage Design.* New York: H. Bittner, 1950.

Serlio, Sebastiano. *The Books of Architecture.* New York: Benjamin Blom, 1970.

Drama

Bentley, Eric, ed. *The Genius of the Italian Theatre.* New York: New American Library, 1964.

Clubb, Louise George. *Italian Drama in Shakespeare's Time.* New Haven: Yale University Press, 1989.

Herrick, Marvin T. *Italian Comedy in the Renaissance.* Urbana: University of Illinois Press, 1960.

Radcliff-Unstead, Douglas. *The Birth of Modern Comedy in Renaissance Italy.* Chicago: University of Chicago Press, 1969.

C H A P T E R

6

General Events

Elizabeth I crowned

1558

Arts Events

Longleat House

1568   1570

Nicolas Hilliard's portrait of Queen Elizabeth I

Theatre History Events

Elizabethan Theatre in the English Renaissance

A strange sight greeted people passing by a muddy construction site near the River Thames in London in early 1989. Protesters, including some of England's most famous actors, stood near the roadside holding sides saying "Don't 'doze the Rose." From a small shack nearby, pamphlets were distributed urging people to join the cause. Earlier that evening Vanessa Redgrave had silenced the applause during her curtain call at a London theatre to ask people for their support. This flurry of activity was not prompted by nuclear development nor was it done to benefit the homeless. It was all in response to a discovery made by construction workers a few weeks earlier.

In the process of digging the foundation for a new building, workers had discovered some old foundations some two meters beneath the paved surface. Because the area was one of some historical significance, archaeologists were called in, and it was decided that the workmen had actually found the foundations of the Rose theatre. Built in 1587, the Rose was the first of four famous playhouses built on London's south bank at the end of the 16th century. The builder at first had planned to continue digging, but due to the outcry by historians and performers, a compromise was reached that delayed construction while historians studied the site and eventually allowed preservation of the site, in the basement of the next building.

As historians began to study this discovery and relate it to previous facts and opinions, a second startling event occurred. On October 12, 1989, the

Francis Drake's voyage	Plague hits London	Elizabeth I dies		James I dies		English Civil War
1577	1588 1592–1594	1600 1603		1625	1649	1642–1660
	Spanish Armada defeated	East India Company			Charles I executed	

	Spenser's *The Faerie Queene*			
	1590	1597		
	Francis Bacon's *Essays, Civil and Moral*			

The Theatre built	Admiral's Men and Chamberlain's Men united	King's Men, Second Blackfriars		
1576 1583	1594 1599	1609	1613	
Queen's Men Company	The Globe built	The Globe burnt; Shakespeare retires		

foundations of the original Globe theatre, Shakespeare's "home" theatre, were discovered. Although only a small portion of the Globe was accessible, it was quickly evident that the two theatres were quite different from each other, and both offered challenges to accepted theories of architecture and performance. Suddenly the whole field of Elizabethan theatre study became new and vital. Public interest has always been keen on Shakespeare's theatre and Renaissance England; now some of that interest can focus directly on the spot where Shakespeare's plays were first performed.

The Renaissance in England is generally referred to as the Elizabethan period because Elizabeth I reigned as queen from 1558–1603. This period of English theatre history, probably more than any other, attracts the interest of modern American readers and audiences. Professional Shakespeare festivals are held annually across the country, including those in Oregon, New Jersey, California, New York, Pennsylvania, and Stratford, Canada. Several theatres in the country were designed to look like the original Globe theatre of Shakespeare's time, including the Old Globe in San Diego and the Oregon Shakespeare Festival Theatre in Ashland. In colleges and high schools everywhere, Shakespeare appears in courses, productions, and required readings. More books have been written on Hamlet than on most historical figures. The appeal of the theatre in Elizabethan times is to be found in the vital and active society of England, in the popular appeal of all the arts, in the inventiveness of the theatre artists, and in the imagination of the playwrights.

SOCIAL IDEAS

London in 1601 was a port of trade, the location of major courts of law, and the home of Parliament. A rapidly growing city of some 200,000 people, it included a diversity of social classes and types who mingled freely in the streets and theatres. Farmers from the surrounding lands of Kent encountered tradesmen, merchants, apprentices, guildsmen, lawyers, and noblemen. The city officials of London controlled much of city life, but Queen Elizabeth ruled the lands outside the city. Londoners were connected to a complex set of social and economic institutions, including city courts of law and national regulations and medieval guilds and capitalistic markets.

The typical Englishman who could read and write was frequently reminded of his place in the social and metaphysical scheme of things. In poetry, drama, and nonfictional works of the period, a systematic and symmetrical world view was articulated to explain human nature. Whether this concept was envisioned as a wheel, a chain of being, or a system of degrees, humankind was clearly at the center of a carefully defined set of relationships. Human activity was associated with the movement of the planets, the changes of the seasons, and the cycle of life from birth to death. Each activity was related to every other activity and to everything around it. Each month of the year, for instance, had its own flower and stone as well as its own personality type. Men and women were regarded as mirrors of the planets and their changing relationships, giving rise to the popularity of astrology. Humankind belonged to a great chain of being that extended from the angels to the beasts, implying that humans had elements of both within them. Every component of human activity could be divided into its parts, and these parts then related to the parts of other systems. Not surprisingly, such a desire for organization also gave great attention to mystical matters, superstition, and the occult, which seemed to violate the natural order. Although the degree of authority granted to such systems undoubtedly varied from person to person, a pervasive desire to organize experience is evident throughout the period. Nowhere is this more evident than in the Elizabethan conception of humours.

Humours

Humours is a theory of human nature that recognizes four basic dispositions, or humours, in human personality. Frequently, individuals are identified by the dominant humour in their own system. Choleric people, associated with the basic element fire, are hot and dry, lean and slender, covetous, ireful, hasty, brainless, and foolish. Sanguine people, associated with air, are hot and moist and given over to amiable merrymaking. Phlegmatic people, associated with water, are cold and moist, heavy, slow, sleepy, and ingenious. Melancholic people, associated with earth, are cold and dry, heavy, covetous, malicious, and slow. Each of these is in turn related through the four basic elements of matter to the planets, the seasons, and the stages of life. Each could also be extended to human virtues, flowers, stones, the days of the week, and the months of the year. Although in our modern era of individual psychology it may seem absurd to place all people into four categories and then link them to all other things in the universe, the Elizabethans were at the very least making distinctions between the personalities of individuals. They were also acknowledging that the individual is not isolated in the universe, but is connected to a wonderful, vast, and ordered system of creation.

Religion

Most Englishmen also belonged to a church. Here again, change and conflict are apparent, for religious beliefs were not universally shared. Henry VIII had broken England's ties with the Catholic Church in 1534, and the ideas of the Reformation had been brought to England by John Knox. This religious independence was a strong prop to the nationalism that developed, particularly during the reign of Elizabeth I.

The Anglican Church, which Elizabeth reorganized when she became queen, was dominant. Some Catholics continued to practice their religion, but they were suppressed by social or political sanctions. Another segment of society, however, was vocal and outspoken in its disagreements with the Church of England. The power of the Puritans was disproportionate to their numbers in the population, for they were heavily concentrated in the cities. They advocated more emphasis on the scriptures and less on church rituals. They wanted the scriptures read in English. They believed that the Bible should be interpreted in the light of personal experience. They abhorred excess in anything, especially in sensual matters, such as food, clothing, sex, and entertainment. As a result, they frequently served as the butt of theatre jokes, probably more for their opposition to the theatre than for their actual influence over national policy.

Elizabeth used the Puritans as a balance against the Catholics in her realm, but she was probably not unaware that the end result of their beliefs meant an end to her royal prerogatives as head of the Church. Their power and numbers increased after Elizabeth's death, until they succeeded in deposing Charles I in 1642.

The new reformed view of religion also affected the economic realm. The Bible taught that "the good shall prosper." It was a simple feat of logic then to realize that those that prospered were, therefore, good. And it was easier in the new era of trade for many Englishmen to prosper.

Capitalism

Even if the Londoners of 1601 were secure in their church and their world view, they still confronted a dynamic economy. The economy of Elizabethan England was a pattern of older medieval institutions and beliefs onto which were being grafted the ideas and practices of a new class of capitalists. The older pattern was agrarian, with up to 90 percent of the population attached to the land in a system of manor, village, and open fields. Guilds organized all the major trades and insured that competition and

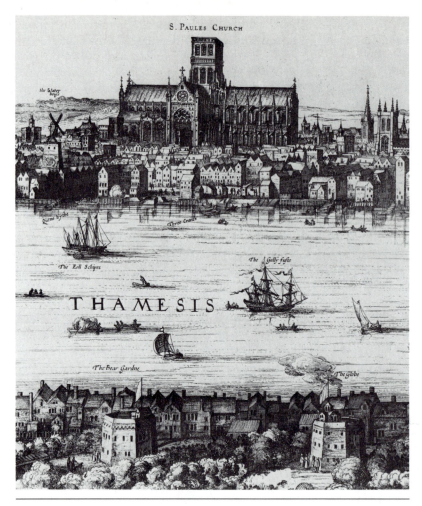

London from Bankside about 1616, showing the Globe and the Bear Garden in the background.   *Courtesy Guildhall Library, Corporation of London*

individual initiative never threatened a balanced but static economy. Individuals could distinguish themselves in such a system by improving their status (rising to the head of a guild, for instance) but not by changing from one class to another.

Under the emerging capitalism of the Elizabethans, a division developed between those who owned the means of production and those who were hired to work those means. A few people accumulated wealth that exceeded their needs, and they began making investments and speculating in trade. Joint stock companies were formed to create the capital for large-scale adventures, especially in international trade. Several industries and some crafts expanded their markets to national and international scale.

The impact of these changes was considerable and was the subject of national regulation as well as theatrical comment. The nation as a whole experienced a period of prosperity, even luxury for some people. New goods, especially food, were available to a segment of the population that had the extra money with which to buy them. Usury was rampant, with financiers and bankers charging outrageous interest on loans. Speculation became common for those with sufficient money, and the idea of making money for its own sake spread.

Puritans reacted to this new economy with disdain for the abominations of luxury. Some playwrights dramatized these new merchants and often depicted their greed satirically. Neither Puritan nor playwright could stop the growth of capitalism, however. It contributed to the Elizabethan sense that the world was rapidly changing and expanding.

Adventure and Exploration

A final reason for the sense of dynamic change and activity characteristic of Elizabethan England was the growth of new markets and new wealth as a result of exploration. The most famous of the explorers, Sir Francis Drake (1546–1596), once realized a profit of some 4,700 percent on one of his voyages. Not only did men like Drake, Sir Walter Raleigh (1554–1618), and Sir John Hawkins (1532–1595) bring new wealth into the country; they also established England as a nation of importance on the seas. English national pride and confidence reached new heights with the famous defeat of the Spanish Armada in 1588. The sense of exploration, discovery, and patriotism fostered by these adventurers found its way into the drama of Elizabethan England.

The Renaissance "Problem"

The Elizabethan world seemed particularly aware of a potential conflict in its own philosophy. While it shared the humanistic optimism in the potential of human beings and the ability of a society to "civilize" the animal nature of humans, it also recognized that the full potential of the human is rarely, if ever, achieved. Many Elizabethan artists pondered this apparent dual nature of the human. The Elizabethan spirit, while nearly always remaining vibrant and energetic, also encompassed the sense of this "dark side" of life: the limitations on the exuberance of being alive.

The social history of the Elizabethans gives the impression of a nation discovering new forms of organization and economic activity at all levels of society while maintaining traditional forms and ideas. The conflicts between the old and new did not divide classes as much as they cut across and created new classes. As a result, change could be felt at all levels of society. This change is one source of the vitality of Elizabethan theatre, for the social dynamism of this change was reflected in plots, characters, and themes.

ARTS IDEAS

Another reason for the vitality of Elizabethan theatre can be found in the arts of the period. What distinguishes arts in the Elizabethan period from the Renaissance arts on the Continent is that they were popular arts, enjoyed by most classes of society. Even private entertainments for the wealthy were performed by people who the next day might perform for an audience made up of lower classes. Royalty did not believe that it owned the arts, but recent studies suggest that it used the arts to prove its status. The rising merchant class was not yet sufficiently accustomed to its wealth to expend it on arts activities that would reflect its power. As a result, the arts were for and by any Londoner with even a small income and an open mind.

Music

Nowhere is this popular feature of the arts more evident than in music and dance. Music was a part of life for all Elizabethans, from Elizabeth herself, who played the virginal, to merchants who encouraged their daughters to play the lute, to villagers who listened to the town fiddler at fairs and weddings. Music filled the streets, with hawkers singing ballads and airs for a living. Drake frequently took a small orchestra with him on his sea voyages. Church music remained an important part of the Anglican service, despite the objections of some Puritans. Jigs and morris dances were common at community or family festivities. The jigs were incorporated into all early performances of comedies, when the clown would perform a song-and-dance routine at the end of a play.

Painting

The visual arts did not flourish to the same extent as music, but the same broad appeal to all classes can be discerned in the Elizabethan preference for crafts over art. Comparatively few examples of museum art can be found from the period, for people generally were not acquisitive; that is, they did not seek to acquire paintings for the sake of ownership. The era, in fact, produced only one portraitist, Nicholas Hilliard (1547–1619), whose chief profession was that of a goldsmith. It is interesting to compare the arts under Elizabeth with the arts under her successors. The Stuart monarchs, who believed in royal prerogatives and the divine right of kings, encouraged a courtly art designed to demonstrate their importance and lifestyle. Charles I (1600–1649), for instance, appointed a court painter, Anthony Van Dyck (1599–1641), one of the leading artists of the 17th century. But under Elizabeth, no such actions were undertaken.

The arts in Elizabethan England were shared by all classes. Distinctions of ownership, rank, or status were, in comparison with the Italian and French Renaissance, minimal. The theatre as well was for all the people.

ELIZABETHAN THEATRE

No single history of this period is possible, for the theatre of the Elizabethan age was extremely varied and included public and private performances, indoor and outdoor theatres, the history plays of Shakespeare and the lyric poetry of the masques, fully professional actors and troupes of young boys, and audiences who ranged from commoner to queen. This variety resulted in a dynamic and fluid theatre world that was a vital component of Elizabethan culture.

Occasion

The most common occasion for performance was based on the economic principle of supply and demand. Plays were written and performed to attract audiences and sell tickets, and performances were scheduled when it seemed likely that a sufficient audience could be gathered. Because the theatre buildings were not roofed, performances were given in the early afternoon. Theatres typically performed six times per week, with a given play being performed as long as it could draw an audience. When audience support slipped, a new play would be presented, or perhaps further performances of a particularly popular older play would be offered while the new play was being prepared. Occasionally, theatre was performed at the demand of the queen, or particular pieces were written for special court occasions.

Theatres could be closed for a number of reasons. Plays were rarely performed on Sunday and never during the Lenten holiday. Occasionally an outbreak of the plague would close the theatres; in 1592–1593 all theatres were closed for an extended period due to the severity of the disease.

Location

Our knowledge of the Elizabethan performance space is extremely problematic. Until 1988, one could make certain generalities about Elizabethan theatres, although even then questions went unanswered. Existing theatre contracts for The Fortune and The Hope provided some information, but both were incomplete and sketchy. Other sketches or descriptions were also incomplete and even contradictory. Despite all of this, scholars had made some basic assumptions about the theatre until two discoveries in 1988 and 1989 brought many things into question.

In December 1988, contractors demolishing an old building discovered the foundations of the Rose theatre that existed in Elizabethan times. Preliminary investigations indicate that the theatre may have been 14-sided, smaller than previously thought, and with the shape of the stage significantly different from traditional interpretations. It is clear also that some major alterations were made shortly after the original building had been completed, resulting in a horseshoe shape for the interior. Consequently it is difficult to decide which form is "typical."

The discovery of a corner of the original Globe theatre added more new information. The small percentage of the structure that is available to historians (more than 90 percent lies underneath a building from the later, Georgian period) contrasts greatly with the discoveries at the Rose. The Globe may be 18- or 20-sided and seems to have had a huge stage. In fact, it seems possible that the entire Rose theatre would have fit inside the Globe. Many legal difficulties face those who wish to study these sites more closely, and no one knows when, or if, complete studies of the two sites will be possible.

What, then, can be said about the Elizabethan performance space? Performance sites for Elizabethan public theatres were outside the city proper, on the far side of the River Thames. This was partly done to avoid building or censorship restrictions that might be imposed by the city. These structures were specifically built for theatre performances, although some seemed to be suited for bear-baiting and other events as

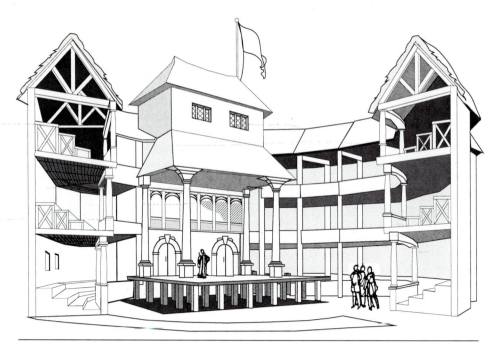

A conjectural sketch of an Elizabethan theatre (c. 1595) based on an existing contract.

well. It is assumed that the structure was only partially roofed and that the interior approximated a circle in shape. The audience areas included the "pit," an open section at ground level where some of the audience stood, and two or three floor of galleries, so that the theatres seated as many as 2,000 people for a performance. The stage was a simple raised platform with a roof called the heavens covering part or all of the acting area. The stage was raised five to six feet from the floor, but the size of the acting area is one of the areas under dispute. Traditionally the stage was thought to be approximately 23 feet deep by 43 feet wide (about the size of many traditional theatre stages), but it now seems that the Globe stage may have been as large as 36 feet by 53 feet. (If this is true, then concepts of acting style may have to be reconsidered.) The back of the stage was situated against one of the sides of the building, and the stage extended part way into the ground-floor audience level. A "tiring house" for the actors was located behind the stage.

Controversy exists concerning the stage area itself. Stage directions in plays of the period give evidence of an upper and a lower playing area and suggest the existence of doors in the tiring house wall. Traditionally, it is accepted that two doors were present, one on each side at the rear of the stage. It is possible that the upper playing area was a balcony that extended the full width of the stage at the rear of the acting area, between two windows located above the doors. This location might have been used for the famous balcony scene in *Romeo and Juliet* or for an army general to address his troops. It allowed for the separation of two characters, a situation that seems to happen regularly in the plays. The lower area beneath the balcony may have been a curtained portion of the stage between the two doorways. When the curtain was opened, the area would have been used to indicate interior scenes of a more intimate nature. This seems unlikely since this area would not be readily visible to all parts of the audience. It is hoped that the new discoveries will provide further information.

Plays were performed in three other locations in Elizabethan London. Occasionally a troupe was commanded to perform at court, where a temporary theatre would be established. Inns-at-Court and some traditional inns were also used. In addition, some indoor "private" theatres, such as The Blackfriars (1608), did exist. Located in a fashionable residence area, these theatres were often converted from a previously existing large room, although some structures were constructed as theatre. Typically, a permanent screen was built at one end of the room, with archways or doors opening onto a low platform that served as the stage. Substantial decoration existed, but we cannot determine if it was originally part of the room or was added for performance. Although audiences would have been seated downstairs as well as in the galleries, in most other ways the environment would have been similar to that of an outdoor theatre. One critical difference between the indoor and outdoor theatres was the price of admission: the cost of entrance to indoor theatres was as much as six times the cost of entrance to the Globe.

Performers

A central reason for the success of Elizabethan theatre was the creativity of artists who presented the plays. The vitality of the theatre derived from its dynamic society and its popular appeal to a broad section of London, but these factors only provided the right circumstances. Imaginative artists were needed to adapt to the circumstances and create effective entertainments.

ELIZABETHAN PLAYHOUSES

Playhouse	Date	Principal Occupants
The Theatre	1576	Chamberlain's Men (later King's Men), Shakespeare, Burbage
First Blackfriars	1576	Children of the Chapel Royal
Curtain	1577	
The Rose	1587	Admiral's Men (later Prince Henry's Men) Henslowe, Alleyn
The Swan	1596	Games, bear baiting
The Globe	1599	Chamberlain's Men
The Fortune	1600	Admiral's Men
Second Blackfriars	1600	Chapel Boys, King's Men
The Red Bull	1605	"Red Bull Company" (Worcester's Men)
Whitefriars	1608	Children of the Queen's Revels
Bear Garden (Hope)	1614	
Cockpit	1617	Winter home of adult companies
Salisbury Court	1629	Winter home of adult companies

The barriers against these artists were considerable. Long before the first permanent theatres were built and even after that time, vagabond actors roamed the countryside, traveling from fair to fair or manor to manor in hopes of finding an audience that would pay to see their juggling, pantomimes, and short plays. At country fairs they could most likely be found on booth stages or simple platforms with a curtain at the rear to hide the actors before their entrances. This kind of experience was invaluable, for it undoubtedly taught actors how to work with and hold an audience.

Other artists got their training in the schools and universities, where students and teachers performed, in Latin, the plays of Terence and Plautus. In the 1580s, several Cambridge students found their way to London to earn their living by writing plays, a notion that earned them the title University Wits. This academic drama influenced Elizabethan theatre by introducing classical stories and techniques into playwriting.

The artists, however, faced considerable opposition. City officials objected to actors because they brought crowds together that were dangerous to public health or civic behavior. Puritans objected to the presentation of plays for various reasons, and some people in the royal court were concerned that playwrights might present politically seditious ideas. The result of this consternation was a close control of actors in Elizabeth's reign, much of it through the role of the Master of Revels. In 1572, this position was given the power of stage censorship. In 1583, the Master of Revels selected the 12 best actors from all the other companies and organized the Queen's Men. By 1589 the Master was granting licenses to produce particular plays, and following the plague of 1592–1593 it was his favoritism that led to the dominance of two companies of actors, the Lord Admiral's Men and the Lord Chamberlain's Men.

Companies could be formed only if they held the patronage (support) of a wealthy nobleman, and then they could perform only in areas controlled by the queen. Since London was under the control of more conservatively minded men, performances were usually prohibited. Also, plays could not be performed within city boundaries unless they had received a license from the Master of Revels.

The best way to earn a reasonably secure income, then, was for a group of actors to band together under the patronage of a nobleman and perform in a permanent theatre just outside London. It is to one of these companies, the Lord Chamberlain's Men, that Shakespeare belonged. In 1594, two acting companies were formalized out of the membership of the Queen's Men. The actor Edward Alleyn and the financier Phillip Henslowe formed the Lord Admiral's Men, while the Lord Chamberlain's Men were organized around the family of James Burbage (1530–1597). Each of these companies included major actors, minor actors, a playwright (who was often an actor as well), apprentices, and a number of young boys who played the female roles, with a total of approximately 25 members. A distinction was made in the company between sharers, or those with a financial interest in the company, and the hired actors. Among the sharers in the Chamberlain's Men were James Burbage, the company's manager, and Shakespeare. Burbage had built The Theatre, the first permanent theatre in England, in 1576. When the lease on the land expired, that theatre was torn down and the materials were used to build the Globe. The construction of the Globe gave the Chamberlain's Men a permanent outdoor theatre for their exclusive use and solidified their prominence in the theatrical world. Under James I, the company became the King's Men, the leading company in England, a position they held until the Civil War in the 1640s, when all theatrical activity was banned.

Despite the periodic injunctions against their work, actors were able to establish some degree of personal and professional self-respect. Few theatre people became wealthy, but those who were sharers were able to accumulate some financial independence, earning perhaps twice as much as a skilled worker. Hired actors, on the other hand, were dependent for their financial well-being on the whims of weather, public health (the plague), fire, and patronage. They toured outside London in small groups with whatever scenery and costumes they could transport, and they faced opposition wherever they went. As any modern actor who has toured knows, the experience has its less than artistic moments.

Another type of company was also performing in Elizabethan England. In the private theatres, plays were performed by companies of young boys trained in cathedral schools as a part of their education in elocution and literature. These young troupes performed poetic dramas in which the emphasis was on the beauty of the spoken word. Trained as choristers, the young actors had great vocal skill and became very popular among the upper class. In *Hamlet* Shakespeare refers to the boys' troupes with disdain, and for a brief period a substantial rivalry existed between the two types of performing companies.

Actors in the public companies, such as the Chamberlain's Men, usually received their training as apprentices in the company. They often played the women's roles while still boys, or they studied the parts of young lovers, to which they would naturally be assigned once they achieved maturity. It is probable that actors took a particular "line," or type of role, and played that in most of the productions. Once an actor took a role, he usually kept it. An actor was expected to appear in many different plays in a single year, sometimes as many as 40, with half of those being new plays.

Debate rages today over the style of acting employed by the Elizabethan actor, but some general comments can be made. The rapid turnover of plays suggests that actors relied on the words to individuate each character, rather than relying on particular moments of realistic insight. Gestures were almost certainly used to indicate meaning, and the new discoveries concerning the size of the stage would support a conclusion that a dynamic use of both voice and gesture were necessary to communicate. Elizabethan plays are very long, and yet apparently they were played in a fairly reasonable amount of time (two–three hours). This rapid delivery suggests that the actors seldom paused for effect or emotion. They limited stage business to what is called for in the lines, and their gestures were indicative but not demonstrative. The jokes made about actors who stalked the stage while roaring their lines indicate (1) some actors did in fact "tear a passion to tatters," and (2) that such a histrionic style of acting was less appreciated with each decade. By the time *Hamlet* was performed, the man most associated with the bombastic style, Edward Alleyn (1566–1626), had retired, and the leading tragedian of the day was Richard Burbage, whose style was regarded as more naturalistic. Alleyn introduced the major characters in Christopher Marlowe's plays, while Burbage first performed major Shakespearean roles, including Richard III, Hamlet, Lear, and Othello.

In the early years of established playing (the 1570s and 1580s) the most popular

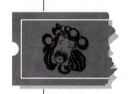

A TRIP TO THE
GLOBE THEATRE,
1601

*I*t is London in the spring of 1601. A merchant and his family are finishing their noon dinner, always the largest meal of the day, but today it is an excellent opportunity for the merchant to see the proof of his recent speculations in trade. One of his sons is off with another family, where he lives while being tutored with five other boys his age. The elder son, apprenticed to his merchant father, sits sullenly at the table while the others finish. He has endured the meal conversation—ranging from the parliamentary debate over monopolies to blessings that the Earl of Essex's bid to overthrow Elizabeth failed—but his heart is elsewhere. He has been given permission to miss the play at the Globe and go instead to a football game north of the city walls. His mother keeps reminding him how dangerous the game is, for there are few rules and frequent injuries. Several city officials have tried to suppress the game because it commonly ends in rioting, she reminds him. The merchant, his wife and daughters, and three servants leave their house within the city limits and head for London Bridge. As they cross a street corner, they ignore a Puritan berating those headed for the theatre. A nobleman with his train of a dozen servants noisily bustles toward the Thames River, where he will make a show of hiring a boat to ferry himself and his servants across the river to the theatre district. Crossing the bridge, with the Tower of London behind them on the left and St. Paul's Church on their right, the merchant's wife cries out that she sees the flag flying from the top of the Globe, confirming that a play will be performed this day at two o'clock. As they leave the city limits, the merchant instinctively reaches for his purse to make sure that it isn't stolen by pickpockets.

Once across the bridge, the group becomes more excited. They are now outside the city and therefore beyond the jurisdiction of the city officials. Although this makes it possible for theatrical groups to present their plays freely, it also creates a sense of danger throughout the area. The merchant's group separates itself from those in the crowd who are going the extra hundreds of yards across the open field to a bear-baiting garden, or further along to the Swan Theatre. At the Globe he points the servants toward the entrance to the pit. After making sure they each have the one penny admission charge, he directs his wife to the exterior stairs leading to the galleries, where he will pay 2d (two pennies) to climb to the second level, but not 3d for the top or third gallery.

By now, over 2,000 people have jammed into the theatre. Food and drink are being served by wandering hawkers, and the midday sun is heating up the pit, made warmer by the closeness of the crowd. The young daughter wonders whether the play could be as interesting as the spectacle of all these people, even though she is anxious to see the famous Mr. Burbage. Suddenly, she jumps, crying out in surprise at the sound of a trumpet. The play has begun. The action moves swiftly. This play, which might take over six hours to read aloud at home, is delivered by the actors in about three hours. There are no scene or act breaks, and one scene begins literally before the previous scene has ended. In spite of the large auditorium, the girl is amazed at how close she feels to the actors. The plot is complex, but the girl follows the story easily, becomes emotionally involved with Hamlet's plight, and is very impressed by the handsome young actors. When Ophelia enters the stage, the young girl is amazed at her beauty and must remind herself that the actor is actually a young boy.

The play is full of sudden discoveries. The audience is surprised and delighted when Hamlet stabs a curtain at the rear of the stage and the body of Polonius slumps forward. They also enjoy the use of a trap or hole in the stage platform itself, used by the grave digger during his scene. The duel at the end is staged very realistically, and a silence falls over the auditorium for the final lines of the play. And like all theatrical effects, the best is saved for last: the audience greatly enjoys the firing of a cannon from the top of the tiring-house when the body of Hamlet is carried from the stage.

After the play the family moves swiftly to be sure to cross the bridge before darkness falls. The girl's father begins another lecture on the flaws in young Burbage's acting, comparing him to other actors, but the girl hears not a word. She can find nothing wrong with the handsome young actor at all.

actor was Richard Tarleton (d. 1588), who specialized in clown or fool roles. He was an acrobat, a juggler, a musician, a dancer, and an expert fencer. He used all his skills on the stage in written parts and in the jigs he performed at the end of a regular play. His successors, both of whom performed with the Chamberlain's Men, were Will Kempe (d. 1603) and Richard Armin (1568–1615). By 1610, popular tastes had shifted to the extent that, although comedies were still crowd favorites, the leading actor was no longer a clown, but the tragedian Richard Burbage.

The use of scenery was minimal, because the plays tended to shift rapidly from one site to another, and elaborate scenery would have been unmanageable. Instead, lines of dialogue indicated the location of the action and simple props and furniture were used to complete the effect. Costumes were an important visual element, even though most costuming was in Elizabethan style rather than that of the period of the play. There is evidence, however, that special costuming was used for ancient clothing,

Richard Burbage, Elizabethan actor.
From the Dulwich Collection

classical figures, ghosts, and witches; for some aspects of race or nationality; and for some traditional figures such as Robin Hood, Falstaff, and Henry V.

Under James I, masques became more popular, reflecting the different tastes of the Stuart monarchy. Masques were theatrical pieces with extravagant costumes and scenery designed especially for them; they were written in verse, but music and dance and spectacle were their chief attractions. Masques were similar to the interludes of the Italian Renaissance, although the absence of specially designed theatres limited their scenic possibilities. Nevertheless, Inigo Jones, who had studied the Italianate scenery, became famous for his designs of Stuart masques. Jones utilized various of the design concepts that had been developed in Italy, including perspective settings, periaktoi, apparati for flying, and various methods of changing scenery. He also designed highly elaborate and fanciful costumes. Masques were very expensive and sponsored only by the court or the nobility.

Audiences

The actors together with the resident playwright performed for a varied and knowledgeable audience. Although royalty could attend plays at any of the theatres, special performances were given for the queen (and later the king and his family under James I and Charles I) on holidays and festive occasions. Under Elizabeth, patrons of the companies each wanted their own troupe to perform as a mark of distinction and preference for both the patron and the company. Such performances were usually given in the Banqueting House in Whitehall.

The court preference for masques indicates the increasing split between popular entertainment and court spectacle and is often regarded as one reason for the gradual

A lady in costume for a masque, c. 1610. *Courtesy Victoria and Albert Picture Library*

decline of the theatre. However, it should be noted that James I (1556–1625) was an avid theatre-goer and attended plays 17 times during one year, while Elizabeth saw only 5 performances. James's successor, the ill-fated Charles I, attended 25 performances one year.

The elite class obviously formed the audience for court performances, including masques, and they also provided the audience at the indoor or private theatres. Recent studies indicate that the privileged class also formed the bulk of the audience at public theatres. Although all classes of society attended, most commoners were unable to attend frequently, due simply to the cost of a ticket. Also, most would have been unable to attend the daily matinees, since they would be at work. However, the privileged class in London included a wide variety of people, including the traditional aristocracy (some of whom had little money left), newly wealthy merchants, country landowners in town for legal or financial reasons, the sons of wealthy families, students, and various other types, so the audience was highly varied in terms of intelligence, education, and manner. Given that an estimated 20,000–25,000 people attended the theatre each week in this city of some 200,000, it seems evident that many people attended regularly. Even though the privileged class formed the major part of the audience, the theatre represented one location in Elizabethan England where a cross section of the populace gathered in relative equality.

Standards of Judgment

The primary basis for judging a good play in Elizabethan England was the financial report, for, as in the commedia dell'arte, Elizabethan players were dependent on the audience for their support. Actors were paid on a share basis, and playwrights were paid only after a play was successful, so capturing the public's attention and approval was a major goal for all companies. The theatre in the Elizabethan period had its opponents, however, and several authors published attacks on it, most notably for its immorality, its lack of Christian virtues, and its support of idleness. In addition, some concepts, such as the famous "Advice to the Actors" from *Hamlet*, appear within the plays.

The major literary critic of the period, Sir Philip Sidney, writes of poetry and literature in general more than he writes specifically of the theatre, in part because he wrote before the flowering of the great literature of the Elizabethan period. (Shakespeare would have been in his twenties when Sidney published "The Defense of Poetry" in 1595.) Sidney defended the use of literature for moral instruction, countering the conservatives who attacked the theatre as lewd or indecent. He included comedy, which, he claimed, demonstrated the low conduct of human beings so clearly that anyone watching it would avoid such behavior in life.

The playwright Ben Jonson used the prefaces to his plays to express his theory of comedy, including the development of "humours" discussed at the opening of this chapter. He also argued against the restrictions of the classical rules concerning number of acts, the use of a chorus, and the unities of time and place, but defended the need for unity of action. He defended the playwright's right to portray the truth of society, claiming it was "the office of a comic poet to imitate justice and instruct to life, as well as purity of language, or stir up gentle affections." Jonson is also among the first critics of Shakespeare, finding some of his work ridiculous but concluding that his virtues far outweighed his faults.

Jonson and Shakespeare are two of the best-known writers from the Elizabethan period, but this was an age of tremendous invention and variety in dramatic writing. The achievements of Elizabethan playwrights were certainly a major factor in the success of the theatre in Elizabethan London.

DRAMATIC LITERATURE

In few other eras has the invention of the theatre artists been as evenly matched by the imagination of the playwright. Elizabethan playwrights gave to the theatre dramatic worlds as dynamic as the society in which they lived. Their characters grew beyond medieval simplicity to a new renaissance complexity. They pursued themes of freedom, self-discovery, the nature of the soul, revenge, and justice, as well as the relation of the individual to an uncertain world. Their imagery encompassed nature and animals, the cosmos and angels, the social and political realities of the court, and domestic and family concerns. This review of Elizabethan drama will focus on three forms: histories, tragedies, and comedies.

Histories

Although few of the history plays are commonly produced today, their importance to an understanding of Elizabethan drama is central, for they provide excellent examples of the dramatic techniques associated with the period. Histories had been a part of the

A Global Perspective

Yoruban Egungun Festivals

*P*reparation began early for the annual Egungun Festival, held in late January in many Yoruban settlements in West Africa beginning in the 17th century. An oracle was consulted to determine the precise date for the festival. Friends and relatives were invited from other towns. Young men began preparing elaborate masquerade costumes, while adults ventured into the jungle at night to obtain magical powers.

The festival began with dances by women of the cult carrying wooden images ("eba" masks) symbolizing fertility, peace, and unity. On the second day, dancing and singing spectators proceeded to meet the Egungun males as they proceeded to the house of the chief. The featured performers enacted rites of magic, impersonated animals, and carried out mimetic actions. Each actor perfected his own performance and performed solo, but they shared certain techniques.

They spoke in guttural sounds unlike normal speech, using soft bananas and palm oil to soften the throat to make the sounds possible. Elaborate costumes were used to disguise the human figure, completely covering the performer but allowing full use of arms and legs. A basket-like apparatus was worn on the head and covered with a hood to extend the height of the individual. The resulting nonhuman figure performed to the accompaniment of drums and gongs, accompanied by the singing and dancing of audience members.

Performances occurred over a two-week period, with a single masquerader usually taking up an entire day with performances at various locations in the town. Since the performer had been granted sacred powers by some other members of the cult, other performers, and audience members were not allowed to touch the performer or to imitate the guttural sounds. Egungan ceremonies continue to be held in Yoruban communities, but the competition of modern entertainments has reduced their popularity and influence.

drama prior to 1575, but they were usually based more on legend than fact, and they often combined elements from classical mythology and the Bible.

The significance of the Elizabethan history plays is that they added a new dimension to human nature, giving it human historical perspective in contrast to biblical certainty. Instead of seeing human history as inevitably linked with God's judgment in the afterlife, history becomes its own framework with its own value judgments. The actions of a king, for instance, are evaluated not by the king's reward in heaven, but by his impact on his court and kingdom.

In addition, the histories reflect the movement of Elizabethan plays away from medieval narration and toward Renaissance drama. Much of medieval drama told a story in the past tense. Elizabethan plays, in contrast, create the world of history and present the actions of humans in that world. The world of the play becomes then, metaphorically, the world of the audience, which is drawn into the action as if it were happening now.

Marlowe.   Of the writers of histories, the works of two in particular are still produced today. Christopher Marlowe, whose spicy and adventurous biography will delight any interested student, wrote several successful plays before his untimely death. In his tragedy *Tamburlaine* (1587–1588) he polished a style that he adapted to his later history of the early English monarch Edward II. Edward's sexual and political preference for his best friend upsets his wife, the nobility, and the kingdom. Blinded by his own passionate sense of self, Edward fails to see either the plots against him or the threats to social stability his actions arouse. The action of *Edward II* thus occurs on two simultaneous levels. One is the political level of the impact of a rash and imprudent monarch on the well-being of a nation. The other, more interesting dramatically, is the struggle of an individual to exteriorize his internal feelings. History becomes drama because the political level is in conflict with the personal one, necessitating an ultimate confrontation between the two that results in Edward's brutal murder.

Shakespeare.   Several of Shakespeare's history plays are still produced. The source of their appeal lies partly in Shakespeare's ability to accomplish the same Marlowian dramatic conflict between personal disposition and public necessity. In addition, Shakespeare fills historical England with dozens of rich secondary characters who represent all stations of life, from nobility to thieves and murderers. While Marlowe's accomplishment was his creation of the historical hero, Shakespeare's was the creation of a composite historical England. This is best realized in *Richard II* (1595); *Henry IV, Parts 1* and *2* (1597–1598); *Henry V* (1598); and *Richard III* (1593).

Mention of a few of the characters will suffice to convey Shakespeare's historical England. There is the villainous hunchback, Richard III, who wants to overthrow the monarchy because he is bored by peace. There is the calculating, distant Henry IV and his equally calculating son, Prince Hal. There is the hot-tempered Hotspur *(Henry IV, Part 1)*, whose desire to win honor is balanced against the great clown figure, Falstaff, a man who doubts honor is worth much because it can't mend war wounds. There is John of Gaunt *(Richard II)*, who gives the most eloquent description of England in all of literature. There are the soldiers surrounding Henry V before the historic battle of

THE LIFE OF
SHAKESPEARE

Who was this man whose plays have dominated Western literature for more than 300 years? Where did he develop his insights into human nature? What were the sources of his genius? Scholars have rightly asked these questions, but sadly there are few certain answers. He left no diaries and few personal records. His contemporaries were equally indifferent to biographical information, for the only comments they have left us are about his plays. Occasionally they indicate that he was well-liked. What remains for the Shakespeare biographer, then, are public records and documents such as his birth and death records, wills, legal actions, and some references in the documents of the Chamberlain's Men (later the King's Men).

William Shakespeare was born in Stratford-upon-Avon in 1564, probably on April 23. His father, John, was at various times a constable, an alderman, and a bailiff, which suggests he was trusted by his community. His mother, Mary Arden Shakespeare, was the daughter of a well-to-do farmer in the area. The couple had eight children, four boys and four girls. John went into debt sometime in the 1590s, fell on hard times, and died in 1601.

Although few specific details are known about Shakespeare's youth, some presumptions can be made based on the educational practices and lifestyle of Elizabethan England. Shakespeare must have studied the Bible and the Anglican Book of Common Prayer. His grammar school education would have included a strong emphasis on Latin. He was probably apprenticed to his father, who was a glover (one who made gloves).

In 1582 William must have walked frequently from Stratford to a cottage outside the town, where Anne Hathaway lived, for they married in November of that year. Anne was eight years older than her husband. Their first child, Susanna, was born in May of the following year. In 1585 twins were born to the Shakespeares, Judith and Hamnet.

Virtually nothing is known of Shakespeare's life between 1585 and 1592, but in the latter year we find him in London writing *Henry VI*. It is most likely that he arrived in London prior to 1592, since it is believed that a jealous playwright's reference to an "upstart crow" is to Shakespeare. By 1594, Shakespeare was an

continued

established writer, for he completed several plays by that year, including *Richard III*, *The Taming of the Shrew*, and *The Comedy of Errors*. In addition, he found a patron who supported his writing of the extended poem "Venus and Adonis," which was to have considerable popularity for over a decade.

Shakespeare's theatre activities were extensive. In addition to writing some 36 plays, he collaborated on at least 2 others, served as an actor in the Chamberlain's Men, and held a share in that company. Not a great deal is known about either his capabilities as an actor or even the frequency with which he took on roles. It is probable that the company perceived his role to be that of playwright and did not expect him to play major roles in their productions. However, he is known to have acted in *Hamlet*, *As You Like It*, and at least one of Ben Jonson's plays.

Shakespeare's share in the Chamberlain's Men must have involved him in some theatre management activities. During his years as a shareholder, the company lost its lease on The Theatre, built the first Globe theatre, purchased the Blackfriars Theatre in 1608, and built the second Globe theatre in 1614, after the first Globe had burned on June 29, 1613. Whatever responsibilities Shakespeare may have had as sharer, he reaped some profit from his work. By the time he retired to Stratford sometime after 1606, he had accumulated enough money to buy New Place, one of the largest homes in Stratford, purchase several acres of land, and make other investments.

It is tempting to see Shakespeare in Stratford in 1611 writing *The Tempest* and putting his own retirement thoughts into the character of Prospero, who "abjures the world" and all its problems. Shakespeare's last years are, however, largely a subject of conjecture. Records indicate that he was living in Stratford with his family and engaging the life of a landowner there, but little else is known. He died on April 23, 1616, at the age of 52.

Agincourt. And there is the suffering wife of Richard II, who plays her minor part in the deposition of her husband with dignity, beauty, and tragic self-awareness.

The basic pattern of the histories depicts the move from an ineffectual ruler to a powerful and commanding ruler, reflecting Shakespeare's nationalistic ideas and his need to please the monarchy. His characters seem to be aware that they are like players on the stage of history. Many, including Richard II and Henry VI, wish at the end that history had assigned them more modest roles. In their soliloquies they stand aside from their deeds and ponder the meaning of their lives. Their thoughts make the audience aware of history and the small place each individual has in it. When this central truth is removed from a historical framework and concentrated in the actions and lives of fictitious individuals, Elizabethan tragedy is born.

Tragedies

Elizabethan tragedy is characterized by a solitary complex character who encounters an alien, hostile world that eventually overwhelms him and those around him. The typical hero expresses himself in poetry because his emotions and perceptions are too acute for ordinary language. The character's own psychological depth is equaled by an expansive, complicated world with a dozen or more distinct characters. Three tragedians illustrate the variations of this general pattern.

Marlowe. Marlowe's tragedies each focus on one central character whose passion for freedom or knowledge dominates the play. The heroes are typically Elizabethan in their pursuit of the limits of human reason and human nature. *Dr. Faustus* (c. 1589) is an account of the legendary scholar who makes a pact with the devil. The question posed by Faustus is whether, having given his soul to Mephistopheles in exchange for knowledge of things beyond human reason, he can repent his error and be received into heaven. Although church bells and angel's voices assure him of God's forgiveness, Faustus is unable to confess his sins. Marlowe's vision of reality in this play is dark, brooding, and ultimately cynical. Nevertheless, he fashioned one of the most enduring characters in dramatic literature.

Thomas Kyd. Much of Thomas Kyd's work has been lost, but one play is worth mentioning because it was extremely popular in its time, and because it is an indicator of the future direction of tragedy. *The Spanish Tragedy* (c. 1589) is a tale of ghosts, murder, revenge, and death told with the Elizabethan convention of using acting as a metaphor for human life. While two characters (a ghost and Revenge) watch with us the audience, a tale unravels of a man seeking revenge for the wrongful murder of his son. The play is full of court intrigues and corruption, of mad scenes, and of plays within the play. *The Spanish Tragedy* has obvious parallels to *Hamlet* (with the father-son roles reversed), and the subject of revenge against a corrupt nobility becomes prominent in the writing of the Jacobean period.

Shakespeare. It is impossible to summarize the features of Shakespearean tragedy, for each creates a distinctive world, self-enclosed yet universal has absorbed the minds of scholars and the hearts of audiences. Included in his list of tragedies are some of the most frequently studied and produced plays in literature: *Romeo and Juliet* (1595), *Julius Caesar* (1599), *Hamlet* (1601), *Othello* (1604), *King Lear* (1605), *Macbeth* (1605), and *Antony and Cleopatra* (1607). Nevertheless, some general features can be identified that reveal Shakespeare's genius.

The plots are complex, composed of several incidents across an expanse of time and involving a dozen or more characters. Each plot involves a single action that is the motive force for all the incidents and characters. For instance, Hamlet seeks to avenge his father's murder, Macbeth seeks to seize and hold the crown of Scotland, and Lear wants to receive the respect he feels he deserves.

Most of the plays contain a subplot or a set of secondary characters who extend the meaning and impact of the play to all human activity. These subplots can be for tragic perspective as in *King Lear* (Gloucester), for character contrast as in *Hamlet* (Fortinbras), or for comic comparison as in *Othello* (the gulling of Roderigo).

Major characters, by their steadfast opposition to the world around them, push their self-knowledge beyond predictable surface rationality to the emotional depths of passion, greed, lust, despair, madness, and the like. In each play, themes and images are developed that are particular to the actions of that play. However, the action invariably is extended to the social/political order, to nature and the cosmos, to family relationships, and to personal integrity. Pride and ambition are common emotions, revenge a frequent motive, and madness a common outcome. All of these become themes in the plays.

Jacobean Tragedy. The period after the death of Elizabeth in 1603, extending up to the establishment of the Commonwealth in 1642, is labeled Jacobean. The tragedies of this era are different in tone and outlook from those of the Elizabethan period. The death of the popular queen, the resistance to the ruling Stuart family, and the waste and intolerance of James I undermined the optimism of the earlier age. The world of Jacobean tragedy is rotten with evil. Characters are motivated by personal lust and greed to wreak revenge on an unjust world. While Hamlet could ponder death at the graveside of Ophelia and then continue his revenge against his uncle, later plays of the period remain at the graveside. Humanity is sick, having gorged itself on freedom from all social control. Characters despair that freedom has won them nothing more than lustful and bloody appetites that cannot be satisfied. Hamlet placed humankind near the angels in his famous "What a piece of work is man" speech. Jacobean tragedy, on the other hand, compared humankind to the basest of animals in the great chain of being. When a reasonably honest woman enters this world, as does the heroine of John Webster's *The Duchess of Malfi,* she is humiliated and debased before being murdered by her own brother.

The plays of Jacobean tragedy are occasionally produced today, especially *The Duchess of Malfi, The Revenger's Tragedy* (author uncertain), and several plays attributed to Francis Beaumont and John Fletcher. They will probably remain of interest as long as people share the view of Marlowe's Mephistopheles:

> Hell hath no limits, nor is circumscrib'd
> In one self place; but where we are is hell,
> And where hell is, there must we ever be . . . (II.i.122–124)

Comedies

In the middle 1500s, comedies were fashioned from the medieval humanistic plays, from the shepherds and other comic characters of the cycle plays, and from readings of Terence and Plautus in the schools and universities. Several of the plays take place in rural settings where love can romp freely among shepherds; such plays are described as pastorals. Romances are plays in which young lovers unite at the end to insure the continuity of society. The best early writer of romances was John Lyly, who wrote for the boy players. Though few of these early plays are performed today, in their day they outnumbered tragedies in performances by three to one.

Shakespeare. As with tragedy, Shakespeare is the touchstone of comedy, especially in the theatre, where productions of his plays outnumber all others combined, including those of the considerable Ben Jonson. *A Midsummer Night's Dream* (1595–1596), *Twelfth Night* (1600–1601), *The Taming of the Shrew* (1593–1594), *As You Like It* (1599–1600), and *Much Ado About Nothing* (1598–1599) remain in the repertory of most major acting companies in England and the United States. Again, it will suffice

The Swan Theatre, Stratford-upon-Avon (England), a contemporary theatre built to stage Elizabethan drama.   *Courtesy Shakespeare Centre Library, Joe Cocks Studio Collection*

here to summarize the salient features of Shakespeare's comedies rather than attempt to summarize each major work.

The standard movement of the plot is from the city to the countryside (to discover natural innocence) and then back for a festivity of some kind that unites young lovers and insures the continuation of society. There are usually two or more sets of lovers who are mismatched or misunderstood. They are surrounded by clowns and fools and by friends and foes who enjoy making fun of their love.

Thematically, the comedies are unusual for they are generally quite cynical. They end as one expects—with the triumph of love—but not before wickedness and deceit have had their day. Malvolio is bullied *(Twelfth Night)*, Kate is rather cruelly tamed *(The Taming of the Shrew)*, Bottom is turned into an ass *(A Midsummer Night's Dream)*, and Proteus betrays his best friend in order to win his friend's beloved *(Two Gentlemen of Verona)*. In Shakespeare's last plays—*Cymbeline* (1609–1610), *The Winter's Tale* (1610–1611), and *The Tempest* (1611–1612)—reconciliation of the generations is a central theme. Fathers are reunited with daughters and rulers with their kingdoms. Goodness and trust ultimately prevail.

Theatrical imagery in the plays includes several songs and dances in each show, clowning and fooling, and broad physical humor. In fact, true appreciation of the plays is best obtained in the theatre, for there the mistaken identities, disguises, and play-acting all come alive with the wit and verbal imagery associated with Shakespeare's plays.

Jonson.   Most of Jonson's works were written in the Jacobean period. Although he wrote some tragedies and several masques, his fame today rests with his comedies. The plays including *The Alchemist* (1610), *Volpone* (1606), and *Bartholomew Fair* (1614)—are strikingly different from Shakespeare's in several respects. Jonson wanted a drama that attended as much to the mind as to the eye and ear. He used the theatre to express his disdain for the fools of life, and he hoped his audiences would be taught as well as delighted by his works. By the time he wrote his last major comedy, *Bartholomew Fair*, he had amended his determination to instruct his audiences, but the subject of the play—human failing exposed to the world—suggests he remained steadfast in his efforts to expose the follies of human nature.

The world of Jonson's comedies is noisy, active, and vital. It is an urban world, with the action taking place on or near the streets of London. The traffic of characters includes charlatans, cheats, pickpockets, gullible old men, pompous Puritans, presumptuous soldiers, and conniving lawyers. People are ruled by dominant humors, leading them to expose their own greed, selfishness, religious hypocrisy, and ignorance. Jonson's view of human nature is pessimistic: when human errors are corrected, they are often corrected by those whose errors are even greater.

In spite of this stark vision of reality, Jonson's plays have much to commend them. They are superb constructions of multiple characters engaged in parallel actions. The theme of human folly is fascinating, for his subjects are the same as those of comedians in all generations. His imagery is often as rich as that of other poets. In

Ben Jonson.   *Courtesy National Portrait Gallery*

performance, Jonson gives to the theatre a rare vitality: characters bound on and off stage like acrobats, displaying the best (or worst) of their talents, and then making way for another group to entertain us.

Citizen Comedy. Not all the comedies of the period were as dark as Shakespeare's or as cynical as Jonson's. Citizen comedies operated according to a fairly strict social code that guides the moral behavior of the characters. Most of the characters are tradesmen or apprentices; they know their place in society and they are proud to fulfill whatever function that place demands. Citizen comedies, including *The Shoemaker's Holiday* (1599) by Thomas Dekker, and Thomas Heywood's *The Four Prentices of London,* appealed to the new merchant class and those around them who wished to uphold the virtues of the trades and guilds.

CONNECTIONS

Most periods of Western history have left, as legacies to future generations, characteristic theatre practices that have been adopted by theatre artists of other times and cultures. So rich is the theatre of the Elizabethan era that its writers and staging practices and architecture have been virtually copied in this century. Some of the replication has occurred because theatre historians have wanted to re-create the original experience of performing Shakespeare's plays. Beyond this arcane interest lies a greater appeal: the vitality of performed Elizabethan drama is as evident today to audiences as it must have been in 1600.

One indication of this contemporary vitality is the variety of interpretations given to Shakespeare's plays in production. Many theatre companies and universities seek to recreate the plays as they would have been done at the Globe. Designers usually expand this concept by creating bare stages with several levels and platforms and by designing costumes rich in historical detail. Innovative production concepts in the 20th century are not uncommon, however. For the 1984 Olympics in Los Angeles, the Théâtre du Soleil of France performed Shakespeare in French with a performance style similar to that of the Kabuki drama of Japan. Peter Brook, one of the world's leading directors, once produced a version of *The Tempest* that retained less than 50 lines of the original and included characters Shakespeare never created. In the 1970s, England's Royal Shakespeare Company produced *A Midsummer Night's Dream* in an all-white circus set with the actors saying their lines while swinging on trapezes and doing acrobatics. Dame Judith Anderson toured America in the role of Hamlet when she was over 60 years of age. The Oregon Shakespeare Festival envisioned Cassius in *Julius Caesar* as a Latin American revolutionary.

The list of interpretations is endless. It demonstrates the potential in the texts for the director and designer. Because each play creates its own world through words and action, the worlds can be re-created in several ways as long as they remain coherent to those words and actions. New interpretations can give fresh meaning to well-worn lines. They can suggest parallels to the world of the audience. Also, they can demonstrate that the themes of the plays are applicable in all ages for all humankind.

Elizabethan theatre and drama remain popular today for several reasons beyond the desire of theatre artists to find new interpretations. The complexity of human experience in the plays seems to conform to the sense of life of many people today. The spectacle—music, dance, pageantry, pantomime, clowns, swordfighting, and crowd scenes—remains visually stimulating and theatrically effective. There is the continual surprise in Elizabethan drama: an insightful metaphor coming from an unexpected source, a suddenly revealed personal truth, a song in the midst of tragedy, or a quiet moment before a battle. In all these ways, Elizabethan theatre and drama are as vital and dynamic today as when they were first written.

SOURCES FOR FURTHER STUDY

Social/Art/Philosophy Background

Greenblatt, Stephen. *Renaissance Self-Fashioning.* Chicago: University of Chicago Press, 1980.

Hart, Roger. *English Life in Tudor Times.* New York: G. P. Putnam and Sons, 1972.

Hussey, Maurice. *The World of Shakespeare and His Contemporaries: A Visual Approach.* London: Heinemann, 1971.

Knights, L. C. *Drama and Society in the Age of Jonson.* New York: J. J. Norton and Company, 1937.

Smith, Lacey Baldwin. *The Elizabethan World.* Boston: Houghton Mifflin Company, 1967.

Tillyard, E. M. *The Elizabethan World Picture.* New York: Vintage Books, n.d.

Theatre History

Bentley, Gerald Eades. *The Profession of Player in Shakespeare's Time.* Princeton, N.J.: Princeton University Press, 1984.

Brockband, Philip. *Players of Shakespeare.* Cambridge: Cambridge University Press, 1985.

David, Richard. *Shakespeare in the Theatre.* Cambridge: Cambridge University Press, 1978.

Dessen, Alan C. *Elizabethan Stage Conventions and Modern Interpreters.* Cambridge: Cambridge University Press, 1984.

Gurr, Andrew. *The Shakespearean Stage: 1574–1642.* New York: Cambridge University Press, 1980.

Leacroft, Richard. *The Development of the English Playhouse.* Ithaca, N.Y.: Cornell University Press, 1973.

Schoenbaum, S. *William Shakespeare: A Documentary Life.* New York: Oxford University Press, 1975.

Shapiro, Michael. *Children of the Revels.* New York: Columbia University Press, 1977.

Styan, J. L. *Shakespeare's Stagecraft.* Cambridge: Cambridge University Press, 1967 (1981).

Wyckham, Glynne. *Early English Stages.* New York: Columbia University Press, 1981.

Drama

Barish, Jonas A, ed. *Ben Jonson: A Collection of Critical Essays.* Englewood Cliffs, N.J.: Prentice-Hall, 1963.

Barber, C. L. *Shakespeare's Festive Comedy.* Princeton, N.J.: Princeton University Press, 1959.

Bock, Philip K. *Shakespeare and Elizabethan Culture.* New York: Schocken Books, 1984.

Bradbrook, M. C. *The Growth and Structure of Elizabethan Comedy.* Baltimore: Penguin Books, 1955.

Donaldson, Ian, ed. *Jonson and Shakespeare.* Atlantic Highlands, N.J.: Humanities Press, 1983.

Hallet, Charles A., and Elaine S. Hallett. *The Revenger's Madness.* Lincoln: University of Nebraska Press, 1980.

Nicoll, Allardyce. *British Drama.* 5th ed. London: George C. Harrap, 1962.

Weitz, Morris. *Hamlet and the Philosophy of Literary Criticism.* Chicago: University of Chicago Press, 1964.

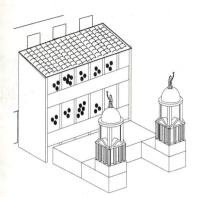

C H A P T E R

7

The Golden Age of Renaissance Spain

The room and the atmosphere were both cold on an April day in 1600 as the ten men entered and found seats around a table. Four of them were members of the King's Council, the immediate advisors to Felipe III. The others were men of the Church, including the king's confessor and the Archbishop of Granada. The topic of the day was a familiar one: the theatre. Although the king had been persuaded as recently as 1598 to close the theatres, more liberal forces had been persuasive and once again *comedias* were performed daily in the city.

Firmly the theologians recited their case against the plays, finding them not only unlawful, but a mortal sin. "All manner of plays other than religious presentations in the churches should be outlawed immediately and permanently," the archbishop stated. The king's councillors, themselves patrons of the theatre and knowing the king's affection for the drama, refused to support such a recommendation. "The *comedia* is not, in itself, sinful. We simply need to provide proper guidelines for the producers," they insisted. The two sides debated for several days, and finally a compromise edict was written and forwarded to the full meeting of the King's Council.

The edict decreed that plays would be allowed as long as the subject matter was not evil or licentious and all immodest dances were eliminated. As a means of controlling the immorality of the performances and the performers, only four companies of licensed players would be permitted. No more than two

Isabella and Ferdinand	Carlos V Emperor of Holy Roman Empire	Felipe II king		Felipe IV king
1469 1478	1519	1556–1598	1588	1621–1665

Inquisition begins

Armada defeated

Escorial built   Velásquez

1541–1614	1563–1584	1547–1616	1559–1660	1605

El Greco   Cervantes   Don Quixote

	Corral de la Cruz			Calderón de la Barca
Lope de Rueda		Lope de Vega		
1510–1565	1579 1583	1562–1635	1584–1648	1600–1681

Corral del Principe   Tirso de Molina

companies would be allowed in town at any given time, and no company could perform more than one month out of the year. To further protect public morals, women would not be allowed on the stage, monks could not attend, and no performances would occur during Lent or on several other holy days. Furthermore, women must be separated from men in the audience, and any play must be presented before a committee for approval before public performance.

The King's Council agreed to several portions of the edict, but rejected the ban on women performing since it seemed less sinful for women to appear on stage than for boys to dress as women. To appease the theologians, women were permitted to act only if their husbands or fathers were present in the theatre. The Council also maintained their right to rule on the number of companies, choosing to license eight instead of four. With these modifications, the edict became law, although the effectiveness of the law was thrown in doubt by the issuing of similar edicts in 1603, 1608, and 1615.

The struggle between Church and State for control of the theatre is a direct reflection of the political, social, and cultural life of Spain. United in their rejection of the

Reformation, the two monumental forces were just as frequently in direct opposition on social issues. This dynamic interplay between the religious and the secular lies at the very core of Spanish culture.

SOCIAL IDEAS

At the middle of the 16th century, Spain was a dominant world power carrying tremendous prestige through its mastery of the seas and its worldwide exploration. Additionally, Spain was the Western European bastion of the Catholic Church. Significantly, the pressures of these two roles greatly determined the growth and development of culture during the Spanish Renaissance.

The Christian Project

The history of Spain as a nation can be dated from the marriage of Ferdinand and Isabella in 1469. This union of the ruling families of the two independent and rival kingdoms of Castille and Aragon provided a sense of political and religious unity that never has waned. From this union, a continuing conquest or usurpation of other lands led to the country we now call Spain.

The rule of these two sovereigns is characterized by the "Christian project"—the preservation of Spain for those of true Roman Catholic belief and the casting out of infidels. Although the medieval history of Spain is of particular interest because of its multicultural, multireligious population, the Christian project marks the end of such cultural diversity.

Determined to rid Spain of heretics, the crown received permission from the Pope in 1478 to form an Inquisition. In 1492 all Jews were ordered to convert to Christianity or leave Spain. The same order was applied to Muslims in 1502. Fear that such converts were not truly converted and might be following heretical religious practices in secret led to the persecution of numerous *conversos.* Begun as a court to punish heretics, the Spanish Inquisition developed into the source of standards of approved behavior for Spanish Catholics, encompassing social as well as religious concepts. As the only "nationwide" political structure for many years, the Inquisition maintained tremendous influence in Spain.

The sense of Spain as the home of orthodox Catholicism was reconfirmed when in 1519 Carlos I (1500–1558), King of Spain, became Carlos V, Emperor of the Holy Roman Empire. The feeling intensified during the reign of Felipe II (1527–1598), beginning in 1556. Throughout the 16th century, the religious spirit of Spain became pervasive. Religious activity increased, including the founding of many confraternities that had both social and religious functions in a community. Numerous devotional books were published and became extremely popular, and the sense of "mission" to Spain's new conquests in America added urgency to belief. The rise of Protestant thought in countries that were traditional enemies of Spain brought a patriotic fervor to the Counter-Reformation, resulting in a sense of political and social unification based around orthodox Catholic religious belief. Not only Spaniards, but Spain itself, found a sense of identity in its Christian aspect. Although relationships between Crown and Church (and most especially Crown and Pope) were not always cordial, the interrelationship of church and state is a key element in the development of Spanish culture.

Expansion and Withdrawal

During most of the 16th century, Spain was without question a leading power in the world. Unified earlier than much of Europe and bolstered by tremendous riches returning from overseas exploration, Spain's influence and presence were dominant in European affairs. Spain controlled most of South America, all of Central America and Mexico, and significant portions of North America. In addition, most of the Pacific Islands, including the Philippines, were settled by Spaniards and remained Spanish possessions until the end of the 19th century. When Felipe II came to the throne in 1556, Spain's horizons seemed unlimited, and so did the responsibilities such a position presented. In time it was the weight of these responsibilities that eventually led to Spain's fall from its position of world power.

When Felipe II became King of Spain, he did not become Emperor of the Holy Roman Empire; that position went to his uncle, Ferdinand I. The rise of Lutheranism in the Low Countries and the rule of Henry VIII in England concerned Felipe greatly, for both events represented a tremendous loss to the Catholic Church. As various European countries, particularly France, began to place secular advantage ahead of sacred duties, Felipe II began to view Europe with suspicion and gradually began a withdrawal from European affairs. In 1559 he banned Spanish students from attending most foreign universities and began banning certain books. Gradually a practice of political isolation developed, and this was coupled with the growing orthodoxy of thought demanded by the Inquisition.

Felipe's personal behavior reflects the focus of the nation. Forced by continued English raids on the Low Countries to wage war against England, Felipe suffered the indignity of the defeat of the Spanish Armada (1588), and with it went Spain's control of the seas. Disillusioned with political developments, he turned his attention inward, focusing much of his energy on the completion of El Escorial, a magnificent palace/tomb built on instructions of his father. In his later years, Felipe withdrew more and more to the Escorial, spending his time in study and meditation.

This tendency toward isolationism had multiple effects on Spanish culture. First, oddly, it led to a veritable "explosion" in the arts as painting, literature, and drama seemed to blossom almost in defiance of political developments. But it separated Spain from many of the cultural developments that Europe experienced in the 17th century. The result is a remarkable cultural outpouring during the "Golden Age" and the development of a perception of Spain as somehow outside the mainstream of Western culture. This has become known as the Black Legend.

The Black Legend

The concept of the Black Legend was popularized in 1914 when Julián Juderias attempted to address the perception, shared by most of Europe and the Western world, that Spain was somehow different, that the Spanish character and government were still trapped in the spirit of the Inquisition and were somehow less advanced than others.

THE MOORISH
INFLUENCE
IN SPAIN

*F*rom the 9th century until 1502, the Islamic Moorish culture of Northern Africa was a dominant force in Spain. The rapid spread of Islam following its inception in the 7th century included the conquest of much of Spain, and for 700 years Islamic, Judaic, and Christian influences were all part of Spanish culture. Only in 1502 did an edict force all Muslims to leave Spain under the threat of the Spanish Inquisition.

Since Western-style drama was prohibited by the Islamic rejection of the creation of human idols, the Moorish influence is most easily noted in Moorish architecture (including mosques, mosaics, and elaborate geometric designs) and by the spread of scientific and mathematic concepts developed by the Arabs. However, artistic influences were also felt through the fields of philosophy, poetry, and shadow drama.

It is worth noting that the "Dark Ages" of Western culture coincided with the Golden Age of Islamic culture. During this period, many of the Greek and Latin classics were translated into Arabic, including the works of Aristotle. Indeed, many of the earliest Latin versions of the Greek classics available in Europe were re-translated from the Arabic.

Perhaps the most influential concept introduced was the idea that life is transitory and may be an illusion. Early Arab poets questioned the power of reason, suggesting that all of life may be a dream in which phantom thoughts are mistaken for reality. Although little study has been done in this area, it is evident that such thoughts are influential in the paintings of El Greco and in the plays of Calderón.

"Spanish" became equated with primitive, ignorant, cruel, fanatical, and ruthless. Spanish culture was seen as medieval and church-bound. The result was an even greater separation of Spain from the rest of European culture. What was even more important, some critics suggest, was that this perception of Spain, which arose as early as the late 16th century, affected Spain's own self-perception and self-confidence.

Whether such a "legend" grew from envy of Spain's wealth and power, from a lack of knowledge, from religious animosities, or from national rivalry is an interesting question but is ultimately unimportant. The importance of the legend lies in its effect on Spanish culture and the way it affected our perception of Spain today. Perhaps the lingering effect of the Black Legend led to the exclusion of Spanish theatre from many history texts and blocked the type of cultural interchange that has characterized other Western dramatic forms.

It must be noted, however, that the Black Legend had little effect on the cultural development of 17th-century Spain. As that country was still riding the crest of her powerful position in the world, the "Golden Age" witnessed an outpouring of artistic creation, including the development of major artists in painting, literature, and theatre.

ARTS IDEAS

The interdependence of religious and secular elements is reflected in the arts as well. An interest in the elements of life that lie beyond rational perceptions are carefully balanced by an awareness of secular responsibilities.

Painting

El Greco (1541–1614). The religious focus of Spanish painting is clearly illustrated in the work of El Greco. Born in Crete in 1541 and trained in Venice, El Greco moved to Spain in 1576. The subjects of his paintings range from the burial of a Spanish count, to the resurrection of Christ, to his famous landscape painting of Toledo. Regardless of the subject, El Greco's paintings maintain a mystical, religious quality. El Greco combined the Venetian's extraordinary use of color with his own religious sense to produce paintings that seem almost to glow with an inner light. An outward sense of tranquillity is often juxtaposed with an inner fervor and the play of mysterious forces that transcend the visible. In *The Penitent St. Peter* (1598–1600) the apostle clasps his hands in sorrowful penance, his eyes turned toward heaven in supplication. The mood of the piece is somber, yet his robe is mysteriously illuminated, almost glowing in the darkness of the picture. In the background one small angel is softly illuminated, offering a sense of hope in a moment of spiritual torment. Painted during the height of the Counter-Reformation, El Greco's works capture the religious intensity of the times. Not content with the Renaissance interest in perspective and verisimilitude, he focuses instead on the unseen, but vital and powerful, realities of the spiritual realm.

Velásquez (1599–1660). The paintings of Diego Velásquez are generally considered to be Spanish masterpieces, and they serve to illustrate several key aspects of Spanish culture of this time period. In contrast to El Greco, Velásquez almost totally ignored religious figures or issues in his paintings. He was hired as a court painter fairly early in his career, and Velásquez's paintings tend to be portraits. None of these, however, is simply a portrait, for each strives to capture a particular moment in time through a virtuosic use of space and light. In typical Spanish style, too, Velásquez resisted the latest trends in artistic circles, choosing instead to focus on his own

The Penitent St. Peter by El Greco.   *Courtesy The Bowes Museum, Barnard Castle, County Durham, United Kingdom*

personal style. Finally, Velásquez's paintings often embody the Spanish interest in secular achievement and the approval of the royal crown.

Generally considered Velásquez's masterpiece, *Las Meninas* (*Maids of Honor, 1656*) illustrates these concepts well. Deliberately secular, the picture depicts an artist (Velásquez himself) at work when he is interrupted by the five-year-old princess and two of her ladies-in-waiting, accompanied by two dwarfs. The painting is charming in its content as one of the dwarfs pokes his toe at a sleeping dog while the ladies-in-waiting attend to the princess.

The biggest surprise in the painting is the unexpected presence of the king and queen, seen reflected in a mirror. Some critics claim Velásquez included them in order

Las Meninas (The Maids of Honor) by Velásquez.   *Courtesy Museo del Prado, Madrid*

to illustrate the status of an artist at court. Whatever the personal motive, the inclusion of the royal couple also serves as metaphor of the ever-present reality of the royal throne in Spanish life.

The two great artists, El Greco and Velásquez, represent the two dominant aspects of Spanish culture: the continuing dominance of religious orthodoxy, and the undeniable importance of secular life. The presence of these two elements and their interplay provide the unique quality of Spanish culture of the Golden Age.

Literature

Cervantes (1547–1616).   Certainly the most popular work produced during the Golden Age is Miguel de Cervantes's *Don Quixote* (1605). Cervantes himself actually experienced the transition from the medieval to the Renaissance ages (he rode in the

Last Crusade), and his novel is both his rejection of medieval concepts and a nostalgic recognition of things lost in any such transition.

Most students are familiar, at least in part, with the character of Don Quixote, the crazy Spanish would-be-knight who rides the roads of Spain searching for wrongs that need to be set right. His perception causes the problems: he thinks that windmills are giants, barmaids are princesses, and barbers are hostile warriors. As we laugh at his delusion, we simultaneously recognize that the Renaissance (and modern) vision of life as simple reality, despite all its advantages, includes the loss of a certain grandeur and adventure. Don Quixote effectively quells the medieval sense of chivalry and conquest, replacing it with a slightly rueful recognition of cold reality. As Calderón will echo in a later play, life is not a dream, and even though dreams offer certain treasures, the reality of existence must be faced.

Cervantes was also a playwright, although not particularly successful. He was best known for his *entremeses*, short comic pieces performed between acts of a play.

SPANISH GOLDEN AGE THEATRE

Just as the culture of Spain developed out of a battle between Renaissance "progress" and Church traditions, the theatre also attempted to straddle dichotomies. Devoted to custom and pragmatic effect, it remained vitally interested in classical rules. Popular with a wide cross section of the populace, it maintained a fiercely philosophical and intellectual outlook. Simultaneously commercial and aesthetic, as with all of Spain, it strove to find a proper balance between the religious and the secular.

As in Italy, Spanish Renaissance theatre was actually two traditions: the *auto sacramental*, a religious play written for the Feast of Corpus Christi, and various forms of secular drama. Although both religious and secular dramas were written by the same authors and performed by the same actors, each style utilized a unique form of presentation.

Occasion

The occasion for the performance of the *autos sacramentales* was the celebration of the Feast of Corpus Christi. At the beginning of the 17th century, it was traditional in Madrid for four *autos* to be chosen from those submitted by the various acting companies. Written specifically for the occasion, and mounted at great expense and with great care, the dramatic presentations were the highlight of the theatre year and were sources of civic pride as well as important religious occasions.

The *autos* formed only a portion of the total celebration, which was expanded during the 17th century to encompass eight days. Typically it included a huge procession, giant figures, secular plays, dances, singing, and magicians. It was an event of great civic pride as each municipality attempted to outdo its neighbors. At the center of the festival, however, was the *auto sacramental* that provided the religious focus for the celebration.

The total number of performances varied from year to year. On occasion, a premiere performance was given privately for the king and his family. Two or three additional performances were scheduled for various state and municipal officials, and one or two public performances were usually given as well. The *autos* might then be performed in the public theatres, or *corrales*, before going on tour to outlying communities. In terms of time, energy, and talent invested, the *autos* represented a significant endeavor for an acting company.

In contrast, the secular drama was a fully commercial enterprise, with acting troupes licensed to perform for a specified length of time in each city. Typically, performances were given all year, except during the Lenten season, with fall and winter performances daily at 2:00 P.M. and summer and spring performances at 4:00 P.M. Although each theatre performed only three to four times each week, in the larger cities of Madrid and Seville the presence of two companies guaranteed daily performances. Sunday was a particularly popular day for theatre-going, and the re-opening of the theatres after Easter was one of the major social occasions of the year.

Location

Other than the scripts themselves, the theatre space provided the greatest contrast between the performance of the *autos* and the secular plays. *Autos* were performed on an open, unadorned platform with a large decorated *carro* situated on either side. These

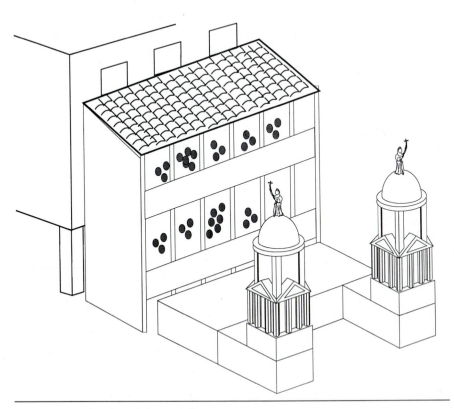

A conjectural drawing of the use of *carros*.

A TRIP TO THE
THEATRE DURING THE
GOLDEN AGE

*F*inally, it is Sunday, church is over, and a married couple is heading toward the center of town to the theatre, fulfilling a promise the husband made many months before. They had hoped to go during the summer but the theatre had been closed for two months due to an outbreak of plague, so instead they had waited until today. It is still warm, but it is now fall, and so the theatre will open at 2:00 P.M. They hurry to make sure they get to the theatre early.

At the theatre, the man pays their admission prices and says goodbye to his wife at the stairway leading to the *cazuela*, the women's seating place. He has saved just enough extra to buy himself a reserved seat away from the commotion. The first time he had come to the theatre he had stood in the center of the grounds among the commoners and had been unable to see much or hear anything of the play. People around him talked incessantly, and twice he had to stop men from fighting.

The play begins typically, with a single actor speaking the introduction. As the actor rambles on about the nature of theatre and the behavior of women in the audience, the man's eyes wander to the box seats and above them to the special third-floor boxes. One of these, he knows, belongs to his patron's family, but he is unable to see the occupants who sit discreetly back from the rail.

The play will deal with the medieval wars between the Moors and the Christians. The man loves this time period, for life in those times seems so much more adventurous and romantic, with passionate love affairs, duels, and forbidden dreams. He knows several ballads that tell this same story, but the playwright has added greatly to the plot. The opening scene hints at incest between the two attractive leading actors, and the entire story of romance and generous self-sacrifice creates a world completely unlike daily life.

The intermission is the time the spectators have looked forward to most of all, for the *entremés*, which is performed between the acts, is almost always hysterically funny, and today's satire about a mean old man who is cuckolded by his young wife is no exception.

As the conflict mounts in Act II, the actors are completely convincing, and one even climbs several ladders to the third-floor gallery in his attempt to escape. Members of the audience seem to identify with one side or the other and loudly cheer their favorites. Although people can scarcely hear a word, it is easy to follow the action.

As the final act begins, a commotion ensues in the *cazuela*. All eyes turn from the stage as many in the audience remember a recent scandal in which a young man had been found in the *cazuela* crawling around looking up the skirts of the ladies. The commotion dies down after a few minutes, and the spectators turn their attention back to the stage, where the action is proceeding as though nothing had happened. The play's ending is both sad and happy, and some in the audience wonder whether they were supposed to side with the Moors or the Christians, since both had attractive as well as negative qualities. However, the final *entremés* is rousing, and the final songs and dances are exceptionally lively, and the couple leaves the theatre in a good mood.

---

carros were mobile platforms that could participate in the procession prior to the performance of the *auto*. The impressively decorated *carros* served multiple purposes within the performance. Besides their obvious use for entrances, exits, and discoveries, the *carros* also housed rooms for musicians, changing, sound effects, and various types of machinery. Huge serpent heads with flaming breath, earthquakes, and various flying creatures are among the special effects called for by the *autos*. The carts could be turned to create a change in scene, and complex engineering allowed elaborate changes in shapes, multiple acting levels, ropes and pulleys for ascensions and descents, and other mechanisms. Although at some performances a seating structure was erected for the nobility, public performances were apparently performed to a standing audience.

In the second half of the 17th century the playwrights were even more demanding. Many *autos* of this time period are written for four *carros* and by 1692 the *carros* were fully 16 feet long and as much as 32 feet high. Indeed, there is some speculation that the size of the *carros* eventually became unwieldy and unsafe, with the result that by 1705 the *autos* were moved to the indoor theatres.

The secular theatre was performed in permanent theatre spaces known as *corrales*. The two major theatres of Madrid, the Corral del Príncipe and the Corral de la Cruz, were opened in 1579 and 1582, respectively. Both were essentially remodelings of existing inn yards, and they retained the traditional rectangular shape. Over the years, the Corral del Príncipe was improved until it reached its final form around 1630.

The *corral* occupied the yard behind a three-story facade, and it utilized the three neighboring structures as well. The facade served as the entrance and the back wall of the theatre. The stage was placed at the far end of the yard, and in time the neighboring building on that end was used to expand the backstage area. The buildings on either side provided "box seats" from rooms on the second and third floors.

The stage was a flat floor approximately six feet in height measuring 28 feet wide by 25 feet deep. A curtain hung at the rear provided two side entrances and an "inner"

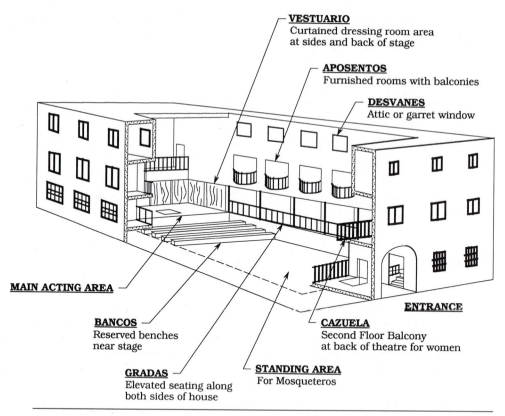

VESTUARIO
Curtained dressing room area
at sides and back of stage

APOSENTOS
Furnished rooms with balconies

DESVANES
Attic or garret window

MAIN ACTING AREA

ENTRANCE

BANCOS
Reserved benches
near stage

CAZUELA
Second Floor Balcony
at back of theatre for women

GRADAS
Elevated seating along
both sides of house

STANDING AREA
For Mosqueteros

A conjectural drawing of a *corral*, Spain's permanent public theatre of the 15th, 16th, and 17th centuries.

acting area at the rear of the staged was formed by two pillars supporting a partial roof. As many as seven trap doors were built into the stage floor for special effects and a corridor or balcony above and behind the stage was used as an acting space for scenes ranging from balconies to a mountaintop to heaven. The area above the corridor contained stage machinery used for flying effects.

Audience seating was segregated by social class and gender. Public seating for men was available in rows of elevated seats *(gradas)* placed perpendicular to the stage along the side of the yard. Standing room for the commoners, or *mosqueteros*, was placed between these seats in front of the stage. Women were seated at the rear of the yard on the second floor in the *cazuela*, an area partitioned from the men and eventually even guarded. Three levels of box seats provided additional private seating. In many cases, these seats were actually rooms in the adjoining houses. Women were allowed to sit with their escorts in the box seats.

It has been estimated that open seating was available for 900 men and 400 women, with 475 people accommodated in boxes and 160 seats available in the third-floor boxes reserved for clergy, placing a total audience of nearly 2,000 in a fairly small space. Both in their origin and their final form, these theatre structures bear a remarkable similarity to the playhouses of Elizabethan England.

Performers

Although both the *auto* and the secular plays utilized scenic effect, the performances were dominated by the actors. Typically on the wrong edge of social respectability, the actors of the Spanish stage nevertheless enjoyed considerable professional status. Records list hundreds of names; however, we know little more about any individual performers, although records of the companies do exist.

Theatre companies were organized by actor-managers *(autores)* licensed by the city. The *autor*, once he was licensed by the city officials, contracted with a local hospital/charity that owned the theatre and supported its charitable work by renting the space to acting companies. (This was frequently a positive association for the theatre in terms of its social acceptability.) Each manager hired a company of 10–20 performers, musicians, and others. As early as 1550 women appeared on the Spanish stage, despite numerous attempts to outlaw them, and a company would typically include 3–4 women. An actor was usually hired to perform a particular type of role (leading man, old woman, and so on) and was hired for the entire season. Actors were paid well: a bit player earned as much as the average worker and a leading actor could earn more than three times as much. Unexpected closures of the theatre due to weather, plagues, fiestas, or periods of official mourning could be costly to the performer, however.

The questionable morality generally attributed to actors existed in Spain as well, and many regulations attempted to preserve a sense of honor. Only married women were allowed to be actresses (even widows were excluded), and only husbands were allowed backstage. Officially, actors were denied the sacraments of the Church, although such decrees do not appear to have actually affected practice.

Very little is known about the actual acting style. Certainly the plays and the theatres indicate that a certain formality would have been a part of the style, with voice and posture probably being the most important elements of an actor's performance. The presence of the *comedia* troupes at the turn of the century and the admiration expressed for them also indicates a possibility that the physicality of the *comedia* performers was adopted into the acting style. Several writers, including Lope de Vega (1562–1635), wrote treatises that praise a naturalistic style, arguing that the audience needs to identify the actor with real life. Unfortunately, the tone of the commentary isn't clear, and we don't know whether these writers are describing the way acting was or the way they thought it should be.

Perhaps the real star performer of the Spanish theatre was the author. Playwrights were extremely well known and were frequently befriended by nobility and even royalty. Lope de Vega, the most successful of the playwrights, was capable of earning nearly twenty times as much as a common laborer. However, when a playwright sold a play to an *autor*, all rights were relinquished and the author received no further payment. Such a procedure helps to explain why an author such as Lope wrote hundreds of plays during his lifetime and continued writing until his death.

Scenery for the *autos* was included entirely in the *carros*, with the emphasis on special effects rather than representation of a certain locale. In the *corrales* simple props were the most common scenic technique, although in later years some simply painted flats may have been used.

Costuming for both types of theatre was elaborate, for although historical accuracy was not a concern, garments did indicate social status and character types. Elaborate and rich garments were the rule, even though each actor was responsible for his or her own costumes. Some nationalities who were known to local audiences were dressed appropriately. Moors, for instance, were dressed in turban and robe. Romans, Greeks, or Poles wore the Spanish national costume, however, despite the pleas of some critics. When a script required women to cross-dress, they were allowed to wear male attire only above the waist, since appearing in doublet and hose was thought to be indecent.

Audience

Obviously this type of performance left a great deal to the audience's imagination, and those attending the Spanish theatre seem to have been more than willing to do their share. A typical audience represented a wide cross section of the populace, including commoners, merchants, nobility, and the clergy, although on fiesta days and Sundays one saw a greater representation of the working class. Most of the descriptions of audience behavior focus on the *mosqueteros*, or commoners, who stood in the patio, and the women who were literally locked in the *cazuela*, a segregated seating area for women on the second floor at the rear of the theatre. The *mosqueteros* were known to be highly vocal in their praise or displeasure. A good play or performance was greeted with cries of "Victor!" while a bad play met with hissing or worse. The women also expressed their opinions clearly—at times pelting the stage with fruit or noisily jangling keys or other rattles.

Action frequently erupted in the audience. Arguments among spectators were not uncommon, and despite a guard at the door, men were known to frequent the *cazuela*, either to flirt or, on more than one occasion, to set some mice free among the women's feet. The general picture is one of a very lively audience freely reacting to the play and to each other. Only the critics, scholars, and academics grouped in the front chairs so they could hear well seemed to mind the free-spirited activity.

Standards of Judgment

In truth, the audience was one of the major critical voices of the period. The public approval of a play determined its success or failure. Even a play approved at court could fail miserably if it failed to interest or entertain the public. Among the "regulars," certain individuals apparently developed status as arbiters of taste, so that the *autores* would attempt, unsuccessfully, to bribe them to guarantee their approval.

A journal from 1679 tells of a shoemaker whose influence was very great. Playwrights sought his approval before they offered a piece to an acting company, and during the first performance, other members of the audience watched the shoemaker carefully to determine how they should behave. If he laughed, they laughed. If he yawned, they yawned. If he was ultimately displeased, the audience reacted accordingly and the play was doomed.

The power of the audience, however, did not deter critical and scholarly writers from attempting to delineate the rules and procedures for good theatre. For the most part, these represent attempts either to subjugate the Spanish theatre to classical rules or to bend the rules to accommodate Spanish traditions.

The earliest critic to publish his writing was Bartolomé de Torres Naharro, whose preface to *Propolladia* (1517) is the first piece of theoretical writing on the drama in Europe. Essentially an interpretation of Aristotle, Naharro ultimately confides that he finds the rules too long and too ponderous. Comedy, he states, is merely an interesting juxtaposition of the ordinary and the exceptional. This tendency to interpret rules loosely is common among some Spanish critics, to the vexation of others.

Alonso Lopez Pinciano's *Philosophía antigua poética*, published in 1596, represents an attempt to find a compromise between Aristotelian theory, the writings of Horace, and Spanish tradition. Pinciano defines the genres of tragedy and comedy according to custom. He adopts Horace's call for a five-act structure, a limitation on the number of characters, and the demand for a suitable ending in which evil is punished and virtue is rewarded. He expands Horace's demand for a 24-hour time period to three days for comedy and five days for tragedy, noting that modern man takes longer to find virtue than did men of the classical eras.

One of the most violent criticisms of contemporary drama is contained in *Don Quixote*. Cervantes attacks Spanish drama for embracing nonsense and lewdness, exhibiting a lack of concern for verisimilitude or decorum, and tolerating character inconsistencies that make a mockery of verisimilitude. He further attacks the fact that virtue is not rewarded, nor is vice punished as authors pander to the tastes of an uneducated public.

Lope de Vega provides one of the most complete statements in an essay written at the order of the Academy of Madrid. He identifies the dual nature of Spanish theatre: the desire for art, and the need to please the audience. The result is a mixture: de Vega dismisses demands for pure genre and finds the combination of tragedy and comedy a pleasurable variety. He is pragmatic about time, urging that the action of a play be completed in as little time as possible. He warns against the use of impossible things or inconsistent characters, and advocates a focus on honor, virtue, and wit. He acknowledges that his own plays fall short of classical precepts, but defends them and himself for having written plays of his own time destined to please the people who came to see them.

Lope de Vega's pragmatism is typical of critical writings of the 17th century, as critics sought to find a middle ground between the demands of art and the popular appeal of the Spanish theatre. Various changes in the demands of the classicists were defended in terms of progress. Renaissance Spain was not Classical Rome, and the proper theatre of one demanded rules other than those that were written for the classical cultures. Tirso de Molina (1580–1648), another playwright, claimed that verisimilitude, in its attempt to imitate nature, cannot follow any rules since nature follows no rules. The role of the Spanish playwright was to transform history and nature through imagination. The result, naturally, was a drama and a theatre unlike any other.

The *Auto Sacramental*

The *auto sacramental* or *auto* is one of two dramatic genres unique to Renaissance Spain. Akin to the mystery and morality plays found in medieval England and other parts of Europe, the *auto* was a religious play in one act that focused on the movement of a human being from a state of doubt to a state of belief. Similar to the development of the medieval drama throughout Europe, the *autos* developed as a part of the celebration of the Feast of Corpus Christi.

Records indicate the celebrations, including floats, music, and dance, began in various cities in Spain during the 14th century. Although these processions included floats with characters depicting various biblical stories, these were tableaus rather than drama. Drama apparently became a part of the celebrations during the middle years of the 15th century. The basic purpose of the plays was to add to the sense of celebration surrounding this important church event and to bolster the faith of the devout. Although the *autos* were not evangelical materials seeking converts to Christianity, some critics see the *auto* as one of the Catholic Church's most valuable weapons in the battle against the perceived threat of Reformation heresy.

Autos could be based on biblical stories, folklore, or other mythologies. Sometimes they were allegorical, but this was not a requirement of the form. From the very beginning, they included various secular elements that added variety and interest to the drama. This combination of religious and secular elements gave the form its particular appeal and power.

Lope de Vega's *Prodigal Son* is a retelling of the familiar biblical parable. His dramatization included the addition of several new allegorical characters. An opening section, not part of the biblical tale, depicts Prodigal in discussion with Youth, who convinces Prodigal that love, women, and gambling belong to the young, but they all require money. Prodigal agrees and, as depicted in the biblical story, departs from home with his father's money. The playwright greatly enlarges the depiction of Prodigal's journey away from home, introducing characters such as Lascivious, Delight, Gaming, and Success as Prodigal's companions. A banquet scene depicts Prodigal enjoying his life fully as he and Delight fall in love to the accompaniment of a musical chorus that not only praises their love but also hints of problems to come. When Prodigal finds himself employed as a swineherd, he decides to return home, where he is accepted with open arms. In a later *auto* based on the same story, the author introduces another character, Inspiration, who counsels Prodigal to repent and seek out the true riches of his home and family.

The *auto* adds considerable drama to the biblical story. The psychological processes of temptation and repentance are clearly presented in scenes with Youth and Inspiration. The joys of sin are vividly represented, allowing the spectator to identify fully with the choices presented to Prodigal. The solution of the story, however, as Prodigal repents and is rewarded for his repentance, clearly follows the teachings of the Catholic Church.

Autos were extremely popular, and each year witnessed several new compositions. The form became more and more polished, and the last *autos* of Calderón de la Barca (1600–1681), written in the mid-17th century, incorporate very skillful poetry, dramatic imagery, complex intellectual thought, and music, all woven in a tightly unified and highly effective dramatic form.

Comedia

The development of the *comedia* in Renaissance Spain must not be confused with the Italian commedia dell'arte. The Spanish *comedia* was a form of dramatic literature that was clearly the dominant form of the time. A *comedia* may be defined as a play that is (1) structured in three acts; (2) written in verse with metrical changes made as is suitable to the action; (3) focused on a dynamic plot structure rather than on character developing; (4) organized around a prevailing theme, often love or honor; and (5) characterized by a mixture of comic and tragic circumstances, usually, but not always, resolving happily. The focus of the *comedia* is nearly always the relationship between the individual and society, and the plays frequently explore the relationship between reality and pretence or role-playing

The plays, though written for commercial purposes, often deferred to Catholic thought or were carefully manipulated to support the concept of royal rule and loyalty to the throne. Within this limitation, however, the playwrights of the *comedia* explored a wide-ranging variety of subjects and situations—from historical subjects to mythology to folklore. The result was a vast body of plays that on the surface seem similar to one another in tone and structure but provide a striking variety of ideas.

Lope de Vega.   Considered a national hero at the height of his popularity, Lope de Vega was the author of at least 800 dramatic works, and some estimate that he may have written nearly 1800 plays. Over 450 plays, including both *autos* and *comedias*, exist today, in addition to volumes of poetry and essays. Given this extreme popularity, one is surprised to find that de Vega's personal life was one of scandal, intrigue, and disappointment. Born the son of an embroiderer, he always considered himself a writer, but circumstances forced him into a bewildering series of adventures. He was secretary to a long line of nobles, was arrested for libel and exiled for a period of time, was married twice, had three long-term (and public) affairs, fathered at least 12 children, served as an officer in the Inquisition, sailed to defeat with the Spanish Armada, and finally took vows of priesthood while openly having yet another affair. These contradictions and tensions are clearly a part of his drama, and, to many, the struggle between his appetites and his moral vision serve as a metaphor for the average Spaniard whose Renaissance appetites were checked on either side by the need to conform to the expectations of Church and Crown.

Lope de Vega's most famous drama is *Fuenteovejuna*, or *The Sheep Well* (1612–1614). In a small town suffering under the tyranny of a cruel overlord, Laurencia, the daughter of the mayor, is assaulted by the tyrant Comendador and is saved only by the valiant efforts of her fiancé, Frondoso. At their wedding, the comendador reappears, attacks the mayor, and has Frondoso and Laurencia taken prisoner. The males of the village cower in fear of reprisal, but Laurencia escapes, finds them, and, with an

COURT THEATRE
UNDER FELIPE IV

*T*he reign of Felipe II was not a prosperous time for the theatre, but under the governance of Felipe III theatre became a necessary part of all state festivities. Not only were public performances supported and encouraged, but special performances were frequently commanded by the court. Felipe III's delight in stage spectacles led to a great growth in the role of design and machinery in stage productions. Under Felipe IV, this tendency reached unheard-of heights.

Felipe IV had first appeared in stage plays as a child—his first recorded role was Cupid—and his interest in theatre continued throughout his life. In 1626 he brought over a noted Italian designer, Cosimo Lotti, who introduced the highly developed Italian style of perspective painting and use of stage machinery. When a vacation palace, the Palacio del Buen Retiro, was built for Felipe in 1633, Lotti took advantage of the setting to produce spectacles on a huge scale. Since the theatre built as part of the palace was not finished until 1640, Lotti staged a series of outdoor spectacles on the lake that was at the center of the grounds. These magnificent pageants lasted up to six hours, ending at 1:00 A.M., and featured one dazzling show of spectacle after another. One production featured a stage constructed seven feet above the lake's surface, waterfalls, a chariot drawn by giant fish, at least seven ships, and stars that rose into the heavens. All of this was lighted by some 3000 lanterns as the king watched from a gondola floating in the lake. This production was repeated for several days with the public invited to attend the final stagings.

After Lotti's death, Felipe hired Baccio del Branco as his successor. Branco's ambitions were equally large, and his reign as court designer featured larger productions with casts of more than 70 performers. Effects indicated in his drawings included a gigantic Atlas who appeared on one knee with the world on his shoulder. After the opening of the play, this Atlas stood fully erect and then sang.

Following Felipe IV's death in 1665 the court theatre continued, but never again did it achieve such heights. Gradually underminded by the failing economy of Spain and protests against such lavish expenditures on luxuries, the theatre scene was further devastated by the death of Calderón de la Barca in 1681. Finally, the death of Carlos II in 1700 ended not only the court drama of Spain but the reign of the Hapsburg family as well.

impassioned speech, urges them to act against the tyranny and to save Frondoso. The townspeople band together and kill the comendador. A judge questions each of them, asking each to identify the murderer. Despite extreme methods of torture, each replies "Fuenteovejuna killed him." The judge reports that either the king must kill them all or pardon them all, and he chooses the latter, although noting that the crime was a serious one.

Structurally, *Fuenteovejuna* is typical of the *comedia* style. The episodic form presents a string of "adventures" depicted without clear connection in time or space. The mixed tone of rustic comedy juxtaposed with serious thought and idyllic love set against tyranny and torture is also a key element of *comedia* writing. Characters are rather stereotypical, and the concept of honor serves to bind the play's elements together. The play ends happily with a "deus ex machina" scene reminiscent of Molière in which the king provides a suitable solution.

Fuenteovejuna is compelling drama on several levels. Perhaps the most noticeable aspect is the central character, Laurencia. Women not uncommonly take on heroic stature in Spanish *comedia*, usually through adopting male behavior patterns. Although such drama in no way mirrors the reality of life for the women of Spain, the creation of such powerful female figures is an interesting aspect of Spanish *comedia*. The woman typically returns to her traditional role of lover and/or wife when the crisis is past; nevertheless, such images of women who are active and powerful were subversive to the status quo and undoubtedly very popular among some women in the audience and attractive and provocative to the men.

Of further interest is the political dimension of the play. Lope de Vega clearly indicates that the evil comendador is a supporter of the Portuguese king in his struggle with the new "Catholic Queen" Isabella and her husband, Ferdinand. The demise of the tyrant is paralleled by Isabella and Ferdinand's victory and ascension to the throne and denotes the new power of the Spanish throne as well as the decline of feudal control.

PLAYWRIGHTS OF SPAIN'S GOLDEN AGE

Torres Naharro, Bartolomé de	1485–1520	*Propolladia* (1517)
Vicente, Gil	c. 1460–c. 1539	*Play of Grace* (1518)
Rueda, Lope de	1509?–1565	*The Delightful* (collection, pub. 1567)
Cueva, Juan de la	1550–1610	*Tragedy of the Seven Princes of Lara* (1580?)
Vega, Lope de	1562–1635	*Dog in the Manger* (c. 1613)
		The Sheepwell (c. 1613)
		The Knight of Olmedo (c. 1625)
Molina, Tirso de	1580–1648	*The Trickster of Seville*
		Prudence in Women
Alarcón y Mendoza, Juan de	c. 1580–1639	*The Suspect Truth*
Calderón de la Barca, Pedro	1600–1681	*The Painter of His Dishonor* (1648)
		The Mayor of Zalamea (1642)
		Life Is a Dream (1635)

Many *comedias* have a political dimension, although some appear more critical than supportive of the reigning government.

Lope de Vega's dramatic skills were not confined to one type of drama. He wrote both rustic and urban comedies, comedies of manners, satire, historical drama, and tragedy. Although some critics question the overall quality of his work (and some of his plays do appear to have been written hastily, probably to meet production deadlines), in his best works Lope de Vega produced work of tremendous vitality, charm, and power.

***Tirso de Molina* (1580–1648).**   One of Lope de Vega's followers as a dramatist was Tirso de Molina, a pseudonym for a monk, Fray Gabriel Téllez. Although he was extremely popular, Molina's career was cut short when political difficulties with the court of Felipe IV led to his banishment from Madrid to a distant monastery, effectively ending his dramatic writing.

Molina's works comprise the full range of Spanish drama: religious plays, saints plays, comedies, plays of intrigue, and heroic drama. His religious plays mirror Lope de Vega in his ability to introduce significant secular allure into a drama that at heart focuses on religious aspects. His retelling of the biblical story of the rape of Tamar by her half-brother, Amnon, *La Venganza de Tamar (Tamar's Vengeance),* is dramatically

Linus Roache as Don Juan in a recent production by the Royal Shakespeare Company. *Courtesy Shakespeare Centre Library, Joe Cocks Studio Collection*

effective largely because of Molina's ability to dramatize the sensual temptation and psychological despair of Amnon before and after his crime. Adding to the effectiveness of this drama is one of Molina's most developed talents—his ability to write powerful women's roles. In this case, Tamar, nominally the victim of the piece, is intellectually dominant and verbally superior to all the men. Amnon's attack is therefore the triumph of brute strength over a superior person, making the rape even more tragic.

Molina's ability to evoke powerful women is best seen in *La Prudencia en La Mujer (Prudence in Women)*, a historical drama in which a powerful, intelligent noblewoman successfully defends her kingdom while her sons are still children. Successful as wife, mother, and queen, Maria is not without doubts or flaws. However, her intelligence combined with her noble spirit allow her to overcome her enemies. This play has evident political commentary. At the time of its writing, Felipe III had recently died, and Felipe IV was only 16. The dangers that such a situation can present to a kingdom already perceived as tottering are clearly outlined in the drama. Although the use of a woman as the controlling force avoids direct commentary, the play clearly parallels the then-existing political situation.

Molina's most lasting contribution to Western literature was the creation of the character of Don Juan. Developed through several hundred years as the ultimate romantic trickster, Molina's Don Juan is a nearly perfect villain. Appearing in *El Burlador de Sevilla (The Trickster of Seville)*, Molina's character delights in seducing women and then dishonoring them. A duchess, a peasant woman whom he promises to marry, his best friend's mistress, and a bride-to-be are all his victims. He openly acknowledges his activity, but since he is successful, he assumes there will be no penalty. He is a man above the law—in Faustian fashion, he chooses to defy the laws of man and God, scorning the possibility of punishment.

At the close of the play he mocks a statue of the father of his final victim, a man who died attempting to defend his daughter's honor. Upon Don Juan's invitation, the statue appears at dinner that night, silently observing Don Juan's attempts at sarcastic humor and wit. He, in turn, invites Don Juan to dine with him the next evening. After a meal of scorpions, vipers, and gall, the statue offers to shake hands. Don Juan accepts, is crushed in the grip of the stone hand, begs for forgiveness, and is finally swallowed up into a crypt as the chapel bursts into flames.

Although the play is nicely structured and is evidence once again of the Spanish ability to combine adventure and religious drama, it succeeds largely on the basis of the dynamic, towering portrait of this individual human being who chooses to pit himself against all of creation. Adopted and altered by a multitude of authors in the following years, Molina's fictitious creation, Don Juan, has become a part of Western folklore.

Calderón de la Barca (1600–1681).

Usually ranked with Lope de Vega as one of the two greatest dramatists of the Golden Age, Calderón de la Barca was born in 1600 to low nobility, was educated in Jesuit schools, and studied at the university level as preparation for entering the priesthood. A variety of personal and family reasons forced him to change his mind about taking religious vows, and he turned instead to the stage at the age of 23. Highly successful, he authored more than 400 stage works, of which more than 200 survive.

As with the other dramatists studied, Calderón did not limit himself to one genre and successfully authored *autos*, comedies, love intrigues, serious drama, and elaborate mythological plays in the tradition of the Italian Renaissance that are early forms of opera. Although Calderón was a master of each of these forms, it is his serious drama that is most often studied today.

Certainly Calderón's best-known play is *La Vida es Sueño* (*Life Is a Dream*, 1635). The tale of a young prince locked away since birth, because foreboding astrological signs and the death of the boy's mother convinced the father that the boy would bring ruin upon the kingdom, *La Vida es Sueño* is a philosophical play that explores several themes. The divine right of kings, the nature of reason and passion in human existence, the role of divine providence and chance in human affairs, and the ever-present concept of honor are all a part of this complex drama. When the prince, Segismundo, is brought out of the prison, his father decides to allow him to rule for one day to see if he is capable. Segismundo's early responses are all passionate—he insults women and kills men—but as the play progresses he develops his use of reason and prudence to become, at the end, a perfect prince. In traditional Spanish fashion, echoing the structure of the *autos*, the play traces a man from ignorance through doubt to belief.

Adding an unexpected layer to the play is the king's attempt to convince Segismundo that his freedom is a dream, so they can take away his power if necessary. At one point Segismundo ponders whether he is awake or dreaming, only to decide that since he cannot know it doesn't make any difference—he must therefore act as he will. To a 20th-century reader, this question of truth and illusion seems undeniably modern.

An additional characteristic of Spanish drama exemplified in this play is the *gracioso*, or comic figure. In this case, Clotaldo, the prince's servant and tutor, not only has the innate wisdom often given to these rustic figures, but also offers pointed comic perceptions at times of high seriousness in the drama, thus demonstrating the mixed tone so common in Spanish drama.

The darker side of Calderón's vision is illustrated by his three plays that deal with wife-murder. In each of these, *El médico de su honra* (*Physician to His Own Honor*, 1635), *A secreto agravio, secreta venganza* (*Secret Insult, Secret Revenge*, 1636) and *El pintor de su deshonra* (*Painter of His Dishonor*, 1648), a husband, convinced that his wife has been unfaithful, kills her to preserve his honor. The plays are stark in their portrayals of human beings caught in the web of social expectations and honor codes that leads them unerringly to the point of violence. The status of the women, utterly powerless and perceived as possessions of the husband, is in stark contrast to the powerful women of Molina's plays.

Calderón also was one of the earliest authors of the *zarzuela*, a musical theatre form of allegorical presentations, usually performed in the open air before a palace of civic building.

By the time of his death in 1681, Calderón had firmly established himself as the leading dramatist of Spain. The secular masterpieces most studied today are all from the early period of his life. His later years were devoted to the writing of *autos sacramentales* (including at least two each year for the last 20 years of his life) and musical court entertainments.

A Global Perspective

Sor Juana Innes de la Cruz (1648–1695)

*A*mong the most unusual figures of Renaissance drama is Sor Juana Innes de la Cruz, the illegitimate child of a Mexican nobleman (or possibly a priest) and a commoner. Raised by relatives in Mexico City, she showed an early promise for intellectual affairs. She served several years at court, but at the age of 19 entered a convent, apparently to avoid marriage, which she felt would be too restrictive. Although the convent required vows of poverty and cloistering, such rules were not strictly enforced, so that Sor Juana was able to maintain some personal wealth and even had a servant during her first year in the convent.

Sor Juana's literary output includes a considerable amount of poetry, theory, a feminist autobiography, songs, and both secular and religious plays. The plays are strongly resistant to the dominant society. *Love Is the Greater Labrynth* contains a strong plea for equality for all persons regardless of social standing (or gender), which ran directly counter to the absolutist government's position. *The Divine Narcissus* was an attempt to bridge Christianity and native religious practices, noting similarities in human sacrifice and Christian communion.

Many of Sor Juana's works were destroyed during the revolutions of the 19th century. Only in recent years has rising critical interest resulted in the rediscovery of her unique talents.

CONNECTIONS

The connections between Spanish Renaissance theatre and contemporary theatre practice are less evident than those previously discussed. Spanish culture tended to remain insolated from the rest of Europe, and less exchange between theatrical forms took place. As a result, many of the plays from this period seem unusual to the modern reader.

Certainly Spain provided the major dramatic influence in Latin America, where the *autos* and the *comedia* became central dramatic forms. The Catholic Church utilized *autos* and adaptations of native rituals as conversion tools, and Spanish plays were the models for early theatrical ventures in the cities of Latin America.

For the most part, the rest of Europe and America ignored Spanish culture, but the Don Juan figure was adopted from Spanish literature and is still found in contemporary film and television.

SOURCES FOR FURTHER STUDY

Social/Art/Philosophy Background

Haraszti-Tkacs, Marianna. *Spanish Genre Painting in the Seventeenth Century.* Budapest: Akademiai Kiado, 1983.

Kamen, Henry. *Golden Age Spain.* Houndmills, U.K.: Macmillan Educational, 1988.

Linehan, Peter. *Spanish Church and Society 1150–1300.* London: Variorum Reprints, 1983.

Marias, Julian. *Understanding Spain.* Trans. Frances M. Lopez-Morillas. Ann Arbor: University of Michigan Press, 1990.

Mariejol, Jean H. *The Spain of Ferdinand and Isabella.* Trans. Benjamin Keen. New Brunswick, N.J.: Rutgers University Press, 1961.

Norea, Carlos G. *Studies in Spanish Renaissance Thought.* The Hague: Martinus Nijhoff, 1975.

O'Connell, Marvin R. *The Counter Reformation.* New York: Harper & Row, 1974.

Payne, Stanley G. *Spanish Catholicism.* Madison: University of Wisconsin Press, 1984.

Smith, Bradley. *Spain: A History in Art.* New York: Doubleday, n.d.

Theatre History

Allen, John J. *The Reconstruction of a Spanish Golden Age Playhouse.* Gainesville: University Presses of Florida, 1983.

Harter, Hugh A., and John D. Mitchell. *Staging a Spanish Classic: The House of Fools.* Midland, Mich.: Northwood Institute Press, 1990.

McKendrick, Melveena. *Theatre in Spain: 1490–1700.* Cambridge: Cambridge University Press, 1989.

Rennert, Hugh. *The Spanish Stage in the Time of Lope de Vega.* New York: Dover Publications, 1963.

Shergold, N. D. *A History of the Spanish Stage from Medieval Times Until the End of the Seventeenth Century.* Oxford: Oxford University Press, 1967.

Surtz, Ronald E. *The Birth of a Theater.* Princeton, N.J.: Princeton University Press, 1979.

Dramatic Literature

Arias, Ricardo. *The Spanish Sacramental Plays.* Boston: Twayne Publishers, 1980.

Bushee, Alice. *Three Centuries of Tirso de Molina.* Philadelphia: University of Pennsylvania Press, 1939.

Hall, J. B. *Lope de Vega: Fuenteovejuna.* London: Grant and Cutler, 1985.

Jones, R. O., ed. *Studies in Spanish Literature of the Golden Age.* London: Tamesis Books, 1973.

Kennedy, Ruth Lee. *Studies in Tirso.* Chapel Hill: University of North Carolina Press, 1974.

Larson, Donald R. *The Honor Plays of Lope de Vega.* Cambridge, Mass.: Harvard University Press, 1977.

Parker, Alexander A. *The Mind and Art of Calderón.* Cambridge: Cambridge University Press, 1988.

Wilson, Edward M. *Spanish and English Literature of the 16th and 17th Centuries.* Cambridge: Cambridge University Press, 1980.

Wilson, Margaret. *Spanish Drama of the Golden Age.* Oxford: Pergamon Press, 1969.

Wardropper, Bruce. W., ed. *Critical Essays on the Theatre of Calderón.* New York: New York University Press, 1965.

Classicism in
the French
Renaissance

General
Events

Arts
Events

Theatre
History
Events

Hôtel de
Bourgogne Théâtre

1548

The month of May 1664 was a busy time at Versailles, the great palace of Louis XIV, King of France. The king had become enamored of a new mistress, and a week of entertainment was planned in her honor. The event, to be held outdoors on the beautiful grounds of the palace, would include water sports, tournaments, ballets, concerts, dances, banquets, and theatre.

A carnival atmosphere suffused the area, with elegantly dressed courtiers and their ladies filling the palace and the grounds with all kinds of merry-making. Since the king's affection for the young woman was no secret, many of the events seemed to encourage the idea of love and love-making. Two light comedies were presented with great success, but on the final evening the bright young playwright Molière produced a new play, *Tartuffe,* which satirized religious hypocrisy. In the atmosphere of revelry and freedom that the week had produced, the king was delighted by the play. However, the Queen Mother was not amused, nor were her devoutly Catholic friends, for the play seemed to present the devout as fools, easily duped by a clever fraud. To please her, the king forbade further performances of the play. A rewritten version was performed five months later, but it once again met with outrage. Suppressed for four more years, only a successful production in 1669 preserved this classic comedy, which has been a favorite of theatre audiences ever since.

	Thirty Years' War	Louis XIII dies		Mazarin dies		Government to Versailles		Louis XIV dies
	1618–1648	1642	1643	1654	1661	1683	1685	1715
		Cardinal Richelieu dies	Coronation of Louis XIV			Louis exiles thousands of French Protestants (Huguenots)		

French Academy established			Academy of Music established	Palace at Versailles
1629–1635		1644	1665	1669	1661–1688

	Descartes' *Principia philosophicae*	Bernini to Paris

	Théâtre du Marais	Molière's troupe to Paris		Comédie-Française
	1634	1636–1638	1658	1659–1660	1680
		Le Cid controversy	Salle des Machines	

The French Renaissance, encompassing most of the 17th century, is one of the great periods in French literature and the arts. It is especially notable in the drama for two reasons that are the twin subjects of this chapter. The first is that it encompasses the genius of Jean-Baptiste Poquelin, know as Molière (1622–1673), considered by many to be the greatest writer of comedies of all time. In France, he is the pinnacle of dramatic literature and the chief model for comedy in drama. In spite of the difficulties of translation, Molière's plays are read and performed in English to this day. Possibly, he is performed throughout the world with more frequency than any other Renaissance writer except Shakespeare.

The second focus of this chapter is classicism, the literary and artistic style that returns to the Greek and Roman classics for rules and guidelines by which to analyze literature. Beginning with the Renaissance, France was embroiled in a recurrent aesthetic battle over the prescriptions of the Ancients (or classical writers) against the programs of the Moderns (those who rejected the principles of the past). Not only did this battle shape the history of French literature to the present day, it also stands as a case study of the reasons other societies at various times have elected to return to the Greeks and Romans for their artistic models. In France, the classicist argument began with the dominance of Cardinal Richelieu (1585–1642), the chief adviser to King

Louis XIII in the 1620s and 1630s. It reached fruition under the absolutist principles of the remarkable Sun King, Louis XIV (1643–1715).

SOCIAL IDEAS

Absolutism

In 1670, Louis XIV's sun shone more brightly than at almost any other time in his 72-year reign. For almost a decade, he had ruled without a prime minister, making all important decisions by himself. His plans to build the greatest palace in the world were well underway at Versailles. He was not yet engaged in expensive and exhaustive foreign wars. He was not plagued by bad harvests or bread riots. He was still young, energetic, and enthusiastic. Government and society focused on him and reflected his glory.

Louis XIV was an absolute monarch. He reigned with the divine authority of God, and no one on earth could question him. He accumulated all power into his hands and forced an identification of the future of France with the future of Louis. If Louis is wealthy, was the reasoning, then France is wealthy. His famous remark, "L'état c'est moi (I am the state)," was indeed for him a literal truth. He once told the French Academy, "Gentlemen, I entrust to you the most precious thing on earth, my reputation." The comment summarized Louis' policies of state and the arts.

The impact of absolutism on the court and nobility was, as might be imagined,

Louis XIV, a bust after Bernini, c. 1665. *Courtesy Samuel H. Kress Collection,* © *1992 National Gallery of Art, Washington*

profound. People vied for the approval of the king through flattery and mimicry. Those who came into money used it to follow the fashions of the court. Absolutism also created a social hierarchy with those who were closest to Louis at the top, those who had the ear of those close to Louis next in line, and so on. Anyone who could, or could effectively pretend to, have been at the king's bedchamber when he arose in the morning (and there were always several there to applaud Louis when he awoke) presumed to have influence and power for that day. Quickly, therefore, the world of Louis' court became a world more of appearance than reality.

On some people this appearance was surely ridiculous, for they would exaggerate the current fashions in order to prove their standing in society. On others, this appearance gained what in our time would be called style, for they wore their masks with gentility and honesty. These latter were known as the *hommes honnête* (roughly translated "honest men"), who engaged life with ease, confidence, and a degree of learning. They prided themselves on knowing something well, but not on working at it or practising it.

Another facet of absolutism was the increasing support for the belief that the universe is subject to rational laws. This idea, developed in the following century and discussed in Chapter 11, assumes that the universe is coherent, that all the parts interrelate, and that the individual mind can and should understand these relationships.

Toward the end of his reign, Louis became more conservative. Laws were passed restricting the freedoms of the populace. When the treasury itself became strapped by the building of Versailles and recurring warfare, entertainment became less important in the court of the Sun King, and finally Louis turned entirely away from the theatre.

ARTS IDEAS

One aspect of absolutism was its impact on the arts. Like the Italian rulers in the century before him (Louis was related to the Medicis), Louis knew that the arts were a powerful expression of his status, wealth, and good taste. He therefore encouraged the arts in ways that would add to the glory of his reign. The arts were organized to prove that the reign of Louis was the zenith of Western culture. Louis himself was symbolically linked with the gods of Greek mythology. The stories of Greek and Roman literature were retold. The rules of ancient writers were followed. All of this was done to prove that in the reign of Louis XIV, writers could continue the traditions of the past and raise them to new artistic heights. The term for this emphasis on the classics is classicism.

Classicism

Absolutism in politics had a stringent variation of classicism as its equivalent form in the arts. Classicism determined appropriate subject matter and prescribed rules for composition. It also located power in the hands of a few people appointed by the king to exercise authority in his name. Cardinal Richelieu had created the French Academy of Language and Literature in 1635 to foster the improvement of French literature. Within two years it was used to determine what was good literature in a celebrated battle over the merits of Pierre Corneille's play *Le Cid.*

The criteria for excellence in that debate were the rules for dramatic construction written by Aristotle and Horace but interpreted by the French Academicians. The play was condemned because it did not sufficiently follow what the Academicians believed were principles of good writing established by the Ancients. The Academy ruled that the play failed to meet the standards of any recognized form but seemed to blend tragedy, tragicomedy, and pastoral. Furthermore it violated the idea of verisimilitude by packing too much action into one day and by allowing a woman to marry a man who had recently killed her father. The message to the writers of the day was evident: write according to the rules, or your plays will not be approved.

Painting

In art, a similar form of classicism took hold. Painters devoted themselves primarily to battle scenes, heroic actions, and religious themes because these reflected the grandeur of the age. Composition and technique were to be based on examples from the past. Nicolas Poussin (1593–1665) summarized the ideas of the classical artists, including the other master, Claude Lorraine (1600–1682), when he demanded that painting limit itself to events that were stately, severe, and grave. He believed that, when depicting a serious subject, the painter must improve on nature: an event should not be portrayed as it actually happened but as it would have happened if nature were perfect. For Poussin and others of his time, the artist must reflect the great moral principles of the past.

Music

In music, Jean Baptiste Lully (1632–1687) used his organizational and directorial skills to secure for himself a virtual monopoly over all music productions for the court. Lully directed the musicians and dancers in the comedy-ballets performed for the court, including *The Would-Be Gentleman* (1670), for which he also wrote the incidental music. He also composed several operas that became the models for future French opera. Most of his operas are allegorical and mythological and permit several scene changes and numerous ballets. Regardless of their setting, however, the purpose of the operas was nearly always evident: to glorify the king. Lully's success lay in his ability to wed the characteristics of absolutism with those of classicism. He produced models of correct musical dramatic structure while at the same time employing large choruses and brass choirs to hail the king's achievements.

Entertainments for the Court

The entertainments for which the court of Louis became renowned were made possible by the arrival in Paris in 1645 of Giacomo Torelli (1608–1678). Torelli had designed the sets for several operas in Venice, and the remarkable speed with which he could change sets gained him the nickname the Great Sorcerer. Torelli had designed an intricate system of counterweights, attached to scenery, and connected with ropes to drums below the stage. As the drums turned, the ropes would also turn, causing the scenery to shift. The fluid and rapid actions, all hidden from the view of the spectators,

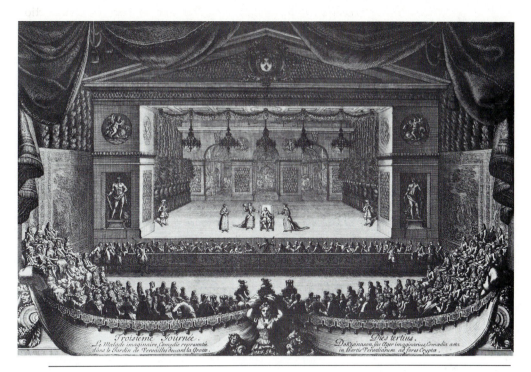

A performance of *The Imaginary Invalid* at Versailles, 1674.   *Courtesy Harvard Theatre Collection*

were a source of wonderment in both Venice and Paris. The French were so taken with his designs that the Théâtre du Marais and later the Hôtel de Bourgogne were remodeled to accommodate machinery similar to Torelli's.

Torelli's settings illustrate the preference for mythological subjects characteristic of classicism. Designed in perspective, they frequently included celestial scenes permitting costumed actors to move across the skies on clouds or chariots, and ocean settings allowing for the depiction of moving water and ships gliding across the stage. Especially popular were magic scenes set in enchanted palaces and islands where all sorts of stage effects could be introduced into the action with textual justification.

The challenge for writers was to write texts that accommodated these visual effects. Just as modern films often suffer because the special effects overwhelm the action, the problem for most plays was that their long set speeches were static in comparison to the spectacular effects Torelli invented. Often the plays were not part of the set changes. New forms of drama had to be devised to integrate these effects.

Ballet d'entrées were dances that contained more pageantry than drama or movement. They involved large numbers of people, all costumed symbolically and appropriately to match the set. The dancing was often based on court dances of the time or on pantomimes with minimal movement. They were popular throughout the early years of Louis' reign, for they allowed members of the court to participate. Louis was especially fond of appearing in the final scenes of such ballets, for he fancied himself an excellent dancer—and, of course, the chance to play a Greek god was not an opportunity to be missed.

Those who best integrated set changes and dramatic action included Pierre Corneille (1606–1684) and, most particularly, Molière. Molière collaborated with Lully and several others in devising entertainments known as comedy-ballets. They were a unique blend of music, dance, spectacle, and lively comic action. After a musical overture, the action of the play would proceed until a character would call for entertainment. When the music and dance were completed, the action would continue. In *The Would-Be Gentleman* (1671), for instance, Jourdain calls for entertainment to impress his guests at a party and to win the affections of a lady with whom he is infatuated. The entertainment is provided, of course, by the music and dance teachers who were in Act I.

FRENCH CLASSIC THEATRE

The 17th century in France was a period in which many techniques were developed that would influence theatre for years to come. In theatre architecture, in performance style, and in dramatic literature, innovations developed during this time period have become the standards of today.

Occasion

France in the 17th century witnessed essentially two occasions for performance: the specially convened court play given on special days and the more-or-less regularly scheduled public theatre. Although the earliest performances may have been given at universities, the first recorded performances occurred in approximately 1552 on a stage erected in a hall of state for the court's pleasure. However, the dominant performance occasion of the 16th century was the royal entry or festival, many of which had "pageants" as a part of the festivities.

In contrast, public performances did not become popular until after the turn of the century. The Confrérie de la Passion, a group organized in 1402 to produce religious drama, held a monopoly on all theatre productions in Paris. Although the Confrérie did mount some productions in its theatre, the Hôtel de Bourgogne, the public theatre was not a strong force in French culture during the 16th century. Commedia troupes performed in Paris in the last quarter of the century, but no regular public performances were given in Paris. Les Comédiens du Roi (The King's Players), founded by Valeran Lecomte (fl. 1590–1613) in 1598, was the first regular company of high quality established in Paris and, naturally, its success spawned a number of rivals. Soon public theatres were giving regular performances, usually three days each week. By the 1660s five companies were performing regularly in Paris—3 drama companies, a commedia company, and an opera—and as many as 200 companies were performing throughout France. By 1700, however, as a result of Louis' growing conservatism and interest in the centralization of power, two organizations had gained a royal monopoly in Paris. The Comédie-Française was the national theatre for the spoken drama, and the Opéra served the musical theatre.

A Global Perspective

Tibetan Mystery Plays

Sometime during the 17th century, Tibetan mystery plays became distinct from religious ritual. Performed by a group of laymen (no females participated), the plays were less religious, and more devoted to entertainment, than earlier plays had been.

Held in late summer, the Harvest Festival (Yonnehecham) occupied four or five days of celebration centered around a series of dramatic presentations. The plots of the plays, either historical stories or mythological tales, were secondary to the performance, and dance was more important than the recitative or dialogue. Accompanied by drums and cymbals, the introduction was a masked dance summarizing the plot. The main drama included long musical recitatives followed by danced segments. Between regular scenes, short comic caricatures of daily life were performed. The final section was a procession of the players through the audience in an appeal for gifts. Plays were lengthy, sometimes requiring two days.

All three sections featured an integration of music, dance, masks, elaborate costumes, and dialogue. Plays were performed under a cloth supported by poles in the middle of a clearing especially devoted to this occasion. Location was established by symbolic means: a square of cloth indicated a home, and tree branches stuck into the ground created a forest. Costuming was colorful and elaborate. Colors indicated status and character type, and an elaborate flowered headdress indicated a female character.

The festival was an important event for the community, and is still performed in modern Tibet. Upper-class members of the audience pitch tents surrounding the performing area and live there throughout the festival, with elaborate banquets and social events filling the evening hours. The lower classes walk to the festival grounds each day and stand in the hot sun to witness the performances. For all participants, the festival is a welcome break in their daily pattern and a preparation for the harvest season to follow.

Location

Although performances were held at court, outdoors, in fair booths, and on street corners, the first permanent playhouse in Paris was the Hôtel de Bourgogne, the home of the Confrérie. It was a rectangular room with seating galleries on three sides and a platform stage at one end. Facing the stage at one end of the room was an ampitheatre-style bank of seating. The floor of the room, or *parterre*, was without seating, and the total capacity of the theatre was approximately 1,600. The stage was raised approximately 6 feet from the floor and had an actable opening of approximately 25 feet. No proscenium arch was present, although the galleries adjoining on each side provided a semblance of an arch.

Companies that didn't want to pay the fee required to perform at the Hôtel found various existing buildings suitable for theatre. Indoor tennis courts were nearly ideal. The rectangular rooms had existing galleries on at least one side and a small row of windows under the roof provided some natural light. Some additional seating and a small platform stage were all that were required to create a suitable environment for drama.

One theatre typical of the period was the Théâtre du Marais. Originally a tennis court, in 1645 it was remodeled closely after its predecessors—it was rectangular, with seating much like that of the earlier theatres. Influenced by Italian designs, it had a permanent proscenium arch and a raked stage. At the rear of the stage was a raised balcony or platform that was 13 feet above the stage floor and extended the full width. Controversy about this "upper stage" centers around its use in staging. The balcony itself does not appear in extant sketches of theatre scenery. However, some historians think that the balcony was used as an acting area or to support special effects when various personages appeared in the air.

Subsequent developments resulted in larger stages and larger auditoriums. The Salle des Machines, built in 1662 for the Italian designer Gaspare Vigarani (1586–1663), had a stage that measured a full 140 feet deep to provide space for the elaborate machinery installed, and a U-shaped auditorium to provide better sightlines. Fully half of the building was devoted to technical apparatus. This interest in mechanical apparatus clearly reflected the absolutist concept of a designed and orderly world. In 1690, however, the opening of the Comédie-Française demonstrated a return to a simpler stage and minimal machinery. The seating capacity was 2,000, with five rows of benches actually sitting on each side of the stage.

Performers

The French classical theatre provided a situation in which performers were able to utilize their talents fully. Often supported by the nobility, designers and actors developed high degrees of skills and were granted individual recognition (and frequently financial reward, too) for their achievements.

During the early part of the period, scenic design was largely in the medieval style with a series of mansions arranged around the edge of the stage. However, with the introduction of Italian designers in the 17th century, design became a major factor in performance. Fortunately, the scene design of this period was recorded in the

A TRIP TO THE
PALAIS-ROYALE,
1670

*I*t is morning, but not too early for the company's manager to arrive to begin preparations for the Paris opening of another of his own plays. Molière is the inspiration for his troupe of actors and friends, for he is their leading actor and their chief playwright. As such, he is also the source of their financial security. He takes his responsibility seriously, far too seriously the company knows, for he is in poor health, and the long hours he devotes to his work take their toll. He doesn't have to be at the theatre this early, but the first Paris performance of one of his successful comedy-ballets is opening today at two o'clock and he wants to insure that everything is ready.

He checks with the candle snuffers, to remind them of their cues to come out and cut the candles. He makes certain that the prompter has all the latest changes he has made in the text. He walks over to a man who is busily checking all the stage machinery. The man is directing his crew through a scene change, and Molière decides not to interrupt him. Molière's friend La Grange arrives at the theatre to check on the people who will sell tickets. Meanwhile, Molière goes backstage to join other company members in preparing for the performance.

Just at that same moment, three young courtiers demanding to see and be seen have barged their way into the auditorium. They make their presence known by loudly praising or condemning Molière and his competitors at the Hôtel de Bourgogne. They make plans to attend the Hôtel's production of Corneille's *Bérénice;* having just seen Racine's version of the same story two days earlier, they are determined to disrupt the performance of Corneille. Backstage, Molière assembles his company, just as the traditional three knocks of wood are heard on the stage floor. The audience quiets, the curtain rises, and the play begins.

During the play, the audience is in high spirits, enjoying the play greatly and demonstrating their approval at every opportunity. The three courtiers move around the *parterre,* partly to see and be seen, but also to be in a good location to cheer a particular phrase or comic bit. They banter among themselves on occasion, but mostly they watch the play, enjoying Molière's famous wit and the talent of the performers.

At the end of the play, Molière addresses the audience to tell them of the

continued

next performance of this play and to announce the performance of Corneille's *Bérénice* that the courtiers had discussed. He thanks the audience for their kind attention and hopes that they will return again soon. For their part, the courtiers agree that the play is indeed delightful, and they rush out to their favorite salon (or private party) to report their judgment. After all, this is the age of classicism, and aesthetic discussions are often more important than simple enjoyment of a performance.

Mémoire of Laurent Mahelot early in the 1630s, providing detailed sketches and information on types of scenery, specific designs, and machinery.

The first Italian designer to visit Paris was Giacomo Torelli (1606–1678), perhaps the most famous designer of his time. Torelli introduced perspective painting and the chariot-and-pole method of scenery changing to the French theatre, creating a great public demand for scenic beauty. Gaspare Vigarani, hired in 1662, worked extensively with flying apparatus, further developing the audience's taste for mechanical marvels. It is reported that for one performance, Vigarani flew the entire royal family and their attendants onto the stage. The French theatre adopted the whole range of Italian mechanical marvels with enthusiasm. Eventually the person who controlled the machinery, the *machiniste*, had a dominant role in any production and was viewed as a major artist.

Toward the end of the century, this tendency was countered by the work of Jean Berain *père* (1637–1711) and *fils* (1678–1726), a father-and-son team that introduced a quieter style based on a single design for each set, although mechanical effects were still used. Eventually this resulted in a stock approach to scenery. The *palais à volonté* provided an exterior background of suitable grandeur for tragedy. The *chambre à quatre portes* provided a domestic interior for comedy. The taste for spectacle was still evident, however, and the opera became the home of spectacle, music, and ballet.

Lighting and costumes were also important aspects of a performance. Lighting utilized both candles and oil, with chandeliers placed at the front edge of the stage and smaller light sources placed between the wing flats as necessary. The use of polished metal reflectors, spring-loaded candleholders to provide a steady flame, prisms, and colored water indicate the desire to modulate the lighting and provide a flattering effect.

Because of the dim lighting, costumes were often made of metallic cloths and decorated with tinsel and jewels. Costumes were expensive, and the actor provided all costumes except "uniforms" for soldiers and priests. Estimates indicate that a sizeable portion of an actor's salary was needed to buy the necessary costumes, although gifts of used clothing from the nobility were not uncommon.

Stock costumes were developed for tragedy. The *habit à la romaine* was used for male and female characters in tragedy. The tightly fitted top with flaring sleeve was worn over a short, stiff skirt for the men or a longer skirt for the women. Tights and boots completed the ensemble, and some small changes might have been used to

A drawing of a 1581 production using a modified medieval style of scenic presentation.

indicate a specific geographic location. Comedy utilized contemporary dress, although some stock characters might have used recognizable garb and/or masks.

The dim lighting was probably responsible for the white makeup base the actors wore. Dramatic lining and the use of rouge allowed the actor to outline features boldly and effectively.

The drama of the period placed strict limitations and great demands on the actors. The small stage, with much of the available space taken up by scenery, allowed little room for movement or physical expression, so actors were required to base their performance on vocal technique. Tragedy required great vocal power and emotional range, usually performed in a declamatory style. Montdory, one of the most famous tragic actors, destroyed his career by overstraining his voice. Comedy asked for a more natural style and physical expression. When Molière directed his troupe in a scene—as he illustrated in his play *The Versailles Impromptu* (1663)—he demanded truthfulness. The actors must enjoy their roles, but they cannot forget the human dimensions of the character.

PRINCIPAL PERFORMERS IN 17TH-CENTURY FRANCE

Molière's Company

Béjart, Madeleine	1618–1672	
Béjart, Louis	1630–1678	
deBrie (Catherine Leclerc)	1630?–1706	
DuCroisy (Philibert Gassot)	1626?–1695	
LaGrange (Charles Varlet)	1635–1692	
Molière, Mlle. (Armande Béjart)	1642–1700	

Théâtre du Marais

Champmeslé, Mlle. (Marie Desmares)	1642–1698	(also at Guenegaud)
de Villiers, Mlle.	?–1670	
Montdory (Guillaume Gilberts)	1594–1654	

Hôtel de Bourgogne

Jodelet (Julien Bedeau)	c. 1590–1660	(also at the Marais)
Montfleury (Zacharie Jacob)	1600–1667	
Turlupin (Henri LeGrand)	c. 1587–c. 1637	

Valleran's Company

Bellerose (Pierre le Messier)	c. 1592–1670	
Valleran-Le Comte	fl. 1590s–1610	
Venier, Marie	fl. 1590–1619	

Comédie-Française

Baron (Michel Boyron)	1653–1729	(also at Bourgogne)

Actors in this period experienced an unusual stability. Organized by companies, each actor was a "sharing" member of the company and received a set portion of the income. Women were acting in France as early as 1530 and were full-share members. Typically one member served as manager and received extra shares for the added responsibility. The manager chose the plays (or wrote them), cast the performers, and scheduled rehearsals and performances.

Members of a troupe knew one another well; some of them performed together for over a decade. They generally played the same type of roles and developed a particular style associated with that "line" of characters. The playwright often wrote the parts to fit the actors, further strengthening the association between the actor and the characters. The entire company functioned as a family, with shared responsibilities to ensure a good performance.

Audience

Although the audience in the early years of the period was broadly based with members of all classes attending, the patronage of the king and the "literary" quality of the theatre produced an elitist atmosphere in the theatre, and a majority of theatregoers were upper class. Figures indicate that althought the theatres were large, they were typically only 25–40 percent filled on a given day, indicating that a substantial portion of the public did not attend the traditional theatre in Paris. A secondary, smaller, and less literary form of theatre growing out of performances at fairs was given at irregular intervals in Paris and was popular with the middle class. In the provinces, theatre appears to have maintained its broad-based appeal, possibly because the performance situation was less formal and structured.

Standards of Judgment

Popular appeal still had some effect on the theatre, and Louis' approval was an absolute necessity, but additional standards of judgment were developed by the French Academy. This body of artists, appointed first in 1635 and still in existence today, was a group of 40 men appointed by the court and charged with the development of the French language. Their writings became the classic French definition of "good taste."

Classicism, also called neoclassicism in reference to this time period because it was technically a new or neoclassical tradition, dominated the arts in the French Renaissance. The term is often used to mean strict adherence to rules established by Aristotle and Horace and interpreted by scholars and academics. However, such a narrow interpretation misses the cultural context of classicism. The preference for the "Ancients" was partly an effort to move the arts away from medieval pageants and practices. It also was a reflection of the desire to enhance the beauty and importance of the French language. It was an indirect means of extending the concept of absolutism into the arts. Before all these, however, it was a way of imposing on the arts a perception of reality that was shared by Louis, his court, and many of the intellectuals of the period.

The vision of reality of classicism is that the world is not perfect, but that it can be encouraged toward perfection. Classicism envisions a civilized way of life structured around a social ideal that includes tolerance, moderation, charity, and appropriateness in all things. It reflects a world in search of moral and ethical organization as much as social organization. Regularity, order, and symmetry are among its guiding principles. Above all, classicism presumes that characters in literature and people in life have moral dimensions. The more noble an individual—and the court of Louis associated nobility with social rank—the greater the scope of their morality.

Verisimilitude. Two particular demands on dramatic literature emerge from this view of life and the arts. First, plays must adhere to *verisimilitude;* that is, the events of a play, and characters' reactions to them, must occur as they could in life (not as they did in life, for that would deprive them of the perfecting techniques of the playwright). If a play obeys this principle, the audience is able to learn the moral lessons of the action and apply them to their own lives.

Playwrights made several adjustments to Greek drama to meet the prescription of verisimilitude. They reduced or eliminated long choruses, since people in real life do not speak in unison. They minimized the use of the soliloquy, giving each major character a confidant or close friend in whom the character can confide his or her innermost thoughts. Also, they insured that characters were consistent in their emotions, never saying or doing something that would surprise the audience.

Bienséance. The second critical principle of classicism was *bienséance,* a word never carefully defined, but meaning approximately the same as the English word *proprieties.* Plays must not offend the sensibilities of the audience. They must be morally uplifting. They must never include any form of violence on stage. Characters and their actions must be appropriate to their station in life. They must not use offensive language or be caught in situations that compromise their morality. In sum, characters must behave as one would wish them to behave in life.

The Unities. These principles of verisimilitude and proprieties were often debated, but neither created as much controversy as a set of rules known as *the unities.* The classicists believed that all plays must obey the unities of time, place, and action; that is, the play must focus on a single action in a single location over a period not to exceed 24 hours. The justification for the unities, apart from the belief that they were advocated by Aristotle, was that the audience would not believe in the verisimilitude of the play unless the unities were followed. If there was more than one set onstage, the audience would know that it was in the theatre instead of believing for the moment that the location was as in life. A play lasting more than 24 hours clearly creates a break between dramatic time and real time, again making the audience aware it is watching a play. No 24-hour period, they continued, includes more than one major event. Therefore, the play must contain no action that is not a part of the main story line.

One final set of rules imposed by the classicists had to do with purity of forms. Each form of drama was to remain distinct and exclusive. Tragedy must be unremitting in its tragic tone, it must deal with nobility or rulers, and it must be written in the purest form of verse. Comedy was reserved for the lower classes and for shepherds, whose happy way of life (!) prohibited any tragic moments. Since the lower classes were not as educated as the nobility, reasoned the classicists, comedy must never be written in verse. Molière's tendency to ignore this rule led to one of the chief complaints against his plays.

To modern readers, these rules may well seem stringent and unnecessary, if not somewhat illogical. It is clear, too, that few dramatists were able to write within these strict limitations. However, the purposes of the classicists were distinct: They wanted to establish standards for what is good in the arts and in literature, standards based on the best models of the past (the "Ancients"). They wanted to improve on life, not merely report it. In doing so, they would then assist in the general growth of civilization, something that would reflect on the greatness of Louis XIV and his reign. Thus, the establishment of these rules insured adherence to a central authority and sustained aristocratic control of the populace.

DRAMATIC LITERATURE

Monsieur Jourdain is an exasperating student. His fencing instructor begs him to realize that the goal in fencing is to give and not to receive. His music teacher tells him of the beauties of pastoral music, but Jourdain thinks that means he should sing a song about falling in love with a sheep. When his philosophy instructor introduces him to logic, Jourdain decides that the words of logic aren't pretty, and he'd rather learn something else. He has trouble with poetry, so the instructor suggests prose. "What is that?" Jourdain asks naively. When the instructor tells him, Jourdain's eyes grow wide and he exclaims, "For more than forty years I have been speaking in prose and didn't even know it!" The reason Jourdain is such a poor student is that he doesn't really want to learn anything. He just wants to know what will impress people. His striped clothes are lined in lime green and orange and festooned with dozens of colorful ribbons and bows. His hat is covered with great feathers. Everyone who comes to see him can't help but laugh at the way this man struts about the stage like a proud peacock. The more they flatter him, the more he exaggerates. After two acts of *The Would-Be Gentleman*, there has yet to be a dramatic story line.

The Would-Be Gentleman by Molière is a delightful satire on those who try to outdo their neighbors in the latest fashions. It is also a theatrical confection filled with music, dancing, singing, and broad physical humor. As such, it was perfectly suited to the tastes of Louis XIV and his court. They believed that they were living in the greatest of all ages for France, a French Renaissance. They wanted entertainments that reflected that Renaissance, either by emulating the style of the ancient Greek and Roman writers or by creating new works designed to please a wealthy and powerful monarch. It may be argued whether *The Would-Be Gentleman* fits the first category; there is little doubt that it succeeded in the second.

Although Molière is the author from this period who is most successful in modern production, several other authors were prominent playwrights of the time. While Molière was somewhat of a rebel, two writers in particular distinguished themselves within the classical tradition.

Corneille (1606–1684)

Pierre Corneille began his playwriting career during the reign of Louis XIII, during which time he advanced the form of comedy, wrote several tragicomedies, and found himself embroiled in one of the great literary disputes of the century.

Corneille was attacked by the Academy for errors in his play *Le Cid* in 1637. He stopped writing drama for a few years, but then began again, eventually proving himself one of the two great tragedians in the reign of Louis XIV. Although many of his later dramas were based on Roman stories, *The Cid* will serve as an illustration of his work.

The Cid is the story of a young couple, Rodrigue and Chimene, whose fathers are bitter enemies. When Rodrigue's father succeeds in winning an honor at court, Chimene's father shames him in a duel, forcing Rodrigue to revenge his father's honor, even though it means killing his lover's father. The dramatic interest of the play centers first on the internal conflict within the hero between loyalty to his father and love for Chimene. After Rodrigue has killed Chimene's father, the interest shifts to her plight. She continues to love Rodrigue, but wishes his death in order to restore the honor and dignity of her family name. When Rodrigue wins a battle that saves the kingdom and earns him the title The Cid, the king refuses to risk losing his best soldier in a duel of honor. He decrees that the couple will separate for a year, during which time Chimene can mourn for her father, and then the couple must wed.

The play realizes several classical elements. It is a tragedy about nobility written in verse. It takes place within 24 hours in a single location (the court). It creates believable reactions on the part of the characters who hold to their feelings without sudden changes. Also, it involves a moral dilemma with no easy solution, requiring the audience to learn from the situation. However, it breaks the unity of action in several ways, chiefly by including another woman who secretly loves Rodrigue. As such, it was denounced by several classicists.

The Cid also illustrates several of Corneille's own characteristics. The focus of the play is a romantic love interest set in the context of a power struggle, in this case between the lovers' fathers. The psychological motivation holds great interest, as the characters struggle with the potential consequences of difficult alternatives. The play's ending is also representative of Corneille. Many of his plays are tragicomedies in that they deal with tragic situations, but they end happily. Corneille's characters are imbued with reason; when they yield to the logic of their situations, they move the plays from tragedy to joy. That they can recognize this logic is both a mark of Corneille and of the classical period in which he lived.

Racine (1639–1699)

Jean Racine was able to work within the classical tradition with less controversy than Corneille. His plots are simple, centered on a single moral problem shared by (usually) three characters. Often his major characters are trapped between personal desires and public responsibilities. They all behave appropriately, however, even when they are driven to madness and despair. They recognize their responsibility to society, and they never satisfy their own needs at the expense of their station in life. Racine's characters express themselves with language notable for its rich imagery, measured verse, and intensity of emotion. These qualities are exemplified in his greatest work, Phaedra.

Phaedra is in love with her stepson, Hippolytus, who in turn loves Aricia. Phaedra is anxious to die because she cannot live with her guilt, even though she has told no one except her confidante. When news arrives of the death of her husband, Theseus, Hippolytus's father, the confidante convinces Phaedra to reveal her love to Hippolytus. She does and he is horrified. No sooner is the secret revealed, however, when the husband returns home, alive. To save herself, Phaedra accuses Hippolytus of loving her, rather than the reverse; to avoid accusing his stepmother, Hippolytus leaves, but not before his father lays a curse on him. Phaedra confesses, but it is too late: Hippolytus is killed by a sea-monster, fulfilling the curse. Phaedra commits suicide, and Theseus is left alone.

The play observes all the unities, verisimilitude, and the proprieties. It presents a moral dilemma in which sin is punished. The greatness of the play, however, is not in its adherence to classical rules. The passion of Phaedra is magnificently realized. The confessions of the characters are filled with emotion. The language of the play is rich in imagery and is beautifully structured. Most of all, the play is filled with tension: between Phaedra and her confidante, between passion and duty, between fire imagery and water imagery, and between ordered propriety of the characters and the passion of their emotions. Racine thus realized the values and expectations of the classicists, but his plays are not merely formally correct. They are powerful dramas by virtue of their plots, characters, themes, and imagery. Other plays by Racine that reflect these characteristics include *Andromache* (1667) and *Bérénice* (1670).

Molière (1622–1673)

One man stands apart from the tragic classicism of his day. Although he wrote one serious play and performed in many of Corneille's works, Molière was at heart a writer of comedies. His 10 one-act plays are models of comic invention, developing a single situation with clever climaxes and contrasts of characters. His comedy-ballets masterfully integrated music, dance, and visual spectacle into their humorous situations. His 12 five-act plays are depthful studies of the follies of humankind. Among the latter works still performed today are *Tartuffe*, *The School for Wives* (1662), *The Misanthrope* (1666), *The Imaginary Invalid* (1673), and *The Miser* (1668).

One source of Molière's genius is his ability to adopt the best elements of those around him. He adapted the commedia dell'arte tradition popular in France (Italian players were frequently housed in Paris throughout most of the century). He observed

Molière as he appeared in the role of Cesar in *The Death of Pompee*.
Courtesy Harvard Theatre Collection

THE LIFE
OF MOLIÈRE

*I*f theatre were a religion, Molière would easily rank as one of its saints. His combined talents as actor, playwright, director, and company manager are unequaled in the history of Western theatre. His impact on the development of comedy is rivaled only by that of four or five others. What is most appealing about Molière, however, is the commitment, responsibility, and vision he brought to his craft. He was more than the leader of an acting company in France; he was and is a symbol of what it means to be a theatre professional.

Jean-Baptiste Poquelin's father was a furniture dealer and upholsterer. Jean-Baptiste was born in 1622. He attended the Jesuit Collège de Clermont, where he studied with the boys of prominent families and undoubtedly learned the court etiquette that would help in his later years with Louis XIV. Although it was presumed that he would take over his father's business, Jean-Baptiste studied law, receiving his law degree in 1641. At precisely the time when his future career seemed evident, Molière fell in love with Madeleine Béjart. She was an actress, a playwright, and a member of a prominent, if poor, family of actors. Despite his father's efforts to keep him in the law profession, Jean-Baptiste took the stage name Molière and joined the Béjarts in 1643. (It was common in the 17th century for French actors to adopt a name other than their own when they entered the profession.)

Molière and 11 other actors, including Madeleine, reorganized themselves under the name The Illustrious Theatre. After a year in Rouen, the troupe performed for a year (1644–1645) in Paris, performing mainly the tragedies of Corneille. The season was a failure, resulting in bankruptcy for the troupe and a brief imprisonment for Molière.

From 1646 until 1658 the company toured the provinces, performing a varied bill of fare, including the tragedies of Corneille, comedies in the style of the Italian players, and several one-act comedies by Molière. Partly through a schoolboy friendship, Molière in 1650 secured the patronage of the Prince de Conti, who helped give the troupe some financial security while it performed in the region around Lyons. During this period, Molière directed his first full-length comedy. When the Prince de Conti underwent a religious conversion, he withdrew his support of Molière's company in 1656. The company was forced to look elsewhere for support.

They returned to Paris in 1658, performing for the king in October. After a modest reception for their tragicomedy, the company performed a Molière one-act, *The Doctor in Love*, to end the evening. It won the praise of the king and his brother. The latter offered the company his patronage, and the king ensured that the company could share the Petit-Bourbon theatre on alternate days with the Italian Players. Molière's success encouraged him to write more comedies, each one further securing his reputation and fame.

In 1662, Molière married the 19-year-old Armande Béjart, who was either Madeleine's sister or daughter. As Molière's success grew, his rivals at the Hôtel de Bourgogne sought every opportunity to attack him. They circulated reports that Armande was in fact Molière's own daughter. Other detractors insisted that Armande was having affairs beyond her marriage and that Molière was still in love with Madeleine, while yet others accused him of homosexuality. In 1663, Molière responded to his critics in *The Versailles Impromptu*. Playing himself, he offered his critics the right to do whatever they wished with his plays and his acting, but he begged them to leave his private life alone. They did not do so. In that same year, Molière gained other critics when he produced *The Critique of The School for Wives*, a discussion of the reaction to a play he had written the previous year. Many courtiers believed Molière had specifically ridiculed them in the play, and they attacked him bitterly.

Although the king came to his rescue in 1664 by standing as godfather to Molière's first child, the playwright embroiled himself more deeply in controversy with *Tartuffe*, a play about religious hypocrisy. So vicious was the reaction to the play (one churchman called Molière "a demon") that the play was withdrawn. Despite the obvious public interest in the play and repeated efforts by Molière to secure the king's permission to restage the play, it was not performed again until 1669.

Throughout the 1660s, Molière continued to write and produce plays, take the lead in most of the productions, direct the company's fortune, and keep the king happy by assisting in the writing of several court entertainments. He fell seriously ill in 1666 and for a time stopped acting and left his wife. The respite was brief, however; he was back at work full-time within a few months. Despite continuing illness, he kept the fortunes of his company alive with his new works.

Finally, in 1673, he performed for the last time in his own last play. Molière died hours after performing the lead in *The Imaginary Invalid*. The company had known of his illness and tried to prevent his performance, but he insisted that their financial security was dependent on him. Molière was denied a church burial because actors were not allowed the sacraments, and only a special request by the king allowed his friends to bury him at night on February 21. The people whom he had supported and to whom he had quite literally given his life were with him at the last.

the comic writings of Corneille and Paul Scarron (1610–1660). He learned from the comic actors of his day—especially from Jodelet, whom he later employed. To these he added his own perceptions of the human condition. The result is the pinnacle of French comedy, and as fine a comic writer as Western culture has known.

In his early plays Molière created a character derived from the commedia, the tricky servant. This character was usually a valet, always cunning, energetic, acrobatic, and inventive. For the part, Molière wore a mask and a simple clown-like costume. After he became established in Paris, however, he created a new character with some of the same characteristics as the valet, but more subdued, reflective, and self-absorbed. This figure—ranging from Alceste, who hates all humanity *(The Misanthrope)*, to the self-centered hypochondriac Argon *(The Imaginary Invalid)*—is invariably someone who lives in his own world surrounded by a self-created fantasy. He exaggerates and puffs up his fantasy world until it is the only reality he can see. The humor derives from the exaggeration (we laugh at Jourdain's pretensions to intellect and culture, for instance) of the character and from the conflict within his fantasy world.

A daughter or son hopes to marry, but the father-figure (a father, a guardian, an uncle) prevents it because he is consumed by his own passion. A relative or friend can be counted on to urge the character to adopt a more normal approach to life. The plays end comically because the central character either reforms or, as in the case of Jourdain, is fooled by the young lovers and forced to consent to their marriage.

This story line and character summary are only the frameworks of Molière's comedies. Molière's understanding of human nature forces the audience to see itself in the central character. Most people experience miserliness, religious zeal, or jealousy at some time in their lives. Molière's genius is that he creates those feelings in a single character without making the person such a fool that we deny the character's relationship to us. He succeeds in this because he gives the characters depth and dimension, making them ridiculous in some situations, but sensible and sensitive in others.

Molière's themes are a reflection of this interest in human nature. He presents and emphasizes the follies of humankind, especially the pretensions of the courtiers surrounding Louis. He pokes fun at those who think they are talented when they have not worked to develop their talent. He satirizes those who feel themselves to be more important than they really are (especially husbands who think they are kings in their own homes). He attacks those who are self-centered and those who are hypocritical. In short, he presents human nature with all its pretensions exposed for the world to see.

Molière's relationship to neoclassicism is not direct because he is writing in a form (comedy) that was not regarded as highly or importantly as tragedy. As a result, he had somewhat more freedom to express himself. Nevertheless, his comedies do reflect the classical spirit of the age. The plays almost always obey the unities. His characters ultimately seek moderation and good sense within a moral and ethical world. It is a world ruled by a benevolent king who brings all problems to a happy resolution. In the case of *Tartuffe*, the king must directly intervene to prevent the destruction of a family through the misguided rule of an ineffectual autocrat. Finally, however, Molière's world is a world filled with exaggeration but not to unbelievable extremes. Molière may use a slapstick to hit a pompous character, but when he does so, the

A costume rendering for Elmire in a contemporary production of *Tartuffe*.
(Design by Alexandra B. Bonds.)   *Courtesy Alexandra B. Bonds*

character feels the pain. In this human dimension, Molière created a model for many
future authors.

Molière died following a performance of *The Imaginary Invalid* in 1673. His
company remained together under the leadership of his wife, but they were forced to
leave the Palais-Royale by Lully. They transferred to the Théâtre Guenegaud, where
in 1680 they were reorganized as the Comédie Française. In 1689 the Comédie moved
to its own theatre, where it continued to produce the great plays of the French
Renaissance. Although it has moved to different theatres, the Comédie continues to
perform today.

Molière was, as P. T. Barnum might have said, a tough act to follow. For over
a century after his death, only one French playwright achieved part of the same
eminence in comedy as Molière, and few critics regard Pierre Marivaux's sentimental
comedies as rich in invention or language as Molière's. Molière, the favorite of Louis

XIV, was the model against whom all future comic playwrights would be judged. His universal appeal, rich theatricality, honest characterization, and catalog of human foibles have made him popular both on French stages and throughout the world.

CONNECTIONS

The classical French theatre created many models that would provide inspiration for future writers and practitioners. The French models of both tragedy and comedy dominated European culture for many years following the close of the period, and the production standards of the French theatre also provided a cohesive model for theatre production that influenced future developments.

The classicist hold on French tragedy continued, with some difficulties, until the 1820s. Sentimental dramas appeared in the 1700s, but critics regarded them as secondary to the classical tragedies of the 17th century. The plays of Corneille and Racine were produced by the Comédie-Française, often with the same style and blocking as when they had been first performed.

The enduring appeal of classicism is not confined to France. Every age and country has scholars who prefer the models of the past to the uncertain directions of the future. The return to the classics provides society with an image of continuity and a location in history. Classicism establishes a particular conception of heroism that is inspirational regardless of the age. It also appeals because of its implied rational and ethical universe. In the 20th century, when so many artists depict a world of chaos and godlessness, classicism offers a moral framework governed by order and aesthetic rationality. For many people, the appeal of that framework is irresistible.

The plays of Molière remain extremely popular in the Western world, particularly the rhymed verse translations by Richard Wilbur. Productions of Molière's plays have been adapted to virtually every time period—from a Victorian *The Miser* to a 1920s *Misanthrope*.

SOURCES FOR FURTHER STUDY

Social/Art/Philosophy Background

Clark, Priscilla Parkhurst. *Literary France: The Making of a Culture.* Berkeley: University of California Press, 1987.

Goubert, Pierre. *Louis XIV and Twenty Million Frenchmen.* Trans. Anne Carter. New York: Vintage Books, 1970.

Harth, Erica. *Ideology and Culture in 17th Century France.* Ithaca, N.Y.: Cornell University Press, 1983.

Lewis, W.H. *The Splendid Century.* New York: William Morrow and Co., 1953.

Mitford, Nancy. *The Sun King.* New York: Harmony Books, 1966.

Muchembled, Robert. *Political Culture and Elite Culture in France.* Baton Rouge: Louisiana State University, 1985.

Theatre History

Arnott, Peter. *An Introduction to the French Theatre.* Totowa, N.J.: Rowman and Littlefield, 1977.

Mittman, Barbara G. *Spectators on the Paris Stage in the 17th and 18th Centuries.* Ann Arbor, Mich.: UMI Research Press, 1984.

Phillips, Henry. *The Theatre and Its Critics in 17th-Century France.* Oxford: Oxford University Press, 1980.

Scott, Virginia. *The Commedia Dell'Arte in Paris.* Charlottesville: University of Virginia Press, 1990.

Wiley, William Leon. *The Hôtel de Bourgogne: Another Look at France's First Public Theatre.* Chapel Hill: University of North Carolina Press, 1973.

Dramatic Literature

Bermel, Albert, trans. *One-Act Comedies of Molière.* 2nd ed. New York: Frederick Ungar Publishing Co., 1975.

Brereton, Geoffrey. *French Comic Drama from the Sixteenth to the Eighteenth Century.* London: Methuen and Co., 1977.

———. *French Tragic Drama in the Sixteenth and Seventeenth Centuries.* London: Methuen, 1973.

Cook, Albert. *French Tragedy: The Power of Enactment.* Chicago: Swallow Press, 1981.

Guicharnaud, Jacques, ed. *Molière: A Collection of Critical Essays.* Englewood Cliffs, N.J.: Prentice-Hall, 1964.

———. *Seventeenth Century French Drama.* New York: Modern Library, 1967.

Howarth, W. D. *Molière: A Playwright and His Audience.* New York: Cambridge University Press, 1982.

Knight. R. C., ed. *Racine: Modern Judgements.* London: Macmillan and Co., 1969.

Lough, John. *Seventeenth Century French Drama: The Background.* Oxford: Clarendon Press, 1979.

C H A P T E R

9

The Traditional
Theatres of Japan

General Events		Kamakura Period
	1185–1333	1192

Yoritomo named shogun

Arts Events		Tale of the Heiki
		c. 1200

Theatre History Events		Kan'ami
		1333–1384

It is only 8:30 A.M. on a Tuesday morning when Yukio Nakiyama leaves his small apartment in the Ginza district. As on most days, he heads first to the studio of his samisen teacher for a short warm-up lesson. Because the program scheduled for today is physically demanding, he also stops by his dance teacher's studio and asks for an early lesson in preparation.

He arrives at the theatre at 10:15 and checks in, making sure he has arrived on time. If he had not checked in 30 minutes before curtain, a substitute would have gone on in his place, and he would have been responsible for paying the substitute. Changing from his shoes to the traditional slippers, Yukio pauses a moment at a small Shinto shrine. He passes the star dressing rooms, some of which have been used by the same family of actors for generations, walks down a hall lined with boxes of costumes, and climbs the stairs to the third floor, where less important actors are located, along with the musicians. At the end of the hall is a large room where the male wigs are kept. From the moment he enters the dressing room, he enters the world of Kabuki and begins to place himself in the Edo period (1600–1868). He dons a complete set of traditional underwear, including a loincloth, an underrobe, and a cotton kimono. Because today's opening piece requires him to sit nearly motionless in the traditional kneeling posture for 40 minutes, Yukio spends a few extra moments doing physical exercises, repeating patterns devised in the 18th century. The traditional makeup for the

Muromachi Period		Japan closed to outsiders	Tokugawa Period
1333–1600	1545	1641	1600–1868
	First European contact		

	Ihara Saikaku, novelist	The Way of the Samurai	
	1642–1693	c. 1660	1644–1694
			Basho, haiku poetry

Zeami	Okuni, beginning of Kabuki	Chikamatsu Monzaemon	
1401	1363–1443	1603	1653–1725	1717
Kadensho			Kabuki indoors

role is applied, perhaps using a photograph or a piece of art to provide both information and inspiration. Next an elaborate wig is donned with the aid of a hairdresser, and finally the many-layered costume completes the transformation from modern man to Kabuki actor. Yukio stops by the dressing room of the star actor to pay his respects by kneeling in the doorway and offering a formal greeting, and then he moves backstage, picking up props as needed. At 11 o'clock the familiar sound of the clackers signals the beginning of the performance, and Yukio and his fellow actors repeat a production first designed in 1751.

The theatrical tradition of Japan offers interesting contrasts and similarities to Western theatre. Although the theatre of Japan can trace its beginnings to a much earlier period, the flowering of Kabuki, Japan's most popular form, occurred during the 16th century. The study of the two great theatrical forms—Noh and Kabuki—offers insights into a wide-range of techniques, revealing the theatre's unique place in Japanese society.

Japanese social traditions have been more enduring than those of much of Western culture. Although Japanese culture has responded to the changing world, it has also managed to retain a vital connection with the past.

Religion

The traditional Japanese approach to religion is unique and revealing. Many Japanese actively embrace more than one tradition, including both Shinto and Buddhism, as well as the philosophy of Confucianism. Indeed, today it is possible for a Japanese to embrace both Christianity and Buddhism, finding essential truths in both belief systems.

The close relationship between man, gods, and nature has functioned as a key element throughout Japanese thought. Humans might attain enlightenment in Buddhism, and they might become *kami* or divine spirits in Shinto. In both systems, man, god, and nature are closely related and in many instances identical.

In Shinto, this unity is expressed through rituals, charms, and purification that are used to mark multiple events of human experience ranging from harvest rituals to healing. It is further enhanced by religious festivals that serve as a unifying link between individual homes and groups of people, creating a spiritual unity among certain groups. These festivals frequently involve musical, dance, and dramatic elements.

Shinto is not practiced only through festivals and rituals, however. Although daily or any formal worship may or may not be a part of one's normal activities, the full range of daily activities possesses religious connotations. The center of religious practice is the home, and honor to one's family, living or dead, is essential.

The concepts of Buddhism—particularly Zen Buddhism, which is most favored in Japan—focus on intuitive knowledge gained through meditation as opposed to rational intellectual cognition. The goal is to reach one's true character, which frees one from the painful trappings of life and allows one to act simply and truthfully. Based on rigorous self-discipline, Zen advocates a life of austere simplicity. As Richard Storry has pointed out, the simplicity of Zen is in perfect accord with the unadorned natural quality of Shinto.

Daily events and interactions among people are governed by the precepts of Confucianism. Japanese Confucianism, adapted from the Chinese, stresses submissiveness to authority, reverence for the past, love of learning, courage, and correct treatment of others. Such regulations mesh well with both Shinto and Buddhism, providing a powerful force in the shaping of Japanese culture.

The focus on the spirituality of all life and the lack of clear distinction between the religious and the secular are important factors in Japanese cultural history, and both strains of thought have had great impact on the cultural life of the country.

The Samurai Code

Many concepts found in Japanese society were developed in the code of behavior developed by the samurai, trained warriors who had their beginning in the 10th century CE as a military serving regional lords but who eventually came to dominate the

Japanese ruling class. While they were originally viewed as barbarians useful only for military might, the samurai learned civilized ways as they gained power, integrating knowledge of courtly life with their ruthless warrior spirit.

The word *samurai* is written with a symbol that means "one who serves," and the core of the samurai spirit is loyalty, to one's lord above all, and also to one's father and to oneself.

A concept of honor is also present, particularly in the need for the samurai to repay any obligation—positive or negative. The samurai's lord was repaid for his generosity with loyalty. The samurai's enemy was repaid with swift and brutal revenge. Other elements of honor included a stoic suppression of emotion when it might conflict with duty, a strict code of behavior, and readiness for death, either in battle or through ritualized suicide *(seppuku)*.

The samurai's most prized possession—indeed it is referred to as the *soul* of the samurai—was his sword. The samurai sword was at once a religious expression, a symbol of one's duty, and a powerful weapon. A master craftsman forged the sword in strict accordance with Shinto principles and rituals. Once forged, the sword was used in the service of one's master, thus fulfilling the Confucian ethic of loyalty. And finally, it was properly used in a manner influenced by the study of Zen Buddhism in which a state of *munen*, or "no thought," readies the samurai for combat. The way of the samurai thus crystallizes the combination of Shinto, Zen, and Confucianism. For 700 years (1100–1800) the samurai were a dominant factor in Japanese society, and the concepts they engendered have not fully disappeared even in modern Japan.

ARTS IDEAS

Aesthetics

Several key aesthetic concepts that are uniquely Japanese have had an impact on the presentation of the theatre. As with most aesthetic concepts they are difficult to define literally. However, certain elements are essential to an understanding of the Japanese theatre forms.

Aware is a sensitivity to nature, an appreciation of a supreme creative force that flows through all things in the universe. Such an appreciation allows the artist to identify with nature, although this identification often carries a sense of sadness in the perishability of all beauty. *Aware* allows the artist to find beauty in the ordinary.

If *aware* finds significance in that which is nominally meaningless, *okashi* finds amusement in that which is nominally meaningful. It is an objectivity that gives a new perspective to subjective experience and is related to Western concepts of satire and irony.

Miyabi, a term closely associated with early medieval times in Japan, is a sense of refinement, a subtlety in color, expression, and action that was an ideal of the court society. Although it was originally connected with the aristocrat and the intellectual, the sense of *miyabi* has been transmitted throughout Japanese culture. Even today, employees may be granted a day off to view cherry blossoms in peak bloom.

Sabi is the recognition of beauty in that which is old or faded. In *sabi* there is no regret over perishability; instead, objects or individuals are cherished because they are old. The worn utensil for the tea ceremony is valuable because it is worn; a withered branch is equal in beauty to one in full vigorous bloom.

Yugen is a concept that is key to the theories of the Noh drama. Various scholars have identified it as an obscure beauty, or inward truth. It carries a sense of the ideal, but without negating the particular. The realm of *yugen* is an intuitive, momentary understanding of beauty and its relationship to truth. As such, it is the ultimate aim of artistic creation.

The Tea Ceremony

When the host greets a guest at the head of the garden path leading to the teahouse, the first gesture is the offering of water for cleansing or purification. This is the first step in creating the refined and chaste world of the tea ceremony *(cha-no-yu)*. In every carefully prescribed step, the tea ceremony creates a unique world, totally separated from the normal experience of life.

Paralleling the teachings of Zen, the central concepts of the tea ceremony are simplicity and purity. All earthly concerns for ambition, status, and material wealth are put aside. Guests are seated without regard to social position, and conversation avoids any mention of earthly concerns, especially politics and religion. The decoration is austere, with only a few objects adorning the tearoom. Although the teahouse and the utensils may be made from the very best materials, they are without ornamentation. Perhaps only one scroll or one vase containing only one branch will serve as decoration, inviting the guest to focus on each object rather than superficially noticing a wealth of decoration. Similarly, the utensils are plain, avoiding any materialism or display of wealth. Although tea utensils are prized possessions in modern Japan (and some are museum pieces), frequently it is the used, tarnished, or broken utensil that is most valuable.

In modern practice, the tea ceremony is taught down to the smallest detail, with specific rules governing every moment—from the sending of invitations, through the arrival of the guests, the making of the fire, the brewing and partaking of the tea, and the ending of the ceremony. The intent is to lead the participant to an awareness of the underlying beauty in the simplest of acts or objects *(wabi)*. Indeed, in the writings of the masters of the tea ceremony, participants are urged not to become involved in the procedure or in the trappings of the ceremony. "Make tea and drink it" is the urging of one master. However, to do so one must free oneself from all concerns dealing with the outside world. It is this freedom that is the ultimate goal of the tea ceremony. It is through this freedom that life and art are united, however briefly.

Woodblock Prints *(ukiyo-e)*

The Edo or Tokugawa period (1600–1868) of Japanese history was characterized by the growth of a wealthy middle class and almost complete isolation from the rest of the world. The result was the development of several unique styles of artistic expression, including *kabuki* and *bunraku* theatre and *ukiyo-e* or woodblock prints.

Woodblock printing, centered entirely in Edo (Tokyo), represented a change from the elitist art of earlier Japan and was developed to meet popular tastes. As such, it was

A woodblock print of a Kabuki actor.

important that the price be kept low and that multiple copies be produced for sale. Indeed, for many years woodblock prints were virtually ignored by art patrons and critics, being regarded as low class and ordinary.

A woodblock, rather than being the distinct creation of one artist, was produced in most situations by four separate craftsmen: the painter, the woodcutter, the printer, and the publisher—and each played an important role. The painter selected the subject and provided the drawing. The woodcutter did the actual engraving and was responsible for the detail and precision of the final product. The printer had great influence in the coloring of the print, and the work of these three was totally dependent on the publisher who sponsored the product and distributed the results.

Woodblocks were also considered "low class" because the favorite subject matter was not China or Japanese history or even nature. Instead, woodblock artists focused on life in Edo, particularly life in the entertainment district. Pictures of the beautiful women of the teahouses were the most popular, although the actors of the *kabuki* theatre were also featured. Other prints depicted charming young girls of ordinary background. In later years, woodblocks were used to portray the scenery of Japan and the life of the ordinary Japanese citizen. Although these prints do not appear realistic by current Western standards, they presented a degree of realism unknown in earlier Japanese art.

The woodblock prints of the Tokugawa period covered a wide range in both subject matter and technique. They are characterized by a strong sense of line, by figures that are supple and active, and by a use of color that ranges from delicate to bold. In contrast to traditional Japanese arts, they provided the middle class with an art form that was accessible, enjoyable, and relevant to their own lives.

THE NOH THEATRE

As with many forms of theatre, the Japanese Noh drama emerged from a blend of earlier forms, including dance, music, and mime. Among these were such traditional forms as the Shinto *kagura* ritual dance, and artistic forms such as *bugaku*, a Chinese music/dance form that utilized masked dancers and was imported along with Buddhism as early as 500 CE. These two were blended in the ancient courts of Japan and were adopted as part of the official court music, *gagaku*, in 701. In contrast, *sangaku* performances, also imported from China, were a more populist art form, featuring mime, acrobats, juggling, magic, and dance. This form blended with a rural harvest dance form, *dengaku*, and became *saragaku*. Early descriptions of the Noh describe puppet shows, dances, fortunetellers, and, in particular, mime pieces based on traditional or mythical stories.

Saragaku, the direct forerunner to Noh, was developed between 800 and 1300, with various elements from the other forms being included to meet popular demands. The form of Noh that is preserved today is the result of the teachings of the actor Kan'ami (1333–1384) and the development of those ideas by his son Zeami (1363–1443). Although there is no one specific moment at which the various contributing forms coalesced into the Noh, it is the work of these two men that contributed most to the development of the form that is still performed today.

Occasion

The Noh drama has, from its earliest development, been associated with shrines and with the nobility. Troupes of actors were hired by various shrines and temples to perform various ceremonies and rituals. As a bonus, these troupes were also allowed to tour the area under the jurisdiction of the particular temple or shrine. Thus, performances were held not only at specific calendar celebrations, but also on ordinary days when the troupe toured from village to village.

Before Kan'ami's time, the performers were essentially itinerant wanderers who were accorded little social respectability. Because Kan'ami's performance (and Zeami's beauty) caught the eye of the shogun, or local military ruler, Yoshimitsu, they were given a place at court. Thus, the key event in the development of Noh occurred under full royal patronage with the protection and the material support of the court. For this reason, Noh has always carried with it a sense of elitism; however, Noh has always been popular with commoners as well.

In 1603, a victorious shogun utilized a Noh performance to celebrate the occasion and adopted it as the official court drama. For the next 200 years, Noh was frequently a part of political and ceremonial occasions such as the inauguration of a new shogun, promotions, coming-of-age ceremonies, and births. During the same period, Noh troupes were occasionally given permission to perform short seasons of plays for paid admissions, performing for large crowds of commoners who traveled great distances to see the legendery performers.

Following the overthrow of the shogunate regime and the restoration of the emperor in 1867, Noh troupes suffered from their connection with the shogun and gradually disbanded due to a lack of financial support. Only a decision to utilize the Noh to entertain visiting officials from the West revived the art form. Gradually the Noh became a part of all official ceremonies, and the preservation of the art form became an aim of the government and an artistic cause among prominent families.

Throughout its history, Noh has managed to combine both a courtly and a commercial function. More important, it has managed to survive and is performed regularly today in Tokyo, Kyoto, Osaka, and Nagoya.

Location

Originally, the location of a Noh drama was not of major significance. It was performed at court and was also performed in the countryside in various localities and under widely varying circumstances. Gradually, specific shrines and courts began to establish spaces that were dedicated to Noh performances. The oldest surviving Noh stages date from approximately 1600, and it is those stages that have been the models for the established form of the Noh stage.

The stage is an important aesthetic aspect of Noh, and its simple beauty sets the tone for the performance. The stage is a raised platform, approximately 19 feet square and nearly 3 feet high. The space beneath the unpainted, polished cypress wood floor is hollow, since the resonance of foot-stomping is important to the performance. Sometimes empty jars are placed under the stage to increase the resonance. A "bridge" or passageway called the *hashigakari* connects the back of the stage to the offstage area. A pillar at each corner of the stage supports an ornate roof. A small added section of flooring is placed stage left to hold the chorus. The only decor is a stylized painting of a pine tree on the back wall and three small pine trees placed along the *hashigakari*.

The auditorium and the stage are symbolically separated by a narrow band of material that surrounds the stage. Although this is typically gravel or small rock, at one famous traditional theatre the sea flows between the audience and the stage. The

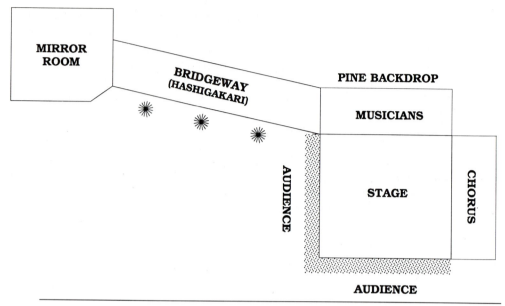

The Noh stage.

audience sits both in front of the stage and next to the stage-right side. There is no seating at stage left since the chorus would block the view. Originally, the seating was almost like a small room with comfortable box seats complete with refreshments. Today, seating is Westernized, although some theatres still retain remnants of the earlier tradition.

Performers

The Noh is a combined performance by actors and musicians. Noh musicians play flutes and various drums. Strictly trained, they provide entrance and exit music, underscore the dancing, and accompany the singing of the actors and chorus. The chorus, composed of 8 to 10 men, serves both as accompaniment to the action and actually, on occasion, to provide the vocal part of the main actor's performance when the dance section is considered too difficult to allow the performer to sing as well.

The core of the Noh performance, however, is the main actor, or *shite*, and the secondary performers, *tsure*, *waki*, and *kyogen*. Only male performers appear in classical Noh, although parallel female troupes apparently have existed from time to time. Currently, five schools of Noh—Kanze, Hosho, Komparu, Kongo, and Kita—are active, and they represent the totality of professional Noh performers.

Trained from infancy, the typical Noh actor will debut at the age of 5, begin formal training at the age of 7, and will likely perform a major role by the age of 16. Traditionally, membership in one of the professional schools is available only to the sons of the actors. Other classes for amateurs are taught, however, and the amateur study of Noh is quite popular in Japan.

The actor's training is based essentially on imitation of the master. Movement and vocal patterns are imitated precisely, with no attention to understanding the subtleties of the poetic metaphors. As an actor progresses, he is gradually introduced to the secret texts that have been handed down through the generations of the schools. Control of these secrets is in the hands of the *iemoto,* or head of the school, and it is only with his approval that they are shared with a young performer.

The Noh performer's life is devoted to the study of Noh, and every day begins with practice, whether or not a performance is scheduled. Each movement and each vocal phrase is performed in a specific manner. The vocal parts include prose sections that are delivered in a sonorous, chant-like voice. Other poetic sections are sung. Both require remarkable vocal skill, for the range of pitch and texture demanded of the Noh performer far exceed those for Western performers. Movement is equally complex; each *kata* or movement pattern has to be precisely performed. More than 200 *kata* are used in the contemporary repertoire. Even the typical Noh walk, in which the heel never leaves the floor, requires exceptional concentration. Further study is necessary to correctly wear the elaborate costumes and to create expression while wearing a stylized mask.

Zeami's classic writing, *The Kadensho,* speaks at length about the development of the Noh performer, moving from a superficial style to a more simple style to a truly spiritual style of performance. The movement along this path of development is a spiritual journey, accomplished through reflection, discipline, and concentration.

As an actor progresses in skill, he attempts more difficult roles. Some actors will never perform *shite* roles but will specialize in *waki* or supporting roles. Progression is based not only on talent, but on experience. Some of the most difficult roles are considered impossible for another under the age of 50, even though the part may be that of a young woman.

Although there is no scenery, some stage props are used in performance. Sometimes these are small bamboo constructions used to represent a mountain, a cart, or a small hut. At other times they support a black curtain behind which the actor can suddenly disappear. These are brought on stage when needed by stage assistants *(koken)* and removed when no longer required. Hand props may range from a hat to a sword, but the most important is the fan. Specific fans are created for specific roles and the handling of the fan is intricate and symbolic. Other players use simpler fans, usually bearing the crest of their specific school.

Central to the aesthetic effect of the Noh performance are the masks worn by the *shite.* Approximately 50 styles of mask are in current use, each carved by an artist from cypress wood from the valley of Kiso. This wood is floated down the river to Tokyo and stored for six years in a mixture of salt and fresh water before it is carved. Traditional masks exist for each of the major roles in the Noh repertoire; however, enough variation occurs in the individual renderings that the choice of mask can affect the mood of the entire performance. The expressions of the masks tend to be subtle and enigmatic, allowing the skill of the actor to actually suggest changes in expression.

The mask is considered the key to the performance and is treated with reverence. Before a performance, the actor sits in the greenroom before a mirror, contemplating his own appearance. At a signal, his assistant presents the mask. The actor offers a salutation to the mask and then, as the tradition states, "The mask is not put on the face, but the face should be thought of as being put into the mask." From this moment, the actor considers himself "in performance" even though he may not enter for several minutes.

A Noh play in performance.

Completing the aesthetic impression of the Noh performance are the costumes. Huge, elaborate, and heavily decorated, they provide much of the spectacle of the Noh performance. Although the feet are always covered by the traditional white *tabi*, or cloth sandal, other Noh costume elements are spectacular. Originally patterned after regular clothing, they developed gradually into the showpieces used today, with luminous colors and elaborate brocade patterns being prominent. Although costumes are traditional, some leeway in color and pattern is allowed for the individual interpretation of the role, and the actor is allowed to select the specific garments he will wear. Some elements, however, are essential, since the color of a particular item of clothing can provide essential information about social class or standing. A wig completes the costume.

A traditional Noh performance includes five plays, plus several *kyogen*, or short comic interludes. As such, the entire program may last many hours. Since modern audiences are not prepared for an eight-hour theatre experience, contemporary performances usually contain only three plays and one *kyogen*. The overall effect of a Noh performance is impossible to describe to anyone who has not seen it. The pace is exaggeratedly slow, the words are undecipherable (often even to the aficionado), the music is strange to Western ears, and the play itself is essentially without the concept of dramatic action. A Noh performance is serious, meditative, and subtle. As an artistic form, it parallels the tea ceremony, offering a studied withdrawal from the activity of daily life to a tranquil, dignified contemplation.

Audience

Throughout history, the nature of Noh audiences has changed from era to era. In Noh's earliest form, performances incorporated specific elements to please particular audiences, and audience reaction may have ranged from devout silence at a shrine ritual to noisy participation at a rural performance. Early court audiences were known to eat and drink as they watched, allowing the Noh to serve as the centerpiece for a social occasion.

A contemporary Noh audience is usually a curious mixture of tourists and connoisseurs. It is not unusual to see students of Noh following the performance in the text, much like music students at opera performances in New York. These audience members are aware of each subtle variation in the performance. Such subtleties are not evident to the tourist audience, many of whom find the demands of Noh exhausting. The atmosphere at a contemporary Noh performance has been compared to that in a cathedral, characterized by a respectful silence and austerity. Certainly early descriptions of audiences moved to tears seem odd to a modern viewer, for whom the Noh may present a historical or intellectual experience, but rarely an emotional one.

Standards of Judgment

Contemporary standards of judgment are based on exhaustive study of the various critical writings on Noh that have been preserved over the past 600 years. The most influential is Zeami's *Kadensho*, which focuses heavily on the actor's performance. Two elements are essential: *monomane*, or the representation of the appearance of things, and the achievement of *yugen*. That actor was most successful who could incorporate both the reality and the spirituality of a character. In this, Zeami echoes the Japanese thought on the inseparability of the natural and the divine.

Perhaps most central is Zeami's belief that the focus of performance is the audience, and the audience is the final arbiter of excellence. It is not the actor who experiences *yugen* but the spectator. Zeami believed that even the most rustic spectator could appreciate *yugen*, and it is the spiritual quality, not the virtuosic display of technique, that determines the superior performance.

THE KABUKI THEATRE

If Noh managed to serve both the nobility and the commoner, Kabuki has no such pretensions. Kabuki from its beginnings has been a commoner's theatre, and its virtuosic and dynamic form of theatre offers a sharp contrast to the austere and simple beauty of the Noh.

Early forms of Kabuki appeared in the 17th century, at approximately the same time as the Noh was adopted as the official drama of the shogunate government. Responding to the new era of peace and freedom following the victory of the

Tokugawa family, various dance troupes, that had traveled in obscurity in the provinces, descended upon the capital, Edo. Among these was a company headed by a woman named Okuni.

Okuni's company was one of several women's companies known in the country at that time. Forced to live as itinerant performers by the strict Buddhist edict against female performers, most of the women were also prostitutes. Okuni's presentation of short mime-dances, popular songs, and dances were immensely popular and were given the name *Kabuki*, meaning "avant-garde." In a relatively short time, women's troupes were common. Typical "plays" dealt with ways in which prostitutes approached their clients or similar subjects; suggestive movements and bawdy lines were common. Outbreaks of violence among spectators arguing over the favors of the performers brought the performances to the attention of the officials, who outlawed the women's troupes. In their place, the officials licensed a form of Kabuki performed entirely by young boys. The sensual appeal of the dancing was associated with homosexuality (as were many of the plots), and this form was also banned. A compromise was reached in 1652 that allowed men to perform with a shaved forelock (thus removing the sensuality of the young boys). Sensual subjects were banned, and only nonsensational plays were allowed.

From this humble beginning, the art of Kabuki developed, although the transition from "burlesque" to "culture" was gradual. Through the development of its own theatre structure, the rise of the playwright, the influence of other Japanese theatre forms, and finally the establishment of performance norms during the 18th century, Kabuki remained a popular art. Only in the modern period, with the introduction of Western forms, did Kabuki become a "classic" theatre.

Occasion

Kabuki remains popular with many Japanese today and is performed regularly in the large cities. Indeed, the Grand Kabuki has toured worldwide and is internationally recognized as one of the major theatre companies of the modern world.

Location

The earliest performances took place on bare platforms, and the earliest theatre structures were essentially outdoor theatres. Originally the stage was similar to the Noh theatre, with a bare thrust stage surrounded by the audience on three sides, including box seats along the side walls. A temporary roof covered the stage, but the central audience area was uncovered. All audience members sat on tatami mats, although some may have had pillows available. Only in 1700 did the Kabuki move indoors.

The most unique feature of the theatre was the *hanamichi*, a raised pathway that reached from the stage-right front of the stage to the back of the auditorium, passing through the audience. In earlier theatres, a second *hanamichi* was used on the other side of the auditorium, and the two were sometimes connected by a third. In today's Kabuki theatres, only one *hanamichi* is used, but it is an essential feature in performance as many important aspects of Kabuki performance utilize it. The *hanamichi* allows the closest possible rapport between the actor and the audience, and this relationship is the core of Kabuki.

As early as 1758 Kabuki theatres used a revolving stage to assist in difficult scene changes or to show simultaneous action. Several stage lifts were also commonly used, including one on the *hanamichi.* These are maintained in today's Kabuki theatre, along with systems for flying various apparatus (and performers).

On stage left a small elevated platform is used for those plays that call for a narrator and his accompanist. Stage right, a long narrow window cut in the wall provides visibility from the musicians' room, although some Kabuki plays call for the musicians to appear on stage.

As these scenic devices became more important, the theatre was enlarged to contain them, and the Kabuki-za, the traditional home of Kabuki in Tokyo, serves as an example. The stage of the Kabuki-za is 93 feet from side to side, almost double that of a typical Western proscenium stage. To hide the machinery that is now an integral part of the Kabuki, a proscenium-style stage was adopted late in the 18th century. The *hanamichi* is 5 feet wide and extends 65 feet to the back of the auditorium. Thus an actor can walk in one direction for a total of 158 feet, or half the length of a football field. The stage contains three large traps, each capable of moving an entire setting. The auditorium of the Kabuki-za seats 1,078 on the ground floor (all in Western-style chairs), with room for 1,522 more in the mezzanine and balconies.

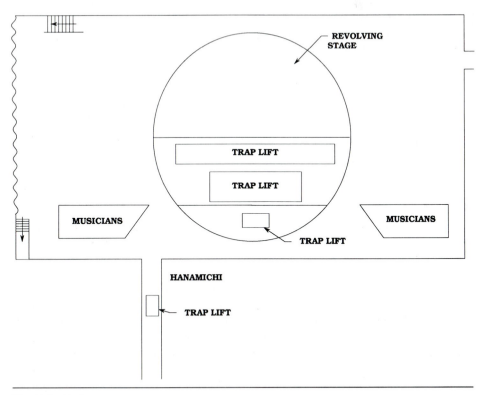

The Kabuki stage.

Performers

As with the Noh, the Kabuki performance is based on the combined effects of musicians and actors. However, the use of music in the Kabuki is more complex and varied than in the Noh.

Several types of music are used in a Kabuki performance, and sometimes more than one at the same time! The dominant instrument is the *samisen*, a stringed instrument similar to the mandolin. Additional music comes from a large assortment of percussion instruments, including various drums, gongs, cymbals, and wooden beaters. In addition, flutes are occasionally used along with various special sound effects.

Music is used for a variety of purposes in a Kabuki performance. It may indicate weather, describe a location, establish basic character traits, or provide background for certain types of action (especially fight scenes). The integration of music into the plays and the dynamic relationship of the actor and the music is one of the key aesthetic elements of Kabuki.

In Kabuki plays borrowed from the *Bunraku*, or puppet theatre, an important role is played by a narrator who is accompanied by a shamisen player. Sitting stage left apart from the action, the narrator may explain action, may interpolate comments into the action, or on occasion may speak the words for the actor.

In any form of Kabuki performance, however, the central element is the actor. Indeed, it may not be an exaggeration to say that the form exists to display the talents of the actors. Although the total effect of Kabuki relies on the talents of various artists, it is the actor who is foremost and it is the actor's virtuosity that distinguishes a great performance from an ordinary one.

As in the Noh, Kabuki actors often are the descendents of other performers, although this is not a requirement any longer. Normally trained from an early age, Kabuki performers begin their careers playing small roles and gradually advance through more and more difficult parts. Only after proven success is an actor allowed to attempt a leading role. Several famous actor "names" have been passed down through the generations. Only through demonstrated excellence can an actor be given one of these names.

Kabuki actors, who are all male, tend to develop their reputation based on one of three performance categories. The *aragato*, or "rough" style, is focused on masculine vigor and power, mirroring the samurai code. Although Kabuki performers do not wear masks, the *aragato* makeup is frequently a striking "painted mask." The costume is huge, creating a figure literally larger than life. The *aragato* voice is high-pitched and strong, and, on occasion, high points of emotion are expressed in nonsense syllables, relying on the vocal skill of the actor. Movement is large and strong, and performances of major *aragato* roles are known to be physically exhausting.

In contrast, the *wagato* style is based on delicacy. Often the *wagato* hero is beautiful and a much-sought-after lover, but irresponsible and spineless. Used most often in more realistic plays, the style relies on an elegant and refined style. The *wagato* voice is soft and melodic and the movement pattern tends to appear feminine.

Certainly the most unique performer by Western standards is the *onnagata*, who portrays female roles. The intent of the *onnagata* is to create an image of ideal femininity. In earlier days, an *onnagata* lived the life of a woman even offstage, keeping care not to exhibit masculine habits and forced to keep his married life secret. Although such extremes are not practiced today, the *onnagata* performer must master a complex series of postures and movements, be a master of Japanese dance forms, and utilize a highly cultivated vocal technique. The unusual appeal of these performers is an essential quality of Kabuki.

The basic patterns utilized by an actor are known as *kata*, as they are in the Noh theatre. Although these typically refer to physical gestures and vocal techniques, they also extend into production elements. In contrast to the subtle *kata* of the Noh theatre, the Kabuki *kata* are bold and vivid, reminiscent of the techniques of the woodblock prints. Developed over a long period of time, they have become traditional and codified, with the same *kata* always used in a particular play.

The most memorable of the *kata* are *mie*, vigorous movements followed by a sudden freeze. Used to underscore the emotional highlights of a play, *mie* are also an opportunity for an actor to demonstrate his skill. The *mie*, held for several seconds, nearly always prompts wild exclamations of approval from the audience. *Mie* is usually associated with *aragato* roles, although quieter forms are used in other styles as well.

Roppo is a movement *kata* normally used for exits and entrances, often done on the *hanamichi.* Literally translated as a "six directions" movement, it is an exaggerated

An *onnagata* in performance.

swaggering walk, often executed in huge, bounding strides with the arms swinging wildly.

Shichisan acting takes place on the *hanamichi* at a spot seven-tenths of the way to the stage, thought to be the strongest acting position. Frequently used for entrances, the character uses *shichisan* to introduce his character to the audience through various movement *kata* including *mie*, dance, or dialogue. The seven-three position, as it is called, is also used for final moments prior to exists and to reveal reversals in character.

Kata also exist in reference to vocal techniques, sound effects, costumes, makeup, and scenic effects. Sudden changes of costume are used to effect a transformation in several plays. On a subtler scale, the use of a different color in a particular costume can indicate a change in the interpretation of that role. Scenery *kata* include sudden appearances or exists using stage traps and lifts. Although *kata* are traditional and tend not to vary, established stars have introduced new *kata* as a means of distinguishing themselves from other performers.

Makeup, costume, and scenery are also notable elements of the Kabuki perform-ance. Makeup ranges from the traditional white face of the *onnagata* to the highly stylized *kumadori* makeup of the *aragato* warrior, with multicolored lines outlining the features of the face. Costumes may be a simple monk's robe, an elegant kimono, or a huge multilayered fantasy with eight-foot sleeves. Scenery ranges from a simple but beautifully painted backdrop to a full-sized temple capable of supporting a fight scene on its roof. A traditional scenic device is the use of a revolving stage introduced in the 18th century. Traps, including one located on the *hanamichi*, are used for sudden appearances and disappearances. To the Western eye these technical elements may be dazzling. In each case, however, they are designed to showcase the actor, the true focal point of Kabuki performance.

Audience

Kabuki has always been an art form of the middle class, and from the beginning the relationship between actor and spectator was direct and immediate. The physical arrangement of the theatre placed the actor and the spectator in close contact, with some box seats actually adjoining the stage. Since the repertoire of plays was standard and *kata* dictated the essentials of the performance, the focus of the audience was on the performer. Critical booklets were printed that discussed both the performing and the private lives of the actors, and audience members were highly knowledgeable about individuals and about levels of performance. This focus on the individual actor led to the development of performance conventions. During the play, an actor might pause to welcome another actor back to the city or to introduce a newcomer. At times, a member of the audience might interrupt the action to praise one specific actor, and clubs of enthusiasts developed who would sit together singing songs in support of their favorite. When an actor received an honorary name, a formal announcement and ceremony was held between acts. One of the few audience behaviors to survive until modern times is the spontaneous shouts from enthusiastic viewers. At critical moments, after a *mie*, or during an exit, devoted fans were likely to shout out the actor's name, much as a Western opera fan might shout "Bravo!" after an aria.

Perhaps of more importance, however, was the audience's familiarity with the plays and their knowledge of the art form. An informed and discriminating audience is essential to Kabuki. Because they knew the plays and the standards of performance, members of the audience were able to recognize subtle variations and express approval or disapproval. In this way they contributed to the constant growth of Kabuki as actors sought new ways to involve and please their viewers. There is some concern that today's audience is no longer as perceptive, and that therefore less motivation exists to prod the modern actor to perfect his art.

Standards of Judgment

Two levels of judgment apply to the performance of Kabuki. Formal judgment of an actor is given by the troupe's leader. The company governs the actor's progression through the lesser roles, and also determines his ultimate status. However, the primary standard of judgment in Kabuki has always been the approval of the audience. There is no written critical standard that serves as a model for Kabuki performance; tradition serves as a guideline, and actors are frequently compared to earlier actors. However, the ultimate judge is the spectator. As long as the audience continues to attend, and as long as the audience is pleased, then Kabuki is successful.

DRAMATIC LITERATURE

Noh

The literature of the Noh theatre defies almost every tradition of Western drama. It is often without evident conflict, is not dependent on character development or psychology, and rarely follows a pattern of complications followed by resolution. To the Western reader or viewer, the drama of the Noh theatre seems to be concerned with remote events that tend toward the supernatural. The plays, developed from an ancient poetic structure, incorporate intricate reference to other works; subtle wordplays, poetic shadings, and powerful imagery serve to translate interior emotion into words. The complexity of the literature makes them fully accessible only to the connoisseur, but the beauty and strength of the stories make them effective for less knowledgeable audiences as well.

The Noh plays developed from several sources: ancient Japanese and Chinese poetry, Buddhist works, other literary sources, and folk tales. Introduced by an orchestral passage, the plays usually center around a visit to a particular place and the relating of a story connected with that locale. During the telling of the story, the central character reveals that he or she is actually the person the story is about and frequently returns in a final section to sing and dance that character's lament.

Sotoba Komachi, credited to the author Kan'ami Kiyotsugu, tells the story of Ono no Komachi, a beautiful woman poet. She refused to meet with a man in love with her unless he visited her home one hundred nights in a row. He died before completing the task. In the play, two priests come across an ugly old woman who reveals that she was once beautiful. When the priests accost her because she is sitting on a holy spot, Komachi engages the priests in an intellectual discussion and proves surprisingly astute.

B U N R A K U

A second form of theatre developed during the Edo period alongside Kabuki. Although created to please the same middle-class audience and sharing Kabuki's interest in contemporary life and strong emotions, the Bunraku theatre presents these same elements through puppetry.

The puppets of the Bunraku are approximately one-third life size and require three operators. The puppet heads are works of art, created by a very few master craftsmen. Most of them are careful re-creations of original versions. The heads are mounted on a central rod, and string mechanisms allow the puppeteer to move the eyes, the eyebrows, and the mouth as well as the right hand. Sometimes as many as five masks may be used for one character to illustrate changes of emotion. Some masks are designed for transformation characters and have special mechanisms that allow the mask to distort its face, grow horns, or expose the teeth.

The chief actor, wearing elevated shoes to make him taller than his assistants, controls the head and the right hand. The first assistant controls the left hand, and the second assistant manipulates the feet. The chief actor appears dressed in black, without a hood, relying on his artistry to create such a life-like performance that his own presence will be forgotten. The two assistants, also dressed in black, wear black hoods.

The narrator and his samisen player are central to the presentation of Bunraku, for Bunraku is essentially illustrated story-telling. The narrator both provides narration of events and speaks the recited dialogue of the individual characters. The vocal range is impressive as the narrator moves from the high-pitched voice of a young woman to the deep bass sounds of the warrior. The emotional nature of the plays also demands total command of the singing/chanting style of the Bunraku narrator, who must master not only the lyrical sounds typical of travel scenes but also the guttural wails of an enraged samurai.

The plays, many of them written by the master playwright Chikamatsu Monzaemon (1653–1725), cover a wide range of topics both domestic and historical, but most are based on situations that arouse extreme emotion. The central action is usually a conflict between duty and affection; battles and/or sacrifices are not uncommon endings. Actually, Kabuki and Bunraku share many plays, although each form alters a given script to focus on its own strengths.

Although the nature of Bunraku allows magnificent visual effects, many spectators are amazed at the life-like quality of the puppets. The skilled puppeteers, supported by the virtuosity of the narrator, create a world of their own, with a sense of realism that is absent from the Kabuki stage.

She reveals that she was once Komachi and they express regret that such beauty could turn to such ugliness. Komachi suddenly reappears as her lover and retells the torture of his travels and his death. In the final stanza, Kabuki laments the torture of her possession, vowing to do good deeds in the future so she can find peace.

The story only hints at the nature of the drama. Many lines are extended poems, and on occasion the chorus speaks for the leading character. The result is a collage of voices and sounds creating a unique dramatic form.

Traditionally, Noh plays are divided into five categories determined by the subject matter: God plays, warrior plays, woman plays, miscellaneous plays (including contemporary plays and plays of madness or obsession), and demon plays. A complete Noh program consists of one play from each category, although most modern performances feature only two or three plays.

Kabuki

The literature of the Kabuki stage include adaptations from the repetoire of the Noh, plays originally written for the puppet theatre (Bunraku—see insert), and plays, either historical or contemporary in subject matter, written especially for the Kabuki.

Plays adapted from the Noh literature contain more dance than the other forms. *Kanjincho*, based on the Noh play *Ataka*, is based on the story of the legendary hero Yoshitsune, who, disguised as a monk, attempts to escape the villainy of his brother. His loyal retainer, Benkei, assumes the role of the leader of the group. When the party is stopped at a guard station, the guard is suspicious and submits them to several tests, which Benkei, surprisingly, is able to pass. When one of the guards seems to recognize the master, Benkei seizes a stick and beats his master, an unthinkable act. The guard actually recognizes Yoshitsune, but, moved by Benkei's loyalty, allows them to pass.

In the Kabuki version, the emotional qualities of the play remain fully intact, but the emphasis is on the opportunities the script provides for exciting acting. One of the tests put to Benkei is reading the list of his supporters. This is performed in an *arogato* style, which allows the actor to utilize a vast range of vocal and physical expressiveness as Benkei summons all of his mental and emotional powers to create the imaginary list. Similarly, the scene in which Benkei whips his master is extremely emotional. The combination of music and dance, emotion and restraint, pathos and comedy are typical of this style of Kabuki play.

Chushingura is one of the most famous of the Kabuki plays adapted from Bunraku.

It is based on an actual occurrence in 1703, when 46 retainers of Lord Naganori avenged the death of their master by killing the man who had forced him to commit suicide. *Chushingura* was almost immediately adapted for the stage, but was not performed in the Bunraku theatre until 1748. Although the Kabuki version is much shorter than the 10-hour version for puppets, the essential story remains the same.

The hero of the Kabuki play is called Yuranosuke, and during the course of the action the actor playing that role is allowed to display great virtuosity. Yuranosuke in one scene pretends to be a pleasure-loving fool, in another a stupid samurai, in others a drunk, a lover, and a hero, all the while plotting revenge. The play offers many dramatic moments ranging from a full-scale battle to a duel fought on a bridge. In a horrific scene typical of this category of play, Yuranosuke discovers the dagger that killed his master and licks the blood off it. In the climatic moment of the play, Yuranosuke suddenly plunges his sword through the floor, killing the villain who is hiding below.

Among the plays written for the Kabuki stage, *Narukami* is an example of a play set in an earlier historical period. Narukami, a priest, in an attempt to bring suffering upon the emperor, has imprisoned the dragon god of rain at the foot of a waterfall. Princess Taema is sent to seduce Narukami so that the spell will be broken, thus relieving the drought that plagues the land. When she arrives, she asks to be Narukami's disciple. She pretends to be ill and he is moved by her beauty to abandon

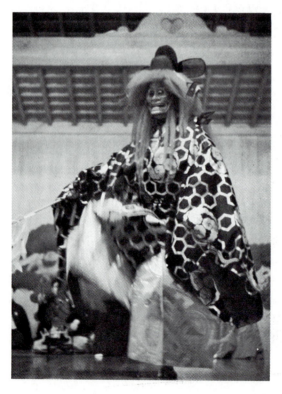

A Kabuki play in performance.

his prayers and take care of her. He drinks sake with her and falls asleep, allowing Taema to cut the rope and release the dragon god. Narukami is transformed into a demon by his rage. He flings his sacred books around the stage and then leaves in search of Princess Taema.

Narukami provides an example of the eroticism found in certain Kabuki plays. It also provides the sort of magnificent climax—the transformation of the priest into a demon—which Kabuki audiences seem to love. Although the play is charming and delightful in its early sections, it is the power of the final scene and the famous *roppo* exit that have made this one of Kabuki's most popular plays.

Sukeroku was also written for the Kabuki stage, but in the 18th century, and it was based on a contemporary story. It was first performed in 1713. Set in front of a high-class bordello, the play deals with a fashionable commoner, Sukeroku, who is searching for a lost sword. He begins to pick fights with people to force them to draw their swords. His attempts to teach his brother to fight are comical, as are the scenes in which they force passersby to crawl between their legs. Finally, he finds the sword and decides to ambush the man who has it, to take the sword away. In the final scene, Sukeroku kills the man, hides from a group of pursuers in a vat of water, and then makes an exciting escape over the rooftops.

Although the play seems to lack the depth of others, the sumptuous costumes, the elegance of Sukeroku's opening dance performed on the *hanamichi*, the combination of adventure and comedy, and the exciting ending provide great entertainment values, and *Sukeroku* remains one of the most popular plays in the Kabuki repertoire.

As was the case with the woodblock prints, Kabuki succeeds through broad strokes, vibrant colors, and a sense of excitement and realism. Because it is accessible to all classes, focuses on popular tales of adventure, comedy, and beauty, and is presented by virtuoso artists, Kabuki has remained a vital artistic presence in Japan until the present day.

CONNECTIONS

The theatres of Japan were first "discovered" by Western dramatists and directors near the beginning of the 20th century. The Irish playwright W. B. Yeats used his knowledge of Noh texts and a limited viewing of Japanese dance to create symbolic, ritual drama; Asian theatre influences are reflected in the symbolist and surrealist movements as well. Antonin Artaud included the Japanese theatre among forms that influenced his development of the "Theatre of Cruelty," and later directors—including Jacques Copeau and Jean-Louis Barrault—have incorporated it into their training and production methods. In particular, the poetic nature of the drama, combined with the emphasis on controlled, expressive gesture, has become a foundation of Barrault's work, which he has expanded into the use of masks. Although the line of influence is less easily traced, the ritualistic nature of such works as *Marat/Sade* and Peter Shaffer's *Equus* also reveal the impact of Japanese concepts on Western theatre. Similarly, the spare, nonactive nature of the plays of Samuel Beckett reflect the simplicity and philosophical nature of the Noh. In general, exposure to Japanese theatre has awakened a sense of style that

A costume rendering for a modern Kabuki-style presentation of Euripides'
The Bacchae at the University of Oregon. (Design by Alexandra B. Bonds.)
Courtesy Alexandra B. Bonds

has served contemporary authors, choreographers, and directors to seek a physical
representation other than a mimicry of external reality.

SOURCES FOR FURTHER STUDY

Social/Art/Philosophy Background

Fukukita, Yasonusuke. *Tea Cult of Japan.* Tokyo: Japan Travel Bureau, 1955.
Keene, Donald. *The Pleasures of Japanese Literature.* New York: Columbia University
    Press, 1988.
Malm, William P. *Nagauta, The Heart of Kabuki Music.* Rutland, Vt.: Charles E.
    Tuttle Co., 1963.

Munsternberg, Hugo. *The Arts of Japan.* Rutland, Vt.: Charles E. Tuttle, 1957.

Storry, Richard. *The Way of the Samurai.* New York: G. P. Putnam's Sons, 1978.

Tsunoda, Rysaku, Wm. Theodore De Bary, and Donald Keene. *Sources of Japanese Tradition.* New York: Columbia University Press, 1958.

Turnbull, Stephen R. *The Book of the Samurai.* London: Arms and Armour Press, 1982.

Ueda, Makoto. *Literary and Art Theories in Japan.* Cleveland: Western Reserve University Press, 1967.

Wilson, William Scott, trans. *Ideals of the Samurai: Writings of Japanese Warriors.* Burbank, Calif.: Ohara Publications, 1982.

Yamamura, Kozo, ed. *The Cambridge History of Japan.* Cambridge: Cambridge University Press, 1990.

Theatre History

Ando, Tsuruo. *Bunraku: The Puppet Theatre.* New York: Walker/Weatherhill, 1970.

Arnott, Peter. *The Theatres of Japan.* New York: St. Martin's Press, 1969.

Brandon, James R., William P. Malam, and Donald H. Shiveley. *Studies in Kabuki.* Honolulu: University Press of Hawaii, 1978.

Dunn, C. J., and Bunzo Torigoe, eds. and trans. *The Actor's Analects.* New York: Columbia University Press, 1969.

Ernst, Earle. *The Kabuki Theatre.* London: Secker and Warburg, 1956.

Keene, Donald. *Bunraku.* Tokyo: Kodansha International, 1965.

———. *No.* Tokyo: Kodansha International, 1966.

Motokiyo, Zeami. (J. Thomas Rimer and Kamazaki Masakazu, trans.) *On the Art of the No Drama.* Princeton, N.J.: Princeton University Press, 1980.

Scott, Adolphe Clarence. *The Kabuki Theatre of Japan.* London: Allen & Unwin, 1955.

———. *The Puppet Theatre of Japan.* Rutland, Vt.: Charles E. Tuttle, 1963.

Dramatic Literature

Brandon, James R. *Kabuki: Five Classic Plays.* Cambridge, Mass.: Harvard University Press, 1975.

Keene, Donald. *Battles of Coxinga.* London: Taylor's Foreign Press, 1951.

———, trans. *Chikamatsu Monzaemon: Four Major Plays.* New York: Columbia University Press, 1961.

———, ed. *Twenty Plays of the No Theatre.* New York: Columbia University Press, 1970.

McKinnon, Richard N., ed. and trans. *Selected Plays of Kyogen.* Tokyo: Uniprint, 1967.

Nakamura, Matazo. *Kabuki: Backstage, Onstage.* Trans. Mark Oshima. Tokyo: Kodansho International, 1988.

Richie, Donald. *Six Kabuki Plays.* Tokyo: Hokuseido Press, 1963.

Ueda, Mokoto. *The Old Pine Tree and Other Noh Plays.* Lincoln: University of Nebraska Press, 1962.

C H A P T E R

10

English Theatre, 1660–1800

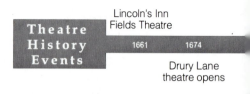

General Events	Restoration of Charles II
	1660

Arts Events	Milton's *Paradise Lost*	
	1667	1675–1710
		St. Paul's Cathedral

Theatre History Events	Lincoln's Inn Fields Theatre	
	1661	1674
		Drury Lane theatre opens

It should have been a great theatrical success, one that would amaze the audience with its spectacle and establish a new fashion for ballet and stage design. The leading actor and manager of the English stage, David Garrick (1717–1779), had arranged to import a French ballet for performances following his productions at the Theatre Royal in Drury Lane. The ballet, entitled *The Chinese Festival,* had awed and thrilled audiences in Paris, thanks to its 60 richly costumed dancers, stunning scene changes, and innovative dance patterns. Garrick's difficulties in getting the production's producer, Jean Georges Noverre (1727–1810), to agree to terms, however, were nothing in comparison to what would follow. By the time the company arrived in London in 1755, relations between England and France had deteriorated badly. War was a distinct possibility, and anything French was considered suspect. Patriotic feelings were running so high that Garrick published a playbill explaining that Noverre was Swiss and so were most of his company (to which one audience member later responded, "Swiss, what the devil do we know of Swiss! A Swiss is a foreigner, and all foreigners are Frenchmen; and so damn you all!"). Garrick's efforts were to no avail.

The first performance of *The Chinese Festival* was given on November 8, 1755. With the king in attendance, the audience confined itself to stamping, hissing, and shouting, "No French dancers!" Garrick decided to wait until November 12 before presenting the ballet again, believing that tempers would

Charles II dies — 1685
English Bill of Rights — 1689
"Glorious Revolution" — 1688
George I of Hanover — 1714
George I dies — 1727
George II dies — 1760
Stamp Act — 1765
American independence — 1776

Locke's *Essay Concerning Human Understanding* — 1690
Defoe's *Robinson Crusoe* — 1719
Swift's *Gulliver's Travels* — 1726
Handel's "Messiah" — 1741
Fielding's *Tom Jones* — 1749
Gainsborough's *Blue Boy* — 1770

Jeremy Collier's attacks — 1698
Covent Garden Theatre — 1732
Licensing Act — 1737
de Loutherbourg arrives in London — 1771
Garrick retires — 1776

cool. Instead, the number of opponents increased, and their determination to stop the show was greater than before. The hissing was worse; fights ensued, and one man was thrown over the gallery onto the main floor (the pit). Despite the debacle, Garrick continued to present the ballet. For a few days it appeared he might succeed in winning over the audiences. Then, on November 18 an observer saw the following: "The riot was very great, the Gentlemen came with Sticks . . . and the rout went on." One man was pelted with an apple when he tried to speak, others dodged fruits and vegetables being tossed onto the stage. Supporters and opponents of the production battled with drawn swords for control of the pit and the stage (the actors were hiding behind the scenery). "One [side] would not give way to the other, and they seemed to be pretty equally balanced: at last, after much mutual abuse, loud altercation, and many violent blows and scuffles, the combatants fell upon that which could make no resistance, the materials before them. They demolished the scenes, tore up the benches, broke the lustres and girandoles, and did in a short time so much mischief to the inside of the theatre, that it could scarce be repaired in several days."

A riot at Covent Garden protesting the price of tickets. *Courtesy Victoria and Albert Picture Library*

The Chinese Festival riots were not the only ones in London theatres in the 1700s, though the extent of the destruction that week was rare. Audiences in that century clearly felt that they had the right and the freedom to express themselves vocally and physically about the plays, the performers, and even the managers' policies. Events at the London theatres were a barometer of social attitudes and feelings. When the aristocracy controlled the theatres in the late 1600s, they wandered around on the stage, discussed the worth of the plays for all to hear, including the actors, and generally preferred to see actions that reflected where they went and what they did. Beginning around 1690, these "wits" and "milords" abdicated the theatre and were gradually replaced by a rising middle class. This new audience demanded a wide range of theatrical delights for their hard-earned money; they wanted to see their middle-class values rewarded in the plays, and they fully expected the theatre to adhere to their wishes.

The English theatre 1660–1800 is a reflection of (and on) society of that time. Its social function seems to have been to cater to the tastes of a dynamic social structure that was begrudgingly making room for more people as the economic and political systems evolved from a rigid monarchy to the Industrial Revolution. The study of the period must therefore begin with a brief description of the social structure of England after 1660.

SOCIAL IDEAS

The Restoration of the monarchy in 1660 brought to the throne a monarch who believed in the divine right of kings. Charles II (1668–1685) and his successor, James II (1633–1701), used the prerogatives of an absolute monarch to place all power in themselves and in the friends and relatives of their court. Charles particularly enjoyed the social trappings of the monarchy, including theatrical entertainments. This exclusivity was not popular, however. After only three years as king, James II was forced to flee to France. England began to move away from royalty as the center of its social structure.

When George I (1660–1727) was brought from Hanover (Germany) to become king in 1714, his lack of knowledge of both the English language and customs forced him to rely on the advice of his ministers. These men wasted no time in sharing their power with their relatives and friends. By the middle of the 18th century, some 200 families controlled most of the land and power in England. They used Parliament to establish the kind of social and economic structure most advantageous to themselves and their relatives.

Control and manipulation of parliamentary power was only one means by which these families maintained their wealth and status. An equally effective method was to require that all large family estates remain intact. Laws of inheritance prohibited all estates from being divided for distribution among heirs. Thus, the eldest son or next of male kin waited for the death of his father to inherit the family estate and much of its fortune. During the wait, the son was dependent on the father (or a guardian) for living expenses. Daughters held no rights to an estate and therefore were dependent on a suitable marriage for their future welfare. To many families, a daughter's chief asset was therefore her marriage prospects, for a convenient union could insure her financial security and bring new money or land to the family.

As power shifted to parliamentary leaders, interest in the behavior of the nobility was replaced by interest in these landed gentry and wealthy merchants. Many plays of the 18th century present wealthy families caught up in domestic squabbles, while others show the rising merchant class engaged in the making of money. It is impossible to prove a direct causal link between the changing composition of the audiences and dramatic characters, but a correlation exists.

The social structure of England was therefore aristocratic but not courtly. As merchants increased their wealth, they were begrudgingly admitted into the social elite, usually through marriage. One result of this was that English drama shifted from the playful indifference of courtiers to the work ethic of the merchants. Two ideas in particular were championed by this new power elite: reason and sentiment.

Reason

Isaac Newton (1642–1727) symbolizes 18th-century English thought. To every problem he brought the rationality of controlled experimentation and repeated observation. He searched the world for explanations, and he found logical order wherever he looked. His investigations of the material universe included the study of light (*Opticks*, 1704), the measurement of the moon's orbit, the laws of motion of the planets around the sun, and gravity. In his application of mathematics to problems of motion, Newton conceived of the universe as an intricate but regulated coherence. The universe took on the image of a magnificent clock, a mechanism of balanced parts that interrelate according to discernible principles. In place of a God of Mystery whose work passes all understanding, God's relationship to His creation was that of a kind of engineer who made occasional necessary adjustments in the machine He created.

Like Newton, John Locke (1632–1704) replaced confusion and mystery with regularity and reason. He wrote of God, nature, man, government, and politics, and his thoughts concerning human understanding influenced English thought for a full century. Locke argued persuasively that the power of reason is at the core of human nature. "Reason must be our best judge," he wrote, "and guide in all things." He was an advocate of common sense, and he opposed the religious emotion that had swirled through England during his youth. He shifted the focus of intellectual inquiry from unknowable matters of faith to discernible patterns of social conduct.

Sentiment and Sentimentality

Newton and Locke provided persuasive justification for adherence to rationality. Some writers became strict empiricists, rejecting all phenomena that could not be proved with the senses. Had the rampant rationalism of the age been left unmodified, the popularity of the drama would have probably diminished. Plays are not philosophical essays; they communicate the emotional structure of characterization as much as the logical and linguistic capacities of the individual. The individual who drew the connection between reason and feeling was the third Earl of Shaftesbury (1671–1713). As much as anyone, he helped establish the basis for sentimentalism, or the dramas of sensibility.

Central to Shaftesbury's writing is the idea that moral goodness, beauty, and emotion are all associated with one another. He believed that beauty in human action has the same impact on the soul as does the beauty of the art world: it generates feelings of pity and kindness within us. When we see a beautiful action, we are moved by that action, he reasoned. Moreover, these feelings induce us to do that which is good and right in our own conduct in order to retain those positive feelings as long as possible.

Shaftesbury's ideas were the basis of an entirely new justification for the drama. If the drama can evoke feelings of pity and kindness in the audience, then it is a beautiful act that is morally good. To achieve this effect, the characters of the drama must engage in sensible and just action themselves. They must be examples of good conduct to insure that the appropriate feelings are created in the audience. This in turn means that the morally good characters must have a situation that allows them to act in a morally beautiful manner. They need to prove their goodness to themselves and to the audience.

Thus, dramas of sensibility usually have a virtuous individual who acts to reform or save another individual who has lost his or her virtue. In comedy the reformation or salvation is successful, while in tragedy the wayward individual fails to follow the example. The tragedy is always unnecessary and unfortunate; the audience feels pity for the poor soul who failed to follow his senses.

While in exile at the court of Louix XIV, England's Prince Charles—later to be King Charles II—developed a French taste in art, fashion, and theatre. Of the artistic developments in the 18th century, the most important in relation to the theatre were in music and literature. In both areas, forms that had been developed on the Continent became popular in England and developed unique English characteristics.

The Novel

In literature, the newly developed novel form became extremely popular. Written narrative was not new to England; there was a long tradition of writing, particularly poetry, stemming from the medieval period. The development of the novel, however, introduced several important characteristics to British literature.

The first novels to develop widespread popularity were romances imported from France. The appeal of these delicate tales of passion are recorded by the famous diarist Samuel Pepys (1633–1703), who notes his wife's fascination with them and her tendency to retell the stories to him *ad infinitum.* The focus on the life of everyday people, free from classical allusions, is one of the hallmarks of the novel. Early writers such as Daniel Defoe (1661–1731) and Jonathan Swift (1667–1745) wrote successful prose fiction that introduced all the major elements of the novel: verisimilitude, a natural language, fully developed characters, and a seriousness of purpose.

It remained for Henry Fielding (1707–1754) to incorporate these elements into one work of art. Successful as a playwright as well, Fielding has a reputation today that is based on his great novel *The History of Tom Jones, a Foundling* (1749). This rollicking tale of the life of a young man is filled with characters from all walks of life, as Tom's travels lead him from one adventure to another. Characters possess both virtues and vices, and if virtue is triumphant, it is simply through human choice. Fielding illustrated the writer's ability to create an absorbing fictional world peopled by fascinating characters who were completely recognizable to the reader.

Opera

Throughout the Restoration, operas were a popular form of theatrical entertainment, from *The Siege of Rhodes* by Sir William Davenant (1606–1668) through the dramatic operas of John Dryden (1631–1700), so-called because they moved the story forward through spoken dialogue rather than recitative. Italian operas were also popular until the patriotic zeal of the English audiences reacted against them in the 1720s. The oratorios of George Frideric Handel (1685–1759) took the place of both dramatic and Italian operas.

Although traditional opera was popular in the early part of the period, the most popular opera of the 18th century was actually not an opera in the traditional sense at all. It was the ballad opera *The Beggar's Opera* (1728).

Ballad Opera

The ballad opera was an acted dramatic work for voices and instruments that relied on popular songs and airs for its musical sources. The lyrics of the melodies were changed to fit the dramatic action. The origins of the ballad opera can be traced to 16th-century jigs, but the first and most successful of them was *The Beggar's Opera* by John Gay (1685–1732). Performed at Lincoln's Inn Fields, through 69 songs and dramatic scenes it told of life in the criminal underworld of London. The lifestyles and attitudes of the poor, the downtrodden, and the wicked were contrasted with the easy life of the rich. The opera succeeded because it viciously satirized the double standard of the British class system, in which gentlemen's crimes were excusable but beggars' crimes were punished with death. The show ran for a month, an incredible run for an age that still saw most plays close after a dozen performances, and it spawned hundreds of imitations over the next century.

THE RESTORATION THEATRE

Prior to the return of Charles II, a knight or his Puritan counterpart would not have attended the theatre at all. During the Commonwealth (1642–1660), theatrical activity was banned. Theatre houses were shut down, and actors could be arrested. Some performances were given either in secret or through bribery of officials, but these works would have been given few performances. Activity began to increase near the end of the period, due particularly to William Beeston (1606–1682), who trained a company of boy actors; and also to William Davenant, who produced operas (considered musical entertainments, not theatre pieces). In 1656, Davenant's production of *The Siege of Rhodes* used Italianate scenery in a public performance for the first time. Nevertheless, the English theatre was in a state of uncertainty and disarray when Charles was restored to the throne in 1660.

Occasion

With the return of the king, theatre was reestablished as a social event, aimed primarily at the nobility. But even before the king landed in England, a struggle ensued over the right to produce plays. Sir Henry Herbert (dates uncertain) reestablished himself as Master of the Revels and issued licenses to three companies, including one to Beeston. The king, however, granted two other men patents to produce plays. Davenant formed the Duke's Company and Thomas Killigrew (1612–1683) the King's Company. Despite efforts by Herbert's licensees and others, Davenant and Killigrew secured the king's support as the only men authorized to produce plays in London. The men built and used a variety of theatres in the first years of the Restoration as they endeavored to turn their patents into lucrative business ventures. Despite their monopoly, they could not prevent financial and personal problems from jeopardizing their security. Killigrew, not as devoted to the theatre as Davenant, was a poor manager, and his company was absorbed into the Duke's Company in 1682. The United Company performed in Drury Lane for 13 years, until internal dissension led to a split and returned London theatre to the pattern of two predominant theatre companies.

Throughout this period, theatre functioned as a commercial enterprise, performing whenever appropriate to draw an audience. Regular theatre seasons featured performances on as many as five nights a week; fewer performances were given during the summer.

Location

In the early years of the Restoration, several theatre buildings were used, and performances were also given at court, at outdoor fairs, and at concert halls and inns of court. The indoor public theatres have attracted the most historical attention, however, because they established a tradition for theatre structures that is still in evidence today. Both Davenant and Killigrew first performed in theatres converted from tennis courts—Killigrew at the Vere Street Theatre and Davenant at Lisle's Tennis Court in Lincoln's Inn Fields. The stage was placed at one end of the rectangle and the audience faced the stage or sat at the sides. Davenant constructed the Dorset Garden Theatre in 1670, and Killigrew built a theatre at Bridges Street, Drury Lane. When the latter burned in 1672, Killigrew began construction of what was to become the most famous theatre in English history: the Theatre Royal, Drury Lane.

The Drury Lane is typical of its period. The auditorium contained the pit (or flat seating area in front of the stage), boxes arranged in a semicircle around the pit, and two galleries containing two rows of seating. The upper galleries were generally used by "ordinary people," as one commentator of the day reported, while the boxes were reserved for the wealthy and the aristocrats. The pit was particularly popular among the young wits, who relished the opportunity to display not only their sharp minds but also their elegant clothing. Other young wits sat on the stage itself, and a few periodically crossed it to show off their new clothes. That the courtier could sit and walk on stage suggests that he saw no distinction between the fiction of the play and the fiction of his life; both were inventions for his entertainment. Estimates of the number of people who could attend a performance at Drury Lane vary, but the number was most likely around 650 and certainly did not exceed 1,000.

The stage itself was about 34 feet deep, divided in half by the proscenium arch. This meant that the scenery was confined to the rear half of the stage. Side doors provided entrances to the forestage or apron. Action usually took place on the apron, because candlelight provided the only illumination, and the actors would have been seen more distinctly near the front.

Performers

Among the most notable developments in the performance of theatre during the Restoration was the increased interest in scenic display. The use of stage machines or movable scenery began in earnest with William Davenant. Machines, previously confined to the masques performed privately for the court, became a popular means by which a producer would attract a large interested audience. The sides of each stage behind the proscenium were fitted with grooves into which could be slid wings or flats with painted scenery, thus giving rise to the name "wing-and-groove system." Backdrops covered the rear of the stage. The limited size of the Restoration theatres meant that the scenery systems were less complex than those on the Continent. Nevertheless, the addition of trapdoors and flying machines meant that the Restoration theatre could produce a dazzling visual spectacle. A production of *Psyche* in 1675 at the Duke's Theatre included furies rising and sinking, Venus descending in a chariot, and various characters flying in and out of clouds. The famous Restoration diarist Samuel Pepys, who attended the theatre frequently, often commented that the scenery of a play is "very fine indeed and worth seeing" (sometimes more so than the play itself).

The remaining elements of the visual picture were very different from what audiences of today expect to see. Costumes were not specifically designed by a single person for a particular production as they are today. Rather, the company or the actors themselves owned and wore those items of clothing that most effectively presented the actors to the audience. This meant that the fashion of the day was worn in a play when the play was set in ancient times. There were some attempts at indicating time or location, but generally the addition of feathers, hats, or other accessories were the key indicators of the location of the action. The fact that the costumes were seldom representational, however, does not mean that they were shabby or undistinguished. Records indicate that considerable moneys were spent on new materials for stockings, shoes, capes, and fabric. When new costumes were made, the producers frequently highlighted this point in their advertising.

Lighting was achieved with candles both in the auditorium and on stage. The candles in the auditorium remained lit throughout the performance. Those on stage could be snuffed for night scenes, but the effort to relight them was cumbersome and the effect was probably not often used. Visibility with such lighting was somewhat limited, and Pepys complains frequently that his eyes hurt for trying to see in the dim candlelight.

Much of the attention during this time period was focused on the performer, both on and off stage. Actors held an ambivalent status in society. Their profession was no longer illegal, and leading actors achieved popular reputations among theatregoers. Actresses particularly drew the attention of the audience, since the first women to perform on an English stage appeared in 1660 or 1661. Their popularity, however, had a price. The women were a cause for gossip and rumor about their personal attachments to members of court. The salaries were seldom more than what an industrious, uneducated Londoner could make elsewhere, and, given the limited number of performing companies, the total number of professional actors in London has been estimated to have been less than 100.

Actors usually specialized in certain character types, a practice that encouraged the development of standard bits or acting habits that could be used by the actor regardless of the role. Especially in comedy, actors tended to play the same character regardless of the play, much as was customary in vaudeville in the 20th century. Variation from one role to another was minimal. Specific detail for a particular character was not crucial. Because many of the plays were written for a specific company with particular actors in mind for each major role, the development of unique qualities for each role was not necessary, and actors could rely on their best attributes. Actors were known for their personality, not for their range of character. Excelling in this system was Thomas Betterton (1635–1710), noted for his tragic roles and his formal style of

Thomas Betterton, Restoration actor.
Courtesy Harvard Theatre Collection

delivery. Nell Gwynn (1642?–1687) and Anne Bracegirdle (1671–1748) are two women who established themselves in comedic roles. At the end of the Restoration, the dramas of the period fell into disfavor, but the tradition of fine acting continued throughout the next century.

Audience

Considerable dispute has focused on the makeup of the typical Restoration audience. For years, scholars felt that the Restoration theatre was a "closed club" with only a very small elite segment of the populace in attendance. This produced an image of performance in which "in jokes" were popular and in which the atmosphere approached that of a huge ball or social occasion.

Recent scholarship, however, disputes such an interpretation, holding that the audience probably contained a cross section of the population. Admittedly, the upper class would have dominated due to their access to leisure time and funds, but at any given performance a variety of people would have been in attendance. Indeed, many of the moral attacks on the theatre were based on the presence of prostitutes in the audience. But whatever the makeup of the audience, those in attendance felt free to express themselves about the play, or one another.

Studies of audience behavior, including excerpts from diaries of the period, indicate that much of the attention of the audience was on one another as well as on the play. It was equally important to see and to be seen, and dress and deportment were essential considerations when attending the theatre.

Standards of Judgment

The critical writing of the Restoration focuses largely on the neoclassical concepts of tragedy as developed in France. Those who found the French example compelling were vocal in their criticism of "modern" developments and even found grounds to censure Shakespeare. The premiere writer of criticism was John Dryden, himself a serious playwright. Dryden's works illustrate the Restoration concern for finding a way to demonstrate appropriate admiration for the writing of the ancients while allowing their own personal tastes in theatre to emerge. Of particular concern for the serious dramatist were the restrictions placed on authors by the unities. Having inherited the complex dramas of Shakespeare, these authors found it difficult to limit their action to one single plot. Similarly the demand for unity of place seemed unnecessary given the new ability to create plausible locales through the wonders of Italian design. Finally, the neoclassic demand for purity of genre denied the mixture of comedy and tragedy, a long-standing English tradition in the drama. The final decision appears to be one of compromise in which, Dryden claims, the judgment of the playwright should be respected.

Comedy was also a concern for the critics of the day. One focus of their concern was whether comedy should provide "delight" or "instruction." A loudly expressed view roundly condemned the comic theatre for its moral bankruptcy. Jeremy Collier (1650–1726), in his pamphlet "A Short View of the Immorality and Profaneness of the

Anne Bracegirdle, Restoration comic actor, as "The Indian Queen." *Courtesy Harvard Theatre Collection*

SOME PROMINENT ENGLISH ACTORS, 1660–1800

Restoration Actors

Barry, Elizabeth	1658–1713	tragic actress
Betterton, Thomas	c. 1635–1710	best of Restoration actors
Bracegirdle, Anne	c. 1663–1748	played comedies of manners
Doggett, Thomas	c. 1670–1701	"low" comedian
Gwyn, Nell	1650–1687	famed for affair with the king
Kynaston, Edward	c. 1650–1706	played heroic roles

18th-Century Actors

Barry, Spranger	c. 1717–1777	specialized in romantic heroes
Booth, Barton	1681–1733	tragic actor
Cibber, Colley	1671–1757	playwright, played fops
Cibber, Susanna Maria	1714–1766	played only serious roles
Clive, Kitty	1711–1785	singer, noted for high comedy
Garrick, David	1717–1789	considered greatest actor
Kemble, John Philip	1757–1823	notable also as manager
King, Thomas	1730–1805	played comic old men
Macklin, Charles	c. 1700–1797	introduced "serious" Shylock
Oldfield, Anne	1683–1730	comic and tragic actress
Pritchard, Hannah	1711–1768	Garrick's leading lady
Quin, James	1693–1766	considered dignified, solemn
Siddons, Sarah Kemble	1755–1831	considered greatest actress
Woffington, Margaret	c. 1714–1760	famed for "breeches parts"

English Stage," admits the talents of English authors but condemns their purposes, finding that Restoration plays laughed at serious matters, portrayed lewdness without censure, used foul language, abused the clergy, and rewarded vicious behavior. His opponents noted the stage's potential to instruct humans and censured Collier for his attempts to ruin the theatre.

It is difficult to ascertain the affect of these writings on the individual audience member or even on the management of the theatres. Certainly throughout this period's early years, Restoration comedies were popular and successful on the stage, and only over a period of time did the tone of the drama change.

18TH-CENTURY THEATRE

Just as the Restoration—that celebration of liberation from the Puritans—began with the ascension of Charles II to the throne, the end of that period must really be considered to date with his death in 1685 and the ascension of his brother, James II. James's devout Catholic faith was at least part of the reason his rule began in dissension and went steadily downhill. One source notes that he "committed every stupid error that was possible," including intriguing with the French king, attempting to pack Parliament with his supporters, and persecuting Protestants. His actions aroused great opposition, and at the invitation of Parliament, William of Orange invaded England and began the "Glorious Revolution," which ended with his being crowned king in 1689. For the first time, Parliament had named the king, breaking the power of "divine right" and signaling the growth of the power of the people. In addition, the new king and queen were moderates, and brought with them a new sense of conservative morality and domesticity. These two elements—the growing strength of the middle class and a conservative morality—were highly influential in the development of the theatre during the 18th century.

Occasion

Theatre remained a commercial enterprise, and the occasion for performance was greatly influenced by a new audience. The changing audience of the day was perhaps best reflected in an account by playwright/critic John Dennis (1657–1734). Dennis noted that the theatre was empty of "originals" and that the audience was characterized by a dull uniformity. He noted that there were three uneducated types of people attending plays: younger brothers who could not be educated due to the high taxes, people who had recently come into money, and foreigners. These, he maintains, lacked the leisure to enjoy good drama, and the ease and serenity of spirit to appreciate it.

The new audience influenced the theatre in several ways. Plays were required to meet their more conservative moral standards, which resulted in rejection of most of the drama written between 1660 and 1690. No longer were the scandalous Restoration plays popular, and there seemed to be little appetite for new plays. Instead, the audience preferred older plays, particular those of the Elizabethan period. Records from the period indicate almost no new dramas were performed between 1697 and 1703.

Additionally, the new audience brought with them a taste for diverse entertainments, and the theatre began to include musicals and dances as forepieces, entr'actes, and afterpieces. At times, it seemed the audience came more to see these entertainments than the drama. Although the impact of this change was not immediate, such events began to put new standards on the drama as it strove to compete with the alternative forms.

The question of who would rule England became paramount in the following years. Queen Anne (1665–1714), the second daughter of James I, became ruler upon the death of William. Although she mothered 17 children, none survived, and thus, upon her death, it was necessary for Parliament to use the Act of Succession to crown the nearest Protestant relative of the Stuart family, ignoring the traditional claims of the descendants of James II, who were Catholics. It is through this complicated system of politics that George, a young German prince, became King of England. George realized that he was likely to be unpopular with at least one-half of the populace, and he essentially refused to rule, never bothering to learn English and spending most of his time in Hanover. Instead, he vested full authority in his Cabinet, largely in the person of Robert Walpole (1676–1745), who continued as the chief or Prime Minister through the reigns of George II and George III, retiring in 1742.

During this period, the growth both in the numbers of the middle class and in the economic power they wielded resulted in a great increase in the audience available for theatre presentations. A new form of drama, termed "exemplary" or "sentimental" comedy, became popular. This form reflected the middle-class values of virtue, chastity, and modesty, and suddenly theatre was an attractive enterprise.

A new, enlarged Covent Garden opened in 1732, and in the following years several individuals, determined to share the wealth suddenly available to theatre managers, questioned the legalities of the patents issued to Davenant and Killigrew. Unlicensed theatres began to open and close at a bewildering rate, challenging the authority of Parliament to restrict them. This alone was enough to cause concern among the government, but a second development occurred that forced Walpole's hand in taking firm control of the theatre in England. Satirical dramatic works ridiculing government officials began to appear. In the plays of Henry Fielding (1707–1754)— including *Tom Thumb, or The Tragedy of Tragedies* (1730), and *Pasquin* (1736)—this satire focused directly on Walpole, and his reaction was swift.

The Licensing Act of 1737 was enacted by Parliament to provide adequate means of control over the theatre. In fact, it resulted in a system of prior censorship that would remain in effect for more than 100 years. Under the provision of this act, no play could be performed for profit that had not previously been licensed by the Lord Chamberlain. Further, the king's powers to license theatres were restricted to the district of Westminster, effectively limiting theatre once again to Drury Lane and Covent Garden.

The effect on the theatre was drastic. Between 1740 and 1747, Drury Lane performed only one new drama, and Covent Garden performed only four. Clearly, in a restricted, repressive atmosphere there was not enough reward to attract authors to playwriting.

It did not take long for the theatre to find ways to circumvent this new restriction, however. In 1740 one theatre charged admission to hear a concert, with a play presented as a "free added attraction." Other ruses included the offering of free plays to those who bought a dish of chocolate or attended an "Action of Pictures." However, new theatres were closed as frequently as they appeared. The repeated closing of the New Wells Theatre so discouraged a young actor/manager named William Hallam (d. 1758) that he organized a young troupe and sent them to America under the leadership of his brother, Lewis (1714–1755), where they became a major contributor to the fledgling theatre of the New World.

Such massive changes in the control and the audience of the theatre and the demands they created led to changes in the areas of production as well, and architecture, staging, and acting all were forced to change to accommodate the new audience and the new drama.

Location

Theatre architecture in the 18th century can be characterized essentially by an increase in size to accommodate the large new audiences. Christopher Rich (?–1714), a leading theatre manager at the turn of the century, was one of the first to decrease the size of the forestage, removing one of the proscenium doors and several feet of acting space in order to allow more patrons into the pit. This arbitrary action was highly unpopular with the actors (particularly since Rich did not share the additional income with them), but other theatres were remodeled in the same manner, and some even went further. The original Drury Lane held approximately 650 persons. When a new Covent Garden was built in 1732 it held 1,440 people, and when a new Drury Lane theatre was designed in 1794, the seating capacity was 3,611. The new building was so large that it occupied the area on which the original theatre was built and the land that had held several other neighboring buildings as well. In the original Drury Lane theatre no member of the audience was more than 36 feet from the front of the stage. In the new theatre it was nearly 100 feet from the front of the stage to the back of the auditorium.

This increase in the size of the auditorium was echoed by an increase in the size of the stage. Although the forestage remained foreshortened, the stage behind the proscenium increased greatly in size, at least partially to accommodate the new style in scenic design. The public taste for spectacle had been developed through the presentation of pantomimes and similar diversions, and it did not take long for enterprising managers to include this element in the presentation of drama.

Drury Lane theatre.   *Courtesy Victoria and Albert Picture Library*

Performers

Spectacle, of course, was not entirely new to English drama, for the Stuart court masques had been imaginative and lavish productions. However, such presentations were not seen during the Restoration, at least in part because spectators were seated on benches on stage. However, with the lack of new drama available, it soon became financially expedient to present new scenery. New scenic artists were required to make this possible.

One of the earliest developers of this new art was Jean-Nicolas Servandoni (1695–1766), a designer for the Paris Opéra who was hired by Christopher Rich to design for Covent Garden. This introduced England to the new style of perspective design, and further developments followed. The most influential of these new designers was Philippe de Loutherbourg (1740–1812), whose work for Garrick revolutionized English design. Aided by Garrick's decision to ban spectators from the stage area, de Loutherbourg increased the dependence on illusion through painting, three-dimensional construction, and lighting techniques. [See insert, p. 228.]

Costuming also began to develop an interest in pictorial accuracy, and some of the earliest attempts can be found in the productions of David Garrick (1717–1779), who at least tried to distinguish plays written before 1642 from those that followed the Restoration. During the 18th century the earliest books concerned with fashion were published, but their influence on stage dress was slight. Fashionable dress was still the most common costume, and since theatres could not always meet the standards, most of the major performers maintained their own wardrobes, wearing for a particular performance the clothes they felt most favored their own personal appearance without regard to the character being portrayed.

In the absence of great playwrights, the actor became the dominant artist in the theatre. This was at least partly due to the interest in actors' private lives introduced during the Restoration. However, it was also partly due to the changes in acting style. At this time most character interpretations were traditional and varied little from actor to actor. In the first half of the century Colley Cibber (1671–1757) and Thomas Doggett (1670–1721), among others, were noted for high and low comic characters, respectively. Anne Oldfield (1683–1730) was the leading actress of the time. Her burial at Westminster Abbey is a clear indication of the new social status that was enjoyed by performers.

Occasionally an unusual, bold choice by an actor could arouse audiences to enthusiasm or to riot. Charles Macklin (1699–1797) brought to the stage an incredibly dogged and fiery personality filled with wit and cynicism. He once killed an actor over the possession of a wig, and even infuriated other actors by improvising comic business on stage during a scene. Macklin created a furor with the first tragic interpretation of Shylock in 1741, introducing a sense of emotional reality and seriousness.

At the same time, David Garrick revolutionized acting with his demand for an acting style based on a direct observation of life, shunning the vocal pyrotechnics of his predecessors. This style included a more natural vocal pattern, a mobile face, expanded use of movement and pantomime, and a variation of pace and intensity that was realistic and dramatic. [See insert, p. 229.] Garrick was ably supported by some fine actresses, among them the gifted comediennes Kitty Clive (1711–1785) and Peg

PHILIPPE DE
LOUTHERBOURG

When Philippe de Loutherbourg arrived in London in November 1771, at the age of 31, he was already an established painter in his native France. At Garrick's request de Loutherbourg presented an elaborate proposal to alter and improve the lighting, scenic, and mechanical systems at the Drury Lane. According to his plan, he would oversee all such operations, do some painting himself, and design costumes. In effect, he was proposing that he serve as a master designer, unifying the scenic effects in ways previously unknown.

Throughout his 10 years working with Garrick at the Drury Lane, de Loutherbourg was constantly experimenting. Together he and Garrick gradually abandoned the stock scenery that was in common use at the time and designed new scenery for specific productions. Rather than symmetrical side wings, de Loutherbourg used multiple free-standing pieces that allowed him to develop a greater sense of depth and texture. Often these depicted actual locations in London and throughout England that were thought to be so effective that an individual viewing them might actually be deceived.

De Loutherbourg's use of light was also revolutionary. Placing the lights in the wings instead of in candelabra over the stage, he perfected the use of tinted cloth and glass to produce subtle variations of color. This allowed him to depict changes of light from dawn to midday and created quite a rage among audiences for sunset and moonrise effects. The popularity of these effects is illustrated by one record that indicates that a new play was composed in great haste, specifically to make use of new scenery devised by de Loutherbourg. He was so successful that by 1776 even the French and Italian scenographers began to copy his techniques.

De Loutherbourg remained at the Drury Lane until 1781, when he resigned due to a salary dispute with the new owner, Sheridan. He devoted the next several years to his own miniature theatre, the Eidophusikon, a stage six feet by eight feet, for which he designed *Various Imitations of Natural Phenomena*, including an Italian seaport, Niagara Falls, the coast of Japan, and a view of Milton's conception of Hell. These scenes were accompanied by music and sound effects and were extremely popular.

Although he was generally recognized as the finest designer in England since Inigo Jones, de Loutherbourg designed only rarely after 1781. He devoted some years to his interest in mysticism and alchemy (including some failed attempts at faith healing), and then returned to his career as a painter until his death in 1812.

DAVID GARRICK

*D*avid Garrick, born in 1717, first demonstrated his acting skill to schoolmates with his ability to peek through the keyhole and mimic the private affairs of the schoolmaster and his wife. His first appearance in a play was as a substitute for an ailing actor, but it was only after his mother's death in 1740 that he dared join a small theatre company performing in Ipswich. During this time, he carefully hid his career from his family, acting under an assumed name. His London debut occurred in the part of Richard III at Goodman's Fields theatre in October 1741, for which he was billed only as "a Gentleman who never appear'd on any stage."

His performance that night electrified the audience, and the press commented that the "reception was the most extraordinary and great that was ever known upon such an Occasion." Even this success did not convince his family that this was an appropriate career, but the absence of their approval did not deter him. In six short years he had moved from unknown actor to the highest position in London theatre. Alexander Pope summed up Garrick's supremacy as an actor when he wrote "that young man never had his equal, and he never will have a rival."

Theatre was an all-consuming passion for Garrick, who demonstrated exceptional skill in all areas of theatre practice, gaining fame as an actor, a manager, and a playwright. As an actor he objected to the stiff, declamatory style of the time. He became noted for a naturalness of expression that was based on conversational vocal patterns, facial expression, movement, sudden shifts of mood, and a revolutionary use of pause to break up speeches. The total effect was a "realism" unknown prior to his appearance. On one occasion an individual who had come to London to do business with Garrick was invited to the theatre the night before his appointment. He so totally believed Garrick's characterization that he left London the next day refusing to do business with such an unsavory character.

As a manager, Garrick was equally innovative and successful, working in all facets of theatre to insure the success of his productions. He was noted for his ability to alter scripts to make them successful by deleting objectionable wording, rewriting scenes to make story lines more clear, shortening the playing time, and injecting stage business into otherwise passive scenes and long speeches. He rehearsed his casts much longer than had been done previously and even invited young apprentices to his estate during the summer for intensive training. He was

continued

among the first to no longer allow patrons on stage or backstage during performances. He instituted many reforms in scenic practices, including inviting Philippe de Loutherbourg to England, where together they instituted new concepts in lighting and new heights in realistic depictions of scenery. Garrick also spent a great deal of attention and money on costumes, insisting on new garments of the finest quality and at times venturing into the beginnings of historical costuming. In addition, he was an astute businessman, and the records of the time demonstrate his skill in attracting audiences and negotiating the most favorable deals with actors and authors.

Garrick retired from the stage in June 1776, by which time his influence and reputation had spread through France, Germany, and Italy. Although there was distressing news from America about the incipient revolution, Garrick's retirement was the most newsworthy event at the time. At his final performance, he spoke to the audience "in so pathetic a Manner as drew Tears from the Audience & himself & took his leave of them for Ever." Three years later he died, and Samuel Johnson wrote: "I am disappointed by that stroke of death which has eclipsed the gaiety of nations and impoverished the public stock of harmless pleasure." By ignoring the protests of his family, Garrick had found his own path and firmly established himself as one of the leading figures of the stage.

David Garrick and Mrs. Cibber in *Venice Preserv'd.*   *Courtesy Victoria and Albert Picture Library*

Woffington (1714?–1760), who was noted for her performance of "breeches" parts. The leading tragic actresses were Hannah Pritchard (1711–1768) and Susanna Cibber (1714–1766). Garrick was not without male rivals, either, for Spranger Barry (1717?–1777) was generally considered superior to Garrick in romantic roles. At the end of the century, John Philip Kemble (1757–1823) and his sister, Sarah Kemble Siddons (1755–1831), popularized a more formal and classical style of acting characterized by dignity, grace, and beautiful vocal work. Well-suited to the larger auditoriums, it was this style that would continue to hold the stage until the advent of the Romantic Era.

Audience

The relationship between an actor and the public was intense, and the period was marked by intense rivalries in which the theatregoers acted as judge and jury. The choice of plays, changes in casting, ticket prices, and even styles of performance were frequently the reason for riots as the audience firmly established its rights to demand satisfaction in the theatre. The power to control the theatre which had originally rested with the king had moved through Parliament and the Lord Chamberlain squarely into the hands of the paying public.

Standards of Judgment

Although the paying public exercised considerable influence on the theatre, critics continued to pass judgments and establish standards. While the debate about the authority of the ancient critics continued, new critical concerns developed about the nature of comedy. Concerned with the development of a sentimental style of comedy in which tears of sympathy and joy replaced laughter as the typical result, playwright Oliver Goldsmith (1728–1774) determined to reestablish "laughing comedy" as the proper style. In an essay entitled "A Comparison between Sentimental and Laughing Comedy," he notes that comedy has become the dominant form, replacing the earlier emphasis on tragedy. He asserts that the role of comedy is to focus on normal life, but that an examination of life's follies is preferable to a detailing of its calamities, which should be the role of tragedy. He claims that the fastidious manners of the age and the tendency to address only the virtues of humans threaten to banish humor from the stage entirely. It is this stance that led to the writing of Goldsmith's famous comedy *She Stoops to Conquer* and paved the way for the comedies of Richard Brinsley Sheridan (1751–1816).

DRAMATIC LITERATURE

Poor Sir Peter Teazle. Six months ago he married a young girl from the country and it made him the happiest of men. As soon as she saw the latest fashions of the beau monde, however, Lady Teazle became infected with the worst social excesses of the London aristocracy: she invented gossip, ridiculed friends, and spent her husband's money. Of late, she has compounded her extravagancies by keeping company with wits and scandalmongers who enjoy destroying reputations of honest folk. To make matters worse, another young lady in Sir Peter's life seems obstinately set against his wishes—his young ward Maria prefers the carousing Charles for her husband over Sir Peter's choice, Charles' brother Joseph. Charles spends his money on his friends for parties that go on for days. Joseph presents himself to society as a man of sentiment, always feigning dislike of any excessive conduct and appearing to all around him as a perfectly correct young man.

If truth be known (and eventually it is!) Joseph is attempting to seduce none other than Lady Teazle with the argument that all wives of London husbands should have a lover. Suddenly, Sir Peter is at the door. Then Charles arrives. In a scene rarely equaled in comedy, Joseph tries to divert Sir Peter's suspicions onto Charles. He hides Sir Peter in a closet, then tries to get Charles to admit he likes Lady Teazle. The trap fails. Imagine Sir Peter's surprise when he steps out of the closet to apologize to Charles, only to discover his own wife hiding behind a screen at the other end of Joseph's room. Sir Peter fears he has lost his wife, Lady Teazle is certain she has lost her reputation, and Joseph fears he has lost his chance for a delicious affair.

Richard Brinsley Sheridan's *The School for Scandal* (1777) is both a popular comedy and a superb example of 18th-century English drama. The comedy lies in its depiction of the scandalmongers, led by one Lady Sneerwell, who puff up their own reputations while inventing stories about people they've often never met. In scintillating language and witty dialogue, the play humorously describes the rules of London's fashionable world. In addition, the play resolves its several story lines in a manner that is both comedic and satisfying. Husband and wife are reunited after Lady Teazle realizes her behavior has been foolish, the scandalmongers are banished from the stage (if not society), Charles and Maria become engaged, and Joseph is exposed as a villain. By his disposition of each character, Sheridan tells the audience what he thinks of their manners and behavior. The audience has a good time in the theatre, and it learns something of the consequences of living according to the world of fashion rather than the truth of the heart.

English comedy from 1660 through the 18th century is often a commentary on social behavior. Characters identify codes of conduct by which they live, and the playwrights dramatize the consequences of those codes. The lifestyles of town (London) and country are contrasted, leading the characters to ask themselves which of the two they prefer. The manners of other characters are also contrasted: the older generation and the younger, pretended wits and truly clever individuals, those who are honest in love and those who aren't, users and abusers of social rules, aristocrats and citizens. The plays are dramatically effective because of the intense conflicts that arise from these juxtapositions. Behind these conflicts, however, is a question that is as important for the audience as it is for the characters: how should a person behave in

A TRIP TO THE THEATRE ROYAL, DRURY LANE, 1777

Standing in the outer lobby of the Theatre Royal in 1777, a young man, waiting for his friends to join him, overhears several conversations. In one corner stand two landowners. Both are members of Parliament, where they have become good friends of the playwright, and they are anxious to see whether Mr. Sheridan is as good a writer as he is a debater. A London tea merchant marches through, declaiming loudly enough for all to hear on the subject of the rebellion in the American colonies. His lecture is interrupted when a young gentleman wearing a pale pink waistcoat and sporting a new two-foot-tall wig on his head passes by outside. Virtually all conversations stop while people watch and comment on this latest fashion of London youth. Most of the talk in the packed lobby is reserved for theatre gossip. Several people wonder aloud to friends whether the great Drury Lane can survive now that its most famous actor, Mr. Garrick, has retired.

When the doors to the auditorium are opened, more than 1,000 seats are quickly filled in anticipation of the performance of *The School for Scandal* by Richard Brinsley Sheridan. The young man takes a seat with his friends on the padded benches in the "pit." Before the play begins, however, an orchestra in the pit immediately in front of the stage plays several selections while the audience visits, paying only scant attention. Then an actor appears and delivers a prologue signaling the beginning of the play.

The play is a tremendous success, for although the sets are the same used in several performances during the past months, the plot and characters are delightful. There is little noise other than laughter and applause from the crowd during the performance. Between acts, the dance company attached to the Drury Lane performs, and several songs are sung. Following the play comes an epilogue and then a two-act afterpiece. Announcements about forthcoming productions are given to end the evening. In all, the entertainments have lasted about five hours.

Leaving the theatre, the young man and his companions discuss the audience as much as the play, condemning the servants in the heavens who threw orange peels at the stage, but commenting admiringly on several of the young women in attendance. Despite the late hour, the streets are full of carriages as playgoers begin a late-evening round of social gatherings.

society? English plays of the 18th century are constant reminders that individuals have a choice in their rules of conduct.

In two forms of comedy in particular—the comedy of manners and sentimentalism—18th-century playwrights challenged their society and at the same time created effective theatre. The comedy of manners presented the latest social fashion, making fun of those who failed to follow the fashion or those who followed it to excess. Sentimentalism presented what ought to be rather than what is in fashion. It focused on the moral conduct of its characters.

Comedy of Manners

Since at least Aristophanes, comedy has been a difficult pursuit: to make audiences laugh requires a situation familiar and close to the audience's yet sufficiently removed from theirs that it is not threatening. Laughter further requires an object of the humor, usually someone whose actions vary from the audience's expectation of normal behavior. The someone doesn't have to be in the play (he or she can be simply referred to, as when a comedian imitates someone famous), but the humor can be developed more easily if the person is on stage engaging in the behavior that the audience finds abnormal. By contrasting that person with someone who represents the norm, the abnormality is emphasized and the humor increased. The comedy of manners contrasts the manners or behavior of those who stray from the social norm in some way with those who represent approved behavior.

Strictly interpreted, any comedy is one of manners, but in the Restoration, the comedies focused so specifically on social codes of conduct that the term is usually associated with this time period. In play after play of the late 17th century, the following characteristics can be found: a wealthy young man (or men) seduces one or more young ladies, one of whom is usually married or betrothed to someone else at her father's insistence. During the seduction scenes the lady decries the young man's forwardness, while he complains about her shyness, enabling both to discuss what they think is appropriate behavior for young ladies and gentlemen. Frequently, a second couple will be involved, further complicating the plot and extending the discussion. To expand the discussion beyond the lovers' situation and into the world of fashion, politics, and society, another character is often introduced who exaggerates everything current in society: he or she tells the most outrageous gossip, wears outrageous clothes, and pretends to know far more about human behavior than is obviously the case. This "third" character (after the two lovers) has little to do with the resolution of the lovers' situation; however, it is customary for such characters to think themselves so magnificently attractive that they try to win away the lovers for themselves. More important to the lovers' plight is a fourth character, either a parent figure or a spouse, who holds some legal claim on one of the lovers. This person temporarily prevents the lovers' union by insisting that the new fashions of the lovers will make for a bad marriage.

Within this framework, considerable variation could occur. During the Restoration, the strong preference of the audience was for sexual plays in which the lovers attempt to engage in an affair without getting caught. Restoration playwrights created a vision of reality in which everyone in society is driven by some sexual motivation. Everyone pursues everyone else regardless of their marital status or their age, and the only approved manners are those that result in successful sexual encounters. Those manners that divert people from this game of love are chided, for the way of the world is love, and a rather loose conception of love it is.

What keeps comedies of manners from becoming comedies of immorality is that the plots, characters, and ideas are all presented with intelligence, wit, and the veneer of supreme confidence. Characters are nothing in this enclosed world unless they can express themselves with grammatical intricacy and clever imagery. Similes and extended metaphors abound in the language of the play. Characters whose behavior may be offensive to the modern reader are fascinating because of their linguistic brilliance. Often it is more important for them to make a witty remark at the expense of another than to be accurate in the observation.

Several playwrights wrote in this style, a few with considerable success. William Wycherly (1641–1715) wrote four plays in the 1670s, including *The Country Wife* (1675) and *The Plain Dealer* (1676). In the former, Horner has devised a method of having all the ladies he wants with no fear of being suspected by their husbands: he convinces the town that he has become impotent while in France. The heroine, a country girl jealously guarded by her foolish old husband, finds herself ensnared by Horner's charms. What separates Wycherly from many of his contemporaries is the range and effectiveness of his language, including a famous scene in which the ladies insist on inspecting Horner's china, an obvious sexual metaphor.

William Congreve (1670–1729) wrote four plays at the end of the century, but *Love for Love* (1695) and *The Way of the World* (1700) are most frequently read today. Despite its confusing and complex plot, *The Way of the World* is a masterpiece of scintillating wit and extended metaphors. It has all the characteristics of a comedy of manners, but it is notable for an especially intelligent and clear-sighted heroine, Millamant, who is quite the match for her hero, Mirabell. He is a subdued, more sober version of the rake, and the pairing of this sensitive hero with a strong heroine gives the play its unique quality. When they decide to marry, it is not out of a need for conquest or gratification. It is the result of a brilliant and witty contract reached after each has asserted his or her independence of mind and lifestyle.

Others who wrote in a similar style included Sir George Etherege (1636–1692), John Dryden (1631–1700), Sir John VanBrugh (1664–1726), and George Farquhar (1677–1707). Other types of comedy in the Restoration were variations of the comedy of humors—with Thomas Shadwell (1642–1692) the most famous writer in this style—and the comedy of intrigue. The latter often included the same characters as the comedy of manners but focused on the unraveling of a complex incident for its tension. Among writers of a comedy of intrigue, Mrs. Aphra Behn (1640–1689) effectively used the potential of stage action and theatricality in such plays as *The Rover; or the Banish't Cavaliers* (1677; second part, 1681) and *Sir Patient Fancy* (1678). [See insert, p. 236.]

Although the comedy of the period has been the chief legacy to modern theatre,

APHRA BEHN

"That Which I Dare Not Name"

"*I* see no reason why women should not write as well as men." Thus wrote the first woman playwright in the English language, Aphra Behn. While she knew that women are the equal of men, most literary critics and historians in later centuries were less sympathetic to her gender. They believed that her work was inferior to that of a man and therefore made no effort to record with accuracy the facts of her life. Nor did they preserve the place she must have had among her contemporaries. Although most of what is known of her is only reasonable conjecture, she is nevertheless one of the most intriguing figures in all of English letters.

Aphra Behn was born in 1640 at the dawn of the Oliver Cromwell era. Sometime after the Restoration of Charles II in 1660 she went to Surinam, in South America. There she gathered the materials for what is arguably the first novel in English, *Oroonoko.* The story is that of a black man whose honest character is tested by deception and intrigue in both white and native society. It is remarkable for its opposition to the treatment of humans as property and for its celebration of a black man as the hero in a white society. Because it is based on Behn's own experiences in Surinam, Behn must have been one of the first white women to journey into the Amazon wilderness.

She returned to England, but soon went to Holland as a spy for the king. Her loyalties to and service for the king and his family gave her introduction to the leading wits of the new court. She wrote at least 15 plays, several books of stories and poems, and even a letter concerning dramatic criticism and literary theory, something truly unheard of for a woman in the period. She died in 1689 and was buried in Westminster Abbey, a rare honor for any literary figure.

The plays of the early Restoration are filled with sexual intrigue and innuendo, and Aphra Behn's are no exception. The titles alone suggest the focus on love and sexual union: *The Amorous Prince* (1671) and *The Dutch Lover* (1673). The plays often refer to the power and beauty of love; their conflicts center around social restrictions that inhibit love. They are as frank as those of her contemporaries, although coming from the pen of a woman they were considerably more scandalous. Behn, unlike some of her male counterparts, did not write only of the sexual mores of her society. She opposed forced marriages, spoke out on the politics of the time (once being arrested by the king's men), and attacked the critics who preferred more classically oriented themes and treatments.

After her death, Behn's reputation diminished. The 18th century did not appreciate the openness of Restoration drama, and those plays by a woman were all the more unseemly. Direct personal attacks on Behn were common. A critic in the 18th century described her as being "qualified to lead the playwrights of her day through pure and bright ways, but she was a mere harlot, who danced through uncleanness, and dared them to follow." Only in the last 20 years has criticism begun to wipe away the sexual politics of other ages and look anew at her work. This attention has also led to the discovery of two volumes of plays by Margaret Cavendish, published as early as 1603, and to other plays by women during this period, including Elizabeth Polwhele's *The Frolicks* (1671); *The Spanish Wives* (1696) by Mary Pix; and *The Wonder: A Woman Keeps a Secret* (1714), one of many successful plays by Susannah Centlivre. Recent research continues to uncover successful plays by women during this period, with Katherine Phillips, Catherine Trotter, and Jane Wiseman among the prominent playwrights.

the Restoration was not without other forms of drama. John Dryden's *All for Love* (1678) is a tragedy based on Shakespeare's *Antony and Cleopatra*, and his *The Conquest of Granada by the Spaniards* (1672), although not truly tragic, is a serious verse drama. Another writer known for serious works during this time is Thomas Otway (1652–1685), whose most famous work is *Venice Preserv'd* (1682).

Sentimental Comedy

What most offended critics of the comedy of manners is that the heroes were ultimately removed from the world around them and completely self-sufficient. They were neither dependent on their society for its charity nor on God for salvation. There was no religion in these plays: ministers, often in disguise, appeared only to bless a union quickly before the couple changed their minds. Characters were careless of the example they set for others. They were independent in the full sense of the word: they had no responsibility for others and no responsibility to some higher authority.

To many critics, this was simply intolerable. So-called moralists like Jeremy Collier and the adherents of Shaftesbury's views argued against the irreverence, hypocrisy, and immodesty of Restoration comedy. Increasingly, they were supported by theatre audiences. The more austere monarchy of William and Mary and the influence of John Locke furthered the demands for a different kind of comedy, one filled with sentiment, good judgment, and a sense of responsibility to God and society. The result has become known as sentimental comedy.

It is rare to see a sentimental comedy performed today because the concepts of comedy underlying it differ from the modern in several ways. The plays present exemplary characters whose actions are a model of behavior for the audience. To be good examples, they must have a moral problem that by its solution will demonstrate their goodness. Characters are seldom ridiculed or banished, therefore, for that would be uncharitable. The successful resolution of the problem lies in an application of charity and forgiveness. Comic endings are not meant to be humorous, but uplifting. Usually they include a repentance, followed by tears of reunion. Sir Richard Steele (1672–1729) went so far as to assert that comedies should make people cry, not laugh. The playwright was not satisfied to create an effective dramatic world; his responsibility extended to the audience, for the final test of the play is its impact on the behavior of the audience.

The play titles alone indicate the intention of the sentimental style: *The Careless Husband* (1721), *The Lady's Last Stake; or The Wife's Resentment* (1707), *The Conscious Lovers* (1722), *The Sick Lady's Cure* (1707), and *The Tender Husband* (1705). Invariably there is a wayward hero wed or betrothed to an all-suffering heroine who trusts in the ultimate goodness of her man and endures four acts of shame and unhappiness until she can win him over in the fifth act. One or both of these characters usually has a trusting and loyal friend who encourages reform in the hero and endurance in the heroine. Servants either loyally follow their masters or foolishly mimic the hero's bad habits. In sentimental comedy, women are idealized and the class structure is rigidly asserted.

Two playwrights wrote the most effective and popular sentimental comedies. Colley Cibber is credited with helping to establish the sentimental trend in such plays as *Love's Last Shift; or The Fool in Fashion* (1696) and *The Careless Husband*. The goal of the latter plot is the reform of a wayward husband who is having an affair with the maid and about to have one with Lady Graveairs. His wife knows of his behavior but refuses to confront him for fear she will appear jealous. For most of the play, the characters simply talk, play cards, or go off to eat. Although the husband's inconstancy is repeatedly shown, the wife refuses to confront him, hoping that her good example will win him over. Finally the husband's realization that his wife has known about him all along forces him to realize how careless he has been with his love and with her honor. He reforms and encourages others to follow suit.

Sir Richard Steele wrote the most famous plays of the style, including *The Accomplish'd Fools* (1705) and *The Conscious Lovers* (1722). His plays reflect his desire to bring his audience to tears of happiness. He avoids mocking wayward characters, choosing instead to focus on the gentle resolution of all domestic problems.

Later Comedies

By mid-century, a balance had been achieved in many instances between the laughing comedies of the Restoration and the tearful comedies of sentimentalism. Most plays allowed for the broad physical humor of the actors, yet retained resolutions of sentiment and moral rectitude.

Richard Brinsley Sheridan wrote two of the most enduringly popular comedies of all time: *The Rivals* (1775) and *The School for Scandal* (1777). Sheridan's effectiveness lies in his ability to combine the best of both Restoration and sentimental comedies. His characters are caught up in matters of love demanding immediate resolution, and they are witty enough to make us laugh at their situation. In the end, they assert their good natures over the false fashion of Lady Sneerwell and her school of scandal. Oliver Goldsmith wrote another of the great English comedies, *She Stoops to Conquer; or, The Mistakes of a Night* (1773), which succeeds in creating a laughing comedy, as its author had hoped. Other comic playwrights in the last part of the century include Hannah Cowley (1743–1809), who wrote *The Belle's Strategem* (1780), and John O'Keefe (1747–1833), author of *Wild Oats* (1791).

Other Dramatic Forms

During the Restoration, heroic tragedies were popular. They were written in elevated language and presented heroes with few of the passions of the average person. Just as the comedy of manners became sentimentalized, the heroic tragedy was also modified to account for the tastes of the 18th-century audience. In 1731, George Lillo's (1691?–1739) *The London Merchant, or The History of George Barnwell* was produced. It was striking in its use of an apprentice as the hero, its use of prose in tragedy, and its pathetic tone for the life of a mere ordinary Londoner. It has many sentimental characteristics: a pure and suffering heroine, a trusty and loyal friend, an honorable merchant, servants who follow their masters, a wayward hero, and a villain who uses the customs of society to her own benefit.

Afterpieces, as their name suggests, were short pieces presented after the full-length play. They provided variety in the evening's entertainment. By mid-century, three types of afterpieces were standard: farces, pantomimes, and musical entertainments. Farces were usually stories with bizarre and broad comic characters who delighted the audience with physical humor—slapstick, mugging, pratfalls, horseplay, and exaggerated imitations. Some of the farces were actually more akin to short sentimental comedies, including those written by the actors Samuel Foote (1721–1777) and David Garrick. Pantomimes were visual spectacles combining dances, music, and scenic effects. Their lineage includes puppet shows, fairy tales, and Italian commedia. Other afterpieces were musical entertainments and combinations of farces, pantomimes, and comedies. The ballet *The Chinese Festival* discussed at the beginning of this chapter was one such musical afterpiece.

Together, these afterpieces illustrate how the English stage had become the home of nonliterary entertainment. In the Restoration, playwrights prided themselves on their ability to fashion a well-turned phrase and unravel a complex plot. By the 1780s, however, the popularity of afterpieces, the demand for pantomimes, and the personal appeal of dozens of actors had transformed audience tastes from literary merit to theatrical excellence. It would be nearly a full century before a truly great English dramatist would appear who could be the equal of Wycherly, Congreve, and Sheridan.

CONNECTIONS

Several contributions to modern theatre emerged in this period. The rectangular shape of the theatre house, first used in the tennis court theatres, is still in use in American theatres and movie houses. The introduction of new scenic devices created a demand for visual realism that would appear in the next century. The lighting advances of de Loutherbourg first made theatre artists aware of the possibilities of that art form. Garrick's acting style changed the history of English acting and began a tradition that can be seen in the work of Sir Laurence Olivier.

In dramatic literature, new forms were created that are still being used by modern writers. The comedy of manners has become a staple of modern comedy, including the English drawing-room comedies of Noel Coward and the American urban-lifestyle plays of Neil Simon. *The Beggar's Opera* and the pantomime are the ancestors of the American musical comedy. Domestic tragedy and sentimental comedy together provided the antecedent elements of television soap operas.

The soap opera has many characteristics, chief of which is an all-suffering woman who is victimized by the inconstancy of the man she loves. Other prominent soap opera characters are an evil woman out to destroy the reputations of honorable people, trusting friends who always have time to listen to the heroine, men who know how they should behave but keep failing in spite of themselves, an older woman who is a guardian helplessly observing her loved ones make mistakes, and a businessman or professional whose chief function is to act as a reminder that life includes making money.

The themes of the soaps are also sentimental. To add to Alexander Pope's adage, soaps teach that to err is human; to forgive, divine—but to forget is impossible. Life is filled with travail, and one can never expect to find permanent happiness. Most people have good intentions, but they are persuaded by their own weakness to make the wrong decision. In the world of soaps, one must pay for one's past mistakes; wrong decisions bring punishment. As in sentimental drama, one of the worst crimes one can commit is to lie. People are accepted for who they are, provided they always tell the truth. But when people cannot trust each other, the fabric of society is stretched.

Of course, soap operas are different from sentimentalism in structure and imagery. The soaps usually run an hour a day, every weekday of the year, necessitating different handling of expositions and climaxes. The imagery reflects the modern American lifestyle, though as in sentimentalism it tends to be upper-middle-class Protestant and largely Anglo-Saxon. Nevertheless, the origins of soaps can clearly be traced to the plays of Cibber, Steele, and Lillo.

The Restoration began by being supremely satisfied with itself. The Bloody Revolution and the ideas of Newton and Locke strengthened the self-confidence of the aristocracy. The political system, the economy, and the class structure remained as these aristocrats wanted for the better part of another century. In that time, English drama changed very little. On the Continent, however, the calls for liberty, fraternity, and equality created the demand for new political forms of drama to accompany them.

SOURCES FOR FURTHER STUDY

Social/Art/Philosophy Background

Falkus, Christoher. *The Life and Times of Charles II.* London: Wiedenfeld and Nicolson, 1972.

Jones, J. R., ed. *The Restored Monarchy, 1660–1688.* Totowa, N.J.: Rowman and Littlefield, 1979.

Morrah, Patrick. *Restoration England.* London: Constable, 1979.

Reay, Barry. *Popular Culture in Seventeenth Century England.* London: Croom Helm, 1985.

Redwood, John. *Reason, Ridicule, and Religion: The Age of Enlightenment in England, 1660–1750.* Cambridge, Mass.: Harvard University Press, 1976.

Skilton, David. *The English Novel.* New York: Barnes and Noble, 1977.

Smith, Robert A. *Eighteenth Century English Politics: Patrons and Placehunters.* New York: Holt, Rinehart, and Winston, 1972.

Theatre History

Avery, Emmett, and Arthur H. Scouten: *The London Stage, 1660–1700: A Critical Introduction.* Carbondale: Southern Illinois University Press, 1965.

Gilder, Rosamond. *Enter the Actress: The First Women in the Theatre.* Boston: Houghton Mifflin Co., 1931.

Hogan, Charles Beecher. *The London Stage, 1776–1800: A Critical Introduction.* Carbondale: Southern Illinois University Press, 1968.

Holland, Peter. *The Ornament of Action: Text and Performance in Restoration Comedy.* Cambridge: Cambridge University Press, 1979.

McAfee, Helen. *Pepys on the Restoration Stage.* New York: Benjamin Bloom, 1916.

Nicoll, Allardyce. *A History of the English Drama, 1660–1900. Vol 1: Restoration Drama.* Cambridge: Cambridge University Press, 1952.

Price, Cecil. *Theatre in the Age of Garrick.* Oxford: Oxford University Press, 1973.

Stone, George Winchester. *The London Stage, 1747–1776: A Critical Introduction.* Carbondale: Southern Illinois University Press, 1968.

Styan, J. L. *Restoration Comedy in Performance.* Cambridge: Cambridge University Press, 1986.

Summers, Montague. *The Restoration Theatre.* New York: Macmillan Co., 1934.

Dramatic Literature

Hume, Robert. *The Development of English Drama in the Late Seventeenth Century.* Oxford: Clarendon Press, 1976.

Hynes, Samuel, ed. *English Literary Criticism: Restoration and Eighteenth Century.* New York: Appleton-Century-Crofts, 1963.

Loftis, John, ed. *Sheridan and the Drama of Georgian England.* Cambridge: Harvard University Press, 1977.

Marshall, Geoffrey. *Restoration Serious Drama.* Norman: University of Oklahoma Press, 1975.

Rothstein, Eric. *Restoration Tragedy.* Madison: University of Wisconsin Press, 1975.

Wilson, John Harold. *A Preface to Restoration Drama.* Boston: Houghton Mifflin, 1965.

C H A P T E R

11

The 18th Century in Europe

General
Events

Louis XV
1715–1784

Arts
Events

Theatre
History
Events

Bibiena family
prominent
1700–1770

The small theatre of Jean-Baptiste Nicolet (1728–1796) seemed a petty target for the cultural aristocracy of Paris. Nicolet had begun presenting simple entertainments at the local street fairs. His ingenuity had led him to puppet shows, and finally to the presentation of short dramatic pieces in a rented hall. To please his working-class audience, he included ample amounts of humor and even added acrobats and dancers as well as musicians. His group performed materials directly descended from the commedia dell'arte and pieces discarded from the Opéra-Comique as well as original sketches. As Nicolet's presentations began to develop great popularity, he drew the interest of the Comédie-Française and the Opéra.

Traditionally, the use of speech and "regular" art forms was forbidden in the smaller theatres. Nicolet argued that he was not in competition with the larger theatres; he was providing entertainment for a new audience, for the laboring class that composed nearly half of Paris's population at the time. A petition from the legitimate theatres in 1762 urged the authorities to deny the minor stages the use of either song or speech, limiting their activities to pantomime, acrobatics, and dance. Nicolet responded that his theatre contributed to civic order, and he suggested that the smaller theatres served to civilize the lower classes and to instruct them in such matters as morality and manners. In 1766 a governmental ruling decreed that Nicolet could perform no play "in either the French or the Italian manner." This regulation was apparently unsuccessful, for in 1768 a firmer order forbade Nicolet to use

Timeline

Maria Theresa	Frederick the Great	Catherine the Great	Louis XVI	Steam engine	French Revolution	Joseph II
1740–1780	1740–1786	1762–1796	1774–1792	1775	1789	1780–1790

Bach: Brandenburg concerti	Encyclopédie	Voltaire's Candide	Gluck's Orpheus	Klinger's play *Sturm und Drang*, Adam Smith's *Wealth of Nations*	Mozart's *Marriage of Figaro*	Haydn's 12 symphonies
1721	1751	1759	1762	1776	1784	1791–1795

Gottsched, Neuber	Goldoni calls for end to commedia dell'arte	Founding of Hamburg National Theatre / Lessing's Hamburg Dramaturgy	Barber of Seville
1727–1739	1750	1767 1768	1775

any play belonging to either the Italian or French actors or even any scene from them, and restricted him to "buffooneries or parades," and those only after permission from the authorities. Later years saw additional restrictions through excessive taxation (up to 25 percent of his income), limited times of performance, and reduction of repertoire. None of these was successful, however, and Nicolet and other "boulevard" theatres continued to prosper. Finally, recognizing that the smaller theatres had created an audience too diverse and too large to be served by the aristocratic theatres, the authorities relented, allowing smaller theatres to perform plays upon payment of exorbitant fees to the organizing theatres. Although the aristocratic institutions of the 18th century fought to maintain their ascendancy, the rise of the middle class appeared unavoidable.

Cultural images of 18th-century Europe offer a bewildering array of contrasts and contradictions. The age is often labeled the Enlightenment for the prominence of its philosophers and its optimism about social progress. The German philosopher Gott-fried Leibniz (1646–1716) exuberantly declared "that everything is for the best in the best of all possible worlds." Yet, absolutist monarchs dominated the map of Europe, the slave trade flourished, strict censorship inhibited many of the great artists, and philosophers could as likely find themselves in jail as in an aristocrat's salon.

Representative of the connection between the Enlightenment and the theatre is Johann Wolfgang von Goethe, whose influence on both the thought and the theatre of his time was such that he will appear in this and succeeding chapters. He was a scientist in his work on color theory; he greatly influenced the musical compositions of Ludwig von Beethoven; he dominated Germanic literature; and he participated in civic affairs. In the theatre, he was an author, a producer, and a prototype for the modern director.

Terms such as the Enlightenment and the Age of Reason have been commonly applied to the 18th century to highlight the rational discussions of social problems that characterized intellectual thought and several royal courts. Philosophers influenced monarchs and ideas shaped revolutions. Men and women of property would take long walks to acquaint themselves with their contemplative natural surroundings. Aristocrats even took to having their portraits done in Greek or Roman clothing to emphasize their connection to the greatness of past civilization.

SOCIAL IDEAS

The Enlightenment is commonly defined as a period that emphasized the exercise of enlightened reason. It was not so much a doctrine of ideas as a method of pursuing ideas. Rigorous intellect without attachment to superstition or bias was its hallmark. Many in the century were convinced that rational problem solving could sweep away the emotional traditions of the past and usher in a new age of progress.

Intellectual optimism was certainly one of the chief characteristics of the age. Denis Diderot (1713–1784) conceived of the idea of a vast encyclopedia that would bring together the great writers and ideas of the time. Diderot's agenda was to demonstrate the power of the mind to reason clearly. Begun in 1747, the *Encyclopédie* became a testament to the range and depth of human rationality. As such, it was a threat to the monarchy of Louis XV, who had several of the later volumes banned. The *Encyclopédie* had no consistent point of view. For example, Baron Montesquieu (1689–1755) argued for the retention of the monarchy as a rational organization of society, while Jean-Jacques Rousseau (1712–1778) saw little more than corruption in the society around him. Nevertheless, the work as a whole was a monument to the enlightened approach of the age to the concept of humankind.

To the philosophers of the 18th century, reason meant more than intellectual facility. It was common sense and clarity of thought. It was contemplation of human nature without any political or religious system that would seek to control the mind. Freedom of conscience lay at its core. Reason was therefore a concept that could engender social and intellectual unrest because it could be appropriated by the middle-class merchants of Holland and the colonists of the Americas as well as by the rulers of empires and tiny duchies.

Reason fanned the winds of change. Faith in the individual capacity to think led to a distrust—or in some cases hatred—of the social structures of the day. Rousseau declared that "man is born free and everywhere is in chains." Thomas Jefferson

(1743–1826) in the *Declaration of Independence* asserted "that all men are created equal, that they are endowed by their Creator with certain unalienable Rights. . . ." Jonathan Swift (1667–1745) wrote viciously against the poverty of Dublin. Thomas Paine (1737–1809) wrote, in *Common Sense*, of the urge to liberty. These and dozens of other writers set the stage for the French and American revolutions that in turn would usher in a new era in European thought.

Voltaire (1694–1778)

No philosopher held sway over Europe more than Françcois-Marie Arouet, known as Voltaire. A historian, satirist, novelist, playwright, and scientist, Voltaire was an adviser to Louis XV of France (1710–1774) and Frederick the Great of Prussia (1712–1786). His support of both political freedom and enlightened despotism (absolute rule by a monarch who is enlightened by reason) typifies the contradictions of the century. It also meant that he could be and was imprisoned by the very despots who sought his advice.

Voltaire was committed to freedom of thought. He attacked any idea or system of thought that limited a person's capacity to think. Some of his best writing is reserved for his ridicule of human foolishness and absurdity. His most famous work, *Candide* (1759), demonstrates the folly of unbridled optimism. Taking Leibniz's quotation given earlier, Voltaire fashioned the adventures of a young man whose tutor insists to him that this is the best of all possible worlds. The young man encounters one tragedy after another, always seeking to justify events in order to retain his optimistic faith. After having justified an earthquake, a rape, and a murder, the absurdity of his tutor's position becomes increasingly evident to Candide. The novel concludes that all individuals must forgo political, religious, and philosophical dogma in favor of "cultivating our own gardens." This final image is usually interpreted to mean that human beings must throw off all intellectual chains that prevent them from seeing the world clearly.

Kant (1724–1804)

If Voltaire represents the skepticism of the 18th century, Immanuel Kant is representative of the search for an intellectual framework within which to hold the ideas of the age. While other writers focused on the limitations of social structures, Kant examined the foundation of the enlightenment itself: reason and its uses. His *Critique of Pure Reason* (1790) and other writings explored the ways human beings think. He was especially attracted to the imagination and its powers of resolving contradictions such as the real and ideal, general and particular. His thinking evolved through his writings, and any short summary is impossible. He deserves mention, however, for the rigor of his thought, and his influence not only on his contemporaries, but on the Romantic philosophers who would follow him.

ARTS IDEAS

Europe in the 18th century is a study in contrasts: the drive toward popular revolution is juxtaposed against the increasing power of absolutist monarchies; the conviction that reason and sensibility can create a new, perfect social order is balanced with the irrelevant and irreverent follies of the aristocracy. In the arts, the clean, cool lines of neoclassical art coexist with the exuberant brush strokes of baroque and rococo style, while in music the baroque exploration of sounds and forms gives way to classical restraint and conviction. Yet even these generalities are tenuous because many of the artists of the period contained conflicting creative tendencies within their own work. Nevertheless, 18th-century artists capture in sound and image the same lifestyles and themes that playwrights and theatre artists portray on stage.

Music

The century includes two of the greatest composers of Western music, Johann Sebastian Bach (1685–1750) and Wolfgang Amadeus Mozart (1756–1791). Bach's compositions, especially for the organ and for choral groupings, came in the first half of the century, while Mozart's works were written entirely in the second half. Their distinctive styles provide insight into the stylistic contradictions and the range of musical tastes of the period.

Bach's work is commonly labeled baroque to associate it with the elaborate interiors of early 18th-century churches and the monumentality of European royal residences. However, Bach's prodigious output was so great that no single label appropriately captures his musical contributions. With the exception of opera, Bach placed his imprint on virtually every form of music then known. While working as a music director and organist, he composed music steeped in his Lutheran faith and filled with rigorous complexity.

Bach delighted in the fugue, a musical form shaped around the passing of a melody from one voice to another and combined to create counterpoint (the simultaneous playing of two or more discrete voices.) He wrote more than 300 cantatas, short oratorios that set a short religious text to music. His *St. Matthew Passion* (1728), on the other hand, is a large-scale choral and instrumental setting of the crucifixion of Jesus as found in the Gospel of St. Matthew. In a work of astonishing scope, passages of the gospel are given musical expression through the choice of vocal soloist, organ, instrumentation, or chorus. Of greatest importance to Bach, however, is the religious message; the *Passion* ultimately celebrates a deep and abiding faith in the New Testament.

When Bach died in 1750, his musical style had gone out of vogue. The quick rhythms, inventions of form, the terraced dynamics, and especially the religious impetus of his work were no longer popular. The fresh winds of reason demanded a musical style with clarity and pure musicality. The size of the orchestra was increasing due to the invention of new instruments, and brass and woodwinds joined the strings to create a new sound more compatible with the Enlightenment. This sound was later labeled classical and is most closely associated with Mozart and the classical symphony.

Mozart's life has been popularized in recent years by a play and a movie entitled *Amadeus.* Highly fictionalized, the story line captures some of the tragedy of Mozart's personal life. A child genius who began writing musical compositions at the age of three, Mozart was constantly under the shadow of financial ruin and a series of authority figures who attempted to shape his life and music. The popularity today of his operas, symphonies (lengthy compositions for an orchestra), and concertos (compositions for a solo instrument and orchestra) tend to obscure the constant struggle for acceptance he endured through most of his life.

As with Bach, Mozart wrote brilliantly in so many different forms that it is difficult to select one or two as examples. The sonata form, however, is representative both of the musical style of the period and of the kind of rational shaping of an idea that is associated with the Enlightenment. The sonata form has three parts, an exposition in which an idea is stated and usually repeated, a development in which the idea is explored musically by moving it from one voice to another and varying its components, and a recapitulation in which the idea and some of its variations are repeated or summarized. The sonata form, which can be used in any musical composition whether for symphony or solo instrument, has a simplicity to it; yet its structure allows for infinite variation simply by changing the musical idea. Mozart used the sonata form in many of his works. To it, however, he brought a musical invention that astonished his contemporaries. His ability to combine sounds, harmonies, and musical ideas was unmatched, even by his contemporary Franz Joseph Haydn (1732–1809).

Mozart's operas reflect the developing interest in that musical theatre form after the middle of the century. If his mind was searching for new ideas to express musically, he found a home for those ideas in opera. In *The Marriage of Figaro* (1786), he pursues with rich tones and sonorous melodies the joys of love, including the passionate uncontrolled love of youth and the gentler, mature love of the middle-aged. He explores in rhythms and harmonies the foolishness of those in love, and he resolves that foolishness in forgiving vocal ensembles. His world, like that of the 18th century, is dominated by aristocrats. But like the free thinkers whose ideas intrigued him, Mozart places in this aristocratic world a rejection of human foolishness regardless of the social class. In another opera, *Don Giovanni*, his version of the Don Juan character is an unrepentant villain, a man who beds all women and discards them without feeling. Yet Mozart sends Don Giovanni to a smoke-and-fire-filled pit at the end while the victims of his adventures sing, "Mark the end of Don Juan! Are you going to Heaven or Hell?" In *The Magic Flute* (1784), he sends lovers on a symbolic quest for truth in love. Before their love can be consummated, they must learn the meaning of that love.

The 18th century, then, was a period of incredible musical invention and creativity that reflected the contrasts of the era. It was a period in which composers sought to express their convictions about life in their work, whether through the Lutheranism of Bach or the naturalism of Mozart.

Visual Arts

Contrasts of a different order mark the visual arts. The subjects of 18th-century oil painters reveal a shifting perspective on social life. At the beginning of the century, the elegant and aristocratic subjects of paintings by Antoine Watteau (1684–1721) reflect a world of easy dalliance and social indifference. In addition to capturing the lifestyle of the early 18th-century aristocracy, Watteau is also noted for his paintings of the Italian commedia dell'arte actors in Paris.

Upper-class frivolity is chronicled later in the nude bathers of François Boucher (1703–1770) and the jilted lovers of Jean-Honoré Fragonard (1732–1806). The end of the century is noted for a return to a heroic classicism in Jacques Louis David (1748–

The Swing by Fragonard.   *Courtesy The Wallace Collection*

1825) and his political and moral calls to sacrifice. The aristocracy has met the guillotine and the winds of change have blown their lifestyle off the canvases of artists, replaced by a glorification of the Napoleonic ideal and the Greek and Roman models that were to become the basis of a new social order.

One of the great chroniclers of the irreverent and irrelevant lifestyle of the French aristocracy was Fragonard. The titles of his paintings alone convey the dominance of the goddess Venus over this elaborate world: *The Lover Crowned, The Lover Spurned, The Kiss, The Lock*. Often melodramatic in their placement of figures, Fragonard's paintings show his subjects engaged in the eternal pursuit of pleasure. They do not work; their concerns are conquest and sensual pleasure. Amidst a lush overgrown natural world that begs secret meetings and hidden affairs, lovers toy with each other and delight in delaying the inevitable.

In contrast, David's work is noted for a coolness, a distancing from any emotions inherent in the action of his paintings. The lines of his figures are distinct, the compositions are carefully staged, and the lighting and atmosphere are focused on illuminating a message of self-sacrifice and heroic abandon. *The Oath of the Horatii* (1784–1785) paints the story of three men taking an oath to avenge their country's honor, even though their women's families will suffer. The women are grouped to the side of the action to diminish the importance of their tears. The lighting focuses instead on the great dedication demanded of the men. Evidently, the Napoleonic era ushered in a new political order, one that called for a commitment to one's nation before one's class.

It would be inappropriate to leave this summary of the arts of the 18th century without acknowledging the audiences for these arts. As the century progressed, the arts were increasingly performed for a wider social spectrum. Folk melodies began to appear in the work of serious classical composers, the size of the orchestra demanded larger performance spaces, and this in turn generated a search for new audiences. The gradual disappearance of the aristocracy in the paintings of the period are the result of a new clientele for oil painting: the bourgeoisie, which sought to glorify its own values against those of an outmoded and outworn titled class.

EUROPEAN THEATRE OF THE 18TH CENTURY

The impetus of new modes of thought developed in the Enlightenment, rapid political changes, and the general sense of confidence that characterized the 18th century in Europe, all were reflected in the theatre of the day. New forms of theatre, new methods of organization, and continued changes in styles of performance created a lively and constantly changing theatrical scene.

Occasion

A key aspect of theatre developments in the 18th century was the diversity of offerings. While traditional theatre companies maintained the formal presentation of theatre on a regularly scheduled basis, theatre also was part of other social occasions.

In Paris, the Comédie-Française, the Théâtre-Italienne, and the Opéra maintained a typical commercial schedule, and other theatre companies founded during this century in most of France's larger cities followed their example. The theatrical season lasted from November to May and featured nightly performances. The two drama institutions performed a rotating schedule of plays throughout the season while the Opéra tended to perform one production as long as it was popular. Performances were scheduled in the early afternoon during the first part of the century but shifted to late afternoon (4:30 or 5:00 P.M.) later on, possibly as a response to the new theatres performing "on the boulevard."

These boulevard theatres, as they came to be known, were outgrowths of theatrical performances that were part of the fairs of Saint Germain (spring) and Saint Laurent (later summer-fall). Originally monologues, pantomimes, and acrobatics, the success of the performances gradually led into the development of various dramatic forms. As these events became more and more popular, they were also presented on the Boulevard du Temple, a traditional recreation area, eventually establishing year-

EARLY THEATRE DEVELOPMENTS IN GERMANY

*T*he development of a legitimate theatre in Germany during the 18th century was not the first sign of a theatre tradition. Although the lack of national unification, the absence of a common language, a continuing series of wars, and the relative isolation of many of the kingdoms delayed the arrival of a German drama, three different dramatic traditions were evident throughout the 17th century and even earlier.

In most of the larger centers of population, the court theatre featured touring troupes of Italian opera singers or French comedians. As early as 1652 a theatre was built in Hamburg, and Vienna had an elaborate opera house in 1668. These companies performed in their native languages and were extremely popular. The financial and popular support of the court and upper classes made opera the most common form of theatre until the middle of the 17th century.

Theatre also had a long tradition in the schools of the region. Protestant schools first, and Jesuit schools later, used theatre as an educational tool and as a public-relations endeavor. The Jesuits, particularly, made theatre an important part of the curriculum. Although performances were typically given only once a year, these performances were one of the highlights of the school year and were performed for an invited audience of dignitaries. Eventually, some of the Jesuit academies even built fully equipped theatres for the presentations, which gradually grew to include as many as 100 participants. The dramas, written by professional scholars, were written primarily in Latin, but musical interludes and ballet were also frequently a part of the performance. The texts were usually biblical and always told a story of Christianity triumphant.

More important in the development of the spoken drama were the professional touring companies found in nearly every city. Itinerant troupes had long been present, but the arrival of troupes of English acting companies during the late 16th century and throughout the 17th century provided the momentum for this theatrical tradition. The English companies, forced out by the intense competition of the Elizabethan period or seeking some form of income while the English theatres were closed between 1642 and 1660, performed a full range of English plays, including Shakespeare. To keep an audience, they gradually added bits of dialogue in German and focused on clowns as a means of ensuring audience appeal. Occasionally, a German player would be added for specific bits, and as the English departed, German troupes took their places.

The traveling players usually performed at fairs or other festivities. Frequently operating in a given province with the permission of the ruler, they proclaimed themselves the "court theatre of . . . ," although they probably never performed for royalty. Actors had no training and were usually young people with no other prospects for employment. The life was difficult, for they were poorly paid, traveled long distances, and were considered among the lowest classes. Scripts were rough and crude, and many parts were improvised.

Changes in the fortunes of these troupes were gradual. The troupe of Johannes Velten (1640–1695) represented a new level of accomplishment. Velten was university educated, and several of his actors were university men as well. Velten is credited with introducing the works of Molière to the German stage and with developing a more realistic and polished style of acting. He included women in his troupe in the English style, and one list indicates he had as many as 85 plays in repertory at any one time.

The plays presented by these companies tended to be crude farces dependent on physical acting and special effects. They mixed tragedy and comedy indiscriminately and were described by one participant as "amusement for the mob." A familiar part of the drama was the participation of a German clown who frequently mocked the main drama. Gradually this character was combined with elements of the Italian Harlequin and the English clown figures to create Hanswurst. Formalized in the work of J. A. Stranitzky (1676–1726) in about 1710, Hanswurst was a stocky peasant type, recognizable by his pointed beard, red jacket and trousers, and a conical green hat. He became a great favorite with audiences and was a dominant figure on the German stage for most of the century.

It was the touring companies that provided theatre to most of the people of the region, and it would be touring companies that provided the foundation, in the 18th century, for the establishment of a German theatre tradition.

round performances in that location. These presentations were extremely popular with lower- and middle-class audiences, and even the aristocrats seemed to take delight in venturing out occasionally to the boulevard. Gradually, different theatre groups developed specialties, so that on a given evening a theatre patron could choose from musical performance, mime, dance troupes, or comedians doing imitations of the latest successes at the traditional theatres. One form developed by the boulevard, the *opéra-comique*, proved so popular that the Opéra claimed it for its own. Before the end of the century, all opera companies were producing comic opera, at times even maintaining a separate company of performers to produce this new genre.

The success of the boulevard theatres alarmed the traditional theatres, who sought further legal action to restrict the upstart companies. Various rulings were enacted that attempted to preserve the status of the official theatres. At first attempts were made to ban boulevard performances completely or to schedule them only when they did not compete with the traditional theatres. When these failed, regulations were passed that barred the boulevard theatres from performing any of the classical plays or any plays in verse, since such performances were obviously beyond their abilities. Further, no impersonation of the aristocracy was allowed, and no political subjects could be addressed, since these performers had no knowledge of such matters on which to base their work. Various other rules were gradually developed that attempted to create a distinct separation on social class lines, and also to preserve the distinction between "art" and "entertainment." Clearly, the social contradictions and tensions of the age were to be found in the theatre.

In Saxony and other Germanic kingdoms, touring companies and amateur groups had long been the dominant theatre form (see insert on early German theatre, p. 250) with performances scheduled on a haphazard schedule determined largely by audience interest. In contrast with French attempts to preserve the literary theatre from the inroads of the popular theatre, the German experience is the creation of a literary theatre to replace popular entertainment. The stated goal of the new literary theatre was to improve the quality of theatre as part of a growing sense of cultural nationalism, to create a "German" language and culture.

The first major contributors to this movement were Johann Gottsched (1700–1766), and Johann Neuber (1697–1756) and Carolina Neuber (1697–1760), who joined forces in 1727 to produce theatre in Leipzig. Gottsched had already stated his interest in developing the German language to replace the Latin currently used in the schools and the French that was the language of the courts. The theatre, he contended, offered a unique ability to reach a large number of people in a unique way.

The Neubers were professional actors who had recently founded their own acting company and had some success in attracting a higher-class audience by performing verse plays in costumes on loan from the opera. Gottsched's literary reforms, which focused on adherence to classical tradition and the use of the theatre as a moral institution, were supported by Neuber's theatrical reforms, which focused on high standards of performance, regular rehearsal, and exemplary personal lives.

The company was only partially successful. Attempts to improve the repertoire were tempered by the need to attract audiences and the lack of available plays. Few good German plays existed, and audiences were accustomed to the traditional characters of the old-style comedy. Gottsched and Neuber incorporated numerous translations of French drama, including tragedy, classical comedy, and the popular sentimental plays. As a means of compromise with audience tastes, they frequently performed afterpieces, which were short improvised farces. Even a public ceremony in which the Neuber troupe banished Hanswurst from the German stage had little effect, and the intended reform fell short of its goal. Clearly, however, Gottsched and the Neubers were instrumental in creating a literary theatre in the German language that would be the basis of further developments when touring diminished, actors became more skilled, and permanent theatres were developed.

Similar goals led to the founding of the Hamburg National Theatre in 1767. The theatre was the project of J. F. Löwen (1729–1771), a literary figure and drama critic. Löwen's thesis was that the German theatre was hindered by existing conditions of performance, including the preponderance of touring companies, the poor quality of the actors, the failure of officials to provide support, and the lack of good German

CAROLINA NEUBER

First Lady of the German Stage

*T*he development of the German theatre was largely the result of the blending of the literary trends of the day with the traditional theatre tradition. One of the key figures in the success of this development was a fiery, outspoken, and dynamic woman, Carolina Neuber.

Born in 1697 and raised by a tyrannical father after the death of her mother, Carolina joined the theatre as a means of escape. After a failed elopement at the age of 15 ended with imprisonment, a second attempt at the age of 20 succeeded. This time her companion was young Johann Neuber, and the two of them found employment with the Spiegelburg Acting Troupe, a wandering company of itinerant players. Eventually they were married.

Carolina was an instant success on the stage. Her beauty and intelligence were great assets, and she soon developed a solid repertoire of comedy roles. Throughout her career, her key attribute as an actress was her versatility. She would ultimately perform successfully in French tragedy and in improvised farce, and was particularly successful in breeches roles.

After moderate success with several touring companies, the Neubers decided to form their own company, and shortly thereafter they had a fortuitous meeting with Gottsched, the leading literary critic of his day. They agreed to join forces, with both sides determined to improve the sorry condition of German theatre.

Existing records suggest that one of Carolina's major responsibilities was the political manipulation of officials. She composed numerous poems in tribute to various civic leaders and members of court, and wrote most of the company's requests for support or permission to perform. Her independence in this regard is demonstrated by an occasion in which she repudiated an agreement made by her husband, claiming it was meaningless since she had not signed it, an unusual claim for a woman of this time. This strength and determination are equally evident in her reforms of theatrical practice.

Determined to raise the social and artistic levels of the actor's art, she demanded regular rehearsal, careful designing and execution of stage business, and attention to the demands of verse. She demanded that all members of the company be able to read, since performing scripted drama required quick memorization.

continued

Offstage she was equally zealous, supervising even the public behavior of the troupe. The actresses of the troupe roomed with her and spent their nonperformance time sewing costumes or otherwise preparing for performance. The men of the company also took their meals with Frau Neuber and were expected to help with scenery and other duties during the day.

Together Neuber and Gottsched intended to create a legitimate German theatre equal to those in other European countries, but they were handicapped by a lack of excellent scripts. They introduced numerous French plays in translation and presented Gottsched's own writings, but were unable to find a theatrical form that was both enlightened and attractive to the German audiences. In an attempt to discredit the crude German comedy that still commanded the stage, the company staged a ritual "exorcism" of Hanswurst. In a classic *pas de charge* Carolina, dressed as Minerva, attacked and overcame Hanswurst, who was then slaughtered, mourned by the Devil, and carried off stage while the company rejoiced. Even this failed to persuade German audiences, who still demanded their traditional comic fare. After more than 10 years in which they were financially successful but considered themselves still short of their larger goals, the Neubers and Gottsched quarreled and parted company.

In her later years, Carolina repeatedly formed companies and returned to the stage, but without much success, working in Vienna for a time and also in Russia. On one occasion, her company's work (and a beautiful young actress) attracted a university student, Gotthold Lessing. He became friends with the Neubers, and his first play was performed by Carolina and her actors. Carolina never suspected that one unnoticed performance actually fulfilled her life goal. Although the comedy was only mildly successful at the time, she had introduced to the German stage the playwright who would be instrumental in establishing a legitimate German theatre.

Unfortunately, Carolina's life did not end on a note of triumph. After a period of repeated failure on the stage, she died impoverished, alone, and unnoticed. Denied a church funeral, she was buried in the churchyard only because friends passed the coffin over a wall at night. Only in later years would her contribution to the German stage be recognized.

dramatists. A true German theatre required a location in a major city (he hoped for Berlin, but accepted Hamburg), a nonprofit organization, a salaried full-time director, an academy for training, decent salaries, a pension plan, and prizes for authors of excellent plays. Surprisingly, he found a group of businessmen willing to support his venture in Hamburg, and he attracted Gotthold Ephraim Lessing (1729–1781), an established critic and playwright, to participate as well. Although the project lasted only two years, it had a major impact on German theatre. Lessing's *Hamburg Dramaturgy* (1768), published as a periodical during this period, became a standard document of theatre criticism, and the concept of a "national" theatre greatly affected the development of German theatre.

The 18th century was a time of transition in the theatre as the old division between aristocratic and popular forms of theatre began to weaken. Although opera and ballet were clearly defined as upper-class diversions, the spoken theatre appealed to all social classes and two patterns of response are evident. Either the aristocratic theatre attempted to redefine the boundaries or attempts were made to bridge the differences between the two. Each of these responses is evident in the development of theatre structures, style of performance, and the written drama during this century.

Location

Theatre buildings were essentially the province of the established aristocratic theatres, and changes evident in buildings constructed during this period reflect the desire to preserve the aristocratic nature of the theatre experience. Although concerns for safety resulted in some buildings being constructed of brick rather than wood, and architects and critics debated whether the circular or the horseshoe shape was acoustically preferable when building an auditorium, major changes in theatre structures were based on economic and social factors.

Economic concerns, as well as the growing interest in spectacle, led to an increase in theatre size. Typical theatre structures of this period included three to five galleries or balconies surrounding the "pit"; capacity ranged as high as 4,000 spectators. The stage space increased proportionally, with deep stages and large backstage areas providing room for vistas, crowd scenes, and special effects.

The division of the galleries into tiers of separate boxes, rather than open seating areas, increased the sense of social distinction, and the additional of private suites of rooms adjoining the boxes provided additional social prestige for those who could afford them. The final removal of standing room in the pit was an additional "civilizing" factor, and in some theatres these seats were usurped by the monied set while the lower-priced ticket holders were sent to the uppermost tier.

Lavish decoration in the theatre also attested to the social prestige of the traditional drama. Baroque and rococo decoration was often extensive, featuring huge columns, grand staircases, and intricately carved walls. Large public areas, waiting rooms for servants, and even covered porticos for coaches were further features of the large auditoriums.

Despite these changes in the audience area, little change occurred in the stage itself. The chariot-and-pole remained the standard device for scene-shifting, with additional scenic support offered by trapdoors, flying machines, and various sound effects. The art of perspective painting continued to dominate stage design, and new concepts in perspective painting required the addition of free-standing units at the rear of the stage to replace the traditional drop. However, the most significant change was in size, as monumental scenes of palaces and city squares became popular. The increased scale of the spectacle can be seen in a new theatre built in Bordeaux, France, in 1780, which featured 12 sets of wing flats (rather than the usual four) to accommodate the scenic spectacle.

Not all theatres were so magnificent. Many theatre companies continued to use older auditoriums, and nontraditional companies such as the boulevard theatres performed in converted spaces which frequently offered only a bare platform and extremely crowded conditions for performers and audience alike. The trend, however, was to larger and more ornate auditorium spaces, particularly as the theatre and its performing space became part of the national or civic cultural pride.

Performers

In a theatre in which the size and elegance of the spectacle were important considerations, it seems logical that designers were among the most important performers. Such was certainly the case in the 18th century. A vast majority of the leading designers were Italian, but their work was seen in every part of Europe.

Foremost among these was a remarkable family of designers. The Bibienas spanned four generations and produced designs throughout Europe, even journeying to Russia. The Bibiena style, a descriptive term still in use today, was characterized by tremendous perspective skill and an ability to render huge scenes filled with rococo decoration that still maintained a sense of rhythm and grace. Among their most important innovations was a move from straight-on perspective based on two vanishing points to *scena per angolo,* or angled perspective, in which the scene is perceived from one side rather than from the front and the perspective is based on multiple vanishing points. This eliminated the symmetrical stability of earlier designs and introduced a new element of movement and tension to the stage picture. In addition, it eliminated the rear vista that had dominated scenic design, so that the scene vanished into the wings, allowing the audience to imagine the continuation.

Eclectic in their approach, the Bibienas borrowed freely from Greek and Roman sources, managing to incorporate various elements in a harmonious whole. As tastes changed during the century, the Bibiena family adjusted their work as well, so that later designs began to reflect a neoclassical tendency toward linearity and harmony to replace the elaborate rococo designs of the early part of the century. Although the family members worked closely, with one member frequently contributing to another's project, they were not secretive about their techniques and even published detailed descriptions of their methods. As a result, numerous imitators flourished and the Bibiena style became the standard for design throughout Europe.

The critique of neoclassicism that characterized the Enlightenment relaxed several long-standing traditions in theatrical design and created a growing interest in historical accuracy and the creation of mood to support the drama. At the Paris Opéra, Jean-Nicolas Servandoni (1695–1766) introduced the full range of the Bibiena style, coupling it with an interest in creating actual locations rather than imaginary locales. He was particularly noted for a series of performances in which nonspeaking actors functioned as foreground for his settings, which represented actual locations that the audience might recognize.

A similar development occurred in costuming practices. For the first half of the century, the traditional practice of wearing fashionable contemporary clothing was maintained, although a trend toward more and more elaborate dress developed. Leading actors and actresses owned extensive personal costume collections of great monetary value while lesser actors wore garments maintained by the acting company. Traditional costumes, such as the *habit à la romaine,* and costumes for certain of Molière's comic characters, were also continued with little concern for any consistency in the costume style in a given production.

A Global Perspective

Court Theatre in Sweden

Although theatre in Scandinavian countries is usually ignored by traditional European histories, Scandinavia shares the dramatic heritage of Europe, with liturgical drama being performed during the medieval period, followed later by school dramas sponsored by the Lutheran Church, and later still by a gradual development of dramas based on local history.

The 18th century in Sweden provides a good example. In the 17th century, Queen Christina encouraged the theatre, importing opera and commedia dell'arte troupes and sponsoring amateur ballets. A troupe of French players was in residence by 1710, and the Royal Tennis Court was converted into a theatre to provide a home for the players.

A royal troupe, the Royal Swedish Stage, was founded in 1737, and their success led to the construction of the Drottningholm Court Theatre in 1766. Discovered in 1921 after more than 100 years of disuse, the theatre offers a remarkably well-preserved example of an 18th-century baroque auditorium. It was designed with a very deep stage and elaborate stage machinery (a member of the Bibiena family designed at least one show there), and was provided with traps, moveable wings, a rudimentary fly system, and machinery for cloud and wave effects. Also in prime condition at the time of the discovery were 30 complete stage sets by major artists of the period.

This theatre was at its height during the reign of Gustav III (1771–1792), when Drottningholm hosted elaborate summer festivals of opera, ballet, and theatre. The king, himself the author of several plays, revived the Royal Dramatic Theatre and dedicated it to the performance of Swedish plays. His death in 1792 was a setback to dramatic developments, and Sweden's first important dramas were not written until the middle of the 19th century. At the close of the 19th century, Swedish drama gained international attention with the writings of August Strindberg.

In 1753 the leading actress of the Théâtre-Italienne, Marie-Justine Favart (1727–1772), played a peasant woman wearing a linen dress with bare arms and wooden shoes, displeasing some critics; several years later she insisted that all performers be dressed in Chinese fashion for a play set in China, with her own clothes actually being imported from China. The author Voltaire and two actors, Mlle. Clairon (1723–1803) and Henri LeKain (1729–78), also encouraged historical accuracy in costuming, with Clairon noting that "costume contributes much to the spectator's illusion . . . [and] one must above all arrange his garments to suit the characters."

Their reforms were only partially successful, however, and for the remainder of the century costuming continued to be an unruly mixture of styles. In the printed script for *The Marriage of Figaro*, the most successful play of the century, the author, Beaumarchais, delineates the costume requirements, stating that all clothing should be in the "Old Spanish" style. He goes on to describe specific costume pieces, including prescribed style and color for each character.

Mlle. Clairon in a "Chinese" costume for Voltaire's *L'Orphelin de la Chine.*
Courtesy Bibliothèque Nationale

The interest in historical style and a more "realistic" costume paralleled developments in acting. Throughout the 18th century, the acting style moved away from the declamatory style of the previous era toward a more natural presentation. The style was firmly established in the 1720s when Michel Baron (1653–1729), the leading actor of the 1680s, returned to the stage at the age of 65, presenting a style that was described as familiar but noble, creating illusion "to the point of making you imagine that the action unfolding before you was real." Both Baron and the actress Adrienne Lecouvreur (1692–1730) were noted for their attention to detail and subtleties of performance. A different approach was noted in the work of two actresses who dominated the French stage after Mme. Lecouvreur. Marie-Françoise Dumesnil (1713–1803) and Mlle. Clairon were both famous for the passionate strength of their performances, although Mlle. Clairon modified her style toward the end of the career to include more subtlety and constancy of character. The inconsistency of their performances—some moments were riveting, others very weak—contributed to the growing discussion about the proper technique an actor should utilize for performance. [See insert, "The Paradox of Acting."]

The actor LeKain (1729–1778) was the dominant performer after 1750. Although he possessed neither the handsome face nor the riveting voice expected of actors, his skill in performance overcame these deficiencies. Critics of the day noted his skillful preparation, his ability to utilize his talents to the fullest, and his intelligence. Although

FAMOUS "FIRSTS": THEATRE IN COLONIAL AMERICA

1598	A *comedia* performed by Spanish military in what today is Texas.
1665	*Ye Bare and Ye Cubb*, first record of a play performed in English.
1699	First license to perform plays granted to Richard Hunter in New York. No record of performance exists.
1700	Assembly of Pennsylvania prohibits plays and other entertainments.
1714	*Androborus:* first play published in America.
1716	First contract to build a theatre recorded in Williamsburg, Virginia.
1736	Formal opening of Dock Street Theatre, Charleston, South Carolina. Students at William and Mary College present a series of plays.
1750	Touring company from England (Murray and Kean) opens in New York.
1752	First American appearance of Lewis Hallam and his company.
1758	Lewis Hallam, Jr., joins with actor David Douglass to form a united company that becomes known as The American Company.
1767	First professional performance of a play written in America: *The Prince of Parthia* by Thomas Godfrey.
1774	Resolution by Congress against extravagances, including plays. First of a series of patriotic verse dramas and satires by Mercy Warren, Hugh Brackenridge, and John Leacock.
1787	*The Contrast*, by Royall Tyler. First performance of a play by an American, about Americans, performed in America.
1794	Opening of Chestnut Street Theatre in Philadelphia, America's first fully equipped playhouse.
1798	Opening of the Park Theatre in New York.
1800	National Theatre is first theatre in the newly established capital city.

Chestnut Street Theatre, 1794.   *Courtesy Hampden-Booth Theatre Library*

he was not capable of the emotional heights of Dumesnil or Clairon, he managed to command the stage for many years. In Germany, Konrad Ekhof (1720–1778) championed the natural style. Ekhof's goal was to imitate nature so clearly as to make it appear that actions and words were being performed for the first time.

Later in the century, Friedrich Schröder (1744–1816) became the leading actor of the Romantic style. He excelled in the natural style as a member of the Hamburg National Theatre, but embellished his performances with a careful exposure of each character's contradictory characteristics, adding great range to his portrayals. He was particularly successful in the *sturm und drang* plays that allowed him to fully display his talents at portraying the extremes of human emotion.

Audience

Despite the serious efforts of designers and actors to create a more vital and modern theatre, records of audience behavior at the time create some doubt as to whether anyone would even have noticed or cared. Critics writing about the audience either describe a social event in which no one paid attention, or complain about the passive audience which the new theatres had created.

Descriptions of the opera, in particular, depict audience members inviting others to visit them in their boxes during the performance, serving meals, and participating in gambling games. It was a sign of social aptitude to know which parts of the performance were the most interesting, and only at those moments would one stop to pay attention. Some boxes even had shutters that allowed the occupants to close off the distraction of the stage.

Other critics describe the change that occurred in audience behavior after seats were put in the pit area. Denis Diderot (1713–1784) wrote longingly about the former days when the audience freely responded to the action on stage, shouting their approval or displeasure and becoming thoroughly engaged with the performance. He and others deplored the lethargic audience that sat in calm, cold silence and went away without ever making connection with the stage.

Only one aspect of audience behavior seemed to meet with general approval. In 1759 the Comédie-Française permanently barred spectators from being seated on the stage. Actors were delighted to have additional freedom to perform, designers rejoiced at the ability to expand the spectacle, and critics also approved a decision that provided equal access to the performance for every spectator.

Standards of Judgment

It was those same critics that provide a sense of the standards of judgment that were placed on theatre performance in their time. Not surprisingly, critics in the early part of the century support the neoclassical ideal, but the thrust of the critical writings of this century is toward a new concept of theatre.

Voltaire was among the first to question conservative readings of Aristotle. After witnessing performances of Shakespeare in England in which nearly every Aristotelian precept was broken, Voltaire began to conceive of a way to expand the theatre without violating Aristotle's rules. While maintaining the concept of the unities, he urged a drama based more on action than on words, and one that would admit a great range of behaviors within its definition of decorum. If art is to imitate nature, he argued, then any part of nature should be admissible as long as the representation is done in good verse and with proper style.

Diderot agreed with Voltaire's stand but chose to question the need for the strict genres of tragedy and comedy as defined by Aristotle. He questioned whether a tragedy has to deal only with persons of stature, noting that "whether or not the victim of passion is famous, whether or not his ruin is dazzling, the lesson is no less general in import." He urged acceptance of the new domestic tragedy, a form that was particularly popular among the middle class. At the same time, he questioned whether comedy need only reveal vice but whether it might not celebrate virtue, picturing the simple and good lives of ordinary people.

The playwright Beaumarchais (1732–1799) also defended the concept of serious drama as distinguished from tragedy. This new dramatic form, he contended, demanded a different style of performance. It required simplicity, truth, and a focus on action. Its aim was "to carry me far from the backstage world and to make it impossible for me to remember the banter of actors and machinery of the theatre even once during the performance." Indeed, Diderot's instruction to the actor to "imagine on the edge of the stage a large wall that separates you from the audience" is one of the earliest formulations of the concept of the "fourth wall" that is a key dramatic concept of the 20th century.

Louis-Sébastien Mercier (1740–1814) urged acceptance of a form that moved beyond that envisioned by Beaumarchais and Diderot. Noting that the aim of theatre

THE PARADOX
OF ACTING:
REASON VERSUS
EMOTIONALITY

*D*ebate has raged for years over acting technique. One of the most constant arguments is whether the actor should actually feel the emotion of the character or whether the actor's job is simply to reproduce the appearance of the emotion. One of the earliest and most provocative formulations of this question appeared in the writings of Denis Diderot.

A self-styled bohemian writer who was imprisoned during his youth for inflammatory writings, Diderot became one of the leading intellectual figures of the 18th century. His critical writings, his plays, and his leadership in the compilation of the *Encyclopédie*—a work intended to contain all modern knowledge—are all clearly the products of an Enlightenment man with absolute faith in the power of human reason.

His discussion of "The Paradox of Acting" begins with a statement that the an essential skill for the actor is judgment. An actor must have "in himself an unmoved and disinterested spectator." He states that an actor who depends on sensibility or emotion is unreliable and will perform well on some occasions but fail completely on another. He cites Clairon as an example of a studied actress who is always effective, and Dumesnil as an example of an actress who may have a moment of startling effect but be unable to carry it through the whole performance. The key, Diderot claims, is the ascendancy of the head over the heart.

When a person acts, she observes herself the whole time. She is not experiencing the emotion but rather is carefully detailing the truthful appearance of that emotion. The exact reproduction of a rehearsed intention produces art. The actor who relies on emotion will tend to develop mannerisms and become repetitious as compared to the actor who creates each role from fresh observation and carefully crafts a unique apparition. Versatility distinguishes the true artist. "Extreme sensibility makes for middling actors; middling sensibility makes the ruck of bad actors; in complete absence of sensibility is the possibility of a sublime actor," he writes. The triumph of reason and intellect allows the person to create the finest art.

Diderot's position provoked long-lasting debate. This very issue was at the center of a famous theatre debate between Henry Irving and Coquelin in the 19th century and still continues among actors today.

is to incite moral behavior, he then proposed that the effect of the theatre is based on emotional impact, not moral content. He agreed that the artificial separation of comedy and tragedy was a denial of a reality in which laughter is sometimes bitter and tears are sometimes joyful. He, too, defended the new form of serious drama and called for total abolition of the concept of genre, which he felt serves to inhibit the playwright from depicting the world as people actually experience it.

The interest in depicting the world as emotionally experienced is key to the writings of Friedrich Schiller (1759–1805). In a preface to his play *Die Räuber* (1781), he stated that a play that intends to teach morality "must unveil crime in all its deformity and place it before the eyes of men in its colossal magnitude." Writing early in his career, Schiller defended drama that depicts men who are neither good nor bad, but mixed. The purpose of drama is to present the full range of experience in a manner that will affect the audience, for the final end of drama is emotion. Such an emphasis on emotional truth was a clear indication of the close of the "Age of Reason."

DRAMATIC LITERATURE

Much of the dramatic literature of the 18th century was written as a reaction to the bourgeois theatre that had become increasing popular. Two popular forms of plays, the *drame* and the *comédie larmoyante*, both were sentimental dramas that relied on extreme emotions for dramatic effect. The *drame* frequently featured a tortured heroine whose life was defended through quarrels and duels, and some even ventured into the realm of horror. The *comédie larmoyante*, or "comedy of tears," was similarly based on the peril of an innocent woman and her eventual salvation through her own moral goodness and the efforts of those around her. Gross, irreverent farces were a third type of popular drama; they parodied serious comedy through the use of stock characters, songs, and special effects.

Many critics deplored the lack of new drama, noting that theatres were filled either with irrelevancies, revivals of old plays, or dull imitations of the classics. Throughout Europe authors responded to this challenge, seeking to create a drama that reflected the issues of the time. Some chose to refine old models; others chose to completely break from tradition. The result was a wide-ranging group of plays that sought to explore the possibilities and the limitations of the Enlightenment.

Marivaux

Born Pierre Carlet, the author known as Marivaux (1688–1763) left few clues about his personal life. A student at the Faculty of Law in Paris in 1710, he began writing in 1715 and adopted his pen name in 1716. During his career, he wrote more than 30 comedies, with his most successful work being done with the Comédie-Italienne in Paris. Married, he was the father of one daughter who joined a convent when Marivaux's financial position—he lost a great deal of money financing ventures in Louisiana—precluded her being able to attract a proper suitor. He wrote prolifically as a novelist, essayist, and playwright, and was elected to the French Academy in 1742.

Today we consider Marivaux a "classic" writer, but in his own time he was classified with the "moderns" who rebelled against the strict classicism in vogue among the educated. His writing is notable for its realism couched in a highly refined style. His interest in the minute psychological distinctions in human behavior, and the delicate quality of his writing, led critics of the time to invent the term "marivaudage" for writings that were excessively refined.

Marivaux was heir to a rich theatrical tradition. The tragedy of Racine, the masterful comedy of Molière, and the joyous romps of the commedia dell'arte were all important influences, and his plays demonstrate a successful combination of all three. Rejecting any theatrical excess, whether the boldly stated passion of the fashionable "comedy of tears" or the lewd and boisterous buffoonery of the commedia, Marivaux fashioned a unique and elegant comedic form.

In the midst of the "Age of Reason," Marivaux was fascinated with the concept of love and its ability to override all social considerations. His characters usually exhibit a nobility of feeling that contrasts with the growing cynicism of the age. This was not, however, his only concern, and his plays subtly criticize social, political, and philosophical issues of his day.

In one of his earlier plays, *The Double Inconstancies, or The Inconstant Lovers* (1723), a simple couple, Silvia and Harlequin, are engaged to be married. The prince, commanded by law to marry one of his own people without damaging her feelings, is in love with Silvia but is forced to woo her rather than command her hand. A series of devices including disguise, lies, and deceit are used to separate Silvia and Harlequin. In the end she marries the prince and Harlequin marries a woman of the court. In both cases, however, the matches are "natural"—Silvia's unfettered grace is suited to the nobility of the prince, while Harlequin's clumsy truthfulness is matched by the simple manner of Flaminia.

There is a dark side to the play, for essentially it relates the story of a seduction, carefully managed and manipulated by the prince. To Marivaux's credit, he manages to recast the story in a comic vein that leads to a happy ending.

Marivaux also included social commentary. The decayed morality of the aristocracy (portrayed in the paintings of Watteau) is repeatedly assailed by both Silvia and Harlequin, and Harlequin dismisses the pretensions of the court as meaningless. At play's end the manipulation of power, all questions of honor, and even the power of reason are futile. As she declares her love for the prince, Silvia silences Harlequin, saying, "My heart is too full. One cannot, it is true, reason with me any more."

Marivaux's ability to combine the elegance of high comedy with the characters and situations of the commedia marks the uniqueness of his contribution. Today his plays, including *The Game of Love and Chance* (1730) and *The False Confessions* (1737), are a regular part of the repertory of most European theatres, but he has not yet been popularly produced in the United States.

Beaumarchais

The plays of Beaumarchais (1732–1799) are rarely produced today, but they are widely known as the basis of two of the world's most popular operas: Rossini's *The Barber of Seville* (1816) and Mozart's *The Marriage of Figaro*. Originally written as plays, the two works are vital comedies that utilize traditional plot situations and familiar characters but are enlivened by the author's quick wit, deft phrasing, and mastery of characterization.

Beaumarchais's life—containing as it does court intrigues, international scandal, semi-secret involvement in the American revolution, law suits, and exile—could itself easily become the plot of an implausible play. His lasting reputation, however, is based on his skills as a playwright.

The two plays upon which Beaumarchais's reputation is based are in many ways highly traditional and reminiscent of earlier French comedy. The plots are essentially commedia tales, and the character types are familiar as well. Beaumarchais's ability to transcend character types and create multifaceted humans brings reality and vitality to his plays. In particular, it was his creation of the self-confident individual struggling against the restraints of a restrictive society that both displeased the king and aroused all of Europe.

The Marriage of Figaro (1784) is a sequel to *The Barber of Seville* (1775), in which a young barber, Figaro, aids a young count in stealing a beautiful young woman away from a possessive, tyrannical ward. The second play, however, focuses clearly on the barber Figaro. The count is now Figaro's master and, bored with his marriage, has designs on Figaro's intended bride. Various side plots provide added interest as would-be-wives turn out to be mothers, music teachers are identified as fathers, and eventually everyone ends up properly paired.

Elements to displease the king are evident in the play's subtle attacks on the power of authorities. Figaro questions the motives of the count, and the means of advancement at court, and describes politics as the ability to deceive, neglect, and promise.

Scandal is evident in Beaumarchais's inclusion of a young boy who is in love with every woman he sees, and the hint that one of the women might possibly respond. Attacks on the English and on lawyers are present as well, albeit the attacks are in good humor. Even more scandalous, however, is a series of speeches on the role of women in society. Delivered in a court setting by an older woman, the speeches describe women as the mere playthings of men's passions, condemned to a life of servitude glossed over with respect. The actors of the Théâtre Français suppressed these lines in performance, but Beaumarchais reinstated them when the play was published.

The play is most notable for a remarkable monologue delivered by Figaro in Act IV. Faced with the loss of his bride to the count, Figaro mourns his situation. He damns the count for having advantages simply by virtue of his birth. He rages against restrictions on liberty. He bemoans a world in which everyone is a swindler and in which honesty is unrewarded. Finally he questions his fate, observing himself as a toy of fortune who is unsure even of his own identity.

Beaumarchais cannot leave a play at such a point, and by the end all is restored. The final song offers several possible conclusions—that the clever man will win, that the strong man will win, that the woman will win—but concludes it isn't terribly important anyway.

Although the works of Beaumarchais maintain a light tone, they are not pure farce, for beneath the intrigue and the gaiety, Beaumarchais revealed a tinge of sadness, a human vulnerability, and the growing sense of longing and unrest that presaged the coming of the French Revolution.

Goldoni and Gozzi

In Italy, two playwrights found prominence in their attempts to create new forms of Italian comedy to replace the old forms of erudite comedy and commedia dell'arte. Although both Carlo Goldoni and Carlo Gozzi turned to the commedia dell'arte for their inspiration, they wrote very different plays.

Carlo Goldoni (1707–1798) was born in Venice, the son of a physician. He dabbled at playwriting as a youth (actually stowing away with a company of strolling players at the age of 14), but was trained as a lawyer and practiced law until the age of 40. Although he was married and successful, Goldoni could not refuse an offer by a leading theatre company in Venice to be their resident playwright. Leaving behind his practice, he returned to Venice in 1748 and during the next 14 years wrote nearly 200 plays. The jealousy and vicious attacks of critics forced him from Venice in 1762, and he moved to Paris to write plays for the Italian Players there, living the final 30 years of his life in exile.

Goldoni's first successful play was *The Servant of Two Masters* (1753), which used written dialogue and scripted action to recapture the spirit of the traditional commedia. Carefully plotted, using the traditional characters, filled with invented and inventive *lazzi*, and completely proper in its language and situations, the play is a monument to the commedia tradition. However, even in this early play certain of Goldoni's tendencies are evident. His ability to expand the commedia characters into full human beings adds depth to the piece, and the casual realism of his language and situations provide a sense of verisimilitude lacking in the old form. These talents were more fully realized in later works.

Mirandolina, also written in 1753, is representative of Goldoni's best work. The simple story of a young woman innkeeper who uses the full range of her intelligence and charm to subdue an avowed woman-hater, the play introduces stock characters who have been fully developed into contemporary citizens, an independent, self-confident and intelligent heroine, and an economical story line.

Goldoni was a natural optimist—he once had to move his law practice because potential clients found his demeanor too cheery. His plays exhibit this attitude, choosing to focus on the joys and tribulations of the daily life of ordinary people. However, even Goldoni's optimism cannot hide his social position. In a later play he notes that "Nature, that common mother, regards us all as equal. And the day will come when one pudding will again be made of both great and small." Such words will later be echoed in the cries for revolution that fill the end of the century.

Carlo Gozzi (1720–1806) was born to the nobility and staunchly defended his position throughout his lifetime. A founding member of a conservative academy dedicated to the preservation of Italian culture, Gozzi actually became a playwright to oppose the writings of Goldoni. Objecting to Goldoni's changing of the traditional commedia structure into realistic social comedy, and objecting also to Goldoni's politics, he challenged him, claiming that he could attract a greater audience to see a children's fairy tale than Goldoni could entice to the theatre with his new comedy. Although the challenge was preposterous (one critic compared it to telling Sheridan that "Jack and the Beanstalk" would outdraw *The School for Scandal*), Gozzi proceeded to write the first of his "Tales" for the theatre.

Gozzi's plays are an amazing combination of melodrama, farce, and myth, often combining literary allusion, physical comedy, and Oriental aspects in a single scene. In a typical plot, order in a kingdom is threatened from outside and order is restored through some type of magic.

In *The King Stag* (1762) the kingdom is threatened by the evil king's favorite, who gains possession of a secret entrusted to the king by a magician. Using the magic, he transforms himself into the king and attempts to seduce the king's bride. However, the magician himself returns and restores order to the kingdom. The virtuous are rewarded, the evil are punished, and the status quo is preserved.

The story is fantastical as a laughing statue aids the king in choosing a bride, humans are transformed into stags, and a parrot transforms into a magician. Complex characterizations are replaced by spectacle. Maintaining the Italian Renaissance love of scenic display, Gozzi provides multiple opportunities for magnificent costuming, vistas, and special effects. Scenes in which the peasants chase a bear across the stage, beautiful stags transform into human beings, and a flying parrot is captured after a chase offered remarkable opportunities for designers and tremendous delight for audiences.

Gozzi was not without a social agenda. His plays restore the classical concepts that the nobility are suited to serious drama and the lower classes are comic, even though they are all contained within the same play. Rarely performed today, Gozzi's dramas offer a strong counterpoint to those of Goldoni and enlarge our knowledge of Italian culture in the 18th century.

Two aspects of Germanic drama are of particular interest during this time period. Although very different in their philosophies and in their drama, each represents a significant contribution to the drama's attempt to define the relationship between classical values and the rising individualism of the epoch.

Lessing

Gotthold Ephraim Lessing (1729–1781) was the son of a Lutheran pastor. From an early age, however, Lessing displayed great curiosity in a wide range of endeavors, including foreign languages and theatre. His first play was produced in 1748—a fact that led his father to call him home from the university immediately. Various attempts to focus his education on medicine all failed, and eventually he gained employment as a critic for an academic journal. His most prominent work was as the resident playwright and critic for a new theatre founded in Hamburg in 1760. In 1770 he became librarian to a duke and remained in that post for the remainder of his life.

Although his greatest fame was as a critic, Lessing authored many plays that are significant in the development of the drama. *Minna von Barnhelm,* his most successful comedy, was written in 1767. It tells of a Prussian officer who falls in love with a Saxon woman but is forced to flee under the shadow of a scandal. Despite the formidable obstacles of his personal sense of pride, a bungled scheme to change his attitude, and the destruction of a letter redeeming his honor, the two lovers are reunited.

The play is labeled a comedy only because of its happy ending, for its tone is essentially serious throughout. In fact, Lessing's drama is surprisingly realistic in its portrayal. Set in a contemporary time period immediately following the Seven Years' War, which made Prussia the dominant force in the area, the play uses common German

Gotthold Emphraim Lessing.   *Courtesy Deutsches Theatermuseum*

names, fully developed middle- and lower-class figures, and language that varies to suit the occasion. *Minna von Barnhelm* is frequently viewed as Lessing's dramatization of the unification of Germany as the two opposite sides overcome multiple obstacles to secure their ultimate union.

Sturm und Drang

A contrasting movement in German theatre of the late 18th century is a group of plays classified as *sturm und drang*, or "storm and stress." It was a youthful rebellion against the limitations of dramatic tradition. Most of the writers were more intent on breaking rules (and occasionally stunning the audience) than in writing effective plays. Their plays are noted for multiple scenes, emotional outbursts, attacks on social values, and violent actions. Both Johann Wolfgang von Goethe (1749–1832) and Friedrich von Schiller (1759–1805) wrote a play in the *sturm und drang* style. Goethe's *Götz von Berlichingen* (1773) is the story of a medieval knight who, through 54 scenes, involves himself in robbery, war, political intrigue, and family love. Its dramatic unity derives from its adventuresome atmosphere and the vitality of its characters. Similarly, Schiller's *Die Räuber* (1782) relies on adventure and historical settings for its popular appeal. In both plays, the focus is on a hero who is an outcast from society and whose downfall is caused by his inability to sustain a totally idealistic perspective. Like others in the storm-and-stress style, these plays exhibit several new qualities including no unity of time or place, a corrupt society, political intrigue, and references to a sense of personal freedom. Although the *sturm und drang* movement was short-lived and ultimately unsuccessful, rejected even by Goethe and Schiller in their later works, it provides a foundation for the concept of Romanticism that will arise in the next century.

CONNECTIONS

The dominant art form of the 18th century was music. Bach, Haydn, and Mozart contributed their masterworks to this century, and the popularity of symphonic music was paralleled by the popularity of opera. Today both symphonic music and opera remain dominant art forms and attract large crowds as well as substantial and continuing financial support from individuals, corporations, and governments. Nearly every major city, and many smaller cities as well, maintains a resident professional symphony orchestra, and resident opera companies are also found in most municipalities in Europe.

The opera, in particular, provided the most auspicious locale for the presentation of the grand spectacles that were so popular during the 18th century and that remain a major aesthetic element of opera and theatre today. The dramatic size of the opera lent itself to huge stages and magnificent scenery, and this tradition is maintained today in major opera houses throughout the world. The appeal of spectacular scenery is clearly evident in theatre practice today, not only in contemporary opera but in the musical theatre as well, where huge sets, mobile scenery, and magical changes are a key component of the theatrical presentation.

"Atrio Regio," a scenic design attributed to Francesco Bibiena. *Bibiena, Atrio Regio. Louvre. © Photo Réunion des Musées Nationaux*

The 18th century also marked the development of a clear concept of "culture" as opposed to "entertainment." The division between upper-class art forms and those reserved for the middle and lower classes became distinct during the 18th century and remains intact today. The concept of "culture" referring only to those art forms validated by the aristocracy affects our own 20th-century view of art in which a distinction is made between real culture and popular culture.

Theatre frequently finds itself somewhere on the dividing line, not quite as clearly aristocratic as the opera, the ballet, or a museum, but not as much of a popular entertainment as rock concerts or the cinema. The struggle to define theatre's role began in the 18th century and remained a focal point for the next 200 years.

SOURCES FOR FURTHER STUDY

Social/Art/Philosophy Background

Anderson, M. S. *Eighteenth Century Europe.* London: Oxford University Press, 1966.
Besterman, Theodore. *Voltaire on the Arts.* Oxford: Clarendon Press, 1974.
Harris, R. W. *Absolutism and the Enlightenment.* London: Blanford, 1967.
Jones, Stephen. *The Eighteenth Century.* (Cambridge Introduction to the History of Art.) Cambridge: Cambridge University Press, 1985.
Richter, Petyon, and Ilona Ricardo. *Voltaire.* Boston: Twayne, 1980.
Robert, David. *Art and Enlightenment.* Lincoln: University of Nebraska, 1991.
Robinson, Paul. *Opera and Ideas: From Mozart to Strauss.* New York: Harper and Row, 1985.
Ruston, Julian. *Classical Music: A Concise History from Gluck to Beethoven.* London: Thames and Hudson, 1986.
Woloch, Isser. *Eighteenth Century Europe: Tradition and Progress.* New York: Norton, 1982.

Theatre History

Beiger, Agne. *Court Theatres of Drottningholm and Gripsholm.* New York: Benjamin Blom, 1972.
Bruford, M. A. *Theatre, Drama, and Audience in Goethe's Germany.* Westport, Conn.: Greenwood Press, 1974.
Carlson, Marvin. *The German Stage.* Metuchen, N.J.: Scarecrow Press, 1972.
————. *Goethe and the Weimar Theatre.* Ithaca, N.Y.: Cornell University Press, 1978.
————. *The Italian Stage.* Jefferson, N.C.: McFarland & Company, 1981.
Durham, Weldon B., ed. *American Theatre Companies 1749–1847.* New York: Greenwood Press, 1986.
Lessing, G. E. *Hamburg Dramaturgy.* New York: Dover Publications, 1962.
Oenslager, Donald. *Stage Design: Four Centuries of Scenic Invention.* New York: Viking Press, 1975.

Ogden, Dunbar, trans. *The Italian Baroque Stage.* Berkeley: University of California Press, 1978.

Prudhoe, John E. *The Theatre of Goethe and Schiller.* Totowa, N.J.: Rowman and Littlefield, 1973.

Rankin, Hugh F. *The Theatre in Colonial America.* Chapel Hill: University of North Carolina Press, 1965.

Root-Bernstein, Michele. *Boulevard Theater and Revolution in Eighteenth-Century Paris.* Ann Arbor, Mich.: UMI Research Press, 1984.

Williams, Simon. *German Actors of the Eighteenth and Nineteenth Centuries.* Westport, Conn.: Greenwood Press, 1985.

Dramatic Literature

Bermel, Albert, and Ted Emery eds. *Carlo Gozzi: Five Tales for the Theatre.* Chicago: University of Chicago Press, 1989.

Brereton, Geoffrey. *French Comic Drama.* London: Methuen & Co, 1977.

Gozzi, Carlo. *Useless Memoirs.* London: Oxford University Press, 1962.

Haac, Oscar A. *Marivaux.* Boston: Twayne Publishers, 1973.

Lamport, F. J. *German Classical Drama.* Cambridge: University of Cambridge Press, 1990.

————. *Lessing and the Drama.* Oxford: Clarendon Press, 1981.

Lob, Ladislaus. *From Lessing to Hauptmann.* London: University Tutorial Press, 1974.

Reidt, Heinz. *Carlo Goldoni.* New York: Frederick Ungar Publishing Co., 1974.

Simons, John D. *Friedrich Schiller.* Boston: Twayne Publishers, 1981.

VanCleve, John Walter. *Harlequin Besieged.* Bern: Peter Lagn Press, 1980.

C H A P T E R

12

Romanticism,
1780–1850

Prior to the opening performance, sections of the script had been leaked to the press, where they served as cannon fodder in the literary war between the classicists and romantics. Even the author was reportedly fearful of the play's reception, and he convinced the theatre management to give him some 400 of the 1500 tickets to distribute among his friends. Those who wanted them trouped daily through Victor Hugo's home, aware that a ticket to the opening night of *Hernani* was a symbol of membership in a new literary movement that was enveloping all Europe.

At one o'clock that afternoon, Hugo's friends lined up outside the theatre where they were pelted by classicists intent on provoking a riot. The management opened the doors at three o'clock, letting in the 400 Romantics, and then promptly locked the theatre. An impromptu party in the darkened auditorium occurred, punctuated with poetry readings and testaments to Romanticism. When the rest of the audience was admitted at seven o'clock, the theatre was in disarray. The auditorium was littered with garbage, and the Romantics were in a state of excitation like a crowd before a football game. Conservative aristocrats were shocked and the actors were terrified, but the Romantics were delighted and smug. These young men who were the center of attraction wore brightly colored clothing and long hair; a mixture of students, artists, writers, and sons of wealthy families, they expressed themselves freely and loudly. The unofficial head of this energetic group for the day was

Napoleon crowned Emperor	War of 1812	July Revolution in France	Revolution in European cities
1804 1806	1812 1815	1830	1848
Holy Roman Empire ends	Battle of Waterloo		

Arc de Triomphe	Mary Shelley's Frankenstein	Hugo's Hunchback of Notre Dame	Dumas' The Count of Monte Cristo
1806	1818 1823	1831 1832	1844
	Beethoven's Ninth Symphony	Berlioz's Symphonie Fantastique	

Théâtre National de l'Opéra-Comique	Goethe's Faust, Part One	Gas lighting at the Opéra, Paris	Hugo's Hernani
1801	1808 1812	1822	1830
	Present Drury Lane theatre erected		

Théophile Gautier (1811–1872). He was wearing pale green trousers, a pink satin doublet, a black coat, and a wide-brimmed hat resting atop a head of long ringlets reaching to his shoulders. The more the typical Comédie audience of conservatives commented on Gautier's appearance, the more he exulted in the evening's activities.

Before the first sentence was finished, some people in the audience were hissing. The opening speech brought catcalls. The entrance of a new character a moment later occasioned shock and disbelief. By the end of the first scene, the audience was bitterly divided between those who hailed the production as the harbinger of a revolution in the theatre and those who found the play distasteful and offensive. Arguments broke out during the intermissions and spilled over into the next acts. The actors felt helpless—no matter what they did, the audience remained in a virtual uproar throughout the five acts. At times the audience and the actors were more aware of individuals in the house than they were of the stage action. By the time of the final dramatic action, people were out of their seats, shaking their fists at the stage, demanding that such plays be banished forever, and crying shame on the actors who had played in it. Others were wildly enthusiastic, congratulating the author on his success, and telling one another that they were witness to the dawn of a new theatrical era. Whether the play was regarded as a success or failure, the first performance of Hernani on February 25, 1830, was a night to remember.

The riot at the first performance of *Hernani*.   *Courtesy: Musées de la Ville de Paris © by SPADEM 1992*

Because the Comédie was the symbolic home of classical French theatre, the victory of the Romantics in this theatre was the artistic equivalent to storming the Bastille. Conservatives were furious with the management of the theatre for agreeing to produce the play. Romantics rejoiced in the triumph of their new form. The triumph was short-lived, however, for the age of the Romantics upon the stage was essentially over in 10 years.

Two rebellions were afoot in France in 1830, one literary and artistic, the other social and political. The first was the romantic rebellion, and it introduced a new set of aesthetic ideas into the arts world. Traditionalists despised the aesthetic anarchy of *Hernani*, while Romantics hailed the playwright's refusal to follow the established conventions. The second rebellion was a continuing struggle between the French monarchy represented by the reigning Charles X (1757–1836) and an increasingly restive bourgeoisie. The king's opponents treated *Hernani* as a public forum for their hatred of the censorship and restrictions of Charles X's rule. Five months after the play opened, Charles was deposed.

No definition of Romanticism is possible, because for many artists it was a reaction against something rather than a movement for something. Romanticism was a by-word for artistic exploration, and each writer strove to place his or her unique stamp on his own work. As a result, the period is one of engaging contradictions, most noticeable in the range of individual styles of the various artists. The rise of a popular theatre (see the next chapter) is balanced by the inner search of the Romantic individual. Reactions against Romanticism, especially in the Germanic states, are as evident as many of the new approaches to the arts. This chapter reviews the Romantic interlude in European cultural history, but the full impact of the ideas discussed here is best seen in the context of the material in Chapter 13.

SOCIAL IDEAS

War, Revolution, and Nationalism

The Romantic era is dramatically framed by two major revolutions: the French Revolution in 1789 and the rebellions throughout Europe in 1848. In between, most of Europe, the Americas, and South Asia were engaged in major warfare at least some time during that 60-year period. Much of Europe battled against Napoleon, ending at Waterloo in 1815. Britain fought, at various times, with the United States (War of 1812), India, Burma, Afghanistan, and China (Opium War); and Russia and Turkey battled with their neighbors when not fighting with each other.

Internal revolts occurred in several countries. Demands for constitutional rights led to revolts in Spain and Portugal in 1820 and to the Russian Decembrist revolt in 1825. In central Europe the weavers rebelled in Silesia in 1844, demanding better working conditions and decent pay. In 1848, revolts broke out in Venice, Berlin, Milan, Rome, and Paris. Louis Philippe (1773–1850) abdicated the French throne; Ferdinand I (1793–1875) abdicated in Austria; and the papal premier was assassinated in Rome.

Nationalism swept across Europe and Latin America. Simón Bolívar (1783–1830) freed much of South America. Cries for release from foreign domination led to national movements in Poland, Hungary, and the Slavic countries. The battle for Greek independence against Turkey captured the imagination of much of Europe. Meanwhile, national movements in Italy, Switzerland, and Germany sought to unite nations divided into small city-states and duchies. Switzerland succeeded in becoming a federal union, but Italy and Germany did not achieve union until several years later.

These several wars, revolutions, and nationalistic movements had consequences beyond the loss of human lives. The wars created heroes and villains whose legends were quickly adopted into the folklore of their nations. The revolutions undermined the baroque legacy with its strict rules and closed social systems. New debates began concerning the rights of humankind and the relationship of the individual to the state and to society. The absence of rules ended the aristocratic dominance of the arts and ushered in a period of experimentation, growth, investigation, and artistic freedom.

To develop national pride, many artists studied and rediscovered their country's rich folk traditions, including tales, dances, and songs. Through all these trends, the cry of freedom was heard: freedom from cruel and unjust invaders, freedom from oppressive regimes, freedom from untenable working conditions, and freedom from internal and unnecessary political divisions. The battles were bitter, but to the combatants the stakes were nothing less than personal and national survival.

Imagination.   For the Romantics, reason insufficiently explained the way the mind works. It could not account for emotional attachments or sudden inspirations. Some other process of the mind was operating in these instances. That process must be important, Romantics argued, because it was natural; that is, it was free of any outside laws or regulations. The term they used for that process was *imagination.*

To the Romantics, imagination is a mental process involving several functions. It has the capacity to organize the sensory impressions it receives from nature. It creates a coherent vision from the jumble of perceptions constantly bombarding it. It also attaches feelings and responses to these perceptions. By virtue of these emotions, imagination invests the world with meaning and significance. In other words, our emotions help the external world make sense, *and* they give it meaning. In addition, imagination abstracts from the world around it: it can select a few images to represent the whole; it can perceive within an image processes that do not appear to the senses, or it can attribute qualities from one image to another.

To this point, the concept of imagination suggests a love of the external world and a joy in the contemplation of it. It suggests also an open acceptance of the visionary powers of the individual. However, a few of the Romantic writers went even further. They believed that in reaching out to the world and experiencing beauty, an individual would create inner feelings of love. Love is the attachment of the self to the perceptions of beauty in the world; it harmonizes the self with the external world. Love is not self-satisfaction; it is a union with nature and the universe, and therefore with God or the Universal Being. Imagination is therefore much more than a flight of fancy. Imagination is the core of a person's being, the spiritual force that gives the individual meaning in his or her life.

The concept of imagination was the basis for the Romantics' understanding and experience of the world. It gave prominence to the contemplation of nature. It led people to express themselves freely and openly. It encouraged individuals to explore and expand their own imaginative capabilities. It championed the relationship between beauty and truth. It also gave new meaning to concepts of the self and of nature.

To the Romantics, Nature is more than a physical entity operating according to immutable and knowable laws. An organic and dynamic entity with its own coherence, Nature is a unified complex of interrelated components deriving its meaning from the whole rather than from the parts. In other words, Nature is the landscape, not the farms that make up the land of the landscape. Infinite and variable, it cannot be apprehended in a single thought or moment. An ever-changing phenomenon of growth, decay, and rebirth, it is a vast swirl of infinite change. In those moments when the Romantic can experience the dynamic whole, the process is exhilarating and magnificent. When the infinity of nature overwhelms the artist, however, the emotional mood that follows is one of despair, uncertainty, or great sadness.

The Romantic Self is alone in the world, dependent only on him/herself to know the meaning of truth. There are no set rules or principles as in the Age of Reason, nor can one's perceptions and beliefs be subjected to rational discourse by a group of philosophers. Each person experiences the world differently. In the Romantic era, the world loses its center: the Holy Roman Empire comes to an end in 1806, absolutist monarchies are deposed or overthrown, and the immutable laws of reason are unable to explain the private emotions of each person. The individual is cast adrift in a sea of uncertainty.

The Romantic hero who emerged from this developed in one of two directions. The confident or successful hero accepted his social condition and enjoyed his solitude. He established his own principles of behavior and adhered to them regardless of the consequences. On the other hand, the tragic Romantic hero could not withstand the emotional despair in his life. He wandered the world in search of stability, acceptance, or permanence. He was a social outcast who knew he could never find peace in this life, but he could not help feeling cheated nonetheless.

In its philosophical orientation, then, Romanticism was a departure from the Age of Reason. It replaced the Reason with Imagination as the chief faculty of the human mind. It rejected the Newtonian depiction of the universe as clockwork, substituting a dynamic, unknowable universe. It placed the individual outside the social structure.

Liberty Leading the People by Delacroix.   *Delacroix*, La Liberté Guidant le Peuple. *Louvre.* © *Photo Réunion des Musées Nationaux*

Literature

The concept of Imagination, Nature, and the Self encouraged artists to explore new artistic territory. In all the arts, there was a virtual explosion of activity. Romantic literature is filled with some of the most popular characters in Western culture—Frankenstein, William Tell, Ivanhoe, Joan of Arc, the Count of Monte Cristo, Don Juan, the Hunchback of Notre Dame, Faust, and the characters of many fairy tales. The settings are exotic, historical, and mysterious. The actions are adventurous and extensive, usually involving some sort of a quest. The honor of the hero and heroine are demonstrated through great sacrifice and physical feats. The predominant themes are freedom, personal honor, national pride, and loyalty to one's principles. When love is involved, it often remains unattainable, but nonetheless beautiful and pure. The popular imagery of Romantic novels includes dungeons and medieval castles, mountains and inaccessible locations, sunsets and sunrises, oceans and lakes, and darkness and light.

Because Romanticism placed faith in the symbol as the creative link between the self and the external world, the era was a period of tremendous productivity in poetry. Shelley, Keats, Wordsworth, Coleridge, Southey, Burns, and Byron dominated English letters in the first quarter of the 19th century. In Germany, Schiller, Novalis, and Friedrich von Schlegel also wrote Romantic poetry.

Music

As in literature, Romanticism in music was characterized by expansion of the classical modes, introduction of new themes and techniques, a passionate exploration of tone color, and the development of new forms to express a range of emotions. Music became a national and nationalistic expression in many countries by drawing on folk melodies and popular dances. It was often programmatic; that is, it told a story that was included or summarized in the program. Melody was more important than form and structure, making the music easy to listen to for those without musical training.

Three composers in particular illustrate some of the characteristics of Romantic music. Franz Schubert (1797–1828) in his *lieder* provided short musical settings of German Romantic poetry. Hector Berlioz (1803–1869) in his *Symphonie Fantastique* (1832) expressed the feelings of a young man who drugs himself in a fit of amorous despair. Frederic Chopin (1810–1849) wrote piano compositions that symbolized Romanticism in music. His sonorous melodies, dripping with despair and melancholy, require great technical virtuosity in performance.

In 1827, the Englishman Charles Kemble brought his troupe of actors to perform in Paris and greatly influenced not only music but the entire Romantic movement in France. Kemble's troupe performed several Shakespearean plays, which excited the Romantics because the plays broke neoclassic rules. Their excitement fueled the burgeoning interest in new modes of expression that broke traditional codes. Berlioz particularly was influenced by the Kemble troupe because he fell in love with one of the actresses, and it is that love affair that led to the *Symphonie Fantastique*.

Painting

The Romantic era was saturated with artists, not all of great quality, who sought to express their intense feelings by elaborating specific moments and symbols that captured a special emotion or idea. At their best, they reached that level of moral reflection envisioned by Wordsworth and Shelley in their concept of imagination. At the very least, they articulated a new vocabulary of images rich with meaning for themselves if not for others. Each artist painted the world as he or she experienced it, and it became difficult to put any two artists in the same "school" or artistic movement.

In England, for instance, John Constable (1776–1837) depicted the English countryside with a vitality and spontaneity that reflected his deep reverence of nature. J. M. W. Turner (1774–1851), the other pillar of English Romanticism, was preoccupied with sunrises and sunsets, with the ocean, and with cataclysmic events of nature such as fires and avalanches. In France, Eugène Delacroix (1799–1863) let his powerful imagination range from political paintings on behalf of liberty (*Massacre at Chios* and *Liberty Leading the People*) to several canvases based on images from his trip to Northern Africa. In Spain, Francisco Goya depicted the ravages of war, injustice, starvation, and poverty. In *The Third of May, 1808*, for example, he paints the stunned horror of Spanish peasants being slaughtered by French troops allegedly for having started an uprising the day before. In Germany, Caspar David Friedrich (1774–1840) used soft hues, symmetry, and majestic settings to convey his conviction that God is in nature. In

The Third of May, 1808 by Goya.   *Museo del Prado*

virtually all his landscapes, there is a presence beyond the natural facts of physical reality. Humankind is a minor observer of a great panorama, an occasional intruder on scenes of contented beauty.

The Romantic era was a great emotional river that occasionally flooded its banks and overwhelmed whole sections of Europe. Its presence awakened faith in the mysteries of life that surpass the understanding of reason. It encouraged individuals to give free rein to their emotional moods, even to the point of fainting in public. It led to excesses of political zeal that were often doomed to failure. Yet, it was also a period in which the artist became a philosopher and a political spokesman. The arts, drama included, were a primary mode of communicating ideas as well as feelings. When a lady went to the theatre, at least in France, she experienced the play as an artistic statement and as a political symbol as well as an entertainment.

THEATRE AND ROMANTICISM

During this Romantic period, theatre was flourishing throughout Europe, and developments in France, Germany, and England were particularly influential on later periods. Romantic theatre was not the only theatre of its time, and the Romantic aesthetic was never dominant. Conservative theatres continued to perform and flourish with presentations that were still in the mainstream tradition of the Enlightenment, while others experimented with the new perspective. Romantic plays were not performed for special occasions or in unusual places: when produced they were part of a regular theatre season.

Performers

Romantic plays were typically filled with great spectacle and numerous scenes, and new scenic practices required to meet the demands of these plays. At first there was resistance to the emphasis on visual splendor. Baron Taylor once angered critics simply by producing a play that required scene changes within an act. The popularity of special effects and grand scenery was irresistible, however. At both the Comédie and the Opéra, plays were often selected because they called for novel events such as an active volcano or a flaming stairway. Louis-Jacques Daguerre (1789–1851), who later invented the daguerrotype, created the diorama that was adapted to the theatre as the panorama. It was a huge painted canvas that was attached to upright rollers at either side of the stage. By turning the rollers, the canvas "unrolled" from one side of the stage to the other; to the audience it looked as though the scenery was moving, but it was only the painting on the canvas that was changing.

More important to scene design was the work of Pierre Luc-Charles Ciceri (1782–1862), who specialized in realistic depiction of historical settings, exotic locations, and ancient ruins. Ciceri designed huge sets with great columns, walls, and stairways. He worked for both the Comédie, where he designed the sets for *Hernani*, and at the Opéra. At the latter, he achieved his greatest triumph: the setting for the opera *Robert le Diable* in 1831. For that work he designed an elaborate and complex medieval cloister that was remembered for decades. As Romanticism had given rise to unusual and dramatic settings in painting, so had it led to the same in the theatre.

To match the pictorial splendor of Ciceri's sets, new and imaginative costume practices were required. Some actors had their own costumes made, at times asking Romantic artists for their assistance. The huge sets at the Opéra, however, required large casts to fill the spaces, and this necessarily entailed some organization in the costuming of the crowds. Several costume designers became prominent in the 1830s. Paul Lormier, for instance, designed some 700 costumes for *La Tentation* (1832), based on the paintings of the late medieval artist Hieronymous Bosch. He was equally capable of re-creating scenes from historical painters or imagining a world of fantasy.

In lighting, the Comédie was still using oil lamps and footlights when *Hernani* was produced. Side-lighting provided some opportunities for theatrical illusion, but general illumination remained the standard until the 1840s. At the Opéra, gas lighting was installed in 1822, allowing for much greater control over intensity and atmosphere. The revolution in lighting techniques and designs was to come later in the century and is discussed in the next chapter.

As would be expected of the Romantic era, the acting style at the performance of *Hernani* was expressive and emotional. Hugo's stage directions specifically call for histrionic displays of despair and anguish, and the hero's quick and extreme emotional transitions ensured that the actor displayed great range in his performance. The action even calls for a character to stand downstage with his back to the audience, something that was still regarded as offensive at the end of the century. The usual stage picture at the Comédie was for the major characters to align themselves in a semicircle and then step forward for their lines. It was not unusual for an actor to omit lines in performance if the script asked them to go beyond their limits. Some actors even refused roles in Romantic dramas.

The Romantic style of acting was more successful in theatres other than the Comédie, because traditions were less entrenched. The most popular Romantic actor was Frédérick Lemaître (1800–1876), who performed at both the Odéon and Porte Saint-Martin between 1830 and 1850. Lemaître impressed audiences with his natural style and his unique interpretations of many roles. His spontaneity on stage convinced audiences that he was hearing the lines for the first time, something not common at the time. He also initiated many of the great Romantic roles including Kean, Napoleon, and Romantic adaptations of Hamlet and Othello.

Audience

The audience for Romanticism was essentially the same as for the other mainstream theatres, composed of upper-class people of developed artistic taste. It was not unusual at the performance of a Romantic play for numerous "Romantics," self-styled aesthetic revolutionaries, to attend to give the playwright their full, vocal support. The situation at the opening night of *Hernani* was one of the most volatile in the history of theatre.

Standards of Judgment

Since opinion was so dramatically divided and most critics either praised the new form or completely rejected it, the standard of judgment that prevailed is not easily deter- mined. The appeal of Romanticism was emotional rather than logical, and its power came largely through its disruption of accepted theatre values. As with many avant- garde movements, one of the major evaluators of success was scandal. To many of its supporters, a Romantic play was successful if it outraged the conservative theatre community, forcing reevaluation of existing standards and thereby promoting change and growth.

DRAMATIC LITERATURE

Romanticism was a truly European phenomenon, affecting Great Britain and most of the Continent. The general characteristics of the style varied from one nation to another according to several factors, but some aesthetic assumptions were generally shared.

Romantic drama considerably modified the classical model of dramatic structure. What guided the playwright was the exploration of some emotional state, not the imitation of action. Either a single emotion was intensified, as in poetry, or the hero experienced a full range of emotions in a variety of situations. Romantic writers, therefore, broke the traditional unities of action, place, and time, extending the action wherever and whenever it suited their pursuit of emotional description.

The central characters in typical Romantic dramas are the heroes or heroines who are in pursuit of their true selves. Only their emotions can be trusted (because they are natural) as guides to that true self. They may challenge the greatest evil, love the most beautiful person, conquer the most imposing obstacles, or break the most cherished social laws. In all of these, success is less important than the experience of the emotional consequences of their actions.

To keep such a central character from being simply a bizarre social aberration, the playwright usually gives the hero a noble purpose and an honorable intent. He is like us, the audience, because he has the same fantasies and dreams (perfect love, social justice, exceptional courage, personal freedom), but he goes beyond us by actually pursuing these dreams. Invariably his search pits him against a corrupt society in need of change, thus warranting his actions.

The freedom of the soul as expressed through multiple emotions and experiences is the dominant theme of Romantic plays. To universalize this, the hero's freedom can be achieved only by changing the world around him. This opposition of hero and society (or society's ruler) gives the playwright considerable latitude: by placing emphasis on the social corruption, the play becomes predominantly political and philosophical; by focusing on the hero, the play becomes introspective and reflective. In either case, tragedy almost always follows, because society cannot accept the implied anarchy in the hero's individualism.

The Romantics' belief in the moral dimensions of imagination led them to treat imagery as an end in itself. In Romantic drama, characters can invest a single moment with extended poetic significance. Especially in English Romanticism, mostly written by poets, pages of dialogue will be devoted to description rather than exposition or action. Spectacle often overwhelms the action altogether (Romantic writers were frequently ahead of then-current theatre practice in envisioning stage events that were simply not practical at the time). Music is also used to communicate mood and feeling and to heighten the emotions of a scene. Imagery does not replace or supersede plot (that will not occur until the Symbolist movement at the end of the 19th century), but it receives greater attention than had become customary in sentimental dramas and neoclassic works of the 18th century.

Two giants of German drama before 1900 are among the earliest to be associated with Romanticism. Although both wrote in several literary styles, they are most associated with Weimar classicism, which is covered in the next chapter. However, both Johann Wolfgang von Goethe (1749–1832) and Friedrich von Schiller (1759–1805) produced at least one major work in the Romantic style. Goethe's most ambitious drama is the two-part *Faust*, with Part One published in 1808 and Part Two in 1831. Part One is often labeled Romantic by critics, while the second is regarded as classical. Even though there are many Romantic characteristics in the first part, Goethe himself rejected the Romantic label for his work. The Faust legend, with its intellectual hero who makes a pact with the devil in order to learn the secrets of the universe, is reworked by Goethe to illustrate several ideas. The search for salvation, the renunciation of one's sins, the limitations of human knowledge, and the power of creativity are but four of the many themes critics have found in the play. The Romantic overtones in these themes is apparent.

Only in *William Tell* (1804) does Schiller write a drama that critics regard as Romantic. The famous scene of Tell shooting the apple from his son's head occurs in Act III, but the bulk of the drama tells of the rebellion of the Swiss against foreign rule and corrupt aristocrats. From the opening scene, in which Tell risks his life to ferry a peasant across a lake during a terrible storm, the play is filled with heroic adventures. Night-time conspiracies, reports of injustice, and two conversions to the Swiss rebellion by a man and woman who find love together in the cause of freedom dominate the action. William Tell himself is a Romantic hero in his folk origins, his solitary lifestyle, and his determination to uphold his honor and reputation. He is the savior of the Swiss, willing to do whatever he must for freedom and justice. He does not seek adventure or honors, but he always responds to calls for assistance. The imagery of the play is also Romantic: lakes, storms, mountains, thunder, light and dark, dungeons and deer. The dominant image in the play is a circle representing unity, strength, and infinity. Schiller died the year after the play was produced.

In the same year, Ludwig Tieck (1773–1853) wrote *Kaiser Octavianus*, a sprawling study of Christianity. Tieck was one of the few German Romantic writers who wrote drama. August Wilhelm von Schlegel (1767–1845) contributed to the movement by translating many of Shakespeare's plays, thus sustaining that writer's popularity in Germany and keeping his nonclassical style before German audiences. Other Romantics wrote plays, but many of them were never intended for production and few of the others were successful.

Heinrich von Kleist (1777–1811) wrote several plays that have some Romantic qualities but are primarily concerned with the neoclassic conflict between love and honor. Georg Büchner (1813–1837) wrote just three, one of which (*Woyzeck*, 1836) shows influences of storm and stress and Romanticism in its break with dramatic conventions. Christian Friedrich Hebbel (1813–1863) began his career as a Romantic but turned instead to prose, real-life characters, and domestic situations to present his conflicts between the old and new order.

French Romantic plays were in verse, usually with historical subjects. They were expressions of romantic love in which the hero and heroine are prevented from realizing their love by some external force. They were rarely theoretical or philosophical. The characters want freedom to express themselves, but they do not discuss the meaning of freedom. They believe in honor and justice, but the social or philosophical significance of those terms seldom matters. The core of French Romantic drama is the expression of the soul in love and honor.

When Victor Hugo (1802–1885) published the "Preface" to his historical drama *Cromwell* in 1827, he contributed to a growing momentum on behalf of Romanticism. His "Preface" was a plea on behalf of nature against art. He opposed the classical rules for writing—especially the unities of time, place, and action. He developed the theory of the Grotesque, insisting that ugliness in life is as worthy of poetic attention as beauty. In the same year that this artistic manifesto appeared, Charles Kemble's acting company arrived from London to produce Shakespeare's plays and send the liberal Parisian audiences into ecstasy. In 1828, Hugo's *Amy Robsart*, based on a novel of Sir Walter Scott's, was performed. The following year several Romantic works appeared. The traditionalists decided to make their final stand against the movement with the opening of *Hernani.*

The play is set in Spain in medieval times. The hero is an outcast, a rebel with

Douglas Fairbanks, Jr., in *The Black Pirate.*   *Courtesy Museum of Modern Art/Film Stills Archive*

a grievance against the king, Don Carlos. The king's father took Hernani's estate and sentenced him to death. Hernani's hatred is fueled when he discovers that the king loves the same woman he does, Doña Sol. Hernani's goal in the play is to love freely and passionately, something he cannot do unless he seeks revenge against the king. When he is with Doña Sol, he is consumed with revenge and the impossibility of their love ever being consummated. Doña Sol is in many ways a minor character. She loves Hernani but has little time to express it because she is interrupted by his despair or the king's arrival. She lives in the castle of an extremely honorable and honest old duke who protects Hernani when the king comes for him, simply because the code of honor to protect a guest must be followed. In exchange, Hernani offers his life to the duke at any later time. All problems appear to be solved when the king becomes the Holy Roman Emperor. He pardons Hernani and unites him with both his estate and Doña Sol (she is now beneath his status). The happy reunion is spoiled, however, when the duke comes for his pledge. Hernani balks at suicide, but Doña Sol shows him his only course of action by drinking the poison first, and Hernani then joins her.

Hugo succeeded with *Hernani* because of the play's dark, swarthy, and courageous hero, and its moments of self-reflective humor. He had mixed success with his other plays in the 1830s. *Marion Delorme* (1831) and *Ruy Blas* (1838) were popular, but *The King Amuses Himself* (1832), an outright attack on the monarchy, and *Don Juan de Marana* (1835) were not.

Alexandre Dumas *père* (1802–1870) is today known for the swashbuckling heroes in his novels *The Count of Monte Cristo* and *The Three Musketeers*. His Romantic dramas were often as popular as Hugo's, however. He assisted the Romantic passion sweeping Paris in 1829 with *Henry III and His Sons* and *Christine*. He also wrote a Romantic drama in modern dress, *Antony* in 1831, and dramatized several of his novels. His *Mademoiselle de Belle-Isle* (1834, usually translated as *The Great Lover*) is one of the few successful Romantic comedies to be written in the period.

Romanticism never completely left the Paris stage in the 19th century. Even after 1843, Dumas *père* continued to write plays, and a revival of Romantic drama came at the end of the century. Edmund Rostand (1868–1918) wrote the most enduringly popular Romantic play in 1897, *Cyrano de Bergerac*. The brilliant swordsman and poet with the extremely long nose is a tour de force for actors. Cyrano's love for the most beautiful woman in France in spite of his deformity, and his ability to write poems while sword-fighting, is a virtual catalogue of French Romantic characteristics.

English Drama

Romantic drama did not fare well in England. Despite the presence of several great actors to interpret them, few English plays between 1790 and 1840 achieved critical acclaim. Virtually none of them is performed today. The great poets of English Romanticism wrote plays, but only those of Shelley and Byron are at all effective.

Percy Bysshe Shelley (1792–1822) wrote *The Cenci* (1819) and *Prometheus Unbound* (1820). The first is filled with the horrible deeds, passionate declamations, political intrigues, and acts of revenge found in many Continental plays. *Prometheus* is more of a dramatic poem, because the visions and celestial beings that visit the hero could not be effectively realized on stage.

George Gordon, Lord Byron (1788–1824), insisted that his plays were not meant for production. His sense of dramatic action and characterization was sure, however, and his plays were occasionally performed because they were excellent vehicles for star actors. Byron's heroes are often in search of peace of mind; they are troubled by their past, their fears of those around them, or their premonitions of the future. Injustice is rampant in the societies of his plays, but there is little hope that it can be eradicated. The hero wishes only to escape it all. In *Manfred* (1817), the hero wants only to commune with the isolation and beauty of nature. In *The Two Foscari* (1821), the Venetian ruler and his family are content to die at the hands of unjust political enemies, if only they can witness the natural beauty of their beloved city before death. *Werner* (1830) thinks he will find peace when his life-long enemy is murdered, but his recurring premonitions are justified when he learns that it is his son who is the murderer.

CONNECTIONS

The contributions of the Romantic era to 20th-century theatre and film should be evident. Historical dramas, sprawling epics, breathtaking adventures, and exotic travelogues are all indebted to Romanticism. The musical comedies of Rodgers and Hammerstein are Romantic in their love of nature, their unabashed expression of emotion, and their heroes who are at odds with their societies. Other examples of Romanticism in musicals are *Man of La Mancha*, with its outcast hero following an impossible dream; *1776*, which romanticizes the signing of the Declaration of Independence; and *Hair*, with its call for a new age by breaking down the traditions of the past. American films of the 1970s and 1980s featured heroes removed from their surroundings, solitary and sullen. They are reluctant but determined defenders of justice, caught up in adventures in spite of themselves. Other films glorified antisocial behavior with heroic stature, ranging from *Bonnie and Clyde* and *The Electric Horseman* to *Gandhi*.

In television, many of the successful miniseries have romantic elements, especially *Roots*, *Shogun*, and *The Thorn Birds*. In the 1950s and 1960s, many popular series centered around Western heroes who were solitary men with a strong sense of justice and a knack for getting into dangerous adventures. The Romantic myth of the American cowboy also appeared in many of the most popular Hollywood Westerns, including *Shane*, *High Noon*, and *The Lone Ranger*.

Typical of contemporary Romanticism is the movie blockbuster trilogy beginning with *Star Wars* (1977). The story is of Luke Skywalker, who learns to trust "the force," his natural instincts, while combating injustice and evil in a corrupt universe. He races from one adventure to another, all of them in exotic locations with dozens of bizarre characters, and all of them requiring him to test himself in increasingly difficult circumstances. Luke is a standard romantic hero in that he is someone like us (a youngster who wants to discover himself but whose parental authority wants him to stay at home), who holds values the audience would like to see realized. The society he finds himself in is as corrupt as any imagined by Hugo or Byron: the Empire is a cold machine of automaton-like people determined to crush any rebellion against authority. The imagery is Romantic in its love of spectacle and theatrical gadgetry, its contrast of natural feelings and impersonal machines, and its location of the rebels' stronghold in the only thickly forested area seen in the movie. Notably, Luke and his heroine, Leia, are not as interested in romance as in justice and adventure; by the third film in the series, their love has been eliminated altogether. Romanticism may not have produced many great plays in the 19th century, but its traditions clearly spawned many popular works in the 20th.

SOURCES FOR FURTHER STUDY

Bowra, C. M. *The Romantic Imagination.* New York: Oxford University Press, 1961.

Carlson, Marvin. *The German Stage in the Nineteenth Century.* Metuchen, N.J.: Scarecrow Press, 1972.

Daniels, Barry V. *Revolution in the Theatre: French Romantic Theories of Drama.* Westport, Conn.: Greenwood Press, 1983.

Donohue, Joseph W., Jr. *Dramatic Character in the English Romantic Age.* Princeton, N.J.: Princeton University Press, 1970.

Draper, F. W. M. *The Rise and Fall of French Romantic Drama.* London: Constable, 1923.

Driver, Tom F. *Romantic Quest and Modern Query: History of the Modern Theatre.* New York: Dell Publishing, 1971.

Einstein, Alfred. *Music in the Romantic Era.* New York: W. W. Norton, 1947.

Engell, James. *The Creative Imagination: Enlightenment to Romanticism.* Cambridge, Mass.: Harvard University Press, 1981.

Fairley, Barker. *A Study of Goethe.* Oxford: Oxford University Press, 1947.

Goethe, Johann Wolfgang von. *Goethe on Theatre.* Trans. John Osenford. New York: Columbia University, 1919.

————. *The Sorrows of Young Werther* and *Novella.* Trans. Elizabeth Mayer and Louise Bogan. New York: Vintage Books, 1971.

Kelly, Linda. *The Young Romantics.* New York: Random House, 1976.

Le Bris, Michel. *Romantics and Romanticism.* New York: Sira/Rizzoli, 1981.

Lister, Raymond. *British Romantic Art.* London: G. Bell and Sons, 1973.

Peyre, Henri. *What Is Romanticism?* Trans. Roda Roberts. Tuscaloosa: University of Alabama Press, 1977.

Rossini's
Barber of Seville

Arts
Events

1816

Gas lighting
at Drury Lane

Theatre
History
Events

1817   1823

Kemble's
King John

The 19th Century: The Growth of Popular Theatre

His farewell performances had begun almost two years ago. He played for the last times his most famous roles and made his final appearances at various theatres outside of London. Now, at the Drury Lane on February 26, 1851, he was giving his "last time forever" interpretation of Macbeth. Astute observers could comment to the growing crowds outside the theatre that this performance was the end of an era, for the star was associated with the playing of classics at a time when the London stage was becoming inundated with visual and musical spectacle at the expense of the written word. Other critics could counter that the innovations of the man who had brought them together that night were transfroming the English theatre. He had restored Shakespeare's scripts to the original form, eliminating 18th-century editions that removed the Fool from *King Lear* and added love scenes to the tragedies. He had markedly improved the audience environment in the theatre by banishing prostitutes from the theatres altogether, by placing individual seats or stalls in the pit instead of benches, by numbering the seats to allow for advance reservations, and by eliminating the puffs or journalists who advertised the plays with extravagant claims. As an actor, a director, and a manager he had demanded of and for the theatre the dignity and importance he felt it deserved. On this special evening, the affection of theatregoers for this man was never in doubt: thousands of people queued up to get the

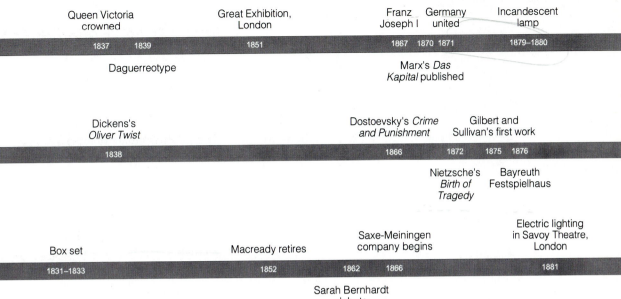

Queen Victoria crowned		Great Exhibition, London		Franz Joseph I	Germany united		Incandescent lamp
1837	1839	1851		1867	1870	1871	1879–1880
	Daguerreotype				Marx's *Das Kapital* published		

Dickens's *Oliver Twist*			Dostoevsky's *Crime and Punishment*		Gilbert and Sullivan's first work	
1838			1866	1872	1875	1876
				Nietzsche's *Birth of Tragedy*	Bayreuth Festspielhaus	

						Electric lighting in Savoy Theatre, London
Box set		Macready retires		Saxe-Meiningen company begins		
1831–1833		1852	1862	1866		1881
			Sarah Bernhardt debuts			

unreserved tickets for the pit and gallery. Some 2,000 more had purchased tickets in advance. The unlucky ones would stand in the theatre lobby or outside in the cold air throughout the evening. All wanted to be a part of the event that marked the end of the career of one of the most famous tragedians of the 19th century, William Charles Macready (1793–1873).

The theatre that night was probably filled with the literary elite and the aristocratic social set, for Macready, to them, was the last of the "classic" actors. However, most London theatres were filled with clerks, tellers, and tradesmen who cared little for intellectual ideas or literary excellence. They were hard-working citizens of the Industrial Revolution; their chief concerns were making money in an emergent mercantile economy and sustaining the family in a time of social upheaval. They packed the theatres nightly. By their purchase of tickets to different kinds of drama and their demonstrable ovations for particular plays, they virtually created a new concept of theatrical entertainment. No longer filled with poetry or literary allusion, presented in a simple and unaffected acting style, and based on shameless emotional appeal, the theatre of the 19th century reflected the attitudes of a rapidly changing world.

The Industrial Revolution

In 1851, England celebrated the Industrial Revolution with the first international fair dedicated to trade and industry. The Great Exhibition of the Works of Industry of All Nations was a festival in honor of economic progress and industrial wealth. It celebrated Britain's economic achievements and honored the machine as the source of Britain's national status. Not to be outdone, the French offered their tribute to industry in 1867. As with the earlier English exhibit, the French version displayed the excesses and extravagances of huge machinery and industrial equipment. The exhibit intended to honor industry, but a side effect was to remind the average spectator that an economy built with such machinery was necessary to the welfare and future of the nation.

These two exhibits heralded the benefits of industrialization, but the price paid for the new economy was a social transformation of nearly unprecedented dimensions. At the top of the economic scale, wealthy merchants challenged the power of the old estates. They created and managed companies of clerks, and factories of workers, who were enlisted for the manufacture of products they seldom saw or could little afford. Speed of delivery and volume became determinants of business success, encouraging managers to force employees to work harder for longer hours. More workers meant more volume, and workers were brought together in increasingly larger work configurations.

No precedents existed for dealing with the squalid urban conditions that resulted from this social disruption, especially in England. There were no child labor laws, no social security plans, no union regulations or unemployment compensation plans to protect the workers from economic despair. Starvation, slums, orphans, and disease became facts of daily life. Yet, no social theories existed to deal with those effects. A new concept of social justice was needed to provide governments with guidelines for correcting the situation.

Social Justice

The shocking urban conditions of the century could not be ignored. Except in the most reactionary duchies of central Europe, where the Industrial Revolution would not arrive until the end of the century, politicians and social thinkers had no alternative but to attempt some solution for the destitution and deprivation of the poor. England, the nation in which the Industrial Revolution occurred earliest, produced some of the earliest proposals for the political reform of the social system, notably the ideas of Jeremy Bentham (1748–1832), John Stuart Mill (1806–1873), and Robert Owen (1771–1858). It also produced a moral liberalism that preferred educational and moral reform to political change. Both movements were fostered by writers like Charles Dickens (1812–1870), who drew attention to the conditions of the poor. In France, several other theories of social change also appeared, most particularly socialism.

All of these movements illustrate the social environment of 19th-century drama.

They help to explain why, for the first time in centuries, plays were written that chronicled the plight of the poor. They provide a background to the value structure of melodrama and social drama. Also, they offer an explanation for the preoccupation with social justice that pervades all the dramatic forms of the era.

English Liberals of the 19th century advocated a system of government based not on kings or individuals, but on laws that would apply equally to all people. They believed in individual freedom for everyone, regardless of social status or historical circumstance. They believed that economic and social progress is possible only within the context of personal liberty. In addition, they advocated fair parliamentary representation to insure that all groups and individuals could participate in the making of laws.

Moral Reform

Political Liberals wanted to improve the social conditions of the workers and the poor by changing the laws and social structure that governed them. Other 19th-century writers, however, insisted that change could occur only within the individual. They advocated moral reform of the individual, devising several ingenious if naive plans to that end. Some insisted that education could mold the young, but others relied on pamphlets extolling the virtues of hard work and perseverance. Their tactics may have varied greatly, but the moral reformers were in general agreement that social justice was a problem in England and that something needed to be done about it. Their concepts of charity, sympathy, and hard work became the moralistic dynamos that drove the heroes of virtually all the melodramas of the period. Among the moral reformers were Samuel Smiles, who wrote *Self Help* (1859), and Thomas Hughes, who wrote *The Manliness of Christ* (c. 1880).

Socialism

Today the concept of socialism is so closely associated with the names of Karl Marx (1818–1883) and Nikolai Lenin (1870–1924) that it is easy to forget that the term existed prior to and independent of Marx. The experimental communities of Robert Owen are examples of the early efforts to rid society of the competition and inequality generated by the free-enterprise system. Before Marx, socialism attempted to achieve social justice by promoting cooperation among workers and ensuring greater equality in living standards. It often had strong religious overtones, equating social justice with the kingdom of God. In the case of the French socialist Saint-Simon (1760–1825), it meant a science of society in which social managers would operate the nation by applying tested laws whose exact effects would be known. In such a system, Saint-Simon declared, private enterprise and the unhealthy consequences of competition would disappear.

The theories of Karl Marx are too complicated and controversial for discussion here. Marx's theory of alienation, however, was to have considerable impact on writers and thinkers over the next century. It is therefore worth summarizing. In an industrial economy, Marx argued, humans are alienated from the product of their work because of the subdivision of labor, which has reduced their tasks to the completion of small repeated actions. These tasks are independent of the person completing them because they can be undertaken by anyone; thus, if human beings fit the mold of a job the job is not suited to humans. Also, this separation of the individual and the job alienates the workers from one another because they all know that they can be replaced by someone else. They must compete with one another to do a job any one of them could do, rather than work together to create a product they are proud of. As a consequence, a person's work is undertaken only because it provides subsistence, not because it is pleasurable or satisfying. Humankind thereby becomes alienated from its own nature.

In the context of the drama, the importance of Marx's concept of alienation lies in the attention it gives to the workers' lifestyle, the economic environment of the individual, and the sense of entrapment felt by the worker. It exemplifies, along with the ideas of the liberals and moral reformers, the concern of 19th-century social thinkers for social justice. The era was inundated with calls for awareness, charity, reform, and revolution. Theatres responded by offering plays that elicited sympathy for victims of social injustice. Dramas seldom proposed revolutionary solutions to social problems, but they often championed the cause of the downtrodden and the unfortunate.

The Rulers

The prominence of the middle classes in Europe is reflected even in the leading monarchies. Queen Victoria (1819–1901) of England, Emperor Franz Josef (1830–1916) of Austria-Hungary, and Louis Philippe (1773–1850) of France were all conservative in dress and manner. While the 18th century had been one of "great" rulers—Catherine the Great (1729–1796) of Russia, Frederick the Great (1712–1786) of Prussia, and Queen Maria-Theresa (1717–1780) of Austria-Hungary—the 19th-century rulers were almost bourgeois by comparison.

Victoria lent her name to the family morals of middle-class England; to be Victorian is to be dowdy and restrictive or solid and respected, depending on one's view. Her lifelong attachment to her dead husband, Albert, was a symbol of feminine respectability to the 19th century. In France, Louis Philippe gave up his military uniforms to don the black clothing of a merchant. And in Austria-Hungary, Franz Josef ran his country from 1848 to 1916 almost as if it were a family business. His austere lifestyle combined with his close monitoring of the civil service gave him the appearance of a chief bureaucrat.

ARTS IDEAS

Visual Arts

Several artists in the mid-19th century reacted against Romanticism with an emphasis on naturalism and scenes of daily life. As the industrial revolution helped spawn the rise of the middle class and a concern for political and economic rights, visual artists focused increasingly on the countryside for their subjects.

Jean-François Millet (1814–1875) reflects this trend in his depictions of the life of the French peasant. Millet reveals the peasant at work in the fields, sowing, harvesting, digging, and herding animals. What makes his work notable is a distinct subjectivity Millet brings to the subject: through shading, lighting, and the positioning of his

The Sower by Millet. *Courtesy Museum of Fine Arts, Boston*

figures, Millet invests his peasants with a somber dignity. He imbues them with gravity and grandeur. The figures are rarely happy, yet they retain a noble determination that seems to praise their hard work and hard lives. Today Millet's depictions seem sentimentalized to some critics, but his work nevertheless reflects a growing awareness of the real world beyond the classicism of David or the romanticism of Delacroix.

Musical Theatre

During the 19th century, the theatre achieved a level of popular acceptance unprecedented in Western Europe since the Renaissance. Musical theatre contributed significantly to this popularity. Italian opera became identified with the national movement for Italian independence and unification. The operetta, a lighter and more comical form than its older antecedent, became a staple of musical theatre in London and Paris. Audiences who didn't appreciate the foreign and classical references of opera could delight in caricatures of their own lifestyles. A survey of 19th-century theatre would not be complete without mention of the contributions of Giuseppe Verdi, Jacques Offenbach, and the English team of William S. Gilbert and Arthur Sullivan.

***Giuseppe Verdi* (1813–1901).**   Verdi's work spans more than a half-century: his first success was in 1839 and his last, *Falstaff*, came in 1893. In between he composed at least a half-dozen of the most enduringly popular operas of all time. In a two-year period alone, from 1851 to 1853, he penned *Rigoletto*, *Il Trovatore*, and *La Traviata*. His music, which he asserted was written only for the masses and not for the critics, adapted some of the greatest Romantic stories to operatic form. From Shakespeare he took the stories of Macbeth, Othello, and Falstaff; from Schiller he adapted *Joan of Arc* and *Don Carlos;* from Hugo he took Hernani and Rigoletto (based on *The King Amuses Himself*); and from Byron he used *The Two Foscari.*

These stories, however, were only the framework. He heightened the dramatic impact of the incidents, he enhanced the emotional settings with musical atmosphere, and he added psychological complexity to the characters. Verdi's music was equally effective in solo arias for his tragic heroines and in robust marches for his processionals. He could devote most of an entire act to three characters to explore their motivations or he could create spectacular theatre with grand ball scenes or African parades. In short, he was a true composer for the theatre, writing something for everyone while retaining musical vitality and integrity.

***Jacques Offenbach* (1819–1880).** Jacques Offenbach made no pretensions to serious purpose; he wrote music to delight and divert his audiences. When his stories took place in the palaces of the gods, Offenbach used the occasion to spoof the antics of the heavenly creatures, not to assert cosmic truths. He reduced the schemes of the gods to the petty level of ordinary reality. In the process he charmed the bourgeois Parisian audience and established a musical theatre form that would help lead eventually to the American musical. Offenbach did not invent the French operetta, which first appeared about 1850, but he was easily its most famous composer. Working with the librettists Jacques-Fromental Halévy and Henri Meilhac, Offenbach fashioned the characteristics for which the operetta became known: sections of dialogue alternating with musical numbers, satirical versions of classical myths, vibrant dance music, low comic interludes, and an irreverent vision of reality. Regardless of the location of the play's action, his characters were always distinctly French and bourgeois. In *Orpheus in the Underworld* (1858), *Fair Helen* (1865), and *Parisian Life* (1866), among many others, Offenbach and his librettists poked fun at the lifestyle, customs, and institutions of Napoleon III's France. Combined with the composer's infectious rhythms, clever melodies, and simplified but effective orchestrations, the stories captivated their audiences. His later works were not well-received, but his contributions to the musical stage are nevertheless important.

***Gilbert* (1836–1911) *and Sullivan* (1842–1900).** William S. Gilbert first collaborated with composer Arthur Sullivan in 1875 in *Trial by Jury,* a light but effective commentary on the English justice system. The two men, although very different in temperament, elicited the best from each other. Together they produced the most successful operettas in English history: *H.M.S. Pinafore* (1878), *The Pirates of Penzance* (1879), *Patience* (1881), *The Mikado* (1885), and *Yeoman of the Guard* (1888). All of their collaborative efforts were produced by D'Oyly Carte (1844–1901), who built the Savoy Theatre to house their work. After several quarrels preceding *The Grand Duke* in 1896, the pair permanently split. Their stories and lyrics brought Victorian society to life: its customs and manners, its laws and judicial system, its moral values, and, above all, its hypocrisy and its inept officials. Whether the plays take place in Japan or Italy, they are thoroughly Victorian. The operettas are commentaries of the people inhabiting the streets and the newspapers of London in the 1880s. *Patience,* for example, captures with vicious clarity the aesthetes who were parading around London with refined airs and pompous attitudes in 1881.

In sum, the arts reflect a response to the demands of a new, less aristocratic audience. The middle class wanted subjects that reflected its values and tastes, and the arts responded.

19TH-CENTURY THEATRE

Theatre history in the century is essentially a study in commercialization. As social and economic developments created a new class of people with both enough money and some leisure time, enterprising producers devised an astonishing array of theatrical activities to entice this new audience.

Occasion

Theatrical presentations included not only drama and the musical-theatre forms mentioned earlier, but circuses, animal acts, vaudeville, minstrel shows, puppet shows, and various other para-theatrical forms. In each case, however, the occasion for performance was the commercial opportunity it presented. Not surprisingly, the commercial possibilities of theatre required changes in the methods of organization and regulation.

England and France. The gradually diminishing role of the "official," "state," or "patent" theatres in France and England corresponded to growth in the number of alternative producing organizations. In Paris, restrictions were loosened so that by mid-century more than 25 theatres were producing on a regular basis. In London, rather than the 2 theatres mandated by the 1660 law, more than 20 theatres were part of the London theatre scene.

These new companies did not easily compete with the established theatres, and a second change is found in the new forms of entertainment developed to enable them to draw audiences. In France, the boulevard theatres continued to produce new playwrights and experimental dramas, significantly aiding the growth of melodrama. In London, the minor theatres introduced the *burletta,* a form similar to comic opera, which allowed clever managers to adapt traditional scripts that regulations forbade them to produce. Even Shakespeare's plays were presented as burletta with interpolated songs, or as melodrama with just occasional chords of music added, to distinguish them from traditional drama. This confusion ultimately resulted in the Theatrical Regulation Act of 1843, which repealed the Licensing Act of 1660 and established legal equality among all theatres.

The United States. In the United States, New York established itself as the center of theatrical production with more than 25 established theatres operating there by 1875. In addition, permanent theatrical companies were found in Philadelphia, Charleston, Boston, Chicago, St. Louis, New Orleans, Providence, and even San Francisco.

With no significant theatrical legislation, a wide variety of theatrical forms became established. Many members of theatre audiences were not fluent in English, for immigrants from many nations comprised the population. Therefore, the traditional drama, performed in English and with an emphasis on the spoken word, was, with few exceptions, popular only among an educated elite. To attract the other audience, some managers produced variety entertainment featuring singers, dancers, comics, animal acts, gymnastics, and other features. In its early days, these variety entertainments or vaudeville were considered vulgar and frequently were performed in saloons or beer halls. Only at the end of the century did Tony Pastor (1837–1908) seize the opportunity to make vaudeville a family entertainment, eliminating bawdy elements and stressing wholesome entertainment. Pastor's success spawned imitations, and soon a complete vaudeville circuit was formed, presided over by B. F. Keith (1846–1914) and E. F. Albee (1857–1930). Their success with a string of theatres located throughout the East resulted later in the century in even larger circuits that stretched from coast to coast.

The term *burlesque* is often associated with vaudeville, but the 19th-century form of burlesque was not the "exotic dancers" of this century. Originally, burlesque was a parody of an existing script, echoing a tradition that goes back at least as far as classical Greece. The first major modern success in the form was a parody of *Hamlet* presented in 1811. During the middle part of the century, burlesque managers incorporated a new trend that first occurred in melodrama and began to rely on the exposed female leg as a major attraction. Gradually the presence of scantily clad females became more important than the parody, and burlesque became a variety entertainment featuring songs, comics, skits, and dances, always featuring a large group of beautiful young women. Only in the 20th century, however, did it become the striptease with which we associate the term today.

Further competition for the variety performers was provided by the popularity of minstrel shows. Although African-American performers had been featured in some solo acts previously, the performance of a character named "Jim Crow" by Thomas D. Rice (1806–1860) enhanced the popularity of blackface performers—white actors who blackened their faces with cork to portray comical black caricatures. The Virginia Minstrels were the first troupe to provide a full evening of minstrel performance in 1843, and the Christy Minstrels made their debut the next year and established the minstrel show as a major form of entertainment.

The traditional minstrel show featured a series of ballads, musical performances, and soft-shoe dances interrupted by satirical exchanges and playful insults between the interlocutor who sat in the middle and the two "endmen." The mood was casual and upbeat, and the show offered many performers a chance to exhibit special talents, so that each show contained something to interest nearly any spectator. Soon many others troupes were formed, and minstrel acts became popular throughout the nation and even in Europe. Eventually African-American artists formed their own minstrel troupes, resulting in a strange self-caricature as African-American artists wore blackface to successfully portray the expected image. Both burlesque and minstrelsy achieved their greatest success in the 1870s and eventually dwindled into minor forms.

The first African-American acting troupe in America was formed in 1821 by James Brown. His African Grove, located in New York City, presented a repertory of plays including the works of Shakespeare and the first known American play written

A cover for a sheet-music collection of songs from the Christy Minstrels.   *Courtesy Houghton Library, Harvard University*

by an African-American, Brown's *King Shotaway.* The leading actor was a West Indian, James Hewlett, but it was Ira Aldridge who moved from the African Grove to international fame in Europe. [See insert, p. 308.]

The various influences of the century seem to merge in the production of *The Black Crook* in New York City in 1866. Musical entertainment had been a part of theatre throughout the century, with orchestral numbers and specialty acts often performed before and after plays or even between acts; ballad opera had also been introduced from England. However, *The Black Crook* introduced a new type of theatre. A flimsy melodramatic plot served as an organizational core for the production, which featured a large cast of beautiful women (wearing "no clothes to speak of" according to one newspaper's account) surrounded by magnificent spectacle. Although many contemporary critics scorned the play's vulgarity and indecency, it was a tremendous success with the public, playing more than a year in one theatre. Many historians consider *The Black Crook* to be the forerunner of the American musical theatre.

When the additional presence of the circus, a lecture series, and touring solo artists is added to this bustling theatrical scene, the result of the commercial emphasis on theatre is evident. Although the spoken drama continued, it now had to compete with a whole range of entertainments that were easily understood, visually interesting, and emotionally exciting.

Obviously, the traditional theatre was forced to respond. In the competition for the audience's attention, theatrical producers were forced to abandon the concept of repertory performance and focus more on single popular attractions, and particularly on star performers. The 19th century marks the beginning of the tradition of the "long run," in which a play is presented as long as it draws an audience, rather than being presented for a limited run in repertory with other plays. It also marks the rising dominance of the star performer rather than the play as the major box-office attraction. These two new practices proved disastrous for many local companies as producers abandoned the concept of a permanent repertory company to bring in touring shows and stars.

Germany and Russia.   Theatre in Germany and Russia did not respond as quickly or as fully to commercialization. In Germany the concept of a state or national theatre, newly born in the 18th century, was maintained, although private commercial theatres existed as well. The most common arrangement was a small theatre company attached to a specific court that provided significant financial support, although the specific patterns of responsibility varied in each locale.

The most influential court theatre of the early century was located in the small principality of Weimar, a town of only 6,000 residents. The duke and duchess had witnessed theatre in Berlin and Austria and determined to form their own company to replace a hired company that had fallen out of favor with the populace. The duke engaged Johann Wolfgang von Goethe (1749–1832) to form the company in 1791, and for the next 18 years Weimar witnessed a unique theatrical phenomenon.

Goethe determined to forge a new type of theatre that would restore the classical traditions of German theatre. Beginning with a short four-week season, the theatre soon expanded to a Weimar season from October to June and a summer season in a neighboring village in July and August. Performances were given three times weekly, and the repertoire included a mixture of popular plays, new dramas, classical plays, and opera. Goethe gradually built a permanent company of actors who were all experienced in the clean, classical style he preferred. With the aid of the author Friedrich von Schiller (1759–1805), who worked with the company from 1798 to 1805, he established a regional reputation for his company. Despite this critical and aesthetic success, however, Goethe was forced to include melodrama and musical theatre in his weekly schedule in order to meet expenses, with the popular forms representing nearly 70 percent of the performances.

Through the mid-century, Germany experienced a growth in popular theatre similar to those in France, England, and the United States as various forms of musical and variety entertainment developed to please the growing middle class. Political upheavals that began in 1848 finally resulted in the unification of Germany in 1871, and a new trade law removed all restrictions on the establishment of new theatres. This precipitated a rush to open new houses, and more than 90 were opened in Germany during the next two years. In the midst of this rush of commercial enterprise, the efforts of a great composer resulted in a major theatre festival clearly divorced from the demands of commercialization.

Richard Wagner (1813–1883) was famous throughout Europe as a composer, and his dream was to produce a theatre festival. He was determined that this festival would not be in an urban center, for he was determined it would be a special event attended only by those who came together for that express purpose. He chose the small town of Bayreuth in central Germany and in 1876 produced his first festival. The massive effort—featuring Wagner's own operas in magnificent productions, with more than 300 performers—was successful but still ended heavily in debt, and only in 1882 was the second festival produced. Although Wagner did not live to see the festival become a national institution on a regular basis, the inspiration of Bayreuth led to the establishment of numerous "theatre festivals" throughout the world in future years.

The Russian theatre, given its foundation by Peter the Great (1672–1725)—he decided to import Western concepts in the early 18th century—was firmly attached to the centralized government and the upper classes. A national theatre was founded in 1756, and by the end of the century theatres were also part of the estates of the feudal barons. The companies, comprised of serfs or slaves, were trained in ballet and music and performed for visitors or on special occasions. In the state theatre and on the provincial stages, theatre was performed as a tribute and as a testament of loyalty. Although the court regularly supported theatrical performances and most state theatres maintained regular seasons of performance, until 1882 a law prohibited private theatrical enterprises. Only those theatres established, supported, and controlled by the government were allowed to operate.

Location

The need to attract large audiences for commercial success, the continuing interest in spectacle, and the aesthetic ideals of key individuals resulted in changes in theatre buildings during this century. The most significant trends can be identified in four theatres: the Paris Opéra, the Drury Lane theatre in London, Booth's Theatre in New York City, and the Bayreuth Festival Theatre in Germany.

The Paris Opéra, which opened in 1875 as a showcase of the French government, illustrates the continuation of the baroque concepts of grand and elegant theatrical spaces for the aristocracy and the growing dependence on size and scope of technical production. Designed to outdo the new Vienna Opera, the Paris Opéra was conceived on a grand scale and was perhaps more notable for its elegant public areas than for its auditorium or stage. Huge staircases, enormous foyers, and luxurious decor provided a sense of national prestige. A library, a restaurant, a magnificent ballroom, and a school of dance were contained within the building, emphasizing it's function as a cultural center. The auditorium seated nearly 2,200 people in a traditional horseshoe configuration. Modern innovations in the building included heating and ventilation systems, full plumbing, and a completely electric lighting system (installed in 1881).

The Drury Lane theatre, constructed in 1812 to replace a building that burned

SELECTED 19TH-CENTURY PLAYHOUSES

Chestnut Street Theatre	1794	Philadelphia
St. Pierre Theatre	1807	New Orleans
Covent Garden Theatre (enlarged)	1809	London
Drury Lane Theatre (rebuilt)	1812	London
Park Theatre (rebuilt, original 1798)	1820	
Maly Theatre	1824	Moscow
Princess Theatre	1836	London
Bolshoi Theatre (present site)	1856	Moscow
Ford's Theatre	1862	Washington, D.C.
Crosby's Opera House	1865	Chicago
Vienna Opera House	1869	Vienna
Booth's Theatre	1869	New York
Opéra (present site)	1874	Paris
Festspielhaus	1876	Bayreuth, Germany
Madison Square Theatre	1879	New York
Metropolitan Opera	1883	New York
Wyndham's Theatre	1899	London

down in 1809, provides a good example of a tendency to maintain traditional theatre structure but enlarge the seating capacity to increase revenue. It also provides an early glimpse at changes in theatre structure designed to aid the development of realism.

The 1812 theatre did not differ greatly from its predecessors. It was designed to hold some 3,200 persons to meet the demands of the box office, and a circular design was selected for the seating areas to provide the best sightlines for patrons. Four stories of open boxes and two galleries surrounded the pit area, which was furnished with benches. Six sets of wings and machinery for flying were provided in the stage area.

As a means of increasing income, comfortable chairs were placed in the front rows of both the pit and the galleries, creating additional seating for privileged patrons and altering the traditional seating patterns. Great care was taken to keep the classes from mingling, however, and a separate means of entrance and exit was devised for those wishing to sit in the new "orchestra stalls" so that they would not have to mix with the lower classes. At the Haymarket Theatre, constructed in 1840, the apron of the stage vanished behind the proscenium wall, eliminating the proscenium doors and creating the style of proscenium theatre that became the standard throughout the 20th century. This development in stage architecture closely paralleled the growing trend toward realistic staging.

In the United States, Booth's Theatre opened in 1868 to house the productions of Edwin Booth (1833–1893), and it further illustrates the adaptation of theatre architecture to promote the presentation of realistic stage pictures. Seating was essentially on one floor, with only a few boxes located next to the proscenium wall. The proscenium doors were eliminated and all acting took place within the stage frame. The stage was not raked and neither was it grooved, so that flats could now be placed in any position on stage, greatly increasing the opportunity for stage design and for the addition of three-dimensional stage pieces. An elaborate trap system provided a means of quick scene changes, and a 75-foot fly gallery was one of the first in the United States. In Booth's Theatre and others built at this same time, the focus is not on decor nor on the audience areas. Rather, the theatre structure is modified to accommodate new aesthetic concepts.

The Festival Theatre (Festspielhaus) in Bayreuth, built in 1876, represents radically innovative concepts in theatre building, although the major innovations occur in the auditorium rather than on the stage. Wagner's intent, and that of the theatre designer, Gottfried Semper (1803–1879), was to design a theatre in which the action on the stage was clearly the focus of every member of the audience. To accomplish this, a double proscenium was built with a sunken orchestra pit placed out of audience sightlines between the two. This removed the possible distraction of the orchestra and created a "mystic gulf" between stage and audience that enhanced the reality of the stage illusion. To avoid the unnecessarily high proscenium that had developed to accommodate the four-high rows of boxes and galleries and to provide proper perspective for every spectator, the seating was placed on one sloping floor with rows of seats running in a fan shape the entire width of the auditorium. The rows were placed far enough apart, in what is currently called "continental seating," that central aisles were eliminated (and since Wagner would not seat latecomers, none was needed). Thirteen hundred spectators could be accommodated in this fashion, and a royal box and several flanking boxes at the rear of the seating provided places of privilege for 300 additional guests. The central chandelier was eliminated and discreet house lighting was provided at the sides of the auditorium. During performances, the house was entirely darkened to further ensure focus on the stage.

Although the stage contained no innovative structures, the adjustments to the

The Festspielhaus at Bayreuth.   *Alinari, Editorial Photocolor Archives*

front of the house increased the effectiveness of the technical presentation. The result is a theatre that represents the culmination of 19th-century trends. Democratic in its audience arrangement, it represents the final collapse of the class distinctions found in older, segregated seating. The emphasis on sightlines and the creation of the distinct separation between actor and audience clearly support the creation of a complete and unified illusionistic stage. The "mystic gulf" makes the "fourth wall" even more pronounced and clearly promotes the development of stage realism.

Performers

Even though the commercial nature of the theatre and the new theatre buildings both supported the development of a theatre form that would attract the new middle class, the major source of new ideas in the theatre came from the individuals who controlled the theatres. In most cases, these were versatile theatre people, skilled in several areas of theatre production. The most common combination was the actor-manager, but toward the end of the century playwrights took on managerial duties, and eventually the role of manager became separate from other theatrical duties.

These men and women took over the management of theatres and concerned themselves with both the financial and artistic aspects of their productions. They instituted new managerial policies affecting prices, seating arrangements, and the general comfort of their audience. They reformed the staging of bold old and new plays. They experimented with the newest special-effects equipment. They competed with one another for the best designers available. They also became the first stage directors: they attended to detail in the performances of their major and minor actors, and they imposed a single artistic vision on their productions. Many of them were only partially successful as managers, for audience affections changed frequently. Many others were not at all successful as actors. Nevertheless, they were responsible for the bulk of the changes in theatre practice in the 19th century.

English theatre during this period is in many ways the story of successful actor-managers. John Philip Kemble (1757–1823) was the leading actor in London from 1790 until he retired in 1817. In addition, he served as manager of the Drury Lane from 1788 until 1802, and of Covent Garden from 1802 until 1817. His attention to detail in scenery and costume, his demand for quality and consistency from the performers, and his use of spectacle to support the plays of Shakespeare made his the dominant theatre in England. His brother, Charles (1775–1854), was manager of Covent Garden from 1817 to 1832. Although less successful than John, Charles is noted for emphasizing historical accuracy in some of his productions. His production of *King John* in 1824 is regarded as the first to use historically accurate costumes for a Shakespearean history play.

The emergence of Lucy Bartolozzi (1797–1856) as a prominent actor-manager must have surprised every person in the London theatre world except the young singer/actress herself. Known as Madame Vestris, she had established a successful career as a singer and an actress, but her greatest success had been as a burlesque performer, and most of the critical response had focused on the beauty of her legs.

Regardless of her background, in 1830 she took over the management of the Olympic Theatre, a smaller theatre that produced minor dramatic forms, including melodrama and burlesque. By surrounding herself with talented artists, including the playwright/designer J. R. Planché (1795–1880) and her future husband, Charles Mathews (1776–1835), she soon elevated the Olympic to a new degree of popularity and acceptance. Mme. Vestris is frequently credited with the popularization of the interior "box set," which eliminated any wing entrances by creating three walls of a room complete with doors and windows.

Charles Kean (1811–1868), the son of one of the most famous actors of the century, was well regarded as an actor himself, but in retrospect his staging practices have overshadowed his acting ability. Kean, appointed Master of the Revels by Queen Victoria in 1848, managed the Princess Theatre from 1850 to 1859; his social standing, coupled with his management techniques, brought new respectability to that theatre. He staged elaborate productions with as many as 13 different sets requiring 140 stagehands for a single production. He hired several of the great scene painters of the period to create romantic landscapes and accurate locations, insisting on careful research and even travel abroad to ensure accuracy. He failed, however, to achieve his desired illusion completely, for his actresses, including his wife, Ellen Tree (1806–1880), continued to wear the petticoats then in fashion.

Kean refused to hire star performers, feeling that they worked against the unity of the production, and he took great care to locate his stage crowds and give them appropriate business. In his control of the production, his desire for accuracy in historical presentation, and his emphasis on a unified whole, Kean anticipated many trends of the later 19th century and laid a foundation for 20th-century theatre concepts as well.

The development of pictorial realism on the stage was further enhanced by the management of Squire Bancroft (1841–1926) and his wife, Marie Wilton Bancroft (1839–1921), at the Prince of Wales Theatre between 1865 and 1871. Greatly influenced by their resident playwright/director Tom Robertson (1829–1871), the Bancrofts emphasized ensemble performance and realistic stage settings, even in comedy. The drawing-room settings of the plays, the understated style of performance, the detailed use of props and incidental business based on normal, everyday activities all added to the totality of the illusion.

The role of actor-manager was equally important in theatres throughout Europe and the United States. In Germany, Goethe's work at Weimar went beyond the traditional role of author and/or producer. Beginning in approximately 1798, Goethe researched each production carefully. His interest in detail is evident in a letter addressed to Schiller about their joint production of *Macbeth* (1800), which had played the previous season. For future productions, he listed 28 suggestions, ranging from "Make the symmetrical blocking of the witches more subtle" to "A deeper bell tone must be created." Further remarks center on the table settings at the banquet, the color of Banquo's makeup, and even the possible additional of an extra monologue for Malcolm. Goethe did not hesitate to prescribe specific rhythms or intonations for the actors as he strove to create his image of the play.

Heinrich Laube (1806–1884) at the Burgtheater in Vienna had similar goals and methods. A talented actor-coach, he introduced a new style of unaffected realism to the Vienna stage that stressed ensemble performance and the inclusion of casual, natural business. Laube introduced the box set to the German stage, but his most important innovation was to increase the number of rehearsals from the usual five or six to nearly twice that number, not only rehearsing the actors in their line readings but taking time to carefully develop appropriate movement.

The French actor-manager Adolphe Montigny (c. 1812–1880) played a similar role in the French theatre. Montigny was quite resourceful in breaking old traditions and introducing new ideas. He placed furniture specifically so it would disturb traditional patterns of moving and posing on the stage. He insisted that actors sit when it was appropriate to the scene and that characters talk to one another rather than to the audience. He scattered properties around the setting, which he then used as motivation for character movement within the play. His goal was to thoroughly break the French classical tradition of performance and introduce a new, realistic style.

America produced the man who was, perhaps, the first successful nonacting theatre manager: Augustin Daly (1838–1899). Known as the "autocrat of the theatre," Daly controlled every facet of a production. Actors complained of his "countless rehearsals" in which Daly trained each moment of the performance of each actor to create the ensemble effect he desired. Each piece of scenery, property, and costume was personally approved by Daly, and lighting was also under his control. A good judge of talent, he personally oversaw the careers of his actors and imposed fines on actors who were late or who were discourteous. He prohibited any contact between his actors and the press, but he wasn't above employing a reviewer as a means of influencing opinion. A good businessman as well, Daly was the first to initiate Wednesday matinees and the idea of a subscription series. Daly's company was the first American troupe to successfully tour in Europe, and eventually he opened his own theatre in London.

The appearance of the actor-manager and the growing importance of these people in theatre production are strong indications of a changing theatre aesthetic that proposed that realistic performance, with acting, scenery, costume, and the drama all contributing to a unified impression, was the goal of theatre. Major contributions to this new aesthetic were made by the leading actors and scene designers of the 19th century.

The 19th century began with a titanic clash between the classical styles and the new emotionalism of the Romantic movement. For the first half of the century some actors still clung to the old formal style of the classical heritage, while others used the impetus of the Romantics to search for a new style of acting to blend with the growing trend toward realism in the theatre. As always, some individuals found a style uniquely their own, distinguished by their own personality rather than by similarities to others.

The classical style of acting relied extensively on elocution and the vocal skills of the performers. Sarah Siddons (1755–1831), John Philip Kemble's older sister, dominated the English stage for many years with her grand manner, her eloquence, and her intelligence. Her brother was perhaps the most classical of actors, with each moment of his performance carefully composed, intelligent, formal, and poetic. In both cases, careful study of the script allowed these actors to find novel interpretations, but these discoveries were communicated through intelligence and the voice. Another advocate of the classical style, the Italian actor Tomasso Salvini (1829–1915), combined the careful planning of the classic performers with a more natural simplicity and greater range of emotion. He gained an international reputation when he toured Europe

DION BOUCICAULT
(1820–1890)

*D*ion Boucicault was a star—someone who attracted an audience as much by his personality as by the performance. His first play, *London Assurance*, was produced at Covent Garden in 1841 when he was just 21. In 1852 his career in London was disrupted by his flagrant affair with the actress Agnes Robertson, an affair that caused Charles Kean to void his contract. Undaunted, Boucicault took Agnes to America, where they had a string of successes. By 1860 he was back in London with an international reputation and enjoying the great success of his latest play, *The Colleen Bawn.*

Defiant and independent, he possessed energy and concerns that were at least partially responsible for new copyright laws in the United States and for a system that resulted in royalty payments to authors. Boucicault was tireless in his efforts to give his brand of theatre wide acceptance. He reduced the entertainment of an evening to a single play in order to give attention and focus to it. With *The Colleen Bawn* he instituted a new system in London that altered theatre history. Instead of sending a star on tour throughout the country, he sent a company that could perform one play only. The play became the attraction, then, and the actors were subordinate to it.

Boucicault is often overlooked in the annals of theatre history because many of his plays (he wrote nearly 200) have not been successfully performed in the 20th century. In their time, however, his plays were tremendously popular, and his contributions to theatre in a variety of fields deserve notice.

and England, relying on a handsome face and body, a natural grace, and a powerful and well-modulated voice to enthrall audiences who could not understand a word of the Italian he spoke.

In America, Charlotte Cushman (1816–1876) adopted the classic style as well, relying on her strength and dignity to produce powerful performances of strong female characters such as Lady Macbeth. The leading actor of the American stage during this time period, Edwin Booth, also remained faithful to the classic style. Booth's acting was always elevated and he shunned the new, realistic plays. Based on a careful balance of intellect and emotion, faultless elocution, and a graceful carriage, Booth's performance revealed extensive textual analysis that allowed him to bring continual nuance to his performance of a given role.

In contrast to the classical style, the emotional style relied on intuition and emotional commitment. In England, Edmund Kean (1789–1833) provided the only challenge to the reputation of John Philip Kemble during the Romantic period of English theatre. His fiery, unpredictable style dominated the London stage from the end of Kemble's era until his own death in 1833. He was regarded as an intuitive actor who followed his instincts spontaneously. He was alternately brilliant and expressive, then subdued and withdrawn. Critics described his abrupt transitions, unexpected and elongated pauses, and sudden shifts from grandeur to simplicity, and the English author Coleridge once observed: "to see him act is like reading Shakespeare by flashes of lightning." Audiences found his style irresistible and he was a huge success both in England and on tour.

A refined version of Kean's style characterized the performances of the French actor François-Joseph Talma (1763–1826). A rebel against the power of the Comédie-Française, Talma's early performances were filled with passionate outbursts of emotion and attempts to create a true portrayal of nature, so that one critic described his work as "pathological realism." Accused by traditionalists of going beyond the boundaries of his art, Talma adjusted his style as he matured, seeking to find a balance between the discoveries of his intuition and the ability of his intelligence to control those discoveries.

This balance between intuition and analysis, between sensibility and intellect, between physical expression and elocution, was the goal of those actors who aspired to a new "natural" style of acting. The Russian actor Shchepkin (1788–1863) was a leader in this approach. He urged the study of human beings to understand their social background as a necessary part of the actor's work. The actor's goal, according to Shchepkin, was the elimination of self and total absorption into the action of the scene so that the audience's presence went unnoticed. With these concepts, he clearly paved the way for the development of the 20th-century acting style formulated in the writings of Konstantin Stanislavski.

This style of performance was also characteristic of the American actor Joseph Jefferson (1829–1905). Although his historical fame is based on his creation of the part of Rip Van Winkle, which he performed regularly for some 30 years, Jefferson's 71-year career included a wide variety of parts. Jefferson valued spontaneity, but he also recognized that control was essential, and he constantly sought the perfect balance between the two.

Some performers managed to achieve prominence on the stage through personal magnetism or a unique style of performance that defies categorization. Among them is a man generally regarded as the first great American actor, Edwin Forrest (1806–1872). In his preparation, Forrest adopted many of the methods of the natural style of acting, relying on observation as the foundation for characterization. He visited old men's homes and asylums before playing Lear, and spent time with a Native American tribe before portraying a chief. In performance, however, Forrest's bearing and manner were reminiscent of the classical style. For an audience, Forrest's most notable attribute was the size and power of his performance. A handsome man with a large and muscular body, he used his athletic style and a powerful voice to overwhelm audiences with an acting style that one critic referred to as "muscular." In scenes of combat, he was known

Edwin Forrest as Spartacus. *Courtesy Hampden-Booth Theatre Library*

to become so involved and excited that other actors actually feared for their safety. He was in many ways the prototypical American: muscular, independent, rough, and powerful. As one critic summarized: ". . . take him all for all, we shall not look upon his like again."

Henry Irving (1838–1905), generally considered the finest actor on the English stage during the second half of the century and viewed by many as the greatest actor since David Garrick, managed to utilize nearly every known acting style to achieve his success. In the melodramas that first catapulted him to fame he utilized full emotional release and involvement to the extent that some criticized him for tasteless excess. Since he did not possess either great physical beauty or a great voice, Irving used any style, any device necessary to affect his audience. He believed that great actors were remembered for single, startling moments that revealed character or text in a unique and startling manner, and utilized his intelligence and analytical powers to create such effects, frequently stirring an audience to applause or to total silence with a single word or just a look.

Constant Coquelin (1841–1909) refused to accept the new concept of natural acting, maintaining that the theatre demanded something larger than life. A master of acting technique, Coquelin portrayed a wide range of roles ranging from Tartuffe to domestic tragedy and achieved his greatest fame in the role of Cyrano de Bergerac.

No one has been able to pinpoint the first appearance of an African-American on an American stage. Certainly theatre of a sort was created in the songs, religious and secular, of African-Americans. The tradition of African-American song and dance in restaurants and gambling houses was well established by the middle of the 18th century; but though African-American characters appeared in plays as early as 1767, there is no record that African-Americans were allowed to perform them.

In 1821, however, James Hewlett, a West Indian, founded the African Theatre Company. Originally begun as a means of avoiding police regulations against a Negro Ice Cream Parlor called the African Grove, the performances of the African Theatre Company became very popular, with *Richard III* their most popular piece. The performances eventually attracted white audience members, who were asked to sit in the rear of the theatre when their raucous behavior disrupted the performances. In response, the police repeatedly raided the theatre, often arresting actors in the midst of scenes, and one night in 1823 a gang of white men wrecked the theatre.

Although no record clearly ties him to the African Grove, Ira Aldridge went to school nearby and very likely was a participant in the performances. Little is known about his early years, although evidence now indicates he was born in New York City, probably in 1807. Following the closing of the African Grove, he spent a year observing the theatre through a backstage job on Broadway and then sailed to Britain, where he is believed to have attended a university in Scotland. Armed with a letter of introduction from his Broadway employer, he found his way to the theatre scene in London and appeared in 1825 in one of the smaller theatres. Billed almost immediately as the "African Tragedian" or the "African Roscius," he was rarely referred to as an American, even when he performed *Othello* for the first time in 1826.

Aldridge was given a warm reception by critics and audiences and toured successfully throughout the provinces of England, gradually increasing his repertoire. Critics described his acting as "realistic," without stage tricks or exaggeration, and he was praised as "exceeding all the great actors of the day." Eventually his repertoire included nonblack roles, including the great Shakespearean characters—Macbeth, Lear, and Shylock. He performed at Covent Garden, replacing Edmund Kean, who had become ill. He toured successfully in Belgium, Germany, Austria, Switzerland, France, and Turkey and appeared triumphantly in Russia in 1857 and again in 1862. One Russian critic commented that "after Aldridge it is impossible to see Othello performed by a white actor, be it Garrick himself."

He was a complete success as an actor and in his personal life as well. He was married first to the daughter of a member of England's Parliament; following her death—she was his senior by many years—he married the daughter of a Swedish baron. His fame became so great that theatres were able to charge double the normal price for his appearances. Aldridge received awards from several governmental figures, was invited to perform for royalty, and inducted as a member of several learned societies. In every respect he was one of the major theatre figures of the mid-century, and yet he remained a mystery to his native country. In 1867, while touring the Continent, he died in Poland, still planning a tour of American theatres that had never witnessed his talents. Ira Aldridge was ignored by historians as he had been by American producers and critics; only in recent years has his full story become a part of American theatre history.

Insisting that acting was the work of an artist, he deplored the new style of "imitating nature" and strove to create a reality that corresponded to nature but presented it in a unique way.

The minor forms of theatre produced notable performers, too. Often these were essentially variety performers who relied on their personal magnetism and charm for their success. Prominent among these was Charlotte Crabtree (1847–1924), who began her career as an entertainer in the California mining camps and eventually became a nationally known star. Whatever role she played, it was always the same character, but the character was presented openly, honestly, and with great personality. She was a talented singer, a passable dancer, and an accomplished banjo player, and plays were rewritten or new plays created to allow her to incorporate these skills in her performances. This personality style of acting became extremely popular as audiences began to expect entertainment that was energetic, quick-paced, pleasing to the eye, and accessible.

The appeal to the eye was not left only to the physical attributes of the performers. The demand for historical accuracy begun earlier was pursued with new zeal, and the emphasis on special effects ranging from natural disasters to huge battle scenes clearly demanded new styles of scene design. Many talented and innovative individuals responded to this challenge.

William Capon (1757–1827) was a principal designer for John Philip Kemble at both the Drury Lane and Covent Garden. A painter by training, Capon created sets that were noted for their size and elegant style combined with a new interest in historical accuracy. He was particularly successful at creating Gothic backgrounds for the plays of Shakespeare. His designs became part of the theatrical stock at Covent Garden and were used until late in the century.

Pierre Luc-Charles Ciceri (1782–1862) contributed similarly to theatres in both America and France. As a youth he moved to America and did his first work in New York City. His designs for the opening of the new Park Street Theatre were praised for their size and elegance, although some disapproved of the excessive $60 budget he was allotted. Ciceri returned to Paris in 1806 and in 1810 became head designer at the Paris Opéra. There he was the principal artist for the Romantic productions, designing spectacular environments and special effects. Eventually, he formed his own design studio with numerous assistants, effectively establishing scenic design as a commercial venture.

A colleague of Ciceri, Louis-Jacques Daguerre (1789–1851) is generally credited with introducing the use of the panorama to the stage, although his most notable achievement was the diorama, an independent entertainment form. The panorama in its earliest form was a circular painting that totally surrounded its audience, allowing them a 360-degree view. Daguerre expanded this concept to create his diorama, which opened in 1822. The diorama was set in a long, narrow auditorium, with the diorama itself, measuring 45 feet by 75 feet, located more than 40 feet in front of the audience.

The diorama utilized painting on transparent linen that was modulated through adjustments in multidirectional lighting, resulting in an illusion of change. A later development utilized painting on both the front and back of the cloth so that even more detailed changes could be portrayed. In the theatre, the panorama was used as a backdrop to indicate movement that the stage could previously not suggest. A huge painting was mounted on a spool at one side of the stage and attached to an empty spool on the other side. By rolling the painting from one spool to the other, the designer could suggest a moving panorama behind the actors, thus enabling the theatre to portray chases, carriage rides, or other similar effects realistically.

A similar response to new developments was needed of costume design as well, and the work of J. R. Planché (1795–1880) is typical of the period. In 1823, Planché convinced Charles Kemble to stage a production of Shakespeare's *King John* in historically accurate costumes, marking the first time that the London stage had presented a historical view of the medieval period. Planché further insisted that costumes be designed for every member of the company, not just for the leading roles. The venture was expensive, but the production was very popular and returned the management its investment so that similar productions followed. The designs were a triumph for Planché as well and the drawings for the costumes were actually published.

As the spectacle of scenic production grew, more and more mechanical devices were required to make them practical and useful. In New York, Steel MacKaye (1842–1894) introduced a mechanical marvel at his Madison Square Theatre in 1879. MacKaye designed a complete double elevator stage with two complete stages arranged one above the other and operated by hydraulics. When one stage was in use, the other stage was one floor above or below being set with an entirely new scene; complete changes of three-dimensional scenery could occur in approximately 20 seconds. Although the intent was to disguise the process of scene changing, the device was so unique that the audience frequently remained after the performance for a demonstration of the elevator stage. MacKaye's work marks an early development in a trend that was to become a dominant force during the 20th century.

The elevator stage designed by Steele MacKaye at the Madison Square Theatre. *Courtesy Museum of the City of New York*

All of these scenic achievements were enhanced by new developments in stage lighting. The introduction of gas lighting at the beginning of the century made the stage lighting brighter, more even, and capable of more complete control. The control of intensity allowed the auditorium to be darkened thus providing greater brightness and clarity onstage. (Some historians think that the brighter light was a major influence in improving the quality of scenic painting.) The development of a control device known as the gas table allowed all light in the theatre to be controlled from one position, greatly increasing the ease of adjustments. Although the basic purpose of stage lighting was general illumination, investigations in the development of color mediums continued. The introduction of limelight, an intense light with a very precise focus, effectively introduced the concept of a spotlight to the stage and by midcentury limelight was used to highlight the principal actors at important moments in the play. The introduction of safer, more efficient, and more sophisticated instruments for gas lighting indicated great possibilities in stage lighting, but they were eclipsed with the introduction of electricity in the 1880s.

Audience

The growing preference for realism over poetry, for entertainment over art, for personality over character was all engendered by the new theatre audience that developed during this time period. They demanded melodramas and social dramas for serious entertainment, and improbable farces and operettas for comedy. They loved spectacle, special aquatic dramas, plays with real horse races, or dogs who saved the heroine in the last act. They witnessed changes in musical theatre as the operetta, which satirized the stories and style of traditional opera, gained wide acceptance in both France and England. In Italy, Verdi and other composers wrote operas that achieved tremendous mass appeal. In short, they demanded the creation of a popular drama intended to attract large audiences.

Reports of audience behavior vary greatly. One critic attending the minor theatres of England was appalled at the casual attitude and disrespect shown by spectators for the performance onstage; spectators responded openly to the players and occasionally pelted them with pieces of orange. A noted author visiting a regular theatre was disappointed at the utter passivity of the audience that laughed well at jokes but remained emotionally distanced from the action onstage. Another noted that those in the cheaper seats in the top galleries were ideal spectators who keenly focused on the action and openly expressed their reactions, while those in boxes seemed utterly disinterested and paid little attention to the stage.

On occasion, 19th-century audiences became more than spectators. One of the most famous occurrences in American theatre history was the Astor Place Riot in May 1849. The English actor William Macready and the American Edwin Forrest had engaged in a long-term petty rivalry based on Forrest's perception of ill-treatment during a tour in London. In response to his perception that Macready had been behind the poor reception, Forrest attended a Macready performance in Edinburgh and blatantly hissed the English actor's performance. The feud between the two was a common topic in newspapers in both countries and lasted for many months.

Four years later Macready journeyed to the United States for his farewell tour, receiving notably negative receptions on several occasions as fans of the American actor expressed their dislike of the sophisticated British actor, a response conditioned at least in part by growing anti-British sentiment in the United States. On May 8, Forrest fans filled the Astor Theatre and literally booed Macready off the stage. An aristocratic theatre group, appalled at this behavior, convinced Macready to perform again on May 10 and bought all the tickets themselves. A full-scale riot evolved as a crowd estimated at 10,000 people gathered outside the theatre and began to throw rocks. Eventually an infantry regiment was called to quell the disturbance, and several people were shot. Panic erupted, and more people were killed or injured as the crowd tried to disperse. Macready escaped the theatre, and the country in disguise and never returned. Although such happenings were very rare, the new dominance of the middle-class audience cannot be questioned. The theatre had become entertainment for all and could no longer be considered a pastime of the elite.

Standards of Judgment

Such a revolutionary change in theatre practice required new standards of judgment as well, and 19th-century criticism reflected the changing aesthetic. In England and America, one notable trend was the appearance of journalistic criticism. Much of the critical writing of the period appeared in newspapers or journals. Such criticism was usually written in response to one particular performance and printed as soon after the performance as was possible. This style of criticism tended to focus on the actors and scenery rather than on literature or the nature of drama.

William Hazlitt (1778–1830) was the leading English critic during the early years of the century. Noted as an essayist and lecturer on a wide range of topics, Hazlitt's theatre writing appeared mainly in various periodicals published between 1813 and 1818. While maintaining that a clear distinction of tragic and comic genre produced the best results, Hazlitt valued drama that created characters who were utterly unique and yet recognizable. One of the first critics to champion Edmund Kean, Hazlitt favored Shakespeare over the new melodrama but was able to appreciate the new achievements in spectacle.

George Henry Lewes (1817–1878), a failed actor and sometime playwright, also wrote for journalistic publication. Lewes deplored the critic's need to pass immediate judgment on a play or a performance, recognizing that time and consideration often changed first impressions. His writing was utterly sincere and frank, and he always gave the reasons for his judgment. This wasn't enough for Charles Kean, however, and after one particularly unfavorable notice, Kean revoked Lewes's free admission pass. Lewes's role as a critic was not to establish a standard, but simply to share his own perceptions and reactions.

In France and Germany, criticism continued in its traditional form as various critics, including leading playwrights, published essays, prefaces, and lectures in which they presented a literary standard by which theatre could be judged. The German author Georg Büchner (1813–1837) was one of the earliest critics to promote a concept of theatre as the re-creation of history. The purpose of drama, Büchner wrote in 1835, was "to come as close as possible to history as it actually happened." It was not the theatre's role to present a moral stance but simply to mirror the actual world.

A similar stance was taken by Alexandre Dumas *fils* (1824–1895). In his preface to his international success, *La dame aux camélias* published in 1851, Dumas went to great lengths to point out that the play was based on the actual life of a Frenchwoman. Dramatists, he insisted, have no need for imagination, for their only obligation is "to observe, to remember, to feel, to coordinate, and to restore. . . ." Although he maintained the need for the theatre to present such ideas in an artistic style, his views clearly indicate the rising tide of realism in the theatre.

Gustav Freytag (1816–1895), in his *Technique of Drama* (1863), presented an outline for dramatic structure that remained dominant throughout the 19th and 20th centuries. Freytag considered the drama to be an accurate depiction of human experience, but the experience needed to be structured to have dramatic impact. Basing his work on Aristotle, Freytag proposed a dramatic structure composed of an introduction, an inciting event leading to a rising action, a climax, a return or fall, and a catastrophe. He demonstrated that this pattern was an accurate analysis of the work of the great dramatists and suggested that this pattern should guide the work of playwrights and actors alike.

Standing directly opposed to the rampant growth of realism was Richard Wagner (1813–1883). Wagner considered drama to be the supreme form of art, for it was drama that allowed a person to "broaden out his own particular being . . . to a universally human being." This can be accomplished, Wagner maintained, only through the ultimate combination of all art forms. Wagner envisioned a *Gesamtkunstwerk*, a master artwork of

A Global Perspective

Latin American Theatre in the 19th Century

*T*heatre did not arrive in the New World with the European settlers; dramatic rituals existed in nearly every community before their arrival. Early settlers utilized puppet dramas for entertainment, and priests soon learned to use the drama as a means of spreading Christian doctrine. The continued arrival of colonists brought more and more European influence, resulting in a thriving and diverse theatrical scene by 1800.

In Argentina, a military victory over the British in 1808 was celebrated in plays, as was the resulting independence from Spain in 1810. Both events thus provided an impetus for the growth of theatre in Argentina, and in 1817 the Society of Good Taste in the Theatre was formed to promote theatrical activities. Theatres performed the European repertory (Molière, Voltaire) as well as musical works, and the circus was also popular, but local work was also promoted. *Juan Moreira* was the first highly successful play, combining elements of the circus with a melodramatic story that pitted the heroic *gaucho* (cowboy) against villainous soldiers.

The earliest record of theatre in Chile dates from 1663, but the birth of a truly Chilean theatre dates from the early 19th century, when plays were viewed as an educational tool in the newly independent country. Plays based on national history were encouraged, but the European repertoire was still favored. Translations of Sheridan's *The Rivals* and Hugo's *Hernani* were popular, and local comedies were also developed. Juan Rafael Allende, Chile's first great playwright, wrote 17 plays ranging from the Spanish musical form, the zarzuela, to patriotic drama.

Mexico's theatrical history started early with permanent roofed theatres being built as early as 1597 (well ahead of Madrid), and an established dramatist, Juan Ruiz de Alarcón, who gained fame when he moved to Spain in 1613. By the 19th century theatre was not confined to Mexico City. Permanent companies were working in Guadalajara, Zacatecas, and Yucatán and the national budget contained a subsidy for theatre. Productions ranged from European imports to Mexican plays dealing with political issues, and included comedies of manners. Manuel Eduardo de Gorostiza, born in Mexico but educated in Spain, was the most noted playwright of the period, and he is credited with introducing the style of the Spanish Golden Age into Mexican drama.

the future. It would be created by fusing dance, tone, and poetry into a single expressive whole. Such a unity would free each element to achieve new creative heights unattainable when each was grounded by its own limitations. Musical drama became the ideal form for the master artwork because it included all three sister arts. This theatre form is not a re-creation of nature but the ultimate creation of human imagination. In this respect, Wagner continued the concepts of the Romantics, and the contrast between the Romantic and the realist concepts frames theatrical events of the next epoch.

DRAMATIC LITERATURE

History is seldom tidy. Artistic movements rarely have a definitive beginning or end, and they are always accompanied by countermovements of one kind or another. This is especially true of Romanticism, which was itself an artistic revolt. One of the great periods of classicism occurred in the midst of the European passion for Romanticism. Because it was centered in one city, it has gained the name Weimar Classicism. Between 1790 and 1820 two men in particular produced some of the monumental works of German literature.

Johann Wolfgang von Goethe's prodigious output included plays, novels (his story *The Sorrows of Young Werther*, when published in 1774 did much to popularize the Romantic movement in Europe), operettas, and several scientific experiments. As head of the Weimar Court Theatre from 1791 to 1817, he virtually revolutionized German theatre.

After his experience with the Romantic style, Goethe embraced a literary style more akin to classicism than either *sturm und drang* or Romanticism. *Egmont* (1787) tells of a prince who stands for local justice against the tyranny of the Spanish overlords. Long set speeches and extended discussions of proper conduct dominate the first acts of the play. Egmont agrees to go to the palace of the Spanish representative, where he is imprisoned and put to death. That a trap had been laid for him is obvious, but adventure is not the purpose here. Goethe uses the entrapment to write a discussion between the representatives of political repression and popular liberty. Just before his execution, the spectre of Liberty comes to Egmont in his sleep, giving him the courage to face death.

Friedrich von Schiller differs from Goethe in his more conservative adherence to traditional values of womanhood, family life, and morality. His women are suffering heroines, noble wives, and waiting lovers. His characters long for and extoll the joys of family love. In *Mary Stuart* (1800), in which Queen Elizabeth is the villain against the heroic Mary, Elizabeth is never calculating or cruel. Schiller uses Elizabeth's historic indecision on whether or not to condemn the Catholic Mary for treason as an opportunity to show the courage and stamina of women. The formal poetic style, the measured rationality of Elizabeth, and the controlled emotions of Mary place the play in the classical mode.

Melodrama

French melodrama was nurtured in an era of exceptional emotional violence. The Revolution, the Reign of Terror that followed, and the nation's preoccupation with the fortunes of Napoleon created an atmosphere in which adventure, matters of personal honor, and violent tragedy were commonplace. Patriotic zeal dominated the battle-fields; personal glory appeared on stage. Life on the streets was governed by intrigue and conspiracy; life in the theatre came to match it.

Guilbert de Pixérécourt (1773–1844) filled his plays with violent and direct actions, characters with little subtlety, and an unrelenting justice that strikes the heart of the villain in the end. Pixérécourt established many of the conventions associated with melodrama in both France and England. He pitted virtue against villainy, with life, love, and security at stake. Conflicts abound in his plays, and, unlike in classical tragedy, they are all presented onstage for the audience to witness. Each act ends in some kind of climax that portends doom, and most of these climaxes involve special effects or physical action. To modern audiences, these plays may appear ludicrous, but at a time when the stately poetry of classic tragedians was still the standard of excellence, the plays of Pixérécourt were fresh and appealing.

The most popular German dramatist of the period was August Friedrich F. von Kotzebue (1761–1819). Not only did his melodramas, of which he wrote more than 200, achieve immense popularity in Germany, but he was translated into several languages and became the most popular playwright of the period throughout Europe. English translations helped spawn the rise of melodrama in England. Of these, the most popular were *The Stranger* (1798) and *Pizarro* (1799), adapted by Richard Brinsley Sheridan.

Of the hundreds of melodramas written after Pixérécourt, most have several elements in common. Melodrama presents idealized human beings in conflict with a hostile environment. Several characters in the play, usually including a young girl and a mother-figure, are just, honest, and virtuous. They expect little from life because they are comfortable in the belief that their adherence to moral virtue is its own reward. In their determination to be good even at the cost of their lives, an atmosphere of inevitability is created. Melodrama is a world of destiny in which it appears preordained that goodness will win after great struggle. Of course, the blocking character to this destiny is some form of evil incarnate. His (or her) badness derives from selfishness, greed, and lechery, usually in that order. The evil person is not alone, however; his negative qualities are recognized to be a part of human nature. Life, then, is a struggle to overcome all the base instincts that are hostile to goodness and virtue.

Melodrama is a theatrical art form, not a dramatic one. The tight moral range of the vision of reality limits the thematic possibilities. The separation of good and evil into distinct characters renders subtle characterization impossible. However, what the plays lack in thought, they compensate with visual and aural spectacle. The characters use pantomimic gestures to express themselves as fully as possible. The conflicts are realized in heroic struggles with lots of challenges, duels, and circus-like feats. Scenically, the plays alternate between the security of domestic settings and threatening natural landscapes. Special effects abound, with ghosts appearing from nowhere, walls disappearing, ships getting tossed about on the ocean, and factories exploding in flame. Each action is accompanied by appropriate music in the style of the silent movies of the 1910s and 1920s. Dancing and singing are common. The productions are calculated to draw the audience into the action and never give it time to reflect on the logic of the circumstances. Melodramas may not be thematically complex, but they are theatrically rich.

A TRIP TO THE
ADELPHI THEATRE,
1860

*T*he audience crowding into London's Adelphi Theatre at Christmastime 1860 bustles noisily, anticipating a great evening of theatre. *The Colleen Bawn* by Dion Boucicault had been a success in New York earlier in the year, and the author and his wife, the stars of the production, are playing the major roles here as well. Queen Victoria herself has already seen the show, and it is rumored she will attend again soon.

The auditorium is filled with middle- and lower-class people freshly scrubbed for an evening out. They are all excited about the play they are going to see, because although they attend Shakespeare, they adore the new melodramas. They delight in the richness of the decor in the auditorium. The Adelphi Theatre, with its ornate molding and rich curtains, is a beautiful room, and visiting such a place is part of the excitement of the evening. Well-dressed patrons move to their places in the more expensive seating areas as the lights dim in the auditorium and the orchestra begins to play.

For the first several minutes, the audience takes in the idyllic setting showing a small home on the banks of a beautiful river. Every word and every movement of the actors seems so real that the audience forgets they are in a theatre. The play is full of terrible happenings. When the final scene of the second act reveals a cave under large rocks surrounded by the waters of the lake, no one questions how the scenery has been constructed to show a lake, but everyone is concerned about the heroine's safety. Suddenly, the hero climbs onto a rock and dives into the water to save his beloved Eily, and many in the audience gasp aloud as he disappears from view.

The ending of the play is unbearably sad as the hero nobly surrenders the heroine, allowing her to marry her true love. As the heroine bursts into tears of happiness on the final line, the audience smiles through their tears as they applaud the performance. A silly afterpiece is presented following the main play, but many in the audience do not stay, knowing that they must get up early next morning to go to work.

A N N A   C O R A
M O W A T T
(1 8 1 9 – 1 8 7 0)

*H*er childhood years should have signaled that the life of Anna Cora Mowatt would produce some remarkable events. By the age of 10 she had read the complete plays of Shakespeare, at 15 she was married to a young lawyer, and she had published poetry by the time she was 18 years old. Health problems did little to deter her work, and when her husband suffered financial difficulties, she became a public "reader," or elocutionist. Unable to maintain the rigors of that career, she returned to her writing, publishing magazine articles, biographies (including one of Goethe), and a series of books on domestic issues. A close observer of society, she frequently entertained friends with her witty comments on New York's fashionable set, and when a friend suggested she write a play about it, she immediately responded.

Four weeks later *Fashion* was complete, and the friend presented it to the manager of the Park Theatre, who scheduled it for performance one week later. The play had been mentioned in the papers, and for the opening night on March 26, 1845, the theatre was filled with the cream of New York society, quite a switch from the usual middle-class clientele. The ladies of the night had been banished for the evening, and an unusual number of women were in attendance, even sitting in the pit. (Anna was to continue to attract female audiences throughout her career.)

Fashion is a comedy of manners in the style of Sheridan, although it is completely American. Set in New York City, it depicts the efforts of Mrs. Tiffany to gain acceptance among the fashionable elite. She is surrounded by the incompetent (her black valet, her rustic sister, her husband, and a farmer friend), the would-be fashionable (a young man-about-town and a would-be poet), and the truly fashionable (Count Jolimaître). Mrs. Tiffany's efforts to arrange a marriage between Jolimaître and her daughter are destroyed when she discovers that the count is actually a former valet who is engaged to her own maid. Beyond this difficulty, however, her husband has been forging notes to cover her extravagances, and only the gracious generosity of the farmer, Adam Trueman, saves them from complete disgrace. The entire play has a light tone, although melodrama does intrude occasionally and at times the play is pure farce. The public loved it, however, and the critics were also impressed. The poet/critic Edgar Allan Poe wrote, "We are delighted to find, in the reception of Mrs. Mowatt's comedy, the clearest indications of a revival of the American drama."

When further financial difficulties developed and no second play was forthcoming from her pen, Anna decided to become an actress. Friends and associates were shocked, certain that this was an act of mad desperation. Anna had experience in public performance from her days as a "reader" and was a woman of great beauty and charm, but she was totally inexperienced in the world of theatre. When a producer/friend scheduled her debut for New York City, Anna was aghast, for she had been certain she would be allowed to begin her career in a smaller venue. With only three weeks before the performance, she began working daily with an established actor, spending four hours daily on vocal drills and also studying fencing and beginning to exercise on a regular basis. Only two actual rehearsals had been scheduled, for the other actors had played the roles before. On the day before the performance, the cast went through a complete run-through, and a brief review was held the morning of the performance. Anna had provided her own costume at no little cost, and once she had learned how to handle the pats of butter, coloring, and cork used for makeup, she felt prepared. However, when she reached the stage she was taken aback at the new furniture and the props she was expected to use. She delayed the curtain briefly to gain some control and then ordered the curtain to rise. The performance was a triumph and at the final curtain the audience rose to its feet, showering the stage with flowers.

Despite recurring health problems, Anna continued her acting career for nine years. She played a variety of roles, including Shakespearean ones, throughout the United States, and was very successful in London as well. When her husband died in 1851 she continued to perform, but she retired from the stage in 1854 to marry a wealthy Southern gentleman, William Ritchie.

Never fully accepted by Ritchie's family because of her Northern connections and her theatrical background, she left him in 1861. She lived in Europe for most of the rest of her life, with only one brief return to the stage with an amateur theatre group. She died in London in 1870.

Eugène Scribe and the Well-Made Play

A second form of popular drama in the 19th century also began in France. Some two decades after Pixérécourt began writing melodramas, Eugène Scribe (1791–1861) developed a style known as the *pièce bien fait,* inadequately translated in English as the "well-made play." Scribe's tight play structure and conservative values provided a reassuring vision of reality. He decried the ill effects of money on marriage and the family, preferring traditional values of breeding and class status. His vision of reality was upright, conservative, and moralistic. He believed in the family structure and attacked anything that might threaten its security. He was bitter in his denunciation of people who marry for money, but he was also cautious of passionate romance. He was certain that hard work and financial economy were the bedrock of a successful marriage.

Given this perspective, the dramatic structure that Scribe evolved in plays such as *The Glass of Water* (1940) and *Adrienne Lecouvreur* (1849) was careful and meticulous. His plays open with exposition, often revealing a piece of information that will become important later. Two characters then become locked in a battle of wills, or else a major character is tempted to make an error of judgment. Either one of these situations could destroy family and personal reputations. A series of calculated reversals occurs, in which new information arriving by letter or messenger constantly alters the expectations of the characters and keeps the audience uncertain of the outcome. Invariably, characters make mistakes in judgment based on false information; the audience knows the truth but must sit helplessly and watch the characters try to unravel the situation themselves. In comedies, these mistakes are the source of one of the great comic devices in the theatre (when two characters listen to the same story and interpret it completely differently). Through some grand contrivance (the reappearance of a long-lost relative, for instance) the fates of the characters are resolved to everyone's satisfaction. Through the entirety of the drama, however, the motive force has been the logical and persistent drive toward resolution. The reversals and contrivances are so rapid that the audience has little time to question the validity of the proceedings. When it ends, the play may not have given the audience much to think about, but it has also given them little time to think.

Dumas *fils* and the Social Thesis Play

The third form of popular drama in the mid-19th century was the social thesis play, also known as social drama in England. Social dramas focused the dramatic action on a specific problem in society. Typically the problems had to do with courtesans, financial speculation, or marriage problems. Whereas Scribe and Pixérécourt relied on action and theatrical plot devices, social dramatists used the plays to present their views of society's problems. Action was secondary to idea; the play's outcome was the result of the argument of the play rather than a consequence of the action. Thus, a character might be shot at the final curtain even though there had been no preparation for the murder; the playwright simply didn't want the character's attitudes to succeed.

Alexandre Dumas *fils* (son) opened the theatre to discussion of social problems in his 1851 drama *La dame aux camélias*, or *Camille*. The problem Dumas dramatized was the treatment of courtesans by French society. Marguerite Gautier, the lady of the camellias, is portrayed as a woman of good heart and kind intentions who pushes her youthful admirer, Armand Duval, away from her because she knows that society will not accept a union between her and a respectable family. Yet, like the Romantic heroines who preceded her on the Parisian stage, she dreams of an ideal love free of social restrictions and demands. Dumas thus gives credibility to Marguerite's dilemma. Society is to blame for the tragic situation that prevents Marguerite from ever finding the happiness she deserves. In Armand's father, who ultimately forces the couple apart, the morality of the age is personified. That he says and does what most in the audience would have done forces the audience to confront its own values. By weighting all the action in favor of Marguerite, the audience is led to reach the conclusion Dumas wants: that its values are wrong. The opening night audience at the Vaudeville Theatre was overcome with emotion. Even the actors were swept up by the moment: when Armand exited at the end of Act IV, the actor

UNCLE TOM'S CABIN

*R*arely has the theatre world witnessed a phenomenon to rival the appearance of *Uncle Tom's Cabin* on the American theatre scene. Harriet Beecher Stowe (1811–1896) published her novel in 1851, and from then through the remainder of the century *Uncle Tom's Cabin* was a dominant feature of theatre in the United States.

An instant sensation from the moment of its publication, *Uncle Tom's Cabin* appeared in dramatic form within one year. Since copyright laws were lax, various versions appeared, none of them authored by Mrs. Stowe. At one time five playhouses in New York and five more in London were performing the play simultaneously. By the end of the century, 500 companies were presenting the play across the country, and popular productions were staged throughout Western Europe. George Aiken (1830–1876) authored the most successful version, and his company performed the play for a period of 35 years.

The subject of all this excitement was an episodic, sentimental melodrama depicting the life of Negro slaves. The characters are now part of American folklore: the gentle kindly old slave, Uncle Tom, who passively accepts evil treatment by his master, Simon Legree, and is ultimately murdered; the young black girl, Topsy, adopted and converted by a white woman; the brave young wife, Eliza, who eludes her pursuers to join her husband in Canada and eventually escapes to Africa; and Little Eva, the gentle young white girl who befriends Uncle Tom but dies in childhood.

The plot was perfect for a theatrical melodrama. Enterprising producers added bloodhounds to pursue Eliza as she crossed the ice floes to escape her white pursuers. Choruses sang religious music to underscore the most sentimental scenes. And Uncle Tom's ascent to heaven to be reunited with Little Eva at the close of the play allowed great use of theatrical spectacle. One New York production featured 18 sets, more than 200 performers, and several species of animals onstage.

Clearly, Mrs. Stowe intended the play as an indictment of slavery, and her book was the first in history to depict African-Americans sympathetically. It immediately sparked a response, and the play was banned in many areas of the South. Unfortunately, the style of production tended to stereotype the characters. The black characters were usually played by white people in blackface (only in

continued

1878 did the first African-American actor play Uncle Tom), and the minstrel tradition prompted the creation of caricatures. Revisionist versions of the play changed the ending, eliminating Uncle Tom's murder and depicting him as a happy old man living under the rule of a loving master. Gradually, the play lost its social impact and the characters were transmuted into familiar figures of vaudeville and early films.

Historians note that *Uncle Tom's Cabin* clearly had an impact on social feeling during the years prior to the Civil War. Beyond that immediate effect, the stereotypes that the play created continue to impact our society in the closing years of the 20th century.

playing Armand, Charles Fechter, nearly pulled the set down in his frenzy, and Marie Doche, playing Marguerite, fainted.

Dumas had second thoughts about his glorification of the morality of Marguerite, and he began retracting his public stance in 1854 in *Diane de Lys*, and again in 1855 in *The Demi-Monde*. However, his more conservative plays were never as popular as his story of the courtesan with a heart of gold.

Feydeau and Farce

Georges Feydeau (1862–1921) began writing humorous monologues in 1880; he kept his readers and audiences laughing until his last play in 1916. Of Feydeau's most successful plays, *Hotel Paradiso* (1894), *A Flea in Her Ear* (1907), and *Keep an Eye on Amelie!* (1908) are probably the most frequently produced in the United States today. In all of his plays, however, Feydeau was an impish jester in the temple of love. For him, love had none of the tragic despair of the 18th century or the unrelieved *angst* of the 20th century. It was, instead, a trifle, a bonbon, a temporary escape from a dreary existence. Unlike the social dramatists who preceded him, Feydeau found the love triangle a dramatic jack-in-the-box that could explode with surprises in all directions. His cads, those middle-aged (and older) men who hope to entice women into brief but elegant affairs, were likeable rather than villainous. Audiences laughed with them because of their honesty, their simplicity, and their genuine need to experience something positive in their lives. Feydeau's women were sometimes naive, but seldom innocent. They too were in need of an amorous release from their banal existences. The humor of the love chase in a Feydeau play is the result of everyone being both chaser and chased at the same time. Everyone is escaping someone else and hoping to fall into the arms of another person. That they rarely succeed is Feydeau's final comment on love—it may make the world go round, but the world usually ends up right where it began.

Just as Feydeau is indebted to the social dramatists for his subject matter, he is indebted to Scribe for his initial sense of dramatic construction. What Scribe used to build intrigue and reversals, however, becomes in Feydeau's hands the technique of farce. His plays begin with a simple proposition (a man wishes to have an affair, for instance) and gradually build up the momentum of a train. First, the man endeavors to escape the watchful eyes of his wife or neighbors. While planning his rendezvous, he encounters other characters, each of whom becomes ensnared in his plans. By the end of the first act, Feydeau's stage is generally filled with a dozen or more characters all unwittingly embarked on an adventure that will bring them into embarrassing contact with one another. In the second act, the characters are trapped in their own devices, caught in a hunting lodge or a nearby hotel where they hoped to make their assignations. They appear and disappear in closets and hallways with bewildering speed, each encounter timed to the very second before their schemes are discovered. (Gunshots are fired, but no one is ever hurt; men boast of saving their honor, but they only lose their clothes; and little children prove to be impudent interruptions in the game of love.) Public officials appear who are outraged by the whole situation, but they are ultimately so confused by the situation that they cannot arrest anyone. In the final act, all the characters return to their homes and their original partners, presumably to begin the mad chase again after they have caught their breath.

Farce is rooted in wish fulfillment: characters pursue socially unacceptable goals in the guise of respectability. The fear of being exposed is avoided at the last second, fools and bullies are made more foolish by their actions, and disorder and chaos overwhelm the world in an anarchic thrust against social convention. Individualism confronts a world of mechanical logic and nearly succeeds in asserting itself. Because farce is comic, the playwrights orchestrate these fantasies to elicit the maximum humor from them. By keeping the stakes low (no one is ever going to be really shot or lose her husband) and generating an atmosphere of playfulness with buffoon characters and physical jokes, the playwright ensures that the incidents of the play are all taken in jest. When these same devices are used to threaten the stability of society, farce becomes melodrama.

Wagner and Music-Drama

Just as the works of Goethe serve as an extension of the classical movement, the works of Richard Wagner become a summation of the Romantic spirit. He drew on the characteristics of Romantic music and drama, and yet he extended them so far beyond their original intents that he created his own unique operas. His musical dramas were peculiarly distinctive in their choice of thematic materials, their use of the orchestra, their handling of the singers, and their overall conception. Wagner stands astride the century like some artistic demon imposing his will and his theories on the shape of his operas, dwarfing everyone around him except the Italians.

After two minor works in the 1830s that took their musical subjects from the then-current German opera tradition, Wagner first received acclaim in 1842 with two operas, *Rienzi* and *The Flying Dutchman*. He followed these with two strongly Romantic works, *Tannhauser* (1845) and *Lohengrin* (1846–1848). He then became embroiled in the political upheavals of 1848, during which time his theories of art and society developed. He published his two monumental books, *Artwork of the Future* and *Opera and Drama*, in 1850 and 1851. He then turned back to the theatre, where he determined to realize his theories in a new operatic form of his own creation. He dismissed traditional characterization, creating instead characters of mythic proportions. He rejected realistic or historical story lines, substituting Teutonic myths and symbolic ideas with minimal narratives. He used the stage as a gigantic arena for the conflict of the most elemental forces in human nature. Gods clashed with mortals, and human beings struggled for a vision of eternity. The sacred and profane were pitted against each other, testing the meaning of love on a scale simply not imagined by any Romantic before him.

Tristan and Isolde (1865) is a love story with almost no action. The two lovers are sensuously trapped by their erotic passions. The opera explores musically their struggle to find love in death. A magnificent love theme captures the lovers' yearning in its now-famous use of unusual harmonies. With chromatic richness and continuous musical invention, the extended work is unprecedented in its exploration through sound of the dimensions of illicit love.

Wagner's epic *The Ring* (1869–1876), a cycle of four complete operas, illustrates the demands of his *Gesamtkunstwerk*. The cycle's narrative—the least important element in the work—tells of a magic ring in the possession of three Rhine maidens. It is stolen first by an evil dwarf, then falls into the possession of the god Wotan; it is recovered by the epic's hero, Siegfried, and is eventually returned to the Rhine, after bringing destruction to those who possessed it. The Ring cycle has been subjected to extensive critical scrutiny. All kinds of symbolic significance have been attached to its images, characters, and incidents. A summary of its meaning is impossible. Wagner wanted to create works that reached levels of meaning untouched by other writers. By abstracting and symbolizing his musical dramas, he achieved his goal, at least to those who became his devoted followers.

CONNECTIONS

In the 19th century, theatre became the most popular art form in Western Europe. Never before had it appealed to such a broad social spectrum. Never before had English actors become sufficiently respectable to be knighted. In addition, several developments occurred that influenced theatre, film, and television in the 20th century.

The period between Romanticism and the plays of Henrik Ibsen established many of the conventions that would become part of the realistic style of the 20th century. The rise of realism was neither gradual nor consistent, but several factors led to its existence. The spectacular sets and special effects of the melodramas and pantomimes generated a demand for more realistic scenic devices. The box set enclosed the theatre space and for the first time created the illusion of a real interior location on stage. The directorial and managerial policies of Vestris in England and Montigny in France were also significant, because they began using real props and decorating their sets with real household objects. Realistic detail also emerged from the determination to re-create the historical locations of Shakespeare's plays. Gas lighting and then electricity made possible greater control over atmosphere and mood. The directorial policies of Macready, Kean, Irving, Montigny, and others diminished the opportunities for star actors to stand out from the other actors. Taken together these were the first steps in the direction of the realistic style that would be the standard of post–World War I drama.

A second 19th-century trend was the rise of the modern director. The characteristics of the director today include someone who is in charge of the total production, who is responsible for creating the environment of the play, and who communicates the ideas of the play through the actors to the audience. Few men prior to Kemble held such authority. By 1900, however, most productions had a director with such responsibilities. The care in the presentation of promptbooks that held all the blocking and technical cues began with Kean and others. Both Kemble and Kean sat with the actors and worked through each moment of the play to their satisfaction. Irving and others demanded long rehearsals with attention to every detail of the stage action. The managerial policies of Kean and Irving particularly were so clearly defined that productions could be identified as having been under their care. Audiences began to go to a play to see what the manager/director had created as much as to see the actors or the outcome of the play. Directorial experimentation with old texts did not really begin until the next century, but the role of the director was well defined by the time Irving retired from the stage.

In addition to the rise of realism and of the modern stage director, the dramatic forms of the 19th century also continued to be popular into the 20th century. Melodrama appeared in several silent movies of the 1910s and in the swashbuckling adventures of the 1920s. Melodramatic characteristics also continue in use in the movies today, especially the reliance on unusual special effects, the underscoring of lurid music in horror stories, and the heroic deeds of space adventurers. The melodrama was also the historical bridge between sentimentalism and the television soap opera. Whenever members of society feel that they are basically good but the world around them is not, melodrama will appear in the theatre arts.

Scribe and the techniques of the well-made play can still be found in the situation comedies and action-adventures of commercial television shows. His reliance on a repeated set of structural characteristics lends itself to writers who must come up with a new script every week. Many of the well-made play characteristics are evident in these shows: they begin with a straightforward exposition showing a murder or identifying the problem, and the simple incident is then extended across time by sudden reversals in the characters' expectations. Plot devices that lead to unexpected events are more apparent than internal changes in the characters. The stories contain some secret known to the hero and the audience but not to the villain (a man has a bionic arm or drives a computerized automobile, allowing the audience to share in the secret and enjoy its final revelation). Finally, the vision of reality of most sitcoms is that life is a string of occurrences-turned-adventures that contain simple moral truths understandable to almost anyone. All of these elements first appeared in Scribe's works.

The operettas of Offenbach and of Gilbert and Sullivan also are important because of their influence on the development of musical comedy. Offenbach's stories of romance set to vivacious dance rhythms, his smooth orchestrations, and lovely melodies all had an impact on the American operettas of the 1910s and 1920s. Gilbert and Sullivan revived the connection between satire and musical theatre that had virtually disappeared after the Licensing Act of 1737. Gilbert's lyrics, with their topicality and erudition, were the model for lyricists from Gershwin and Porter to Sondheim. The continued revival of their works is the ultimate testament to the greatness of Offenbach and of Gilbert and Sullivan.

SOURCES FOR FURTHER STUDY

Social/Art/Philosophy Background

Barzun, Jacques. *Darwin, Marx, Wagner: Critique of a Heritage.* Boston: Little, Brown and Company, 1941.

Brahms, Caryl. *Gilbert and Sullivan's Lost Chords and Discords.* Boston: Little, Brown and Company, 1975.

Grout, Donald Jay. *A Short History of Opera.* New York: Columbia University Press, 1947.

Kemp, Tom. *Industrialization in Nineteenth Century Europe.* London: Longman Press, 1985.

Letwin, Shirley Robin. *The Pursuit of Certainty.* Cambridge: Cambridge University Press, 1965.

Mayer, Arno J. *The Persistence of the Old Regimes.* New York: Pantheon Books, 1981.

Sigsworth, Eric M. *In Search of Victorian Values.* New York: St. Martin's Press, 1988.

Weaver, William. *The Golden Century of Italian Opera from Rossini to Puccini.* London: Thames and Hudson, 1980.

Theatre History

Bruford, W. H. *Theatre, Drama, and Audience in Goethe's Germany.* Westport, Conn.: Greenwood Press, 1950.

Carlson, Marvin. *The French Stage in the Nineteenth Century.* Metuchen, N.J.: Scarecrow Press, 1972.

————. *The German Stage in the Nineteenth Century.* Metuchen, N.J.: Scarecrow Press, 1972.

————. *Goethe and the Weimar Theatre.* Ithaca, N.Y.: Cornell University Press, 1978.

Donohue, Joseph. *Theatre in the Age of Kean.* Oxford: Basil Blackwell, 1975.

Kelly, Linda. *The Kemble Era.* New York: Random House, 1980.

Mander, Raymond, and Joe Mitchenson. *A Picture History of the British Theatre.* London: Hulton Press, 1957.

Rankin, Hugh F. *The Theatre in Colonial America.* Chapel Hill: University of North Carolina Press, 1965.

Richards, Kenneth, and Peter Thompson, eds. *Essays on 19th Century British Theatre.* London: Methuen, 1971.

Rowell, George. *Victorian Dramatic Criticism.* London: Methuen, 1971.

————. *The Victorian Theatre 1792–1914: A Survey.* 2d ed. Cambridge: Cambridge University Press, 1978.

Southern, Richard. *The Victorian Theatre: A Pictorial Survey.* New York: Theatre Arts Books, 1970.

Wilson, Garff B. *A History of American Acting.* Bloomington, Ind: University of Indiana Press, 1966.

————. *Three Hundred Years of American Drama and Theatre.* Englewood Cliffs, N.J.: Prentice-Hall, 1973.

Dramatic Literature

Gerould, Daniel, ed. *Melodrama.* New York: New York Literary Forum, 1980.

Hemmings, F. W. J. *Alexandre Dumas: The King of Romance.* New York: Charles Scribner's Sons, 1979.

Kaufmann, Friedrich. *German Dramatists of the 19th Century.* Freeport, N.Y.: Books for Libraries Press, 1970.

Lob, Ladislaus. *From Lessing to Hauptmann, Studies in German Drama.* London: University Tutorial Press, 1974.

Montague, C. E. *Dramatic Values.* London: Chatto and Windus, 1941.

Pronko, Leonard C. *Eugene Labiche and Georges Feydeau.* New York: Grove Press, 1982.

Taylor, John Russell. *The Rise and Fall of the Well-Made Play.* New York: Hill and Wang, 1967.

C H A P T E R

14

General Events

Confucianism
state philosophy

BCE 202   CE 50

Buddhism and
Taoism popular

Arts Events

Theatre History Events

The Traditional Theatres of China

DENISE CHUK

On March 12, 1935, at the invitation of the Soviet Union's All-Union Society for Cultural Relations with Foreign Countries (VOKS), a Peking Opera troupe, led by the famous Mei Lan-fang, arrived in Moscow. The troupe was warmly received by a committee that included K. S. Stanislavski, V. I. Nemirovich-Danchenko, W. E. Meyerhold, and S. M. Eisenstein. The Chinese company opened a three-week season in Moscow and Leningrad. Those who went to the performances and the discussion sections following the shows included Maxim Gorky, Alexi Tolstoy, Erwin Piscator, and Bertolt Brecht. Eisenstein, who had seen Japanese dramas before, commented on the difference between Japanese and Chinese drama, and described Peking Opera as an ancient theatrical art that combines movement, music, and costumes into one. With the cooperation of Mei, Eisenstein directed and filmed a few scenes from a play, *Rainbow Pass,* to show this foreign form of stagecraft.

Although this was not the first time Peking Opera was performed in a foreign country, as Mei and his company had toured Japan in 1919 and the United States in 1930, it was the Russian tour that finally established Peking Opera's position as a

T'ang Dynasty	Yuan Dynasty		Ch'ing Dynasty
618–907	1279–1368	1368–1644	1644–1911
	Ming Dynasty		

Block printing introduced	Tu Fu, poet		Tung Ch'i-ch'ang, landscape painter
CE 590–618	701–762 712–770		d. 1636 1700–1800
Li Po, poet			"Romance" novels

Dance/music forms		Tsa-chu	Beijing Opera
618–907		1279–1368 1368–1644	1644–1911 1844–19664
		Chu'an-ch'i K'un ch'u	Mei Lanfang

relevant and unique artistic form of theatre in the consciousness of Western literary and theatre people. This synthetic form of theatre, with many of its styles and concepts passed down from its remote ancestor in the 13th century, has withstood many political and cultural challenges, such as the Cultural Revolution in China in the 1960s and the rising popularity of the drama and films from the West, and is still entertaining the masses, albeit a decreasing number, both in China and in the Republic of China on Taiwan.

CULTURAL IDEAS

To truly appreciate the form and content of Chinese drama, we must first acquire some understanding of the historical and cultural heritage that shapes such a particular art form.

Confucianism or *Ju Chia (Ru Chia)*

Contrary to the popular Western misconception, Confucianism is no more a Chinese religion than Platonism is a religion in the West. Rather, it is a system of ethical, moral, and social beliefs first advocated in detail in the *Analects*, a collection of the teachings of Confucius (551–479 BCE), and later in the teachings of Mencius (372–289 BCE). Confucianism concerns itself not so much with philosophical or metaphysical issues

Peking Opera in performance.   *From* The Beauty of China: International Theatre. *Published by the Han Kong Corporation, Taiwan, 1980*

("One does not know what is life, how can one know about death?"), but the questions of an individual's virtue and place in society. Several concepts are key to the makeup of a virtuous person:

Jen (human-heartedness) is the kind of virtuous love that is at the core of every good deed. Confucius believes that *"jen* consists in loving others" (*Analects,* XII, 22). Although such love comes in different gradations, as in the case of a father who would love his own child more than he would the neighbor's child, one should extend such love until one can not only treat the young in one's family as they should be treated, but also extend this treatment to the young of other people's families. Thus, *jen* in a larger sense can be used to denote not only love, but all the virtues combined. A "man of *jen*" therefore is a man of perfect virtue.

Yi (righteousness) is doing what ought to be done without the motivation of profit. It is imperative that one does not choose to do something because it can be beneficial to the doer, but rather because it is the right thing to do for its own sake. When a person returns a lost wallet to its rightful owner, the action will not be regarded as true *yi* if the person in his mind is expecting a reward or even praise of his character.

Chung (loyalty and conscientiousness to others) and *shu* (forgivingness and altruism) are ways of practicing *jen.* A person should do to others only as that person would expect others to behave in return. Hence one should serve one's superior in exactly the way one expects to be served by one's subordinates. If everyone practices *chung* and *shu*, with *yi* as the formal guideline, then *jen* will be very easy to obtain.

The practice of such virtues results in a society in which everybody does deeds according to their name and station in society. Hence, within the microcosm of a family structure, a father loves his children as a father should; a child acts filially toward the parents, respecting and obeying all their wishes. Such relations can then be extended to the larger social and political scene, when one always treats one's friends and neighbors properly, and the ruler sets good examples for his people and rules benevolently, and his subjects offer him unquestioned loyalty. By upholding such a network of interpersonal and social relations, Confucianism helps bring about a society that is harmonious and stable.

Taoism or *Tao Chia*

Like Confucianism, Taoism is not a religion but rather a philosophy. Through the centuries, however, some Taoist beliefs degenerated into a sort of superstitious religious practice, and it is this practice that is frequently referred to as *Tao Chiao*, or the Taoist religion. The terms *Taoism* and *Tao Chia* (the School of Tao) refer to the philosophical teachings of two people: Lao Tzu (c. 604 BCE–c. 531 BCE), author of *Tao-Te Ching* (the *Book of Tao*), and Chuang Chou or Chuang Tzu (c. 369 BCE–c. 286 BCE), author of *Chuang Tzu*. The true dates of the men and their authorship of the books are debatable; nonetheless, the beliefs we call Taoism have been a very influential force in the Chinese psyche. Unlike Confucianism, whose teachings are centered in moral and ethical issues, the fundamental concern of Taoism is rather metaphysical, as illustrated by the following key concepts:

Tao (the Way) is the most important term in Taoist beliefs, yet it is also difficult to describe, as it is something that is unnamable. The very beginning of *Tao Te Ching* discusses Tao as such:

> Tao that can be comprised in words is not the eternal Tao,
> Name that can be named is not the abiding name,
> Wu, the unnamable is the beginning of Heaven and Earth,
> Yu, the namable is the mother of all things.

Once we think we know what Tao really is and name it, it is immediately transformed and degraded into a fixed aspect of the full potential and thus ceases to be the true Tao. Therefore, the name *Tao* is simply a designated sign with which we speak of this otherwise unnamable Way and does not imply that it has any namable attributes.

Constancy is the nature of the law of Tao. Though things in this world are ever changeable and constantly changing, behind them all lies a *ch'ang*, or constancy that is unchangeable, and the mutability of the world is exactly a manifestation of this *ch'ang*. To understand this is to be able to avoid the emotional distress and sufferings caused by ignorance of the law of nature.

Relativity and *Reverses* are two important manifestations of the way of Tao. Things that exist in the manifested world are all relative in nature, because all words and concepts are merely built upon a finite point of view that is relative and alterable. The famous incident when Chuang Chou dreamt that he was a butterfly and then woke up only to doubt whether it was truly a man named Chuang Chou dreaming that he was a butterfly or a butterfly dreaming that it was a man named Chuang Chou shows the relative nature of all our perceptions. Also, when a thing develops certain extreme qualities, it is invariable that those qualities will revert to become their own opposites. So, in every action there is implied its counteraction; the hollowness or "lack" of a spoon is exactly the reason why it becomes useful.

Wu-Wei (Nonaction) does not imply abandoning action altogether, for choosing nonaction is also an action. Rather, *wu-wei* implies doing less to interfere with the law of Tao, acting without artificiality, and restricting action strictly to what is necessary and what is natural. A person that understands the principle of *wu-wei* is meek, humble, and content. When expanded to a social and political scale, the Taoists believe that the more restrictions and prohibitions there are, the poorer people are. Thus the wise head of the country should rule with *wu-wei* and should not govern through the formal machinery of government.

Chinese Buddhism

Buddhism reached China around the first half of the first century CE. Due to many similarities shared between Buddhism and Taoism, Buddhism in China has been "Tao-ified" first superficially, and then in true essence to form a kind of "Chinese Buddhism." Some general concepts in Buddhism include:

1. *karma* (or *Yeh* in Chinese), which designates deeds, actions—including what an individual sentient being speaks and thinks;

2. *samsara* (or *Ying Kuo* in Chinese) is the *ad infinitum* cause and effect of the *karma;*

3. *avidya* (or *Wu ming* in Chinese) is the fundamental ignorance that leads to all suffering. This can be helped by achieving *bodhi*, which means enlightenment;

4. *nirvana* (or *Nieh Pan* in Chinese) is emancipation from *samsara*, thus escaping suffering altogether and achieving a Buddha-like nature.

In both Taoism and Buddhism, then, there is a distinction between *Yu* (being, the namable) and *Wu* (nonbeing, unnamable). The method of approaching the highest state of existence is also similar between the two: through constant negation until the final denial of denial, emptying out the concept of emptiness, one can finally be closest to the one that is not namable.

A great part of Chinese aesthetic, moral, and social structures, as well as a basic view of life and reality, have been shaped by Confucianism, Taoism, and Buddhism, and often by a mixture of the three. The respect for moral courage and virtue, the firm belief in social order and propriety in individual behavior, the ability to discern superficial realities from more permanent ones, and the philosophical acceptance of misfortune in life, together with a persistent interest in the otherworldly—all have found their ways into the traditional theatres of China.

DEVELOPMENT OF THE DRAMATIC FORM

Chinese drama originated from various sources. Probably as early as 300 BCE, the shamans used their dances to entertain the gods. Later, there were court jesters, horn-buttings, and acrobatic variety shows to entertain the people. It was probably not until the North Ch'i Dynasty (386–589 CE) that music, dance, and some form of story-telling were combined. Prince Lanling of North Ch'i was also said to be the originator of mask-wearing, as he was recorded to have worn a fierce-looking mask in battle to cover up his handsome face. Hence a mask is also known as *Tai-mien*, or *Daimien*, which means "substitute face."

Compared to other forms of literature, drama was a relatively late-comer in Chinese literary history. A true form of theatre did not develop until the 13th century. However, in the T'ang and Sung Dynasties, various forms of dramatic entertainment flourished and helped shape the form of Chinese theatre in later periods.

The T'ang Dynasty (618–907 CE) was one of the most brilliant political and cultural periods in Chinese history. One of its emperors, Hsüan-Tzung (Xuanzong, also known as Minghuang, c. 712–756), was credited with having established the first drama academy (the Pear Garden, or Liyuan) in China. The T'ang Dynasty saw the popularizing of several forms of dances and dramatic presentations that it had inherited from earlier times. Among these forms, the *ts'an-chün-hsi*, or adjutant plays, are especially worth mentioning. These plays presented two types of roles: the adjutant, who was a relatively dimwitted official, and the "grey hawk," the witty character who played many comic tricks at the expense of the adjutant. These plays bridged the development from mostly song and dance to a more dialogue-oriented type of performance.

The Sung Dynasty (960–1279) had two important forms of dramatic skits: *tsa-chü* and *nan-hsi*. Sung *Tsa-chü* used northern music in its performance while *nan-hsi*, or southern plays, used southern music. So began a long tradition of the split of Chinese theatre into two forms, according to the type of music used in a play.

The Yüan Dynasty (1279–1368) and the Yüan *Tsa-chü (Zaju)*

The Yüan Dynasty saw the development of the first true form of theatre in China. Several political and social factors contributed to this development. The first and most important factor was that the Yüan Dynasty was founded and ruled by Mongolians, who were culturally far less advanced than the Han Chinese they had conquered. They preferred popular oral literature over the more refined poetic tradition of the Chinese, and they had no respect for the scholar class, displacing them from the traditional top place on the social strata to the next to the bottom position, just barely above the beggars. For 80 years during their rule (1237–1314), they also banned the civil service examination that had always been the center of focus for scholars, as it was the one most direct way for a scholar to promote himself. As a result, displaced scholars were no longer isolated as an elite class, but were forced to mingle with the common people. They also had to direct their creative energies to things other than the preparation for the examination. As the dramatic form provided them with the most freedom and space for expression, many scholars chose playwriting as a new focus. Participation by the scholar class in drama injected a new creative energy from the literati and raised the level of drama to a more serious and legitimate position.

The dominant type of Yüan drama was the *tsa-chü (zaju)*. Inheriting music and songs from its predecessors, *tsa-chü* combined music, songs, speech, and dancelike movements with well-developed plots and characters into a dramatic whole. It usually had a structure of four *chê*, or acts, sometimes with a shorter unit called *hsieh-tzu*, or the wedge that served as a prologue or an interlude. Such divisions also showed a well-defined musical structure, as each act was composed of a set of usually 10 or more melodies from one musical mode. *Tsa-chü* based its music on the 28 modes of the T'ang Dynasty, but only 9 of those were used. Each mode corresponded to a particular mood, and, frequently, a mode was chosen to match the plot and action. Hence, in the Yüan *tsa-chü*, music no longer existed outside of the story, but was integrated into the story of the play itself. *Tsa-chü* employed a variety of instruments including stringed instruments such as the Chinese lute *(p'i-p'a)* and the three-string guitar *(san-hsien)*, wind instruments such as the side-blown flute *(ti-tzu)*, as well as percussion instruments such as drums, gongs, and clappers as accompaniment. There are also records showing that sound effects such as cock-crowing, the sound of a parrot, wind blowing, and thunder were being used to strengthen the mood of the play.

Tsa-chü contained both lyrics and prose speech. Only one rhyme per act could be used in the lyrics, which were sung by only one character—a very unique feature since, in other forms of drama, normally more than one person can sing. Prose was used mainly in dialogues, as well as in monologues in which a character would describe the past, or introduce the present situation, or introduce himself to the audience. This practice of characters introducing themselves has become an important convention in Chinese drama since then.

Other important *tsa-chü* conventions that were inherited by later forms of Chinese drama include typified character roles and the nonrealistic use of costumes and makeup. Although type characters such as the adjutant and the grey hawk of the adjutant plays, or the *mo* and *ching* of the Sung plays already existed before Yüan, it was in the *tsa-chü* that a more complex role system evolved. There were four main types of characters: *mo* (male roles), *tan* (female roles), *ching* (comic or villainous roles), and *ch'ou* (clowns). Many of these main types could be further divided into some lesser types. The *tan* role, for instance, could be divided into eight different categories, depending on the age and personality of the character. Such development of role types attests to the fact that the content of the *tsa-chü* did evolve from simple skits to more complex plots and richer stories.

Not a great deal of confirmed information is available concerning the use of costumes in *tsa-chü*. However, from what is known, it can be safely assumed that the stylized and rich costuming in Chinese theatre was already prevalent in the performance of *tsa-chü*. There was no concern for historic accuracy in costumes; rather, they were used to differentiate various types of characters, such as military and civil, young and old, rich and poor, good or evil, noble or base, foreign or Chinese. Such symbolization of costumes did not hinder the richness of varieties. We know, for instance, that in one play there were 46 kinds of male headgear, 7 kinds of female headdresses, 47 kinds of male garments, 7 kinds of female garments, 6 kinds of male scarves, and 6 kinds of male girdles used. Sometimes famous individuals had their own distinct costumes and could be immediately identified by what they were wearing. Likewise, makeup was also employed stylistically instead of realistically. There is evidence that the famous painted-face in Chinese theatre already existed in *tsa-chü*, although the colors and patterns were more subdued and were less elaborate and gorgeous than the look of its future descendants. For the most part, only black, white, and cinnabar were used, with other colors occasionally used for some specific characters. In most cases, faces were painted to designate a questionable character, as in the case of the female role with painted face (*hua-tan* and *ch'a-tan*). Stylized beards were also being used, and there was no attempt at making them realistic.

Both men and women acted in *tsa-chü*, and they could also be cross-cast, where women would play the *mo* roles, and men the *tan* roles. Actors had very low social status in general, and there is speculation that they had to wear some special dress offstage to indicate their profession. However, they could be very popular and well-loved by the audience, and could support a decent living through their profession, although we also know that actresses frequently were engaging in prostitution on the side. Actors also had the obligation to answer official calls and perform at official banquets any time they were summoned.

From written records referred to in poems, plays, as well as a wall painting on a temple wall in Shansi province, we can speculate on how *tsa-chü* might have been staged. There were two kinds of stages: those in permanent theatres and the temporary makeshift stages frequently found in temples or any large open space. From the time of the southern Sung dynasty on (beginning of the 12th century) there had been permanent theatres capable of holding a substantial audience. The stage was frequently raised and surrounded by railings. Even the makeshift theatres were mostly roofed. There was a backstage area, as well as an area off one side of the stage that was called *yüeh-ch'uang*, or the "music crib." This was probably where the female performers sat when they were not performing, and they might be playing some form of clappers, drums, or cymbals. As many of the actresses were also prostitutes, it is suspected that this was the place where they were on display for their potential customers. Drapes and hangings covered the back and frequently the sides of the stage. A table and several benches served as the only set on stage. While a permanent theatre had benches for the audience, most audiences just stood around a temporary stage. Many other activities such as gambling, eating, and drinking were carried on at the same time as the performance on stage.

On the day before a performance, members of the troupe would go around town hanging colored paper notices everywhere to attract an audience. On the day of the performance, banners, flags, and back-curtains were hung before the show began. Right before the performance, the theatre door would be opened, and someone would stand next to the entrance yelling for attention. The audience would be let in once a fee was paid. Occasionally, the performers would list all the plays that they could perform, so that the audience could request the ones they would like to see.

A *tsa-chü* performance seems to have contained more than just the scripted material, but this is not indicated in the plays themselves. Before the play, there frequently were some opening speeches or songs that were unrelated to the plot, but were addressed to the audience for their favors. Frequently, music, dance, and other variety shows were inserted in between acts. Sometimes, in one of the later acts, the dramatic action would be interrupted by a person outside of the play summing up or commenting on the plot to please the audience and to solicit more tips and rewards for the performance. Occasionally, song and dance would follow the conclusion of the play to see the audience off.

Ming Dynasty (1368–1644): *Ch'uan-ch'i (Chuanqi)* and *K'un-ch'ü (Kunqu)*

The growing political and social unrest toward the end of the Yüan Dynasty eventually ended Mongolian rule in China in 1368. Replacing it was the Ming Dynasty, a regime that ruled for the most part with a most autocratic and centralized government. Playwriting and theatre, along with all other forms of literature, were under heavy supervision and censorship. The scholars, with their prestigious social position as well as the civil service examination restored, were no longer interested in or willing to express dissatisfaction or to deliver social criticisms. They in effect monopolized the writing of plays, since it was only acceptable for men with great literary and musical knowledge to attempt to do so. All these factors led to very different forms of drama in the Ming Dynasty, of which the most important ones are the *ch'uan-ch'i* and the *k'un-ch'ü*.

With the fall of the Yüan Dynasty, the popularity of the *tsa-chü* also declined, and it was gradually replaced by *ch'uan-ch'i*. This term, literally meaning "transmission of the marvelous," was first used to designate the marvel tales of the T'ang Dynasty. In drama it was originally used to refer to a type of drama that flourished at the end of the Yüan Dynasty and that had its origin in the southern plays of the Sung Dynasty. *Ch'uan-ch'i* varied from *tsa-chü* in several ways. While *tsa-chü* was limited to four acts per play, *ch'uan-ch'i* had no limitations on either the length or the number of acts or scenes allowed in one play. Frequently, a *ch'uan-ch'i* could have 30 to 50 scenes, and the plays were definitely longer. Hence, stories and plots could be more complex. Lyrics could be sung by more than one character, in the form of solo, duet, or chorus. While *tsa-chü* used only one mode and one rhyme in one act, a scene in a *ch'uan-ch'i* could contain songs from different modes, and rhymes could be changed at will. *Ch'uan-ch'i* also placed more emphasis on prose speech, and in this sense it was a more rounded drama than the *tsa-chü*.

As in all forms of classical Chinese drama, characters in a *ch'uan-ch'i* were differentiated into major role types, including *sheng* (male roles), *tan (dan)* (female roles), *ching (jing)*, *ch'ou*, and *tsa* (clowns). A typical *ch'uan-ch'i* would open with a prologue, usually performed by the *fu-mo* (a secondary *sheng* type), who would deliver two poems, the first one generally with a *carpe diem* theme, and the second one an argument of the plot. Sometimes in between the two poems there could be a question and answer dialogue where the *fu-mo* asked about the title of the play, and a voice offstage gave the answer. The prologue always ended with a title quatrain. After the prologue, the *sheng* would begin the dramatic action itself. The *tan* and other lesser characters would

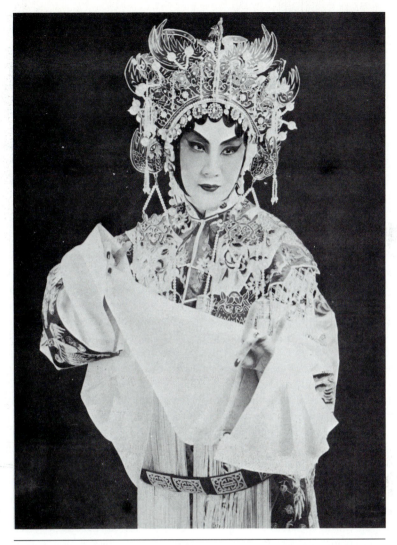

A female *(dan)* figure from Peking Opera. *From* The Beauty of China: International Theatre. *Published by the Han Kong Corporation, Taiwan, 1980*

enter the play in the scenes that followed. Each scene had either a four-character or a two-character title to describe the content of the scene, but sometimes the title could have three or five characters. In general, each scene ended with an exit poem, usually containing four lines, each with either five or seven characters. Even if such exit poems were omitted in the rest of the scenes, the end of the last scene would always contain a poem to sum up the spirit or the message of the play.

Although there were some brilliant *ch'uan-ch'i* written during the period between the Yüan and Ming Dynasties, with the task of playwriting mainly in the hands of the literati, who were either too preoccupied with the civil service examination or too stifled by the moral and literary correctness to be truly creative, *ch'uan-ch'i* in the Ming Dynasty had generally declined into a kind of closet drama. The plays demonstrated a broad range of literary and musical knowledge at the expense of dramatic interest and structure. Thus, they became tedious and frequently unperformable. The failure of Ming drama as a whole was only avoided by the timely rise of *k'un-ch'ü*, a new musical form that instilled new life into the stagnated *ch'uan-ch'i*.

The rise of *k'un-ch'ü* is one of the most important events in the development of Chinese drama. Until this point, music in drama had always shown a split between the north and the south, with the *tsa-chü* representing the northern music and the *ch'uan-ch'i* the southern sound. It was not until *k'un-ch'ü* appeared that the two sounds could be combined into a unique and pleasant sound. Playwrights very quickly learned to make use of such new sounds in their plays, and from then on, Chinese drama was dominated by *k'un-ch'ü* for 250 years.

In the middle of the Ming Dynasty (second half of the 15th century) there were four popular types of southern music: *Haiyen*, which used clapper, drums, and percussion to accompany soft and quiet singing; *Yuyao*, which employed a fast tempo and a practice of inserting "parenthetical songs" (explanatory passages in colloquial language to elaborate on more literary lines); *Yiyang*, a very popular form of songs with no accompaniment except drums and gongs, an offstage chorus that joined in at the end, or inserted parenthetical songs; and, lastly, *K'unshan*, a soft and simple music that underwent many improvements and eventually become the dominating *k'un-ch'ü*.

K'un-ch'ü's success is generally attributed to the innovations of Wei Liang-fu, who lived roughly around the early to late-middle part of the 16th century. With the help of a friend who was an expert in the northern songs, Wei set out creating a new sound based on the melody of *k'unshan*. His contributions were in two areas: in music, he created an extremely smooth and delicate tune, accompanied by a side-blown bamboo flute *(ti-tzu)* and a clapper or a fan to beat time. For fuller accompaniment, he added percussion and used both string and wind instruments such as the lute, moon-guitar, side-blown and straight flutes, and *sheng* (a kind of pipe with 13 reeds); in singing, he taught and advocated accurate and proper enunciation of words and delivery of lines.

Wei's innovation was quickly adopted by Liang Chen-yu (1520–1580), who was himself a musician and also a playwright. He wrote a very successful play *Wan Sha Chi (Washing the Gauze)* in which the new music was used. From then on, the term *k'un-ch'ü* no longer was used to merely refer to the musical form, but to this new dramatic form that wedded *k'un-ch'ü* music with the *ch'uan-ch'i* form. Before *k'un-ch'ü*, *tsa-chü* was the name for the drama using Northern music, and *ch'uan-ch'i* for the drama using Southern sounds. After *k'un-ch'ü*, however, the term *tsa-chü* was used to refer to shorter plays, whereas *ch'uan-ch'i* was used to refer to those that were longer.

The role categories of *k'un-ch'ü* again could be divided into four main categories: *sheng*, *tan (dan)*, *ching (jing)*, and *ch'ou*, each subdivided into many types. Because of the refined music and literary elegance of *k'un-ch'ü*, it also began to emphasize refined body movements and subtle facial expressions to underline the meaning of the words and to enhance the melody. For the role of *ch'ou*, for instance, an actor had to learn 27 kinds of foot placement and movement in standing and walking, 37 kinds of special finger, hand, and sleeve movements, as well as many other techniques pertaining to the character of a clownish figure. Such meticulous attention to the postures, gestures, and movements of the actors formed what became the renowned stylized acting of Chinese theatre. An actor needed to learn the fundamentals of acting and singing through hard work and practice, and was frequently tutored by retired actors or even playwrights.

Continuing the tradition from Yüan drama, Ming performances used elaborate costumes that were neither historically accurate nor realistic. Many designs were eclectically based on patterns from previous dynasties. The function of costumes was to please the eye as well as to establish the identity and social status of the characters. Makeup was also employed in the same manner, using nonrealistic face-painting either to enhance the beauty or to indicate the physical and moral qualities of the character. The more simplistic face-painting of the Yüan period was expanded, and the designs were gradually extended to cover the whole face. More colors were also used to indicate different characters: red was for loyal generals, purple was for loyal officials, yellow was for scheming characters, black was honesty and seriousness, while blue suggested mischief and arrogance.

There were several types of acting troupes in the Ming Dynasty. The court-supported troupes were selected and controlled by the Imperial Academy of Music. They performed at court on special occasions and sometimes also staged public performances. Outside of court, there were two kinds of companies: the private troupes kept by rich and powerful households and the professional ones that either were stationary or toured extensively. Members of a private troupe were normally servants, slaves, and concubines, and they would have to perform other household duties when they were not entertaining their lords and masters. Independent troupes recruited their members from towns and areas mainly of the south, frequently from poor families. In some smaller traveling companies, all the members of a family would be involved in some way.

Plays were performed on various types of stages. There were two public theatres associated with court performances, with large, well-decorated, storied buildings. In the private sector, plays were performed in courtyards, halls, and temples. If the stage was not raised, it would be marked out by a red carpet, with the musicians at the back of the carpet. A raised stage would have railings all around and would be open on three sides. Later, even such stages would be covered with the red carpet, which became almost a synonym for the stage itself. In general, actors would enter from stage right and exit stage left. Again, except for the use of a number of hand props, scenery generally was not used, since the flexibility of having no scenery fit better the rapid scene and location changes required by the scripts, as well as the general symbolic aesthetic of the theatre. However, we do have records of some productions that experimented with scenery. The play *Mu-lien Chiu Mu (Mu-lien Saves His Mother)* was said to have been performed on a big stage set up on a military parade ground; it lasted for three days and three nights. A hundred booths around the stage were set up for women in the audience. The production had to hire some 30 to 40 extra actors to perform all kinds of acrobatic feats such as fighting, tumbling, rope-walking, and leaping through fire. Scenes of the supernatural under-world were represented vividly, with various apparatus for torture, such as a mountain of knives, a huge pot of boiling oil, sword-sprouting trees, trenches full of blood, and grinding axes. The audience was said to have been rather frightened by such scenes, and thousands of pieces of paper sacrificial money were burnt to appease the ghosts. In another play about a T'ang emperor traveling to the moon, a black curtain on stage was withdrawn to reveal a moon—a round disc complete with curling clouds surrounding it. The Moon Fairy sat in the middle of this moon, along with two other customary denizens of the moon in Chinese myth—Wu Gang, whose eternal task was to hack at a cassia tree that kept growing back, and a White Rabbit, who used a pestle to pound medicines.

Ch'ing (Qing) Dynasty (1644–1911) and Peking (Beijing) Opera

Like the Yüan Dynasty before it, the Ch'ing Dynasty was established by non-Han people. The Manchus, a tribe who dwelled mainly to the northeast of China, toppled the faltering Ming Dynasty and conquered the whole country in 1644. Unlike the Mongolians, however, the early emperors of the Ch'ing Dynasty soon realized that brutal suppression alone would not eliminate Han resistance; they therefore tried to assimilate with the people they conquered and learned to respect and even embrace Chinese culture with enthusiasm. Instead of drastically disrupting the existing social structure, the Manchus more or less continued the long social, cultural, and literary tradition. The result was that the Ch'ing Dynasty as a whole was generally committed to imitating and duplicating the excellence of the past.

In drama, the beginning of the Ch'ing Dynasty saw a split between two styles of theatre: the elegant school of *ya pu*, mainly represented by *k'un-ch'ü*, and the popular school, or *hua pu*—a collective name for all the unrefined forms of drama popular among the common people. What we now commonly know as Chinese Opera or Peking (Beijing) Opera was in fact a synthesis of part of the *k'un-ch'ü* tradition with several forms of the *hua pu*. After a bitter struggle for popularity and legitimacy, Chinese Opera eventually dethroned the long reigning *k'un-ch'ü* and became the dominant form of drama in China. At present, the term *Chinese Opera* is still used as a synonym for the classical theatre in China.

Several factors contributed to the decline of *k'un-ch'ü*. Ever since the innovations of people like Wei Liang-fu and Liang Chen-yu, the development of *k'un-ch'ü* had consistently moved toward the refined and the artistic, with its playwrights mostly being the scholarly types who were more interested in demonstrating their knowledge than concerning themselves with dramatic effects. The plays grew in length to the point where only fragments could be performed, thereby marring whatever little was left of dramatic structure. The words became so elegant and refined that it was difficult for nonliterary persons to understand. As a result, *k'un-ch'ü* grew more and more distant from the taste of the common people. As many attractive elements of *k'un-ch'ü* were quickly adapted and absorbed by its opponents from the popular camp, *k'un-ch'ü* itself was left with mere words to read and beautiful music to be sung until it ceased to be a true performable dramatic form.

At the same time, many popular regional forms competed for the support of the common people as well as the favor of the aristocrats. Among them, the *yiyang* continued its quiet popularity since the Ming Dynasty; the *kao*, a sub-form of *yiyang*, that can still be found in many regional drama to this day; the *pang-tzu* and the *ch'ui*, believed to be also related to the *yiyang*; the *hsi-p'i* and the *erh-huang*, which combined to become the major component of Chinese Opera; and the *ch'ing*, which was sung at a very high pitch. Several stood out as the most successful. In 1779, Wei Ch'ang-sheng, a popular performer of the *Ch'ing* school, went to Peking to participate in the grand celebration of the 70th birthday of the emperor Chien Lung (Kao-tzung). His innovations in the *tan* roles brought him tremendous success. To enhance the femininity of the roles, Wei popularized the habit of wearing small clogs *(ts'ai ch'iao)* to imitate very tiny female feet—an object of obsessive delight for men in the Ch'ing Dynasty. Wearing these false feet, actors would have to walk in a very seductive, wiggling manner. To beautify their faces, false hairpieces were employed to redefine the shape of the face. These practices were then passed down to the Chinese Opera, and are still in use today.

In 1790, the year of Emperor Chien Lung's 80th birthday, many troupes again traveled from the provinces to Peking for the celebrations. Among them, the troupes from Anhui province became the chief vogue. By the 1810s, four of them known as the Four Great Anhui Troupes had established an absolute position in the Peking theatre world. Their major strength lay in their ability to incorporate various styles to create a more successful new form. Aside from refined acting technique, they also rekindled the audience's interest in acrobatics. They brought with them the *erh-huang* style of music. Later on it was joined by the *hsi-p'i* style, which was accompanied by string instruments such as the *hu-ch'ing* and the moon guitar, and could be played with a wide range of beats. Performers thus had the advantage of being able to change keys easily as well as to alter the tempo and the rhythm. Together, *hsi-p'i* and *er-huang* (known as *p'i-huang*) laid the foundation of the Chinese Opera.

Chinese Opera therefore can be looked at as the direct descendant of the Anhui troupes, from whom it also inherited the spirit of adopting successful elements from various styles of drama. Following the long tradition of character types since the Yüan drama, Chinese Opera has a highly developed system that consists of four major role types, each with very well-defined subtypes. *Sheng* (male roles) can be divided into *wen-sheng* (civilian types) and *wu-sheng* (military types). *Wen-sheng* again can be subdivided into *lao-sheng* (older male), *hong-sheng* ("red male," refers mainly to the role of Kuan Kung, whose face is completely red), and *hsiao-sheng* (younger male), which in turn consists of *shan-tzu sheng* (young male with fan), *chih-wei sheng* (young male with pheasant feathers on his headgear), and *wa-wa sheng* (young child). *Wu-sheng* has two different types: *ch'ang-k'ao*, who has the temperament and pose of a military general, and *tuan-ta*, who is agile and skilled in acrobatic movements. *Tan* (female) can be divided into *lao-tan* (older woman), *ch'ing-i* (a virtuous and decorous woman, who chiefly excels in songs and elegance), *hua-tan* (a coquettish and vivacious woman who excels in movement and expression), *hua-shan* (a type between *ch'ing-i* and *hua-tan*), *tao-ma tan* (literally the sword-and-horse *tan*, a military female who is also good at singing, expression, and movement), *wu-tan* (a military female who usually does not sing), and *ch'ou-tan* (a clownish old woman), who is also called *ch'ou p'o-tzu* or *ts'ai-tan.*

The elaborate painted-face, which has become the trademark of Chinese Opera, actually is used mostly by the role *ching (jing).* There are two major types of *ching: ta hua-lien* (literally "big flower-face") and *erh hua-lien* ("second flower-face"). *Ta hua-lien* has a simple face-painting pattern and can be divided into *he-t'ou* (black face) and *t'ung-ch'ui* (character holding a *t'ung-ch'ui,* a round-headed weapon made of copper).

Painted-face *(ching)* role.   *From* The Beauty of China: International Theatre. *Published by the Han Kong Corporation, Taiwan, 1980*

Erh hua-lien has a very complicated pattern for face-painting. The category *ch'ou* (clown) can also be divided into the *wen-ch'ou* (civilian) and the *wu-ch'ou* (military), and can play both good and evil characters.

Chinese Opera has also developed a highly evolved and eclectic system of music and accompaniment. The orchestra plays two types of accompaniments, the *wen-ch'ang* and the *wu-ch'ang* (which refer more to the quality and feel of the music than whether it is a civil scene or military scene, as the words *wen* and *wu* would seem to indicate). Drums, gongs, clappers, and cymbals are used in the *wu-ch'ang*; *ti-tzu* (side-blown flute), *hu-ch'in* (two-stringed Chinese violin), *erh-hu* (a lower-pitched *hu-ch'in*), *yüeh ch'in* (moon guitar with four strings), *san-hsien* (three-stringed guitar), and the *so-na* (a loud Chinese horn) are used in the *wen-ch'ang*. The player of the one-sided drum leads the music section; he has complete control of a play's pace and tempo. There are three important elements of the music. The drums and gongs are used to control the rhythm of the actors' speech and movements, denote the general feel of the scene (whether it is tense or relaxed), and dictate the pace of the action. They also create sound effects such as the sounds of water, arrows, oars, birds, and animals. The *wen-ch'ang* musical tunes or melodies are also very important in that they coordinate with the movements of the actors and highlight the plot and the situation. There are six main types of tunes: holy and solemn tunes, feasting music, dance music, military sounds, sounds that are festive and joyous, and sounds that are sad and melancholy. Finally, *hu-ch'in, erh-hu,* and *yüeh-ch'in* are used to accompany the aria to enhance the beauty of the songs and the voice.

Chinese Opera costume has become a distinguished and renowned feature of the theatre form due to its detailed and elegant embroidery, its dazzling array of colorful designs, and its combination of aesthetic and symbolic purposes. Continuing the traditional approach toward costumes, Chinese Opera employs its costumes as another language of the stage, to communicate information such as the nationality, social and economic status, age, and personality of its characters. There are several distinct types of costumes for men and women, nonmilitary or military. *Mang* is the official robe worn on very formal occasions. It has a round collar, long "water-sleeves," and rich embroidery. Colors such as red, purple, blue, white, and black are used to further differentiate the wearer's specific rank. *P'ei* is a type of semiformal dress for receiving guests or dealing with official business. It has a lower, V-shape collar and water-sleeves, and is buttoned only at the waist. *Tieh-tzu* is the everyday apparel with water sleeves. For the female, it is buttoned at the collar and the waist; for the male, the front piece overlaps toward the right side, and it is buttoned under the arm. Usually, the *tieh-tzu* is plain, but some current female versions have some embroidery added to them. The role of *hua-tan* does not call for the more graceful water-sleeves, but a *k'u-ao* (blouse and trousers) or *ch'un-ao* (blouse and skirt). Her costume always includes an embroidered sash. *Fu-kuei-i* is the costume for a beggar or a very poor person. It is basically a *tieh-tzu* patched with pieces of silk in different colors. Military roles also have their specific look, which included *k'ai-k'ao* or the armor for state or ceremonial occasions, the *k'ai-ch'ang* for everyday wear, and the *chien-i* for intense fighting scenes.

Depending on the character types, makeup in Chinese Opera ranges from a plain face with little or no makeup to a fully painted face. Usually, the walk-ons and some

A scholar *(sheng)*—here played by a female actor—and a clown *(ch'ou)*.
From The Beauty of China: International Theatre. *Published by the Han Kong Corporation, Taiwan, 1980*

decent, older characters have no makeup. Youthful *sheng* and *tan* roles will have a white face with blushes on the cheeks and red lips. Their foreheads will have to be wrapped in a manner that the corners of their eyes will be raised upward, a look that is deemed beautiful and elegant. A *ch'ou* has a patch of white on the nose and the center of the face; his specific personality depends on the size and shape of the white area. The *ching* role has a fully painted face, some with simple patterns and only one or two colors, while others use a variety of colors and very complex designs of patterns such as a shattered face or a butterfly on the forehead. In general, face-painting follows a scheme that designates the symbolic qualities of each color: red represents loyalty and truthfulness, purple is similar to red but depicts a slightly older person, black represents straightforwardness and strength, blue obstinacy, yellow a cunning and scheming personality. A person with a green face is hot-tempered and stubborn, while gray suggests old age. Gold and silver are used for supernatural beings. Occasionally, masks are also used for some specific characters, usually gods and demons.

Chinese Opera does not require realistic sets. Scenery is normally defined by the words, the movements of the characters, and some very simple props. The main stage properties—a table and two chairs—can be used to represent a multitude of things, such as a bed, a mountain, a court, a wall. Other frequently used props include flags that can represent waves, wind, or storms, depending on the pattern or image on the flags. A stick with multicolored tassels can represent both a whip and a horse, and two flags with a wheel drawn on one side become a chariot.

The very simple requirements of staging with very few or no sets enable Chinese Opera to be very flexible in the use of performance space. From mat-shed theatres to temple stages, from makeshift platforms to tea houses, from fancy court theatres with thrust stages to Western style theatres with proscenium stages, Chinese Opera easily adapts to whatever space it might be performed in. A typical theatre in the Ch'ing Dynasty usually had a square stage with four pillars, about three or four feet off the ground. At the back was a wooden back wall with two openings on either side. The stage right opening was used as the entrance door, and the stage left one as the exit door. Both openings were covered with red embroidered drapes. The pillars were surrounded by low balustrades that were about a foot high. Above the stage between the two front pillars stretched a horizontal bar called *chou-kun*, which was used to assist actors in a military scene to perform acrobatic feats. The orchestra usually would be seated at stage right, with the leader of the orchestra, player of the one-sided drum, sitting in the section called *chiu-lung k'ou*, or "the mouth of the nine dragons." The area was so named because of a legend about how emperor Hsüan-tzung of the T'ang Dynasty used to sit there, on a platform carved with nine dragons, when he directed the orchestra himself.

The auditorium could be divided into several different spaces. *Ch'ih-tzu* (the pond) is the central space in front of the stage. Inside the *ch'ih-tzu* were long tables and benches that faced the two side walls instead of the stage, an arrangement that highlighted the fact that for most audiences of the time play-watching was never a serious and solemn activity that excluded other activities such as chatting with friends and eating and drinking. In fact, most such theatres did not charge an admission fee but rather a fee for tea, and upon entering the theatre one would immediately be offered a pot of tea. *Hsiao ch'ih-tzu* (little pond) referred to the benched space on either side of the stage. Because of its proximity to the stage, it was a coveted area for the more sophisticated and interested in the audience. *Kuan-tso*, or the official seats, were areas upstairs on the verandahs on either side of the stage. They were compartmentalized into rooms that could hold more than 10 people apiece; each space was equipped with low benches, and also with high benches with padded seats that were considerably more comfortable than those in the *ch'ih-tzu*. *Tao kuan-tso* was the area over the entrance and exit of the stage. As one could see little more than the back of the actors from there, it was mainly occupied by actors' relatives or people that did not have to pay.

Chinese Opera performance makes such strict demands on actors that they have to undergo long, strict, and disciplined training. Usually, an actor starts basic training, or *yu-kung*, at a young age. The training includes hours of *shan-pang* (holding the arms horizontally, chest high with elbows pointing out), exercises to increase the flexibility of the waist and legs, and also *ta-pa-tzu*, consisting of five basic weapon routines and some slightly complicated combat moves. No matter what role an actor eventually will study, everyone is required to go through all the basic training to ensure each person has complete control of the body and of every single movement one makes on stage. An actor usually chooses one role type to specialize in, depending mainly on the actor's look, body build, temperament, voice, and natural talent. Training for singing roles includes very strict rules for diction, enunciation, and breathing. Delivery of the lines in speeches is also emphasized in training, for a good delivery can be much more difficult than singing, as proved by the common saying, "A thousand kilos weighs the speech and four ounces the singing." The *tan* roles have to learn *ts'ai chiao*, or walking on the false small feet. For those in military roles, advanced training of the body as well as many daring acrobatic movements will shape the actor into an agile, flexible, and graceful performer who can do incredible feats. Learning to do specific plays involves a direct, line-by-line passing down of tune and movement by the teacher. Hence, the same play can be performed in slightly different styles. A talented actor can also improve on certain styles and thus create his or her own school of style.

As audiences are generally very familiar with the story of the play they attend, a performance is normally judged by its execution rather than the content of the plot itself. Music and dance have always been the most important factors in Chinese theatre; hence an actor is also judged by his or her movements and singing. In an action-oriented scene, the audience looks for flawless and precise execution of difficult movements, as well as well-timed and smoothly choreographed fights. In a less militaristic scene, the gracefulness of the movements, the appropriateness of every gesture, and the quality of the singing are the focus of attention. It is not uncommon to see an audience member "hearing" instead of watching a scene, with eyes closed and head circling and bobbing along the flow of the music. It is also acceptable for the audience to show their appreciation for a particular movement or song well done. Applause mixing with shouts of "*hao*" (good, bravo) can erupt any time during the performance. Such relaxation carries on the tradition of play-watching in tea houses or outdoor stages and is indeed quite different from the more formal experience of Noh or Western opera.

DRAMATIC LITERATURE

Classical Chinese drama derived its stories and plots from various sources: material from oral legends, ancient mythologies, earlier works of history and literature, T'ang Dynasty marvel tales, Buddhist stories. Originality of the plot was never a critical concern; the element of suspense was nonexistent, as the stories and their endings were very well known. A playwright's challenge lay not in inventing the plot but in the language and style in which he chose to retell the story.

In general, Chinese plays can be divided into several categories, according to their theme and subject. *Justice plays* tell the stories either of a wise and just official (with the character Pao Cheng or Pao King as a prime example), or of Robin Hood–type outlaws and bandits who take justice into their own hands. *Romantic love plays* most often deal with the love between a young scholar and either a truthful courtesan or a loyal, virtuous woman. They usually have to go through some hardship and trial, but will triumph in the end. *Taoist plays* reflect the Taoist idea of our worldly being as evanescent and illusory and portray the ideal existence of a person truly in tune with nature. Frequently we will see hermits or reclusive sages as protagonists in such plays. *Buddhist plays* likewise treat the world and its phenomena as transitional, and expound on the doctrines of karma, predestination, and enlightenment, with a strong sense of retribution and cause and effect. *Confucian plays*, on the other hand, emphasize order and propriety in human relations, starting within the family and extending to the country. Forces that contribute to the stability and the functioning of a person in society, such as filial piety, loyalty, and truthfulness, are praised and upheld. *Supernatural plays* express the Chinese people's love for the fantastic and the supernatural, and their view of the very thin demarcation between the natural world of humans and the supernatural world of gods, spirits, and ghosts. Most of the time these themes do not appear alone, but combine with other themes to express, confirm, and uphold the beliefs, world views, and moral systems of the audience.

Tsa-chü

Because the plays of *tsa-chü* have a short length and a stricter form (four acts with an occasional prologue), they generally display a stronger sense of dramatic structure than their successors. As in most Chinese traditional plays, the Aristotelian unities of time and place do not exist in the *tsa-chü*. A play can cover an extended period of time and various locations, and one single line can introduce the passing of 20 years or travel to a far-away place. The language usually combines beautiful poetry with very realistic prose. Due to the political and social conditions at that time, the plays, despite their familiar plots and stories from the past, very often reflected the harsh reality of living under Mongolian rule.

Some of the most famous playwrights include Kuan Han-ch'ing, Wang Shih-fu, Pai Pu, Ma Chih-yüan, and Cheng Kuang-tsu. *Tou-ngo Yüan (The Injustice Done to Tou-ngo)*, written by Kuan Han-ch'ing (c. 1224–c.1297), is one of the most famous plays of this period. Tou-ngo, at the age of seven, was given away by her scholar father to a wealthy widow to be her son's future wife. In return, the father received enough money to go to the capital and take the civil service examination. Seventeen years passed; Tou-ngo, herself now a widow, never heard from her father. One day her mother-in-law brought home a father and a son who had just saved her life. Tou-ngo's stern refusal prevented the two men from marrying the two widows. Thinking that Tou-ngo would comply if her mother-in-law died, the son tried to poison the old woman but killed his own father instead. He then threatened Tou-ngo with a murder charge unless she would agree to marry him. Tou-ngo refused, and she was sentenced to death by a corrupt official. Before she died, she swore that three things would happen if she were truly innocent, and they did: her blood did not spill onto the execution ground, snow fell on that June day when she was executed, and the county suffered three years of drought. Three years later, her father, now a high official, came back and restored her honor by punishing and executing the culprits.

The story itself was from an old tale telling how heaven intervened when a pious women was wrongly accused, and in this play, the heroine herself referred to this myth. Yet, aside from the common themes of virtue and retribution, *Tou-ngo Yüan* is also interesting in several other ways. Using the scenario from an old story, the play reflects the corruption of the society and the officials under the Mongolians, and the sufferings of the helpless people who could only turn to heaven to voice their complaints. Also, though this was probably not intended by the playwright himself, the importance of the civil service examination to the scholar class is ironically shown. Finally, this play is hailed as the best Chinese tragedy by many. Whether or not there is true tragedy in Chinese drama is a debatable question, yet *Tou-ngo Yüan* vividly and powerfully describes the demise of an innocent, virtuous person who has a most unfortunate life from her childhood on. Consider the price she has to pay (her life) for upholding her duty and her integrity; the meager reward (restoring a good name) she has at the end is not enough for it to be termed a happy ending. Hence, in the Ch'ing Dynasty, when happy endings for plays were almost mandatory, *Tou-ngo Yüan* was rewritten into *Snow in June*, in which Tou-ngo's execution was stopped in the nick of time by the timely arrival of a good official.

Ch'uan-ch'i and K'un-ch'ü

Unlike *tsa-chü*, there was no restriction in length or structure for the *ch'uan-ch'i* and *k'un-ch'ü* plays. They therefore were able to cover a more complex story adequately and to include more detail. However, many of the plays (especially the less well-written ones) tended to have very little dramatic structure and became rather episodic in nature. Besides the stories and literature of the past, these plays also drew their plots from the *tsa-chü*, with such alterations as they saw fit. For instance, many would change the ending of a previous play to accommodate the general appreciation for happy endings. As the composition of the plays were in the hands of the literati, many of the plays can be read as literature instead of a dramatic script in that they are rich in beautiful lines of poetry and smooth and witty prose.

Some important plays in *ch'uan-ch'i* include *P'i-p'a Chi* (*The Lute Song*), *Ching-ch'ai Chi* (*The Hairpin*), *Pai-t'u Chi* (*The White Rabbit*), *Pai-yüeh T'ing* (*The Moon Prayer Pavilion*), and *Sha-kou Chi* (*Killing a Dog*). Among *k'un-ch'ü* plays, *Wan-sha Chi*

(Washing the Gauze), *Mu-tan T'ing (The Peony Pavilion)*, *Ch'ang-sheng Tien (The Hall of Eternal Life)*, and *T'ao-hua Shan (The Peach Blossom Fan)* are the most well known and best loved.

P'i-p'a Chi, or *The Lute Song*, written by Kao Ming (c. 1301–1370), was the first important play written in the *ch'uan-ch'i* style. The play adopted a famous folk story about a pious and faithful woman whose husband left home to take the civil service examination, leaving her with his aged parents. When a famine broke out, both parents died. When the woman found her husband, now a high official, he had already married the daughter of an important political figure. The husband rejected the woman and killed her, and he was punished by heaven and killed by thunder. Kao Ming, however, slightly altered the story so that the husband no longer was depicted in such a negative light. He was not responsible for most of his actions. In the beginning, he was reluctant to leave home, yet his parents forced him to go and seek fame and fortune. Later, after he was appointed to a high position, he tried to turn down the position in order to go home, but his request was denied by the emperor. Finally, he tried to refuse the marriage, again to no avail. The play eventually ended happily when his first wife arrived at the capital and met his new wife, who was very sympathetic, and in the end the husband was able to have both virtuous women as wives, with the blessing of the emperor himself.

Although this play is quite long and has 40 scenes, it progresses rather smoothly and is structured effectively. Many scenes are pitched against one another (the success of the husband juxtaposes with the sufferings of the wife), and the conflicts within the characters are vividly conveyed in the most beautiful and effective language. Moreover, it signals a switch in the idea about the function of drama—to praise proper deeds and uphold social and moral values in a positive manner. The characters try very hard to fulfill all kinds of obligations, to their parents, the family, the country. If conflicts should arise from these requirements, they will be solved in the end nonetheless. No wonder this play was loved and praised not only by the mass but also by the aristocrats, including some emperors.

Mu-tan T'ing, or *The Peony Pavilion*, written by T'ang Hsien-tsu (1550–1617), was sometimes criticized for its deviations from the prescribed tunes of the *k'un-ch'ü*. This weakness, however, was amply made up for by the immense power and beauty this romantic play displayed. It is about a beautiful woman who, falling in love with a young scholar she met in her dream, pines away and dies, leaving a portrait of herself. The compassionate judge of the underworld frees her soul and has her body preserved. The young scholar in her dream comes across the portrait and greatly admires her beauty. When the woman's spirit shows up, they have a love affair and the scholar exhumes her body so that she can really live again. They get married and he takes the civil service examination. While waiting for the results, out of pressing poverty, the couple turn to the woman's family for help. The father refuses to believe in such an extraordinary story and only the timely announcement of the scholar's new promotion saves him. Finally, imperial intervention makes possible the reconciliation between the daughter and her grudging father. *Mu-tan T'ing* not only shows the power of love and the very Chinese view of the closeness between dream and reality, but also tells the story in the most refined and polished language. Some of its scenes, such as *Yu-yüan* (stroll in the garden) and *Ching-meng* (the dream), are still among the favorite scenes performed today.

Peking (Beijing) Opera

Strictly speaking, plays from the Peking Opera are usually looked at as playscripts for performance rather than as dramatic literature to be appreciated in reading. Although the language of the lyrics and the poems is elegant and well-polished, some prose speech may use quite colloquial and sometimes even vulgar language and refer frequently to contemporary events and persons. Many of its plays derive their sources

Peking Opera in performance.   *From* The Beauty of China: International Theatre. *Published by the Han Kong Corporation, Taiwan, 1980*

from ancient stories and famous novels, as well as Ming and Ch'ing plays, but new plays have also been written, some of them specifically for a particular actor. In most cases, an individual play may not cover a whole story but rather a famous scene from a story. Therefore, frequently, one story can be written into several plays, and rarely will a Chinese Opera perform a whole story from beginning to the end in one performance.

The Monkey King from the novel *Journey to the West* has been a very popular figure in Chinese literature, and some scenes from this story are quite popular in Chinese Opera. *Ta Nao Tien Kung (Creating Havoc in Heaven)* is a scene about how the not-too-disciplined Monkey King made havoc of the otherwise peaceful and orderly life in Heaven. This play contains many fighting scenes and is especially popular among people who do not particularly care for the slower singing of Peking Opera. Another popular story is about the White Snake, who had acquired the form of a woman and married a scholar. Together with her faithful maid and friend the Green Snake they led a happy life until a meddling monk showed the husband her true form and imprisoned her under a pagoda. A play entitled *Pai-she Chuan (The Story of the White Snake)* contains many famous scenes such as *Chin-shan Ssu* (the Chin-shan temple), and *Tuan-ch'iao* (the broken bridge). Many spectacular uses of symbolic props (as in a flood scene where a terrible tempest is raised by the White Snake's sea-dwelling friends) and movement (as in a boating scene) make this play another favorite among the knowledgeable and unsophisticated audiences alike.

CONNECTIONS

The unique form of Chinese traditional theatre, its nonrealistic aesthetic, its synthesis of music, movements, and speech, and especially its graceful and stylized rendering of realistic actions in acting, offered Western theatre a whole new way of defining acting and theatre. On seeing Mei Lan-fang's performance in 1936, Brecht wrote an essay entitled "Alienation Effects in Chinese Acting" in which he advocated the Chinese style of acting. Although Brecht had some misunderstanding of the Chinese theatre, the symbolic quality and distancing of reality he saw in Chinese acting helped shape and define his own concept of acting style in Epic Theatre. Admittedly, the highly conventionalized context, the language barrier, the loud music, and sometimes the singing still can hinder many Westerners from truly appreciating this art form, but oftentimes a meeting of such great differences can result in very new and wonderful forms of theatre. Shakespeare's plays, many of which can fit quite well into the overall style of the Chinese Opera, have been done many times in a traditional Chinese Opera style. Experiments of less compatible unions can still yield interesting and refreshing results. A good example can be seen in a 1982 production of Ionesco's *The Chairs* in Taipei, where it was performed in the Chinese Opera style. On the one hand, the symbolic situation of Ionesco's characters and their situations were easily communicated through the symbolic tradition of the Chinese Opera. On the other hand, the basic incongruity of the two—*The Chairs* requires a visual overflowing of chairs on stage, whereas in Chinese Opera two chairs can represent many and therefore do not need such crowding of the stage—created a tension that added to the experience of the play. Ionesco himself was in the audience, and he was said to be greatly amused by the result. Like Japanese theatre, Chinese theatre offers the West a new set of aesthetics and a performance style that Eisenstein described as having all the advantages of the principle of realism, yet is guided, as Stanislavski observed, by the laws of the art.

SOURCES FOR FURTHER STUDY

Social/Art/Philosophy Background

Chang, Chi-yun. *The Essence of Chinese Culture.* Taipei: China News Press, 1957.

Fitzgerald, C. P. *China. A Short Cultural History.* New York: F. A. Praeger, 1958.

Fung, Yu Lan. *A Short History of Chinese Philosophy.* New York: Macmillan, 1948.

Graham, A. C. *Studies in Chinese Philosophy and Philosophical Literature.* New York: State University of New York Press, 1990.

Hughes, Ernest Richard. *Chinese Philosophy in Classical Times.* London: J. M. Dent & Sons, 1942.

Liu, Wu-chi. *An Introduction to Chinese Literature.* Bloomington: Indiana University Press, 1966.

Weller, Robert P. *Unities and Diversities in Chinese Religion.* Seattle: University of Washington Press, 1987.

Theatre History

Crump, J. I. *Chinese Theatre in the Days of Kublai Khan.* Tucson: University of Arizona Press, 1980.

Dolby, William. *A History of Chinese Drama.* London: Unwin Brothers, 1976.

Mackerras, Colin, ed. *Chinese Theatre from Its Origins to the Present Day.* Honolulu: University of Hawaii Press, 1988.

Shih, Chung-wen. *The Golden Age of Chinese Drama: Yüan Tsa-chü.* Princeton, N.J.: Princeton University Press, 1976.

Wu, Zuguang, Zuolin Huang, and Shaowu Mei. *Peking Opera and Mei Lanfang.* Beijing: New World Press, 1981.

Zung, Cecilia S. L. *Secrets of the Chinese Drama.* New York: Arno Press, 1980.

Dramatic Literature

Arlington, L. C., and Harold Acton. *Famous Chinese Plays.* New York: Russell and Russell, 1963.

Dolby, William. *Eight Chinese Plays from the 13th Century to the Present.* New York: Columbia University Press, 1978.

Gee, Tom. *Stories of Chinese Opera.* Taipei: Liberal Arts Press, 1978.

Hung, Josephine Huang. *Classical Chinese Plays.* Taipei: Mei Ya Publications, 1971.

Liu, Jung-en. *Six Yüan Plays.* New York: Penguin Books, 1972.

Scott, A. C. *Traditional Chinese Plays.* Vols. I, II, III. Madison: University of Wisconsin Press, 1970, 1975.

C H A P T E R

15

In Search of
a New Theatre,
1880–1920

No one could have predicted the importance of this meeting. Vladimir Nemerovich-Danchenko (1858–1943), successful playwright and teacher of theatre, had arranged to meet with a young, talented amateur, Konstantin Stanislavski (1863–1938). They were to share lunch at the Salvyansky Bazaar Hotel and discuss their ideas on theatre. At 2:00 P.M. on June 22, 1897, they met, acquired a private room, and began a conversation that would change the world of theatre forever.

The conversation began amiably as Nemerovich-Danchenko proposed forming a small theatre company that would include the most talented amateurs from Stanislavski's group and Danchenko's best pupils. The aim was to escape the commercialism of the traditional theatre and explore new styles of presentation. The accord between the two was immediate as each outdid the other with sarcastic observations on the horrible state of Russian theatre. For every problem they noted, one of them offered a suggestion, and Nemerovich-Danchenko was amazed to note that not one disagreement surfaced.

Lunch was finished, coffee had been served, and already it was time for dinner. Still the conversation continued without interruption. Following dinner the two adjourned to the Stanislavski home in the country, still avidly sharing their dreams. They began to draw up a set of regulations for their new theatre. Administrative affairs would have to be secondary to theatrical needs. Stock scenery would not be allowed and the orchestra had to be abolished. Instead of the one dress rehearsal that was then customary, they would have six.

	The Ford		The motion picture		First powered flight			Wireless radio developed		First World War		Gandhi works for Indian independence
		1893	1895	1896		1903	1905		1909		1914–1918	1917	1919

X-rays, wireless telegraphy   Einstein's Special Theory of Relativity   Bolshevik Revolution

Eiffel Tower built   Picasso's *Les Demoiselles d'Avignon*   Kafka's *Metamorphosis* written   International style in architecture begins

1889	1891					1907	1909	1912	1913	1917

First skyscraper   Ballet Russe de Monte Carlo   Stravinsky's *Rite of Spring*

Freie Bühne   Moscow Art Theatre   Abbey Theatre   Futurist movement   Dada movement

1889	1890		1898	1904		1909–1915	1916–1920

Independent Theatre

Scenery and costumes would be prepared ahead of time so that actors would be accustomed to them before the final rehearsals. In every aspect, the theatre would have to demonstrate a sense of excellence. Actors would be disciplined, audiences would be polite, each detail of production would be finely polished. It was possible; they would make it real.

As Nemerovich-Danchenko journeyed back into Moscow in the early morning light of the next day, still energetic after 18 hours of conversation, he carried with him Stanislavski's scribbled notes. Transposed into action, those notes would become a major force as the practices of the Moscow Art Theatre established a new standard for contemporary productions.

Although the founding of the Moscow Art Theatre proved to be a momentous development in theatre history, the actions of the two men were not unusual for the time. The artistic milieu at the turn of the century can be characterized by the rise of the independent artist; painters, musicians, and other artists turned away from traditional methods of communication in an attempt to relate their sense of modern existence. Poetry focused on the simultaneous juxtaposition of seemingly unrelated words. Musicians defied the traditional patterns of tone and rhythm for new connections between sounds and musical accents. Architects discovered the skyscraper and the possibilities of metal and reinforced concrete. Many of these experiments in the arts were limited to a few pioneers, and none of them was introduced without considerable debate and opposition; but there can be no doubt that all of the arts were suffused with a nervous excitement generated by the search for new forms of expression. Because most of those new forms appeared in a rapidly changing society, they gained a social significance greater than the work of artists in any other time in European history since the Renaissance. Whether the artists changed society or reflected tremendous upheavals in their society is debatable; but the work of Ibsen, Picasso, Stravinsky, and dozens of others came to represent all that was happening to Europe at the end of the 19th century.

The term applied by critics and society alike to these new artists and their ideas is *modern.* It may seem strange that the term *modern* is applied to the work of a Norwegian writing 100 years ago or a Russian composer long dead, but as a label for the arts modern implies more than that which is current. It suggests a disinterest in the past and in the values and forms of that past. Technically, any age is modern to its contemporaries, but surprisingly no age before 1880 had ever adopted the term as its own. Other eras always clung to the past as a key to the definition of the present. Whenever a new artistic style had appeared before 1800, it always had references to what had preceded it, either in its imagery or its formal construction. The artists at the end of the 1800s sought (or at least used) new forms, ideas, and techniques. They seemed to reject virtually all the standards of the past, preferring instead to find their own definition of what is right, good, or beautiful. They chose as their subjects the people of their time, from all strata of society; and they talked about issues of importance to those people.

There was, in essence, a disjunction, a kind of cataclysmic break with the past. By 1920, the world had come to look like the projections of these modern artists. World War I had shattered the complacent and benevolent monarchies of Europe. Political authority was transferred to the "people" in many countries, and these people were disenchanted with their governments for having led them into war. Time and space were telescoped by the automobile and the airplane. The effort to establish a worldwide tribunal of justice had floundered. Everywhere new ideas about the nature of humankind were debated, and many of these ideas suggested that individuals really had no control over their destinies. By all accounts of contemporaries as well as of later historians, the world had undergone an incredible change between 1880 and 1920. To appreciate fully the importance and meaning of the theatre of this period, it is necessary to have some idea of what that incredible change really was like, for the world as we know it in the 1990s was foreshadowed in the events of the 1880s.

SOCIAL IDEAS

Social Order

Although society was undergoing a transformation in 1880, not everyone was aware of it. The middle and upper classes lived in a world of social comfort and security, certain in the knowledge of how they fit into an enlightened and forward-looking world. In spite of the poverty of urban slums and the starvation of peasants in central Europe, they held to the conviction that rational people could avoid political or domestic strife through common sense and hard work.

Nevertheless, vast socio-political changes were on the horizon. Political upheavals are commonplace in human history, but in the period from 1880 to 1920 they took on a size and importance seldom seen before. Ancient dynasties fell throughout the world, replaced by governments ostensibly acting by and for the will of the masses. Revolutions occurred in Portugal (1910), China (1911), Russia (1917), and Ireland (1917–1921). The First World War ended the Prussian and the Austro-Hungarian empires. Elsewhere, agitation began for freedom from foreign control, notably in South Africa (1899–1902) and India (beginning in 1909).

The voice of the downtrodden was increasingly heard in Europe's theatres. The impact of World War I on the conscience of Europe cannot be overestimated. What started out as a war that would last until Christmas turned into a bloody nightmare of some four years' duration. What began as a test of national pride and heroism became a muddy quagmire in France and Belgium, where nations pounded each other with heavy artillery and mortar shells for the sake of a few square yards of devastated real estate. What began with crowds demonstrating in the streets of the major capitals of Europe ended with disbelief in the train stations where the wounded returned from the battlefront. What promised to be popular support for each nation's government turned into cynicism (and the first credibility gap between government and people) when soldiers returning from the war revealed that what the governments had been saying was not true. Although the full impact of the war would not be realized until later in the century, it generated a mood of anger and despair in artists in the postwar period.

From this incredible explosion of political events came a number of ideas that greatly influenced the way in which modern dramatists view their characters and their world. Unlike other ages, when the ideas of a time seemed to blend together to create a coherent world view, the ideas of the modern era are disparate, disconnected, and often contradictory. If there is a single overriding impression that the "modern" movement gives, it is that of disagreement among individuals over the nature of human existence.

People reacted against Victorian morality, against the dehumanizing nature of industrialization, against the failure of rationalism to solve the world's mysteries, and against the continuing oppression of various people based on materialistic values. With so many "enemies" it is little wonder that people could not agree on a solution.

Modernism therefore is characterized by a variety of styles and movements, and these occur because there is no longer a single, fixed view of human nature or of God. Examples from science and psychology illustrate the variety of perceptions of the human condition.

Scientific Ideas

***Charles Darwin* (1809–1882).** Charles Darwin's scientific studies generated a storm of controversy regarding the nature of humankind. His theories postulated a world of change, but that change was ultimately orderly and knowable. Writers, including playwrights, debated issues of free will and environmental determinism. They wondered how much heredity influenced behavior. They placed fictional characters in their social surroundings to explain the characters through the environment. Their endeavors were considerably beyond the scope of Darwin's studies, but they gained a notoriety of their own. Artists found themselves forced to articulate their own personal moral order, beginning with the question of whether we live in a moral universe, and extending to the reasons humans behave as they do. On the one hand, this led to a vitality in drama, for there is an excitement about going to the theatre to hear a new point of view, one that is in sharp contrast to what one might have heard the night before. On the other hand, it led to dissension and to plays that are more effective as political tracts than as dramatic events.

***Albert Einstein* (1879–1955).**   If species are in the process of adapting to their natural surroundings, as Darwin suggested, then a corollary is that nature is in a state of constant change. The scientist who developed most fully a new conception of the world to account for the "permanence of impermanence" was Albert Einstein. His theories of relativity provided a model for the universe to replace that of Newton's. Instead of a linear, causal conception of existence and experience, Einstein formulated a space-time continuum without any center or reference point. All phenomena are relative; that is, they vary depending on the space and time in which they are located. Einstein's ideas were, of course, far beyond the abilities of most people to comprehend. Yet his theories gave support from the physical world for the ideas of philosophers who were insisting that characters be judged on their own terms, not on the basis of moral absolutes.

Psychology

Two other sets of concepts affected the development of drama in the 20th century. They derive from investigations into the structure and operations of the mind by Sigmund Freud (1856–1939) and Carl Jung (1875–1961). Freud attempted to understand the motivations for human behavior. He focused on the individual's past experiences, especially those of early childhood. He believed that every event, no matter how idiosyncratic, has an explanation in the complex of the individual's mind. The significance of the event is often not revealed to the individual until the nature of the complex is understood.

Jung, like Freud, was concerned with the subconscious mind, the vast reservoir of images and symbols that never lend themselves to ready analysis. He was interested in the relationship between the overt or external behavior of a person and the interior thoughts that lie behind that behavior. And he was, like Freud, involved in the study of motivation, the reasons people behave as they do.

However, there were fundamental differences between Jung and Freud. While Freud perceived the mind as a tripartite relationship between the id (the agent of pleasure), the ego (the agent of reality), and the superego (the agent of morality), Jung saw an elaborate interrelationship between the conscious and unconscious. This interrelationship is found in psychic processes that can be grasped elusively through symbols and images. Freud's theory was linear in its organization, mechanistic in its operation, and reductive in its conclusions; Jung's theory was holistic in its organization, evocative in its operation, and tentative in its conclusions.

The ideas of Darwin, Einstein, Freud, and Jung are but four of the dozens of important experiments and explorations into nature and human behavior that were carried out between 1880 and 1920. They are unusual in that their impact was profound, but they are typical in their revision of 19th-century thought. After them, few playwrights could write as if the universe contained moral and behavioral absolutes. Instead, the modern theatre came increasingly to reflect a world of uncertainty and anxiety. Each writer created from his or her own particular experience, hoping that it would have meaning for others.

ARTS IDEAS

In the arts world, too, there were new ideas and experiments that changed the way people saw the world around them. In the years leading up to and including World War I, artists developed a wholly new vocabulary for the visual arts.

Painting

Historical paintings, landscapes, the human form and portraiture, and genre painting (or scenes of domestic life)—all were different in 1920 from what they had been in 1880. At the beginning of the period, paintings identified a hierarchy of values through line, color, shape, and composition; human figures bore some degree of photographic resemblance to "real" or live studio models; and the interplay of light and atmosphere distorted perception but did not disturb our sense of recognition. At the end of the period, the certainty of perspective was shattered. Values were presented as if they had no history or connection to a moral order. The human figure was rearranged according to the whim or predisposition of the painter. The viewer was increasingly dependent on knowledge of the painter's personal symbols for an understanding of the painting.

Once the art world overthrew the accepted standards of composition and perspective, which had been operative for 500 years, wave after wave of new schools of thought attempted to dismiss the previous school and implant its ideas on the public mind. For the first time in Western history, the public witnessed not simply a revolution from one style to another, but successive revolutions, tumbling on top of one another with as little neatness as many of the paintings they created. In an effort to secure adherents, many of these new schools resorted to hyperbole and bombast, relying on the technique of shock rather than persuasion. The term *modern* came to mean more than just "recent"; it meant "the latest." With breathtaking abandon, visual artists propelled the world through a kaleidoscopic array of new shapes, colors, symbols, and materials. For the remainder of the 20th century, artists throughout the world would attempt to rework and re-explain the ideas created by these pioneers of modern sensibility.

Realism and Naturalism.   The first movement to affect the arts was realism. Social realism was never a movement with any clearly defined manifesto or theory of human behavior. Yet it serves as a convenient umbrella for the work of many artists in this period. It is best characterized as a concern for the relationship between the individual and social policy. It evokes a tension in the viewer between the legitimate desires of a character and the impossible social situation preventing those desires from being realized. The impact of a social realist work of art is that we, the audience, wish to change the social structure to accommodate characters whose demands on life are forcibly articulated by the writer or artist. The viewer is led away from contemplation of characters' motivations and toward the causes of the characters' tragedy—causes that are found in the social environment.

Chief among the social realists in the visual arts was Kathe Kollwitz (1867–1945), whose work in woodcuts and lithographs are among the most moving and disturbing studies of war and poverty in art history. Emphasizing the stark conditions of life through contrasts of black, gray, and white, she completed a number of studies on peasant uprising, infant mortality, war, and starvation. Her usual subject is a mother, either caressing a starving or dead child or reaching out for help to assist her struggle to survive. Unlike a naturalist painter, who would accumulate details to create a vivid picture of life as it is, Kollwitz is a reductionist. She provides only what is necessary to express an emotional moment. In a series entitled *Weavers* (1895–1898), a study of the German weavers' uprising in the 1840s, she depicted the conditions that led to the peasants' revolt.

Another realist strain in the 1870s and 1880s was naturalism, which found its greatest exponents not in art but in literature. If realism investigated the motivations of characters in their real surroundings, naturalism took this concept to its logical conclusion and made the investigation scientific and objective. It focused on the ramifications of the motivations and detailed as accurately as possible the natural environments of the characters. Unlike social realism, naturalism had a chief theorist, Emile Zola (1849–1902), who argued the case for a science of art and who virtually demanded that art adopt his principles or die. Zola insisted that art must give up its subjectivity, at least as far as humanly possible, and treat the theatre and literature as laboratories for the microscopic analysis of human nature. He railed against the well-made play and its imposition of a false structure on the experiences of life. He preferred to replace surprise twists and climaxes with normal events without apparent structural devices or theatrical moments.

Although he did not agree with the stridency of the social thesis playwrights who demanded action from the audience, Zola nevertheless saw the drama as a social scalpel, cutting to the truth of a situation and exposing it for all to see. Yet he is different from the social realists in the means by which he discussed social problems. He referred to "the inevitable laws of heredity and environment" and he wanted his characters to exist according to those laws, and not according to any personal feelings he himself, as author, might have. The search for a science of art led him to the darker side of

The Weaver by Kollwitz. *From Kathe Kollwitz,* Graphics, Posters, Drawings. *Copyright © 1981 by Random House, Inc.*

life—the world of vice, murder, deceit, and infidelity—in order to demonstrate that all of life is a fit subject for analysis.

Impressionism and Cubism. As with many of the dramatists of the period, the French Impressionists shocked the public into seeing the world differently. They insisted on presenting their own personal (and sometimes private) impression. They forced the viewer to look at a landscape as they had; they did not organize a scene according to principles of perspective. They presented a world of change and flux. They emphasized the importance of the fleeting moment by means of dabs of color, seemingly erratic brushstrokes, and asymmetrical compositions with angular perspectives. Most important, the Impressionists were the first modernists, for they gave modern artists the conviction to present what they see rather than what they think the world expects them to see.

A shocking new way of seeing came in 1907 when Pablo Picasso (1881–1973) painted *Les Demoiselles d'Avignon. Les Demoiselles* is associated with the development of Cubism, an art movement that reorganizes and reassembles reality into geometric shapes, such as blocks and cubes. It is also a significant statement of what artists at the beginning of this century were feeling and thinking. Depicting a parade of prostitutes before prospective customers in a brothel, the painting evokes a disturbing anxiety. The figures have been partially dislocated and distorted. The women express an inhuman, unfeeling quality. The African masks on three of the women and the vacant

Les Demoiselles d'Avignon by Picasso.   *Picasso, Pablo.* Les Demoiselles d'Avignon. *Paris, 1907. Oil on Canvas, 8′ × 7′8″. Courtesy Collection, The Museum of Modern Art, New York. Acquired through the Lillie P. Bliss Bequest.*

stares of the two central figures are haunting and disturbing. The women freely expose their upper bodies but then with shy embarrassment cover their groins, creating a conflicting tension in their purpose. Further, they seem to live in a different world, for Picasso has given the atmosphere around them a drapery-like quality, investing it with substance and shape. The world of the painting becomes, then, the world of the modern: angry, disturbing, and dislocated.

Symbolism.   For some European artists, the world at large was guilty of excessive and misplaced reliance on a descriptive material world for an understanding of the human condition. In their eyes, realism ignored the power of the spiritual and the mysterious. Gathering around the French writer Stéphane Mallarmé (1842–1898) between 1885 and 1895, they sought truth in the transcendental, the abstract, and the unconscious. Their contribution to art and drama was the elevation of the symbol to a place of signal importance in artistic communication. In place of the world of appearances, Symbolists used evocation, allusion, and suggestion to find a poetic truth more in harmony with human experience than the agendas of the realists and naturalists.

Expressionism.   In Germany, from 1905 to about 1925, many of the elements of Impressionism and Cubism found a new mode of organization in what became known as Expressionism. Using the techniques of outline distortion, vivid and expressive color juxtapositions, and personalized perspective, the Expressionists depicted a world that is hostile to the average individual. The painters translated the right of the painter to depict his impression into the right to pursue his sense of the increasing inhumanity of the Western world. In the dramas of Walter Hasenclever (1890–1940), Ernst Toller (1893–1939), and Georg Kaiser (1878–1945), as well as in the paintings of men like Otto Dix (1891–1969), Ernst Kirchner (1880–1938), and Wassily Kandinsky (1866–1944), characters are presented as if ensnared in their own personal nightmares. Reality is distorted to assume the shape of the unconscious. Buildings and bureaucrats loom menacingly over an individual, genuine hopes and desires are perverted into impossibility, and logic and rationality assume a machine-like indifference to personal needs. The Expressionist painters utilized techniques later found in many silent films of the 1920s (including the famous *The Cabinet of Dr. Caligari*): people assume grotesque postures and heavy makeup to reveal their inner natures; physical reality is depicted in a series of machines that wear down the individual; colors reveal more about an individual than shape; light and shadow are methods of accentuating the extremities of human feeling; heavy, bold outlines separate the individual from the world around him.

    The ideas of the Expressionist dramatists were similar: the inner soul is suffocating due to imprisonment and frustration; the social world demands that the individual ignore his or her private feelings and behave according to rigid expectations; the physical world is cold, mechanical, and aggressively hostile; the individual's mind feels out of control to the point that everything in reality becomes an animate expression of the psychic state of the mind, thus blurring and confusing the line between sanity and madness. Finally, the characters almost always sacrifice themselves to demonstrate the impossibility of living in a cruel world.

Futurism.   At the same time that the Expressionist railed against the mechanical quality of life in central Europe, another group of artists took exactly the opposite point of view and developed an artistic cult-worship of the machine. Filippo Tommaso Marinetti (1876–1944) was the founder of an Italian movement that praised new machines, energy, and danger. Futurism made the factory a temple, translated steam and revolving gears into a Gregorian chant, and exalted the machines of the future as the new icons of a prosperous and exciting utopia. If the future was a god presiding over this visionary kingdom, then the past was the devil. Futurists rejected the art of the past, instead constructing new forms and ideas out of the material of the future. Anything that helped to eradicate the old was applauded, and the Futurists went so far as to glorify war, which they called "the world's only hygiene." When the public realized the true horrors of World War I, the Futurists fell quickly into disrepute, but not before they had contributed the idea of action painting to later generations.

In the drama, the Futurists were particularly audacious. They wanted action and reaction. They craved the excitement and danger that an unruly mob could create, and they searched for new forms to express their politics. They used pamphleteering, direct address to the audience, and images of surprise rather than words of rationality. They relied heavily on simultaneous sound poems, a kind of free-association poetry, which struck the rationalists as absurd and nonsensical. Often the scenes of their short plays (called *sintesi*) were experiments in form, ranging from dances in which the performer takes on strange symbolic significance, to investigations into the meaning of time or the absence of location. Marinetti's *Feet*, for example, purports to explore the evocative capabilities of feet by having the curtain raised only far enough to expose the actors' feet as they express reactions to a variety of situations.

Dada.   If the Futurists were angry at the past for inhibiting movement toward the future, the Dadaists, who gained attention in 1916, were even angrier at the present for having destroyed the possibility of the future. As World War I progressed, the artists of Europe were outraged that humanity could allow itself to commit such atrocities as fighting a year-long battle over 50 feet of pasture. When the war-wounded returned to their homes, the full impact of what was happening gradually dawned on everyone who, until that time, had believed that the war was going well and that the troops would be home by Christmas. This realization found expression and momentum in the artists who had gathered in Zurich, Switzerland, to avoid the war. Choosing a name with no meaning to convey their feeling that the world had become a slaughter-house organized by idiots, the Dadaists went even farther than the futurists in their search for artistic forms that would shock their audiences. In art, Dadaists expressed the lack of principle and organization in the world through the collage, that is, the accumulation and presentation of a variety of seemingly unrelated objects frequently mixed with painted images. In the theatre, the Dadaists found their true home, for there they were able to play at will, combining poetry readings (usually of the same non-sense-making variety employed by the Futurists), dances, artists at work, and political speeches—all performed at the same time to confuse, anger, and ultimately revolt the audience.

It is impossible to sustain intense anger for any length of time, however, and within five years the impetus of the Dadaists had been lost. Because they had no proposal for changing the absurdity around them, they tended to drift toward nihilism (a political philosophy that denies meaning or value in anything) or a new art movement, Surrealism (discussed in the next chapter).

Music

The collapse of tradition occurred in music as well. Although Giacomo Puccini (1858–1924) kept alive the Italian opera tradition, other composers were stretching and breaking the harmonic and structural principles that had guided Western music for centuries. Claude Debussy (1862–1918), Camille Saint-Saëns (1835–1921), and Maurice Ravel (1875–1937) explored tone for its own sake, ending commitment to a developed melody line. Igor Stravinsky (1882–1971) shocked the ballet world with his *Rite of Spring* that followed no regular metre. Finally, Arnold Schoenberg (1874–1951) and Alban Berg (1885–1959) removed the last lynchpins of tradition by developing a 12-tone system of composition to replace the tonic scale that had been the foundation of Western music.

Many Europeans simply rejected these movements without consideration, but those people who identified with the avant-garde were caught up in a swirl of controversy. When they went to the theatre in 1890, they were likely to encounter new ideas and unusual stage techniques.

THEATRE HISTORY

Independent young artists were also the prime motivating force for change in theatre. In contrast to earlier times, these people were not actors or playwrights, but rather producers and directors. The new realism that dominated theatre production, and the many reactions against realism, all depended on an organizing artist, one person who determined the overall effect of individual efforts. The producer and the director became the controlling artists in the theatre.

Occasion

Despite the fervor of the new artists at the end of the century, the commercial theatre continued its set course. In France, the theatres of the boulevard were highly successful in presenting melodrama and farce, and the theatres of Germany, despite their aims of creating a literary drama, offered similar fare. In England and the United States, romantic drama and musical spectacle were dominant forms. The operetta, forerunner to the modern musical, was immensely popular, as it combined elements of melodrama with beautiful music and spectacular production. This was the era of the "matinee idol," as star performers became more important than the drama. Theatre had become fashionable and was seen as a polite and entertaining diversion if one had the money and the leisure to enjoy it.

The combination of melodrama, star performers, and technical wonders continued to entertain the theatre audience, and producers saw no reason for change. The long run was now the standard method of presentation, and a successful show might run for 200–300 performances with some even exceeding that number. Tours provided additional income and producers continually sought ways to increase the financial potential of their product.

As the commercial nature and possibilities of theatre increased, the role of the producer became dominant. In the United States, an enterprising group of six men managed to gain nearly complete control of the theatre industry by organizing the vast touring theatre scene. The Syndicate, as the group became known, began in 1896 as a means of providing one central booking office for touring companies and stars. Eventually they controlled access to most of New York's theatres and nearly all touring opportunities, so that a star actor or a producer was forced to contract with the Syndicate. (It should be noted that some of the more forceful stars, including Sarah Bernhardt, Joseph Jefferson, and Mrs. Minnie Maddern Fiske, battled the Syndicate with varying degrees of success.)

The Syndicate was composed of businessmen, not artists, and they used every means to promote their product. They purchased so much advertising that newspapers were compromised into printing favorable reviews. They bribed critics, boycotted organizations that attempted to defy them, and even had people fired if they wrote negative reviews. The Syndicate angered many theatre people, and eventually their power was broken by the efforts of a few successful individuals and the combined efforts of the Shubert brothers. The Shuberts, producers in their own right, eventually controlled U.S. theatre as completely as the Syndicate had, and today nearly every major city in the East and Midwest has a Shubert Theatre, although the Shubert monopoly was eventually dismantled by court order in the 1950s.

Although the Shuberts were more artistically inclined than the Syndicate, their primary interest was in commerce. However, for several young artists, theatre was more than a product, it was an artistic creation. Dissatisfied with the moribund state of theatre, they set up separate companies, often very small and underfinanced, through which they could pursue their artistic goals. Although each differed in its goals and its methods, they were all seeking to redefine the nature of theatre in modern society.

The Independent Theatre movement is a term applied to the creation of private theatres built primarily to stage the works of the new playwrights who after 1880 were experimenting with form and thought. The theatres bore no particular resemblance to one another except in their determination to offer an alternative theatre for the audiences of the major cities of Europe and the United States. They made no attempt to achieve great financial success, focusing instead on their artistic product. As a result, they met with public resistance, financial disasters, and (occasionally) political censorship. Their commitment to the new drama is their chief contribution to 20th-century theatre, however, for they persisted in presenting works that would, eventually, come to rank among the greatest dramas in Western literature. As a result, they provide an important bridge from the 19th to the 20th century.

Théâtre Libre.   André Antoine (1858–1943) founded the Théâtre Libre in 1887. Despite occasional artistic successes, the theatre's debts increased until it was closed in 1896, leaving behind its legacy of 112 plays, all directed by Antoine. He then went on to manage other theatres, but the model for avant-garde theatre that he created with the Théâtre Libre remains his most enduring contribution to theatre history.

A production of *La Terre* at Théâtre Antoine, 1902.   *Photo: Giraudon*

Each play was presented only three times. A dress rehearsal was open to friends of the cast, an opening night was performed for specially invited guests, and a third performance was given for season subscribers. Antoine's innovative financial plan of season subscriptions was but one facet of his importance. It was actually his artistic decisions that made his theatre unique. He sought out French playwrights who could not induce the large boulevard theatres to produce their works. Although most of these works are unknown to modern American audiences, they were a fresh and vital alternative to the standard fare of the day. Further, Antoine produced foreign plays of the dominant writers of the age, including Leo Tolstoy, Henrik Ibsen, August Strindberg, and Gerhart Hauptmann.

The brochure that proclaimed the new theatre described its goal as "truth and exactness" through which the theatre would present to its audiences "the simple gestures and natural movements of a modern man living our everyday life." Whether through genius or insecurity, Antoine gave to each production great care and attention to detail. He insisted on building each set for each play instead of reusing older flats.

He accepted the materialists' belief in the importance of the environment and tried to create the illusion of reality in his productions by refusing to paint objects on the walls when the objects could be found and placed onstage. (His most famous attempt at a realistic set was for *The Butchers* [1888], when he brought actual animal carcasses onto the set.) He worked with the actors to develop a sense of ensemble, encouraging them to ignore the presence of the audience and respond directly to the dramatic moment. Antoine was not the first person to do any of these, but in doing all of them on behalf of significant naturalistic dramas of the period, he established a notoriety for himself and a precedent for the future. Not all of Antoine's productions were naturalistic, in his later works he experimented with various other forms as well. In its dedication to new theatre forms, however, his theatre became the model for independent theatres throughout Europe.

Freie Bühne. In 1889, the Freie Bühne (Free Theatre) was established in Berlin as a counterpart to Antoine's experiment in Paris, and it even used the same subscription methods to avoid the censors and ensure an audience for its productions. The founders of the theatre, led by Otto Brahm (1856–1912), opened their first season with a production of Ibsen's *Ghosts.* Dedicated as it was to artistic merit to the exclusion of commercial possibilities, the Freie Bühne was immediately popular and acquired more than a thousand members within the first five months. The group performed on Sundays because on that day they could obtain the use of a theatre and professional actors were free to participate. The program closed its doors two years later because it had succeeded in proving the viability and popularity of the new naturalism, and then returned in 1892 for one production of Hauptmann's *The Weavers.* During its brief existence the Freie Bühne made some important contributions: it introduced contemporary foreign drama to the German theatre, encouraged young German writers, and introduced naturalistic drama to mainstream German theatre.

Independent Theatre. A third theatre with similar intent was the Independent Theatre, started in London in 1891 with the same opening play as the Freie Bühne: Ibsen's *Ghosts.* For six years, founder J. T. Grein hoped to find new English playwrights, but a majority of the 26 productions were by foreign writers, for Grein could "find" only one playwright whose work was the equal of continental writers of the period. That single playwright was George Bernard Shaw (1856–1950), whose plays will be discussed shortly. The Independent Theatre's major significance lay in its presentation of Ibsen in England and in its espousal of the works of Shaw, two achievements that cannot be underestimated because they permanently altered the direction of English and American playwriting for at least a century.

The Elizabethan Stage Society, founded in 1894, was an independent theatre with a different aim. Under its artistic director, William Poel (1852–1934), the ESS determined to revive Elizabethan conventions and to present Shakespeare in the proper context. The society's productions emphasized the verbal beauties of Shakespeare's plays and attempted to duplicate staging concepts of the Elizabethan age. In many ways, Poel's innovations are the forerunner of the Shakespeare Festivals that have been so successful in England and the United States throughout the 20th century.

Another result of the Independent Theatre's work was a three-year series of plays at the Royal Court Theatre under the management of Harley Granville-Barker (1877–1946) and J. E. Vedrenne (1867–1930). Like other independent theatre ventures, the company was founded to promote new plays of merit. Granville-Barker insisted on an ensemble style of performance that led to uniformly good productions, but the true impact of the theatre was the matinee series, which was used to introduce the major works of Shaw.

Abbey Theatre.   A shared characteristic of each of these theatres was the desire to promote plays of that theatre's own nationality. No independent theatre was more successful in this endeavor than the Abbey Theatre of Dublin. Although Dublin had known professional theatre since the Restoration, when Charles II granted a patent for a theatre in Smock Alley, the Abbey Theatre spearheaded an Irish renaissance in literature by providing production opportunities for some of the finest writers of the 20th century. Founded by Lady Gregory (1852–1932), W. B. Yeats (1865–1939), and Edward Martyn (1859–1923) in 1899 as the Irish Literary Theatre, it was dedicated to the performance of Irish plays, written by Irish playwrights, about Irish life. At first for the most part they produced the plays of Gregory and Yeats, and although these were provocative artistic writings they were not the uniquely Irish voice the company had sought. The addition in 1902 of two talented actors, W. G. Fay (1871–1947) and Frank Fay (1870–1931), greatly improved the performance standards and brought the company new attention. A key turning point in the life of the theatre was May 1903, when the company was invited to perform in London. The simplicity and power of the performances astonished London critics and audiences. Among them was Annie Horniman, a theatre fan and sometime costumer, who offered to provide and equip a small theatre in Dublin for the company. The new Abbey Theatre opened in 1904 and provided the stability the theatre needed. Three years later the company achieved international status with *The Playboy of the Western World,* by John Millington Synge (1871–1909). Recognized today as a great play, at its opening it was a scandal that resulted in full-scale riots on two continents.

Dublin audiences found the depiction of the rural Irish people insulting and the common lower-class language of the play unsuitable for the theatre, and they reacted with outcries, hissing, and threats of violence. One critic referred to it as "a vile and inhuman story told in the foulest language we have ever listened to from a public platform." Such notoriety of course attracted London producers, and the following year the play was staged in London and other cities, where it was acclaimed as a masterpiece. In 1911 the Abbey Theatre took the play to the United States, expecting the large group of Irish immigrants to gleefully welcome their fellows. Instead, they found an immigrant population that shared the views of Dubliners. In Philadelphia the entire company was arrested, and wherever it played it produced an overt response.

The plays of Synge prompted a response among Irish writers and thus the Abbey Theatre achieved its goal. It is one of two prominent independent theatres of this time period that are still operating today. It has weathered controversy and financial disaster partly because it has remained true to its intent to present plays about life in Ireland.

Théâtre d'Art and Théâtre de l'Oeuvre.   In Paris, 18-year-old Paul Fort found the theatre of Antoine very exciting, although he found naturalism itself unsatisfactory. He was intrigued by the work of the Symbolists, and his Théâtre d'Art opened in 1890 to investigate symbolist and other antinaturalist theatre forms. Working with some of the leading painters of the day, Fort utilized a wide range of theatrical effects. Silent tableaus, musical motifs, transparent gauze curtains separating the audience from the actors, and nonrealistic use of color all attempted to create a unique artistic world. Actors minimized movement and used chanting rhythms in delivering their lines. The results were at times highly evocative; at other times they were simply dull. Although rarely successful with critics or audiences, Fort's theatre succeeded in its aim of experimenting with novel means of production and of discovering alternative means of communication in the theatre. Various difficulties with finances, mismanagement, and unfavorable criticism forced the closure of the theatre in 1892.

From his work with both Antoine and Fort, Aurélien Lugné-Poe (1869–1940) had formed his own vision of theatre and brought it to fruition in the work of the Théâtre de l'Oeuvre. The theatre opened in 1893 to continue the work of Fort but was far more successful than Fort had been. The production of Maeterlinck's *Pelléas and Mélisande* was a scandalous success. The play was performed entirely behind a scrim, and the staging utilized muted colors, semidarkness, muttered words, and strange poses to communicate the supernatural quality of the play. Criticism was mixed, but the discussion the production provoked ensured the theatre's success. Lugné-Poe's taste in theatre was eclectic. He presented several of Ibsen's non-naturalistic works, including *Brand* and *Lady from the Sea.* He performed classical Indian drama and the latest writings of Oscar Wilde. His greatest success (although a financial failure) was his 1896 presentation of *Ubu Roi*, by Alfred Jarry (1873–1907); this grotesque, puppet-like morality play depicting the savagery and greed of human beings has since been judged as the earliest forerunner of the absurdist school. From the first moment of the play, when King Ubu's first word is "Shit!", the play outraged the audience, although critics praised the work's originality and power. Jacques Copeau, a young actor in the audience who would soon be a leading dramatic artist, labeled the play "pure theatre," a term which would still be current 100 years later.

Moscow Art Theatre.   The other prominent independent theatre still in existence is the Moscow Art Theatre, founded by Vladimir Nemirovich-Danchenko (1858–1943) and Konstantin Stanislavski (1863–1938). It followed much the same pattern as the other theatres discussed here: a company of actors and artists seeking greater artistic freedom devoted themselves to the new ideas of the time. They had strong directors who molded the productions into a single vision through meticulous preparation; and they encouraged national playwrights whose themes and environments reflected the mood of the country—Anton Chekhov (1860–1904) and Maxim Gorky (1868–1936). Stanislavski scheduled numerous rehearsals for each play and demanded careful research into the actual social conditions of the characters by each actor. The MAT adopted one important variation on the general model when it decided to produce only a handful of plays each season, preparing the plays in rehearsals that sometimes lasted more than a year. Successful shows were retained in the repertory, giving the company time to spend on new productions. The MAT's greatest successes were with the plays of Chekhov; they provided the theatre with a sound financial and artistic base, which it never lost, and in time the Moscow Art Theatre came to represent the highest standards in world theatre. Their visit to the United States in 1923 was instrumental in shaping the course of American theatre, and their influence was felt throughout Europe as well. Stanislavski, however, found much of the work of the MAT disappointing, even when the MAT experimented with non-naturalistic works. Never did he feel that he had been able to overcome the years of tradition associated with major theatrical productions. To counter this development, the theatre began to sponsor Studios in which various directors could pursue experimental goals in the theatre. It was the work in the Studios that led to the development of Stanislavski's famous "system" of acting and provided the opportunity for experimental works by a series of influential directors.

United States Developments.   Even before the visit of the Moscow Art Theatre, the independent theatre movement had reached fruition in the United States. As early as 1912 the Chicago Little Theatre had been formed to promote new plays and young artists. In New York City the Neighborhood Playhouse opened early in 1915, followed later that same year by the Washington Square Players. This last group of young theatre practitioners was determined to legitimize the one-act play and to utilize concepts of the "new stagecraft" from Europe as a means of simple, honest production. They focused on dramas of social import and brought an air of seriousness of purpose to their productions. For three years, until the pressures of World War I resulted in financial difficulties and many of the young actors were called away to military service, the Washington Square Players introduced a new, noncommercial presence to the New York theatre world. Although they produced no significant playwrights, they did provide the stimulus for the formation of the Theatre Guild, a group that would become a major force in theatre in the 1920s.

Provincetown Players.   During the summer of 1915 a different group of young artists began a theatrical venture in Provincetown, Massachusetts. A summer residence for young bohemians, Provincetown offered an ideal atmosphere for a new theatrical venture. Organized by the playwright Susan Glaspell (1876–1948) and her husband George (Jig) Cook (1873–1924), the Provincetown Players was devoted to an ideal of collective creation. Begun as a sort of group-therapy, the group quickly progressed to the writing and staging of new American plays. In their earliest organizational rules, it was expressly stated that the author of a new play selected for production would direct the play and all other members would support the production in some way.

During their second season they discovered a young playwright named Eugene O'Neill, and the success of the theatre was secured. In the fall of 1916 they moved to New York City, and the story from that point to 1922 is one of continued success, a factor that gradually undermined the collective nature of the group. Professional directors were hired, among them Nina Moise and James Light, and the group continued to be successful, with the plays of O'Neill and Glaspell proving to be particularly effective. As members were deemed successful by critics and the public, they received opportunities to join the professional theatre. Finally, the overwhelming success of O'Neill's *The Emperor Jones* in 1922 marked the professional success of the company and its end as a unique organization.

Lafayette Players.   In another part of New York, a unique venture was providing theatrical access to a different group of young artists. Theatre was not new to the black population of Harlem. Bert Williams (1874–1922) and George Walker (1873–1911) had become famous stars of the musical theatre, and their shows provided additional opportunities for young black performers throughout the 1890s. The Syndicate actively suppressed black performers, however, and by 1910 the black actor, with the exception of Bert Williams, was noticeably absent from Broadway. Portrayals of black Americans were part of American theatre—Edward Sheldon (1886–1946) in *The Nigger* (1909) dramatized the powerful tale of a black man passing for white, being elected governor, and realizing that he cannot help his own race from that position. The play spoke openly about the black experience in America, including discrimination and mob violence. However, not one member of the cast was black. One response to this situation was a surge of theatrical activity in the black community.

The Lafayette Theatre in Harlem was the site of many of these developments. A musical revue called *Darktown Follies* was a major hit there in 1913, even attracting white audiences from Manhattan, but many nonmusical plays were successful as well. Ridgeley Torrence's *Three Plays for a Negro Theatre* was produced downtown, which added prestige. In 1919 Lester Walton and Anita Bush organized the Lafayette Players, and for several years this company produced a variety of theatrical works ranging from musicals to dance-dramas. Although no major playwright was discovered, the Lafayette Players served as a training ground for a large number of black performers who went on to success in the theatre and in film and provided a solid foundation for the continuing growth of black theatre in America.

Little Theatre Movement.   The independent theatre movement in the United States was not limited to New York City; small independent companies were founded in Cleveland, Chicago, Boston, and other cities. The community theatre movement brought theatre to small communities across the nation. By 1917 more than 50 theatre companies were in existence in the United States, and by 1925 the number would grow to more than 5,000, including theatre programs in major universities.

The independent theatres made no attempt to please everyone; theatre-going became a matter of taste. The theatre as an institution became a forum for debating the national health and the problems of living in the modern era. It was no longer simply a social event, but an evening of intellectual and artistic stimulation. If modernism meant a break with the past, these theatres were truly modern in their choice of subject matter and in their methods of presentation. Artistically, the independent theatres focused attention on the script, the characters, and the environments, and away from star personalities or stage gimmicks. By World War I, these theatres had successfully introduced new production concepts and new playwrights to the world that formed the framework for 20th-century theatre.

Location

Obviously, the range of theatres that developed during this period resulted in a great variety of theatre structures, and no one building can be viewed as typical. A sense of the variety may be achieved through a study of four: the Hippodrome and the Little Theatre in New York City, the Grosses Schauspielhaus in Berlin, and the Vieux Colombier in Paris.

The Hippodrome, which opened in April 1905, was a commercial venture in every way. Billing itself as "the world's largest theatre," it seated more than 5,000 spectators. The stage, which required more than 5,000 lights to illuminate properly, was nearly 200 feet wide and more than 100 feet deep. A staff of more than 1,000 was required to operate the theatre. The opening show was entitled *A Yankee Circus on Mars*, and it was, in fact, a spectacular revue complete with circus acts. The Hippodrome provided great challenges to producers (it was hard for everyone in the theatre to see, let alone hear), and after the novelty had worn off the theatre was used for vaudeville and eventually for film. It was resurrected in grand style in 1935 for *Jumbo*, a massive musical production based on circus life and featuring full-blown circus acts.

Of similar dimensions, but with an entirely different purpose in mind, the Grosses Schauspielhaus was built in Berlin in 1919 by producer/director Max Reinhardt (1873–1943). Reinhardt had used the circus structures of Germany for his classic presentations, seeking to re-create a sense of the ancient Greek amphitheatre. In his new auditorium, he created a modern equivalent that was designed to produce "primitive grandeur."

The Grosses Schauspielhaus featured a horseshoe-shaped acting area backed by a proscenium stage in an arrangement similar to that of the Teatro Farnese. The stage was equipped in traditional fashion with a revolving stage and a domed cyclorama surrounding it. The forestage and the entire "thrust" stage area could be lowered or raised as desired allowing great flexibility in staging, and three "vomitoria," or tunnels, under the seating provided actors access to the thrust stage area. The audience surrounded the acting area on three sides with the seats stretching in one continuous bank nearly to the ceiling of the huge room, which was topped with a huge dome that partially concealed lighting positions. Reinhardt's hope was to create one space capable of containing both actors and audience in which the grand passions and lofty ideals of classical theatre could be reborn. Although the theatre was hugely successful with audiences, Reinhardt used the theatre for only three years, gradually defeated by difficulties with acoustics and expenses.

The little theatre movement also wanted to bring the audience and the actor into a closer union, but the means of achieving it were in direct opposition to Reinhardt's ideas. The Little Theatre, built in New York City in 1912 was designed to bring the audience closer to the stage so that truly naturalistic staging techniques could be utilized without any need for exaggeration of voice, scenery, costume, movement, or expression.

Designed partly as a traditional proscenium theatre, it featured a flat stage nearly entirely encompassed by a revolve. The revolve itself was thoroughly trapped and a modest fly gallery was included as well. Adequate lighting positions were provided in the ceiling, and panels could be removed to provide the proper angle. Acoustics were a major concern, and an acoustical expert was included on the design team. The auditorium, holding just 299 seats until a balcony was added several years later, was slightly raked to provide good sightlines for each spectator. The overall effect was one of simplicity and intimacy—the hallmarks of naturalistic production.

Even greater simplicity marked the Vieux Colombier, the theatre built to house the theatre company of Jacques Copeau (1879–1949). In an attempt to create a sparse, simple theatre in which the emphasis would be wholly on the actors, Copeau designed a simple, bare stage with no proscenium arch. In its final version in 1920, the front edge of the stage was curved and two curved steps connected the stage to the auditorium floor with stairs at either side of the stage also leading to the auditorium. At the back of the stage, a curved arch formed an "inner below," while two flights of stairs rose above the arch to a central raised platform. Two doorways placed asymmetrically to either side of the central alcove gave access to stairs leading to the upper level, with the stage right door also providing an offstage exit. Although modifications could be made by altering the trapped floor, draping, or additional stage structures, the basic

The Vieux Colombier.   *Photo: Giraudon*

stage unit was permanent and no further stage apparatus was included other than tasteful, hidden placements for lighting instruments.

The success of the Vieux Colombier stage remains open to debate. Some critics found it limiting and an obstruction to creativity. Others found in it a formal dignity that supported the work of the actors. All else aside, the concept of an architectural stage may be seen as an antecedent to the contemporary theatre's use of unit settings; it provided a strong alternative to the spectacle-dominated commercial theatre.

Performers

Directors.   Although new theatre buildings provided the necessary setting for the performance of theatre, the dominant performer of this time period was the stage director. While the importance of this role had been evolving throughout the 19th century, it is during this period that a group of dedicated directors clearly established the dominant role of the director in the 20th century.

The development of the modern concept of the director is generally associated with the work of Georg II, Duke of Saxe-Meiningen (1826–1914). As director of his own court theatre he introduced new concepts of ensemble performance and unified production that have greatly influenced the theatre of the 20th century.

Belasco. Among the most successful of the new breed of directors was a brash young American, David Belasco (1853–1931). Although Brooks Atkinson (1894–1984), noted American critic, dubbed him "the master of mediocrity," Belasco's success in the theatre is undeniable. Born in San Francisco, he began his theatre studies there and came to New York as a stage manager and playwright, becoming an independent producer in 1890. For twelve years he worked under the Syndicate, but in 1902 broke with them, rented a theatre, and finally built his own theatre, the Belasco.

Belasco typifies the new figure of the theatre director. Every detail of every production was under his control. Prolific, eccentric, and energetic, he wrote more than 70 plays and directed nearly double that number. His intricately detailed settings and performances were the peak of naturalistic production. For one play he actually had workmen remove the interior of a room in a boarding house, including the wallpaper, and reconstruct it onstage. For another, he created a precise replica of a Child's Restaurant, complete with food preparation. In lighting, too, he sought for naturalistic effect, using a wide variety of lighting techniques to create appropriate moods on the stage.

In his work with actors he was a complete tyrant. He was a "star maker" who would find young performers, usually women, and train them for several years before allowing them to make their debut. His skill was to identify a particular trait in an actress and then drill her, with arduous and demanding lessons, into perfecting that particular trait. Then a play would be written or adapted to suit her "type," and Belasco would unveil another star. Belasco was equally demanding with all of his employees. He typically rehearsed a play for 10 weeks rather than the now-standard 4, and he insisted on complete precision in every aspect of a production.

Other directors felt that naturalistic production techniques were confining and began to acknowledge the theatricality of the production. These efforts began in part

GEORG II,
DUKE OF
SAXE-MEININGEN
(1826–1914)

*T*he playwright Gerhart Hauptmann saw them perform when he was a boy and recounted later that "no word can measure the extent of the spiritual wealth that these few evenings provided me for my whole life." The *London Times* said that their performance "has certainly never been surpassed at a London theater." For a performance in Berlin, scalpers were able to obtain 15 times the normal price for a seat in the auditorium. The theatre troupe that received such acclaim was not the Comédie-Française nor a leading company of the English stage. Rather, it was the court theatre of a rather modest German duchy, Saxe-Meiningen.

The troupe was not under the direction of a hired professional or noted scholar, but was personally supervised by Georg II, Duke of Saxe-Meiningen. Educated as heir to a title, Georg II demonstrated an early talent for drawing, became an accomplished pianist in his youth, translated and adapted *Macbeth* at age 15, and attended theatre in many cities throughout Europe. Still, he had major political and military responsibilities. Only in 1866 did a period of peace and prosperity allow him to turn his attention to the theatre.

Assisted by his third wife, the actress Ellen Franz, and his trusted assistant, Ludwig Chronegk, Georg II established new standards for theatre performance. He restored classic texts, removing "improvements" that had been made to suit the needs of star performers. He researched historical periods to ensure accuracy in stage settings and costumes. Interior scenes were performed in box sets, often set within a larger exterior setting to allow for simple scene shifts. He experimented with lighting effects, props, sound effects, and makeup to produce the proper setting and atmosphere for the play.

The reputation of the troupe, however, was based above all on their acting style, which came to represent the epitome of ensemble performance. Virtuosity in performance was frowned upon, but each member of the troupe was given personal training. Rehearsals, in most theatres a mere exercise two or three times before a performance, extended from morning to night over a period of many weeks. Rehearsals were done onstage, with staging indicated and in full costume. Cast members not involved in a scene were directed to sit in the auditorium and observe.

Georg II staged each moment of the drama meticulously. His written instructions placed each member of the ensemble in a particular position with a carefully defined relationship to the action of the scene. He was known to use four hours to rehearse a single scene. He was not a tyrant, however; cast members were encouraged to express opinions, and the duke was willing to try any idea that might improve a scene.

His staging broke many rules. Actors moved in normal patterns, looked directly at the person they addressed, and occasionally even turned their backs on the audience. He frequently diverted attention from the speaker, using other characters' reactions to illustrate the impact of the speech. Offstage crowd noises were often used to underscore a scene and provide tension.

The troupe performed lengthy seasons at home and had multiple international tours that included performances in England, Scandinavia, and Russia. Despite his attention to the theatre, Georg II did not create a "toy" for himself to the neglect of his dukedom. Indeed, his rule was a time of prosperity. Saxe-Meiningen was noted for its orchestra as well as its theatre. He continued working with the theatre until his hearing failed, and even then he returned in 1912 to direct a final production. He died shortly before the outbreak of World War I in 1914.

Georg II is generally credited with introducing the modern concept of the director to the theatre. Beyond that, his innovations in staging and acting were influential in the developments after 1880 that significantly altered the nature of theatre in the modern world.

as a result of a basic tenet of naturalism: each production must be true to the environment of the play. From this it followed that directors would develop a new concept for each production, adapting their ideas to the needs of the play. Instead of resulting in naturalistic sets for each show, this eclectic approach created a variety of styles. Directors concluded that the illusion of reality did not necessarily mean physical reality but might refer to an imagined reality as well. Naturalism ultimately provided little creativity because designers and directors would find actual locations of the plays and then rebuild them onstage. What theatre artists wanted was to create the world of the play with their imaginations, not their cameras.

Reinhardt. The eclectic stage director is fully realized in the person of Max Reinhardt (1873–1943), who stated "there is no one form of theatre that is the only true artistic form." Reinhardt felt that each script demanded a different approach, and frequently, for Reinhardt, this meant a different performing space. Reinhardt was trained in naturalistic production at the Freie Bühne, and his later work ranged from a blend of expressionism and naturalism in a production of *Ghosts* (1906), designed by the artist Edvard Munch, to a production of *Oedipus Rex* (1910) performed in a circus building. He directed a production of *Everyman* (1920) set on the stairs of Salzburg Cathedral, and for *The Miracle* (1924) he reconstructed a Broadway theatre to resemble the interior of a cathedral, with a set that measured 200 feet long, 120 feet wide, and 110 feet high.

Rehearsal techniques varied as much as the physical production. Although for each production Reinhardt prepared a *Regiebuch* that contained all details of a given production worked out in advance, he freely made modifications during rehearsals. In smaller works, his directorial method was based on patience and careful attention to each actor, with many instructions given privately to individual performers. For larger works he worked more authoritatively—*The Miracle* required 22 assistant directors; Reinhardt himself worked from a scaffolding while assistants relayed his instructions. In all cases, he made the director the emotional center of the production, relying on his own inspiration, commitment, and enthusiasm to inspire the cast.

Meyerhold. The work of Vsevelod Meyerhold (1874–1940) and other Russian directors sought nothing less than a new vocabulary for the theatre. After working with the Moscow Art Theatre in realism, Meyerhold devoted the remainder of his career to discovering an alternate form of theatre that went beyond mere duplication of reality. For Meyerhold, theatre (and all art) had to be distinct from reality; it should be presented in conventionalized terms so that it was seen and not merely observed. To achieve this, he abolished the curtain, extended the acting area into the audience, eliminated the proscenium wall, and removed the footlights. For actors, he developed a new style called biomechanics, in which conventional gesture expresses concepts or emotions rather than psychologically motivated behavior. Rage might be expressed through a somersault. Evil could be shown by leaping onto another actor's chest. Settings were abstract, symbolic apparatus that accommodated the stage movement.

As director, Meyerhold felt he had complete freedom to interpret a script. He rearranged scenes, juxtaposed moments, and attempted to "fragment" the illusion in any way possible. His constructivism, as this style of theatre came to be called, was the work of a man who saw the director not as a person who shaped a production, but as one who redefined the basic concepts of theatre.

Meyerhold was not the only Russian who attempted to find a way to overcome the dominance of naturalism on the stage. Alexander Tairov (1885–1950), echoing the ideas of Wagner, sought a theatre that unified the arts of movement, rhythm, music, and dance. His productions sought to create archetypal figures rather than specific individuals through the use of music, pantomime, and emotion expressed through gesture, music, rhythm, and words. Tairov's productions were a blend of theatre, opera, and dance, which utilized chanted dialogue and danced pantomime. It was the role of the director to provide a milieu (script, music, decor, and costume) that allowed an actor the fullest expression, and then to mold the actor's work to the unifying concept.

Eugene Vakhtangov (1883–1923) began his career as a disciple of Stanislavski, was briefly intrigued with Meyerhold's work, and then attempted to bridge the differences. His style of theatre, termed *imaginative realism,* was developed at the First Studio, an offshoot of the Moscow Art Theatre established specifically for the investigation of new ideas. Vakhtangov attempted to move away from pure naturalism to a universality achieved through exaggeration and distortion of perceived reality. As director, he modified texts, altered characterizations, and coached actors to begin with Stanislavskian analysis and then distort the character toward a universal type. He died at the age of 39, but even though his career was not of long duration, he established a style that remained influential in the Soviet Union for many years.

Nikolai Evreinoff (1879–1953) shared Meyerhold's interest in theatricality, but he sought not to create a symbolic reality but to theatricalize life itself. His mono-dramas were similar to expressionism in their attempt to unite the audience with the perceptions of the protagonist, allowing each audience member to experience a heightened reality. The most complete realization of his ideal was *The Storming of the Winter Palace*, in which he utilized a cast of some 10,000 citizens to actually re-create a famous historical event.

The extravagance of Evreinoff's triumph stands in sharp contrast to the directorial aims of Jacques Copeau. Outraged by what he termed the "frenzied spirit of commercialization" in the theatre, Copeau founded his own theatre, which he declared to be "the rallying place of all those authors, actors, spectators, who are tormented by the need of restoring beauty to the stage." Copeau, dedicated to a rigorous simplicity, intended to maintain the purity of classical forms while exploring contemporary concerns. The sparse and undecorated stage (see above) was merely a platform for the actor who was the central artist of the theatre.

As a director, Copeau maintained complete control of every element. Exhaustive textual analysis preceded any staged rehearsals, so that Copeau's interpretation was firmly established. During the staging process Copeau was equally dominant, staging each movement and demanding specific results. He wanted actors to break the tyranny of typecasting and to recognize the elevated function of an actor in society. Given this attitude among the artists, Copeau felt the theatre audience would be similarly enlightened. He was apparently successful, for he developed a devoted following and an international reputation.

Designers. Although Copeau's absolute simplicity placed little emphasis on scenic design, the innovative concepts of other directors and theorists required a similar inventiveness from scenic designers. As in the visual arts, the end of the 19th century witnessed both the height and the end of scenery painted in traditional perspective, and brought forth an entirely new conception of the function of scenic design.

In Russia, the work of Leon Bakst (1866–1924) utilized drawing and painting techniques to full effect. Bakst combined his love of Greek art and his interest in Asian design to create fanciful sets and costumes distinguished by their bold use of color, their exotic shapes, and their theatrical expressiveness. Although he was particularly successful in ballet, Bakst's theatre works were also viewed as artistic creations, and his drawings and renderings were as popular as his stage work. His sophisticated eclecticism and bold style were highly influential, and the work of his pupils, notably Natalie Goncharova, maintained the popularity of the style in the Russian theatre for many years.

The tradition of the painted set was also evident in the work of Joseph Urban (1871–1933). Trained in Vienna as a painter and a sculptor, Urban worked in all of the major theatres in Vienna before coming to the United States in 1911. Here he worked for both Flo Ziegfeld and the Metropolitan Opera, besides contributing to the early years of film. Urban was essentially a painter, and his designs remained pictorial and decorative. He was innovative, however, in his techniques. He introduced to the United

States the European style of painting flats while they lay flat on the floor; he experimented with painting mediums to achieve a translucent effect, and he adapted the pointillistic style of painting to introduce the effect known today as spattering. An eclectic, Urban utilized the old *periaktoi* devices and the new concepts of three-dimensional scenery in his attempts to create the proper atmosphere for a production. Possibly due to his style and flair, Urban was more successful with musical and revue productions than with traditional drama.

Alfred Roller (1864–1935) was also trained as a painter in Vienna, but his designs hinted at a new concept of scenic design. Focused fully on the interplay of light and color to create evocative stage spaces, Roller's designs did not reject realism. Rather they relied on a selected or simplified realism in which only a few items were introduced to the stage, but each of them was evocative, detailed, and powerful. Roller utilized mobile scenic towers that could be rearranged and altered with light to form new shapes and movement patterns on the stage. In his interest in the sculptural quality of design he was perhaps the earliest designer to embody the ideas of two revolutionary theorists, Adolph Appia (1862–1928) and Edward Gordon Craig (1872–1966).

Swiss-born Appia found the theatre experience to have a mystical, almost primeval quality. He felt that a play should evoke a response in the audience based on the rhythms of the sound, movement, and design. The focus of the drama was the actor, and the setting should provide the necessary environment for the actor to "tell" the story without extraneous decoration or design. He sought to eliminate the disparity between two-dimensional set walls and the three-dimensionality of the actor. He did this by creating monumental structures made of large step units, full-sized pillars, and multiple platforms. To this he added multidirectional lighting in order to achieve a three-dimensionality in the contrast between light and shadows. His sets were rarely particular or detailed; instead, they were general and universal. The result of his designs often created a feeling of an eternal struggle taking place in the plays; they raised the action above the level of the ordinary into the realm of the archetypal. At the same time, Appia signaled new directions for stage designers in his emphasis on the relationship between light and shadow and on the relationship between the shape of the actor's movement and the shape of the set. Although many of his designs were never realized, they were quite revolutionary in their search for a language of theatrical symbols.

Craig's contributions share many similarities to Appia's. He disdained painted scenery, realistic detail, and enclosed spaces. He wanted a unitary vision onstage in which all elements of the theatre (action, sound, light, line, color, and mass) are equal. He strove for sculptural shapes and open playing areas that would suggest an eternal theatre where majestic deeds occurred. He differed from Appia in his preference for verticality in combination with horizontal lines. Imposing columns, oversized doors, and towering screens often dwarfing the actors were characteristic features of Craig's designs. Craig had even fewer of his designs realized than Appia had, and one major production of *Hamlet* at the Moscow Art Theatre for Stanislavski was a complete failure. Nevertheless, he was an important designer, because he was an excellent polemicist, arguing forcibly in books and articles for his vision of a new theatre. His theories provoked responses from actors, playwrights, directors, and other designers and were a major impulse in the development of our modern theatre.

Actors and Acting Theorists.   The explosion of new ideas in the theatre presented a difficult challenge for the actor. New styles of plays, differing concepts of design, and the presence of the director with a need for a unified impression all demanded new styles of performance.

Not all successful actors felt the need to respond to these new demands, relying instead on their own unique personalities to attract and keep an audience. In England, William Kendal (1843–1917) and Madge Kendal (1848–1935) earned great success in light comedy roles tailored to their abilities. On Broadway, Richard Mansfield (1854–1907) parlayed his strong personality, confidence, athleticism, and a powerful voice into stardom by specializing in offbeat characters such as Dr. Jekyll and Mr. Hyde or Ivan the Terrible; Otis Skinner (1858–1942), William Gillette (1853–1937), and Julia Marlowe (1866–1950) also were part of the "personality school" of acting. Maude Adams (1872–1953), perhaps the first American actress to acquire a loyal following that came to every play she performed in regardless of quality, projected joyful optimism and youth so keenly that her portrayal of such roles as Peter Pan made her the top money-making star in the United States. To preserve her stage image, she avoided any part that included negative elements and steadfastly refused to make her private life available to the public.

The variety of performance styles allowed actors to achieve stardom in very different ways. The careers of Ellen Terry (1847–1928), Sarah Bernhardt (1844–1923), and Eleonora Duse (1858–1924) differed greatly, but each received international acclaim. [See insert.]

Other forms of theatre also created "stars." Bert Williams (1874–1922) began his career in minstrel shows wearing burnt-cork blackface because his own skin wasn't dark enough. He first established himself as a performer with his partner, George Walker, in all-black musical shows that eventually led him to Broadway in 1903. Carefully molding his personal image, Williams created the stage image of a slow-paced shuffling innocent "darky" that eventually made him a star of the Ziegfeld Follies from 1910 to 1919, the first black actor to integrate a white cast.

Vaudeville continued to produce stars who also found their way to Broadway. Joe Weber (1867–1942) and Lew Fields (1867–1941) were childhood friends who began their careers in blackface but soon developed a "Dutch" act based on ethnic humor and physical comedy. As their popularity increased, they began to produce full-length evenings featuring burlesques of current hits that allowed them to utilize the full range of their zany skills.

The first full-blown star of the Broadway musical theatre was George M. Cohan (1878–1942). Trained in vaudeville, Cohan was a skilled playwright and composer as well as actor/singer/dancer. Between 1900 and 1928 he wrote, directed, and starred in a string of plays that all celebrated traditional American values. Cohan himself was the prototypical American. Straightforward, hard-headed but sentimental underneath, cocky and full of energy, both onstage and off, Cohan gave Americans back an image of themselves that they wanted desperately to believe.

Although such performers were financially successful, their skills were not sufficient for the new forms of drama. In the antinaturalistic theatre, the actor was asked to utilize masks, to use dance and vocal music techniques in the presentation of a role, to incorporate pantomime techniques borrowed from the commedia dell'arte, and

TERRY, DUSE,
AND BERNHARDT

*T*he turn of the century marked the climax of the careers of three dynamic women. The Victorian lady Ellen Terry, the unique Italian charmer Eleonora Duse, and the flamboyant Frenchwoman Sarah Bernhardt offer three successful actress in this period.

Ellen Terry (1847–1928) was born into a theatrical family and began acting during her childhood, although she had no notable success until the age of 28. From 1878 to 1902 she performed in the shadow of Henry Irving at the Lyceum, establishing herself as a leading Shakespearean actress. Although she never achieved the notoriety or celebrity of a star, her 69-year career on the stage was marked by consistent quality.

Terry was the embodiment of the Victorian ideal woman. In her physical qualities and her personal manner she epitomized the figure of grace, femininity, and composure that poets and painters had created. To the theatregoing public, she was a work of art. The words most often used by critics to describe her performances were *charm, grace,* and *tenderness.* Although Terry had three marriages and two illegitimate children (one was Edward Gordon Craig), the public and the press chose to ignore this to preserve the stage image she created. She carefully selected roles that suited her natural temperament, always maintaining that beauty could not be sacrificed to realism or effect. This limited her range, but within that range she was unmatched.

Eleonora Duse (1858–1924) was also a member of a theatrical family, but she spent her youth with her parents' traveling company, often walking from one city to the next attempting to find an audience. At the age of 20, her performance in Zola's *Thérèse Raquin* brought her to prominence.

Duse's success lay in her ability to portray the inner tension of her characters, relying on gesture, expression, and her pictorial sense rather than line interpretation. Noted for her understated approach, which was in great contrast to the general style of acting, her sense of restraint and inner torment was ideally suited to Ibsen's rebellious "new woman," and she frequently performed such roles.

After 1887 Duse became her own manager. Temperamental and fiercely competitive, she was a difficult partner and, although she worked successfully with many of the theatrical greats of the period, including Edward Gordon Craig, she never established a permanent artistic home. On tour, she was even more successful throughout Europe and America than in Italy. She retired from the stage in 1909 and established the Library for Actresses in Rome to provide a place for women artists to work, study, and collaborate. Forced to abandon the project and return to the stage due to a lack of funds, she died on tour in the United States at the age of 67.

Sarah Bernhardt (1844–1923) was a self-made international star. A successful actress at the Comédie for several seasons, she broke her contract in 1880 to go in search of better roles and more money. Forced to give up her pension and sued for breach of contract, she immediately signed contracts for American and European tours that more than covered her losses.

Her public image was destined to draw attention. She demanded and received unheard-of salaries and spent money extravagantly. She was accused of issuing false press releases about her mental health so that people would come to the theatre to see for themselves. She was known to faint on the final line of a performance and be carried from the stage, only to return for her bow, supported by the arm of her leading man. She was one of the first performers to allow her image to be used in advertising. In 1899 she opened her own theatre, named after her and decorated with portraits of her previous theatrical successes. The premiere performance featured Ms. Bernhardt in the role of Hamlet.

Her appeal was not entirely based on outrageous behaviors. Her acting talents allowed her to play a wide range of roles, and she enjoyed numerous successes in transvestite or male roles. Her greatest roles were melodramatic heroines in which her physical appeal, her unusual and sensual style of movement, and her vocal skills created dynamic characterizations. Particularly adept at sudden shifts of mood, she kept audiences waiting expectantly for the violent emotional that which characterized her performance. In those moments, Bernhardt was passionate, aggressive, and powerful, the reverse image of the Victorian ideal that Ellen Terry had so beautifully embodied.

perhaps to do gymnastics, juggle, or walk a tight wire. To meet these demands, various theatre artists, including Meyerhold and Copeau, established schools where actors could experiment and develop these new requirements. Since the needs of each individual form were unique, no unified approach was developed.

What was needed for the naturalistic theatre was a theory of acting that would point the actor toward a consistency of interpretation throughout the play and suggest the character's real experiences. The methodology of François Delsarte (1811–1871) attempted to demonstrate that stage expression could be as scientifically designed as mathematics. His theory developed a system based on relaxation, posture, breathing, and script analysis. These elements, according to Delsarte, could be carefully combined in specific poses that would correctly express the desired emotion. Delsarte's method,

Sarah Bernhardt. *Courtesy Victoria and Albert Picture Library*

while breaking new ground for the actor, tended to become rigid and mechanical, and many actors felt the need for a new theory.

Stanislavski. That theory was developed by Konstantin Stanislavski (1863–1938) at the Moscow Art Theatre. Stanislavski prepared for his productions carefully, keeping detailed notes on each line of dialogue and each movement of the actors. He let no stage moment escape his attention, insuring that each was filled with realistic responses from each character. He gave his characters past histories, created the circumstances that led up to the actions of the play, and made the actors visualize the environments mentioned in the dialogue but not seen by the audience. He insisted on asking the question, "What if?"—what if a given action were to take place outdoors in the heat, how would the character respond physically and what sights and sounds would she see and hear? Stanislavski's theory of acting was a virtual science of art, based as it was on observation, investigation, experimentation, and re-creation of the results. Once published, his ideas and exercises became the most influential set of statements of acting in existence. They form the basis for every other theory that has since been developed, either as framework or as point of departure.

It is impossible to summarize his theory because he has been interpreted to mean many things to different people. However, his contributions include at least these:

1. Characters are rational in that they have defined intents or objectives and these various objectives are interrelated, pointing toward a single overriding objective (or superobjective); these intents may not be consciously known by the character, but they must be understood by the actor.

Nemerovich-Danchenko and Stanislavski.   *Courtesy Sovfoto/Eastfoto*

2. Characters are rational because they have reasons for their actions; these motivations are found in the characters' backgrounds and in their actions during the play.

3. Characters, like human beings, are always thinking or concentrating even when they are not talking; therefore, the actor must discover these unspoken thoughts of the character and develop this subtext into a coherent relationship with the spoken dialogue.

4. The actor is a holistic system in which words and actions are mutually expressive of each other; no action should be included by the actor unless it is organic to the intent of the character.

5. The actor must train herself physically to meet the demands of the character; this training includes the ability to command the body and the voice to do whatever is needed and to sustain an intense energy level throughout the performance.

6. The actor must train himself psychologically to concentrate on the internal thoughts of the character, to identify points of contact with the character's world, so that the actor may behave as if he were the character.

7. The actor must treat his art as a serious, spiritual experience in which he enters into the world of the play and sets aside his own feelings and desires of the moment in order to convey the feelings and experiences of

his character; he must accept his art as a holy endeavor growing out of rigorous preparation and faith in the importance of his work.

Stanislavski's work has become the foundation of modern acting. Although many actors during his time and since have defined alternative methods for the actor, the Stanislavski System remains the primary influence on the teaching and practice of acting today.

Audience

The audience for the theatre was as varied as the types of theatre being presented. The commercial theatre in nearly every country had become stylish and was attended by the genteel set. Popular forms of entertainment such as vaudeville and the music halls of London were the choice of the working class, while experimental work such as the independent theatres appealed largely to the artistic and scholarly elite.

Audience behavior ranged from totally passive to the wildly active. Broadway audiences, for example, tended to be chatty, and on several occasions performers stopped the production and directly asked audiences to be quiet. Since the social occasion was more important than the drama, the final act was frequently disrupted by people donning their coats and hats so they could make quick exits to after-theatre activities. Crowd reactions to the experimental theatres ranged from complete outrage to complete boredom. The presentation of *Before Sunrise*, a play by Gerhart Hauptmann (1861–1946), at the Freie Bühne was interrupted in 1889 by a heated dispute between admirers and detractors that included profanity, rhythmic applause, shouting, jangling of keys, and physical threats. The riots that accompanied the Abbey Theatre's presentation of *The Playboy of the Western World* have been described earlier.

The dominant attitude of the theatre audience of this time, however, lay in a search for entertainment. Antoine finally despaired at the Théâtre Libre because the audience was more interested in sensational aspects of the plays than in the social issues presented. Similarly, the critics of the time deplored the success of intellectually vapid drama on the commercial stage, seeking to define a higher standard to distinguish good theatre from mere entertainment.

Standards of Judgment

The standard of judgment for a good play still lay primarily in the box office and the approval of a large audience. Star performances, spectacle, sentimental emotion, and special effects were often enough to make a weak script into successful theatre. Many artists and critics during this period, however, sought a better definition. The concepts they developed marked the boundaries of a dispute concerning the purpose of theatre that has continued until the present day.

The idea that good theatre was popular theatre was not without its own critical adherents. Francisque Sarcey was one of the earliest advocates of this position, writing in 1876 that the primary demand on theatre was that it please its audience. American critic Brander Matthews (1852–1929) supported this view, stating that "the approval of the public is the first proof of worthy success, for there are not good plays save those which have been applauded in the playhouse." Both argued that a simple reproduction of life was not sufficient to move an audience, with Sarcey proposing that a central focus or impression was the primary necessity for positive audience response. This argument supported the rise of the director as a dominant force in the theatre.

American critic George Jean Nathan (1882–1958) agreed that the response of the audience was the primary determinant of a play's success. Not content with the approval of a mass audience determining artistic quality, Nathan felt that the nature of the audience was an important factor in determining a play's worth. Good theatre was "anything that interests an intelligently emotional group of persons assembled together in an illuminated hall." Nathan insisted that good theatre interested the most intelligent people. Lesser theatre interested lesser types. Although this elitism sounds harsh (and one senses that Nathan liked to provoke his audience), similar critical standards are often applied today to distinguish art from entertainment.

William Butler Yeats (1865–1939) was among the first to write that a good play must move beyond the superficial appearance of realism and speak directly to the spiritual dimension of humankind. According to Yeats, bad theatre results when an author thinks of the audience instead of the subject. This theatre focuses on surface reality, character study, and effect. The best theatre replaces seeing with feeling and substitutes imagination for observation. It is not a reproduction of life but a glimpse at ideas that exist beyond temporal existence. This concept was echoed in the writing of Edward Gordon Craig (1872–1966), who suggested that art should not compete with life, but should transcend it. Both Yeats and Craig shared the contention by Vsevelod Meyerhold (1874–1940) that the audience must be creatively engaged by the theatre, that the spectator must ". . . employ his imagination creatively in order to fill in those details suggested by the stage action."

Such idealistic aims for art did not suit George Bernard Shaw, who demanded that the theatre present searching questions about contemporary social problems. Shaw was less interested in method or form than in content. For Shaw there was one method of determining a good play: "If the case is uninteresting or stale or badly conducted or obviously trumped up, the play is a bad one. If it is important and novel and convincing, or at least disturbing, the play is a good one." Shaw championed the work of Ibsen, citing his use of ordinary people, his portrayal of life as it really exists, and his willingness to introduce meaningful social problems to the stage as examples of excellence in playwriting.

The writings of Georg Lukacs (1885–1971) represent not only one of the earliest appearances of Marxian principles in criticism but also the introduction of two concepts that became touchstones of later drama. Lukacs noted that the theatre no longer contained any trace of the festivity or sense of celebration that had marked earlier drama. In its place, he suggested, modern theatre presents a human being isolated from all meaningful structures to the extent that the very struggle to establish one's individuality is dramatic. Both in his recognition of the loss of a communal identity and in his discussion of the alienation of the individual, Lukacs suggested concepts that were central to the development of the theatre in the 20th century.

The tremendous theatrical vitality of the years between 1880 and 1920 significantly affected the theatre as we know it today. Naturalism continues to be the underlying concept of theatrical presentation, and the reactions against it have produced most of the innovations of our time. The concepts of alienation, the communal nature of theatre, the social/spiritual dimension of the drama, and the distinction between art and entertainment continue to be crucial issues in today's theatre. Just as theatre practitioners today continue to struggle with issues and techniques introduced between 1880 and 1920, modern playwrights still find their models in the great plays of that time period.

DRAMATIC LITERATURE

Mrs. Alving is a remarkable woman. She has read the latest books even though her local pastor disapproves. She has finally admitted that her dead husband was alcoholic and unfaithful. She has come to believe that we are all haunted by ghosts, including the ghosts of our parents, the ghosts of our past actions, and the ghosts of our ideas. In the last act of Henrik Ibsen's *Ghosts*, Mrs. Alving confronts the ghosts of her life. Her son Oswald has syphilis. He doesn't know he inherited it from his father. Oswald has also fallen in love with the housemaid. He doesn't realize she is his half-sister by an illicit affair her mother had with his father. In a single hour, Mrs. Alving must make several terrible decisions: Should she tell her son the truth of his illness? Should she approve his incestuous affair in order to preserve the one happy thing in his life? When he has an attack, he begs her to end his misery. Can she help her own son die?

In America in the 1980s, it would be at least mildly surprising that a play would include discussion of the effects of syphilis and incest; for a play to deal with such topics a full century ago was scandalous. It shattered the social tranquillity of monarchical Europe, for it suggested that beneath the facade of Victorian morality and stringent behavior lay human oppression and unhappiness. Over the years that followed the publication of Ibsen's great work, other playwrights would pick up the theme of human misery in the daily life of average people. At no time since the beginnings of theatre in Hellenic Greece had Europe as many great dramatists forcibly articulating the tragedy of the human condition. By the end of World War I, the drama had become for many writers a search for truth and a vehicle for searing social commentary.

As a literary style, "modern" has one common characteristic, that each artist seeks truth from his or her own personal perspective. The meaning of life is variously found in the motivations of characters, in the relationship of society and individuals, in the daily events of less-than-monarchical figures, and in the relationship between subconscious thoughts and conscious perceptions. The personal perspective of the playwright varies with the emphasis given to the role of society, the apparent absence of a moral order, the past experiences of the character, and the degree of satisfaction with

A Global Perspective

The Yiddish Theatre

*T*he Yiddish theatrical tradition began well before 1876—for centuries, storytellers and particularly singers had carried the traditions of the Jewish people from country to country across the world. It was, however, the work of Abraham Goldfaden, beginning in 1876, that began a Yiddish theatre movement that proved highly significant from 1880 until the 1930s.

Goldfaden's plays were not great literature. Silly plots and sentimental songs were his typical fare, and plays were often written as vehicles for established singing stars. At first these plays were shameless corruptions of Jewish history and cheap adaptations of successful plays. However, a serious theatre grew from those beginnings, resulting in a body of plays that helped to preserve a culture. Various folk-types such as the bashful student and the dutiful mother were given concrete form, important ceremonies were repeated and given significance, the songs of the cantor were heard, and the nostalgia for the days of the "homeland" was deepened.

The growing movement resulted in several significant theatre companies. The Vilna Troupe founded in 1916 in Russia had subsidiary companies in Berlin, Warsaw, the United States, and Romania. The Vilna was an international sensation with its production of *The Dybbuk,* a play that toured for years and introduced the actor Jacob Ben-Ami to the world. The Moscow State Jewish Theatre (1917) featured the designs of Marc Chagall, a painter who went on to international fame. The Jewish Art Theatre (1919) in New York City was closely modeled after the Moscow Art Theatre and produced numerous successes in its short life as well as providing early showcases for designers Boris Aronson and Mordecai Gorelik.

Among the prominent playwrights were Solomon Asch and Sholom Aleichem, whose *Tevye the Milkman* became known to the world as the leading character in the musical *Fiddler on the Roof.* Internationally successful for a brief while—eleven plays were translated into Japanese by 1922—the Yiddish theatre nearly disappeared during the persecutions of World War II, but it continues today in small companies throughout the world.

the new directions in which society is heading. Although there are many fine playwrights who are interested in delighting their audiences with romantic fantasies and irreverent comedies, the plays that most influence the 20th century are those that investigate the psyche of the average individual.

Henrik Ibsen (1828–1906)

One of the most significant of these playwrights is Henrik Ibsen. His reputation had spread quietly during the 1870s with his first dozen plays, including *Brand* (1865), many of them written in verse and dealing with the dual themes of the individual's romantic search for truth and the impact of the past on present action.

Peer Gynt (1867), for instance, is a vast, panoramic folktale, covering the progression of an irresponsible young man from teller of stories to adventurer; after traveling throughout the world, he realizes that the truth of his life lies with the woman he loved. What separated Ibsen's early plays from those of his contemporaries was his rigorous determination to find faith in spite of the hypocrisies he saw in legends, religions, and politics. The characters are not satisfied to live without knowing the validity of the beliefs by which they live. In their search for truth they confront experiences and situations far beyond the difficulties confronting other characters of the dramas of the 1860s.

With *A Doll's House* (1879), in which Ibsen shocked the world by bringing the problems of life from the realm of poetry into a middle-class parlor, a stylistic tone was set that would come to typify the popular Ibsen (even though the range of his work is much greater): characters continue their search for truth, but do so in the context of ordinary living. They interweave the habits and rituals of daily existence with events that force them to confront their faith in all that they believe. At times their faith has been naively placed in another person (a wife in her husband, a child in her father); at other times it has been placed in a philosophy (ranging from a restrictive religious code to a freethinking liberalism). In such plays as *Hedda Gabler* (1890), the tragedy is that the object of faith proves unable to avert disaster. The tension of the dramas is in the realization that a life has been destroyed (often literally) because of misplaced faith.

In his last plays, such as *When We Dead Awaken* (1899), Ibsen returned to the mystical symbolism of his early plays while retaining the realistic elements that made him famous. His themes united the earlier interest in human destiny and truth with the relationship of the individual and society. Characters are motivated by forces that seem beyond them, and events occur that suggest that an individual does not have control over his own destiny. Yet they also retain something of the romantic's desire to know the meaning of life, even at the risk of death.

Ibsen was not the first playwright to probe the injustices of his society, but he did so with greater precision and clarity than others. He recognized the potentialities of naturalism, but he did not become lost in the search for realistic detail at the expense of philosophical truth. He presented intelligent characters capable of discussing their problems with the full range of human emotions. He was not the first playwright to realize that tragedy can occur to average people, yet the ability of his average people to feel and discuss their tragedy was greater than that of others. And finally, he never shied away from a difficult dramatic moment, always taking his characters to a point

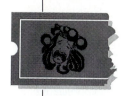

A TRIP TO THE
THÉÂTRE LIBRE,
1890

Some distance from the boulevard in Paris where the major theatre houses are located, a performance is being given tonight of Henrik Ibsen's *Ghosts*. It is the first production of an Ibsen play in France, and the play has already caused considerable interest. Emile Zola (1840–1902), the writer who heralded the advent of realism in French letters, has urged the company's manager to produce the play. The name of Ibsen has been familiar to Parisian intellectuals since his *A Doll's House* was written over a decade ago. *Ghosts* is known to several people because the censors have banned it in Germany. Two months ago, the play was produced in London as the premiere production of J. T. Grein's new Independent Theatre. English critics were not kind, calling the play "malodorous."

Preparations for the play have been under way for months. The company producing the play, the Théâtre Libre, has long been considering a production, but has only recently been able to find a stageworthy translation. Ibsen himself finally sent a copy for his approval. The company manager, André Antoine (1858–1943), finally decides on a production date, despite continuing opposition to the play from some company members. Antoine gives himself the role of Oswald, the young son who has inherited a debilitating social disease from his father. The role of Mrs. Alving, the play's central character, is given to Mlle. Barney, one of Antoine's most loyal company members.

The play will receive one performance only. In order to avoid French censors and to insure capital at the start of the season, Antoine has sold season subscriptions, the first of their kind in Europe. The subscription guarantees admission to the seven evenings of theatre in this, the third year of the theatre's existence. It will be the subscription holders who will make up most of the audience of several hundred. They are people tired of the same plays being performed at the major theatres. They probably agree with Antoine that the theatre is most alive when it is producing new plays. They also agree that naturalism is one of the new directions of the French theatre, for Antoine has established his Théâtre Libre as a home of naturalistic drama. (This has happened almost in spite of himself, for he continues to produce plays of other styles.)

The audience at the performance is, at the least, curious. People know that they will see something that is very different from most Parisian productions. The

continued

major theatres of Paris seat up to 2,000 people; stars like Coquelin and Bernhardt receive applause for a well-delivered speech; the plays are either 300 years old or are predictable well-made plays with few truthful emotions. At the Théâtre Libre, however, the plays are new and occasionally controversial. The theatre is small and intimate. The actors are satisfied to do well even if the audience is not appreciative. The audience is here to be challenged, not complimented.

The production of *Ghosts* is given with the same care as others at the Théâtre Libre. Antoine is meticulous in his preparations, making sure that all the props and furniture are what would actually appear in Mrs. Alving's parlor. He demands that real objects be used to make the play appear as natural as possible. The set designs are created for this production only; Antoine refuses to use sets from other productions. He has eliminated footlights because they are theatrical. When the orphanage burns in Act II, he directs that the lighting effect suggest a real fire.

The actors work closely together. They do not wish to stand out from the text. Instead, they want to immerse themselves in the action of the play. Because Antoine and Barny have performed together for several years, the relationship between the play's mother and son is particularly close. Antoine's own acting is a symbol of the style of acting he advocates: he becomes intensely involved with his character, losing himself in the role for the duration of the performance.

The play is modestly received. Antoine himself admits that many in the audience are bored or confused. The action of the play is discussion, and many people simply are not accustomed to that kind of theatre. Even though Antoine is excited by his own performance, most of the critics attending the play are not enthusiastic. Only a few recognize the potential greatness of the script. Most are intimidated by the unremitting seriousness of the work. Nevertheless, Antoine concludes that the play is the high point of the season. He has lost a considerable amount of money during the year, but he is convinced that he is changing the tastes of Parisian theatregoers and that his artistic crusade will one day triumph. He immediately begins planning next year's productions.

that would demonstrate the consequences of the moral, ethical, and social decisions they have made.

August Strindberg (1849–1912)

August Strindberg was similar to Ibsen in that he began writing plays about historical subjects, usually from Swedish history. And like Ibsen, he became famous with his realistic plays, including *The Father* (1887) and *Miss Julie* (1888). In almost every other way they were different. Strindberg's search led him to probe the inner soul, the hidden motives and fears of the individual. His characters confront each other on an awful plan of complete exposure. Strindberg's conception of realism was less how people may talk in everyday life and more what the real motives of their actions are, to reach these motives and pull them out of the subconscious of the characters. As in *Dance of Death* (1901), Strindberg usually pits against each other two characters who know as much about each other as two humans can know. They taunt one another with this knowledge, alternately threatening to expose and blithely denying any intent to do so. The dramatic result is that the plays seem less realistic than those of his contemporaries. He transformed the parlor into a zone of combat in which elemental forces, such as hatred and fear, anxiety and desire, and masculine and feminine, compete for power and security.

In later works, including *To Damascus* (1898) and *The Spook Sonata* (1907), Strindberg turned from realism completely, creating a world of dreams and nightmares where these primeval forces act out their battles free of realistic detail. Even in these disturbing, antirealist plays, Strindberg wrote of people's desire for security and companionship, and of their dependency on other people for that security. Thus, in *The Dream Play* (1902), when the daughter of a god comes to earth to discover why human beings suffer, she becomes ensnared in the suffocating trivialities of existence. Like other Strindberg characters, she discovers that life is made of opposites: suffering follows joy, and age follows youth. Further, she finds that suffering is a fact of life, not a punishment for past actions.

Strindberg believed that suffering is a fact of life, a condition from which one escapes only at death. As a person, he wanted to believe that the suffering had purpose, that it was a redemption for sins unknown. As a playwright, however, he seldom wrote characters who were able to rest easily with such a faith. Strindberg gave to the modern world the dramatic form of expressionism; he was also the first to articulate the morbid despair that would characterize a great deal of 20th-century drama, and his plays would serve as inspiration for many innovative works.

Anton Chekhov (1860–1904)

Despair of another sort was identified in the plays of Russia's greatest playwright, Anton Chekhov, whose plays, including *The Seagull* (1896) and *Uncle Vanya* (1899), established and secured the reputation of the Moscow Art Theatre. Whereas Strindberg's despair came from irreconcilable conflicts between people, Chekhov's came from the passage of time and the sense of inadequacy in the face of the future. His characters seem caught at a point of indecision between past hopes and expectations on the one hand, and a distant future on the other. The young and the optimistic look to the future with exuberance and confidence, while most of the older characters realize that the future will not bring their past hopes. These older characters are unable to move; they feel helpless and tentative, wondering how they got into their predicament. They in turn are contrasted with realistic characters who remain grounded to the practicalities of daily life, determined to make the best of their situation. The conflicts in his plays are between those who dread the future and those who welcome it, and between those who deal practically with the present and those who don't.

Chekhov believed that the theatre should reflect life; and that in life people eat, drink, sleep, and play cards. Life is not a series of momentous actions, but merely the passage of time. As a result, plays such as *The Three Sisters* (1901) and *The Cherry Orchard* (1904) are filled with people who talk about the past and their hopes for the future, but rarely force one another to action. Yet the sense of inaction onstage is misleading, for in almost every play, a life comes to an end with someone committing suicide offstage. Life, then, is a series of reactions to major events over which we have no control. It is a series of internal monologues spoken aloud to people who often do not respond, except with monologues of their own. It is the destruction of dreams or the breaking of illusions, never with a sense of urgency or great moment, only with a cry or a whimper. Nothing, not even death, has an air of finality for Chekhov; life has the quality of a river, carrying us inexorably to our death.

The emotional experience of Chekhov's plays is ambivalent. If one looks hopefully to the future as a realistic potential, then his plays are a comedy, for they make fun of those who struggle foolishly against the tide. If the future is filled with dread, however, then the plays are tragedies of people losing control of their destinies. Chekhov himself saw them as comedies; Stanislavski, who directed many of them, found them tragic. The fact is that both are correct, for Chekhov is the first playwright of tragicomedy, in which events are both comic and tragic at the same time, depending on the point of view. He recognized the relativity of existence and dramatized moments that are humorous to one character but tragic to others.

George Bernard Shaw (1856–1950)

George Bernard Shaw began writing plays in 1892 and continued until his death in 1950. His greatest plays, including *St. Joan* (1923), *Heartbreak House* (1920), and *Pygmalion* (1914—the basis for *My Fair Lady*), came in the earlier part of the century. At first he wrote because he didn't like the plays that he was reviewing as a journalistic critic. Soon, however, his passion to reform society joined with his remarkable gift of language to produce some of the most intellectually stimulating and theatrically exciting dramas in 20th-century England, including *Candida* (1897) and *Major Barbara* (1905).

Shaw was a reformer. He believed in an English variation of socialism, he advocated changes in the English language, and he was a prolific pamphleteer on dozens of political and social subjects. Usually his heroes and heroines are as committed to some cause as Shaw was committed to causes in his own life. Henry Higgins loves the English language so much that he will convert Eliza Doolittle into a lady. Joan of Arc is so convinced of her voices that she leads the French in battle against the English. Each of his heroes is, however, pitted against another character in the play who is equally determined that the hero will not succeed. Eliza is not about to do what Higgins wants and Joan comes up against the officials of the Catholic Church. The battle between the opposing forces gives Shaw the opportunity to discuss some burning question of human history: will the masses never rise above their station because they can't learn English? Will nationalism tear Europe apart?

Shaw's techniques were developed in part as reaction to the well-made play. He particularly disliked the plays of Victorien Sardou (1831–1908) and even labeled the well-made play "Sardoodledum." The techniques that characterize a typical Shaw play are discussion, wit, and inversion. Shaw believed that the best action was discussion between two articulate characters who can express themselves eloquently. Even his love scenes are discussions; hero and heroine may agree to unite, but only after they have locked wits and declared a draw. Wit is another Shavian feature; characters are funny because they are astonishingly honest. Their ability to remove the facade from each other is both funny and refreshing. In addition, Shaw's plays are often the opposite of what the audience expects. He said that a good play is one in which the hero and the villain are indistinguishable. The typical 19th-century hero is usually the plodding fool of Shaw's plays, while the rakish, debonair man-of-the-world becomes the true hero. The ideal heroine is not a sweet young Victorian lass, but a dynamic and assertive woman. The combination of discussion, wit, and inversion result in popular plays for those who love to hear remarkable people talk about important problems of life, love, and history.

These playwrights are only the most influential of dozens who radically altered the theatre between 1880 and 1920. They are remembered over others because they were the first to raise problems of modern living and because they created new dramatic forms to express those problems. They wrote eloquently of a constantly changing world filled with anxiety and lacking in shared moral principles. They rarely liked what they saw, but they were compelled to present reality as they understood it in hopes that others would see the same truth. They were the first generation of modern playwrights expressing the pain of being alive in the 20th century.

There were, however, other playwrights deserving mention, each of whom wrote at least one play that continues to be read or produced for its theatrical value and significance. Their individual styles further illustrate that the search for truth during the period came in many forms. Oscar Wilde (1854–1900) wrote one of the funniest and most-produced comedies in the English language, *The Importance of Being Earnest* (1895). Wilde delighted in shocking Victorian sensibilities through characters whose brutal honesty about life is at once witty and shocking. Belgian-born Maurice Maeterlinck (1862–1949) championed the cause of symbolism in France, especially in The *Intruders* (1890) and *Pelléas and Mélisande* (1892). He also wrote persuasively on behalf of the Symbolist movement, insisting that truth lay as much in silence as in dialogue. In Russia, Maxim Gorky (1868–1936) penned several plays for the Moscow Art Theatre, but only one of them, *The Lower Depths* (1902), achieved great success. Closer to naturalism than most texts from the period, the play is set in a rundown tenement house where a vast range of what society would call lowlife types struggled for survival. Finally, the German playwright Benjamin Franklin Wedekind (1864–1918) did not gain early acceptance of his plays because of their frank discussions of and emphasis on sexuality, especially in *Spring's Awakening* (1891). His distinctive style also inhibited critical approval, but he greatly influenced the German expressionist movement.

The Drama of Expressionism

The theatrical form of expressionism is easily recognizable in the writings of Georg Kaiser (1878–1945). *From Morn to Midnight* (1912) traces the adventures of an insignificant bank cashier in his quest for the Perfect Woman. He fails to find meaning in family, sensuality, or religion and finally realizes he must discover his own soul. A meeting with Salvation Lass, his soul mate, offers temporary relief, but she then betrays him for a reward. He shoots himself and dies as he is crucified. When the electrical power fails at the final moment the last line of the play sums of the message: "There must be a short circuit in the main." In his last expressionistic play *Gas II* (1920), Kaiser succumbs to the pessimism inherent in the expressionist stance and portrays a world destroyed. Ernst Toller (1893–1939) in his *Man and the Masses* (1920) was unique in placing a woman at the center of the drama, although her attempts to relieve suffering are continually rebuffed by a cold, organized authoritarian State that ultimately executes her. The play presents seven "pictures" in the woman's quest rather than a complete narrative, and the final picture shows her final "confession" to a priest who maintains throughout that humans are essentially evil. In these plays the message is clearly and forcefully presented, sometimes with great dramatic impact and ingenuity. The overriding pessimism of the plays failed to attract a great following, particularly since they were greatly at odds with much of society during the 1920s. The movement lasted only a few years, but the influence of the expressionists was very great during the 1960s.

Irish Renaissance

When the Irish Literary Theatre moved to the Abbey Theatre in 1904, the works of three playwrights were performed on opening night, and all three would achieve international success, each for a different reason. Lady Augusta Gregory (1852–1932), one of the company's founders, wrote plays with the widest popular appeal in Ireland, possibly due to the reliance on peasant stories and folk legends. Her fame rests more on her prominence as a managing director than on her plays. William Butler Yeats, known to the world primarily as a poet, wrote in a poetic style reminiscent both of his own poetry and of symbolist drama. His work is not strictly symbolist, however, for it combines his personal views of the Irish peasantry and their attitudes with legendary characters.

John Millington Synge (1871–1909), however, achieved international fame as a playwright. *The Playboy of the Western World* (1907), as noted earlier, caused riots on two continents. *Riders to the Sea* (1904) is probably the single most produced one-act play in the English language. And *Deirdre of the Sorrows* (1910) reflects the interest of all the Abbey playwrights in Celtic legend and Irish folk history.

Synge was not popular in Ireland during his lifetime, however. His uncompromising look at the ignorance and superstitious mind of the Irish peasant drew the wrath of Irish nationalists. *Playboy* is the story of a man who wanders into a village insisting that he is running from the law because he has just killed his father. What angered audiences was that the villagers did not react with moral indignation to him, but rather sought to establish him as a hero. When he is discovered to be a fraud, they throw him and his father out of town.

The playwrights at the turn of the century were exploring new concepts that dealt with the very nature of human existence. The multiple ideas they advanced would become the foundations for further developments in the drama after World War I.

CONNECTIONS

The contributions of this 40-year period to contemporary theatre and drama are obvious because the concepts of the artists in that period are still practised today. Only two of the independent theatres are still producing, but the concept of avant-garde theatre in small locations away from the major theatres is very evident in Off-Broadway and Off-Off-Broadway in New York City, in the fringe theatres of London, and in hundreds of small theatres in virtually every theatre-producing country.

The plays championed by Antoine, Brahm, Grein, and the others are still produced in regional and university theatres. Their staging practices are now accepted without question; actors are expected to stay in their roles throughout the play; directors are expected to impose a single vision on a production; and set and costume designs are expected to be particularized for each show. The influence of Appia and Craig in design is pervasive, as will be evident in the next chapter. The ideas of Stanislavski are taught in most acting schools and at all universities. Finally, the plays of Ibsen, Strindberg, Chekhov, and Shaw are taught in most drama literature classes and used in scene work in most directing and acting classes.

The influence of Ibsen's dramatic structure is particularly important, for it has influenced television and film writing as well as dramatic writing. He provided audiences with characters of their own social and economic rank, presented issues that affected their daily lives, and articulated their inner feelings eloquently and forcefully. The language is that of ordinary life, yet his characters are always intelligent and capable of expressing themselves to the full extent of their feelings and their ideas. They never wallow in self-pity, but attempt to do something about their situation. That they fail is both the tragedy of the human condition and the weakness of an inadequate social system. Realism had already developed by the time Ibsen wrote *A Doll's House*, but he gave to the theory of realism a social conscience, a roster of fascinating individuals, and an eloquent voice. He was less concerned about the faithful or photographic depiction of reality and more about the real conditions of life as they were experienced by his characters. He brought issues of life and death, of religion and morality, of truth and human destiny to the parlors of middle-class Europeans. The consequence was that he made people realize that such issues do not exist simply in philosophical treatises or ancient dramas; they were issues being lived daily by the people he dramatized. In his search for the truth of what it means to be a human being, he turned away from the answers of the past and focused on the theories of the present as they affect the individuals of the present.

The vast majority of dramas in theatre and many in television use elements of Ibsen's technique and style. They show average people dealing with ordinary problems with universal significance. They rely on aspects of realism, but not on the full, literal presentation of it. They probe conflicts within the family structure, especially those that have a long personal history. They depict characters at the moment of greatest crisis in their lives and discuss the consequences of that crisis on everyone around them. Recent plays also show the influence of Ibsen when they probe the difficulties of finding faith in the modern world. Ibsen identified the path of the future. Others have altered that path to suit their own particular needs, as we shall see in the next chapters, but none will break as much ground.

SOURCES FOR FURTHER STUDY

Social/Art/Philosophy Background

Grossman, Manuel L. *Dada: Paradox, Mystification and Ambiguity in European Literature.* New York: Pegasus, 1971.

Hedges, Inez. *Languages of Revolt.* Durham, N.C.: Duke University Press, 1983.

Hemmings, F. W. J. *Culture and Society in France, 1848–1898: Dissidents and Philistines.* New York: Scribners, 1972.

Hughes, Robert. *The Shock of the New.* New York: Alfred A. Knopf, 1981.

Mayer, Arno J. *The Persistence of the Old Regime.* New York: Pantheon Books, 1981.

Theatre History

Antoine, André. *Memories of the Théâtre-Libre.* Trans. Marvin A. Carlson. Coral Gables, Fla.: University of Miami Press, 1964.

Atkinson, Brooks. *Broadway.* New York: Macmillan, 1970.

Beacham, Richard C. *Adolphe Appia.* Cambridge: Cambridge University Press, 1987.

Brockett, Oscar, and Robert R. Findlay. *Century of Innovations: A History of European and American Theatre and Drama Since 1870.* Englewood Cliffs, N.J.: Prentice-Hall, 1973.

Brown, Frederick. *Theater and Revolution: The Culture of the French Stage.* New York: Viking Press, 1980.

Knapp, Bettina L. *The Reign of the Theatrical Director: French Theatre: 1887–1924.* Troy, N.Y.: Whitson Publishing Company, 1988.

Miller, Anna. *The Independent Theatre in Europe.* New York: Benjamin Blom, 1931.

Mitchell, Lofton. *Black Drama.* New York: Hawthorn Books, 1967.

———. *Voices of the Black Theatre.* Clifton, N.J.: James T. White, 1975.

Rischbieter, Henning. *Art and the Stage in the 20th Century.* Trans. Michael Bullock. Greenwich, Conn.: New York Graphic Society, 1973.

Rudnitsky, Konstantin. *Russian and Soviet Theatre.* London: Thames and Hudson, 1988.

Walton, J. Michael. *Craig on Theatre.* London: Methuen, 1983.

Dramatic Literature

Bentley, Eric. *The Playwright as Thinker.* New York: Meridian, 1955.

Brustein, Robert. *The Theatre of Revolt.* Boston: Little, Brown, and Company, 1962.

Fergusson, Francis. *The Idea of a Theatre.* Garden City, N.Y.: Doubleday, 1949.

Gilman, Richard. *The Making of Modern Drama.* New York: Da Capo Press, 1987.

Strindberg, August. *Open Letters to the Intimate Theatre.* Trans. Walter Johnson. Seattle: University of Washington Press, 1967.

Valency, Maurice. *The Flower and the Castle.* New York: Grosset and Dunlap, 1963.

————. *The End of the World.* New York: Oxford University Press, 1980.

C H A P T E R

16

Theatre in Transition, 1920–1945

Theatre
History
Events

*Beyond the
Horizon*

1920

No one who had gathered at the theatre that evening in 1917 knew quite what to expect. Certainly, several performances in recent years had surprised the theatre audiences of Paris and shocked the critics, and the opening performance of *Parade,* a "realistic ballet," promised to be more of the same. The composer Erik Satie (1886–1925) had been at work a full year on the piece. The author was the young poet Jean Cocteau (1889–1963). In fact, there was no script as such; Cocteau's text was a succession of scenic notes, suggestions of choreography, and some expository explanations of his intentions. The scene designer was a radical young artist named Pablo Picasso (1881–1973), who had accepted the challenge even though his painter colleagues had strenuously objected to such a menial task for a true artist; and the principal performer was the famous mime/dancer Leonide Massine. Many of the avant-garde attended hoping to see something daring and unusual in the tradition of *Ubu Roi* or the hilarious *Impressions d'Afrique* by Raymond Roussel (1869–1937), which featured a trained earthworm playing a zither.

Early descriptions of the event had promised "universal joyousness" for all participants. Picasso's cubist cityscape was revolutionary, but his costumes were outrageous. Huge in scale, the abstract costumes were essentially larger-than-life puppet figures that obscured traditional ballet movements and reduced the movements of the "dancers" to simple, repetitious patterns. Satie's music was similarly repetitious and included sounds from such sources as typewriters and sirens. Few critics made it past the designs and the music

Fascists in Italy; Hitler in Germany — 1922

Lindbergh's solo flight — 1927

1929–1933 — Great Depression

Nazis control of Spanish Civil War — 1936–1939

World War II begins — 1939

United States enters war — 1941

World War II ends — 1945

James Joyce's *Ulysses* — 1922

First surrealist manifesto — 1924

Huxley's *Brave New World* — 1932

Picasso's *Guernica* — 1937

Jackson Pollock's first show — 1942

Copland's *Appalachian Spring* — 1943–1944

Pirandello's *Enrico IV* — 1922

Moscow Art Theatre visits United States — 1923–1924

Group Theatre — 1931

Stanislavski's works published in United States — 1932

Federal Theatre Project — 1935

The Theatre and Its Double — 1938

Oklahoma! — 1943

to comment on Cocteau's story of a series of failed attempts by managers to lure a crowd into the circus tent. The ballet included simple actions such as taking a snapshot, imitations of Charlie Chaplin, and music-hall numbers. Too engrossed in the parade of trivial realistic detail, the crowds ignore the manager's pleas that the "real show is on the inside."

The crowd reacted in outrage to this unfamiliar and unexpected spectacle, and following the performance friends had to protect the artists from a group of women wielding hatpins. Critics were scornful and dismissed the entire production as worthless. Satie's reply to one critic was enough to have him tried for libel, but the influence of this production on future developments in the theatre was an ultimate victory for all concerned. Typical of this time period, the group of artists ignored tradition and created their own "style" of production. Rejecting the tyranny of realism, they sought a new type of theatre that responded to the new vision of the world in the aftermath of World War I.

The challenge of theatre after 1920 was to respond to the implications of global conflict and destruction. Artists committed to an investigation of the meaning of human existence felt compelled to confront the social and psychological consequences of the

The overture curtain design by Pablo Picasso for *Parade*.

greatest loss of lives the world had known. In order to present human characters in a modern perspective, European artists felt they had no choice but to ponder a cluster of unthinkable questions: Is the ability to destroy whole cities and nations within the capacity of each individual? Does the human race have the capability to destroy itself? How does the individual develop a sense of dignity in a world in which human life is of little value? Artists had begun the century hoping to probe the possibilities of new machines and the effects of scientific discoveries. How were they to know or imagine that the machines would become agents of human destruction? Not since the medieval period had artists confronted as directly and immediately the dark side of life.

The loss of faith left few options to writers who used the drama to explore the meaning of existence. Some reacted in anger, striking out at everything around them that they felt contributed to the despair of the 20th century. Others became reformers by offering new social systems or championing particular causes. Still others simply withdrew from the realities of human interaction, preferring to dramatize abstract artistic principles or to fantasize worlds were people could exist as they had in earlier times. The most common reaction of artists, however, was to express the futility, defeat, and hopelessness that gripped Europe through most of the century. Often these writers depicted a universe without moral purpose or structure.

In contrast, the United States was filled with optimism. Feeling that they had saved the world for democracy, Americans sought new artistic forms to express their confidence that the world could be conquered with faith, hope, and American know-how. Until the Depression, the thrust of the theatre was toward comedy in the drama, and invention and exploration in theatrical practices. Even after the Depression, exploration continued, although very much in response to the social and economic conditions in which the theatre existed.

SOCIAL IDEAS

Political Events

No one was prepared for the long duration of World War I (four years), or for the cost of the war (more than 30 million casualties in Europe). Nor were they prepared for the events following the war: the failure of the Paris Peace Conference, an influenza epidemic that killed an estimated 20 million people, and the 10 million returning war wounded who discovered that jobs were difficult to find and medical rehabilitation was inadequate. Communism became a major political force, undermining traditional governmental assumptions. Fascism came to power in Italy under Benito Mussolini (1883–1945) in 1922, and Hitler (1889–1945) began his drive for control of Germany in the same year.

Events after 1930 did not return the world to normalcy. The worldwide economic crises brought on by the Depression focused attention on the plight of the poor. In America unions held strikes and sitdowns at major plants to demand changes in working conditions. In Germany Hitler took power in 1933 in part because inflation had virtually destroyed the German economy. Meanwhile, the world continued to slide toward conflicts around the globe: Japan invaded Manchuria in 1931; the Spanish Civil War broke out in 1936, the same year that Mussolini invaded Ethiopia; and Hitler annexed Austria in 1938. When Hitler invaded Poland in 1939, the world was plunged into a conflagration more horrifying and more global than anyone could have imagined.

Alienation and Anxiety

Given these events, it comes as no surprise that European writers and dramatists responded to world conditions with discussions of alienation and anxiety. The use of the terms actually began in the 19th century with the writings of Karl Marx and the theologian Søren Kierkegaard (1813–1885). Kierkegaard believed that the alienation of the individual is the result of the conflict between universal systems that give the individual a place in a crowd but deny his individuality. Such systems offer the individual a sense of belonging to a logical and rational order, but they deny or dismiss the irrational, subjective forces within the self. The individual is thus alienated from his subjective self and from the world around him. The feeling engendered by this alienation is *angst*, or anxiety, the desire for what one dreads.

The influence of this emotional state on modern drama is incalculably great. Love stories in this century are not about people who come together and then are tragically separated; they are often about people who cannot come together in the first place. Comedies often deal with characters who are so alienated that the world becomes a monster they battle against like Quixote against the windmills. When characters confess their inner state, they reveal a sense of dread that has no apparent cause or explanation. Many modern plays never end with a conclusion at all, because the anxiety of the characters is unrelieved by the action. Alienation and anxiety are the most common emotional states in modern drama.

Existentialism

A second major idea of this period was existentialism, the philosophy that marked a culmination in the study of the individual as an isolated self. Jean-Paul Sartre (1905–1980) formulated many of the tenets of the philosophy that have alternately angered and excited intellectuals since World War II. Sartre concluded that the universe has no purpose, structure, or plan. Instead, there is only existence, the facts of experience. Because there is no order or logic to the universe, life itself has no meaning. There is no external moral authority by which to judge human activity, only the self acting upon the reality around it. That which is good or bad is not so by reference to some outside philosophy or moral construction. It is good or bad only in relation to the situation in which it occurs. Thus, the term *situational ethics* arises, meaning that the judgment of an action or experience must be based solely on the situation surrounding the action, not on any *a priori* assumptions about what is right or wrong.

From this brief description, it is evident that existentialism requires an altered view of tragedy. No longer can the Greek assumptions about reaching and testing the moral parameters of the universe hold true; no longer can the drama teach universal moral principles. No longer can the structure of the dramas assume a cause-and-effect relationship that implies a logical universe. Instead, plays test whether there is any morality in existence. They deal with characters who are on an interior journey in which the external world is merely an intrusion or a testing ground. And they have structures that are circular or nihilistic; sometimes the plays return to the point at which they started, while other times they simply wind down to nothingness.

Those who believe in God will find existentialism alarming or repugnant, for the assumption that the universe has no purpose means in effect that there is no God. However, many of the people who wrote about existentialism were less concerned about atheism than they were about freedom. Because life has no meaning, the individual is completely free in every awful aspect. The ultimate freedom, however, is responsibility for one's own life, and therein lies the anxiety of the modern soul for existentialists. The individual has choice, but he or she also has to live with the consequences of that choice. Despair is the realization that the self is alone in the world, but joy is found in the capacity of the self for its own creation.

The American Dream

While alienation and questions of existence were of concern in Europe, optimism in America led to different consequences. World War I gave the United States a united purpose and a common value, to make the world safe for democracy. The economic activity following the war, particularly in the mass production of consumer goods, added another value that would be shared by many Americans: the desire to have material goods. Politicians promised a chicken in every pot and a car in every garage. Immigrants believed that there was nothing they couldn't achieve if they worked hard enough. The economy was booming, and the fortunes of the average American grew with it. Salesmanship and industry were the creators of standards of ethics and behavior.

The Great Depression burst the bubble of optimism, but the American dream survived in the New Deal promises of Franklin Delano Roosevelt (1882–1945). Roosevelt's administration didn't change the American dream as much as add to it. The New Deal determined to ensure that all Americans, regardless of economic status, had an opportunity to get ahead, and to improve their economic condition by gaining access to the material possessions of a consumer society. American theatre, then, diverged from its European counterpart in its greater expressions of hope and optimism.

ARTS IDEAS

Ideas that influenced the theatre in the 1900s came from the other arts as well as from politics and philosophy. New voices arose to express the postwar experiences of Europeans and Americans. The collaboration of artists from different media in Paris during the 1910s encouraged the exchange of aesthetic concepts from one field to another. Artists and dramatists worked with dance companies and musicians to create new aesthetic visions. Other artists sought new expressions through the interrelation of the arts. Dancers began to speak, actors to dance, painters to sculpt, and sculptors to create architectural environments. This kind of experimentation encouraged artists to work with new materials. It also encouraged borrowing of artistic principles from other media. One result of this collaboration and experimentation was the absence of a dominant artistic style in any of the arts.

Surrealism

Surrealism was an artistic outgrowth of symbolism at the turn of the century. It sought to unleash the subconscious in the artist in order to reveal another reality, or *sur-reality*, beyond the one evident in the physical world. Led by the dominant figure André Breton (1896–1966), the surrealist manifesto of 1924 advocated "pure psychic automatism," an artistic expression void of rationality, logic, order, expectation, or moral preoccupation. Breton urged the use of chance, stream of consciousness, automatic writing, and images from dreams and fantasies to construct a world of truth that exists parallel to the world of reality. Surrealism did indeed unleash a burst of artistic expression—in the childlike lines of Paul Klee (1879–1940), the disparate juxtapositions of René Magritte (1898–1967), the folk images and whimsical farmhouses of Joan Miró (1893–1983), and the disturbing animated fantasies of Max Ernst (1891–1976). In the 1930s, surrealism gave way to a multiplicity of individual styles, including the surrealism of Salvador Dali (1904–1991) and a revival of German expressionism.

Surrealism encouraged European playwrights to create scenes from dreams and

Europe after the Rain by Max Ernst.   *Courtesy Wadsworth Atheneum, Hartford, Connecticut. The Ella Gallup Sumner and Mary Catlin Sumner Collection.*

nightmares with sets and costumes reflective of the humbled connections often found in dreams. It encouraged reliance on imagery—both literary and theatrical—rather than on the language of daily life. It suggested dramatic structures with their own logic rather than with the logic of the scientific world. August Strindberg had pioneered the techniques and intent of surrealism in his expressionistic plays, but the surrealist movement helped to keep them alive.

Abstraction

Abstraction is difficult to define, for it is not a movement with a leader and followers or with a manifesto of prescribed principles and techniques. Nevertheless, it is an important characteristic of the era, affecting particularly the visual arts, but virtually all art forms after the 1920s. Abstraction can take many forms, including the simplification, rearrangement, and distillation of images to their essential components. In this regard, abstraction is like the classicist's search for the ideal in life; it is the opposite of existentialism, insisting that essence precedes existence. The abstract artist isolates pictorial or aural images and lets them stand by themselves in order that the audience may contemplate their "pure" worth or value. The art object (painting, sculpture, music piece, or play) then becomes a vehicle, a means to an end. Although many people think of abstraction as being "too far out," it is usually a conservative trend, preferring the realm of pure thought and contemplation to the idiosyncrasies of ordinary reality.

Each of these general trends reflect the continuing search of the artist for appropriate means of expressing the conditions of the modern world. The absence of stylistic uniformity, combined with the surrealist and abstractionist search for new forms and modes of organization, suggests that artists in this century cannot agree on a single style or set of techniques that fully capture their feelings of anger, withdrawal, and futility.

Jazz and Blues

In music, the interwar years were marked by the spread of popular music, through sheet music, radio, and phonograph recordings. America particularly responded to new sounds so popular that the 1920s gained the title the Jazz Age. Eubie Blake (1883–1983), Fats Waller (1904–1943), Cab Calloway (1907–) and Louis Armstrong (1900–1971) shaped audience tastes for decades to come. Drawing on the experience of African-Americans, especially in the South, jazz and blues artists brought new syncopated rhythms, extended improvisations, and soulful tunes to the world of popular music. Whether in the blues sounds of Billie Holiday (1915–1959) and Bessie Smith (1894–1937), or the appearance of jazz in such African-American musicals as *Shuffle Along* (1921) and *Runnin' Wild* (1923), Americans and the world were treated to a new era of musical invention. If the new era needed vocal expression, it found it in the exuberance of swing for the 1920s and the sadness of soul for the 1930s.

Music was just one facet of what became known as the Harlem Renaissance, a flourishing of the arts in the years immediately following the end of World War I. Writers, scholars, and playwrights as well as musicians made the African-American section of New York City a center for artistic and political expression. Until the Depression and a resurgence of racist sentiment, Harlem was a mecca of cultural activity that would influence African-Americans—and all American arts—through the remainder of the century.

THEATRE HISTORY

Just as the world continued to diversify and fragment, theatre practitioners also sought new and individualistic methods of creativity. The theatrical world between 1920 and 1945 was a time of exploration as independent producers sought to create their own personal visions of the world.

Occasion

The theatre between 1920 and 1945 was a theatre in search of definition. Traditional production methods, although they continued to dominate the commercial stage, were found lacking by many young theatre artists. These actors, directors, and designers were mesmerized by the powerful ensemble of the Moscow Art Theatre, challenged by the ideas of Appia and Craig, and thrilled by the simple beauty of the Vieux Colombier. Both appalled and challenged by social and political situations and eager to embrace new artistic concepts, they sought through a variety of ways to create a theatre that reflected contemporary ideals.

The Commercial Mainstream.   The primary occasion for post–World War I theatre was a night out on the town. Commercial presentation continued to be the dominant occasion for theatre production. The traditional theatre remained organized around the long run, with plays chosen for their ability to attract a large and continuing audience. Although most countries maintained a classical repertoire, a majority of theatre productions were of a more popular nature, with musicals becoming increasingly popular. Performances were given on a regular schedule and continued as long as a suitable number of tickets were sold.

In America, Broadway dominated the theatre more than ever. During the 1920s more than 70 theatres were operating in New York, and they weren't enough to house the productions looking for space. The 264 productions that opened in New York in 1927 are the highest number ever recorded. New York drama critic Brooks Atkinson (1894–1984) described Broadway during this period as "the carnival spirit fantastically commercialized." Neon lights, huge advertising billboards, and several new theatres provided a garish background for crowds of theatregoers dressed in full evening wear who mixed uneasily with peddlers, beggars, and prostitutes. Going to the theatre was adventurous and exciting.

State-Supported Theatre.   Throughout Europe, state-supported theatres continued to flourish. In Germany, municipalities continued their active role in theatrical production, and most cities had a "civic" or "national" theatre that was at least partially subsidized. Both Czechoslovakia and Poland established National Theatres that became viable when the two countries gained independence in 1918. In France, the Comédie and the Odéon continued as the recognized "state" theatres.

In Russia, following the revolution of 1917, the new government at first relaxed control of the theatres and withdrew the favoritism previously shown to the state theatres. The result was an outburst of theatrical activity and the creation of numerous small theatres with a particular aesthetic or political point of view. Only with the rise of Stalin in 1927 did state censorship begin to restrict theatrical activity. Licensing was required by 1930, and in 1934 *socialist realism*, a dramatic form based on the triumph of a socialist hero, was declared the only valid dramatic form. Numerous theatre artists were persecuted, and Vsevolod Meyerhold was imprisoned and probably executed for his refusal to cooperate.

In the United States, a revolutionary attempt at government-supported theatre began following the Depression as a part of President Roosevelt's New Deal. The Federal Theatre Project, although it had a short life span, provided a unique occasion for theatre performance. [See insert.]

The "Other" Commercial Theatre: Variations on a Theme.   For some theatre people, however, advocating commercial success rather than artistic quality was unacceptable. This resulted in a variety of attempts to find a way of maintaining aesthetic quality *and* box-office appeal.

Theatre Guild. The Theatre Guild was one of the first groups to attempt to "civilize" the Broadway experience by placing quality on an equal footing with popularity. Begun by a group of amateurs headed by Lawrence Langner (1890–1962), Lee Simonson (1888–1967), and Theresa Helburn (1887–1959), the Theatre Guild opened in 1920 and proceeded to produce theatre of higher literary quality that was usually found on Broadway, and supported it with equally high production standards. During the first twenty years of its existence, the Guild championed the plays of Shaw and

THE FEDERAL
THEATRE PROJECT

*O*rganized as part of the New Deal under Franklin D. Roosevelt, the Federal Theatre Project was a social-works program that utilized theatre as a means of providing employment, entertainment, and education to the American public. From its beginnings in 1935, the program was developed and directed by Hallie Flanagan (1890–1969).

Flanagan established production units throughout the country, determined to provide at least a subsistence income to the nation's artists while attracting new practitioners and a larger audience to the theatre. During its existence the FTP presented more than 1,000 performances nationwide, ranging from classic dramas to experimental works, from operas to puppet shows, and even a circus. It produced *Everyman* in churches and schools, and an Orson Welles/John Houseman production of *Macbeth* set in Haiti. It sponsored theatre companies for the blind and the homeless, and one production, *It Can't Happen Here,* opened at 21 locations in 17 states on the same day. FTP productions were performed at government functions, highway dedications, and community picnics. Some performances were done in European languages to special audiences, and all–African-American units were developed to perform for African-Americans. Quality was not the issue and apparently it varied greatly, with slap-dash amateurism as likely as thoroughly professional work.

Certainly the most provocative of the FTP's projects was the Living Newspaper. Building on European agitprop models, this project sought to dramatize immediately contemporary social issues and events. Each individual projection was focused on a particular problem: *Triple-A Plowed Under* dramatized the plight of the farmers in the 1930s, and *One-Third of a Nation* focused on the problems of the homeless. Productions used a variety of materials, including actual news reports, history, human-interest stories, editorials, and cartoons. Juxtaposed through inventive staging, including projections, the productions were frequently focused around one individual character, with music providing an important integrating element.

Eventually, the FTP's political focus, which had always been its strength,

continued

became its undoing. Charges that the theatre was dominated by Communists, coupled with a concern about finances, resulted in the cancellation of the project in 1939. For four years it had provided jobs for more than 10,000 people and entertainment and education for millions at a cost to the government of approximately $46 million. As Ms. Flanagan noted, that was very close to the cost of one battleship.

introduced the work of Tolstoy, Strindberg, and Kaiser. Defying theatre tradition, it staged Shaw's *Back to Methusaleh* in three parts, with Part I playing for one week, Part II the next, and Part III during the third week. The Guild's famous production of O'Neill's *Strange Interlude* (1927) lasted five hours, and *Porgy and Bess* (1935) defined a new American opera form. By the mid-1930s the Guild's subscription base was 30,000 in New York City alone, and for those theatregoers the occasion for theatre was a cultural event beyond mere entertainment.

Civic Repertory Theatre. In a similar attempt to upgrade the theatre, Eva Le Gallienne (1899–1991) founded the Civil Repertory Theatre in 1926 in a run-down theatre in lower Manhattan. The company performed true repertory with a permanent company of actors, focusing on the classics. Although it featured superior acting and low prices, the Civic Repertory was never completely successful and closed in 1933, unable to survive the Depression.

The Group Theatre. Even these cultural agendas were insufficient for the brash young people who founded the Group Theatre. Given leaves of absence by the Guild and even furnished with their first play, the Group Theatre wanted to distance themselves from the commercial motive. To them the Guild Theatre was still in the business of selling theatre; they just offered a better product than the others.

Organized during a 1931 summer retreat in Connecticut, the Group Theatre was under the leadership of Lee Strasberg (1901–1982), Harold Clurman (1901–1980), and Cheryl Crawford (1902–1986). When they returned to New York, their premier production of *The House of Connolly* by Paul Green (1894–1981) was unanimously hailed by critics. However, one successful show did not create a successful company, and the next two years were full of struggle and disappointment. Poor scripts, a lack of money, and disagreements over policy contributed to the Group's difficulties through two difficult seasons, although the summer retreats continued to inspire all concerned. Finally, their production of *Men in White*, a play by Sidney Kingsley (1906–   ) in September 1933 established their reputation in New York City as a serious company whose revolutionary new attitudes and practices were creating exceptional theatre. Later productions, many of them of the works of Clifford Odets (1906–1963), cemented the group's reputation as one of the major producing groups in the theatre.

The Group refused to follow typical Broadway procedures. Casts were listed alphabetically with no stars, biographies were eliminated from the programs, and interviews focused on the Group rather than on individual careers. Although disagreements and power struggles were frequent among members, to the outside world they presented a picture of cooperation previously unknown in the theatre.

The organization lasted only 10 years as film opportunities, individual success, financial troubles, and personal difficulties led them in different directions. During that period, however, they provided a model of a permanent company devoted to the ideal of ensemble playing and politically focused drama that still remains an inspiration to many. Members of the Group went on to contribute to American theatre in many fields. Elia Kazan (1909–   ) became a prominent director, Mordecai Gorelik (1899–1990) and Boris Aronson (1898–1980) rank among America's finest designers, and Stella Adler (1903–   ), Lee Strasberg (1901–1982), Robert Lewis (1909–   ), and Sanford Meisner (1905–   ) became America's finest teachers of acting.

The Independent Theatre. Small private theatres remained the home of experimental theatre. In most countries these were small, independently operated theatres, although the licensing acts in England required the Gate Theatre to be organized as a private club rather than a theatre to avoid censorship difficulties.

A dominant pattern of theatre production during this period was a theatre company organized around an aesthetic ideal, producing a limited season of plays. Copeau's Vieux Colombier resumed its activities after the close of World War I, and when it disbanded in 1924—so that Copeau could devote his energies to teaching—several other small theatres were organized along similar lines. Each of these theatres was devoted more to artistic aims than to commercial success, and each attracted a specialized audience.

In London, the Old Vic Theatre was begun in 1915 by Lillian Bayliss (1874–1937) specifically to provide regular presentations of Shakespeare in London. Bayliss targeted a diverse audience, maintaining low prices and frequently scheduling matinees for schoolchildren. In 1923 the Old Vic became the first theatre to have performed all of Shakespeare's plays. Faced with diminishing returns, Bayliss hired Tyrone Guthrie (1900–1971) in 1935, and his innovative productions attracted a large popular following that made the Old Vic a dominant theatre on the London scene.

Repertory theatres were also successful in cities outside London. One of the earliest was organized in Manchester under the financial sponsorship of Annie Horniman (1860–1937), the woman who had also provided financial backing for Dublin's Abbey Theatre. In Birmingham and Cambridge, repertory theatres were highly successful. Barry Jackson's Birmingham Repertory Theatre was eclectic in its repertoire, focusing on talented young actors (including Sir Laurence Olivier and Sir John Gielgud in their youth) and maintaining high production standards during its most successful years between 1913 and 1935. Several Birmingham productions transferred to London after their original run, establishing a pattern that continues today. The Cambridge Festival Theatre, founded by Terence Gray (1895–   ), found an audience among Cambridge students and faculty for a nonrealistic theatre from 1926 to 1933. The highly ambitious Gray produced 24 plays each year, with productions ranging from original interpretations of Greek and Elizabethan plays to highly stylized interpretations of Ibsen. The repertory movement extended throughout Britain, introducing professional theatre performance to a large audience.

Summer Festivals. Another occasion for theatrical performance was the summer festival. Wagner's work at Bayreuth, and the Salzburg festival in Austria featuring the work of Mozart, and a summer Shakespeare festival at Stratford-upon-Avon provided early models. The Stratford festival began in 1879, but was interrupted by the war, and resumed in 1919 under the direction of W. Bridges-Adams (1895–1965) featuring a short season of six plays. The Malvern Festival, another creation of Barry Jackson (1879–1961), ran a short season (two to three weeks) that featured the works of George Bernard Shaw. This festival included morning lectures, teatime talks, and other cultural activities during the day with theatre the main focus in the evening. The success of these ventures would lead to further festivals after World War II.

Location

The diversity of occasions for theatrical performance during this period was paralleled by the diversity of spaces utilized for theatre production. To be certain, the proscenium theatre was the dominant theatre structure of the period. The now-familiar plan of a raked orchestra seating area backed by two balconies became common during this period, and a tendency toward plain decoration rather than the baroque gilt of earlier years can also be noted.

Traditional proscenium theatres continued to be built in New York City. The demand for theatre space convinced two businessmen, the Chanin brothers, to build six theatres between 1925 and 1929. These theatres, along with several built during the 1910s, were standard proscenium spaces with tasteful decor, one or two balconies, and small lobbies. Many of these theatres remain in use today; in fact the period between 1935 and 1970 saw no new theatre buildings on Broadway. The most lavish theatre spaces were built for the cinema. The Roxy, built in 1927, was decorated with marble and crystal throughout. Radio City Music Hall, still in use for spectacular reviews and cinema today, was built as a vaudeville house in 1932. Capable of holding 6,200 spectators, the theatre is now a historic landmark even though it operates daily year round, luring thousands of visitors.

Many theatrical producers/directors, however, found the "picture frame" stage too restricting. Walter Gropius (1883–1969), working with the Bauhaus school of art in 1927, designed a "total" theatre that incorporated arena, thrust, and proscenium stage in one single design based on a rotating audience area. Although the theatre never was built, the concept of a flexible theatre has been a dominant influence in theatre architecture for the past 65 years. The Municipal Theatre at Malmö, Sweden, built in 1944, combines a thrust and a proscenium stage and can be configured to seat three different sizes of audience.

Other individuals, lacking the funding for a completely new structure, altered other spaces to create a theatre suited to their needs. The resulting structures included small chamber theatres such as Reinhardt's remodeled ballroom at the Redoutensaal, an open stage at the Cambridge Repertory Theatre (in which the proscenium wall was removed, allowing free access between audience and stage), and the first modern use of "theatre-in-the-round" by Russian director Nicolai Oplahkhov (1900–1967), followed by the construction of a permanent "arena theatre," the Penthouse, at Seattle's University of Washington in 1935.

Many theatre productions of this era, including most of the work of the Federal

The Penthouse Theatre (Seattle, Washington). *Courtesy of the University of Washington Press*

Theatre Project, operated in "found spaces" such as churches, gymnasiums, or other areas where a temporary stage could be erected for a time. The need for theatre space in New York City led to the construction or adaptation of several smaller spaces to serve as theatres, a trend that would become more popular in later years.

Performers

Frequently the demand for a different theatrical space originated with a director. During this period the modern concept of the director as the primary interpreter of the theatre became standard. The director became the central focus of a production, often influencing every aspect of production from architecture to publicity.

Different directors defined the director's role differently. In France, four young directors, all influenced by Jacques Copeau, formed the *cartel des quatres* as a part of their mission to improve the state of the theatre. Although Louis Jouvet (1887–1951), Charles Dullin (1885–1949), Gaston Baty (1885–1952), and Georges Pitoeff (1884–1939) were each influenced by Copeau, they each developed a unique approach to directing, and the four together illustrate the range of directorial approach during this period.

The Director as Interpreter. Copeau's belief in the primacy of the text was also the basic working premise for Louis Jouvet. Jouvet was experienced in all aspects of the theatre, and utilized his knowledge of acting, design, and technical theatre to create a careful, detailed presentation of the text. His work was based on simplicity of presentation and a focus on the actor's speech to discover each nuance of the text. Jouvet worked closely with the playwright Jean Giraudoux (1882–1944), and the collaboration produced remarkable productions.

The image of the director as servant of the text was fulfilled in England by Sir John Gielgud (1904–   ). Known primarily as an actor, Gielgud began directing in 1930 and was particularly effective with the works of Shakespeare. Gielgud's work focused on the text and the actor, with all elements of the production simple and appropriate. Working with the best of England's actors, he produced numerous memorable productions. His 1936 *Romeo and Juliet*, in which he and Sir Laurence Olivier (1907–1989) traded the roles of Romeo and Mercutio each night, is still justly famous.

The Director as Acting Coach.   Russian-born George Pitoeff began his studies in Russia under both Meyerhold and Stanislavski. He considered the director to be an actor above the other actors who needed to understand every character at every moment. Similarly, Gaston Baty sought to isolate and magnify the actor's work, utilizing a bare stage, evocative lighting, and strong control of rhythms to achieve his desired effects.

A similar approach marked the work of Agnes Morgan (1879–1976), one of the first women to flourish as a director rather than entering the field as a playwright or actress. She studied with George Pierce Baker (1886–1935) at Harvard University, began directing for the Neighborhood Playhouse in 1915, and remained associated with that group until 1927. She then founded her own company, working largely with women and producing plays on Broadway until 1939. During this time she was engaged by the Shuberts to direct on Broadway, perhaps the first woman to function in that role. (Interestingly, her first production, *Maya* [1928], was closed by the police because its portrayal of prostitution was thought to corrupt the morals of youth.) She continued to direct on Broadway and in summer theatres, and also worked as part of the Federal Theatre Project. Beginning in 1934 she was a regular director at the Paper Mill Playhouse in New Jersey.

The Director as Collaborator.   Rather than viewing the text as the focus of a production, Charles Dullin sought to supplement the text to reveal deeper meanings. He was particularly noted for his use of music and abstract scenic design coupled with fine actors. Dullin felt that the theatre was *not* reality and sought to establish the unreality of the theatrical experience. Equally skilled as teacher and director, Dullin trained many of Paris's finest young actors and was also responsible for the first productions of plays by Jean Anouilh (1910–1987) and Jean-Paul Sartre.

A similar approach was taken by George Abbott (1887–), the prototypical Broadway producer/director/author. Energetic and efficient, he brought his unflagging zeal to every production. Highly successful in farce, Abbott also triumphed with musical comedy. He was interested in every facet of a production, and was known to rewrite scripts that weren't working. His trademark was a frenetic pace that captivated Broadway audiences for years.

Tyrone Guthrie took this concept of the director's role a step further. Guthrie was noted for audacity. As the director of the Old Vic beginning in 1935, Guthrie viewed the director as the supreme interpreter of the script, and he frequently shocked his audiences with novel interpretations of famous scripts.

Orson Welles (1915–1985) was the "bad boy" of this period. Just 21 when he made his directing debut in 1936, Welles had already established himself as a performer in his native England and made his Broadway debut as an actor in *Romeo and Juliet* two years earlier. Appointed to direct the Negro Unit of the Federal Theatre Project with John Houseman (1902–1988), Welles gained instant recognition with his voodoo-inspired production of *Macbeth* (1935–1936) set in Haiti. Following their work with the FTP, Houseman and Welles organized the Mercury Theatre. Although the enterprise lasted for only four productions, these included a controversial modern-dress production of *Julius Caesar*. Following the close of the Mercury, Welles did most of his work in Hollywood film. Houseman had a distinguished career as an educator/teacher, as well as a highly popular stint as a television actor in the 1980s.

The Director as Visual Creator.   The discovery of a truth beyond the text served as the quest of Gaston Baty (1885–1952). He considered the tyranny of the word on the French stage an unnecessary limitation on the theatre and focused his attention instead on picturization and visual image. Baty was interested in the creation of mood and atmosphere, and at times added scenes of mime or music to the text, stressing that the power of the visual element of theatre to communicate was at least equal, if not superior, to the power of the spoken word.

Leopold Jessner (1878–1945) of Germany also stressed the visual element of production. Jessner felt that the theatre was obligated to the intellectuals, the educated, and serious theatregoers. He found most of the new drama simplistic, expressing old truths rather than exploring new ideas. To undo this, he focused on producing classic plays with an emphasis on visual production elements. In total control of every detail of the production, Jessner demanded a rhetorical acting style that utilized exaggerated gestures. This style allowed Jessner's manipulation of color and space to be fully effective. Noted for his use of huge banks of stairs *(Jessnertreppe)*, Jessner used broad symbolic strokes in his directing. Movement from the top of a bank of stairs symbolically represented a character's fall from power or grace, and color was used symbolically to represent such vital forces as death, power, and goodness. Jessner did not feel tied to the script, feeling that the director had the right to rearrange the work to support a production concept.

For another German, Erwin Piscator (1893–1966), the theatre was primarily educational, and all of his devices were employed to make a powerful impression on the audience. Overtly political, he used multimedia techniques, including the use of film, projections, and photographs, to communicate the message of his plays. For Piscator, the director was essentially an author who carefully constructed and orchestrated the communication in the theatre. Projected texts or dates could either support or contradict stage action, either suggesting a relation between the two or denying an apparent connection. The distancing nature of such presentations provided the groundwork for the theories of Bertolt Brecht.

E. F. Burian (1904–1959) developed multimedia techniques to a new height in his Czechoslovakian experimental theatre, beginning in 1934. Burian was one of the first directors to integrate the use of film, projections, and live action to create a cohesive impression. Projections served as backdrops to live scenes, actors' recorded voices accompanied filmed scenes, and actors even related physically to projected images. Often working with scripts adapted from novels or other nondramatic works, Burian viewed his role of director not so much as interpreter, but as author.

Certainly, these directors relied on the work of designers to realize their concepts. Many of the designers continued to build on the concepts introduced by Craig and Appia, emphasizing the symbolic/abstract use of scenery. The development of modern American stage design may be said to begin with the work of Robert Edmond Jones (1887–1954), Lee Simonson (1888–1967), and Norman Bel Geddes (1893–1958) in the 1910s. Jones had studied in Europe prior to World War I and returned to the United States to apply the ideas he had learned there. In his early work with director Arthur Hopkins, Jones established a reputation for expressionistic sets that evoke the mood of the action. His book *The Dramatic Imagination*, published in 1941, incorporated his ideas about scene design and theatre in general. Lee Simonson began his career with the Washington Square Players and The Theatre Guild. Both groups produced plays in the tradition of the independent theatres of Europe. They relied on small stages and minimal budgets. As a result, Simonson helped give American design a creative simplicity that would be utilized in little theatres throughout the country. Bel Geddes was particularly influenced by Adolphe Appia. He used steps, platforms, and unusual lighting effects to produce the atmosphere of the stage action.

The term frequently applied to the work of these men and their contemporaries is *new stagecraft*. Although each designer had his own unique orientation, all were collectively known for several principles. First, each wanted to design settings specifically for each individual play. They wanted to find the core experience of each play and visualize it in their designs. They did not want to repeat the work of others or rearrange scenery from other productions. Second, they sought a simplicity in their design concepts. They did not fill sets with realistic detail. Instead they selected only the necessary elements of the scene to suggest location and establish atmosphere. Third, the designers took advantage of the new technology available to them in lighting and set construction. For example, they used directional lighting and backlighting to find new ways of suffusing a set with light.

Jones's design for *Macbeth* in 1921 illustrates these principles. Three oversized masks peer over the action of the play, providing an eerie reminder of the prophecies the witches make to Macbeth. Lighting from these masks alternately isolates Macbeth in soliloquies or becomes more generalized for group scenes. There is low backlighting behind the set to evoke a feeling of mystery and suspense. Shadows are prominent as a result of the careful use of spotlights; their purpose is to capture the night and evil imagery in the play.

Other designers became associated with specific directors and worked as part of a team to create productions. The expressionist productions of the Mannheim Theatre were enhanced by Ludvig Sievert's designs, which emphasized distortion, diagonal lines, and harsh colorings. E. F. Burian relied on the talents of Miroslav Kouril (1911–   ) to create the mysterious black void fronted with scrims and backed with projection screens that allowed his multimedia presentations to function. Motley, a three-woman team composed of Sophia Harris, Margaret F. Harris, and Elizabeth Montgomery, worked extensively with Gielgud in London. Their simple, flexible

Scenic design by Robert Edmond Jones for *Macbeth*.

settings and innovative costuming techniques were mainstays of London theatre for
more than thirty years.

The designs of Caspar Nehar (1897–1962) were essential for the work of Bertolt
Brecht, and Brecht himself noted Nehar's importance in conveying the narrative of the
play. Nehar utilized fragmentary and flexible abstract settings, relying on suggestion
rather than representation. In contrast, he was meticulous with properties, often using
actual items to provide maximum support for the actor. Nehar and Brecht worked
closely, with Nehar actually participating in the analysis of the script and creation of
character, often providing a unique chair or other piece of furniture to accentuate a
specific character trait.

Although the popularity of the repertory company concept placed great emphasis on ensemble performance, and the work of the directors and designers began to gain
public attention, certain individuals still managed to create a personal style that made
them important actors. Most of them were women, and one critic called the theatre of
this time a matriarchy because the female actresses were so dominant.

More and more actors of the period became conversant with the Stanislavski
system as it grew to be the dominant methodology for acting. In Britain, Sir John
Gielgud (1904–   ), Dame Peggy Ashcroft (1907–1991), Dame Edith Evans (1888–
1976), and Sir Laurence Olivier (1907–1989) were four British stars who achieved their
popularity based on excellent performance in a wide variety of roles both classical and
modern. The repertory companies tended not to produce stars, since ensemble was

LEADING SCENE DESIGNERS: 1920–1945

Urban, Joseph	1872–1933
Jones, Robert Edmond	1887–1954
Bernstein, Aline	1880–1955
Simonson, Lee	1888–1958
Schlemmer, Oscar	1888–1943
Gorelik, Mordecai	1889–1990
Bel Geddes, Norman	1893–1958
Nehar, Caspar	1897–1962
Aronson, Boris	1900–1980
Mielziner, Jo	1902–1976
Oenslager, Donald	1902–1975
Basq, André	1909–1973
Bay, Howard	1912–

usually a major goal of the group. However, Helene Weigel (1900–1971), Brecht's wife, distinguished herself in the work of the Berliner Ensemble, and Ludmilla Pitoeff (1884–1939) was similarly important to the work of her husband. Ruggero Ruggeri (1871–1953) established himself in the works of Pirandello in Italy, where Vittorio Gassman (1922–   ) became one of the earliest stars to establish himself both on stage and in film.

Among the unquestioned Broadway stars of this era, Gertrude Lawrence (1898–1952) achieved stardom on the basis of her charismatic stage presence and her energetic charm. Whether in comedy, drama, or musical comedy, the Englishwoman captured Broadway audiences with her magnetic appeal, which allowed her to stand out from the production and to establish herself as the central focus of the action. Not only onstage talents but offstage behaviors contributed to the reputation of Tallulah Bankhead (1902–1968). Much of her fame was based on her scandalous public behavior, although she surprised many critics with superior performances in *The Little Foxes* (1938) and *The Skin of Our Teeth* (1943). Ethel Merman (1909–1984), who made her debut on Broadway in 1930, was the reigning star of the American musical for several decades. Annie Oakley in *Annie Get Your Gun*, Reno Sweeney in *Anything Goes*, and Rose in *Gypsy* were but 3 of 13 starring roles she originated. With her big, brassy voice and confident stride, she helped define one of the strongest female dramatic types on the American stage in musicals by Irving Berlin, Cole Porter, and others. Another star of the musical stage was Florence Mills (1895–1927). First achieving notice in the runaway hit *Shuffle Along*, Mills turned down an offer from the Ziegfeld Follies to tour internationally with an all–African-American review that returned to a Broadway run as *Dixie to Broadway* in 1924. Critics in New York, London, and Paris praised her performances, noting her exceptional voice, her exotic looks, and her consummate technique as a performer.

Exotic good looks and enchanting Russian ways were not the only attributes of Alla Nazimova (1879–1945). Trained in Russia, Nazimova came to the United States in 1905 on tour and decided to stay. She learned English in six months and made her English-speaking debut in 1906. Noted for her emotional range, she worked for the Civic Repertory and for the Theatre Guild, establishing herself as the first notable

St. James Theatre

PLAYBILL
the national magazine for theatregoers

HELLO, DOLLY!

Ethel Merman in *Hello, Dolly!*   *Courtesy Museum of the City of New York*

Stanislavski-trained performer in the United States. She was particularly effective in the plays of Ibsen and Chekhov, although she also received acclaim for her performances in Eugene O'Neill's *Mourning Becomes Electra* (1929–1931).

Katherine Cornell (1893–1974) and Helen Hayes (1900–   ) did not establish themselves as "stars" in the public sense of that word. Instead, they based their reputations on their performances onstage. Cornell was successful in a wide range of plays, including sophisticated comedy, melodrama, and the classics. Her quiet, composed style was frequently described as "graceful" and she excelled in scenes of vulnerability and fragility. Hayes began her career at the age of nine and was a popular actress by the time she was in her teens. Her two most successful roles were as queens: Mary of Scotland in the play by Maxwell Anderson (1933), and Victoria in *Victoria Regina* (1935) by Laurence Houseman. Small in stature, she was able to command the stage with her focus, her clarity of character, and her unshakeable air of dignity.

Of all the Broadway actors of this era, perhaps the most successful were Alfred

Lunt (1892–1977) and Lynn Fontanne (1887–1983). The English-born woman and the Midwestern man had both established themselves as comic performers before their marriage in 1922, but it was as a couple that they captivated Broadway. They were major performers for the Theatre Guild, starring in comedies and dramas. Critics praised their work in Maxwell Anderson's *Elizabeth the Queen* (1930), and audiences loved everything they did. Although they worked separately for a time, after 1929 they appeared only as a team, and it was this sense of intimacy that made their work unique.

The principal male stars of the time were all imported from England. Maurice Evans (1901–1989), John Gielgud, and Laurence Olivier appeared in New York both before and after their reputations were established in London. Two African-Americans, however, made powerful impressions. Charles Gilpin (1878–1930) performed in numerous productions at African-American theatres before his starring role in *The Emperor Jones* (1920) catapulted him to fame. Paul Robeson (1898–1976) was a sensation in the role of Crown in *Porgy and Bess* (1927), but his greatest achievement was as Othello, a role he played in London in 1930, in New York in 1943, and at Stratford-upon-Avon in 1959.

Audience

It seems evident that the diversity of theatre offerings would attract a diverse audience. The mainstream commercial audience continued to consist of largely middle- and upper-class individuals. Attendance at the established theatres in Paris and London, particularly, was a social event requiring certain standards of dress and decorum. The experimental theatres appealed to the intellectual strata and audiences were frequently made up largely of other artists. To some practitioners, it became clearly evident that theatre was unavailable or uninteresting to a great portion of society—namely, the lower classes. The German *Volksbühnen* had been founded at the turn of the century to meet this need, and, in France, Fermin Gemier (1869–1933) had staged huge community pageants in an attempt to involve more segments of the populace. In 1919, Gemier produced a season at a circus-theatre that featured huge spectacular productions that he hoped would appeal to more people. In 1920 the government created the Théâtre National Populaire (TNP) under his direction. Although the early form of this theatre was unsuccessful, consisting largely of reproductions of existing productions produced in a large theatre at low prices, after World War II the TNP would become one of the most successful "people's theatre" experiments.

In the United States, the combination of talking films and the Depression were serious setbacks for theatre attendance and tended to increase theatre's dependence on the upper class. The work of the Theatre Guild, the Group Theatre, and similar organizations focused on an educated audience, even though their lower ticket prices were meant to encourage less affluent members of society. Only with the work of the Federal Theatre Project was a new theatre audience discovered. The FTP was designed for the general populace and the diversity of its style made it accessible to people who generally did not attend theatre. Unfortunately, the abrupt collapse of the project did not allow sufficient time to significantly change the habits of the American audience.

Standards of Judgment

The theatre critics of the period recognized the need for change in the theatre. The tradition of journalistic reviews continued, and financial success defined good theatre in the commercial theatre. For the experimental theatres, however, success was measured aesthetically rather than commercially, and, in response to these works, many critics began to look beyond superficial questions of performance quality and question the very nature of theatre.

For some critics, the essence of theatre lay in its ability to make evident the emotional truth of existence. The expressionist Friedrich Koffka (1886–1941) felt that the role of theatre was to portray the human being as an emotional entity distinct from the rest of the world. Loren Kjerbull-Peterson found that such revelation occurred in the delicate balance between illusion and reality on the stage. Any theatre piece contains elements that promote illusion and elements that deny that illusion. It is through the constant balancing of these two elements that the audience member is led to self-revelation, and it is essentially the work of the actor, not the script, to monitor the balance of the elements to create the proper atmosphere.

Others strove to move beyond the emotional level of knowledge and challenged the theatre to explore spiritual truths. Surrealist playwright Jean Cocteau (1889–1963) called for the theatre to explore a deeper realism than that presented in naturalistic drama, seeking a truth that goes far beyond the reality of daily life. Louis Jouvet (1887–1951) held that the role of the theatre was to reveal the supremacy of the spiritual over the material. The most provocative statement of this position came from Antonin Artaud (1896–1949), a French director/playwright whose works are still highly influential.

For Artaud, the theatre was capable of totally restructuring human existence. Calling for a complete rejection of naturalism, Artaud proposed a theatre that would explore the internal, philosophical, religious aspects of life. Rejecting the tyranny of reason and the written word and inspired by Balinese dancers, Artaud envisioned a theatre based on visual effects, gesture, the exploration of space, and movement that would discover fundamental truths of human experience. His term *The Theatre of Cruelty* referred to the discovery of the fundamental cruelty of existence, the recognition of a darkness that is a vital aspect of human experience but that modern society has long repressed. Such awareness would come through the use of percussion instruments, gongs, hypnotic rhythms, and provocative lighting through which the theatre would develop ritualistic qualities. Artaud did not propose a *katharsis;* one's fate is permanent and necessary. Although Artaud was never wholly successful in integrating his concepts with production, his influence in the middle part of the 20th century is beyond question.

Another type of critic rejected the artistic pretensions of a theatre that sought to explore other dimensions of reality, focusing instead on the theatre as an educational means of changing the world in which we live. Russian filmmaker Sergei Eisenstein considered the theatre a means to guide spectators in their choices. Beyond the superficiality of the plot or characters, the spectator must be made aware of the ideological concepts that underlie the action, and must be led to a proper conclusion about those concepts.

The most complete delineation of this idea is found in the writings of Bertolt Brecht. [See insert.] However, a challenge to Brecht's ideas is found in the later criticism of Georg Lukacs (1881–1971). Although he, like Brecht, rejected the "formalist" or nonrealistic forms of theatre, Lukacs proposed that theatre should accurately present the actual reality of a society in its full historical and social sense. For Lukacs, the theatre was not concerned with the depiction of the contradictory nature of particular moments of existence that suggest that change is achieved through individual action, but instead was concerned with transcending those dualities to present the potential integration of those contradictions. He accused Brecht of presenting incomplete humans through his emphasis on a particular behavior or trait, rather than showing humans as constantly changing and evolving. Brecht and Lukacs maintained a public debate for many years concerning the proper focus of the drama, and in their writings they preview many of the questions that are addressed by Marxist critics today.

Several American critics promoted the concept that the theatre needed to be relevant to modern society and to the full range of political and social issues confronting the United States. Ludwig Lewisohn (1882–1955) in *Drama and the Stage* (1922) identified the need to expand the theatre audience. He challenged theatre to erase the scars of the war by eliminating vengeance as a part of the tragic concept, and also by focusing on the sharing of suffering by a community of spectators. Rosamond Gilder (1891–1986), one of the first women to be accepted as a critic (she was later the first woman elected to membership in the New York Drama Critics Circle) also felt the theatre needed to avoid triviality. She advocated a theatre of significance, closely related to social and political reality, that would stir listeners to action.

The peculiar nature of modern society led to a debate over the viability of tragedy as a dramatic genre in the 20th century. Joseph Wood Krutch (1893–1970) identified a "tragic fallacy" in modern society, arguing that since humans no longer viewed themselves as significant, tragedy in the classic sense was impossible. Francis Fergusson (1904–   ) identified the modern problem with tragic drama as the result of the fragmentation and diversity of society. He agreed that the classical definitions of tragedy no longer applied directly to modern life. The role of the theatre was to present a multiplicity of ideas, laced with ambiguities and unanswered questions that would provide glimpses of answers leading the spectators to a sense of a lost wholeness. Maxwell Anderson (1888–1959) disagreed with modern critics of tragedy. Anderson held that the function of tragedy was universal and beyond temporality. It was a religious affirmation that was the human means of reviving hope in the face of despair; it had been valid for the Greeks and it was equally valid for 20th-century Americans.

Robert Edmond Jones did not enter specifically into the debates of political significance or tragic vision, but his concepts were extremely influential on many theatre practitioners. Jones sought a theatre that had been lost; a theatre that contained a dream, an excitement, a conception of greatness that modern society had consumed. For Jones, theatre was not prose, nor was it journalism. Great theatre was the creation of legend or myth. The best theatre was not theatre that preached or narrated; rather, good theatre was theatre that stirred the dramatic imagination of the spectator.

BERTOLT BRECHT

*T*he Berliner Ensemble is the role model for political theatres, for it created a theatre form that expresses political action without appearing to be elitist or commercial. Bertold Brecht's plays and his conception of theatre heavily influenced the avant-garde theatres of Europe and the United States in their staging, their acting, and their commitment to social change. In theoretical writings and in more than 40 plays and adaptations, Brecht offered an alternative theatre form to experimental artists tired of the confinement of the box set and the causal connection of realistic dialogue. He provided both socialists and communists with methods of presenting and constructing Marxist ideas in the theatre. His first play was written in 1918 and his last great work in 1945, but his greatest impact on others came after World War II, when many of his works were translated into other languages, and when his own theatre company performed his plays throughout Europe. To see the Berliner Ensemble perform, whether at the Theatre am Schiffbauerdamm in East Berlin, where the Brechtian company was housed after 1954, or at the Paris International Festival in 1954 and 1955, where the company won international recognition, was above all to see the ideas of Bertolt Brecht realized in theatrical form. Productions were designed to communicate ideas, and the philosophy behind these designs was intriguing.

Brecht opposed the traditional dramatic theatre, with its emphasis on making the audience feel pity and fear, and its effort to project the audience into the event. He also opposed a causal and careful play structure that leads the audience to a tidy resolution. Brecht believed that the usual dramatic theatre viewed humankind as unalterable and the world as unchangeable. Because Brecht was a revolutionary who saw great suffering and inequality in existing social forms, he quite naturally rejected this theatre. Instead, he preferred what he called epic theatre. He wanted the stage to narrate stories about a new type of human being evolving out of the present social and economic systems. Instead of telling people that their lives are fine, he wanted to make them think about what is needed to change their lives.

All art is political, Brecht felt, and all plays comment on the existing social systems either by tacit support or by critical perception. Brecht believed that a production should comment on the play's action and not immerse the audience in

continued

emotions that would blind them from the truth of the characters' situation. To achieve this, Brecht sought to distance the spectators from the stage events sufficiently so they would ask questions about the play and eventually make decisions. He found various means of maintaining that spectator distance. He had the actors "break character" to address the audience and then return to their role. He found gestures or physical symbols that would reveal truths underneath the platitudes of the character. He placed the action in a distant time or location so that the audience had no personal connection to the events or outcomes of the play. Brecht wanted the actor to believe in the message and truth of the story, not in the psychological continuity of the character; he wanted the actor to involve the audience, not ignore it; he wanted to highlight the contradictions of the character's beliefs, not provide uniformity of emotional structure; and he wanted the actors to feel that they are members of the audience, not superior to it.

Brecht intensely disliked theatre in which the mind is closed while the emotions flow freely. He certainly wanted emotional response from his audiences, but he wanted that response to sharpen the thought processes and to toughen the audience's resolve to action in order to change the injustices identified by the action. Brecht felt acutely the inhumanity of humankind, and his plays demanded that the audience realize that inhumanity and understand the causes of it. Emotion for its own sake would blind the audience to the inhumanity. Therefore he wanted to create an effect that would "make strange" the stage action *(verfremdungseffekt)* in order to keep the problems of the play before the audience's mind.

This brief description only touches the major points of Brecht's remarkable contribution to stage theory and practice, but it provides the background to a Brechtian production. The key was to make each element of such a production remove or distance the audience from the action. First, he made the audience aware of the theatrical event by leaving lights exposed to the spectators' view, by changing scenery during the action, and by keeping the actors in close proximity to the audience. Second, each element—music, costumes, sets, makeup—commented on the action as if a separate voice in a chamber orchestra. Music especially undercut individual moments, pulling the audience away from the words and reminding it of hidden intentions or subtle tensions within a scene. Third, the sets were always spare and essential, never complete and elaborate. True to the proletarian intentions of the scripts, set pieces were carefully researched but never ornate or lavish. Frequently, all set pieces and props for the play were left onstage throughout each scene, again to keep the audience from believing in the realism of the action. Brecht used projections in the form of slides cast on screens placed near the center of the action or at the back. Signs and posters telling the outcome of a scene before it began, or commenting on dialogue as it occurred were also common techniques. The use of projections and posters, which Brecht learned from Erwin Piscator, split the focus of the audience, distanced it from the emotions of the characters, and led it to a clearer understanding of the intent of the play.

Brecht left Germany during the Nazi era, returning in 1948 to direct a production of *Mother Courage and Her Children.* The company of this play became the foundation for the Berliner Ensemble, formed the next year. Although the government provided financial support for the company and renovated the Theatre am Schiffbauerdamm for use after 1954, Brecht complained bitterly that the government was more interested in the propaganda value of having him in East Germany than it was in promoting his productions. Obviously Brecht wanted a theatre for workers, but he estimated that less than 10 percent of his audience were from that class. After Brecht's death in 1956, the Berliner Ensemble continued to grow in international stature, particularly through the leadership of Brecht's widow, Helene Weigel, Manfred Wekwerth, and Joachim Tenschert.

DRAMATIC LITERATURE

Mother Courage is in the midst of a war, pulling her wagon of supplies from one camp to another, desperately seeking to survive on the battlefields that surround her. She doesn't know or care which side in the war is justified; she only knows that as long as the war continues she will be able to eke out a living selling stolen and recovered goods to the soldiers. To her, war is a business proposition. She has little use for empty words like "truth" or "courage" or "valor"; to her, the poor have the only courage because they get up in the morning and put up with rulers and popes. However, Mother Courage will eventually lose all three of her children: one for refusing to reveal the location of a cashbox entrusted to his care, one for looting even though he was a hero, and the third for warning a town of an approaching army. Even though she tried to teach them to look out only for themselves, they each succumbed to the temptation to regard values as more important than personal survival. When the play ends, Mother Courage is dragging her wagon by herself, saying, "I must get on with business."

Bertolt Brecht's Mother Courage is an appropriate symbol for the drama of the interwar years, since most of the characters of the period are struggling for survival in a hostile and threatening world. Some characters respond to the social and economic environments that limit their sense of humanity, others become enmeshed in the uncertainties of existence or withdraw into imaginary worlds. Still others struggle with the traditions and prejudices of their native countries.

Political Theatre of Brecht

Representative of the desire of playwrights to reform their society during the interwar period is Bertolt Brecht, whose theories have already been discussed. Given those ideas, it is not surprising that Brecht's plays focus on the downtrodden, the poor, and the peasants. His characters are forced to struggle to live, and rarely have the opportunity to think of their own dignity or to dream of a comfortable existence. They are victims of the social and economic environments, and they justify theft, graft, and even murder on grounds that it is both the way of the world and the way to survival. Brecht particularly blames capitalism for his characters' weaknesses, asserting that it forces individuals to work against one another, and that it encourages selfishness, greed, and injustice within the individual. (Many English-speaking critics, however, have also found in his plays a cynical world view in which injustice is an inherent component of human nature and not at all the result of the economic system. This is hotly disputed by socialist critics.) The sources and consequences of social and economic injustice are the heart of Brecht's investigation, and he uses the techniques already identified to make the audience think about and respond to the conditions he sees. His ideas are evident in such plays as *Mother Courage and Her Children* (1938), *The Caucasian Chalk Circle* (1944–1945), *The Private Life of the Master Race* (1935–1938), and *The Resistible Rise of Arturo Ui* (1941).

Pirandello (1867–1936)

The search for truth led the Italian playwright Luigi Pirandello to a very different problem, the conflict between truth and illusion. Although his most famous plays, including *Enrico IV* (1922), *Six Characters in Search of an Author* (1921), and *Tonight We Improvise* (1930), come very early in the period discussed here, they are very much the product of the philosophical ferment before World War I. Pirandello used the theatre to express his feelings of doubt and confusion that come from living in the modern world. In other ages, character had always been fixed according to the morality of the times. Pirandello recognized that the concept of personality had lost its certainty in the 20th century, and he sought to present the impact of that loss in his plays. Although his philosophy is often simplistic and muddled, he was effective in dramatizing the emotional consequences of that philosophy. Insofar as the modern world is one of change, Pirandello created characters who responded to that change with panic and fear, anger, and (occasionally) madness. He dramatized human beings who do not always know who they are, who feel isolated from themselves, and who are unable to determine the line between appearance and reality. Additionally, he used the theatre as a metaphor for life by confusing the audience about whether it was watching a play or watching a real event. The trick has since become common, but in the hands of Pirandello it was original and forceful.

Surrealism and Fantasy

Jean Cocteau (1892–1963) established the possibilities of surrealism in the drama. Through a combination of dance, mime, acrobatics, and bizarre visual images (animals climbing out of a camera, talking horses), Cocteau created a dramatic world of magic in which the simple becomes poetic, the mundane is made lyrical, and the fantastical is treated as ordinary. He made no effort to hide the magical devices by which birds suddenly appeared or people walked through mirrors, for his goal was enchantment rather than surprise. Cocteau also used myth like a friendly framework, a comfortable but unobtrusive reminder that important matters are part of some great, inexplicable meaning to life. In such plays as *The Infernal Machine* (1932) and *Orpheus* (1926), he used a means of discovering the relationship of life and death.

Mystery, poetry, and beauty blended in Cocteau's images to create a world distinctly removed from the harsh realities of daily existence. His surrealism was more the result of his desire to escape the drudgery of life than it was due to a belief in the surrealist movement. He mingled ordinary and mysterious images, juxtaposed strange occurrences (a man repairing a window is left suspended in midair, and later is revealed to be an archangel), refused to acknowledge a world of logic or law, and suspended the distinction between this world and the world of death. Cocteau is important as a surrealist dramatist, probably the most successful of them, but his final significance lies more in the fact that he symbolized the desire to escape the unplesantness of life and live in a world without time or fear. Other writers who used some of these same techniques, although with more violent imagery, are Antonin Artaud, Roger Vitrac, and Fernando Arrabal.

The desire to escape into a different fantasy world is found in the plays of Jean Giraudoux (1882–1944). His best-known works include *Ondine* (1930), *Tiger at the Gates* (1935), and *The Madwoman of Chaillot* (1944). His plays are peopled with authority figures from petty bureaucrats to capitalistic scions and Greek gods who are tired of trying to maintain rule, order, balance, and symmetry in life. These characters are opposed or frustrated by a host of beautiful young ladies, young lovers, eccentric women, beggars, and peasants who possess joie de vivre and an invincible determination to appreciate the little things of life. Giraudoux's plays become fantasy melodramas in which good and evil battle each other for control of the human heart. Evil transforms the world into rigid categories, inanimate objects, and indifference; goodness sings the songs of life, paeans to individuality. What saves characters from death or destruction is the desire to express themselves for who they are, to accept the uniqueness of each person, and to find love in themselves and others.

Sartre, Camus, and Existentialism

The increasing dissatisfaction with life exhibited in so many plays became more pronounced in the work of two French existentialists whose plays extended beyond the interwar period. Both Jean-Paul Sartre (1905–1980) and Albert Camus (1913–1960) articulated their sense of the existential condition of the modern individual in essays, books, novels, and plays. Inherently philosophers rather than playwrights, only a few of their plays demonstrate effective use of theatrical conventions. Most of them are read for their insight into the philosophies of the writers rather than for production values. Sartre has been the more produced of the two, with *The Flies* (1943), *No Exit* (1944), *The Respectful Prostitute* (1946), and *The Condemned of Altona* (1959) being his best-known plays. Camus's most famous play is *Caligula* (1938).

Symbolism of García Lorca

Spain's greatest modern playwright was Federico García Lorca (1898–1936), a poet influenced by the symbolist movement. When he began writing plays, Lorca retained both his poetic instincts and his reliance on the accumulation of stark imagery to build emotional intensity. He told stories that have a folk quality to them, beginning them near the climax of a tremendous passion and then extending the fateful tragic conclusion through the use of folk songs and poetic images. Suffused with the Spanish countryside and lifestyle, García Lorca's imagery included knives, guns, and violence, which he associated with masculinity; and flowers, water, growth, blossoms, and fertility, which he associated with femininity. Although the core of most of his plays was a love story with an unhappy ending, the plays gain a richly symbolic quality because García Lorca identified and verbalized the elemental forces that operate in the characters' lives. Not only is there a sense that feminine and masculine are in tragic opposition to each other, but the land is a symbol of the natural forces of life in contrast to the imposed morality of the city and the neighbors. Life is never allowed to flower to fullness because death is destiny, passion overwhelms reason, and those who survive the tragic conflicts of life are condemned to barren, lonely existences. By writing of these forces through symbolic language and stark theatrical images, Lorca gives his plays a universal significance beyond their undoubtedly Spanish background. Representative of García Lorca's work are *Blood Wedding* (1933), *Yerma* (1934), and *The House of Bernarda Alba* (1936).

Sean O'Casey

Another example of reformation in the theatre is found in Ireland in the later works of Sean O'Casey (1880–1964). As early as the 1920s, O'Casey had written eloquently of the economic and political plight of the Irish in such plays as *Juno and the Paycock* (1924), *The Plough and the Stars* (1926), and *Shadow of a Gunman* (1923). O'Casey combined his sensitivity to the Irish peasant with a poetic, expressionistic theatrical style in later plays like *Cock-a-Doodle Dandy* (1949). All of his plays represent a blend of political awareness, desire for change, and use of nonrealistic theatrical styles that are characteristic of European writing.

American Drama

American authors pursued a slightly different objective as they sought to define the basic concepts of American life. Focusing on uniquely American subjects and characters, each author sought to provide an insightful portrait that revealed not only the optimism, but also the dark underside, of the American dream. Of the hundreds of plays produced professionally in the 1920s and 1930s, comedy and musical comedy were the most popular forms. Reflecting the optimism of the first decade and the search for relief from the Great Depression in the second decade, these two forms set the tone for the period. Nevertheless, serious drama had its adherents, including America's first great playwright, Eugene O'Neill.

Musical Theatre.   American musicals existed before the early 1920s, but without a distinct genius to give them shape. The shows of George M. Cohan (1878–1942) were mostly excuses for his songs and dances and patriotic speeches. Other shows were written by a variety of composers who sold their songs to the producer without knowing the storyline. The few critical successes between 1910 and 1927, such as *Very Good Eddie* (1915), *Leave It To Jane* (1917), and *No, No, Nanette* (1925) relied on thin story lines with disconnected actions and characters who were altogether too cute to be believable.

In the early 1920s, a variety of popular theatrical forms contributed to what is today called the American musical. The most important of these was the operetta, a European form of musical with roots in the light operas of 19th-century Paris and Vienna. The operetta is characterized by its reliance on music to sustain audience interest, its emphasis on string instruments, its long, flowing melodic lines, its use of such European rhythms as the march and the waltz, and its tendency to have music accompanying most of the action, including dialogue. The story lines of the operetta were of fairy-tale romances in which beautiful ladies (or daughters of state officials) fall in love with handsome princes and, after a test of loyalty, they live happily ever after. Among the most effective writers of operettas were Rudolf Friml (1879–1972), whose successes include *Rose Marie* (1924), and *The Vagabond King* (1925); Victor Herbert (1859–1924), composer of *The Red Mill* (1906) and *Babes in Toyland* (1923); and Sigmund Romberg (1887–1951), who wrote *Desert Song* (1926) and *The Student Prince* (1924). Other theatrical forms contributing to the musical were the follies, the extravaganza, and vaudeville.

Show Boat (1928) is generally regarded as a critical turning point in the development of the musical because it more carefully integrated the elements of the musical into a meaningful story of American life. Based on a story by Edna Ferber, it combined the music of Jerome Kern (1884–1945) and a book and lyrics by Oscar Hammerstein II (1895–1960) and P. G. Wodehouse (1881–1975), with the producing genius of Florenz Ziegfeld (1869–1932). The plot is long and complicated (the out-of-town tryout lasted over five hours) but focuses on Julie, the daughter of Cap'n Andy, owner of the river boat *Cotton Blossom.* Julie falls in love with Gaylord Ravenal, a hopeless gambler who deserts her and their child in Chicago when the fortunes of the show boat dwindle. Julie is forced to take a job in a nightclub to support herself and her daughter. Many years later, Cap'n Andy is persuaded to start another show boat with Julie's daughter as the star attraction. When the boat docks in Natchez, where the story first began, who should come walking by but old Gaylord Ravenal, who is reunited with his family.

From this description, *Show Boat* is standard 1920s, with its reliance on chance to guide people's lives (Julie and Gaylord fall in love at first sight), its melodramatic characterization of a heroine in distress overcoming all adversity, and its hero who goes wrong but repents in the end. It also had specialty numbers that had nothing to do with the show, including eight minutes of imitations of famous people of the 1920s by one of the leading ladies who was famous for such routines. However, it was innovative and effective in other ways: the integration of the chorus into the action, the opening chorus of African-American dockworkers instead of a chorus of pretty women, the remarkable "Old Man River" with its despairing and turgid vision of reality, the American locations and imagery, the rare treatment of the life of Negroes, the subplot theme of miscegenation, and the richly textured and thoughtfully integrated melodies and rhythms of Kern's music.

In 1931 an American musical won the Pulitzer Prize for best play of the year, signaling the arrival of the "integrated" musical. *Of Thee I Sing* had lyrics that were all appropriate to the action and to the characters who sang them, no superfluous specialty numbers, and actions that were centered on the plot (the election and retention of John Wintergreen as President of the United States on a platform of love). Also, the chorus was composed of characters who were a part of the action, and the story line had a central theme developed through the action (governmental incompetence). The musical was written by George Gershwin (1898–1937) and his brother, Ira (1896–1983), who also scored hits with their *Strike Up the Band* (1930) and *Porgy and Bess* (1935). In the latter, arguably the first American folk opera, the combination of jazz rhythms, opera form, and African-American experience produced a work of unequaled power in the American theatre. George Gershwin's jazz and blues rhythms and harmonies and his difficult vocal ranges blended the qualities of the old operetta with those of the Jazz Age, resulting in a further Americanization of the musical.

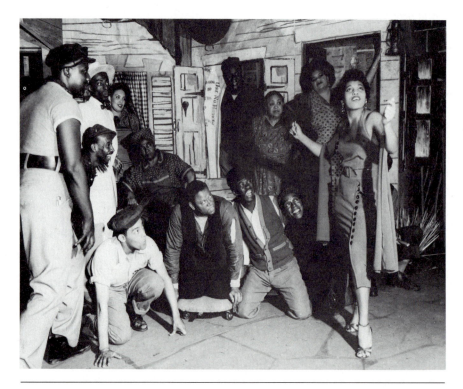

A scene from *Porgy and Bess* as revived in the 1950s.   *Courtesy Lawrence and Lee Theatre Research Institute*

The musical responded to the Depression era in other ways beyond the use of jazz and blues. The most successful writer-composer of the decade was Cole Porter (1891–1964), whose crisp brass sounds and buoyant rhythms expressed the effervescent enthusiasm of his lyrics. One of America's greatest lyricists, Porter wrote of the elegant life of debutantes and millionaires traveling about the world for fun and adventure. His lyrics are mixtures of sophisticated wit, risqué innuendos, topical references, and simple virtues. He extols friendship and loyalty, and his characters always overcome adversity through perseverance, confidence, and honesty. In *Anything Goes* (1934), *The Gay Divorcée* (1932), and *Red, Hot, and Blue* (1936), Porter gave his audiences a reason to have faith and confidence in the future. Destitute characters make it rich, and wealth finds that money is no substitute for love and friendship.

Porter expanded the range of the musical with new character types, popular images from the newspapers, and unabashed exuberance. His story lines were inaccessible to some people because of their emphasis on sophistication, however, and his songs could be transferred from one musical to another without seeming out of place.

Comedy.   Prior to World War II, the most popular American plays were comedies and musicals in which the problems of a happy young couple are dissolved by their love, confidence, and determination. The plays are filled with zany antics, ridicule of authority figures, support of individualism, and wide-eyed optimism. The longest-running show of the 1920s was *Abie's Irish Rose* (1922) by Anne Nichols, which brought together a Jewish boy and an Irish Catholic girl. The conflict of cultures and traditions poses one problem after another for the young couple, but eventually their love overcomes all obstacles.

George S. Kaufman (1889–1961).   George Kaufman collaborated with a number of writers to produce some of America's most enduring comedies. *Beggars on Horseback*, written in 1924 with Marc Connelly (1890–1980), is the story of a young composer whose nightmare about life with his fiancée, the daughter of a wealthy businessman, makes him decide to marry the poor but lovely girl across the hall, whom he really loves anyway. *You Can't Take It With You* (1936), written with Moss Hart (1904–1961), is the model for comedies of the period: a poor girl loves a rich boy, and they learn that love is more important than all the zany antics or stultified manners of their respective parents.

Thornton Wilder (1897–1975).   Wilder's comic vision was less frenetic than Kaufman's. In *Our Town* (1938) he wrote what might be described as the quintessential vision of small-town America. In its division of the play into daily life, love and marriage, and death, Wilder points the audience toward a distanced view of the little habits and activities of ordinary people. With this view, he seeks comfort for his characters and meaning for himself. He raises the mundane exchange of young lovers to an archetypal statement on human interaction. The muted conversations of the deceased of the village suggests that the significance of this life is only because we do not see the fullness of existence. He links the lifestyle of Grovers Corners, New Hampshire, with a cosmic framework that is beyond comprehension yet comforting in its expanse. By eliminating a set, suggesting location with minimal props, and having

A Global Perspective

Improvised Comedy in the 20th-Century Middle East

*T*he history of Middle Eastern countries is dotted with a wide range of dramatic forms, from puppet dramas of the Ottoman Empire in the 14th century to storytellers who performed in male athletic clubs in Iran; from religious epic dramas featuring casts of thousands in the 19th century to improvised comedy that began as early as the 17th century and continues today.

Early forms of improvised comedies were social satires, focusing particularly on foreigners and on the officials of the village. In the style of the commedia dell'arte, troupes traveled from place to place, although some found royal favor and even accompanied ambassadors on official state visits.

Improvisational comedy has survived into the 20th century, and it remains reminiscent of the commedia dell'arte tradition. Performers are often family members, and although widespread touring has been reduced in the age of urban centers, it is still common for a young man to gradually grow up through stock roles until he is ready to perform a leading role.

All performers are male, including the musicians. The central character is invariably a clown figure, often in blackface, who is in conflict with a conservative character, usually a merchant. Other stock characters include a dandy, female characters, and various ethnic types. As is often the case, the clown figure has freedom to approach topics that cannot be discussed in society, and the performances include political references, sexual byplay, and ethnic criticism. Scripts tend to be simple comedy (the clown convinces his companion to balance yogurt on his head as a cure; the yogurt ends up on the companion's face), but some are based on legendary or historical events.

Though originally they were improvised, some scripts have been written down, but performers still maintain license to make alterations to suit the moment, frequently managing to work in references to local situations or recent events. The same story is performed slightly differently by each troupe, and the troupe is free to make variations as needed. Indeed, troupes brag that they can perform the same play in half an hour or three hours, whichever fits the buyers schedule and budget.

Music and dancing are key ingredients—each troupe has its own musicians —but the key ingredients are special bits (*schticks*—like the *lazzi* in the commedia) that may be sound effects, dialects, acrobatics, or pratfalls. Scripts are deliberately manipulated to incorporate these moments, and, following another ancient comic custom, if it works once, an opportunity to repeat the bit is often found.

Although many performers maintain other jobs for financial security, the tradition of improvised comedy in the Middle East continues.

a Stage Manager explain situations to the audience and provide a commentary, Wilder pulls the audience away from the particularities of the action and focuses its attention on the joys of all daily existence. Wilder is also remembered for *The Skin of Our Teeth* (1943) and *The Matchmaker* (original title in 1938 was *The Merchant of Yonkers*).

Eugene O'Neill (1888–1953). Eugene O'Neill received his first attention from the Provincetown Players, who produced his earliest plays. The award of the Pulitzer Prize for his first Broadway play in 1920, *Beyond the Horizon*, established his reputation. He followed the success with a flurry of dramas about people whose faith had been shattered or who placed their faith in false gods: *The Emperor Jones* (1920), *The Hairy Ape* (1922), *Desire Under the Elms* (1924), *The Great God Brown* (1926), and *Mourning Becomes Electra* (1931). Some of these imitated the characteristics of August Strindberg's plays: tortured relationships, intense psychological motivation, obsession verging on insanity, and loneliness twisting into despair. O'Neill's plays frequently identify a young poet, modeled on the playwright himself, who retains his idealism by dreaming of life on the sea or out West. A cancer usually exists within his family, however, and frequently overwhelms him. *Desire Under the Elms* is the story of a farmer who marries a young girl to prevent his sons from getting his inheritance, only to have two of the sons run off West and the third fall in love with his new stepmother. The intense passion of the son and mother and the obvious Strindbergian overtones of the play offer compelling drama.

Even though O'Neill won the Nobel prize for literature in 1937, his reputation went into eclipse. Ironically, it was after he had decided to stop publishing that he wrote his two greatest masterpieces, *Long Day's Journey into Night* (1939–1941) and *The Iceman Cometh* (1939). The first is a painful revelation of family love and tragedy. The Tyrone family lives on the New England coast, where the fog encloses and isolates them from all but their own despair. The mother's addiction to morphine is the catalyst for the exposure of failure in the lives of mother, father, and two sons. In *The Iceman Cometh*, O'Neill's characters are destitute drunkards inhabiting Harry Hope's saloon. Their despair is too great to face the world and their pipe dreams for the future are a sham because they cannot even walk across the street or respond to the suicide of a friend.

O'Neill's work received some of its widest public acclaim after his death in 1953.

By then, the disillusionment of his characters struck a more responsive chord in Americans, many of whom were themselves beginning to question the American dream. Also, O'Neill's characters found their greatest interpreters in the actors Jason Robards (1922–) and Colleen Dewhurst (1926–1992). Through their work, Robards and Dewhurst kept O'Neill's name prominent in the American theatre.

African-American Theatre. The Harlem Renaissance was expressed in drama as well as in music and poetry. The literary leaders of the Harlem Renaissance were highly critical of the popular African-American musicals because of the negative image they projected. Although the musical continued to be the ultimate goal for African-American performers since it offered access and financial reward, a growing body of nonmusical literature came into being as well.

In 1923, Willis Richardson (1889–1977) had the distinction of seeing his plays *The Chip Woman's Fortune* become the first nonmusical African-American play to be produced on Broadway. A simple tale, it presented African-American people in their own setting, with no attempt to sensationalize the story. In 1926, two of his folk plays, *Compromise* and *The Broken Banjo*, were the first productions of the influential Krigwa Little Theatre. *The Flight of the Natives*, produced by the Krigwa Theatre Group in 1927, is an examination of plantation life and urges racial solidarity. *The Deacon's Awakening* (1929) focuses on a conservative father's refusal to allow his daughter to experience the modern world. It is one of the first plays written about African-Americans that did not focus on race, and it is one of the first African-American plays to be openly critical of African-American conservative religion.

Randolph Edmonds, educated at Oberlin, Columbia, and Yale, was instrumental in introducing theatre to the curriculum at African-American universities. To destroy negative stereotypes of African-American people, he was determined that his plays, such as *The Land of Cotton* (1934) and *Earth and Stars* (1946), would present African-Americans in a positive light, possessed of dignity and integrity even in their ceaseless battle against racial oppression.

In the 1930s Langston Hughes (1902–1967) made his debut as a playwright with *Mulatto* (1934). The play tells the story of a young man of mixed blood who kills his white father and then commits suicide in his father's home. The play reveals the tenderness of the relationship between the white man and his "housekeeper," the father's generosity toward the children, and the inevitable tragedy that ensues. A major hit on Broadway, *Mulatto* ran for two seasons and toured successfully as well. Hughes also wrote comedies, musical revues, and "gospel dramas" that combined the gospel spirit and form with drama.

Disillusionment. Other writers in the 1920s who explored the tragic form were Elmer Rice (1892–1967), Rachel Crothers (1878–1958), and Sophie Treadwell (1885–1970). Rice first achieved fame with *The Adding Machine* (1923). In expressionistic form, it tells of an accountant who is fired from his job to be replaced by an adding machine; he reacts by killing his employer. His trial and execution focus the play on its theme of the ill effects of materialism. In 1929, Rice wrote one of the most naturalistic plays in American literature: *Street Scene.* In front of a huge tenement building, an array of city types wander in and out, commenting on the weather and their lives. Their chorus about urban life becomes a backdrop for the tragedy taking place in one of the families.

One of America's first women to write of women's issues, Crothers began her playwriting career in 1904. She successfully wrote and directed for 33 years and scored some 30 Broadway successes, including *The Three of Us* (1906) and *When Ladies Meet* (1932). Her works frequently treated the fragile conditions of American domestic life by creating dynamic female leading characters who challenge accepted limitations on their social and economic lives.

Sophie Treadwell's provocative and experimental plays are best illustrated by *Machinal* (1928), which depicts an unhappy woman whose marriage offers little consolation in an inhuman and mechanized society. Because of its expressionistic technique, it achieved considerable notoriety but little commercial success. In her later plays she nevertheless continued to search for new dramatic forms to express her point of view.

The disillusionment with the American dream gained force during the Depression. Political plays of the period assessed the effects of capitalism and the Depression on the average worker and farmer. Clifford Odets (1906–1963), in his *Waiting for Lefty* (1935), called for changes in the economic system. John Howard Lawson (1895–1977), in *Marching Song* (1937), envisioned the end of the capitalist system altogether. Lillian Hellman (1906–1964) wrote of the greed of a Southern family in the highly successful *The Little Foxes* (1938). She had previously achieved acclaim in 1934 with *The Children's Hour*, a study of the effects of social pressure on two women teachers accused of having a lesbian relationship.

The Federal Theatre Project's "living newspaper," which told of news events during the Depression through dramatic action, brought to life the impact of the economic despair on the lives of farmers in *Triple-A Plowed Under* (1936). The longest-running serious drama in Broadway history, *Tobacco Road* (1933), surveyed the psychological damage of poverty in a sharecropper family. The Depression damaged the dream then and prepared the groundwork for its further demise after World War II in the work of Tennessee Williams and Arthur Miller.

CONNECTIONS

The period between 1920 and 1945 established many of the basic patterns for contemporary drama. Certainly the most influential ideas came from the writings and practice of Bertolt Brecht.

Brecht's ideas on staging, theory, and drama are used by nearly every type of theatre ranging from Broadway to political theatres in Latin America. The episodic structure Brecht championed in his plays has become generally accepted as a dramatic form and is used in many contemporary plays. The exposure of theatrical elements such as lighting instruments is so common in contemporary theatre that it rarely draws comment from critics or audience members. Indeed, Brecht's concepts have become so accepted, so conventional, that they seem to have lost some of their original impact.

Brecht and Piscator were among the first to introduce the concept of multimedia productions. Today, the use of projections is common in the theatre, as are experiments in the combination of theatre and other media. In 1984, Andrew Lloyd Webber's *Starlight Express* used television sets to make the action visible to each audience member, and rock concerts frequently use large-screen television concurrent with live performance. Some contemporary plays integrate film and video segments with live performance. Performance artist Bill Irwin's *Largely New York*, produced on Broadway in 1990, included a segment in which a cameraman shot the action, which was silmultaneously presented to the audience both live and on a video screen. Projections for the future include the use of laser and holograph technology to enhance the potential of multimedia presentation.

Realism has not been abandoned in contemporary theatre, and modified realism remains a dominant style in theatre design. The method-acting style introduced by Lee Strasberg has greatly affected American acting both on stage and on film. Dustin Hoffman, Robert DeNiro, and Meryl Streep are a few of the actors trained in method acting who bring the same sense of interior focus and emotional commitment to their performances.

Perhaps the most influential dramatist is still Eugene O'Neill, who set out the potential range of theatrical styles to which American themes can be adapted. In particular his interest in probing beneath the surface of American family life remains a major feature of American theatre, films, and television. The plays of August Wilson and Tina Howe, films such as *Ordinary People* and *Terms of Endearment*, and television shows such as *Roseanne* continue to explore the positive and negative dynamics of the American family.

SOURCES FOR FURTHER STUDY

Art/Social/Philosophy Background

Breton, André. *What Is Surrealism?* Ed. and trans. Franklin Rosemont. New York: Monad, 1978.

Ensley, Clive. *Conflict and Stability in Europe.* London: Open University Press, 1979.

Friedman, Maurice. *The Worlds of Existentialism.* New York: Random House, 1964.

Fyfe, Albert J. *Understanding the First World War.* New York: P. Lang, 1988.

Gordon, Donald. *Expressionism: Art & Idea.* New Haven: Yale University Press, 1987.

Matthews, J. H. *An Introduction to Surrealism.* University Park: Pennsylvania State Press, 1965.

Read, Sir Herbert Edward. *Surrealism.* New York: Praeger, 1971.

Sandrow, Nahna. *Surrealism: Theatre, Arts, Ideas.* New York: Harper and Row, 1972.

Winn, Ralph B. *A Concise Dictionary of Existentialism.* New York: Philosophical Library, 1960.

Wood, Anthony. *Europe 1815–1960.* London: Longman, 1984.

Theatre History

Brockett, Oscar, and Robert Findlay. *Century of Innovation.* 2d ed. Boston: Allyn and Bacon, 1991.

Brown, Frederick. *Theatre and Revolution: The Culture of the French Stage.* New York: Viking Press, 1980.

Brown, John Mason. *Two on the Aisle.* New York: W. W. Norton, 1938.

Fowlie, Wallace. *Dionysus in Paris: A Guide to Contemporary French Theater.* New York: Meridian Books, 1960

Green, Stanley. *The World of Musical Comedy.* Rev. ed. New York: A. S. Barnes & Co., 1980.

Haskin, James. *Black Theatre in America.* New York: HarperCollins, 1982.

Rowell, George, and Anthony Jackson. *The Repertory Movement: A History of Regional Theatre in Britain.* Cambridge: Cambridge University Press, 1984.

Schumacher, Claude, ed and trans. *Artaud on Theatre.* London: Methuen Drama, 1989.

Willet, John., ed and trans. *Brecht on Theatre.* New York: Hill and Wang, 1957.

Zinder, David G. *The Surrealist Connection.* Ann Arbor, Mich.: UMI Research Press, 1976.

Dramatic Literature

Bentley, Eric C. *The Brecht Commentaries.* New York: Grove Press, 1981.

———. *The Playwright as Thinker.* New York: Meridian Books, 1955.

Edwards, Gwynne. *Dramatists in Perspective: Spanish Theatre in the Twentieth Century.* Cardiff, U.K.: University of Wales Press, 1985.

Guicharnaud, Jacques. *Modern French Theatre from Giraudoux to Genet.* New Haven: Yale University Press, 1967.

Meserve Walter. *Discussions of Modern American Drama.* New York: Heath, n.d.

Olivier, Roger W. *Dreams of Passion: The Theatre of Luigi Pirandello.* New York: New York University Press, 1979.

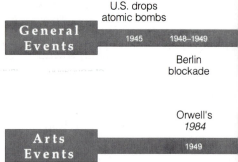

General
Events

U.S. drops
atomic bombs

1945   1948–1949

Berlin
blockade

Arts
Events

Orwell's
1984

1949

Theatre
History
Events

Miller's
*Death of
a Salesman*

1949

Reaction and Recovery, 1945–1968

A man stands at attention, stage center, dressed in a military uniform. Behind him the only scenery is scaffolding. After the lights go down, a spotlight remains on the single actor. Nothing happens for six minutes. A few hippies in the front row try to talk to the actor, but he does not respond. After several minutes members of the audience begin to chat with one another and one man at the back calls out, "Get on with it!" Suddenly several other actors appear, dressed in military style, and begin a silent performance in which they do calisthenics, scrub the floor, and complete other domestic chores. All is done in mechanical unison and the sound of marching feet provides an underlying rhythm. As this action continues, voices from throughout the auditorium begin a group recitation of a poem composed of the words printed on a dollar bill. Without warning, the room is plunged into total darkness. From somewhere among the audience strange Eastern music begins. Actors enter the dark carrying glowing sticks of incense. The actors come very close to people in the audience and the smell of incense is overwhelming.

An actor is revealed sitting in a single spot in the center of the stage. He reads a poem and company members as well as some in the audience repeat phrases in a response reading. It begins quietly with whispered phrases of "Stop the War" and "Freedom Now." Gradually the chants return to a whisper and the actors form a tight circle on stage. They stand shoulder to shoulder as they breathe together and then create a musical mélange of vocal sounds that seem to ebb and flow. Breaking the circle, the actors sit cross-legged at the

Korean conflict — Soviet Union invades Hungary — Berlin Wall built — J.F.K. assassinated — U.S. troops in Vietnam

| 1950–1953 | 1954 | 1956 | 1957 | 1961 | 1962 | 1963 | 1964–1968 | 1968 |

Brown vs. Board of Education — Sputnik launched — Martin Luther King's "I Have a Dream" — Soviet Union invades Czechoslovakia; Martin Luther King assassinated

Hemingway's *Old Man and the Sea* — Boris Pasternak's *Dr. Zhivago* — George Segal's *The Diner*

| 1953 | 1955–1970 | 1958 | 1960–1971 | 1964–1966 |

Pop Art movement — Mark Rothko's art panels for Houston Chapel

Josef Svoboda at Prague National Theatre — Osborne's *Look Back in Anger* — National Theatre, Britain; Open Theatre, NYC — Negro Ensemble Company, NYC

| 1950 | 1953 | 1956 | 1963 | 1965 | 1968 | 1968–1969 |

Beckett's *Waiting for Godot* — Grotowski Polish Laboratory Theatre — The Living Theatre's U.S. Tour

front of the stage. They blow their noses at length, and begin a series of yoga exercises. A convulsive movement leads to a recurring sound that each actor repeats over and over, louder and louder, until their entire bodies begin to vibrate with intensity. Suddenly there is silence, and the actors rise and exit through the audience. Intermission.

This performance of *Mysteries and Smaller Pieces* by The Living Theatre in 1964 is one illustration of theatre's response to the post–World War II world. Alongside traditional offerings, radically new forms of theatre were developed in an attempt to avoid traditional patterns and construct a new and better world.

SOCIAL IDEAS

World War II returned young women and men to the battlefield. The bombing of virtually every major city in Europe in World War II led to the death of civilians, who had previously been safe from the direct impact of war. The Holocaust created the

A TRIP TO THE
THEATRE
IN PARIS, 1953

Great moments in theatre history often pass without the participants realizing the significance of what they have witnessed. The audience members at the Théâtre de Babylone on January 5, 1953, were an exception. From the time they were waiting in line, watching the play's director run to a café next door to find extra folding chairs for the overflow crowd, until the reviews began appearing the next day, the audience had some sense that the first production of Samuel Beckett's *Waiting for Godot* was special. Several factors led to their awareness.

Beckett had finished the play four years earlier. He had been unable to find a director whom he trusted until Roger Blin met with him to discuss the play in 1950. Blin had a great reputation, but little else—no theatre, no company, and no money with which to finance a production. Despite his commitment to the play and a radio reading of part of the script to attract interest, it was not until late 1952 that a theatre was found.

The rehearsal process itself was difficult, as might be expected when a play breaks most dramatic traditions. Several actors who had signed to play Lucky quit. Pierre Latour, playing Estragon, confessed that he never really understood what the play was about. Blin directed the play cautiously, sometimes rehearsing four or five lines for more than an hour. Beckett himself was a commanding presence over the production, always present but seldom explicit in his explanations of the text.

In November, the play was published. The text was now available, and anyone reading it knew immediately that it was unique in the annals of dramatic literature. The play is spare in its dialogue and action. The circular structure of the plot, in which the characters keep returning to the same point, was unusual. The lack of certain information about the characters and their location was contrary to the Ibsenesque structure. How would the play perform? What would the actors do to make the play theatrically interesting? What would be the effect of a play that takes place in a physical void, except for a mound and a tree? These were questions that had attracted journalists and Left Bank intellectuals to the rehearsals and then to the opening night.

The theatre was a converted shop, filled with some 230 folding chairs. There were no back curtains at the rear of the stage, so pieces of cloth had to be sewn together to provide a backdrop. Every production component was done as cheaply as possible. The tree, the single piece of scenery, was made of long coat-hanger wires covered with dark crepe paper. Lighting was provided by three large oil cans with light bulbs—two at the back of the theatre and one offstage to suggest the sun or the moon. The costumes befitted the bum-like nature of the characters: Vladimir wore a long dark coat with unmatched trousers, while Estragon wore a short, nondescript jacket with ordinary trousers. Blin had originally conceived of the play in a circus style, but lack of production funds forced him to the simplest solutions to all problems. That simplicity set the tone for the production and for almost every reading of the play afterward.

The audience's reception was enthusiastic. People wanting tickets would be turned away for the rest of the run. Critics acknowledged the importance of the work. Playwright Jean Anouilh suggested that the play was like watching a philosophical essay performed by clowns. The play did not gain the Paris audience accustomed to classics at the Comédie or musical works at the Opéra, but it was the talk of the arts community.

Beckett was not present for the opening. He preferred to deal with the nerves alone. Nevertheless, when he learned that an actor had modified some stage business on opening night, he quickly wrote to Blin asking that it be changed back to the original. As for the actors and the director, they were immediately besieged with questions about the meaning of the play. Blin wrote to Beckett for assistance with the critics but he never got any. Beckett simply refused to explain his play. The play closed a few weeks later because of prior commitments by the actors. In September, however, Blin revived the production with all but one of the original cast. He then took that production on tour throughout Europe.

specter that an individual's life and death no longer had meaning. The explosion of the atomic bombs in Hiroshima and Nagasaki eliminated the possibility of an individual finding any dignity in death.

The end of the war was both a dream and a nightmare. For some it meant hope for a restoration of normality and a return to the good life. For others, the horror of the Holocaust and the devastating power of the atomic blast at Hiroshima signaled a new era of fear and a frightening awareness of the human ability to destroy everyone and the planet. The end of the war did not guarantee peace. The Berlin blockade of 1948–1949 and the construction of the Berlin Wall in 1961 served as reminders of the continuing tensions between the Soviet Union and NATO countries. Despite periodic protests, the United States and the Soviet Union continued to develop nuclear weaponry. The Cuban Missile Crisis of 1962 underscored the fragility of the peace between the superpowers. The United States placed an embargo on Castro's brand of socialism and endeavored to limit his influence in South America, while the Soviets sent troops into Czechoslovakia in 1968 as they had in Hungary in 1956. The Unites States and the Soviet Union clearly identified spheres of influence that permitted no interference.

European history between 1945 and 1968 was not completely bleak, however.

The Marshall Plan for European economic recovery, the establishment of the European Common Market, the remarkable rebuilding effort throughout the continent after the war, and the ability of nations to sustain their growth despite attacks from extremist groups were all important accomplishments.

At the end of the period, a new postwar generation began to express its political views. In 1968, a youth rebellion occurred in much of Western Europe, reflecting some of the same dissatisfactions as the hippies in the United States. Some young people were content to attend Beatles concerts wearing clothing from London's hip Carnaby Street, but a more serious political and social message was coming from youth protest rallies in Paris and from a violent counterrevolutionary group, the Red Brigade.

In America, a different social culture prevailed in the years following the war. The G.I. Bill of Rights (1947) made the ownership of a home and the right to a college education additional components of the American dream. Americans had fought to protect their lifestyle in the war and they were determined not to return to Depression-style attitudes. Suburbs grew outside of major urban centers, partly as the result of low interest rates available to veterans. Americans wanted their own home with land around it (which for many meant moving to the West); they wanted white-collar jobs rather than laborers' positions; and they elected a president who symbolized a laissez-faire approach to social change and a bulwark of military strength to foreign powers.

Many Americans challenged the American dream because it excluded them. Their dreams had been deferred, to use the phrase of African-American poet Langston Hughes. While the economic fortunes of many advanced, the opportunities for others remained few. Among the groups excluded from the mainstream were the rural poor, who had never really been able to participate in the consumer society; blacks, who had been systematically excluded from society; and women, who refused to accept the role assigned to them in society. More recently, other minority groups identified their exclusion from the nation's image of itself: Hispanics, migrant workers, homosexuals, and the handicapped. By 1968, the question was whether the American dream could expand to include all people and still retain its character.

The challenge to the American dream by minorities is best exemplified by the civil rights movement. The nation had not responded to earlier appeals for equal rights, but the U.S. Supreme Court decision in *Brown vs. Board of Education* in 1954 changed that by declaring that "separate but equal" was not equal. The decision gave judicial support to the efforts of African-Americans to seek redress from injustices done to them. Although the Supreme Court followed its ruling with similar decisions, little change occurred in the lives of most blacks. When in 1955 Rosa Parks refused to sit in the back of the bus in Montgomery, Alabama, as city law required, she sparked a concerted boycott by blacks against the transit company. The civil rights movement had found its key weapon. Economic boycotts were followed by marches, demonstrations, and then sit-ins, in which the demonstrators sat down in the place of alleged discrimination and refused to leave until the situation changed.

Through the legitimacy of its claims and the rhetorical and spiritual eloquence of Martin Luther King, Jr. (1929–1968), the civil rights movement gained in momentum until the middle 1960s. Then, disillusioned with the lack of fundamental changes in their economic situation, many blacks in urban areas took to the streets to express their anger and frustration. In 1965, 34 people were killed in rioting in the Watts district of Los Angeles. Seven people died in a dozen riots in 1966, and New York and Detroit exploded in rioting in 1967. The assassination of Dr. King on April 4, 1968, led to still further racial violence.

ARTS IDEAS

New York supplanted Paris as the center of artistic innovation and excitement after World War II. Prior to the war, visual arts in the Unites States had ranged from the lush desert flowers and Southwestern landscapes of Georgia O'Keeffe (1887–1986) to the idealized versions of American life drawn by Norman Rockwell (1894–1978). After the war, the search for value in art took the predominant form of abstract expressionism. In the social upheaval of the 1960s, a bewildering array of iconoclastic art tested *in Am.* the boundaries of each art form and even the nature of art itself. Since a great many of the artists throughout the time period were American, and since their work influenced what was happening in Europe, this section will treat American arts ideas.

Abstract Expressionism

The term defies simple explanation because it served as an umbrella term for the work of many American artists after 1945. In general, it was a search for value beyond the world of real appearance. It looked for eternal associations between forms and objects rather than ephemeral connections. It was an investigation into the boundaries of traditional art forms while at the same time seeking those modes of expression most appropriate to the modern mentality.

Robert Motherwell (1915–1991) was one of the leading abstract expressionists, with his archetypal shapes and bold, rough lines. Mark Rothko (1903–1970) symbolized what many associate with abstract expressionism: sonorous, somber, and highly formal associations of modulated colors with no evident link to the real world. The artist precluded any realistic connotations by titling his canvases simply as number 1, number 2, and so on. The national imagination was captured, however, by New Yorker Jackson Pollock (1912–1956), who was christened Jack the Dripper by the media. Laying his canvas on the floor, he infused his works with a nervous, frenetic urban energy by dripping, tossing, and flipping paint onto the canvas from all directions.

Many artists sought to clarify the American dream when they tested the distinctions between truth and illusion and between appearance and reality. Jasper Johns (1930–   ) used targets, rows of numbers and letters, and especially American flags, to force the viewer to attempt to distinguish between a sign and a symbol. Covering a painting of an American flag with a waxlike substance called encaustic, he rendered the flag inoperative as a traditional symbol, yet he encouraged the viewer to find new meaning in it. Roy Lichtenstein (1923–   ) painted a portrait of George Washington in the style of American comic strips, urging consideration of the media image of the man and the person behind that image.

WHAAM! by Roy Lichtenstein.　*Courtesy Tate Gallery, London/Art Resource, New York*

Happenings

The search for inherent and eternal American values led to extensive experimentation in the late fifties. Musicians, dancers, dramatists, and artists often worked together to create happenings, chance artworks of loosely structured improvisations. Happenings were spontaneous explorations of objects, spaces, or new ideas. They could be carefully organized preparations for the re-experience of ordinary life (placing ice sculptures on freeways to awaken drivers out of their torpor) or studies by different artists of an artistic concept (such as time or motion).

Dance

In dance, choreography built on the pioneering work of Isadora Duncan (1878–1927), Ruth St. Denis (1878–1968), Ted Shawn (1891–1972), Katherine Dunham (1910?–   ), and particularly Martha Graham (1894–1990). Graham provided a movement vocabulary based on the contraction and expansion of the human form during breathing. She called her works dance/dramas, for they often retold Greek myths with a modern perspective. Merce Cunningham (1922?–   ) explored chance in his choreography, composing pieces in which a movement sequence might be determined by the order in which the movements are drawn out of a hat. He often collaborated with America's premier musical experimenter, John Cage (1912–1992), whose notoriety was assured when he performed a piano solo entitled 4′33″, a study of silence in which the pianist sits down to the piano and never plays a note. Even when engaged in aesthetic speculation, these artists reflected the search for meaning in their lives, something they shared with the dramatists of the period.

Music

In music, American motifs, sounds, and traditions were used in works by Charles Ives (1874–1954), Virgil Thomson (1896–1989), Leonard Bernstein (1918–1991), and especially Aaron Copland (1900–1991), whose "Appalachian Spring" and "Billy the Kid" were studies in American archetypes. American popular music relied heavily on the culture of American blacks for its rhythms and motifs in jazz, blues, and rock 'n' roll. A considerable portion of popular music after 1960 was given over to social statements, frequently critical of the American dream. Folk music gave voice to political dissent in the civil rights and antiwar movements. Country-western expressed the plight of the poor and the rural populations. Music helped shape the youth culture of the 1960s. First with "the King," Elvis Presley, and then with the British invasion led by the Beatles, popular music gave expression to the energy, exuberance, and frustrations of the baby-boom generation. Blending with folk, jazz, Harlem, and Motown sounds, rock 'n' roll made instant world celebrities of Jim Morrison, Jimi Hendrix, Mick Jagger, and dozens of others. Rock also expressed the nihilistic abandon with which many young people faced the future. In general, American artists have been dissatisfied with tradition, usually questioning accepted values. They have been willing to experiment with new ideas and adapt to new situations. They have probed the American conscience, sometimes with care and at other times with indignation, often angering the American public more than pleasing it. Their assessment of the American dream and American values have been accurate, fanciful, or ignorant depending on the artist and on the personal viewpoint of the viewer. Yet these artists have remained determined to say what they believe, and in this they are similar to American theatre artists.

THEATRE HISTORY

The period 1945–1968 witnessed the culmination of one theatrical trend—the dominance of realism. It also witnessed a continued exploration into new forms, new purposes, and new techniques of theatrical production as theatre reacted to the sweeping social developments of the period.

Occasion

National Theatres. Perhaps the most secure theatres were the national theatres that continued to perform in many countries around the world. The oldest of the national theatre companies is the Comédie-Française, founded in 1681. This huge producing organization in 1946 included two auditoriums, 80 actors (only 30 were permanent members, elected into membership just as they were in Molière's day), and more than 400 technicians. Referred to by its critics as a "museum," the Comédie performed a rotating repertory dominated by the classic repertoire, with productions of Molière's plays outnumbering all others by a 3–1 margin. Actors at the Comédie performed a wide range of roles, but the approach was nearly always conservative. The excellence of the company, based on repetition of productions so that they achieved a high degree of polish, continued to draw spectators, although the company depended on its governmental subsidy to survive.

The English Parliament approved the foundation of a National Theatre in 1949, although no company was established until 1962. At that time the existing Old Vic company was named the National Theatre under the direction of Sir Laurence Olivier. Typically, the National produced a broad repertory with the classics featured. Unlike the Comédie, the National did not establish a permanent company, as London's leading actors chose to maintain their freedom and associate with the company for a limited time only. A second national theatre was chartered by the English Parliament when they created the Royal Shakespeare Company under the leadership of Peter Hall (1930–   ) in 1961. Originally the company played half of the year at Stratford and half in London, but gradually both programs grew to be year-round operations. The early years of the company were notable for their experiments in avant-garde productions, including a highly praised and influential production of *Marat/Sade* directed by Peter Brook.

Other national theatres continued to flourish. The Danish Royal Theatre celebrated its bicentennial in 1948, and the National Theatre of Norway celebrated fifty years of production in 1949. The National Theatre of Greece, established in 1932, continued to present European classics and touring companies in addition to traditional Greek drama. In the Western Hemisphere, the Popular Theatre of Mexico also focused on Western classics and plays by young European authors.

The Commercial Theatre.   The commercial theatre continued to be the center of theatrical development, particularly in the United States. The reality of professional theatre as a business is embodied in the theatre of Broadway. The realities of business in large measure shaped the direction of the creative talent employed on Broadway. Investment in a Broadway show is a great risk; relatively few shows that premiere each year are hits and only one or two of these (almost always musicals) produce sizeable profits. Therefore there is a tendency to produce shows that look likely to succeed (often meaning that they fit into the pattern of a previous hit). It also means that shows with artistic merit or critical acclaim are more and more difficult to produce on Broadway because they have limited appeal and therefore might not be able to return their investment.

Nevertheless, Broadway theatre continued to attract top talent and enthusiastic investors. More than 30 theatres with seating capacities above 500 each made up the league of Broadway theatres. At any one time, at least 16 of them had shows in performance. Despite the financial hazards, Broadway remains the center of theatre activity in the United States.

Although each country offered minor differences in terms of organization and costs, the commercial theatres in most countries operated on a similar basis. The primary emphasis was on business, and the demands and limitations of the box office were the principal controlling factors.

Regional Theatres.   One attempt to escape the tyranny of the commercial theatre was the development of permanent, professional acting companies away from the capital cities (or in the case of the United States, New York City) in the hope that these theatres would both broaden the audience base and revitalize the theatre itself.

The movement to decentralize the theatre in the United States began after World War II, when Margo Jones (1913–1955) in Dallas (1947), Nina Vance (1913–1980) in Houston (1947), and Zelda Fichandler (1924–   ) in Washington, D.C. (1949) founded

A SELECT LIST OF MAJOR U.S. REGIONAL THEATRES

Alley Theatre	1947	Houston
Arena Stage	1950	Washington, D.C.
Milwaukee Repertory	1954	Milwaukee
Guthrie Theatre	1963	Minneapolis
Seattle Repertory	1963	Seattle
Center Stage	1963	Baltimore
Actors Theatre	1964	Louisville
Long Wharf Theatre	1965	New Haven
Theatre Atlanta	1966	Atlanta
A.C.T.	1967	San Francisco
Mark Taper Forum	1967	Los Angeles
Goodman Theatre	1969	Chicago

regional theatre companies producing a full season of professional productions with their own actors, designers, and technicians. By the end of the 1960s, the major regional theatre also included the American Conservatory Theatre in San Francisco, the Seattle Repertory Theatre, the Tyrone Guthrie Theatre in Minneapolis, the Goodman Theatre in Chicago, and Actors Theatre in Louisville.

In 1959, the creation of regional theatres in France came about not through the work of individual promoters but through government action. France decentralized the arts in an attempt to provide cultural activities outside Paris. The government established subsidized theatre companies in various large municipalities, hoping that these theatres would develop styles that reflected the cultural heritage and interests of their own audience. In St. Étienne, Jean Daste (1904–) created a theatre that toured throughout the region and performed during the summers in a circus tent in an attempt to reach a working-class audience. The repertoire was not unusual—plays by Molière, Shakespeare, and occasional farces or modern works—but the style was intended to produce a sense of festival and celebration. Roger Planchon (1931–) started his Théâtre de la Cité in a suburb of Lyon. Highly influenced by Brecht, Planchon's work focused on social and political issues. His *Three Musketeers* was pure parody, utilizing images from American western films, puppet shows, and physical comedy to demystify the concept of the popular heroes. In later productions, Planchon experimented with a wide variety of production techniques, including the use of film sequences, simulations of "happenings," and use of nontheatrical space for performance.

A different approach characterized the work of Jean Vilar (1912–1971) at Paris's Théâtre National Populaire (TNP). Working with a government subsidy, Vilar set out to create a ". . . theater of simple effects, without pretensions, accessible to all." Vilar's "region" was those sections of Paris and its surroundings that were not part of the typical cultural milieu. Vilar began with a series of "weekends" in which a full range of programs was presented in various municipal buildings throughout Paris and its suburbs. Determined to build an audience of the working class, he worked with trade unions to arrange special group audiences for his productions at a large theatre. Ticket prices were kept very low, inexpensive meals were available at the theatre, and curtain time was set early to be more convenient for workers who could come to the theatre immediately after work. The production standard was high, although budgets were kept very low. Vilar, using his experience at the Avignon Festival and his training under Charles Dullin, used simple black curtains as backdrops and utilized lighting extensively to create location and mood.

The Piccolo Theatre of Milan was the first regional theatre established in Italy in 1947, and other permanent theatres followed in Rome, Genoa, Turin, and other cities. During the 1960s these theatres, subsidized by regional and municipal governments, represented an attempt to establish a "popular" theatre in Italy, presenting low-cost productions of great plays for an audience composed of the working class and students. The theatres introduced plays of Shakespeare, Molière, and Pirandello, but although they were successful for a period of time, the movement floundered after 1968.

Elsewhere in Europe regional theatre continued to be an effective mode of presentation. German theatre continued to be organized around the regional or municipal theatre dependent on subsidies from local, regional, and national governments. In contrast to the general pattern, established permanent companies were often found in smaller towns in Germany as well as in major cities. In England, too, the repertory theatre continued to function, with as many as 50 regional companies presenting full seasons.

Among the aims of regional theatres were the representation of regional ideals and customs, additional training for young actors, directors, designers, and technicians, and the encouragement of new plays, away from the demands of the commercial theatre centers.

The Independent Theatre Revisited.

However, for many members of the theatre community, even the regional/municipal theatres were too clearly tied to governmental influence and commercial strictures. New York City itself diversified its theatrical activity after World War II, when the League of Off-Broadway Theatres was formed in 1949. Outside the major theatre district surrounding Broadway, these theatres are noted for their more intimate staging of smaller plays (those with fewer sets and technical demands and usually with smaller casts). By definition these off-Broadway theatres seat less than 300, in contrast to Broadway houses, which seat up to 2,000. Plays in these smaller surroundings do not require the financial backing or the extended and extensive popularity of a Broadway production. Some of the best plays by Tennessee Williams and by Eugene O'Neill have received their first professional productions off-Broadway. In the 1950s off-Broadway was noted for companies that ran shows in repertory, many of them classics. In the 1960s, it became the location of single productions that appealed to a limited audience, either because of their subject matter or because they were works by new playwrights.

In France, young producer/director such as Jean Vilar, Jean-Louis Barrault (1910–), and Roger Blin (1907–1984) began to produce what became known as the "New Theatre." Plays were produced in modest physical facilities with little technical support. Often the plays relied on shock value or black humor to force audiences to recognize the condition of humanity. It was these "New Theatres" that housed the earliest productions of the "absurdists," including the first production of Samuel Beckett's *Waiting for Godot* in 1953. Jean-Louis Barrault's Théâtre Marigny, begun in 1946, explored the possibilities of "total theatre." Although Barrault was a full member of the

Comédie-Française, his theatre interests were decidedly avant-garde. Barrault's theatre employed an eclectic mix of theatrical techniques, including music, dance, mime, physical farce, and acrobatics, with physical image more important than the spoken word. Particularly successful with the plays of Claudel, Barrault was appointed director of the state-subsidized Odéon Théâtre in 1959, where he introduced numerous new scripts into a repertoire previously dominated by the classics.

Other theatre also sought to diversify their offerings beyond those available from the subsidized or national theatres. The English Stage Company, under the artistic direction of George Devine (1910–1965) and Tony Richardson, devoted itself from 1957 to 1965 to the introduction of new young English playwrights, such as John Osborne, Arnold Wesker, and John Arden. In Oslo, a group of 19 young actors banded together as the Studio Theatre in 1945 to introduce the techniques of Stanislavski and a modern repertoire to Norwegian audiences. Their production of *Our Town* toured extensively, often appearing before audiences in the northern regions of the country that had never seen live theatre before. In Athens, the Art Theatre, founded in 1942 by Karlous Koun, produced an avant-garde repertory including Williams, Beckett, and Genet until 1959, when it changed its focus to ancient Greek drama. In 1951 the Théâtre du Nouveau Monde was founded in Montreal, producing French classics and introducing new works by French Canadians. The Haiyuza (Actors' Theatre) of Japan, founded at the end of World War II, included a main company as well as several smaller studios to allow experimentation by young practitioners. The Actors' Theatre introduced many Western authors, including Molière, Brecht, and Strindberg to Japanese audiences, and also promoted writings by young Japanese authors.

Theatre Festivals. Another form of commercial theatre that gained popularity during this time period was the "theatre festival." This term has been used rather indiscriminately and often describes events ranging from a gathering of various theatre troupes to a summer theatre designed principally to attract tourists.

The Avignon Festival was established in 1947 by Jean Vilar as one of his many innovative attempts to provide a theatrical experience entirely free of the trappings of commercial theatre. To achieve this, Vilar proposed an annual festival to be held during July, the month when most professional theatre in France were closed. Using a large open platform stage set in the courtyard of a historic palace, Vilar presented visually arresting productions of standard fare produced in a heroic style designed to fill the huge space. Popular from its inception, Avignon quickly developed into a theatre event of international importance. A similar event, the Edinburgh Festival, also began in 1947, and from the beginning included music, dance, theatre, opera, and art, including important performing groups from throughout the world. This international exchange of theatre forms and ideas was a major contribution.

Tyrone Guthrie (1900–1971) provided the model for another festival approach at the Shakespearean Festival at Stratford, Ontario, in 1953. Originally conceived to provide a cultural center to Canadian theatre and to serve as a training ground for Canadian actors and directors, the festival grew into a year-round theatre operation, following the example of Britain's Stratford festival. Other Shakespearean troupes are now located in Ashland, Oregon; in Stratford, Connecticut; in San Diego, California; and at various other locations throughout the United States. A notable example is New

GROTOWSKI'S POLISH LABORATORY THEATRE

*T*he Polish director Jerzy Grotowski (1933–   ) began his small theatre in Opole, Poland, in 1959. In 1965 he moved the theatre to the university city of Wroclaw, where his company was renamed the Polish Laboratory Theatre. During the 1960s his innovative acting techniques and unusual staging of plays caught the attention of prominent theatre artists in Europe. With the publication of his book *Towards a Poor Theatre* in 1968, Grotowski's ideas became the springboard for considerable experimentation in acting theory in both England and the United States. Despite the rigors of his actor training, his ideas remain current in the theatre today.

Grotowski believes that the actor is a spiritual investigator, seeking the meaning of myth and human experience for the audience. The actor is therefore more than an interpreter. The actor is a person who opens himself to the full meaning of a dramatic action in order to share that experience with the audience. To do this, the actor must also be a psychic investigator, someone who seeks to be exposed to the truths of her inner nature. The actor does not choose to read a line, but gives in to the experience of the line. The actor does not accept accumulated methods of reading a line, but instead gets rid of all methods in order to be honest to the line.

The actor in Grotowski's theatre bears an awesome responsibility. Personal responsibility includes knowing and accepting the full meaning of the play's action for his own psychic structure. Responsibility to others in the company involves total exposure of self as they all undergo their own personal investigations. Responsibility to the audience requires recognition that the actor is the audience's means of reaching the full meaning of the play. The result of this responsibility is a moment of truth for the actor and the audience, a moment when the audience and the actor become involved in a collective confrontation with the truth of human existence.

As one would expect from the foregoing, a Grotowski theatre piece is unlike most others. Grotowski created unique actor-audience relationships for each play. He placed the audience outside a box peering in on the action of *The Constant Prince*. He transformed the entire theatre into an interior of a mental institution for *Kordion*; actors moved around the room while the audience sat on the beds or against the wall. Apart from the creation of a unique space, Grotowski employs few traditional theatrical effects. The actor's body and face are his makeup. Costumes are minimal and never ostentatious. Props are employed only if they are extensions of the action.

Perhaps Grotowski's most famous production was *Akropolis,* in which the condemned of a concentration camp build the equipment that will be used to kill them. During the construction, they discuss various stories and myths of Western literature, frequently re-creating them for a few moments, and sometimes changing roles while telling them (Romeo becomes Juliet, for instance). The actors wear no makeup but use the muscles of their faces to express a mask-like horror of their situation. They are dressed in gray rags. They move about the performance with no regard for the audience, which is seated in and around them. They seek no applause or appreciation from the audience. Theirs is a holy task, as they see it, and spiritual and psychic truth needs no reward.

York City, where Joseph Papp first introduced free performances of Shakespeare in Central Park in 1954, and launching a theatre company, the New York Shakespeare Festival, that became a dominant force in the American theatre.

Experimental Theatre. The most influential experiment in theatre during this period took place in Poland under the direction of Jerzy Grotowski (see insert). However, numerous other artists also sought to redefine theatre by adopting different texts, new styles of performance, unusual combinations of art forms, or radical actor-audience relationships.

For sheer experimentation with form and guaranteed controversy, American audiences in the 1960s trekked to off-off Broadway, which was centered around East Greenwich Village. Off-off-Broadway productions were held in cafés, lofts, garages, and churches. It was an alternative theatre to the commercialism of both Broadway and (increasingly) off-Broadway. It was the fringe of theatre activity in that it tested the limits of audience endurance and appeal and questioned the very roots of theatre as an art form. At times outrageous (one theatre called itself the Theatre of the Ridiculous) and at other times intensely reflective (as in some of the plays produced by the Judson Poets' Theatre), off-off-Broadway productions eschewed elaborate staging for actor-audience interaction or performance exploration. Many productions included no stage as such, but transformed open playing areas to suit each action of the play. The audience sat wherever they could find seats, including among the actors themselves. This in turn led to the exploration of new possibilities for theatre, something for which Theatre Genesis, Café Cino, Café La Mama, and American Place Theatre became well known.

Frequently, these theatres developed a script through interaction between the actors and the playwright. Joseph Chaikin (1935–) in his Open Theatre, for instance, would discuss the feelings of the actors about the Vietnam War, then try scenarios about their feelings through improvisation; the playwright would write down what had

A scene from La Mama's experimental production of a trilogy of Greek works.   *Courtesy German Information Center*

happened or what came to mind as a consequence of the improvisations, and then present a script the next day for further testing. Many of the directors and actors in this kind of arrangement preferred to call their works "in progress," because they would continue to evolve even after an audience had been invited. Playwrights who worked in this manner included Megan Terry (1932–) author of *Viet Rock*, and Jean-Claude Van Itallie (1936–) who wrote *America Hurrah*. Similar theatres could be found throughout the world, often existing for only a few seasons, performing with minimal financial or technical support, but experimenting with new concepts of script, performance, and audience-actor relationships.

In England, Joan Littlewood (1914–) launched the Theatre Workshop in London in 1953. It came to represent the spirit of innovation. Featuring the work of new playwrights, including Brendan Behan (1923–1964) and Shelagh Delaney (1939–), Littlewood's early work was highly Brechtian in nature, creating a sense of raw energy unlike typical West End polish and sophistication. The group's most successful piece, *Oh, What a Lovely War!* (1963), was a parody documentary of World War I. Developed by the company during the rehearsal process, the show combined war songs with music hall melodies, military uniforms and commedia costumes, public speeches and gag humor. Slides ranging from war photos to statistics on the numbers of dead and wounded accompanied the action, forcefully presenting the antiwar message of the play.

Similar theatres could be found in many locations throughout the world as artists, many of them young, "set up shop" in storefronts, garages, churches, and other available locations to pursue specific and innovative approaches to performance. For some, the pursuit of art was an aesthetic goal; for others the goal was more attuned to social and political aims.

Theatre of Protest. Theatre productions protesting against various socio-political situations were not uncommon in the theatres of the 1960s, and some theatre groups were formed specifically to carry such protests to the public. These theatres explored the same themes as the experimental theatres, but their expressed aim was to incite social change. In their organizational patterns as well as in their productions, they reacted against the trends of society. Some sought to create a sense of unity within the audience to combat the dehumanization of life, while others deliberately provoked the audience to overcome public apathy and create active response.

The San Francisco Mime Troupe, founded in 1959, utilized commedia dell'arte techniques to mount original works commenting on subjects ranging from the Vietnam conflict to environmental concerns. Performing in public parks and various neighborhoods, the Mime Troupe used high energy, direct audience contact, and physical comedy to present their concerns.

Peter Schumann's New Hampshire–based Bread and Puppet Theatre (1961) evolved out of Schumann's experiments with large puppets as part of dance performances. Utilizing giant puppet figures (as much as 18 feet in height), Bread and Puppet attempted to evoke a sense of ritual celebration, with processions, symbolic imagery, and audience participation being major elements of the production. Gentle in nature, the group's productions typically ended with the sharing of bread as a gesture of unity.

In Paris, the Théâtre de le Commune used Brechtian production techniques in the early 1960s to mount productions of plays by Brecht, Peter Weiss (1916–1982), and contemporary authors. The work of the theatre extended beyond the presentation of the plays, with discussion groups, lectures, public readings, and similar events serving to arouse interest and to direct audience response to the theatre's work.

Luis Valdez (1940–) was a member of the San Francisco Mime Troupe who reacted to the plight of Chicano farm workers in California by organizing a theatre in 1965. He started El Teatro Campesino to encourage workers to join in a general strike protesting the working conditions forced upon the Chicanos; its first formal performances were at weekly union meetings. The short skits, or *actos*, they developed were frequently bilingual and usually comic. Masks, songs, and physical comedy were highlights of these early performances. In 1967 the theatre group separated its activities from the union and established an independent artistic organization.

The Living Theatre. The work of the Living Theatre illustrates the feeling of going to one of these theatres. Started in the living room of Judith Malina (1926–) and Julian Beck (1925–1985) after the war, the Living Theatre's growth and apparent decline reflect the history of alternative theatre in the United States. Despite changes in size and membership during the 20-odd years of its existence, the group consistently has dedicated itself to non-violent revolution, anarchy, the expansion of human consciousness (both their own and that of their audience), and experimentation with form. As the search for theatrical invention and political discussion increased in the 1960s, so did the popularity of the Living Theatre; when events of the streets overtook their political ideas in the late 1960s, their impetus faltered. But their history has symbolized the needs of a portion of America's theatre audiences for challenging ideas presented in nontraditional form.

In 1954, the Living Theatre moved to a loft in lower Manhattan, where they continued their investigation of the function of form through a number of symbolist plays. Their chief aim was to aid the audience to become more than it had expected to be. They wanted a theatre of impact, not somnambulance. With the recently published ideas of Antonin Artaud (1896–1949) to encourage and guide them, they looked for means to disturb the theatre spectators. Until 1959, this impact was achieved through performance techniques rather than through the content of the plays themselves. Between 1959 and 1964 they worked in a theatre seating 169 people in lower Manhattan. Here two of their most famous works were produced, Jack Gelber's *The Connection* (1959) and Kenneth Brown's *The Brig* (1963).

After eviction from their theatre by the Internal Revenue Service, the Becks moved to the coast of Belgium, where their commitment to each other (and their families) and to their anarchic beliefs were steeled. They also developed their own plays through experimentation and improvisation. Their return to the United States in 1968 coincided with social upheaval and a general preference for the new and spontaneous rather than the traditional and tried. Heralded as the embodiment of political theatre, their nationwide tour over the following year included performances of an updated version of *Antigone*, and three plays conceived by the group, *Mysteries and Smaller Pieces* (1964), *Frankenstein* (1965), and *Paradise, Now* (1968).

What brought the Living Theatre to end their tour and leave the United States was not the conservative audience, however, but leftists who argued that if the Living Theatre really believed in what they said, they would quit performing theatre and join the fight in the streets. Without a radical constituency, the Living Theatre no longer had an audience, except for intellectuals curious about their methods and their impact on other theatres. The group left the United States in 1969, some of them going to Brazil, where authorities became unhappy with their calls for revolution. Judith Malina and Julian Beck returned to the United States, and the theatre led a disjointed existence until its revival in the late 1980s.

Teatro de Arena. Brazil's Teatro de Arena did not begin as a theatre of protest. Organized in 1954 by Oduvaldo Vianna Filho but under the artistic directorship of Augusto Boal (1931–   ) beginning in 1956, this São Paulo theatre developed into Latin America's most distinctive theatre by 1968.

In its early years it focused on realism, introducing plays by foreign authors, and then expanding into new realistic plays by developing Brazilian playwrights who dealt with contemporary Brazilian life. Influenced by Brecht, the theatre began to focus more and more on social problems. Beginning in 1962 the group began to produce classics, including works by Molière and Lope de Vega, interpreting the plays to illuminate specifically Brazilian situations. This in turn led to a unique theatrical form that combined historical situations, current events, actual words from speeches given by public officials, and myth to create a moral lesson for theatre audiences. Scripts were developed collectively, with elements of nearly every dramatic style included. Each work was unified by the presence of a narrator who "told" the story and interrupted to provide necessary information. A unique acting system allowed each actor to play each role at some point during the presentation, thus blocking audience identification with the character. This "Arena Contra . . ." theatre, actually a series of plays in which "Arena" commented on a variety of issues, was openly didactic. In the final moments, the chorus of actors directly urged the audience members to take action. Performed essentially without scenery, the "Arena contra . . ." plays were easily taken on tour into small villages and remote locations, and theatre became one of the most effective tools of education in Brazil.

African-American Theatre.   In the 1960s several new theatres were specifically formed in the United States to address the needs of the African-American community. Although several African-American theatres had existed in previous years, they received little attention or financial support from the commercial theatre community. It was difficult for African-American artists to make a living on their work for African-American theatres alone; and there were few employment opportunities outside of these theatres. However, this situation began to change in 1964 with the formation of the Black Arts Repertoire Theatre School in New York. Within four years, virtually all major cities in the United States had theatres that expressed the experiences and the feelings of African-Americans.

Two theatres in particular gained national attention and recognition. The New Lafayette Company founded in 1967 set its mission to be an exclusive African-American theatre. Headed by Robert Macbeth, it has promoted the plays of several African-American writers, including Ed Bullins (1935–) and Imamu Baraka (1934–). The Negro Ensemble Company was formed in New York City in 1968. The artistic director was Douglas Turner Ward (1930–) and the executive director was Robert Hooks (1937–). These men had considerable playwriting and acting experience, as well as the know how to get critical and public interest in new plays and actors. The theatre has championed the work of new African-American playwrights, including Lonnie Elder III (1932–) and Charles Fuller (1939–), and has provided acting opportunities for many young African-American actors.

The search for a true Black theatre was not limited to the United States. In Brazil, Abdias do Nascimento formed the Black Experimental Theatre in 1945 as a reaction to his realization that although half of the population of Brazil was black, he had never seen a black person performing in the theatre. Beginning with a production of Eugene O'Neill's *The Emperor Jones*, the Black Experimental Theatre discovered and presented unknown texts reflecting the black experience and encouraging young authors to write new plays as well, all as a part of the theatre's aim to reclaim a culture that had been destroyed as a result of colonization.

This sampling of theatre groups indicates the tremendous range of theatrical production that developed during this time. period. The new variety of theatres, with diverse reasons for being, and with a wide range of aesthetic and political goals, obviously was accompanied by changes in theatre buildings.

Location

One trend in new theatre construction was the "performing arts center" in which several performing arts rooms were built at one location. Lincoln Center for the Performing Arts opened in 1965 with an opera house, a large theatre for musicals and dance, and a legitimate theatre, the Vivian Beaumont. In the following years similar structures were built in Los Angeles and Washington, D.C. Generally, these buildings were traditional in structure, although their existence was meant to establish a sense of cultural importance. The most significant developments in theatre architecture were the development of various smaller theatre spaces that created new actor-audience relationships.

One of the most influential theatre buildings of this period was constructed to house the Stratford (Canada) Festival in 1957. Rejecting the traditional proscenium stage, the Stratford Festival Theatre features a thrust stage surrounded by a semicircular bank of seats with actor entrances provided through ramps and vomitoria. Although the theatre accommodates more than 2,200 people, the design places all spectators closer to the stage than was possible in a traditional orchestra/balcony arrangement. A permanent architectural set based on Elizabethan theatres was included, featuring a

The Stratford Festival Theatre (Canada).   *Courtesy Stratford Festival*

raised central platform and several entrances. This basic thrust design was also used at the Chichester Festival Theatre in England and at the Guthrie Theatre in Minneapolis.

Other structures were built in reaction to production trends that indicated that no one theatre space was suitable for every play. The Municipal Theatre of Malmo, Sweden, anticipated this trend in 1944 with an adjustable proscenium stage, a removable thrust apron, and partitions that could change the size of the auditorium for individual projections. The Questors Theatre, built for an amateur company in Ealing, England, is also typical of theatres built to meet the new demands. This 1964 theatre featured sliding proscenium screens that allowed the size of the opening to be adjusted to suit a particular show or design. Removable seating in the pit area allowed the acting space to expand into the auditorium, to create either a large apron, a thrust stage, or even a full round. A grid system above the auditorium allowed portions of the seating area to be segmented to ensure proper sight lines. The Loeb Drama Center built at Harvard University in 1960 used computer-controlled mechanisms to manipulate walls, the stage floor, and seating areas to create the desired configuration.

For many theatres during this period, a formal theatre was superfluous. Experimental theatres performed in tiny spaces with 50 seats in Paris, in converted warehouses in London, in lofts in New York, and in parks and city squares in various locations throughout the world. For these groups, the theatre was defined not by mechanical and structural devices but by a gathering of performers and audience.

Performers

The techniques of production were equally challenged by the development of diverse theatrical styles. Designers, directors, and actors were challenged to develop new styles through the use of new and different materials, and in some cases they were asked to redefine the role of each artist in the collaborative creation of theatre.

The director remained the central organizing force in theatre production. For some directors, the opportunity to direct involved functioning as a producer as well. Although Margo Jones's career included Broadway work (she co-directed *The Glass Menagerie* and also directed Maxwell Anderson's *Joan of Lorraine*), her impact on American theatre came from her determination to establish a theatre with a permanent repertory company away from New York. In 1947 she established Theatre 47 (it was renamed each New Year's Eve) and established a pattern for regional theatre development that is still being fulfilled. As a director, Jones was particularly noted for her development of new plays and her interest in theatre-in-the-round at an early date.

Other directors moved from the role of actor into the position of director. Elia Kazan was one of the most successful directors on Broadway during this time. A member of the Group Theatre and Actors Studio, Kazan was noted for the fiery emotionality he achieved through the use of Method acting. The essence of Kazan's directing style lay in the revelation of character, and one of his primary skills was individual actor coaching. Besides such Broadway hits as *A Streetcar Named Desire* and *Death of a Salesman*, Kazan was also successful in directing films.

While a successful career in the theatre led Kazan to film, the reverse was true of Franco Zeffirelli (1923–), whose first experiences were in film and opera. Beginning as a film designer, he began directing opera in 1951. An invitation from the Old

Vic to stage *Romeo and Juliet* was his first major directorial opportunity in the theatre. Zeffirelli's directing was rooted in an overall conception, frequently including major design ideas, which established the proper atmosphere and setting for the play. His interpretations were often unusual, and he became known for his ability to introduce a fresh, modern sensibility into classic works. His successes in Italy, France, England, and America made Zeffirelli one of the first "international" directors.

The theatre career of Roger Planchon (1931–   ) was an indirect result of his interest in poetry and film. Untrained in theatre, Planchon made his first directorial effort with a review-style burlesque of contemporary performance. Planchon interpreted the director's role as the supreme interpreter of the script and felt that every production was an act of criticism. He introduced the term *scenic writing* in reference to the director's responsibility to create images, actions, and even words necessary to make the interpretation effective. Influenced by a wide range of artistic styles, including Jarry, Artaud, the symbolist poets, and Japanese art, Planchon was particularly interested in the power of the visual image. Planchon's primary intent was to force the audience to change its perception of the play, of society, and of itself.

As the concepts of Craig and Appia became generally accepted, the role of the designer became more and more integral to the entire conception of the production. Designers were no longer asked to re-create an existing reality; instead they were asked to participate in the creation of a new reality, focusing more on the establishment of mood and environment than on accuracy.

American scenic designer Jo Mielziner (1901–1976) was an assistant to Robert Edmund Jones before he began to design on his own in 1924. Since that time, he has probably won more awards for set design than any other American, for he was early associated with the work of American playwrights in the 1920s and 1930s. Then, after the war, he designed the original productions of such classic plays as *The Glass Menagerie, Death of a Salesman, Winterset,* and *A Streetcar Named Desire.* Mielzinger's style moved away from the predominantly expressionistic style of Jones toward a "selective realism" that chooses only a few key realistic elements to indicate location and setting. These few components then gain a symbolic significance by virtue of their selection, and become associated with various characters in the play. In *Death of a Salesman,* for instance, Mielziner created a kitchen where Linda, the wife, darns socks, and an upstairs bedroom for the two sons. He then designed an open playing area or medieval platea in front of the kitchen to represent Willy's dream world. Looming over the whole set were the outlines of skyscrapers, suggesting the imposition of outside reality into Willy's private little world.

Oliver Smith (1918–   ) designed sets for Broadway musicals *(The Sound of Music, Hello, Dolly!)* featuring a restrained elegance coupled with technology that produced rapid and inventive scene changes. Boris Aronson (1898–1980), although he was successful in opera, ballet, and serious drama, was also best known for his sets for musical theatre *(Fiddler on the Roof, Cabaret).* Ming Cho Lee (1930–   ) began a career that has extended into the 1990s with his work at the New York Shakespeare Festival, where his skeletal designs created abstract environments for the play.

Jean Rosenthal (1912–1969) was one of the pioneers of contemporary stage lighting; indeed some historians say she invented the position of lighting designer. Her early work included designs for the Mercury Theatre of Orson Welles and John

Scenic design by Jo Mielziner for *Winterset*.   *Courtesy New York Public Library*

Houseman and designs for choreographer Martha Graham, with whom she continued to work throughout her lifetime. Her collaborators noted her talent at script analysis, her sensitivity to nuance, her attention to detail, and her mastery of the "tools" of lighting. One of the first to emphasize the sense of movement in lighting through precise cueing, Rosenthal felt that lighting must be unobtrusive, even though it was a primary contributor to the creation of atmosphere. She successfully designed lighting for dance, opera, musical theatre, and drama; many of this century's most talented lighting designers served their apprenticeship under her.

Such differing forms of theatre placed new demands on actors as well, and a study of the actor during this period might profitably be a study of methods rather than individuals. To be sure, the "star" performer was still in demand. Mary Martin (1913–1990) utilized her vocal skills and vibrant charm to become the most successful musical performer of the period; Olivier continued his sterling career, adding performances in modern plays by John Osborne and Ionesco to a growing list of triumphs in classics. Along with Barrault and Vilar, Gérard Phillipe (1922–1959) was prominent on the French stage, coupling his classical skills with his immense popularity with a young audience. The Danish star Poul Reumert (1883–1968) played a vast range of roles, including Tartuffe, Macbeth, and Peer Gynt; his career culminated with his 75th-birthday jubilee performance in 1958. Ryszard Cieslak achieved international fame through his performances with Grotowski.

During this period of experimentation in all facets of theatre, different styles of acting were developed as well. French actors were frequently trained in mime, following the examples of Étienne Decroux (1898–   ) and Jacques Lecoq (1921–   ). This French focus on physical control contrasted with the English emphasis on vocal technique and intellectual analysis. In America, the Actors Studio continued to develop the heritage of the Stanislavski system. Formed by several former members of the Group Theatre in 1947, the studio provided a place for actors to continually work on their craft. Lee Strasberg became the dominant force after 1948, shaping the teaching around Stanislavski's concepts of sensory and emotional recall to free the actor's own emotions. People differed in their evaluation of the Studio's success. For some, it produced a revolutionary new and exciting personal style of performance. To others, it produced inconsistent actors who were brilliant on one night and miserable on another.

Some forms of theatre seemed to demand an entirely new approach. Judith Malina of the Living Theatre rejected Stanislavski's concepts, striving instead to find a way for the actor to liberate her own personality rather than assuming a character. She wanted a style of acting that was immediate and raw. It would include violence, ugliness, and incredible energy that would be communicated directly by the actor to the audience.

Another approach to acting was developed by Joseph Chaikin (1935–   ) and Roberta Sklar at the Open Theatre. The Open Theatre operated primarily as a workshop rather than as a training center or as a producer of plays. In fact, it avoided productions as much as possible. In contrast to the individualized approach of the Actors Studio, the Open Theatre was a group theatre that worked closely together at all times. Several of their ideas are illustrative of the cultural trends of the 1960s.

Chaikin rejected the Stanislavski concept of superobjective because it suggested that an individual is rational, coherent, and single-purposed. Further, he believed that the actor is a social being who is aware of and responding to a surrounding world; that world presents moral dilemmas that do not resolve themselves through simplistic decisions. A person does not live in isolation, but as a member of a society, and the Open Theatre centered on the group, not the individual.

The company built a sense of ensemble based on close interaction and interdependence. In such a situation of trust, it was possible for the actor to function more freely, escaping the bounds of reason to directly confront life issues. Members took turns serving as director, and the playwright was a member of the group who recorded and developed ideas that evolved out of interaction between the playwright and the company.

The Open Theatre became known for acting exercises that emerged from these principles. They were mostly based on various forms of improvisation, a free and unscripted interaction between actors with a given set of circumstances. The "chord" was an unstructured vocal improvisation to build group unity and sensitivity. Transformation exercises had actors improvising a scene and then suddenly changing their characters to express what they were unable to express as the first character. A timid student interacting with a professor, for instance, might suddenly become a bull and charge the professor, who must quickly decide how to transform herself in order to respond. The purpose of such an exercise was to break the role expectations and easy solutions actors have to situations. The use of improvisation both for actor training and as a rehearsal technique was further developed by Viola Spolin (1906–   ), and her book *Improvisation for the Theatre* was influential with many performers, directors, and teachers.

Audience

The audience during this time is as difficult to define or limit as are the styles of performance. The continued development of national theatres and cultural centers, along with the escalating cost of production at the commercial theatre, created an elite audience for mainstream theatre. The rise of the regional theatre movement increased the total audience for the theatre, but in most cases the regional theatres attracted an upper-class audience from their own geographical region. Various "popular" theatre movements, such as the TNP in France, were successful in developing a working-class audience, although the cinema remained the principal "theatre" for that class.

A significant new audience was developed by the experimental theatres that appealed to a mixed group of intellectuals, bohemians, and students. For some, this remained a small, select group. Grotowski's theater seated very few individuals for any performance, and other theatres developed devoted followers who shared a particular group's artistic or political opinions. Frequently these audiences were younger and included a large number of students. Theatres such as the Bread and Puppet or San Francisco Mime Troupe reached an audience that was not oriented toward the theatre.

Audience behavior varied greatly. At the national and cultural center theatres, evening dress was common and the audience was essentially passive. A performance of the TNP might include well-dressed businesspeople as well as factory workers still in their working clothes. At an experimental theatre, dress was usually casual and audience response could range from intellectual stimulation to political outrage. Not uncommonly, audience members would leave in disgust, engage the actors in argument, or even join in the action on stage.

One result of such divergence was an even stronger dichotomy between "high art" and "low art," and a growing debate concerning the definition of "culture." These arguments were more than philosophical, as frequently the availability of funds from governments or foundations were limited to a certain type of event.

Standards of Judgment

At times, such funding was also linked to "critical approval." Frequently this meant approval by the critics of the daily newspapers, who filed reviews immediately after a performance. These reviewers sought to base their judgments on accepted critical standards, but by nature such reviews were extremely subjective. Approval by certain daily critics was considered essential for the survival of a commercial venture. The responsibilities of these critics has been a subject of controversy in the theatre. One summary of the drama reviewer's responsibilities included the following: good writing to sell copies, serving as a consumer guide, providing valuable feedback to participating artists, providing guidance to the artistic community as a whole, encouraging new artists, and objectively recording performance standards of the day. Often these critics were essentially anonymous figures, and theatre people, recognizing the power of the reviewer in the commercial theatre, frequently challenged their credentials.

Other critics established a body of work that provided commentary on the theatrical experience. Not surprisingly, these writings indicate a wide divergence in concepts of the nature and purpose of theatre. Michael Kirby and John Cage (1912–1992) were among critics (they were also practitioners) who advocated a theatre that defied rationality and relied entirely on chance. Theatre should not be tied to a literary text but should be free to create in the moment of performance. The essence of theatre was its temporary quality, its existence "in the moment," and this should be exploited, not avoided. Theatre was instantaneous creation, not interpretation.

For Armand Gatti, French playwright and critic, the theatre was a means of revolution as originally presented by Brecht. His sentiments were shared by the American Herbert Blau, who condemned the commercial theatre and called for a theatre that would serve to reform societ. Proponents of African-American theatre such as Larry Neal proclaimed a radical position that called for total rejection of existing social values and art. Existing conditions were beyond salvation, he asserted, and a radically new approach was necessary, based on concepts introduced from Third World countries.

This position was in conflict with the concepts of Grotowski, who maintained that the theatre's concern was not with social or political action but with behavior. Theatre for him dealt with essential issues of human existence that transcended political, social, or religious issues, seeking to reveal biological responses that occur under stress. Only through this level of self-understanding could change occur.

One of the most influential critical writings of the period was *The Empty Space* by British director Peter Brook (1925–   ). Brook identified four types of theatre—deadly, holy, rough, and immediate. Deadly theatre, according to Brook, dominated the contemporary stage. In it, culture was equivalent to dullness, and "better" meant polite, tame, easily absorbed.

The holy theatre was theatre that attempted to restore the lost sense of ritual to contemporary culture. The attempt was not to imitate old rituals but to invent new ones. It was not dependent on the spoken word but was based on intense work and dedication.

Rough theatre was a theatre of delight—if holy theatre used a prayer, then rough theatre used a belch. Rough theatre was socially and politically committed and utilized a wide range of theatrical tactics. Rough theatre abandoned the sophistication of modern theatre to return to a more elemental form designed to produce an immediacy of communication with the audience.

Immediate theatre, which Brook favored, was a theatre that challenged accepted values. In this form, the purpose of the artist was to indict society, to challenge accepted values, but this was achieved through a sense of liberation and community. In a clear anticipation of his later career, Brook noted that good theatre was utterly dependent on the specific audience and situation, and that the definition of "good theatre" would continually change.

A Global Perspective

Yoruba Traveling Theatre

*T*he riveting sound of "talking drums," the sound of African melody, dancing that spans the distinctions between ancient and modern: these are only a few of the elements that form the theatrical presentations of the Yoruba Traveling Theatre. Begun by Hubert Ogunde in 1945, the form is continued today by many troupes throughout Nigeria.

Ogunde's popular theatre form resulted from experiments with folk opera, which he modified to reflect the urban life of the Yoruba. The result is an eclectic mixture of elements, including political propaganda, dancing, singing, juggling, and other variety acts. Some of his earlier works (*Bread and Bullet*, 1950) were openly political, and one, *Song of Unity* (1960), was commissioned to celebrate Nigeria's independence. His most famous work, *Yorubu Ronu! (Yoruba Awake!)*, written in 1964, resulted in his being banned from parts of Nigeria.

Duro Ladipo utilized the same basic form as Ogune, but rather than focusing on contemporary society, Ladipo chose to explore Yoruban history. *Oba Koso*, a play in seven acts, is typical of his work. The "opera" utilizes poetry, singing, dance, and orchestra to tell the story of an ancient tribal king, Sango. Unable to control his generals in a civil dispute, Sango loses control in a battle and kills innocent bystanders. In remorse, he hangs himself, but the elders of the society refute the shame of the act, convincing all that Sango has been rewarded for his suffering and become a god. At this glad news, all the people rejoice "Oba Koso!"—"the king did not hang."

The play includes tribal drumming, dancing, solo and choral singing, special effects (Sango can breathe fire), narration, dialogue, Egungan masquerade costumes, and ritual battles. An orchestra of various drums, gourds, bells, and a gourd flute provide constant accompaniment, providing a relentless and exhilarating pace and rhythm.

Some critics scorn the popular theatre form and hold it responsible for the lack of literary growth in Nigeria. The traveling theatres are extremely popular among the people, however, and more than 40 established companies tour throughout the region and appear regularly on television and on film. *Oba Koso* has been performed in remote villages, in university theatres, at the palace of the reigning Yoruba monarch, and on tour in the United States.

DRAMATIC LITERATURE

Two bums stand near a lonely, withered tree, looking out on a barren landscape. They have no purpose except to wait for someone they have never met, someone who may never come. Their conversation goes nowhere because they themselves go nowhere. They consider suicide but aren't sure that they will succeed, or that it will prove anything. They talk, but they always return to the point in the conversation from which they began. They are the representatives of modern drama, the inheritors of those characters who once traversed the Greek stage and spoke to the gods, often as gods. Where Greek actors had to add stature to their demeanors through masks and raised headdresses in order to achieve the size of their characters, modern actors must adorn themselves with tattered clothes and all the despair they can muster. Where once there was a chorus to echo the voices of tragic actors, Vladimir and Estragon in *Waiting for Godot* merely shout to the wind, but nothing returns. The world of modern drama is bleak indeed. Why?

Absurdism

At the end of World War II, no dramatic situation could realistically portray the ghoulish nightmare from which Europe was only awakening. A new form was needed to articulate the absurdity of the human condition. French playwrights found that form in what was eventually labeled the Theatre of the Absurd. There was never a manifesto for absurdism, nor a meeting of the writers who fell into that category. But their work shared the view that life is pointless, whimsical, and cruelly indifferent to human feeling and needs. What separated them from the existentialists was that they relied on theatrical means to express absurdity rather than the logic of reasoned argument. Each play was a theatrical metaphor for the absurdity of life, and the playwrights developed the dramatic possibilities of the metaphor rather than the ideas the metaphor represented. These metaphors were alternately comic and tragic, usually symbolic, and always unusual or bizarre.

Samuel Beckett **(1906–1989).**   The writer whose work is regarded as quintessential absurdism is Samuel Beckett, an Irishman who lived in Paris and wrote in French. *Waiting for Godot* was the cause célèbre of absurdism, receiving international attention for its circular structure, its sense of futility, its images of the world as a void, and its apparent absence of action. Later works, including *Endgame* (1957), *Krapp's Last Tape* (1958), and *Happy Days* (1961), continued to anger audiences because of their bleak perspective on life and their manipulation of the theatre itself. (One could never be sure if Beckett was sometimes making fun of his audience, as in *Breath*, where the curtain rises, a baby cries, breathing is heard, and the curtain comes down.) Beckett's is a world

A scene from the original production of *Waiting for Godot.* *Courtesy Roger Pic, Paris*

without time: characters often have no memory. There is no location: *Endgame* is frequently interpreted as taking place after the destruction of World War III. The world is without logic: a woman is buried up to her waist in *Happy Days* and her husband has become a mole.

Eugene Ionesco (1912–   ).   Romanian-born Eugene Ionesco adds further to an understanding of absurdism, for his is a world in which inanimate objects grotesquely take on a life of their own and in which language is less a means of communication and more an instrument of confusion and uncertainty. Ionesco often takes a single image or idea and extends its theatrical possibilities to its limit. He explores the banality of language in *The Bald Soprano* (1950), which takes place in a typically English cottage with typically English people speaking typically English clichés that have no connection to one another whatsoever. *Rhinoceros* is perhaps the most famous of Ionesco's full-length plays. First produced in 1960, the play is a study of mass psychology and conformity in which everyone but the hero turn into rhinoceroses.

Jean Genet (1910–1986).   Jean Genet is another French writer whose work has absurdist qualities, but whose vision of reality, as expressed in *The Balcony* (1956) and *The Maids* (1947), is ultimately more sinister than that of either Beckett or Ionesco. Genet accepts the absurdist view that life has no meaning, but he pursues an extension of that position, that evil is as valid a way of life as goodness. Genet gives to evil a religious and saintly guise, while stripping goodness of any presumptions to superiority. In addition, he suggests that each role an individual plays in life is merely that—a role, and nothing more. It can be discarded for another because there is no final certainty of anything, including personality. The role is to be filled; it matters not who plays it.

Other Europeans investigated the capacity of the theatre to express the absurdity of life, including Fernando Arrabal (1932–   ), Günter Grass (1927–   ), and Arthur Adamov (1908–1970). Today, their work has lost its initial surprise and audacity. The absurdist view of life was immediately felt as long as one was close to the events that spawned it. Once Europe returned to some degree of economic security, the anger and frustration that underlay absurdist drama seemed petulant and overbearing. The bleak outlook began to give way to other forms of protest and expression. For those who share the metaphysics of absurdism, however, these playwrights remain relevant and vital today.

British Drama

Absurdism was predominantly a French movement with strong advocates in Spain, Germany, and Eastern Europe. Although England's playwrights imitated the absurdists with some notable successes, the concepts of absurdism never took hold. Only David Storey (1933–   ), whose *Home* (1970) is very similar to *Waiting for Godot*; N. F. Simpson (1919–   ), whose *One-Way Pendulum* (1959) offers hilarious images of death; and Tom Stoppard (1937–   ) have found the irrationality and devaluation of language appropriate subjects for investigation. Stoppard loves to combine other dramatic forms with absurdist plots—*Rosencrantz and Guildenstern Are Dead* (1966) is a combination of *Hamlet* and *Waiting for Godot*; *The Real Inspector Hound* (1968) is an improbable match of Agatha Christie and Luigi Pirandello—yet he is only marginally absurdist, for his love of language and his desire to extend the logic of syntax to the logic of the universe are too verbal and thoughtful to fit the genre.

Harold Pinter (1930–   ).   However, England's most consistently acclaimed playwright in the period combined absurdist elements with pungent social satire. The plays of Harold Pinter defy strict categorization, blending as they do elements of absurdism and satire with farce, superrealism, and even abstraction. Many of Pinter's plays take place in a single room inhabited by one or two characters who are about to be replaced by an intruder. The dialogue is realistic yet sparse, and interrupted by long pauses and silences. Characters feel they are on the defensive against sudden attack for hidden motives. The combination of menace and comedy, the intrigue of unrevealed intentions, and the witty dialogue keep his work in the forefront of European drama through such plays as *The Birthday Party* (1958) and *The Homecoming* (1965). Pinter remains active as playwright, director, and screenwriter.

Social Drama.   Pinter is but one of many English playwrights who have contributed to a revival of British drama in the postwar period. In 1956, *Look Back in Anger*, a play by John Osborne (1929–   ), received critical acclaim for its attention to the feelings of modern British men and women. The major character, Jimmy Porter, rants and raves his way through life, critiquing every British institution from the posh newspapers and the monarchy to his own marriage. Ostensibly a love triangle in which Porter's wife is replaced by another woman, who then leaves when the wife returns, *Look Back in Anger* is most effective as an expression of simmering hostility toward a world in which one cannot achieve greatness or feel fulfilled as a person. The play spawned an Angry Young Man movement, a very loose collection of playwrights who addressed the contemporary English social conscience in a variety of styles and personal voices. Included in the group were John Arden (1930–   ) and Arnold Wesker (1932–   ).

Despite the favorable critical reception to the Angry Young Man movement and to the social criticism found in those plays, the vitality of British theatre in the 1960s is demonstrated by the number of playwrights who diverge from this style. Joe Orton (1933–1967) in *Loot* (1960) and *What the Butler Saw* (1966) presented a zany version of black comedy that makes people laugh at destruction and death. Edward Bond (1934–   ) brought horror and violence to the stage in *Saved* (1965) to discuss its social and psychological roots. Simon Gray (1936–   ) in *Butley* (1971) and *Otherwise Engaged* (1975) created characters who seemed incapable of finding direction in their lives.

French Drama

In France, the two most prominent nonabsurdist playwrights were Henry de Montherlant (1896–1972) and Jean Anouilh. Montherlant was most indebted to the style of Jean Racine in such works as *The Master of Santiago* (1948) and *Port Royal* (1954). His focus was the internal struggle between faith and mind.

Jean Anouilh's style and orientation are similar to Cocteau's and Giraudoux's in his love of the theatrical, his use of language, and the refusal of many of his characters to accept the sordidness of life. In plays like *Thieves' Carnival* (1938) and *Waltz of the Toreadors* (1952), Anouilh was frankly theatrical, reminding the audience through various devices that they are watching a play and that whatever may happen on stage is the result of the imposition of the author and not at all something that is possible in real life. The overriding emotional state of the characters is anomie, a vague dissatisfaction with life combined with a sense that one can do nothing about it. Whereas Cocteau created a world of myth and Giraudoux of fantasy, Anouilh's characters reside in a state of bittersweet nostalgia.

This discussion of post-1945 playwrights is by no means exhaustive or even inclusive of all important writers. Each nation had its own spokesmen who articulated the feelings and experiences of their countrymen. Eduardo de Filippo in Italy, Alfonso Sastre (1926–   ) in Spain, Rolf Hochhuth (1931–   ) and Peter Handke (1942–   ) in

Germany, Vaclav Havel (1936–   ) in Czechoslovakia, and Slavomir Mrozek (1932–   ) in Poland are among the writers who enlivened the national theatres of their countries. There was no such thing as a European theatre, but there was a single European experience—world war—and that gave the writers a similar base from which to express their own national perspective. As that single experience faded into memory, newer and more varied styles appeared to give voice to a new generation.

American Drama

The search for the American dream has been a primary subject of American drama since 1920. Playwrights have depicted American life in their settings, characters, and ideas. They have created characters whose dreams are typical of Americans in their situation. Those playwrights who believe in the dreams of their characters naturally tend toward comedy, while those who see little prospect for the dreams write tragedies that probe the causes of failure. These two attitudes—optimism in comedy and disillusionment in tragedy—form two trends of American drama. In addition, African-American writers since the 1950s have formed a third trend. They have expressed the exclusion of minorities from the American dream by developing their own visions of reality.

Comedy after 1945.   When World War II ended, two Broadway hits were still running: *Harvey* and *Life with Father*. The first is a joyful hymn in praise of idiosyncrasy and eccentricity. The second is another look at an American family beset by problems that are eventually overcome through love, compromise, and family unity. In 1946, *Born Yesterday*, by Garson Kanin, used the education of a stock "dumb blond" figure (made famous by Judy Holliday) to end political corruption in Washington, D.C. Other long-running comedies of the period included *Mr. Roberts* and *Teahouse of the August Moon*. At a time when Americans were attempting to realize their dreams in the suburbs through hard work and practical sense, these plays elevated the American soldier to the status of a hero in defense of simplicity, honesty, and virtue.

Neil Simon (1927–   ).   In the 1960s, America's most successful comic playwright secured national recognition with such hits as *Barefoot in the Park* (1963), *The Odd Couple* (1965), and *Plaza Suite* (1968). Neil Simon's early plays usually revolved around two people with incompatible personalities and needs who are thrown together in an unusual situation. The results are filled with physical humor, wit, and social satire. Simon's brisk pace, comic rhythms, and superb one-liners tend to overshadow a recurrent message: in spite of the difficulty in establishing relationships and making them last, tolerance, acceptance, love, and understanding make it possible.

Tennessee Williams (1911–1983).   Williams's first success—and his most enduring one—was *The Glass Menagerie* (1945), with its unforgettable trio of family members caught in the candlelight of their lives in St. Louis. Amanda, with her memories of gentlemen callers; Laura, with her delicate glass animals; and her brother, Tom, with his dreams of escape and withdrawal in movies have become symbols from a symbolic play. Amanda's Southern background suggests the death of Southern lifestyle; Laura's crippled walk and fear of going outside her home evoke feelings of insecurity and fears of the unknown; and Tom's restlessness represents the need to be free and to experience other worlds. The arrival of reality into Laura's world in the guise of the Gentleman Caller and the shattered glass he leaves behind are among the best examples of dramatic poetry in literature.

Like Ibsen and Chekhov before him, Williams found the tragedy of life within the household. His families are composed of individuals struggling for dignity and decency, yet incapable of defending themselves against the truths virtually thrown at them by unfeeling relatives or by a harsh external world. The prototype of this individual is Blanche in *A Streetcar Named Desire* (1947). She lives on the memory of a South that treated women with gentility, yet she has long ago lost her own propriety. She has become an alcoholic and has withdrawn from any reality that may force her to see the truth of her condition. Propelled to a tragic confrontation with the truth by her sister's husband, Blanche goes insane. Williams began his career searching for human dignity in the modern world, as in *The Rose Tattoo* (1951), *Cat on a Hot Tin Roof* (1955), and, to a lesser extent, *Sweet Bird of Youth* (1959). His later plays, however, denied the possibility of dignity altogether and focused on the neurotic reaction to this realization.

Arthur Miller (1915–). The dignity of the individual is also a theme of Arthur Miller, who began his career at about the same time as Williams. Miller found great faith in the individual, no matter his or her station in life. In *The Crucible* (1953) and *Incident at Vichy* (1964) he presented conflicts between individuals seeking to achieve a modest life for themselves, and a society prohibiting the individual from realizing self-worth. The major concerns of Miller's career include moral conscience and social responsibility (*All My Sons*, 1947), family relationships (*The Price* 1968), and the dignity of the average individual in an increasingly overwhelming world.

Death of a Salesman (1949) is Miller's most famous play and an excellent example of his dramatic themes. The story is of Willy Loman's desire to understand the failure of the American dream in his life. Willy followed the American dream. He wanted to be a salesman who traveled from city to city, always known and liked by everyone he met, and always making a great deal of money. He wanted the material goods of a growing America: a car, a refrigerator, and a home of his own. Above all, he wanted a family, including a wife who cooked for him and kept house while he was on the road, and sons who would be well-liked in school and be successes when they grew up. Willy dreamed the American dream, but it didn't come true.

The play presents a complex of interpersonal tragedies. Willy's oldest son, Biff, has lost faith in his father; as a result, he has lost faith in himself. The tragedy of Happy, the younger son, is that he has completely accepted Willy's dream, but it is no more successful for him than it was for Willy. Linda, Willy's wife, has followed the American dream as much as Willy. She sees herself as a housewife who must support her husband through all adversity. Her tragedy is losing the person who gave her life meaning, yet being unable to do anything about it.

Miller continued his pursuit of the dignity of the common man both in later plays and in theatre essays. Even when American theatre turned from disillusionment to despair in the 1960s, Miller continued to dramatize the struggle of the individual to find self-worth.

Before 1960, social criticism by playwrights was usually muted: characters decided their own destinies and not necessarily as the consequence of national trends. As the nation moved into the era of street violence, hippie lifestyles, new moralities, and public demonstrations, however, the tone of the playwrights changed. American institutions, including the cherished family, came under bitter satirical attack, and American audiences weren't sure what to expect when they went to the theatre.

Heading this attack on Americana was Edward Albee (1928–   ), whose short plays *The Zoo Story* (1958), *The Sandbox* (1959), and *The American Dream* (1960) were first performed off-Broadway. Under Albee's incisive, often vicious treatment, the American family became more a hornet's nest than a haven for wounded animals. Confessions were greeted with indifference, insecurity with hostility, and inaction with derision. Albee exaggerated family life until, like a Macy's Thanksgiving Parade balloon, it became grotesque. In *The American Dream*, Albee parodied the family of the 1950s by inverting role expectations and expanding a few qualities of each character. Daddy is ineffectual, impotent, and incompetent; Mommy is talkative, domineering, and opinionated; they can get no satisfaction from anything in life, including clerks, plumbers, and social workers. Frustrated and waspish, they emasculate everyone around them, including their son, the boy they raised to be the American dream. In *Who's Afraid of Virginia Woolf?* (1962), Albee explored the unwritten agreements and unspoken acknowledgments that exist between people. The vitriolic dialogue of George and Martha, who duel for possession of their nonexistent son, reveals their pain of insecurity and incompetence. Albee created other families with hidden secrets and sad truths in *Tiny Alice* (1964) and *A Delicate Balance* (1966).

African-American Drama.   African-American playwrights in America probed the consequences of being excluded from the American dream. Focusing on the psychosocial impact of that exclusion, they created their own dreams for African-Americans and articulated the pride of African-American culture. The impetus for this new drama came from the commercially successful *Raisin in the Sun* by Lorraine Hansberry (1930–1965). Produced in 1959, the play demonstrated to Broadway producers that there was a wide audience for drama about African-Americans. The close family relationships and obvious American dream (the mother wants a home of her own away from the city) made the play popular with all audiences.

In the 1960s, a new African-American arts movement sought to create a theatre for the community that would be different and separate from white society and its interests. Most of the drama of the period was social theatre and its messages were political if not revolutionary. James Baldwin (1924–1987), a successful novelist and essayist, wrote *Blues for Mister Charlie*, one of the biggest off-Broadway hits of the 1963–1964 season. More aggressive in the search for new African-American voices in the theatre was Ed Bullins (1935–   ). Bullins, the resident playwright of the New Lafayette Theatre in New York City, wrote several plays that shocked middle-class white audiences, including *In the Wine Time* (1968) and *Electronic Nigger* (1968).

The work of Imamu Baraka (LeRoi Jones) (1934–   ) is representative of African-American drama in the 1960s. Baraka wrote for African-Americans about black-white relationships. He suffused his plays with the hatred and violence stored in the soul of many African-Americans for decades. *Dutchman* (1964) is a modern adaptation of the myth of a man condemned to float on a ghost ship for eternity. The man of the play

A scene from *Raisin in the Sun* with Douglas Turner Ward and Claudia McNeal.
Courtesy Lawrence and Lee Theatre Research Institute

is a young African-American who is riding on a subway car. A white woman enters and goads him into attacking her. She stabs him, however, and then waits for another African-American man to victimize. The play is unsettling in its implications; its raw emotions and immediate subject matter made it one of the outstanding plays of the decade.

Musical Theater.   When Richard Rodgers (1902–1979) and Oscar Hammerstein II (1895–1960) collaborated on *Oklahoma!* in 1943, they solidified the trend in the American musical toward all-American imagery and story line, archetypical characters, and the sounds and rhythms of American lifestyles. *Oklahoma!* is already a folktale, a story passed from one generation to another, filled with images of a glorious past and moral lessons for an uncertain future. With its cowboys and farmers, its wholesome lifestyle and humorous view of the new and unusual ("Everything's up-to-date in Kansas City"), and its determination to pioneer new land for future generations, *Oklahoma!* captured the spirit of the 1940s. More important, it told a story through songs the audience could immediately follow, with lyrics easily remembered. The choreography of Agnes DeMille was an astonishing blend of ballet and square-dance steps, integrating all the movement into the visual picture of the American West. DeMille's use of dance to promote the action of the story (especially in a famous dream sequence between Laurie and Curley) became standard in future musicals.

Further, Rodgers and Hammerstein established a pattern for the musical that they would use through the 16 years of their collaboration, in *South Pacific* (1949), *The King and I* (1951), *Carousel* (1945), and *The Sound of Music* (1959). The typical plot centers around a couple who are in love but are prevented from coming together by some difficulty presumably beyond their control (race and war in *South Pacific*, race and background in *The King and I*, age and status in *The Sound of Music*). A second couple either sings of idealized love or provides comic relief. A blocking character or villain at the fringe of the hero's society threatens to overwhelm him through bad advice or by taking the heroine for himself. The vision of reality is that nature is alive, beautiful, and filled with song; evil exists in the world, but is confined to a few people who are overcome by love and honesty. (Even in *The Sound of Music*, in which Nazism is the villain, the family escapes because of the love of a soldier for the family's daughter.)

Throughout the 1950s and early 1960s, the structure of the musical changed little, yet the composers and lyricists created some of the most memorable works in Broadway musical history. Alan Jay Lerner (1918–1986) and Frederick Loewe (1904–1988), who had scored a major success with *Brigadoon* in 1947, followed that with arguably the most famous of all musicals, *My Fair Lady* (1956). Leonard Bernstein (1918–1991) teamed with lyricist Stephen Sondheim and book writer Arthur Laurents to create *West Side Story* (1956). Jerry Herman (1933–   ) wrote the music and lyrics for two hits, *Hello, Dolly!* (1965) and *Mame* (1966). Critics praised Meredith Willson (1902–   ) for his *Music Man* (1957), and Jerry Bock (1925–   ) and Sheldon Harnick (1924–   ) for their *Fiddler on the Roof* (1964).

The period also saw the increased importance of the choreographer. Jerome Robbins (1918–   ) had already used dance to tell the story of sections of *On the Town* (1944); when he choreographed *West Side Story*, dance became the chief vehicle of moving the plot forward. The opening dance of the Jets and the Sharks established the use of movement to provide exposition and introduce characters. In every moment of the story, dance extended the lyrics and dialogue and gave new information that could not be conveyed by words alone. So successful was this blend of movement and action that Robbins both choreographed and directed *Fiddler on the Roof*. Since then, many choreographers have directed their own shows and become the central artistic vision for the musical. In fact, by the 1970s, most successful directors of musicals were also choreographers.

Hair (1968) signaled the success of the rock musical; it demonstrated that the musical could adapt to new musical structures and sounds. With its driving rhythms, hard rock beat, electronic instruments, and repeated lyrics, *Hair* moved from off-off-Broadway, to off-Broadway, and then to a long run of 1,750 performances on Broadway. Described as an "American tribal love rock musical" by its collaborators—Galt MacDermott, Jerome Ragni, and James Rado—*Hair* proved its contemporaneity by mentioning many of the issues of concern to Americans in the late 1960s: drugs, new morality regarding sexuality, the generation gap, hippies, peace demonstrations, anti-war protests, pollution, and, of course, long hair. With clever choreography to suggest that everything was spontaneous, the musical parodied everything from Lyndon

Johnson to the Supremes. It did not begin a new wave of rock musicals, for only Andrew Lloyd Webber's rock opera *Jesus Christ Superstar* (1971) and Stephen Schwartz's improvisational *Godspell* (1971) were successful, but it expanded the musical vocabulary of the musical, which in later years would utilize country-western, jazz, and pop music.

CONNECTIONS

The styles and techniques of recent European writers are too current to make any final judgment about their long-range significance. Most of the writers discussed in this chapter are still living or have died within the past 10 years. Further, the conditions that prompted their particular subjects are still a part of world experience, making the predominant responses of anger, reform, withdrawal, and despair very much applicable to current life. Just as there was a shift from withdrawal to despair after World War II, another shift may occur as new playwrights appear.

Therefore it is quite difficult to assess the influence of the period's most prominent style, absurdism, on theatre and the media in the 1980s. An additional difficulty is that absurdist playwrights relied heavily on techniques from the silent-film era. What can be identified as an absurdist technique in the films of Mel Brooks, for example, can also be attributed to the films of Charlie Chaplin, Laurel and Hardy, and the Marx Brothers. Devaluation of language, illogical sequences, bizarre antics, and even the loneliness of the individual can all be found in Buster Keaton or the Keystone Cops. Thus, absurdism today is probably more indebted to its film antecedents than to its antecedents in drama.

The clearest example of absurdism in the media has been the two-year-long television series *Mary Hartman, Mary Hartman*. A late-night parody of soap operas, the Norman Lear–produced series generated the feeling of an absurdist play. Mary was a housewife who sought satisfaction in her clean kitchen with good coffee and a happy family. But the world becomes strange to her when her family is kidnapped, her best friend becomes a country singer, her father is revealed to be the Fernwood Flasher, and her sister has an affair with a priest. She diverts her attention to daily rituals to insulate herself from the chaos of the outside world (the school coach drowns in a bowl of soup at her kitchen table), but these rituals soon assume impossible proportions. She retreats to the kitchen sink, hiding beneath it and hoping no one will interrupt her privacy with still more catastrophes. Later she loses all contact with the outside world and demands that the phone company install a hotline to reality in her house. The hotline seldom rings. Near the end of the series, she visits a toy store, sees a doll house, and crawls in to play house the way she would have liked to play reality. Her life is devoid of purpose, and she must construct a dream world to impose rationality on a world gone crazy.

The movies of Mel Brooks also exhibit many absurdist characteristics, although they are suffused with an overriding sense of joy and abandon that is more reminiscent of silent films. Life to Brooks is a musical comedy; his characters invariably find themselves on stage performing to an unappreciative audience. His movies are filled with visual antics and clowning *(Silent Movie),* disintegration of reality *(Blazing Saddles),* and verbal nonsense *(Young Frankenstein).* A parody of old movies, *Young Frankenstein* also suggests the absurdity of life in its fantastical image of the monster marrying the heroine and settling down to middle-class life. These examples could be multiplied— the film version of Jerzy Kosinski's novel *Being There,* the parody of airline disaster films such as *Airplane,* the humor of Richard Pryor, and the short-lived television series *Police Squad.* All of these are absurdist in their conviction that life is illogical, and the more someone tries to impose logic on it, the more illogical it becomes. However, only *Mary Hartman, Mary Hartman* is close to a true sense of the absurd, for in it the world does not have a happy ending, the heroine will not return to humor us another day, characters die and their loss is painful to others, and insanity appears to be as logical as reality. Ultimately everything can be viewed as absurd, including going to school; however, when the absurdity pains us for its lack of resolution, then it is a likely descendant of the theatre of the absurd. The absurdists would say of reality what Adlai Stevenson once said after losing a presidential election: "I'm too old to cry, but it hurts too much to laugh."

SOURCES FOR FURTHER STUDY

Social/Art/Philosophy Background

Greenberg, Clement. *Art and Culture.* Boston: Beacon Press, 1961.
Hughes, Robert. *Shock of the New.* New York: Alfred A. Knopf, 1981.
Lucie-Smith, Edward. *Art Now: From Abstract Expressionism to Superrealism.* New York: William Morrow, 1977.
————. *Cultural Calendar of the 20th Century.* New York: E. P. Dutton, 1979.
Obst, Linda Rosen, ed. *The Sixties.* New York: Random House/Rolling Stone Press, 1977.
Rosenberg, Harold. *The De-Definition of Art: Action Art to Pop to Earthworks.* New York: Horizon Press, 1972.
Russell, John. *Pop Art Redefined.* New York: Praeger, 1969.
Stearns, Marshall, and Jean Stearns. *Jazz Dance: The Story of American Vernacular Dance.* New York: Schirmer Books, 1968.

Theatre History

Allen, John. *Theatre in Europe.* London: John Offord, 1981.
Bradby, David. *Modern French Drama: 1940–1990.* Cambridge: Cambridge University Press, 1991.
Bordman Gerald. *American Musical Theatre: A Chronicle.* New York: Oxford University Press, 1978.
Brook, Peter. *The Empty Space.* New York: Avon Books, 1968.
Croyden, Margaret. *Lunatics, Lovers, and Poets: The Contemporary Experimental Theatre.* New York: McGraw-Hill, 1974.
Fowlie, Wallace. *Dionysus in Paris: A Guide to Contemporary French Theatre.* Cleveland, Ohio: World Publishing Company, 1967.

Greenberger, Howard. *The Off-Broadway Experience.* Englewood Cliffs, N.J.:
    Prentice-Hall, 1971.

Innes, Christopher. *Holy Theatre: Ritual and the Avant Garde.* Cambridge: Cambridge
    University Press, 1981.

Jones, Willis Knapp. *Behind Spanish American Footlights.* Austin: University of Texas
    Press, 1966.

Kirby, E. T., ed. *Total Theatre.* New York: E. P. Dutton, 1969.

Luzuriaga, Gerardo, ed. *Popular Theater for Social Change in Latin America.* Los
    Angeles: UCLA Latin American Center Publications, 1978.

Rimer, J. Thomas. *Toward a Modern Japanese Theatre.* Princeton, N.J.: Princeton
    University Press, 1974.

Sanders, Leslie Catherine. *The Development of Black Theatre in America.* Baton Rouge:
    Louisiana State University Press, 1988.

Schevill, James. *Break Out.* Chicago: Swallow Press, 1973.

Shank, Theodore. *American Alternative Theater.* New York: Grove Press, 1982.

Ziegler, Joseph Wesley. *Regional Theatre.* New York: Da Capo Press, 1977.

Dramatic Literature

Esslin, Martin. *Theatre of the Absurd.* Garden City, N.Y.: Anchor Books, 1961.

Grossvogel, David I. *The Blasphemers: The Theater of Brecht, Ionesco, Beckett, Genet.*
    Ithaca, N.Y.: Cornell University Press, 1962.

Hayman, Ronald. *British Theatre since 1955.* Oxford: Oxford University Press, 1979.

Taylor, John Russell. *Anger and After: A Guide to the New British Drama.* New York:
    Pelican Books, 1963.

Miller, Arthur. *The Theatre Essays of Arthur Miller.* Robert Martin, ed. New York:
    Viking Press, 1978.

C H A P T E R

18

In Search of a
Future, Post-1968

General Events	First man on the moon
	1969

Arts Events	Solzhenitsyn Nobel Prize for literature
	1970 1971
	Sylvia Plath's poetry; *The Bell Jar*

Theatre History Events	Stephen Sondheim's *Company*
	1970 1971
	Int'l Center for Theatre Research in Paris

No one would have considered it a viable plot for a play, but now a dissident playwright stood on a platform following his inauguration as president of Czechoslovakia. In 1969, the plays of Vaclav Havel were banned in his native Czechoslovakia. Imprisoned on more than one occasion, Havel chose to remain in Czechoslovakia rather than seek exile abroad. Unable to see his plays performed, he arranged for them to be carried to the West and published there. Gradually, his reputation as a playwright grew, as his relationship to the absurdists and the political power of his works gained notice in the West. In Czechoslovakia, his reputation also grew as an outspoken leader of the dissident movement protesting social and political conditions. He was arrested several times during the 1980s, but continued to write his plays. An active participant in the movement that finally led to the overthrow of the Communist government, Havel was elected as the leader of the country and their representative to the rest of the world.

This blurring of the distinction between theatre and the world, between art and life, is one of the primary developments of recent theatre. Faced with a world in which long-standing institutions no longer seemed viable and basic concepts of physics,

Watergate; President Nixon resigns	Americans hostage in Iran	AIDS recognized	Berlin Wall crumbles; Tienanmen Square Massacre in Beijing, China
1973–1974 1975	1979–1981 1981	1983	1989 1991
Vietnam War ends	Columbia, first space shuttle		Soviet Union collapses

	Alice Walker's The Color Purple	Toni Morrison's Beloved
	1982	1987

A Chorus Line opens	Cats opens on Broadway		Producer Joseph Papp dies
1975	1980	1983	1991
	A Chorus Line longest-running show on Broadway		

economics, and ethics were questioned, the theatre responded with new styles of performance that echoed the fragmentation, the lack of linear development, and the uncertainty of modern existence.

SOCIAL IDEAS

Global Revolution

For many, the years 1968 and 1969 were filled with a mixture of extreme emotions, from confident optimism (as expressed by the phrase "the dawning of the Age of Aquarius" and the Woodstock Festival) to despair over political and social concerns (riots in several American cities and on U.S. campuses). In Europe, student and worker demonstrations in Paris focused attention on social dissatisfaction across the Continent. At the time, the left-wing ideology of most of the demonstrators created the image of an impending collapse of capitalism, and some commentators even wrote of concern for democracy. By 1990, however, it was the bastions of communism that had fallen, and freedom and democracy were hailed as the victors of the Cold War.

The collapse of the Soviet Union in 1991 and of the entire Soviet-communist empire in the two years preceding it rank among the most important events not only in this period but in the century. The image of two superpowers with their multiple nuclear warheads pointed at each other had shaped the conscience of a generation of Europeans and Americans, who had come to take the threat of nuclear annihilation as a fact of life. The shape of a new world order after 1991 remains in doubt, but several conditions can be noted: the political collapse of the Soviet Union was at least partly the result of its economic collapse; the economic power of Germany was the nucleus for a European economic community rivaling in size the old Soviet system; Japan had challenged the United States as an economic competitor; and the U.S. economy was forced to undergo considerable reevaluation of its trade policies. In addition, the political map of much of the world was changing: the East bloc countries of Europe struggled with the effects of years of autocratic rule; the former Soviet Union saw nationalistic feuds break out in several former republics; Yugoslavia disbanded; Quebec took steps to separate from the rest of Canada. One revolution that failed occurred in China in 1989, when pro-democracy demonstrators occupied Tienanmen Square but were brutally suppressed by the government. The ultimate significance of all these events remains to be written by future historians; to those living in the period, however, it was unquestionably an era of political and economic turmoil.

Terrorism and Violence

Every age has its violent side, but the period after 1968 was marked by increasing threats to the safety of the individual. Whether on the streets of major American cities (beginning with the inner-city demonstrations in the late 1960s that turned violent), in the air (most notably Pan Am Flight 103 that exploded over Lockerbie, Scotland, in 1988), on the high seas (the cruise ship *Achille Lauro* in 1985), or on the ground (the Iranian hostage crisis of 1979–1981), the world was not a safe place.

Some of the terrorism was politically motivated, as regional or national conflicts were brought to world attention through violent means intended to capture news headlines and force the superpowers and the world community to do something to end the conflicts. The Arab-Israeli conflicts in the Middle East were partly or fully responsible for several assassinations and civilian bombings throughout the region and the Mediterranean. The Irish Republican Army planted terrorist bombs both in Northern Ireland and in England. Basque terrorists in northern Spain were held responsible for several bombings in that region. The Iran-Iraq War, which lasted through most of the 1980s, spawned distrust and hatred between those two countries and served as the backdrop to the Persian Gulf War of 1991, in which the United States intervened to liberate Kuwait from Iraqi invasion.

At home, Americans experienced a different kind of terrorism: the fear of being hurt whenever they left their homes. Women were reminded that it was unsafe to walk alone at night on college campuses and in unlit areas of cities. Gang warfare threatened not only city streets but high school hallways. Crime related to drug activity rose throughout the period. Bizarre cases of multiple murders surfaced periodically (the murder of black teenagers in Atlanta in 1981, or of young men in the Midwest in 1992). Senseless killings by men who opened fire on a crowd of people (a man wanting to kill all feminists who killed 14 women in Montreal in 1990, the 1984 massacre of 21 in a California McDonald's) also received media attention. All these were reminders that the world was not safe, and these events and others like them convinced many people that values and beliefs that had held people together as a community were no longer approved or supported.

Redefinition of the Family

The 1950s image of the American family as a father, mother, and two or three children living together in one house had lost much of its currency by the 1980s. Less than one in four American households could be said to fit that image by 1990. More commonly, children were raised by parents who were divorced and/or remarried, or by single parents. Even more striking was the increased media attention given to domestic violence. The family did not appear to be a safe haven when estimates were published that one in four Americans was abused as a child, and that domestic violence against spouses affected millions of men and women. Television talk shows addressed daily the concern of average Americans that they can't talk with or get along with their partners or other family members.

The media descriptions of the American family may or may not have been close to reality, but some changes were clearly taking place. Politicians of the decade spoke frequently of returning to traditional American values, and religious groups took up the cause of saving the family from what they considered to be dissolution. Those in alternative lifestyles and family structures sought to distinguish structure from values, and urged instead that values can be taught in a variety of familial settings. If nothing else, the debate served to make the image of the American family still more beleaguered than it had been. Since a great many of the most famous American playwrights had focused on the family environment, it is not surprising that the theatre gave voice in myriad ways to the debate over the health and well-being of the American family.

The Individual

In the world described thus far, the individual cannot help feeling insecure, attacked, threatened, lost, or confused. Despite the popularity of heroic figures (Rocky, Rambo, Luke Skywalker, or even the stranded boy in the movie *Home Alone*), the more prevalent image of the individual in America is of someone isolated, uncertain about the future, and disconnected from the past. The women in *Thelma and Louise*, the Southern football coach in *The Prince of Tides*, and the brothers in *Rain Man* are in search of themselves, wandering far from their homes in hopes of finding who they are and what they believe in. Sociologists and psychologists labeled the contemporary individual everything from schizophrenic to narcissistic. As the world became more confusing, many individuals decided to take care of themselves as best they could, even at the cost of those around them. This in turn led to the 1980s being labeled the "greed decade," in contrast to the "me decade" of the 1970s.

The private life of individuals in the 1990s was also subject to fear and uncertainty. AIDS and other sexually transmitted diseases raised questions about casual or promiscuous sexual activity. A woman's right to an abortion was challenged by demonstrators at women's clinics and in the Supreme Court. Sexual harassment in the workplace dominated the news during the confirmation hearings of Justice Clarence Thomas to the Supreme Court.

In those years when the economy was in recession (1974–1975, 1981–1983,

1990–1993) the typical individual either feared for her job or had to seek employment in a difficult job market. The number of homeless in America increased, and virtually every large city in America had a homeless population. For the first time in U.S. history, the generation of the 1970s and 1980s could not look forward to a better economic future than that of their parents. Truly the world was a frightening place for many people.

A bleak picture of the period is only one version of the last quarter century. The era began with a man walking on the moon, and it ended with a decline in the threat of nuclear holocaust. Europe moved toward a political union that seemed to preclude warfare on a continent ravaged by war for 2,000 years. Apartheid appeared to be ending in South Africa. Nevertheless, individuals were confronted by a bewildering and fragmenting world, revealed in the images and ideas of the arts of the post-1968 era.

ARTS IDEAS

Madonna making a video of her life for commercial release, a woman onstage saying she wants to make eunuchs of all businessmen, a sensationalized trial in Cincinnati over a group of allegedly pornographic photographs in a museum of art, the popularity of MTV, buildings with classical columns stuck in front of flat concrete surfaces, dances that combine vogueing and ballet—the arts in the 1970s and 1980s are controversial and, often, confusing. Old and new forms are combined with new technologies to create what some people think are exciting new directions for the arts, but what others call a trivializing of the traditions of the past. The last 20 years have at the very least been controversial, and the term used to refer to many of the artistic endeavors of the period is equally controversial.

In the 1970s a new critical term began to gain currency in the arts: *postmodernism.* Used first in architecture and literature, the concept gradually gained acceptance until by the 1990s most artists and critics at least acknowledged that postmodernism was a way of referring to many of the artistic trends of the period. However, there was very little agreement on the shape or characteristics of the era, and therefore the term *postmodern* remains today controversial in both its definition and its application.

As an artistic critical term, *postmodernism* usually refers to any or all of these qualities: a mixing of different styles from different time periods, a playful or irreverent use of the past without adhering to the values of the past, multiple meanings and moods interspersed through a text or performance, a blurring of the distinction between reality and art, and a self-conscious awareness of being in a performance either by undercutting traditional techniques or by openly acknowledging the audience.

Examples of postmodernism can be found in each of the arts. In architecture, buildings that add false columns, Roman arches, art deco design elements, or playful bright colors to otherwise standard structures would be considered postmodern. In literature, Italo Calvino has written novels in which the storyteller qualifies everything said because he is unsure that it ever happened. In *The French Lieutenant's Woman* (1969) by John Fowles, the storyteller suddenly interjects himself into an otherwise traditional Victorian story and says he doesn't know how to end the novel. In art, postmodern can be most readily identified through the inclusion of classical images in contemporary

Portland public services building by Michael Graves.   *Courtesy Michael Graves, Architect. Photo by Paschall/Taylor*

settings, such as hiding a Mona Lisa in a collage or presenting a classical male nude pose with some modern article of clothing draped over it. In dance, the mixture of styles in the work of Meredith Monk would also be considered postmodern. The opera *The Death of Klinghoffer* (1991) places a very recent news event (the hijacking of the cruise ship *Achille Lauro*) in the context of a form many consider more closely aligned with the 18th and 19th centuries. Robert Wilson (1941–) in his theatre pieces combines the works of several independent artists (musicians, painters, sculptors, dancers), using visual and aural imagery rather than plot structure as an organizing principle. The works are massive in scope—*Ka Mountain* (1972) lasted a full week—and are often performed in slow motion, as Wilson seeks to create a meditative state in the audience.

For many people the end of communist domination in Eastern Europe and the perceived loss of economic dominance by the United States created a feeling that older international structures were no longer valid and that traditions of the past could no longer be helpful since the structures that supported them no longer existed. Postmodern in this context becomes associated with fragmentation and diversity. The increased attention to women's issues in all art forms and the perspectives provided by women directors and writers has broadened the focus of much of the arts on male characters and issues. African-Americans have new voices expressing their cultures in the writings of Toni Morrison (1931–) and Alice Walker (1944–) as well as in the films of Spike Lee (1956–), Melvin Van Peebles (1932–), and others. Latino and Asian communities also have championed artists who articulated their own multiple concerns both within the communities and in relation to the dominant culture presented on network television. New publishing firms have arisen to publish materials directly addressing the concerns and interests of these communities as well as of the gays and lesbians of America.

In the media, postmodern appears in several ways, most notably in a new art form, music videos. In 1981 MTV (Music Television) first broadcast on cable networks; its notoriety was established within four years, and by 1991 it had become so established that its tenth-anniversary celebration included most of the leading artists in the music industry. MTV helped promote the careers of Billy Idol, Michael Jackson, Madonna, and Paula Abdul. With its glitzy, fast-paced format in which most shots last no more than three seconds, MTV acknowledged its connection to the new style when in 1990 it announced an award for the best postmodern video of the year. In film, *Sex, lies, and videotape* is considered postmodern in its self-awareness and recognition of the ways in which our lives can be seen as performance. *My Own Private Idaho* includes in its study of young street hustlers an extended section taken directly from Shakespeare's *Henry IV, part 1.* The films of David Lynch and his television series *Twin Peaks* have a bizarre, uncertain sense of character and event that is characteristic of the period. No longer is there a sharp line between reality and dream states; character motivation becomes frightening or threatening because it is unknowable; values (especially traditional ones) are not worth following because they do not seem to result in positive results.

This rather bleak vision of reality (to some) is hardly characteristic of all human experience or of all arts activities. Countertrends are as evident in the 1970s and 1980s as they are in any other era. Not surprisingly the mass media of film and television continue to portray the human condition as containing a sense of personal dignity and a faith in the future that have always been a staple of their dramatic output. Visual artists continue to work in abstract expressionism more than any new postmodern directions. Popular music has accepted the rise of rap, but the majority of musical groups are white males singing about love. And in the theatre, the romantic and sentimental musicals of Andrew Lloyd Webber have brought more people to Broadway than all dramas combined.

THEATRE HISTORY

Seen up close, history can be a blur. Multiple images of theatre emerged between 1968 and the present, and which of them will have a lasting influence is yet to be determined. Commercial theatre may refer to a group of young college graduates from Illinois State

University forming Steppenwolf Theatre, a small company in Chicago, and becoming a nationally known organization with successful Broadway productions. Conversely, it also refers to huge producing corporations, such as the Nederlanders, which owns several Broadway theatres and is able to exert a powerful influence on theatre production.

Occasion

Regional theatres continue to develop in many countries, including the Scandinavian countries, Italy, Mexico, and the United States. Independent organizations range from The Empty Space in Seattle, Washington, devoted to new plays and avant-garde expression, to the Gruppo Teatro Ottavia, which frequently adapts novels for theatrical presentation, taking the production on tour throughout Italy and performing in any available space. The term *theatre* refers to elaborate musical-comedy presentations featuring operating helicopters, and also to solo performers telling stories from their past. This chapter will offer a series of snapshots of theatrical activity during the past 25 years, seeking to exemplify the diversity of those events.

The Institution: The Royal Shakespeare Company. Large producing organizations continue to be a dominant force in theatrical production. Many are national theatres or large regional theatres that command government or corporate support. Typical of these organizations is England's Royal Shakespeare Company.

The history of the Royal Shakespeare Company originated with the town council of Stratford-upon-Avon, who decided in 1879 to present a play in honor of their most famous citizen and presented the Shakespeare Jubilee. A resident company was founded at Stratford in 1919, and its history records the names of most of England's most famous actors, designers, and directors of the 20th century.

The modern history of the company, and the first use of the title Royal Shakespeare Company, dates from the appointment of Peter Hall as director in 1960. Hall's ambitious leadership resulted in a 1962 season that set a new standard and established the RSC as the largest theatre company in the world: 24 productions involving 500 employees, presented to an audience of more than 700,000. In the next decade, significant productions included Peter Brook's *King Lear* (1962), *The War of the Roses* (1963), *Marat/Sade* (1964), and numerous modern works as well. The struggle to support such a massive undertaking led to the sudden resignation of Peter Hall and his staff in 1968, leaving the leadership to Trevor Nunn, just 28 years old.

Nunn acted immediately to increase the security of the company. Buoyed by the international success of Peter Brook's *A Midsummer Night's Dream* (1970), the company expanded into two smaller theatres (one in London, one in Stratford), added national and international tours, and expanded the repertoire to include more experimental works. Nunn instituted two-year contracts that covered one season in London and one in Stratford to provide stability and continuity. By 1977 the RSC was larger than before, presenting 8 productions in Stratford, 11 at the Aldwych, 14 at the smaller theatres, a season in Newcastle, 2 commercial productions in London's West End, and 2 television contracts. Despite this success, financial demands on such an undertaking were immense, and the company relied heavily on government subsidy.

The RSC's success has been built on its artistry and its versatility. Landmark productions such as the 8-hour *Nicholas Nickleby* (1980) and *Les Misérables* (1988) have been international successes that provided much-needed financial backing. A new building at the Barbican Center, dedicated in 1982, provided a large 1,100-seat auditorium as well as an experimental studio space in a huge complex that included a cinema, a concert-hall, and an art gallery. The political difficulties of managing such a large organization have led to a fairly constant turnover in artistic and administrative staff, and yet the organization itself continues as one of the leading theatre companies of our time.

The Theatre Collective: Théâtre du Soleil.   Based on the experimental work of the Living Theatre and the Open Theatre during the 1960s, some theatre groups organized themselves as a theatre collective in which management and artistic decisions were made by a group rather than by one designated leader. Although their aesthetic and political agendas varied, organizations such as The Performance Group, The Wooster Group, and Mabou Mines developed unique concepts of script development and presentation. Among the most successful of these groups was France's Théâtre du Soleil.

Organized by a group of young French students and theatre artists in 1964, Théâtre du Soleil is a theatre collective devoted to socio-political causes. Although their early work gained them some success, they became internationally noted through the production of *1789* in 1970.

A sketch by Robert Morosco for a Théâtre du Soleil production.   *Copyright Moscoso*

Created by the group without a specific author, *1789* is credited with popularizing the concept of "collective creation." The work began with intensive research by all members of the company, followed by improvisation. No attempt was made at stylistic unity. Some scenes were based on documentary records, while others were pure theatre, seeking to evoke mood rather than historical accuracy. Rather than expressing a particular point of view, *1789* often offers differing perspectives on a single event or person. King Louis XVI is played by several different actors, each of whom accentuates differing aspects of the king's character. At one point the king is portrayed by a hand puppet; at another he is represented by a huge carnival puppet carried in triumph above the crowd.

The play was performed in an open room. The audience stood in the center, surrounded by a series of raised platforms. Action moved rapidly from one area to another, sometimes occurring simultaneously, and frequently intruded into the spectators' area. The triumphant storming of the Bastille was followed by a wild carnival celebration in which the audience could participate. The closing of the play, however, made the group's political message clear as an actor gave a solemn speech declaring that the revolution had managed only to replace the tyranny of the ruling nobles with the tyranny of the rich.

The success of the play was phenomenal. Performed first in Italy, it then played at the group's home base in Vincennes, France, for two years, attracting more than 250,000 spectators. Guided by their artistic director, Arianne Mnouchkine (1934–   ), the group has continued to experiment with various styles, always relying on the membership to define a project of interest. Their home is in a converted munitions factory that dates from the 19th century. Set outside of town and without any of the normal trappings of a theatre—reserved seats, proscenium arch, and so forth—the Cartoucherie provides a unique space for the company's work. Their process as well as their success has attracted an extremely talented company whose skills range from mask-making to composing to design. All of these talents are utilized to devise unique methods of theatrical communication.

Multicultural Explorations: International Center for Theatre Research. Some artists became dissatisfied with the limitations of one particular performance style and sought to achieve a theatrical expression that could overcome limitations of language, custom, and theatrical convention. Eugenio Barba's Teatro Odet, some of the work of Mabou Mines, and the later explorations of Jerzy Grotowski are examples of these explorations. One of the most visible and influential efforts in this field has been the work of Peter Brook (1925–   ).

Following his success in the commercial theatre in England, and the securing of an international reputation with his production of *A Midsummer Night's Dream*, Brook turned away from commercial presentation to focus on research in the nature of theatre performance. In November of 1970 he organized the International Center for Theatre Research in Paris dedicated to an international investigation of the nature of theatrical performance. Recognizing that no theatre exists without an audience, the Center also produces theatrical events. In several instances, the works produced during recent years under Brook's direction have been momentous occasions in the theatre.

In 1973, following 15 months of preparation, Brook took his group of international performers on a tour of Africa. Using a set of improvisational situations without any predetermined direction, the group performed 34 times for audiences in remote African villages. Freed from normal theatrical conventions and audience expectations, they were forced to allow their work to be molded by the spectators. Not knowing traditional Western conventions, the audience didn't recognize the attempt of a young actress to portray a old woman by walking bent over. The audience thought the actress was ill. Time and again, the actors found themselves forced to abandon their expectations and their attempts to manipulate the audience. Only with the most simple and honest actions were they able to communicate.

In 1985 Brook culminated five years of work with his presentation of *The Mahabharata* at the Fête d'Avignon. Based on the Sanskrit epic poem that occupies 18 volumes of verse, the play was written by Jean-Claude Carrière in cooperation with the company. Preparation included research trips to India (including the whole cast for one visit), workshops in Kathakali (a classic Indian dance form), and preliminary performances for children in Costa Rica. For the first production, the theatre was a remote limestone quarry outside of Avignon where spectators sat on scaffolding in front of huge cliffs and an acting area filled with yellow sand with a small reflecting pool of water at the front and a running stream behind. The play began at twilight. Throughout the night, the story of human existence as contained in the ancient epic poem was told in a series of scenes that included storytelling, ritual, classical Indian dance, Shakespearean grandeur, and magical effects. Performed by a multiracial cast composed of 16 different nationalities who all spoke in French, the play culminated in a spectacular battle that ranged to the tops of the cliffs. The play ended at daybreak with the symbolic new dawn providing the philosophical coda to the story.

Brook continues to explore new ground in theatrical production. He followed his

The Mahabharata, directed by Peter Brook.   *Courtesy Mairie de Paris*

work on *The Mahabharata* with successful and innovative productions of *The Cherry Orchard* and *The Tragedy of Carmen*.

Self-expression/Minority Theatres: At the Foot of the Mountain. A key social movement of this period was the continuing emergence of various minority groups. For these people, theatre became a means of self-expression. Through theatre, minority groups were able to validate their experiences, share their cultural tradition, and seek self-definition. Groups such as New York's Pan-Asian Repertory Theatre provided racial definition. San Francisco's Rhinoceros Theatre focused on the issues of the gay community. One of the most vital movements was the growth of women's theatres. Although no one theatre can represent the diversity of approaches represented in these movements, the women's theatre called At the Foot of the Mountain, based in Minnesota, provides an illustration of a theatre devoted to a specific group and to new methods of preparation and presentation.

At the Foot of the Mountain began in 1974 and sought to make theatre more personal right from its founding. Plays were created and performed based on the members' own lives and dealing with their own issues. Although they explored a wide variety of social themes (rape, madness, war), these issues were always approached on a personal basis. Performances were based on a theatrical ritual that included moments in which the audience was invited to participate by sharing their own experiences. In *Raped,* audience members were encouraged to add their own experiences to the play at any point in the action simply by shouting "Stop." Audience responses were stories of personal experience, not intellectual debate, but these additions could support the play, alter its direction, or even provide an opposing idea. In *The Story of a Mother,* the audience was led through a guided meditation that asked them to see the world as their mother saw it. They were then asked to speak in their mother's voices, completing lines such as "I always said. . . ." Audience members were allowed to speak voluntarily, and each evening's response was different. Improvised scenes of bonding and of separation between mothers and daughters followed, and a sharing of bread preceded the final moment. At the close of the evening, each member of the cast and the audience introduced herself by her name and as the daughter of her mother. "I am Jane, daughter of Eleanor."

Social Action: The Experimental Theatre of Cali (Colombia). Socio-political agendas are one of the hallmarks of many theatres, ranging from San Francisco's Guerilla Girls to the wide-ranging explorations of Teatro Campesino, but the movement appears especially strong in Latin America. The Experimental Theatre of Cali (Colombia) began as a government school but soon rejected that affiliation. After its founding in 1955 under the leadership of Enrique Buenaventura, the company utilized self-generated theatre pieces to oppose colonization. Rejecting the structural and technical perfection of the European theatre, Buenaventura sought to develop a theatre based on the direct experience of the audience. Although at first the group produced existing scripts, from the late 1960s they have concentrated on group-generated pieces. Typically, these pieces investigate Colombian history in such a manner as to question traditional interpretations, motives, and implications. Buenaventura is not interested in providing solutions; he sees the theatre as a means of clarifying perception.

Los Papeles del Infierno is a group of one-act plays that are presented in varying combinations, depending on the situation. The audience is shown small segments of stories from Colombian history that document the continued use of violence as a means of gaining or maintaining power.

The segments alternate between realistic dialogue and grotesque satire, between monologue and elaborate ceremony, between drama and farce. In sum, they present a fragmented, ambiguous, and previously mute history that implicates the oppressed as well as the oppressors. The play is not a call for revolution, for no suggestion is given that revolution can erase the past or improve the future. It is a harrowing look at the underside of history and a forced recognition of unspoken truths.

Location

Theatre structures reveal the disagreement among theatre practitioners concerning the cultural position and the social purposes of theatre. The Performance Group made their home in The Performing Garage. Actually a converted factory, the "theatre" was essentially an open room 50 feet by 35 feet with 20-foot ceilings, cement-block walls, and a concrete floor. A smaller room in one corner measured 10 feet by 24 feet and was used for storage and backstage space. A second-floor room of the same approximate size has been used in a variety of ways ranging from office space to lobby to living quarters as well as a separate performing area. Even the roof of the building has been used for performance on occasion. For each production, The Performance Group, guided by resident designer Jerry Rojo, restructured the ground floor and often part of the second floor as well. Platforming, stairs, suspended balconies, and various other structures that were designed to suit the particular performance, served as acting space and seating area, bringing the actor and the audience into a shared environment.

The National Theatre of Great Britain opened its new building in 1976 after a delay of nearly two years. The complex included three separate theatres along with a large shared complex of lobby and refreshment areas. The major theatre, the Olivier, used an open stage surrounded by steeply raked seating for 1,100 spectators. A 900-seat proscenium theatre and a 400-seat experimental theatre provided alternative staging areas. The complex included workshops, rehearsal space, dressing rooms, and administrative offices to serve the massive company. The entire complex was situated alongside the Thames across from central London. Located nearby now are a concert hall and the National Film Theatre.

In Greece, an entirely different approach is represented by the Theatre of the Rocks. Starting with the inspiration of director Minos Volonakis, this project has begun to construct theatres in the abandoned rock quarries of Greece. Volonakis began by investigating 35 quarries in the hills surrounding Athens. He discovered 11 that had excellent natural acoustics and began a campaign to use them for theatre. Choosing one as his first target, relying on the goodwill of a friendly mayor, Volonakis had temporary steel bleachers erected, but more recent plans include an amphitheatre, a smaller theatre, athletic fields, and a park. The idea has gained popularity in several regions of Greece. (Peter Brook's *Mahabahrata* was performed in the Stone Theatre at Petroupoulis.) The result is a group of theatres reminiscent of the classic theatres. Built away from the center of town and thus closer to many people, the theatres are integrated with the environment and serve as a center of community activity.

Some theatre practitioners avoid using theatre buildings, preferring to place the theatre experience within other cultural settings. Theatre presentations in recent years have taken place at midnight among the ruins of an abandoned castle in England, in abandoned railway cars in Yugoslavia, on city streets in Harlem and Milan, in art galleries in Stockholm and Warsaw, and in city parks and school gymnasiums throughout the world. In those situations the term *theatre* refers to the interaction between the actor and the spectator, not to an architectural structure.

Performers

Certain individuals in the past 20 years have created a distinctive approach to theatre that has distinguished their work. Although what effect the artists discussed below will have on future theatre is uncertain, the work they have produced to date has been challenging and significant. Certainly other noteworthy innovations have been made, and others have contributed significantly to the theatre world—these are chosen to provide a range of examples.

The Producer: Joseph Papp (1921–1991). A job as a stage manager for CBS was not an auspicious beginning for an aspiring young theatre producer, and few could have predicted that at his death in 1991 he would be hailed as one of the greatest benefactors of American and world theatre during the 20th century.

He first gained notice when he convinced the city of New York to support free Shakespeare performances in Central Park. This program still exists today and regularly attracts major stars of film, television, and the theatre to perform in its summer presentations. The success of this venture was just a beginning for Joseph Papp, however, and in 1966 he opened the year-round operation of the New York Shakespeare Festival at the Public Theatre in Manhattan. In a building leased from the city for $1 a year, and now converted into five separate performance spaces, Joseph Papp created one of the most innovative and successful theatre operations of the century. His productions have been critically and commercially successful, with several transferring to extended runs on Broadway.

The range of presentations is phenomenal. His successes range from the experimental works of avant-garde director Richard Foreman to a revival of a Gilbert and Sullivan operetta. His Broadway successes include a choreopoem on the experience of black women *(for colored girls who have considered suicide when the rainbow is enuf . . .)* and traditional Broadway musicals. He was an avowed champion of socially significant works dealing with minority groups, the Vietnam War, and AIDS. Devoted to new and talented young American playwrights (David Rabe and John Guare among others), he also introduced works by distinguished foreign authors, including Vaclav Havel and Caryl Churchill. And he also remained devoted to the works of Shakespeare.

Papp was a tireless producer and a passionate defender of his artists. He appeared personally in advertisements, gave numberless interviews, and cajoled money from corporate and philanthropic sponsors. He arranged short runs so that successful Hollywood performers, such as Meryl Streep, could return to the Public Theatre and perform onstage between film commitments. He personally and publicly admonished critics whom he felt were unfair in their judgment of his presentations, and regularly criticized city officials for their failure to support the arts adequately. Through it all, he retained absolute control of the operation of the New York Shakespeare Theatre and made a nonprofit organization the most successful theatre company in town.

The Director: Giorgio Strehler (1921–   ).   Any list of the most prominent directors in Europe in the last half of the 20th century would include Giorgio Strehler. As one of the founders of the Piccolo Theatre of Milan in 1947 and later as the principal director for Théâtre de l'Europe since 1983, Strehler has been successful with a wide range of productions in both drama and opera. His production work has focused on what he terms "research" that involves restaging of works from earlier historical periods. The Piccolo Theatre is known for its interest in traditional Italian theatre, and Strehler's productions of plays such as Goldoni's *A Servant of Two Masters* and Pirandello's *Six Characters in Search of an Author* are generally credited with restoring those authors to the Italian stage.

Strehler without doubt is the dominant artistic center of his productions, with a clear concern for every element in them. His rehearsal technique, however, is collaborative, with all artistic personnel present at rehearsals. Thus an attempt to bring more lightness into an actor's performance is aided by a change in the lighting cue. A need for a certain resonance in footsteps is solved by the costumer who adds steel tips to the toes of the shoes. Although Strehler has ultimate control, he utilizes the skills of his entire production staff. His task is to provide a situation in which they work at their best, either through his inspiration or in response to his demands.

Strehler frequently protests against the limitations that contemporary theatre places on its artists. He insists that there is never enough time to do the work properly. Under modern conditions, he feels, the emphasis is always on technique rather than on underlying matters that affect the work more profoundly. He claims that the emphasis must be on the idea, not the detail, but his work is ultimately composed of details, for without them the idea gets lost completely.

The Director: Trevor Nunn and **Nicholas Nickleby.**   English director Trevor Nunn (1940–   ) has directed a range of works from *Macbeth* to the hit musical *Cats.* In 1979, he began work on a monumental project that would involve 48 actors, 15 musicians, and dozens of stage crew. Some critics have hailed *Nicholas Nickleby* as the theatre event of the century.

The process by which Charles Dickens's novel was translated into an 8-hour theatre production demonstrates Nunn's creative talents as a director. He and co-director John Caird spent three months re-creating and discussing moments from the Dickens classic. During this time, actors were not assigned parts, but shifted roles as scenes would be interpreted by more than one group of actors. The decision was made to tell the full story of the novel, meaning hundreds of characters and an extended performance of about eight hours' playing time. The number of scenes, locales, and situations meant that the actors would have to rely on themselves to "create" a scene, rather than depend on physical scenery to do that job. As the actors invented and tested situations from the book, writer David Edgar transcribed or rewrote them, and then returned them to the actors for further experimentation. The project could have gone on for a decade, but directors Nunn and Caird finally decided to cast the show

A scene from *Nicholas Nickleby*, directed by Trevor Nunn.   *Courtesy Chris Davies, Photographer*

(giving some actors multiple roles) and settle on scenes and specific interpretations. John Napier began redesigning the entire auditorium in which the play would be performed.

In performance, the actors mingled with the audience during intermissions, narrated much of the action singly or in groups, created their own sound effects, and "built" each scene from props and minimal gestures. The production could be seen in a matinee and evening performance with a dinner break, or over two succeeding nights. At first, the critics were only modestly pleased with the production, but the play gained popularity through word of mouth and soon sold out its entire run, and that of a revived run in 1981, and a three-month run in New York City.

The Director: Joanne Akalaitis.   In 1991, Joseph Papp named a prominent, innovative young director, Joanne Akalaitis, as his assistant at the New York Shakespeare Festival. When he died several months later, she inherited one of the most powerful positions in American theatre. Her work exemplifies the innovative, collaborative approach of many women directors, including Elizabeth LeCompte of the Wooster Group and Meredith Monk.

Akalaitis "discovered" theatre after early studies in premedicine and philosophy. Her training included work at Stanford University, at the Actor's Studio in San Francisco, and with Grotowski in Europe. In her successful directing career she has worked at the Mark Taper Forum, the Guthrie Theatre in Minneapolis (she was the

A photo *(above)* and a drawing *(right)* of the accomplished design by Josef Svoboda for *Siegfried.*   *Courtesy Josef Svoboda*

third woman director in the theatre's 25-year history), the American Repertory Theatre, and the Interart Theatre. However, her first association, from 1975 to 1987, was with the innovative theatre group Mabou Mines.

Akalaitis's work with Mabou Mines involved the communal creation of original pieces. Often these were based on other sources or forms that were combined in unusual ways. *Dead End Kids* (1980) utilized stand-up comedy, civil rights documents, and excerpts from the diaries of Madame Curie. Visual, physical, and musical elements were considered equal in importance to the spoken word. Akalaitis is also known as an interpreter of the works of Samuel Beckett and Franz Xaver Kroetz and has produced provocative and controversial productions of Büchner's *Leon and Lena (& Lenz)* in Minneapolis in 1987 and Shakespeare's *Cymbeline* in New York in 1990.

Her rehearsal methods are equally inventive, often using exercises totally di-

vorced from the text to discover images from the actor's own lives that can be incorporated into the play or used as springboards to other ideas. Her approach is highly collaborative, yet she is also known for strict rehearsal discipline.

The Designer: Josef Svoboda (1920–   ).   The Prague National Theatre in Czechoslovakia is best known internationally as the home of the innovative designer Josef Svoboda. Svoboda is associated with the rise of the scenographer, a person who is responsible for the entire artistic vision of the show. Instead of having separate designers for each area (such as lights, costume, and sound), the scenographer envisions a total concept for the production and then coordinates each technical element to achieve that concept. This approach naturally continues the turn-of-the-century trend toward a distinct and unique visual world for each play. Svoboda has in fact insisted that no one style or technique is appropriate for all productions, but that the scenographer must find solutions uniquely and appropriately adapted to each production.

Svoboda's international reputation rests on his imaginative application of new technical devices and equipment to create a kinetic, flexible, and dynamic stage picture. Two productions illustrate the range of his invention. In 1963, Svoboda designed a production of *Romeo and Juliet*, directed by Otomar Krejca. He employed hanging panels and screens that could move in all directions. Platforms and step-units were placed on a variety of treadmills and lifts to enable them to move on and off stage, to be raised or lowered, and to change direction. The result was a malleable, kinetic space that would flow in rhythm with the action.

An entirely different environmental solution was created for Karel Capek's *The Insect Comedy*, a study of different philosophies of human nature through insect behavior. Svoboda's setting relied on two massive honeycombed reflecting surfaces hung at 45-degree angles to the stage floor. By using different images, the actors, of course, could be seen with the eye or through reflection in both of the mirrors simultaneously. The result was a visual distortion of the human body. The actors looked like they were crawling underneath a microscope. Later work has continued to expand the technological sophistication of design.

Svoboda's work, like that of many scenographers in the 1970s, takes the audience into a realm of visual and aural excitement. Through the use of multimedia techniques, particularly groups of screens that move around the stage and on which are projected either stills or motion pictures, he transforms the static picturization of modified realism into an unpredictable and active spectacle. Recent work has used ionized air particles to give physical dimension to light, adding another possibility in the realm of design. To audiences accustomed to video games and the films of George Lucas and Steven Spielberg, Svoboda's ideas are an appropriate direction for the theatre to take. Others are less enchanted, on the ground that technology is replacing ideas. When a balance is achieved, as in Svoboda's work, the result is a theatre concept readily compatible with the visual experiences of computer-age audiences.

The Multimedia Star: Morgan Freeman.

Many of the most successful theatre actors in the United States are unable to make a full-time career out of the Broadway stage. The promise of long-term employment in television soap operas, and the huge salaries offered by Hollywood studios, are frequently too attractive. However, many of these performers return regularly to the stage. Meryl Streep has returned to perform at the New York Shakespeare Festival, William Hurt did Shakespeare in Central Park, Dustin Hoffman performed Willy Loman on Broadway, and Tyne Daly moved from her starring role in the TV show *Cagney and Lacey* to a Broadway success in *Gypsy*. Indeed, the normal profile of a "star" today includes successful performances in all three mediums, and this has been the case with Morgan Freeman.

He didn't start out a star. In fact, Morgan Freeman, didn't really become a full-time professional actor until he was 30 years old. He spent time in the Air Force before enrolling in college at age 25, and for a short while he pursued a career as a dancer. Once the career started, however, he worked in a variety of venues. He was an off-Broadway actor in a play called *The Niggerlovers*, and he was the head waiter/dancer in the all-black Broadway version of *Hello, Dolly!* He was a regular on the public television show *The Electric Company*, portraying a character named "Easy Reader" in shows designed to help young children learn to read; and he was a soap opera star on *Another World.* He toured nationally in *The Gospel at Colonus*, Lee Breuer's pop-gospel version of the story of Oedipus, and he earned Obie awards for performances in *Coriolanus* and *Mother Courage* at the New York Shakespeare Festival. In recent years, he has become a major film star with his performances in *Lean on Me* and *Driving Miss Daisy*.

The ability to work in all three mediums has greatly increased the opportunities for actors in America. It is a significant statement that, despite the differences in time commitment, salary, and the availability of luxury, established performers still choose to return to the stage.

The Actor as Rebel: Kabuki's Ennosuke III.

The essence of Kabuki theatre is the tradition that links it directly to its origins in the 18th century. Rarely has an art form been preserved so carefully through strict adherence to a multitude of performance conventions that dictate the repertoire, the costume, and even the precise gestures of the actors.

Recently this established form has been challenged by an innovative young performer. This challenge does not come from an outsider but from a member of the Ichikawa family, one of the most famous of all Kabuki families. Ennosuke III, the grandson of the master actor Ennosuke II, has introduced a new, modern spirit into Kabuki performances that traditionalists label as "circus." Ennosuke rejects these criticisms, claiming that Kabuki was always adapting to changes in society until the post–World War II revival began treating it as a museum piece. He is determined to revive Kabuki by making it more in tune with the pace and the interests of contemporary Japanese life.

Ennosuke's path to stardom has been unusual. Trained from childhood, he made his debut at the age of eight. In his teenage years, he broke with tradition by insisting on a university education, including study in Western drama traditions. When he became head of the family at the age of 24, he resumed his career, but his innovations brought him as much censure as acclaim. As a performer he is known to ad-lib in performance and share asides with members of the audience, reviving the tradition of clowning that he claims was integral to Kabuki until the mid-19th century. He is known for spectacular acrobatic feats, including the use of complicated machinery that allows him to fly above the audience.

However, his innovations go much deeper than just the sheer intensity and virtuosity of his performances. He has shortened many plays, compressing their five- or six-hour stories into a length more acceptable to modern audiences. He has introduced modern staging techniques, including the use of projections and film. He has staged a collaborative piece with a Peking Opera company, and he has commissioned more than 25 new plays. Breaking with tradition, he employed a fashion designer rather than the traditional family of Kabuki designers, and even used a woman as a set designer. Ennosuke refuses to consider using women as performers, however, feeling that the *onnagata* performers are essential to the Kabuki aesthetic.

Ennosuke's world tours have played before enthusiastic audiences, and he is clearly developing a devoted following in Japan. Whether his innovative approach will remain an anomaly or whether it will change the face of Kabuki remains to be seen.

The Actor Alone: Spalding Gray (1941–   ).   Among the innovative trends of performance in this period was the rising popularity of monologue artists. Some were one-person shows revolving around a particular individual, as in Robert Morse's Broadway performance as Truman Capote in *Tru*. Others featured a single individual playing a multiplicity of roles in a single play, as in Lily Tomlin's performance in *Search for Signs of Intelligent Life in the Universe*. Stand-up comics became extremely popular, whether they were simply gagsters or character performers such as Whoopi Goldberg and Eric Bogosian.

Spalding Gray began his career as a monologue artist after leaving the avant-garde theatre company The Wooster Group in 1979. His current performance style is complete simplicity. In *Swimming to Cambodia*, which was also released as a feature film, Gray recounts his experiences while filming *The Killing Fields*. In a detached, analytical, ironic mood he tell stories about his experiences, interjecting pieces of history and sociological commentary along the way. He does the entire piece seated at a table, using description, dialogue, interior thoughts, and reflective commentary. A thought may send him off on a tangent, creating a fragmentary image of a related concept before he returns to the narrative. Gray creates the image (or the reality) of an individual retelling significant events in his life and attempting to understand them, inviting the audience to attempt to understand them as well.

Gray's work differs from traditional theatre in several important ways. Unlike most theatre performers, he works alone—his theatre is not an interaction of independent characters, and it is not dependent on the concept of dramatic conflict or action. Also defying tradition, he portrays himself rather than a fictional character created by someone else. Finally, Gray's works are created verbally, not in writing. He begins working with a tape recorder until a piece is developed. Then he tapes performances, using those tapes to develop later performances, so that a performance becomes his variation on a variation of a variation, as Spalding Gray portraying Spalding Gray portraying Spalding Gray.

The Performance Artist: Rachel Rosenthal (1926–   ).   Spalding Gray's work is sometimes labeled "performance art," a term popularized during the 1970s and used to refer to a wide range of artistic efforts. In its early days the term referred to such activities as "Lead Sink for Sebastian," in which an amputee's metal leg was melted, or the works of the legendary Chris Burden, who allowed a marksman to shoot him in the arm. Other artists focused on the human body as an art object, incorporated elements of dance, and experimented with combinations of video and live performance. Laurie Anderson created the first full-scale work—*United States*—in 1982, utilizing music, slides, special visual effects, and a range of unusual sounds.

Rachel Rosenthal's background includes acting study with Jean-Louis Barrault, off-Broadway directing, work as an assistant designer at the New York City Opera, and

Spalding Gray.   *Photo by Paula Court*

independent work as a painter, engraver, sculptor, dancer, and improvisational actress. It was only in 1971, however, after a five-year period as a housewife, that she became aware of feminist art and began her current career in performance.

Rosenthal's work is self-generated, whether it deals with concerns for the environment or traumatic memories of her past. Previous works have dealt with her half-sister, death, physical pain, and Chernobyl. In *Death Valley*, she revealed her loneliness, her fears of growing up to be like her mother, her guilty participation in the destruction of the earth by human beings, and the simple power of one human's behavior. The piece is a rambling monologue delivered with abstract physical gestures and with vocal passages ranging from normal conversation to high keening sounds accompanied by a solo violin.

Traps used more theatrical elements than *Death Valley*. Numerous props ranging from a lighted candle to a clutch of eggs, slide projections, recorded voices, sound effects, music, and a mask are used to create this piece. In it, Rosenthal portrays three characters: a monk-like figure, a female warrior, and, apparently, herself in a normal social situation. A series of conflicting situations culminate in the sound of a nuclear explosion, followed by a scream. A final plea urges people to consider the possibility of wholeness through the existence of tenderness and affection.

The combination of disparate images, the presence of the actor as herself, the combination of various art forms, and the abstract quality of the presentation are all common among performance artists. Although the form may encompass such diverse activities as Karen Finley's screams of rage at the agony of the female experience, and the three live people "hung" on the wall of an art gallery in Stephen Taylor Woodrow's "The Living Paintings," the self-conscious performance of self and the integration of the arts continue a tradition begun by the Dadaists. Many of the techniques have been adapted by MTV and rock performers, and the influence of performance art is felt in the traditional theatre as well.

Standards of Judgment

The judgment of what makes theatre "good" or "bad" has become highly specialized and individual. Certainly, commercial success remains one powerful arbiter of theatrical quality, and, in the United States particularly, media critics have maintained their power of determining what is good or bad. However, several other key considerations have surfaced during recent years. In most cases, these new concepts call for a complete revision of the role of theatre in society and in the creation and presentation of theatre.

One important concept of theatre during this period was termed *environmental theatre* by Richard Schechner (1934–   ). He despised the proscenium theater that segregated the actor from the audience and provided only a few good seats. The primary purpose of such an auditorium, he claimed, was to underscore class distinctions based on financial status.

Schechner envisioned a form of theatre that would provide equal freedom to the audience and the actor. Performance would occur in an open space in which actors and audiences intermingled. The shape of the space would be determined by the individual production and would be altered each night by the actions of the spectators. In such an environment, performance could become a social event rather than a passive observation. Artificial conventions of theatrical politeness could be overcome, and active audience participation would be encouraged. In this manner, theatre could lay claim to its uniqueness as a two-way communication system in a world dominated by one-way communication. The best theatre would involve the audience in a unique communicative event in which the audience and the performers had shared responsibilities for the nature of the communication.

The concept of theatre as communication is also the foundation of the theories of Augusto Boal (1931–   ). Boal labeled as "coercive" the Aristotelian theory of theatre that has dominated Western theatre practice since the Renaissance, arguing that the emphasis on the correction or punishment of behavioral flaws served to maintain the political status quo. Such theatre, Boal argues, is a tool of the oppressor, a servant of the powerful.

As an alternative, Boal argues a "poetics of the oppressed." The purpose of such a poetics is to create a theatre that will transform the people from spectators to actors. Rather than delegating power to a fictional character and experiencing change vicariously, Boal's theatre places power directly in the hands of the spectator. In Boal's theatre, the spectator interacts with the performance onstage, either to offer new suggestions on possible actions for the characters or to physically take over the role from the performer. The goal is to free the spectator to act—first in the theatre, and then in society. As Boal states, theatre may not be the revolution but "it is a rehearsal of revolution." Good theatre, to Boal, is theatre that empowers the spectator.

The feminist movement also produced a new consideration of the standards by which theatre should be judged. Through radical reinterpretation (deconstruction) of existing texts to expose patriarchal ideology, feminist critics have questioned the validity and value of the traditional canon of dramatic works. Through new methods of playwriting and performance, feminists have attempted to create a new form of drama: a form that is circular and eternal rather than linear and proscribed; a form that is nondeterminant and open rather than prescriptive and final; a form that is transformative rather than judgmental. Good theatre from a feminist perspective is communal, restorative, and liberating.

A multitude of other methods exists as well (semiotics, reader-response theory, deconstruction), many of them focusing on the definition of theatre, seeking to understand and define the process by which theatre is performed and perceived. Frequently these theories are more interested in how theatre works than in determining which theatre experiences are the most valid or valuable.

DRAMATIC LITERATURE

In an era of fragmentation and diversity, to select one play with which to introduce the dramatic literature of the period would be presumptuous. Most of the other chapters of this book encompass decades that sustain some sense of stylistic coherence (or at least the distillation of history has created such a sense for those periods.) After 1970, however, such coherence is actively avoided by many artists, and theatres in their selection of scripts appeal to particular audiences, rather than to a general, some would say homogenized, audience. On any given weekend in a major American city, a theatregoer could expect to attend a touring company's production of a recent huge Broadway musical, a new work by a member of a racial or ethnic theatre company, a play by an author whose work is just coming to the attention of mainstream critics, or a re-creation of a European classic in a college theatre. This review of dramatic literature is intended to reflect the qualities of fragmentation and diversity rather than attempt to be comprehensive. It begins with the American theatres where the lure of a Broadway or off-Broadway success remains seductive.

United States

In past decades, American playwrights have set aside some of their anger and their obsession with violence and despair. As the United States pulled away from the events of Vietnam and Watergate, a mood of reconciliation and reconstruction entered into the American drama. Michael Cristofer's *The Shadow Box* (1977) is an affirmation of the process of life and death for terminally ill cancer patients. Mark Medoff's *Children of a Lesser God* (1979) explores the pride of the deaf community. Donald Coburn's *The Gin Game* (1978) highlights the love of aging couples. Ntozaki Shange's *for colored girls who have considered suicide when the rainbow is enuf . . .* (1974) honors the beauty of black women.

Lanford Wilson's three plays about the Tally family in Missouri combine sentiment and acceptance while dealing with difficult social and political issues. *The Fifth of July* (1978), for instance, is a story about antiwar activists coming to terms with middle-class and middle-aged life. Wilson's success with that play, with his *Tally's Folly* (1979), with his earlier *Hot l Baltimore* (1973), and with his 1987 *Burn This* rank him as one of the most important playwrights of the period.

August Wilson achieved considerable fame through his ambitious goal of writing a cycle of 10 plays on the experience of black Americans, one for each decade of the century. Each of the first four plays in the cycle received critical acclaim in New York, including *The Piano Lesson*, which won the Pulitzer Prize in 1989. Director Lloyd Richards, former head of the theatre program at Yale, has directed most of Wilson's works.

Fences (1985) explores the personal struggle with death of a black baseball player who was too old to play by the time blacks were allowed in the major leagues. *Ma Rainey's Black Bottom* (1984), set in the 1920s, concerns a black musical group and its exploitation by a racist recording studio. Wilson's greatest accomplishment is his ability to address the social concerns of black Americans (notably racism) in different decades, through the daily lives and struggles and friendships of black families.

In recent plays and films, Neil Simon has allowed the pain of relationships to break through his comedies and share the stage. *Chapter Two* (1977) deals with a middle-aged man whose wife has just died and an actress recently divorced from her husband. The couple come together but only after each has faced personal uncertainty and social pressures. Family relationships have been important in Simon's semiautobiographical trilogy, *Brighton Beach Memoirs* (1982), *Biloxi Blues* (1985), and *Broadway Bound* (1986), as well as in his film *Only When I Laugh*.

The private moment of shared honesty between two people has been a recurrent image in many American plays. Marsha Norman exposes the feelings behind an imminent suicide in *'night, Mother* (1981). *Frankie and Johnny at the Clair de Lune* (1987) by Terrence McNally looks at a relationship between a man and a woman. Craig

Lucas's *Prelude to a Kiss* (1988) tells of a young couple whose wedding day is disrupted when the bride suddenly finds herself in the body of an old man. A. R. Gurney's *Love Letters* (1988) has two actors simply reading letters written to each other.

Many groups in the United States used the drama to express their lifestyles. Gay culture received attention in the off-Broadway play *The Boys in the Band* (1968) by Mart Crowley and the Broadway success *Torch Song Trilogy* by Harvey Fierstein (1982). Gay theatres produced extensively in San Francisco in the 1980s, helping playwrights such as Doug Holsclaw, Larry Kramer, and Robin Swados achieve recognition. Not surprisingly, many of the gay-related plays focused on the impact of AIDS in the gay communities.

Luis Valdez organized the Teatro Campesino, which wrote and produced its own plays about Chicano life. In addition to encouraging the creation of *teatros* in several West Coast communities, Valdez's play *Zoot Suit* (1978) was the first Hispanic work presented on Broadway. Regional theatres produced several plays by Hispanic-American authors, including works by Lynne Alvarez and Milcha Sanchez-Scott. *Roosters* (1987), by Sanchez-Scott, weaves non-Anglo conceptions of time and reality into a story of Chicano values and issues. David Henry Hwang, noted for his highly successful *M. Butterfly* (1986), and David Wan Gotanda (*The Wash*, 1987) are among the Asian-American authors articulating their vision of reality.

The women's movement also found expression in the plays of Susan Griffin, Maya Angelou, Adrienne Kennedy, Constance Congden, Elizabeth Egloff, and dozens more. In fact, by the 1990s it was virtually impossible to talk about a women's theatre as a single force because there were so many disparate voices raising issues and matters of concern to women. Just as the culture had no single voice for women, so the theatres expressed a range of characters and attitudes about society. Beth Henley became famous for a play about three sisters in a southern town, *Crimes of the Heart* (1979), a traditional story line with women in traditional roles. By contrast, Congden's *Tales of the Lost Formicans* (1989) showed the frustrations and anger of women isolated in a world seemingly controlled by aliens.

Just as women playwrights do not confine themselves to the theme of reconciliation and reconstruction, leading commercial male playwrights also continued to mine the darkness of the human condition. David Mamet in *Glengarry Glen Ross* (1984), Sam Shepard in *Fool for Love* (1983), John Guare in *Six Degrees of Separation* (1990), and David Rabe in several plays all have kept alive the traditional theme of disillusionment. As long as there is a need for social commentary, the American theatres will provide it. Through the 65 years of American drama, playwrights have accepted the responsibility to dramatize for the American people the full range of the American experience. The parade of American drama has included the hopes of the American dream, disillusionment with it, and alternatives to it. Playwrights have presented their understanding of the American condition as best they can, trusting that it will strike a responsive chord in the audience. That the chord has been struck so often by so many is a testament to the vitality of American drama.

The Musical

The 1970s and 1980s were a period of formal experimentation in the musical. Poetry and dance were combined in recital fashion in *Don't Bother Me I Can't Cope* (1972). Tributes to jazz music were the basis for *Bubbling Brown Sugar* (1976) and *Sophisticated*

Ladies (1981). Shows that were almost exclusively dance concert included *Dancin'* (1978), while dance was the dramatic motif of *A Chorus Line* (1975) and *Ballroom* (1979). Traditional shows included *Annie* and *Woman of the Year* (1981). A director's dream-world is created in *Nine* (1982), and slides and photographs related the real world of 1950s Argentina in *Evita* (1980).

The world of the musicals in the 1970s lacked the bright joy of earlier years. The goals of the characters were more frequently to change the environment than to win the hero or heroine. The story lines focused on disintegrating relationships and the ruin of countries. The environments of the plays include a whorehouse, a "fly-killing world" *(Evita)*, gangland Chicago, and a foundry works. The conflicts were between haves and have-nots, believers and nonbelievers, and saints and sinners. Themes included injustice *(Chicago,* 1975), heroism *(Pippin,* 1972), feeling left out *(A Chorus Line),* and fame and martyrdom *(Evita).* The world of the musical no longer reflected the simplicity of life and purity of character that brought it to maturity. Some critics believed that the musical, like a human being, had grown from maturity to old age and the cynicism that can accompany that stage of life. More probably, it reflected the concerns of its audience, for the 1970s were hardly a period of restful optimism for most Americans. As in other periods, the musical offered Americans a look at themselves.

No single composer dominated the 1970s in his style and lyrics as much as Stephen Sondheim. Beginning with *Company* (1970), he redirected the musical to more complex musical structures and sounds and toward more thought-provoking themes. Instead of following Rodgers' folk music structure, Sondheim expanded and elaborated melody lines. In place of a standard four-beat musical measure, Sondheim reworked the $3/4$ beat or waltz time into a series of unusual patterns, especially in the 1973 hit *A Little Night Music.* He reintroduced more complex vocal groupings, such as a quintet to narrate the action of *A Little Night Music,* and a multipart chorus in *Sweeney Todd* (1979). He utilized new instruments in *Pacific Overtures* (1976). Finally, his harmonies were dissonant rather than sweet, and the musical accompaniment frequently played in contrast to the melodic line of the singer.

Not only were Sondheim's themes unusual for the musical, but his handling of them as serious literary material was often shocking to audiences. *Company* is a study of marital relationships, but its surprising quality is that there is no plot. Bobby merely wanders from one married friend to another on his 35th birthday, attempting to decide whether he should get married. He doesn't. Along the way he discovers that his married friends aren't as happy as they pretend to be (although he isn't happy in his single life either). The indifference and inhumanity of urban life is described in "Another Hundred People" and the boredom of upper-class New York life is expressed in "Ladies Who Lunch." *A Little Night Music* offers a carousel of relationships whirling around a Swedish garden. That they all end up with the "correct" partner at the end is undercut by the statement that such things can happen only in the mystery of a summer night. The boredom of being a housewife ("Every Day a Little Death") is the same as that of a popular actress ("Send in the Clowns") and a successful lawyer ("You Must Meet My Wife"). Sondheim's *Sweeney Todd,* the most operatic Broadway success since *Porgy and Bess,* presented a view of life as dark as a murder mystery. Life in *Sweeney Todd* is a cruel, vengeful cheat in which the only question is "who gets eaten and who gets to eat." Onstage murders and bodies thrown in furnaces (plus considerably more) are a far cry from the open skies and winking cows of *Oklahoma!,* but the success of the show

A TRIP TO THE
THEATRE
IN NEW YORK, 1975

*T*heatre marquees are lit up with neon signs. Crowds of people push along the sidewalks to get to different theatres. Traffic lurches nervously forward, and a row of taxis and limousines disgorges ladies in evening gowns and men in tuxedos. The spectator is surrounded by an audience for whom opening night is a social event as well as a theatrical one. A good producer has sold the musical to theatre-party ladies, who in turn have sold the title of the show and its stars to organizations and booking agents. Their efforts have guaranteed a solid advance sale. The out-of-town reports on the show are in, and word of mouth has created a demand for more tickets, for the critics have been positive. The show has also had previews and a run off-Broadway for as long as the producer and director felt was needed to make the best possible show and to assure that everything runs perfectly on opening night. Again, audiences who saw the previews have generated enthusiasm by their reports of the work.

When *A Chorus Line* opened on July 25, 1975, it was the culmination of two years' effort by its choreographer and director, Michael Bennett. He convinced the producer of the New York Shakespeare Festival, Joseph Papp, to use the Festival's facilities for a six-month rehearsal of an idea for a musical (shows usually rehearse for about six weeks). The idea was to make a musical about the making of a musical, focusing on the audition process prior to rehearsals. Bennett interviewed dozens of actors about their experiences in professional theatre, their training, their dreams for the future, and even about their childhood. Incidents were blended together to create characters and induce onstage situations. A simple plot emerged: to select eight dancers for the chorus number of a Broadway musical. Those auditioning would tell their stories to the director, who sits in the auditorium and, for most of the show, speaks to them over the sound system, and the winners would be presented in the show's finale.

What the opening-night audience saw was the result of the technical talents of dozens of people. Stage managers relied on carpenters, electricians, sound people, and stagehands to handle all the sets and equipment. Virtually all set changes were made by computerized machines to insure speed and efficiency of movement. Robin Wagner's set design for *A Chorus Line* relied on a row of periaktoi, the three-sided scenic device of the Greeks. One side was dark for soliloquies and quiet moments, a second side was mirrored to capture the glitter of the lights and reflect the image of the audience onto the stage, and the third side was sparkling, used in the finale.

The costumes also were simple during most of the show, until the entrance of the final chorus line, when Theoni Aldredge selected silver and cream colors for the men's tuxedos and for the women's tuxedo variations. The situation of the musical dictated simplicity until the finale for sets and costumes, but Tharon Musser's lighting design required incredible precision. Each character had to have his or her own overhead light for those moments that highlighted that individual's interior thoughts, necessitating the development of computerized lighting control. The use of a straight line for the auditionees in between some of the dance sequences required subtle light changes to provide visual variety. The use of mirrors further complicated the lighting plot, since lights had to be hung to reflect both on the action on the stage and on the action in the mirror, yet not blind the audience in the front rows.

The play opened to critical acclaim, and audiences soon made it the most popular show in New York City. On September 12, 1983, *A Chorus Line* became the longest-running show in the history of Broadway, and the evening was marked by a gala performance featuring more than 300 present and former cast members. *A Chorus Line* succeeded because, like all great plays, it reflected the lives, the feelings, and the dreams of its audience.

must be attributable in part to its similarity to the view of life that people see on television news. Such depressing images are not likely to remain popular, whether they are similar to reality or not. Yet *Sweeney Todd* clearly proved that the musical has the capacity to change with its audience and with the reality it reflects.

In the 1980s the musical began to move away from the despair of the previous decade. The theme of acceptance of self was prominent in several works, including *Cats* (1983), *Dreamgirls* (1982), and *La Cage aux Folles* (1984). The importance of the family was emphasized in *Baby* (1984), *The Rink* (1984), and *La Cage*. The determination to overcome all obstacles was evident in *Dreamgirls*. These shows were not returning to the same values as the musicals of the 1940s. Rather, they were creating a new understanding of these values from the perspective of the 1980s. They were continuing the tradition in which the musical expresses the mood of the nation.

Although the musical is most associated with American artists and American themes, Andrew Lloyd Webber proved to be the most successful composer of musicals in the 1980s and 1990s. Lloyd Webber established his musical signature with the hit *Jesus Christ Superstar* (opened in the United States in 1971). He combines lush, romantic melodies with rich orchestrations to create sounds that are faintly nostalgic, yet fresh and inventive. He often mixes styles from the past with contemporary top-10 rhythms and orchestrations. Lloyd Webber's *Cats* (opened in the United States in 1983) and *Phantom of the Opera* (opened in the United States in 1988) are the most likely productions to replace *A Chorus Line* as the longest-running show on Broadway.

A scene from Stephen Sondheim's *Sweeney Todd.*   *Courtesy Martha Swope Photography*

In summary, the musical is a richly varied art form that responds to its audiences and reflects its time period. It usually envisions the possibilities of the American dream, but has the capacity (at least for Stephen Sondheim) to express the nightmarish world of those dreams as well. As America broke away from its artistic dependence on Europe, so the musical broke away from European story lines and found its own characters and images. As America became increasingly urbanized and responsive to a younger generation, the musical relied more heavily on the urban sounds of jazz and then rock. As the nation passed from optimism to cynicism in the 1960s, the musical moved from the likes of *The Music Man* to *Company*. It evoked the post-Watergate futility of the 1970s in both formal experimentation and story lines. The future direction of the musical will depend on the creative artists who produce it and the national mood it expresses.

Europe

Playwrights in other parts of the world developed individual means of expressing personal views and exploring social issues. In Europe, despite the arrival of the European Community in 1992, diversity remains evident as the result of differing political and social circumstances. The popularity of Vaclav Havel in Czechoslovakia is directly related to the politics of anti-communism and to his role in leading the country away from Soviet domination. Dario Fo of Italy reflects the presence on the continent of radical theatres committed to socialist revolution.

Many German playwrights investigate the moral ambiguities of existence as that nation builds a new economic stability. And in France, where we begin, Marguerite Duras captures the anguish of lost love, a theme that has dominated Parisian stages for centuries.

Marguerite Duras (1914–   ).   Of all the playwrights in Europe in the last 25 years, few have the originality or individual style of Marguerite Duras. Known primarily for her novels (*The Lover*, published in 1984, was a literary and popular triumph) and screenplays (including *Hiroshima Mon Amour*), Duras is seldom produced by American theatres. Her distinctive style has a more receptive audience in her home country, France. Duras weaves an intricate relationship between time present and time remembered; her characters often seem frozen by their inability to escape the past as they remember it. Because the past is uncertain, the present fails to provide answers to the emotional dilemmas of the characters; silence becomes the last refuge of her heroines. Truth, also a focus of dramatic exploration for Duras, is elusive to the point that Duras has frequently rewritten the same story several times and in several media, each time altering the nuances and shadings the characters give to their experiences.

Vera Baxter, or The Atlantic Beaches (1983), reflects these dramatic situations. The title character has been forced to infidelity by her husband, who needs to justify his own infidelity by paying a man to sleep with Vera. In the silences and uncertainties of the situation and the dialogue, a charged atmosphere of self-destruction, panic, and alienation dominates the stage, leaving little room for traditional dialogue or stage action. Instead, the tension lies in the revelations the wife makes, as she gradually brings forth her story from the inner recesses of her soul. The play may not fit the typical structure of American realism, but its reality is nevertheless present in the honest depiction of the landscape of a woman's soul.

Franz Xaver Kroetz (1946–   ).   Because of the strong support for the arts in West Germany, many of Germany's leading playwrights achieved their fame through the production of their plays on television as well as in small state-supported theatres. Despite his strong political stance both in his dramas and in his personal activism, Franz Xaver Kroetz is one such playwright whose work became known throughout his country through television productions. Kroetz's plays usually focus on the average individual, an innocent who is overwhelmed by historical or economic circumstances. Influenced by Beckett, Brecht, and Arthur Miller, Kroetz places dramatic emphasis on the interior struggle of the individual. His condemnation of the economic system, especially the treatment of foreign workers and his critique of the sexual morality of Germany are both themes that are subsumed by the dominant concern with the interior struggle of the central characters.

Mensch Meier (1978) is the story of an assembly-line worker, Otto Meier, who dreams of winning the world model-airplane championship. He and his wife are upset that their son aspires to nothing more than becoming a bricklayer, because they don't want him to end up with as little dignity as they have. Meier sees his fellow workers lose their jobs, undermining his own security. He responds by becoming increasingly violent around the house, causing first his son and then his wife to leave him. By the end of the play he has been devastated by his situation, and he is left onstage, drunk and crying. The conditions at work that are the root cause of Meier's behavior are never presented onstage, except through the disintegration of the main character. Instead, Kroetz focuses on the effects of those conditions as they radically change the lives of a small German family.

***Vaclav Havel* (1936–   ).**   As leader of the opposition to communism in Czechoslovakia, Vaclav Havel was not only the most well known of his country's playwrights; he was also its most popular political figure. When the communist regime fell in 1989, it was Havel who assumed the presidency of the country. It was a remarkable moment for a man who had spent several years imprisoned for his political views, placed under house arrest, and denied travel rights. For 20 years his plays were banned from the theatre. Suddenly theatres throughout Europe and America were interested in the first playwright to hold a leadership role in his country since Sophocles.

During the middle 1960s, the Czech government allowed fairly open discussion of politics in the arts. Influenced by the prominence of absurdism in Europe at the time, Havel wrote several plays that to an American audience appear absurd. *The Memorandum* is the story of a bureaucracy that institutes a new language for all modes of communication. The director of the bureaucracy tries to stop the spread of incoherence that results, but eventually gives in, in a futile effort to retain some sense of humanity in an increasingly ludicrous world. Havel's playful development of memoranda written in "ptedepe" are funny, but the underlying criticism of a system out of control and indifferent to human needs was not absurd to Havel; it was his experience with communism in the 1950s.

In *Largo Desolato* (written in 1984 and performed in England in a translation by Tom Stoppard) the connections between the central character and Havel's life are even more irresistible. A professor has been harassed by the authorities to the point that he has become paranoid, peering out of his keyhole and listening for sounds outside his apartment. A pair of workers and several friends offer advice and insist he is still important to them, but the professor is so consumed with fear that he is unable to write or say anything that will satisfy their need for him to be their hero. The final twist occurs when he learns that the authorities no longer are interested in him because his isolation has succeeded: no one really cares about his opinions anymore.

***Dario Fo* (1926–   ).**   For those audiences who cling to radical politics in the face of the decline of communism and who would find Kroetz too understated, a play by the Italian Dario Fo would certainly fill the bill. The star of a popular television variety show in the mid-1960s, Fo left television in 1968 to commit himself to a theatre of anti-state activism and support of the ideals of the Italian communist party. With several other theatre groups, Fo formed a theatrical organization, ARCI, dedicated to the proletarian revolution. Believing that the media were preventing the truth from reaching the masses, Fo and ARCI determined to create a theatre that would free the public from capitalist control. The theatrical techniques that Fo uses are a combination of strident political rhetoric, commedia dell'arte characters, and slapstick and broad satire. Fo complains that American productions of his plays tone down the political elements and broaden the comedy, thus depriving the plays of their true political power. Certainly some of his work is difficult for Americans to appreciate, since cries for revolution are not echoed in too many quarters of American politics. One play in particular stands out as representative of Dario Fo and his theatrical technique.

Accidental Death of an Anarchist (1970) is based on a true incident in which an anarchist named Pinelli was arrested in Milan and charged with the bombing of a Bologna railroad station. The police report stated that the diminutive Pinelli managed to struggle free from six policemen and jump out the window, yelling "Anarchism is dead!" before falling to his death. A later report by a judicial inquiry concluded that Pinelli had merely fallen out of the window.

Dario Fo uses the two reports to build a drama of farcical cops and political intrigue in which it becomes apparent that the reports are contradictory. The play's appeal to American audiences lies in part in its emphasis on official blundering and dishonesty and on hints of conspiracy that involve public officials. To those who saw the play in Italy, however, the appeal was in the performance of Fo as the central character trying to discover the truth. He combined his skills as a satirist and a farceur with his passionate belief in the politics of the play.

Alan Ayckbourn (1939–   ).   The most prolific commercial playwright in Britain in the period is Alan Ayckbourn, whose first successful London hit was *Relatively Speaking* in 1967. Like Neil Simon in the United States, Ayckbourn established himself as a facile writer of social comedies and then increasingly developed the dark or tragic side of his plays.

Ayckbourn's plays, which number more than 35, are usually produced first at a theatre in Scarborough, where he is artistic director. The popularity of his blend of zany comedy and social satire has led to productions of his plays throughout the United States and most English-speaking nations around the world.

Within the comedic range, Ayckbourn's plays run the gamut from farce (*Bedroom Farce*, 1977) to tragic satire (*Woman in Mind*, 1987). His skill as a writer is in blending seemingly hopeless situations with characters whose indomitable spirit is determined to overcome all obstacles. His female characters are often exhausted by the demands of modern living. Their anger at the indifference of the men around them and their realizations that they are not treated as human beings lead them to extreme measures, including suicide attempts (comically in *Absurd Person Singular*, 1973) and madness (*Woman in Mind*).

Africa

African playwrights also developed international reputations during this period, and developed divergent dramatic approaches to African life. In Portuguese, French, English, and native languages, playwrights used freedom from colonial rule as a catalyst to dramatic writing. Ghanaian playwright Ama Ata Aidoo investigated the acceptance of Western ideas in traditional cultures in *The Dilemma of a Ghost* (1964), and tragically investigated the woman's role in society in *Anowa* (1969). G. Oyono-Mbia has approached the issues of colonialism through satire. Among the writers best known in the United States are Wole Soyinka and Athol Fugard. Wole Soyinka frequently utilizes traditional elements and structures in his plays to dramatize the modern African experience, while Athol Fugard focuses directly on social problems in his native South Africa.

Wole Soyinka (1934–   ).   Born a member of the Yoruba tribe in Western Nigeria, Soyinka received a college education in England before returning to Nigeria. His most highly acclaimed work, *Death and the King's Horseman* (1975), was based on an actual incident in which white colonial officials attempted to interfere with a Yoruba tradition. According to tradition, when a king dies, his Horseman must die to accompany the king. The interference of the District Officer and his wife is further complicated by the return of the Horseman's English-educated son. In a final lyrical sequence, the power of tradition and the difficulty of adapting tradition to change is forcefully portrayed through the Horseman's self-sacrifice. Soyinka indicts the folly of believing that the old ways will automatically work at the same time he opposes wholesale abandonment of traditional ways in favor of modern knowledge.

The most notable aspect of Soyinka's writing is his use of ritual music and dance to accompany the action. In addition, he writes extended poetic sequences that serve to separate the native tradition from the prose sequences depicting the colonial experience. The elements combine to create an epic style of theatre that abounds with theatrical imagery.

Soyinka was awarded the Nobel Prize for Literature in 1986 for a body of work including *The Bacchae of Euripides* (1973), *Opera Wonyosi* (1977), and *A Play of Giants* (1985).

Athol Fugard (1932–   ).   Fugard's international reputation is based on a body of plays that forcefully investigate the social structure of South Africa. His earlier works such as *Hello and Goodbye* (1965) focused on family structures and relationships. *Sizwe Banzi Is Dead* and *Statements After an Arrest* (1972) were developed improvisationally, based on actual occurrences in the actors' lives. His latest plays, including *Master Harold . . . and the Boys* (1982) and *The Road to Mecca* (1984), although still set in South African and depicting issues in that country, have a more universal content. *The Road to Mecca*, a tale of a young white woman returning to the countryside to visit an older woman, develops issues of cultural isolation, individualism, friendship, and trust.

Fugard has been criticized for writing about a black experience that he, as an educated white man, cannot possibly understand. Others, however, have praised his courage in facing issues directly and presenting them to mixed audiences in South Africa and abroad, raising awareness of the societal structures of South Africa and the plight of its black citizens.

CONNECTIONS

As in every time period, the theatre since 1968 has responded to the tensions in society—not always offering solutions, but serving to identify and focus areas of concern and to reflect the experience of the individual. The diversity of forms is indicative of the fragmentation of experience—the way one person sees the world is radically different from someone else's perspective.

Predicting how these theatre developments will affect future playwrights, performers, and audiences would be foolish guesswork, but we can be certain that changes will occur. As philosophers tell us that life is itself a drama, we may question as Herbert Blau does: "If life is the dream, what is the theatre?" As we have seen from this study of theatre history, the theatre is many different things, finding its reality as a part of a larger cultural construct. Eugenio Barba, noting the continued existence of theatre through radical changes in society, has suggested that the theatre is a way to transform personal needs into individual action. He holds out a faith that "our profession gives us the possibility of changing ourselves and thereby of changing society." For practitioners of theatre for thousands of years, this has been the truest hope and the deepest belief.

SOURCES FOR FURTHER STUDY

Social/Art/Philosophy Background

Foster, Hal, ed. *The Anti-Aesthetic—Essays on Postmodern Culture.* Port Townsend: Bay Publications, 1983.

Gaggi, Silvio. *Modern/Postmodern: A Study in Twentieth-Century Arts and Ideas.* Philadelphia: University of Pennsylvania Press, 1989.

Jencks, Charles. *What Is Postmodernism?* New York: St. Martin's, 1985.

Lasch, Christopher. *The Culture of Narcissism.* New York: Warner, 1979.

Lucie-Smith, Edward. *Cultural Calendar of the 20th Century.* Oxford: Phaidon Press, 1979.

Lyotard, Jean-François. *The Postmodern Condition.* Minneapolis: University of Minneapolis Press, 1984.

Theatre History & Dramatic Literature

Few "survey" texts exist of this period. For additional reading during this time period, the student is advised to seek individual books or journal articles dealing with topics of interest. Such books may focus on a geographic area, such as Alba Amoia, *The Italian Theatre Today: Twelve Interviews* (Troy, N.Y.: Whitson Publishing Company, 1977), a type of performance as addressed in Gregory Battock and Robert Nickas, *The Art of Performance: A Critical Anthology* (New York: E. P. Dutton, 1984); a theatre organization such as the Wooster Group as in David Savran, *Breaking the Rules: The Wooster Group* (New York: Theatre Communications Group, 1988); or an individual, as in Laurence Shyer, *Robert Wilson and His Collaborators* (New York: Theatre Communications Group, 1989). A recent trend in publication has been a compilation of interviews such as David Savran's discussions with contemporary American playwrights in *In Their Own Words* (New York: Theatre Communications Group, 1988). Much of the best information is available in shorter articles printed in leading journals. Journals that provide particularly valuable coverage of theatre during this time period include *The Drama Review, Performing Arts Journal, Theatre Journal, Theater Three,* and *Performance.*

Index

Cueva, Juan de la, 157; *Tragedy of the Seven Princes of Lara*, 157
Cunningham, Merce, 444
Curtain Theatre, 119
Cushman, Charlotte, 305
Cymbeline (Shakespeare), 133, 492
Cyrano de Bergerac (Rostand), 285, 307

Dada, 364, 497
Dafne (Peri), 91
Daguerre, Louis-Jacques, 280, 310
Dali, Salvador, 405
Daly, Augustin, 304
Daly, Tyne, 494
Dan, 337
Dance of Death (Strindberg), 393
Dancin', 501
Danish Royal Theatre, 446
Darktown Follies, 372
Darwin, Charles, 357
Dasté, Jean, 447
Davenant, Sir William, 217–220, 225; *Siege of Rhodes, The*, 217–218
David, Jacques Louis, 247–249, 293
Deacon's Awakening, The (Richardson), 434
Dead End Kids (Akalaitis), 492
De Architectura (Vitruvius), 96
Death and the King's Horseman (Soyinka), 508
Death of a Salesman (Miller), 457–458, 469
Death of Klinghoffer, The, 481
Death Valley (Rosenthal), 497
DeBrie (Catherine Leclerc), 176
Debussy, Claude, 365
Decembrist revolt, 275
Decius, 41
Declaration of Independence (Jefferson), 245
Decroux, Etienne, 460
Defense of Poesy, The (Sidney), 126
Defoe, Daniel, 217
Deidre of the Sorrows (Synge), 396
Dekker, Thomas, 135; *Shoemaker's Holiday, The*, 135
Delacroix, 227, 279, 293
Delaney, Shelagh, 452
Delicate Balance, A (Albee), 470
Delightful, The (Rueda), 157
De Loutherbourg, Phillipe, 227, 228, 230; *Various Imitations of Natural Phenomena*, 228
Delsarte, François, 383
DeMille, Agnes, 471–472

Dengaku, 194
DeNiro, Robert, 436
Dennis, John, 224
Desert Song (Romberg), 429
Desire Under the Elms (O'Neill), 433
Desvanes, 150
DeVilliers, Mlle., 176
Devine, George, 449
Dewhurst, Colleen, 434
Dhalang, 106
Dickens, Charles, 290, 490
Diderot, Denis, 244, 261–262; *Encyclopédie*, 244
Die Räuber (Schiller), 263, 268
Dike, 17, 29
Dilemma of a Ghost (Aidoo), 507
Diocletian, 41
Dionysus, 14–15
Diorama, 310
Dithyramb, 16, 26
Divine Narcissus, The (Sor Juana), 161
Dix, Otto, 363
Dixie to Broadway, 418
Doche, Marie, 322
Dock Street Theatre, 259
Doctor in Love, 183
Dog in the Manger (Vega), 157
Doggett, Thomas, 223, 227
Doll's House, A (Ibsen), 390–391
Domestic tragedy, 240
Dominus gregis, 45
Domitian, 41
Donatello, 90
Don Carlos (Verdi), 294
Don Giovanni (Mozart), 247
Don Juan de Marana (Hugo), 285
Don Quixote (Cervantes), 145–146
Don't Bother Me I Can't Cope, 500
Dorset Garden Theatre, 219
Dottore, 101–102
Double Inconstancies or The Inconstant Lovers, The (Marivaux), 264
Douglass, David, 259
D'Oyly Carte, Richard, 294
Drake, Sir Francis, 115–116
Drama and the Stage (Lewisohn), 422
Dramatic Imagination, The (Jones), 416
Drame, 263
Dreamgirls, 503
Dream Play, A (Strindberg), 393
Dr. Faustus (Marlowe), 131
Driving Miss Daisy, 494
Drottningholm Court theatre, 257

Drury Lane Theatre. *See* Theatre Royal, Drury Lane
Dryden, John, 217, 222, 235, 237. Works: *All for Love*, 237; *Conquest of Granada by the Spaniards*, 237
Duchess of Malfi, The (Webster), 132
Ducroisy (Philbert Gasot), 176
Duke's Company, 218
Duke's Theatre, 220
Dullin, Charles, 413–414, 448
Dumas *fils*, Alexandre, 313, 320; *La Dame aux Camelias*, 313, 320
Dumesnil, Marie, 259, 262
Duncan, Isadora, 444
Dunham, Katherine, 444
Duras, Marguerite, 505; *Vera Baxter*, 505
Duse, Eleonora, 381–383
Dutch Lover, The (Behn), 236
Dutchman (Baraka), 470
Dybbuk, The, 389

Earth and Stars (Edmonds), 434
Edgar, David, 490
Edinburgh Festival, 449
Edmonds, Randolph, 434. Works: *Earth and Stars*, 434; *Land of Cotton*, 434
Edo, 188
Edward II (Marlowe), 128
Egloff, Elizabeth, 500
Egmont (Goethe), 315
Egungun Festival, 127
Egypt, 28
Eidophusikon, 228
Einstein, Albert, 358
Eisenstein, Sergei, 328, 421
Ekhof, Konrad, 260
Ekkyklema, 23
El Burlador de Sevilla (Molina), 159
Elder, Lonnie III, 455
Electra (Euripides), 34
Electra (Sophocles), 34
Electric Company, The, 494
Electric Horseman, The, 286
Electric lighting, 324
Electronic Nigger (Bullins), 470
El Escorial, 141
El Greco, 142–145
Elizabeth I (Queen of England), 111, 116, 124
Elizabethan Stage Society, 368
Elizabeth the Queen (Anderson), 420

Gaucho, 314
Gautier, Theophile, 273
Gay, John, 217; *Beggar's Opera*, 217
Gay Divorcee, The (Porter), 431
Gelbert, Jack, 454; *The Connection*, 454
Gémier, Fermin, 420
Genet, Jean, 466. Works: *Balcony, The*, 466; *Maids, The*, 466
George I (King of England), 215, 224
George II (King of England), 224, 375–377
George III (King of England), 283
German theatre (early), 250–251
Gershwin, George, 325, 430
Gershwin, Ira, 430. *Porgy and Bess*, 420
Gesamtkunstwerk, 313, 324
Ghosts (Ibsen), 368, 391–392
Gielgud, Sir John, 411, 414, 417, 420
Gilbert, William S, 294–295, 325. Works: *Grand Duke, The*, 294; *H.M.S. Pinafore*, 294; *Mikado, The*, 294; *Patience*, 294–295; *Pirates of Penzance, The*, 294; *Trial by Jury*, 294; *Yeoman of the Guard*, 294
Gilder, Rosamond, 422
Gillette, William, 381
Gilpin, Charles, 420
Gin Game, The (Coburn), 499
Giradoux, Jean, 427. Works: *Madwoman of Chaillot, The*, 427; *Ondine*, 427; *Tiger at the Gates*, 427
Glaspell, Susan, 371
Glass Menagerie, The (Williams), 457, 458, 468
Glass of Water, The (Scribe), 320
Glengarry Glen Ross (Mamet), 500
Globe Theatre, 114, 117, 119–120, 122, 130
Glorious Revolution, The, 224
Gnaeus Naevius, 53
Godfrey, Thomas, 250; *Prince of Parthia, The*, 259
Godspell (Schwartz), 473
Goethe, Johann Wolfgang von, 244, 268–269, 283, 298, 303, 315, 323. Works: *Egmont*, 315; *Faust*, 283; *Gotz von Verlichingen*, 268; *Sorrows of Young Werther*, 315
Goldberg, Whoopi, 495

Goldfadden, Abraham, 389
Goldoni, Carlo, 266, 490. Works: *Mirandolina*, 266; *Servant of Two Masters, The*, 266, 490
Goldsmith, Oliver, 231, 239; *She Stoops to Conquer*, 231, 239
Goncharova, Natalie, 379
Goodman's Fields Theatre, 229
Goodman Theatre, 447
Gorelik, Mordecai, 389, 411, 418
Gorky, Maxim, 328, 370, 395; *Lower Depths, The*, 395
Gorostiza, Manuel Eduardo de, 314
Gospel at Colonus (Breuer), 494
Gotanda, David Wan, 500; *Wash, The*, 500
Gothic cathedral, 68
Gottsched, Johann, 252–254
Goya, Francisco, 279
Gozzi, Carlo, 266–267; *King Stag, The*, 267
Gradas, 150
Graham, Martha, 459
Grand Duke, The (Gilbert), 294
Granville-Barker, Harley, 369
Grass, Günter, 466
Graves, Michael, 481
Gray, Simon, 467; *Butley*, 467
Gray, Spalding, 495–496
Gray, Terence, 411
Great Depression, 405
Great Exhibition of the Works of All Nations, 290
Great God Brown, The (O'Neill), 433
Greek New Comedy, 47, 56
Green, Paul, 410; *The House of Connolly*, 410
Gregory, Lady August, 369, 396
Grein, J. T., 368, 391, 397
Griffin, Susan, 500
Gropius, Walter, 412
Grosses Schauspielhaus, 373
Grotowski, Jerzy, 450, 462, 485, 491
Grouch, The (Menander), 34
Group Theatre, The, 410, 420, 460
Gruppo Teatro Ottavia, 483
Guare, John, 489, 500; *Six Degrees of Separation*, 500
Guerilla Girls, 487
Gurney, A. R., 500; *Love Letters*, 500
Gustav III (King of Sweden), 257
Guthrie Theatre, 447, 457, 491
Guthrie, Tyrone, 414, 449

Gwyn, Nell, 221, 223
Gypsy, 418

H.M.S. Pinafore (Gilbert and Sullivan), 294
Habit à la romaine, 174, 256
Hair, 286, 472
Hairpin, The, 348
Hairy Ape, The (O'Neill), 433
Haiyen, 338
Haiyuza, 449
Halevy, Jacques-Fromental, 294
Hall, Peter, 446, 483
Hallam, Lewis, 225, 259
Hallam, Williams, 225
Hamartia, 31
Hamburg, 260
Hamburg Dramaturgy (Lessing), 254
Hamburg National Theatre, 252
Hamlet (Shakespeare), 121, 130–131, 296
Hammerstein, Oscar II, 429, 471–472
Han-ch'ing, Kuan, 347
Hanamichi, 200, 203–204, 209
Handel, George Frideric, 217
Handke, Peter, 467
Hansberry, Lorraine, 470; *Raisin in the Sun*, 470
Hanswurst (German character), 70, 251–252, 254
Happy Days (Beckett), 464–465
Harlem Renaissance, 434
Harlequin, 100, 102
Harnick, Sheldon, 472
Harris, Margaret F., 416
Hart, Moss, 431; *You Can't Take It With You*, 431
Harvey (Chase), 468
Hasenclever, Walter, 363
Hashigakari, 195–196
Hauptmann, Gerhart, 367–368, 386. Works: *Before Sunrise*, 386; *Weavers, The*, 368
Havel, Vaclav, 468, 476, 489, 504, 506. Works: *Largo Desolato*, 506; *Memorandum, The*, 506
Hawkins, Sir John, 115
Haydn, Franz Joseph, 247
Hayes, Helen, 419
Haymarket Theatre, 300
Hazlitt, Williams, 313
Heartbreak House (Shaw), 394
Hebbel, Christian Friedrich, 283
Hedda Gabler (Ibsen), 390
Helburn, Theresa, 408